Language Contact in Siberia

The Languages of Asia Series

Series Editor

Alexander Vovin (EHESS/CRLAO, *Paris, France*)

Associate Editor

José Andrés Alonso de la Fuente (*Jagiellonian University, Kraków, Poland*)

Editorial Board

Bjarke Frellesvig (*University of Oxford*)
Ross King (*University of British Columbia*)
Mehmet Ölmez (*Istanbul University*)
Toshiki Osada (*Institute of Nature and Humanity, Kyoto*)
Claus Schönig (*Freie Universität Berlin*)
Marek Stachowski (*Jagiellonian University, Kraków, Poland*)
Yukinori Takubo (*Kyoto University*)
John Whitman (*Cornell University*)
Pittawayat Pittayaporn (*Chulalongkorn University*)
Mark Alves (*Montgomery College*)
Pavel Rykin (*Russian Academy of Sciences*)
Guillaume Jacques (*Centre de recherches linguistiques sur l'Asie orientale*)
Juha Janhunen (*University of Helsinki*)
Anna Bugaeva (*Tokyo University of Science/National Institute for Japanese Language and Linguistics*)
Marc Miyake (*British Museum*)
Wu Ying-zhe (*Inner Mongolia University*)
Elisabetta Ragagnin (*Freie Universität Berlin*)

VOLUME 19

The titles published in this series are listed at *brill.com/la*

Language Contact in Siberia

Turkic, Mongolic, and Tungusic Loanwords in Yeniseian

By

Bayarma Khabtagaeva

BRILL

LEIDEN | BOSTON

Cover illustration: "Rainbow", Buryatia, Bayarma Khabtagaeva, 2015.

Library of Congress Cataloging-in-Publication Data

Names: Khabtagaeva, Bayarma, author.
Title: Language contact in Siberia : Turkic, Mongolic, and Tungusic loanwords in
   Yeniseian / by Bayarma Khabtagaeva.
Description: Leiden ; Boston : Brill, [2019] | Series: The languages of Asia series ;
   Volume 19 | Includes bibliographical references and index. | Identifiers:
   LCCN 2019003875 (print) | LCCN 2019006414 (ebook) | ISBN 9789004390768
   (e-book) | ISBN 9789004385948 (hardback : alk. paper)
Subjects: LCSH: Yeniseian languages–Foreign words and phrases–Altaic languages.
   | Yeniseian languages–Foreign words and phrases–Mongolia nlanguages. |
   Yeniseian languages–Foreign words and phrases–Tungus-Manchu languages. |
   Yeniseian languages–Foreign words and phrases–Turkic languages.
Classification: LCC PM10 (ebook) | LCC PM10 .K43 2019 (print) | DDC 494/.6–dc23
LC record available at https://lccn.loc.gov/2019003875

Typeface for the Latin, Greek, and Cyrillic scripts: "Brill". See and download: brill.com/brill-typeface.

ISSN 2452-2961
ISBN 978-90-04-38594-8 (hardback)
ISBN 978-90-04-39076-8 (e-book)

Copyright 2019 by Koninklijke Brill NV, Leiden, The Netherlands.
Koninklijke Brill NV incorporates the imprints Brill, Brill Hes & De Graaf, Brill Nijhoff, Brill Rodopi,
Brill Sense, Hotei Publishing, mentis Verlag, Verlag Ferdinand Schöningh and Wilhelm Fink Verlag.
All rights reserved. No part of this publication may be reproduced, translated, stored in a retrieval system,
or transmitted in any form or by any means, electronic, mechanical, photocopying, recording or otherwise,
without prior written permission from the publisher.
Authorization to photocopy items for internal or personal use is granted by Koninklijke Brill NV provided
that the appropriate fees are paid directly to The Copyright Clearance Center, 222 Rosewood Drive,
Suite 910, Danvers, MA 01923, USA. Fees are subject to change.

This book is printed on acid-free paper and produced in a sustainable manner.

In memoriam Professor Katalin Uray-Kőhalmi

Contents

Preface XI

1 **Introduction** 1
    1 The Topic of the Research 1
    2 The Database and Sources 2
        2.1 *Yeniseian Data* 2
        2.2 *Turkic Data* 4
        2.3 *Mongolic Data* 5
        2.4 *Tungusic Data* 6
    3 Yeniseian Languages 7
        3.1 *Kott* 8
        3.2 *Assan* 9
        3.3 *Arin* 9
        3.4 *Pumpokol* 9
        3.5 *Yugh* 10
        3.6 *Ket* 10
    4 Studies on Yeniseian-Altaic Linguistic Relations 11
        4.1 *Yeniseian-Turkic Studies* 11
        4.2 *Yeniseian-Tungusic Studies* 16

2 **Turkic Loanwords** 20
    1 Etymology 20
        1.1 *Nouns* 20
        1.2 *Adjectives* 155
        1.3 *Adverbs* 190
        1.4 *Numerals* 195
        1.5 *Verbs* 196
        1.6 *Postpositions* 203
        1.7 *Interjections* 205
    2 Phonetic Features 206
        2.1 *Turkic Vowels and Consonants in Yeniseian* 206
        2.2 *Long Vowels* 246
        2.3 *Consonant Clusters* 249

3 **Tungusic Loanwords** 257
  1 *Etymology* 257
    1.1 *Nouns* 257
    1.2 *Adverbs* 291
    1.3 *Verbs* 293
    1.4 *Particles* 295
    1.5 *Interjections* 296
  2 Phonetic Features 297
    2.1 *The Northern Tungusic Vowels and Consonants in Ket and Yugh* 297
    2.2 *The Development of Secondary Long Vowels from VCV Sequence* 308
    2.3 *Consonant Clusters* 309

4 **Mongolic Loanwords** 311
  1 Turkic Elements of Mongolic Origin in Yeniseian 311
    1.1 *Phonetic Considerations* 311
    1.2 *Morphological Considerations* 315
    1.3 *Semantic Considerations* 317
    1.4 *Loanwords with Yeniseian Suffixes* 318
  2 Tungusic Elements of Mongolic Origin in Yeniseian 319
    2.1 *Phonetic Considerations* 319
    2.2 *Morphological Considerations* 321
    2.3 *Semantic Considerations* 322
  3 Direct Mongolic Loanwords? 322
    3.1 *Kott* 323
    3.2 *Arin* 323
    3.3 *Yugh* 325
    3.4 *Ket* 326

5 **Typical Features of Altaic Loanwords in Yeniseian** 327
  1 Phonetic Peculiarities 327
    1.1 *Disappearance of Vowel Harmony* 327
    1.2 *Diphthongization* 328
    1.3 *Prothesis in Turkic Loanwords* 328
    1.4 *Apocope* 329
    1.5 *Paragoge* 330
    1.6 *Epentheses in Turkic Loanwords* 330
    1.7 *Gemination* 331
    1.8 *Syncope* 332

1.9   *The Loss of Internal Syllables*   332
1.10 *Word-Final -l of Unknown Origin in Altaic Loanwords*   333
1.11 *The Final -t of Unknown Origin in Altaic Loanwords*   334
1.12 *Metathesis*   334
2   Morphological Peculiarities   336
2.1   *Yeniseian Suffixes in Altaic Loanwords*   336
2.2   *The Loss of Altaic Suffixes*   340
2.3   *Change of the Original Word Classes*   341
3   Compound Words   342
3.1   *Compound Words in Yeniseian*   342
3.2   *Turkic Compound Words in Yeniseian*   344
3.3   *Tungusic Compound Words in Yeniseian*   348
4   Semantic Peculiarities   350
4.1   *Change in Semantics*   350

6 **False Etymologies or Coincidences**   359
  1   Turkic Words   359
  2   Tungusic Words   365

Conclusion   369

References   373
Index of the Yeniseian Words   389
    Kott   389
    Assan   392
    Arin   392
    Pumpokol   394
    Yugh   394
    Ket   395
Index of the Turkic Words   397
Index of the Literary Mongolian Words   400
Index of the Ewenki Words   402

Preface

This research is a result of my study of historical Yeniseian linguistics under the supervision of Professor Edward Vajda at the Center for East Asian Studies (Western Washington University, USA) from April to June, 2012 and in March, 2014 at the frames of the Hungarian Eötvös State Fellowship and the Campus Hungary Fellowship. I would like to express my sincere thanks and gratitude to Professor Vajda: without his teaching, and advice my research would not have been possible. I am grateful for support over the years, and, last but not least, for correcting my English.

My deepest gratitude and thanks go to Professor Stefan Georg (University of Bonn, Germany) from whom I absorbed new scientific ideas and methods thanks to his valuable remarks, and for allowing me to profit from his linguistic expertise.

A special word of thank is due to Professor Alexander Vovin (EHESS/CRLAO, Paris), who carefully read my work, offered me valuable suggestions, accepted my work for publication and supported me throughout years.

I sincerely thank Professor András Róna-Tas (Szeged University, Department of Altaic Studies) and Professor Claus Schönig (Institut für Turkologie, Freie Universität Berlin, Germany) for their feedback and valuable comments and criticism, whether by providing advice or discussion.

My equally big gratitude goes to my colleagues and friends for their help throughout all these years: Prof. Marianne Bakró-Nagy (Department of Finno-Ugrian Studies, Szeged University), Prof. Elisabetta Ragagnin (Institut für Turkologie, Freie Universität Berlin), Dr. Veronika Zikmundova, Dr. Veronika Kapišovská and Dr. Rachel Mikos (Institute of South and Central Asia, Charles University, Prague), Prof. Julian Rentzsch (Institute für Turkologie, Johannes Gutenberg-Universität Mainz), Dr. Hans Nugteren (Seminar für Turkologie und Zentralasienkunde, Georg-August-Universität Göttingen), Dr. Sárközi Ildikó (Pécs University), and Dr. Szeverényi Sándor (Department of Finno-Ugrian Studies, Szeged University).

I wish also to thank Catherine Schellenberg for housing accommodations during my stay in Bellingham (USA) in 2012 and 2014.

I with to express my gratitude towards those close to me—my mother Galina Zhigmitovna and my father Abido Cydypovich, my sister Namsalma and my daughter Emese—for all their support.

This book is dedicated to the memory of Professor Katalin Uray-Kőhalmi—Kati néni—to a wonderful person and my esteemed teacher from whom I learnt the basics of Tungusic Studies, Ewenki and Manchu languages. Without her teaching and support this book would not have come into existence. I am very grateful to my fate that I could learn from her.

All inaccuracies and mistakes, of course, are mine.

Bayarma Khabtagaeva
Szeged
May 24, 2018

CHAPTER 1

Introduction

1   The Topic of the Research

The aims of my research involve the investigation of Altaic (i.e. Turkic, Mongolic and Tungusic) elements in Yeniseian. The most important tasks are the clarification of loanwords origin, the determination phonetic changes and, if possible, the chronology of the borrowing. In the recognition of Altaic loanwords in Yeniseian, the historical-comparative method is used.

The earliest documented sources of Yeniseian languages are quite late. The first short lists of Yeniseian words and phrases were compiled at the end of the 17th and in the 18th century by European travelers such as Witsen (1692), Messerschmidt (1720–1727) and Strahlenberg (1730). The paucity of early written sources on Yeniseian is the reason why such an important role is played by the different loanwords from Altaic, Russian or Uralic in the reconstruction of the earlier stages of the history of the Yeniseian languages. The researchers who dealt with Yeniseian mention the Yeniseian-Altaic linguistic interactions (Dul'zon 1968: 13; Róna-Tas 1970; 1991: 18–19; Vajda 2004: 92; Timonina 2004: 135; Georg 2008: 154), but the topic of different loanwords in Yeniseian was not researched exhaustively.

In brief, only the Turkic elements were examined in the papers by Dem'janenko (1973), Timonina (1978; 1979; 1985; 1985a; 1985b; 1986; 2004) and Stachowski (1996; 1997). Stachowski also discussed the Turkic loanwords of Arabic and Persian origin (Stachowski 2006a; 2006b). Vajda recently published a valuable paper on different loanwords (Russian, Uralic and Altaic) in Ket (Vajda 2009). Mongolic and Tungusic elements were not discussed earlier.

The reason for the low number of studies, dealing with loanwords is the fact that the Yeniseian and Altaic languages belong in different language families, and exhibit typological differences. The phonology and grammar of the Yeniseian languages display features that are absent in the Altaic languages. Examples include
– A class division between masculine animate, feminine animate, and inanimate or neuter (Krejnovič 1968b; Dul'zon 1968: 63–68);
– A highly elaborate verbal morphology (Krejnovič 1968a; Vajda 2003: 57–90);
– One of the important distinguishing features is the existence of four tones. Thus, each Ket word contains one of the four tonal units: $\bar{V}$ (half-long, level or slightly rising); $V^{ʔ}$ (short rising-falling, with glottal constriction or "creakiness");

VV (long rising-falling, lower than V́); and V̀ (short, sharply falling), respectively (Georg 2018: 142). When suffixes are added, the distinctive prosodic quality of the root vowel is lost and gives way to a stress-like system involving the first two syllables of the phonological word (Georg 2007: 47–61). For a complete description of word tones, see Vajda (2000).

According to some researchers, the presence of pharyngeal vowels in the first syllable in Tuvan and Tofan, which is absent in other Modern Turkic languages, can be explained by the Yeniseian impact (Rassadin 1971: 22, 93; Werner 1972: 23).

At the same time, the Yeniseian languages share some contact-induced similarities with Siberian Turkic and Northern Tungusic languages (Anderson 2003; Comrie 2003: 8; Georg 2008).

Obviously, the Altaic languages may play an important role in Yeniseian reconstructions, but it is primarily important in distinguishing the early and later layers of borrowings. The resolution in the establishment of the relation of the early Yeniseian-Altaic linguistic contacts is possible if we first separate and examine the later layer of Siberian Turkic, Mongolic and Tungusic borrowings.

The research is planned to establish an historical-etymological survey of a part of the Yeniseian lexicon. This part of the external contacts of Yeniseian provides knowledge for the comparative database of Proto-Yeniseian and Proto-Altaic reconstructions too.

2 The Database and Sources

2.1 *Yeniseian Data*

The main source of my research was the *Vergleichendes Wörterbuch der Jenissej-Sprachen* by Werner (2002/1–3), which contains all of the lexical material published on the Yeniseian languages to date, not only common words, but also personal names and toponyms, and forms reconstructed from the extinct Yeniseian languages. Some data were checked from the monograph of the Yeniseian lexical material of the 18th century, published by Werner three years later (Werner 2005). This book includes full descriptions of all available data, exhaustive glossaries and some corrections of earlier treatments. Another very important source of my work was the *Etymological Dictionary of the Yeniseian Languages* by Vajda and Werner, which is still at a preparatory stage (Vajda & Werner: in preparation). My sincere thanks are due to Professor Edward Vajda, who graciously shared this material and his other unpublished writings with me.

2.1.1 The "Head"

Every Yeniseian word cited has a reconstructed Altaic (i.e. Turkic, Mongolic or Tungusic) form and its morphological structure is given. Curly brackets are used to indicate the Altaic suffix and its literature: **NN**—denominal noun suffixes, **NN/adj.**—denominal noun suffix-forming adjectives, **NV**—denominal verb suffixes, which form verbs from nouns, **VN**—deverbal noun suffixes, which forms nouns from verbs, and **VV**—deverbal verb suffixes, which form verbs from verbs.

In most cases, the works of Erdal (1991; 2004), Clauson (1972: xxxix–xlviii) and different grammars of Siberian Turkic languages (Baskakov 1947; Baskakov & Inkižekova-Grekul 1953a) were used to indicate Turkic suffixes. For Mongolic suffixes, the grammar of Poppe (1964) was used, and for Tungusic, the works of Vasilevič (1958: 639–799), Boldyrev (1987) and Nedjalkov (1997).

Comparative Altaic data are listed from the different dictionaries (see below). The sign '-' among listed data means that the form is not available, it may be present but not found in the considered dictionaries. The lexical meanings, originally given in different languages (mostly in Russian or German), were translated into English. The Cyrillic orthographic forms of Altaic languages have been transcribed into Latin characters. I use the traditional transcription system which is used in most publications on Mongolic and Tungusic close to the transcription used in Turkic Studies (see Johanson & Csató 1998: xviii–xxii). The sign * is used for reconstructed forms.

Finally, the main bibliographical references are listed in chronological sequence. They include the different works dealt with the etymology of Altaic languages as Räsänen (1969), Ščerbak (SF 1970; 1997), Doerfer (TMEN 1963–1972; 1985), Rassadin (1971; 1980), Clauson (1972), Sevortjan (ESTJa 1974; 1978; 1980), Levitskaja, Dybo and Rassadin (ESTJa 1989; 1997; 2000; 2003), Tenišev (SIGTJa 1984; 1988; 2001; 2002), Schönig (2000), Nugteren (2011), Róna-Tas and Berta (WOT 2011), etc. The Samoyedic data were collected from Joki (LS) and Helimski (1997). The Siberian Russian data were taken from Anikin's (2000) and Vasmer's (1986) dictionaries.

The Persian data were collected from the Steingass dictionary (1930), Arabic forms from Wehr's dictionary (1994), the Tibetan words from the reprinted Tibetan–English dictionary by Das (2000). The Chinese data were taken from *The Chinese–English Dictionary* (1979), but if some words are absent from this source I used *Mathews's Chinese–English Dictionary* published in 1931 (Mathews).

Also, I give the bibliographical references of Timonina (1978; 1979; 1985; 1985a; 1985b; 1986; 2004) and Stachowski (1996; 1997; 2006a; 2006b), who specifically dealt with the Yeniseian-Turkic linguistic connections. Additionally, I give the references of my papers (Khabtagaeva 2015a; 2015b; 2015c; 2015d; 2015e; 2017) connected to this research. It is important to note that in many cases my early etymologies were revised and removed from the book.

2.2 *Turkic Data*

The Turkic database is broken down into Old Turkic and Modern Turkic. The Modern Turkic data are grouped according to the classification of Johanson (1998: 81–87). Only three Turkic branches are mentioned: Siberian Turkic, some Kipchak and some Uyghur Turkic languages.

Of the Turkic languages, only Siberian Turkic had direct linguistic contacts with Yeniseian. It seems that two layers may be distinguished: Yenisei Turkic and Altai Turkic. Rare similarities may be observed with Sayan Turkic, Chulym, Yakut languages and Siberian Tatar dialects. A Southwestern branch or Oghuz Turkic, Chuvas and Khalaj were not considered in this research.

Turkic languages		Source
Old Turkic		Clauson ED 1972
		DTS = Nadeljaev et al. 1969
Modern Turkic		
– **Siberian Turkic** (= North-eastern branch)		
– South-Siberian group (= NE^S)		
– Yenisei Turkic	Khakas	Baskakov & Inkižekova-Grekul 1953;
		Butanaev 1999
	Shor	Kurpeško-Tannagaševa & Apon'kin 1993
	Sagai, Koibal, Kachin	Radloff 1893–1911
	Kyzyl	Joki 1953
– Altai Turkic	Literary Altai	Baskakov & Toščakova 1947
	Qumanda	Baskakov 1972
	Quu	Baskakov 1975; Erdal & et al. 2013
	Tuba-kiži	Baskakov 1966
	Teleut	Rjumina-Syrkaševa & Kučigaševa 1995;
		Radloff 1893–1911
– Chulym Turkic		Birjukovič 1984
– Sayan Turkic	Tuvan	Tenišev 1968
	Tofan	Rassadin 1995
– North-Siberian group (= NE^N)	Yakut	Slepcov 1972;
		Pekarskij 1959
	Dolgan	Stachowski 1993
– **Kipchak Turkic** (= North-western branch)		
– Volga-Ural group or Northern Kipchak (NW^N)	West Siberian Tatar dialects	Tumaševa 1992

(cont.)

Turkic languages		Source
– Aralo-Caspian group or South-Kipchak (NW^S)	Kirgiz	Judaxin 1965
	Kazak	Bektaev 1999
	Fu-yü[1]	Zhen-hua & Imart 1987
– Uyghur Turkic or South-eastern branch (SE)	Yellow Uyghur	Malov 1957; Roos 2000.

2.3 Mongolic Data

The Mongolic data are divided into three groups: Middle Mongol, Literary Mongolian and Modern Mongol. Middle Mongol sources are given according to the writing systems. Literary Mongolian is the 'link' between the various Mongolic languages. Modern Mongol languages are given in two groups. The non-archaic languages include Buryat, Khalkha, Oirat or Kalmuck, while from archaic languages were taken only Dagur and Khamnigan data.

Mongolic languages		Source
Middle Mongol documents written in different scripts		
– Uyghur Mongol script	Preclassical Mongolian (13th–15th centuries)	Ligeti 1963, 1965a, 1967; Tumurtogoo 2006
– Chinese script	Secret History = SH (1228 or 1240)	Haenisch 1939; Ligeti 1964, 1971
	Hua-yi yi-yu = HY (1389)	Haenisch 1957; Mostaert 1977
	Zhiyuan Yi yu = ZY (1325/1326)	Kara 1990
	Yi yu = YY (1599)	Apatóczky 2009
– 'Phags-pa script	(1269–1368)	Ligeti 1973; Poppe 1957; Tumurtogoo 2010
– Arabic script	Leiden manuscript (1343)	Poppe 1927
	Ibn-Muhanna = Ibn-Muh. (14th century)	Poppe 1938
	Mukaddimat al-Adab = Muq. (14th century)	Poppe 1938
	Istanbul vocabulary = Ist. (15th or 16th century)	Ligeti 1962
	Rasulid Hexaglot = RH (14th century)	Golden 2000
– Armenian script	Kirakos (1270)	Ligeti 1965b

---

[1] In spite of strong genetic bonds with Yenisei Turkic [NE^S], a Fu-yü language of Manchuria is regarded as a Kirgiz dialect (Zhen-hua & Imart 1987) in the classification of Johanson (1998: 83).

(*cont.*)

Mongolic languages		Source
Literary Mongolian	Lessing 1996; Kara 1998	
Modern Mongol languages		
– Non-archaic	Buryat	Čeremisov 1973
	Khalkha	Bawden 1997
	Oirat	Coloo 1988
	Kalmuck	Ramstedt 1935
– Archaic	Dagur	E = Engkebatu 1984; T = Todaeva 1986
	Khamnigan	D = Damdinov & Sundueva 2015; J = Janhunen 1990

2.4 *Tungusic Data*

Although the classification of Tungusic languages is not definitive, traditionally (cf. e.g. Ligeti 1948; Cincius 1949: 35) Tungusic languages are divided into two big branches. The northern branch (= NT) includes with 51 dialects and subdialects Ewenki, Ewen or Lamut, and Negidal. The southern branch is divided into two groups. The Manchuric group (= SM) consists of Jurchen or Old Manchu, Manchu, and its sole living member Sibe ~ Sibo. The Amuric group (= SA) includes Nanai, Ulcha, Orok, Oroch, and Udihe.[2]

The Tungusic sources of borrowing in Yeniseian were possibly the Ewenki dialects. The bulk of the Ewenki lexical items were provided by the *Ewenki-Russian dictionary* of Vasilevič (1958), which lists even dialectal forms. Additionally, the Ewenki forms were checked in *Ewenki-Russian* and *Russian-Ewenki dictionaries* by Boldyrev (2000; 1994). The other Tungusic data were collected from the Comparative Tungusic dictionary (= SSTMJa) edited by Cincius (1975; 1979). This fundamental source usually mentions the foreign parallel for

---

[2] A new classification of Tungusic languages was recently proposed by Janhunen (2012: 16), where the northern branch includes the Ewenic group and broadened with the Udegheic group, while the southern branch consists of the Nanaic and Jurchenic groups. Accordingly, the Tungusic languages are divided into two branches. The **Northern Tungusic** branch includes the Ewenic group: a) Siberian Ewenic (Ewen, Arman, Ewenki, Neghidal, Orochen and Urulga dialect of Khamnigan Ewenki); and b) Manchurian Ewenic (Mankovo dialect of Khamnigan Ewenki, Nonni Solon, Hailar Solon and Ongkor Solon). The Udegheic group includes Udeghe and Oroch. The **Southern Tungusic** branch contains three groups: a) the Nanaic group (Nanai, Kili and Kilen); b) the Ulchaic group (Ulcha and Orok) and c) the Jurchenic group (Jurchen, Manchu and Sibe).

the given Tungusic word but not Yeniseian. The Sibe material was collected from Zikmundova's monograph (2013).

3 Yeniseian Languages

The Yeniseian language family is represented today only by the three surviving dialects of Ket. Yugh lost its last fluent speaker in the 1970s. Kott disappeared before 1850. Assan, Arin and Pumpokol vanished in the 1700s. Other groups, such as Yarin (Buklin), Yastin and Baikot are identifiable as Yeniseian-speaking from tsarist fur-tax records compiled during the 17th century, but nothing remains of their languages except a few proper names. Other language forms related to Yeniseian undoubtedly vanished before the Russians arrived in the late 16th century.

The Yeniseian languages belong in the Paleo-Siberian or Paleo-Asiatic language group, which also includes the Yukaghiric, the Kamchukotic, the Amuric and the Ainuic languages. This term is conventionally used in linguistics to classify a group of languages spoken in different parts of north-eastern Siberia and some parts of the Russian Far East. The languages of this group are not known to have any genetic linguistic relationship to each other.

The Yeniseian languages have been proposed as connected with the Sino-Tibetan, Burushaski (Karasuk) Caucasian and Nostratic language families (Starostin 1984; Starostin & Ruhlen: online). Vajda recently put forward a hypothesis that the Yeniseian languages display genealogical connections with the Na-Dené languages of North America (Vajda 2010). His results are still debated by linguists, but this question remains open for further discussion (Campbell 2011). Georg considers that the Yeniseian language family should be regarded as isolated, with no known relatives among living or dead languages or language families of the world (Georg 2007: 19–20).

Toponymic evidence indicates that Yeniseian-speaking people once inhabited vast territories of Inner Eurasia. River names with Yeniseian etymologies stretch from Xinjiang and Western Mongolia northward across southern Siberia from the Irtysh to the Angara (Dul'zon 1959; 1962; Vajda 2001: xxvii; 2004: 2).

It appears from Chinese sources that a Yeniseian group might have existed among the peoples that made up the tribal confederation known as the Xiong-nu, who have traditionally been considered to be the ancestors of the Huns. Until the early 1960s, it was generally assumed that the Xiong-nu were ancestors of Turkic or Mongolic peoples. Ligeti (1950) was the first who suggested that the Xiong-nu language may belong to the Yeniseian language family. He compared the Xiong-nu word *sak-dak 'boot' with the Ket sāgdi ~ śāgdi 'id.'. In 1962, Pulleyblank accepted this etymology and presented more credible evidence that the Xiong-nu language is connected with the Yeniseian language family, with more examples from the basic vocabulary (see Puleyblank 1962). The hypothesis was rejected by Doerfer (1973). The topic was recently discussed by Vovin (2002; 2003), who evaluated the arguments of Pulleyblank and suggested that the Xiong-nu might have been Yeniseian or at least some part of the Xiong-nu confederation, its core or elite, and spoke a Yeniseian language. Vajda (2018: personal communication) believes that the core Xiong-nu group may have spoken an extinct branch of Uralic. At the moment, however, all these suggestions are difficult to substantiate in view of the paucity of the data. Nonetheless, it is certain that the Yeniseian languages could be a key factor in the early formation of the languages of the Eurasian nomads.

Very few historical comparative works on Yeniseian are available. They include Sergei Starostin's comparative phonology (1982), his comparative vocabulary (1995) and Georgii Starostin's reconstruction of the Proto-Yeniseian verbal system (1995). Werner's (1990b) comparative phonetics of Yeniseian languages is another important work that must be mentioned. Vajda and Werner's *Etymological Dictionary of the Yeniseian languages* (in preparation) which may open up a new era in the study of Yeniseian languages. Most Yeniseian publications place focus on the Ket language and are of a descriptive character (Dul'zon 1968; Vall & Kanakin 1990; Werner 1990a, 1993, 1997; 2005; Vajda 2004; Georg 2007).

The most recent works on historical linguistics by Sergei Starostin (1982), Stefan Georg (2007: 16–20; 2017: 141) and Edward Vajda (2014: personal communication) divide the Yeniseian languages into at least three sub-branches: Ket-Yugh, Pumpokol and Assan-Kott. Arin is either connected with Pumpokol or Ket-Yugh or represents a fourth sub-branch.

3.1   Kott

The beginnings of Kott studies are linked with the name of M.A. Castrén, a Finnish scholar and a member of the Russian Academy of Sciences, who carried out fieldwork among the Kott people. He compiled a full description of Kott phonology and morphology, the vocabulary which forms the main corpus of the available Kott data (Castrén 1858). On the basis of Castrén's material, Werner published monographs on the Kott language in Russian (Werner 1990) and German (Werner 1997e). The brief grammatical description of Kott was also written by him (Werner 1997d).

In the 17th–18th centuries, Kott was spoken along the rivers Biryusa (a right tributary of the river Yenisei) and the Abakan (in Khakassia), the Mrass and Kondoma rivers (tributaries of the river Tom) (Georg 2007: 17). Georg considers that Kott may be a substratum language of the Yenisei Turkic variety Shor,

INTRODUCTION

spoken nowadays in this region (Georg 2007: 17). From morphological point of view, Kott shows a rather different typological makeup in many subsystems, e.g. a largely suffixing verbal morphology, as opposed to almost exclusively prefixing Ket and Yugh (Georg 2018: 141).

The Kott material indicates the presence of two different Kott dialects. Werner considers them to be Kott A and Kott B (Werner 1997e; Georg 2007: 17).

3.2 Assan

In the classification of the Yeniseian languages, Assan belongs in one sub-branch together with Kott or principally identical with it (Georg 2016: personal communication).

In the 18th century, Assan was spoken along the rivers Biryusa and Usolka (tributaries of the river Yenisei). Material on the Assan language is sparse. A short grammatical sketch with Kott comparisons and lexical data was presented in Werner's monograph (Werner 2005: 122–141).

3.3 Arin

It is unclear to which Yeniseian sub-branch the Arin language belongs. Vajda links it with the Ket-Yugh sub-branch or regards it as a fourth independent sub-branch (Vajda 2014: personal communication).

The language was spoken on both sides of the river Yenisei. It died out in the 18th century, but some lexical data (altogether ca. 400 lexical items) are preserved in the materials of Strahlenberg, Miller and Fischer (Georg 2007: 18). The short grammatical description and lexical data of Arin is available in Werner's work (2005: 142–168).

From a historical phonetic point of view, the Arin data were examined by Toporov (1968). Important Arin archive material of the 18th century was also found by Helimski (1986).

3.4 Pumpokol

It is considered by Georg (2007: 18) that Pumpokol is originally a geographic name: the name of a town and a district in the upper reaches of the river Ket. The etymology of the designation *pumpokol* is connected with the Khanty *pum-poχəl 'grassy village' by Georg (2007: 18) after Anikin (2000: 458).

The place of the Pumpokol among Yeniseian languages is unclear. Most likely, it forms an independent sub-branch (Vajda 2014: personal communication). The total Pumpokol material accounts for approximately 65 words (Georg 2007: 18) and is available in the monograph by Werner (2005: 179–187), who also wrote a short grammatical sketch (Werner 2005: 169–178).

3.5 *Yugh*

In the literature, Yugh is referred to as the Sym dialect of Ket, due to the fact that Yugh speakers lived on the banks of the river Sym, the left tributary of the river Yenisei (Werner 1997c: 187; Georg 2007: 16). In official documents from the 17th century, the Yugh people were referred to as the *d'ukany*, originating from the forms *d'ukul ~ d'ukun ~ d'ukundri*, the designation of the Yughs by the Tungusic people, though the Yughs identified themselves as *kʌnd'eŋ*. In the censuses of the 20th century, they were considered as Ket people (Werner 1997c: 187–188). According to Vajda (2004: 1), citing personal communication from Heinrich Werner, who worked intensively with the last known speakers, Yugh lost its last fluent speaker in the 1970s.

In the classification of the Yeniseian languages, Yugh is included in the same sub-branch as Ket. The full grammatical description and the lexical material were published by Werner (1997c; 1997f).

3.6 *Ket*

In the early literature, the Ket language was referred to as Yenisei-Ostyak. This led to some confusion with the designation of the Khanty people, one of Uralic language family speakers, who were also called Ostyak.

Today, most of the nearly 1,200 Ket live in north-central Siberia, along the middle reaches and tributaries of the Yenisei, in the Turukhan District of Krasnoyarsk Province, where the speakers of the Ewenki dialects are also present. The differences between the three Ket dialects are not very sharp, but the speakers of the dialects distinguish themselves strictly from each other (Kazakevič & Helimskij 2002: 96). In spite of its official status, Ket is nowadays regarded as an endangered language.

The early material on the Ket dialects was collected from disparate sources for the first time and published by Dul'zon (1961).

An extensive compilation of Ket vocabulary can be found in the three-volume comparative dictionary by Werner (2002), who also compiled Ket-Russian and Russian-Ket student dictionaries (Werner 2002a). We owe detailed Ket grammars (phonology, morphology and syntax) to Dul'zon (1968), Vall and Kanakin (1990), Werner (1997), Vajda (2004) and Georg (2007).

From an ethnographic point of view, valuable information on religion, traditions and customs can be gleaned from the different ethnographic works of Russian or Soviet researchers. I should especially mention the name of the Ketologist from Leningrad, Professor E.A. Alekseenko, whose works covered practically every cultural aspect of the Ket people. Beginning in 1959 she published about 40 papers and monographs on Ket culture, based on fieldwork material (e.g. see papers 1960; 1971; 1976 and 1985). One of her important monographs is *The Ket people* in Russian, where various ethnographic aspects of Ket everyday lifestyle were investigated (Alekseenko 1999).

In 1966, Dul'zon published Ket texts: folktales describing everyday activities such as hunting, which were recorded by the author in the different villages where various Ket dialects were spoken (Dul'zon 1966). There were also very important publications on the topic of Ket ethnography, and especially the Ket tribal structure (Dolgikh 1934, 1982). Some folklore and historical-ethnic questions were discussed by Nikolaev (1985). Vajda recently published a valuable article on Ket shamanism (Vajda 2010).

Full information and an annotated bibliography on ethnographic and linguistic works by Yeniseian people and languages published up to 1998 are to be found in the *Yeniseian annotated bibliography and source guide* by Vajda (2001).

4　Studies on Yeniseian-Altaic Linguistic Relations

Before the arrival of Russian traders and travelers, the territory of Central Siberia contained only sparse populations of nomad people who spoke languages belonging in three distinct genetic groups. Most widespread were the Samoyedic languages with Selkup in the southwest and the languages of the Enets, Nenets, and Nganasan people above the Arctic Circle. The central part of the Yenisei watershed was inhabited by the Yeniseian people. The territory in the south, which includes the Altai-Sayan Mountains, was home to several small Turkic-speaking groups, the ancestors of the modern Yenisei-Turkic and Altai-Turkic people. The Yenisei area also contained Ugric people such as the Khanty from the west and the Tungusic-speaking Ewenki from the east. The historical documents indicate that the first meetings between the Russians and the indigenous population date from around 1606 (Vajda 2004: vii–ix).

According to Vajda, by the mid-19th century, only the Ket and the Yugh remained: all their relatives (the Kott, Assan, Arin and Pumpokol) had been absorbed into Turkic, Samoyedic, Tungusic and Russian communities. The South Siberian Turkic people and the western Buryat, one of the Mongolic ethnic groups, display linguistic or ethnic substrates preserved to varying linguistic and ethnic extents from some bygone Yeniseian-speaking population (Vajda 2004: 1).

4.1　*Yeniseian-Turkic Studies*
The Turkic loanwords of Yeniseian were dealt with by Ljudmila Timonina—Werner's pupil. The Turkic elements in Kott were discussed by her in the first

two short papers (Timonina 1978; 1979). Later, she dealt with the unknown element *il-/al-* which is present in Turkic and Yeniseian (1982a; 1982b). Various aspects of Yeniseian terminology as the names of body parts (1985a), the cultural words (1986) and the names of domestic animals (1985b) were also investigated by her. As a result, in 1985 in Leningrad Timonina defended her candidate dissertation on Turkic loanwords in Yeniseian (1985). Her last paper on this topic was written in English and published in the collection of papers *Languages and prehistory of Central Siberia* edited by Vajda (2004). Here, Timonina clearly distinguishes two different periods of borrowings: the early (prior to about 1230 AD) and the later period following the Mongolic invasions that led to major migrations and mixing of Turkic tribes (Timonina 2004: 137). But it should be indicated that a majority of the loanwords presented in these papers designate the later period of borrowing.

The Turkic elements in Yeniseian were also examined by the Polish researcher Marek Stachowski. His two papers discuss several Turkic borrowings including the names of animals and plants, various words connected to kinship terminology and features characterizing people, clothing and household utensils. One of the papers deals with eleven (Stachowski 1996), while the second one covers twenty nine (Stachowski 1997) Turkic loanwords from etymological and phonetic poits of view. Stachowski also discussed the Turkic loanwords of Arabic and Persian origin (Stachowski 2006a; 2006b). Through etymologizing, Stachowski proves the Siberian Turkic mediation in borrowing of Arabic and Persian words to Yeniseian.

In 2001, Stefan Georg wrote a paper mentioning that the well-known Turkic-Mongolic religious term *tängri* 'sky, God' may have Yeniseian etymology. It probably goes back to the hybrid Proto-Yeniseian form **tiŋgVr-* 'high' with the Turkic possessive suffix *-X*. The diversity of Yeniseian religious terms is shown by the Arin word *ajna* 'devil', which was clearly borrowed from Siberian Turkic, but was ultimately of Persian origin (for details, see Stachowski 2006: 179).

Shortly, the Ket–Khakas lexical parallels were discussed by the Khakas researcher Butanaev (1973; 1992). The common words were investigated by him in toponimics, in the terminology of the names of plants, animals, birds and months, and also some shamanic terms.

The research of Karl Bouda (1957) must be mentioned, which was devoted to a short grammatical sketch of Yeniseian languages and gives some lists of loanwords in Yeniseian. Besides of Samoyedic, Finno-Ungric and Russian, the 'eastern' Turkic and Tungusic elements are listed. But most of them should be handled with caution, some of the etymologies are not reliable.

Some new Yeniseian etymologies for Tofan—the language of Sayan Turkic group—were recently proposed by Alexander Vovin (2017). The paper proves that not only Turkic, but the Yeniseian linguistic influence on Siberian Turkic was quite extensive.

4.1.1 The Main Phonetic Features of the Siberian Turkic Languages
As I mentioned earlier, of the Turkic languages, only Siberian Turkic had direct linguistic contacts with Yeniseian. The Yenisei Turkic and Altai Turkic layers may be distinguished. Also, some similarities may be observed with Sayan Turkic, Chulym, Yakut languages and Siberian Tatar dialects (Details for classification, see above the chapter *Turkic data*).

The main phonetic features of the Siberian Turkic languages are the following:

(1) The Turkic original long vowels were preserved or diphthongized in Yakut and Dolgan, while in other languages they disappeared, e.g.
   - Old Turkic *bāy* 'rich' ~ NE^N Yakut; Dolgan *bāy*; cf. YeniseiT: Khakas; Shor *pay*; AltaiT: Altai; Tuba; Qumanda *bay*; Quu; Teleut *pay*; SayanT: Tuvan; Tofan *bay*; ChulymT *pay*; NW^N Siberian Tatar *pay*;
   - Old Turkic *kȫk* 'blue' ~ NE^N Yakut *küöx*; Dolgan *küök* ~ *küöx*; cf. YeniseiT: Khakas; Shor *kök*; AltaiT: Altai; Tuba; Qumanda; Quu; Teleut *kök*; SayanT: Tuvan; Tofan *kök*; ChulymT *kök*; NW^N Siberian Tatar *kük*;
   - Old Turkic *ōt* 'fire' ~ NE^N Yakut; Dolgan *uot*; cf. YeniseiT: Khakas; Shor *ot*; AltaiT: Altai; Tuba; Qumanda; Quu; Teleut *ot*; SayanT: Tuvan; Tofan *ot*; ChulymT; NW^N Siberian Tatar *ut*;

(2) The Turkic original short vowels are represented by pharyngeal vowels in Sayan Turkic, e.g.
   - Old Turkic *at* 'horse' ~ SayanT: Tuvan; Tofan *a^{c}t*; cf. YeniseiT: Khakas; Shor *at*; AltaiT: Altai; Tuba; Qumanda; Quu; Teleut *at*; ChulymT *at*; NE^N Yakut; Dolgan *at*; NW^N Siberian Tatar –;
   - Old Turkic *ot* 'grass, vegetation; hay' ~ SayanT: Tuvan; Tofan *o^{c}t*; cf. YeniseiT: Khakas; Shor *ot*; AltaiT: Altai; Tuba; Qumanda; Quu; Teleut *ot*; ChulymT *ot*; NE^N Yakut; Dolgan *ot*; NW^N Siberian Tatar *ot*;
   - Old Turkic *qat* 'row' ~ SayanT: Tuvan; Tofan *ka^{c}t*; cf. YeniseiT: Khakas *xat*; AltaiT: Altai *kat*; ChulymT –; NE^N Yakut *xat*; NW^N Siberian Tatar –;

(3) There appears a sporadic change of vowel *a ~ *ï* in Yakut and Sayan Turkic, e.g.
   - Old Turkic *āy* 'moon' ~ NE^N Yakut; Dolgan *ïy*; SayanT: Tuvan; Tofan *ay*; cf. YeniseiT: Khakas; Shor *ay*; AltaiT: Altai *ay*; ChulymT *ay*; NW^N Siberian Tatar *ay*;
   - Old Turkic *tart-* 'to pull, drag' ~ SayanT: Tuvan; Tofan *türt-*; NE^N Yakut; Dolgan *tart-*; YeniseiT: Khakas; Shor *tart-*; AltaiT: Altai *tart-*; ChulymT *tart-*; NW^N Siberian Tatar *tart-*;

- Old Turkic *sap* 'handle' ~ SayanT: Tuvan *sïp*; Tofan –; NE^N Yakut *up* ~ *uk*; Dolgan *up*; YeniseiT: Khakas *sap*; AltaiT: Altai *sap*; ChulymT –; NW^N Siberian Tatar *sap*;

(4) The Old Turkic initial *y-* preserved in Koibal and Kachin dialects of Yenisei Turkic, in Quu and Teleut dialects of Altai Turkic, and Siberian Tatar, while it changed to *č-* in Khakas and Shor of Yenisei Turkic, Tuvan and Tofan of Sayan Turkic, changed to *d'-* in Altai and Tuba of Altai Turkic and changed to *s-* in Yakut, to *h-* in Dolgan, in Chulym Turkic it fluctuates with *č-*, e.g.
  - Old Turkic *yat-* 'to lie down' ~ YeniseiT: Khakas; Shor *čat-*; Koibal, Kachin *yat-*; AltaiT: Altai; Tuba *d'at-*; Qumanda *čad-*; Teleut *yat-*; SayanT: Tuvan *čït-*; Tofan *čï^ct-*; ChulymT *čat-* ~ *yat-*; NE^N Yakut *sït-*; Dolgan *hït-*; NW^N Siberian Tatar –;
  - Old Turkic *yōl* 'road, way' ~ YeniseiT: Khakas; Shor *čol*; Koibal *yol*; AltaiT: Altai; Tuba *d'ol*; Qumanda *čol*; Quu; Teleut *yol*; SayanT –; ChulymT *čol* ~ *yol*; NE^N Yakut *suol*; Dolgan *huol*; NW^N Siberian Tatar *yul*;
  - Old Turkic *yǖz* 'hundred' ~ YeniseiT: Khakas; Shor *čüs*; Koibal, Kachin *yüs*; AltaiT: Altai; Tuba *d'üs*; Qumanda *čüs*; Quu; Teleut *yüs*; SayanT: Tuvan; Tofan *čüs*; ChulymT *yus* ~ *čus*; NE^N Yakut; Dolgan *sǖs*; NW^N Siberian Tatar *yüs*;

(5) The devoicing of initial **b-* in Yenisei Turkic, in Quu and Teleut dialects of Altai Turkic, in Chulym and sporadically in Siberian Tatar, e.g.
  - Old Turkic *bāy* 'rich' ~ YeniseiT: Khakas; Shor *pay*; AltaiT: Altai; Tuba; Qumanda *bay*; Quu; Teleut *pay*; SayanT: Tuvan; Tofan *bay*; ChulymT *pay*; NE^N Yakut; Dolgan *bāy*; NW^N Siberian Tatar *pay*;
  - Old Turkic *baš* 'head' ~ YeniseiT: Khakas *pas*; Shor *paš*; AltaiT: Altai; Tuba; Qumanda *baš*; Quu; Teleut *paš*; SayanT: Tuvan *baš*; Tofan *ba^cš*; ChulymT *paš* ~ *pas*; NE^N Yakut; Dolgan *bas*; NW^N Siberian Tatar *baš*;
  - Old Turkic *balïq* 'fish' ~ YeniseiT: Khakas *palïx*; Shor *palïq*; AltaiT: Altai; Tuba; Qumanda *balïq*; Quu; Teleut *palïq*; SayanT: Tuvan; Tofan *balïq*; ChulymT *pālïq*; NE^N Yakut; Dolgan *balïq*; NW^N Siberian Tatar *palïq*;

(6) The Old Turkic consonant *VδV* preserved in Sayan Turkic and devoiced in Yakut, while it represented as *VzV* in Yenisei Turkic and Chulym and as *VyV* in Altai Turkic and Siberian Tatar, e.g.
  - Old Turkic *aδaq* 'leg, foot' ~ YeniseiT: Khakas *azax*; Shor *azaq*; AltaiT: Altai; Tuba; Qumanda; Quu; Teleut *ayak*; SayanT: Tuvan; Tofan *adak*; ChulymT *azaq*; NE^N Yakut *atax*; Dolgan *atak*; NW^N Siberian Tatar *ayaq*;
  - Old Turkic *qoδan* 'hare' ~ YeniseiT: Khakas *xozan*; Shor *qozan*; AltaiT: Altai; Tuba; Qumanda; Quu; Teleut *koyon*; SayanT: Tuvan *kodan*; ChulymT *qozan* ~ *qoyan*; NE^N Yakut *xoton*; NW^N Siberian Tatar –;

- Old Turkic *bäδük* 'big' ~ YeniseiT: Khakas *pözĭk*; Shor *mözük*; AltaiT: Altai *biyik*; Tuba *biyik*; Qumanda *piyik*; Quu *pīk*; Teleut *piyik*; SayanT: Tuvan *bedik*; Tofan *bedĭk*; ChulymT –; NE^N –; NW^N Siberian Tatar *pöyük*;

(7) The Old Turkic initial sibilant consonant *s-* disappeared in Yakut and Dolgan, while in other mentioned Turkic languages it preserved, e.g.

- Old Turkic *sārïǧ* 'yellow' ~ NE^N Yakut, Dolgan *arī̮* 'butter'; cf. NE^S YeniseiT: Khakas; Sagai, Koibal, Kachin, Shor *sarïǧ*; Kyzyl *sārï·γ^x*; AltaiT: Altai; Tuba *sarï*; Qumanda *sarï* ~ *sārï*; Quu *sarū* ~ *sarï*; Teleut *sarï*; SayanT: Tuvan, Tofan *sarïǧ*; ChulymT *sārïǧ*; NW^N Siberian Tatar *sarï*;
- Old Turkic *sän* 'thou' ~ NE^N Yakut; Dolgan *än*; cf. YeniseiT: Khakas *sin*; Shor *sen*; AltaiT: Altai; Tuba; Qumanda; Quu; Teleut *sen*; SayanT: Tuvan; Tofan *sen*; ChulymT *sän*; NW^N Siberian Tatar *sen*;
- Old Turkic *sūt* 'milk' ~ NE^N Yakut *ǖt*; Dolgan *ǖt* ~ *üt*; cf. NE^S YeniseiT: Khakas *süt*; Sagai, Koibal, Kachin; Kyzyl; Shor *süt*; AltaiT: Altai; Tuba; Qumanda; Quu; Teleut *süt*; SayanT: Tuvan; Tofan *süt*; ChulymT *süt*; NW^N Siberian Tatar *söt*;

(8) The Old Turkic intervocalic and final nasal consonant *ń* changed to *y* in the mentioned Turkic languages, e.g.

- Old Turkic *qōń* 'sheep' ~ NE^S YeniseiT: Khakas *xoy*; Sagai, Koibal, Kachin *qoy*; Shor *qoy*; AltaiT: Altai *qoy*; Tuba; Qumanda; Quu *koy*; Teleut *qoy*; SayanT: Tuvan *xoy*; Tofan *hoy*; ChulymT *qoy*; NE^N Yakut –; NW^N Siberian Tatar *quy*;
- Old Turkic *qańaq* 'the skin on milk, clotted cream; sour cream' ~ NE^S YeniseiT: Khakas; Sagai *xayax*; Koibal, Kachin *qayaq*; Kyzyl *xaymax*; Shor *qaymaq*; AltaiT: Altai, Qumanda, Teleut *qaymaq* 'sour cream'; SayanT –; ChulymT *qaymaq*; NE^N Yakut *xayax*; NW^N Siberian Tatar *qaymaq*;

(9) The *vocal—consonant G—vocal* (*VGV*) and *vocal—consonant ŋ—vocal* (*VŋV*) sequences result in a secondary long vowel in the most Siberian Turkic languages, e.g.

- Old Turkic *aǧïz* 'mouth' ~ YeniseiT: Khakas, Shor *ās*; AltaiT: Altai, Tuba *ōs*; Qumanda *ās*; Quu *aǧïs*; SayanT: Tuvan, Tofan *ās*; ChulymT *ās*; NE^N Yakut; Dolgan *uos*; NW^N Siberian Tatar *aǧïs*;
- Old Turkic *aǧïl* 'a settlement or group of tents'~ NE^S YeniseiT: Khakas *āl*; Sagai, Koibal, Kachin, Kyzyl, Shor *āl*; AltaiT: –; SayanT: Tuvan, Tofan *āl*; ChulymT *aǧïl*; NE^N Yakut, Dolgan *ïal*; NW^N Siberian Tatar *avïl*;
- Old Turkic *süŋük* 'bone' ~ YeniseiT: Khakas; Shor *sȫk*; AltaiT: Altai, Tuba, Qumanda, Quu, Teleut *sȫk*; SayanT: Tuvan, Tofan *sȫk*; ChulymT *sȫk*; NE^N Yakut *uŋuox* ~ *umuox*;

– Old Turkic *yaŋaq* 'cheek' ~ YeniseiT: Khakas *nāx*; Shor *nāk*; AltaiT: Altai, Tuba *d'āk*; Qumanda *čāk*; Quu, Teleut *yāk*; SayanT: Tuvan *čāk*; Tofan *ńāk*; ChulymT –; NE[N] Yakut *süŋāx*; Dolgan *hüŋāk*; etc.

4.2 Yeniseian-Tungusic Studies

The research on Tungusic loanwords have not been discussed yet. The supposed Yeniseian loanwords in Ewenki can be explained by geographical, historical and cultural factors.

The territory along the Yenisei inhabited by Kets, is bordered from the east by the Ewenkis and from the west by the Selkups, one of the Samoyedic people. In 1606, when the historical connections between Yeniseian people and Ewenkis are documented, the right bank of Yenisei was settled by Ewenkis and Kotts.

From a cultural aspect, the lifestyle of Ket and Ewenki people had by now become reindeer-breeding. Their original religion was shamanism and they retained the same type of dwellings (Vasilevich & Smolyak 1956: 620; Popov & Dolgikh 1956: 607; Donner 1933: 19–28; 75–95).

According to Janhunen (2012: 47–48), a very small number of identifiable Ewenki cultural items seem to have been transmitted into Northern Ket. Similar items may be present in Yugh, but they have not yet been identified. The researchers who dealt with Ket (Dul'zon 1968: 13; Vajda 2004: 92; Timonina 2004: 135; Georg 2008: 154) also mentioned possible Ewenki-Ket linguistical interactions.

Geographically, the speakers not of all Ewenki dialects, only some of them have had the lingusitic contacts with Yeniseian people. They include those Ewenki people who live along Yenisei river, near areas the Ket people also inhabited. The other Ewenki dialects probably had linguistic contacts with the Yeniseian speakers only in the early period.

4.2.1 The Main Phonetic Features of the Ewenki Dialects

The Ewenki language[3] in Russia has 51 dialects, which can be grouped into northern, southern and eastern branches (Atkine 1997: 115; Bulatova 2002: 270–271):

---

3 The Ewenki language belongs to the Tungusic language family, traditionally believed to form the Altaic language family together with the Turkic and Mongolic languages. The speakers of language live in Russia, China and Mongolia, scattered over a vast territory. In Russia the Ewenki number approximately 37,100. They live in small groups of a few thousand people, very far from each other (Ewenki statistics in 2010: online): the Republic of Yakutia—21,008; the Krasnoyarsk Region—4,372; the Khabarovsk Region—4,101; the Republic of Buryatia—2,974; the Province of Amur—1,481; the Zabaikalsk Region—1,387; the Province of Irkutsk—1,272; the Province of Sakhalin—209 and other Provinces—312. On the geographical position

(1) The northern group:
- Yerbogochen (subdialects: Yerbogachon, Nakanno);
- Ilimpeya (subdialects: Ilimpeya, Agata, Tura, Tutonchany, Dudinka or Khantai);

(2) The southern group:
- The hissing type (sibilant *s*):
  - Podkamennyi (subdialects: Vanavara, Kuyumba, Poligus, Surinda, Taimura or Chirinda, Uchami, Chemdalsk);
  - Nepa (subdialects: Nepa, Kirensk);
  - Vitim-Nercha (subdialects: Baunt, Nercha, Talocha, Tungukochan);
- The hushing type (sibilant *š*):
  - Sym (subdialects: Tokma or Upper Nepa, Upper Lena or Kachug, Angara);
  - North-Baikal (subdialects: North-Baikal, Upper Lena);

(3) The eastern group:
- Vitim-Olyokma (subdialects: Barguzin, Vitim or Kalar, Olyokma, Tungir, Tokko);
- Upper Aldan (subdialects: Aldan, Upper Amur, Amga, Dzheltulak, Timpton, Tommot, Kingan, Chulman, Chulman-Gilyui);
- Uchur-Zeya (subdialects: Uchur, Zeya);
- Selemdzha-Bureya-Urmi (subdialects: Selemdzha, Bureya, Urmi);
- Ayan-Mai (subdialects: Ayan, Aim, Mai, Nelkan, Totti);
- Tugur-Chumikan (subdialects: Tugur, Chumikan);
- Sakhalin.

Literary or Standard Ewenki is based on the Podkamennyi dialect, which belongs to the southern branch.

The scatterred nature of their territorial distribution explains why there is no possibility for developing a real literary language. In everyday life each speaker uses his/her own dialect (Bulatova 2002: 271).

Linguistically, the Ewenki dialects were examined in detail by Vasilevič (1948), who described linguistic peculiarities with texts examples.[4] The biggest

---

of the Ewenki dialects in Russia, see the appended map in Vasilevič's dictionary (1958) and her monograph (1948: 18).

4 The material which was used for this work was based on her early publication, where she published data only on the Yerbogachen dialect of the northern group and the Nepa and the Sym dialects of the southern group (Vasilevič 1934). She clearly distinguishes the northern and the southern groups but pays less attention to the eastern group. According to her, the eastern group presents a mosaic picture and shares typical peculiarities of both groups equally (Vasilevič 1948: 15). It is important to note that only some Ewenki dialects as Yerbogochen, Ilimpeya, Podkamennyi, Nepa, Uchur-Zeya, Selemdzha-Urmi, Sym, Tokmin, Upper

lexical material of almost all Ewenki dialects is found in the dictionary by Vasilevič (1958). Also, the Ewenki-Russian (2000) and Russian-Ewenki (1994) dictionaries by Boldyrev should be mentioned.

The descriptive grammars of the Literary Ewenki language in Russian were written by Vasilevič (1940), Konstantinova (1963) as well as co-authored by Lebedeva, Konstantinova and Monakhova (1985). These monographs mostly focused on phonetics and morphology. The Ewenki grammars in English were prepared by Nedjalkov (1997), Bulatova and Grenoble (1999).

A detailed and good introduction into Ewenki studies in Russia was given by Atkine (1997: 109–114). See also Khabtagaeva (2017: 17–25).

From a geographical and linguistic points of view, the following dialects with their subdialects[5] are the most important sources for a research on Ewenki-Yeniseian contacts:
– the Yerbogachon and Ilimpeya dialects of the northern Ewenki group;
– the 'hissing' Podkamennyi and Nepa dialects of the southern Ewenki group;
– the 'hushing' Sym dialect of the southern Ewenki group.

The main phonetic features of the northern and southern Ewenki dialectal groups are the following:
(1) The original Tungusic consonant *s in an initial and intervocalic positions changed to *h* in the northern group, while in the southern group it changed to *s* and *š*, e.g.
  – 'to know': Yerbogachon, Ilimpeya *hā-*; Podkamennyi, Nep *sā-*; Sym *šā-*;
  – 'very': Yerbogachon, Ilimpeya *hō*; Podkamennyi, Nep *sō*; Sym *šō*;
  – 'you': Yerbogachon, Ilimpeya *hi*; Podkamennyi, Nep *si*; Sym *ši*;
  – 'woman': Yerbogachon, Ilimpeya *ahī*; Podkamennyi, Nep *asī*; Sym *ašī*;
  – 'eye': Yerbogachon, Ilimpeya *ēha*; Podkamennyi, Nep *ēsa*; Sym *ēša*;
  – 'forest': Yerbogachon, Ilimpeya *mōha*; Podkamennyi, Nep *mōsa*; Sym *mōša*;
(2) The original Tungusic initial consonant *h-* in the northern and 'hissing' southern groups preserved, while in the 'hushing' southern group it disappeared, e.g.
  – 'hammer': Yerbogachon, Ilimpeya; Podkamennyi, Nep *halka*; Sym *alka*;

Lena, Tungir and Sakhalin were examined in this work. The dialects of Yakutia and Buryatia were not studied here. The Ewenki dialects of Yakutia (Tokko, Tommot, Uchur, Mai, Totti) were described later by Romanova and Myreeva (1962, 1964).

5 The detailed list of subdialects see below.

INTRODUCTION 19

- 'knee': Yerbogachon, Ilimpeya; Podkamennyi, Nep *heŋŋen*; Sym *eŋŋen*;
- 'road, way': Yerbogachon, Ilimpeya; Podkamennyi, Nep *hokto*; Sym *okto*;

(3) The consonant *g* preserved intervocally in the northern and 'hissing' southern groups, while in the 'hushing' southern group it yielded a long vowel or diphthong, e.g.
- 'in winter': Yerbogachon, Ilimpeya; Podkamennyi, Nep *tuγe*; Sym *tuwe ~ tue*;
- 'fire': Yerbogachon, Ilimpeya; Podkamennyi, Nep *toγo*; Sym *towo ~ tō*;
- 'people, tribe': Yerbogachon, Ilimpeya; Podkamennyi, Nep *teγē*;

(4) The sporadic change of the intervocalic consonant *w*, e.g.
- 'cap': Ilimpeya *abūn*; Yerbogachon *aūn*; Podkamennyi, Nep; Sym *awūn*;
- 'widow, widower': Yerbogachon, Ilimpeya; Podkamennyi *nawun ~ naun*, Nep *nawun*; Sym *naun*;

(5) The sporadic change of the Tungusic consonant sequences **ld*, **nd*, **md* and **rd*, e.g.
- 'meat': Yerbogachon, Podkamennyi, Nep *ulle*; Ilimpeya *ulde*;
- 'skin': Yerbogachon, Podkamennyi, Nep *nanna*; Ilimpeya, Sym *nanda*;
- 'bone': Yerbogachon, Podkamennyi, Nep *giramna*; Ilimpeya *giramda*;

(6) The original initial consonant *ŋ-* preserved in the mentioned dialects, e.g.
- 'long': Yerbogachon, Ilimpeya; Podkamennyi, Nep; Sym *ŋōnim*;
- 'heel': Yerbogachon, Ilimpeya; Podkamennyi, Nep; Sym *ŋiŋtï*;
- 'straight': Yerbogachon, Ilimpeya; Podkamennyi, Nep *ŋuŋne*;

(7) The original initial consonant *ń-* preserved in the mentioned dialects, e.g.
- 'sky': Yerbogachon, Ilimpeya; Podkamennyi, Nep, Sym *ńaŋńa*;
- 'cloud': Podkamennyi, Nep; Sym *ńekte*;
- 'thigh; shine bone': Yerbogachon, Ilimpeya; Podkamennyi, Nep *ńuŋi*;

(8) The original initial consonant *k-* preserved in the mentioned dialects, e.g.
- 'long cutlass on a stick (Russian *пальмá*)': Yerbogachon, Ilimpeya; Podkamennyi, Nep; Sym *koto*;
- 'pot, cauldron': Yerbogachon, Ilimpeya; Podkamennyi, Nep; Sym *kalan*;
- 'many': Yerbogachon, Ilimpeya; Podkamennyi, Nep; Sym *kete*; etc.

CHAPTER 2

Turkic Loanwords

1　Etymology

This section deals with the etymology of Turkic loanwords in the Yeniseian languages. The loanwords are grouped according to word classes, i.e. nouns, adjectives verbs, adverbs, conjunctions, prepositions and particles.

1.1　*Nouns*

1.1.1　Inanimate Nature

Arin *ba[g]akulak* 'mussel' (Werner 2002/1: 109) ← Turkic *baǵa qulaq 'mussel' (cf. Khakas *paǵa xulaǵï*) < *baqa* 'frog' + *qulaq* 'ear':
< *baǵa* < *baqa* 'frog':

cf. Old Turkic *baqa*; NE^S YeniseiT: Khakas; Sagai; Shor *paǵa*; AltaiT: Altai *baqa*; Tuba; Teleut *paqa*; Qumanda; Quu *baka*; SayanT: Tuvan *paǵa*; Tofan *baǵa*; ChulymT *maǵa*; NE^N Yakut *baǵa*; Dolgan –; NW^N Siberian Tatar *paǵa* ~ *maǵa* ~ *maqa* ~ *baxa*; NW^S Kirgiz *baka*; Fu-yü –; Kazak *baqa*; SE Yellow Uyghur *paqa*;

Etymology: Räsänen VEWT 58a; Rassadin 1971: 159; Clauson ED 311b; ESTJa 1978: 40–42; SIGTJa 2001: 179–180

+ *qulaq* 'ear':

cf. Old Turkic *qulaq* ~ *qulqaq*; NE^S YeniseiT: Khakas *xulax*; Sagai, Koibal, Kachin; Shor *qulaq*; Kyzyl *χulaχ*; AltaiT: Altai; Tuba; Qumanda; Quu; Teleut *qulaq*; SayanT: Tuvan; Tofan *qulaq*; ChulymT *qulaq*; NE^N Yakut *kulgāx*; Dolgan *kulgā(k)* ~ *kulgak*; NW^N Siberian Tatar *qulaq*; NW^S Kirgiz *kulak*; Fu-yü *gulah*; Kazak *qulaq*; SE Yellow Uyghur *qolaq*.

Etymology: Räsänen VEWT 298b; Clauson ED 621a; ESTJa 2000: 124–127, 131; SIGTJa 2001: 204–206; Khabtagaeva 2015d: 141

The Arin compound was possibly borrowed from Yenisei Turkic, cf. Khakas *paǵa xulaǵï* 'mussel' (*lit.* frog ear-poss.sg.3). The semantic change from 'frog ear' to 'mussel' surely deserves attention. The Turkic compound is provided with the possessive marker of the 3rd person +*X*, whereas the Arin form has apparently lost it.

Arin **balǥaš bore** 'dirt' (Werner 2002/1: 99) ← Turkic **balǥaš boro* 'dirty (thing)'
< *balǥaš* 'dirty' + *boro* 'grey':
< **balǥaš* 'mud; dirty, dirtiness' < *balqaš*:
    cf. Old Turkic –;[1] NEˢ YeniseiT: Khakas *palǥas* ~ *palǥaš*; Sagai, Koibal *palǥas*; Kyzyl *palyaˑš*; Shor *palǥaš*; AltaiT: Altai *balkaš*; Tuba *balǥaš*; Qumanda *malgaš* ~ *malgač*; Quu *palǥaš*; Teleut *palqaš*; SayanT: Tuvan *malgaš*; Tofan *baᶜlhaš*; ChulymT *palcïq* (R); NEᴺ –; NWᴺ Siberian Tatar –; NWˢ Kirgiz –; Fu-yü *balgaš*; Kazak *balqaš*; SE Yellow Uyghur –;
Turkic → Samoyedic:
    Kamas *balyaš* 'dirt, mud'; Mator *balgaš* 'dirt, swamp, mud'.
Etymology: Joki LS 81; Räsänen VEWT 60a; Rassadin 1971: 158; Clauson ED 333a; Helimski 1997: 214; ESTJa 2003: 102–105; Róna-Tas & Berta WOT 2011: 86–87
+ *boro* 'grey' ← Mongolic *boro* ← Turkic **bōrŏ* < *bōz*:
    cf. NEˢ YeniseiT: Khakas; Sagai, Koibal; Shor *pora*; AltaiT: Altai *boro*; Tuba *bor(o)* 'grey (colour of horse)', cf. *poro* 'grey'; Qumanda *boro* 'grey-brown', cf. *poro* 'grey'; Quu *boro*; Teleut *poro*; SayanT: Tuvan; Tofan *bora*; ChulymT *pora*; NEᴺ Yakut *boroŋ*; Dolgan *boroŋ*; NWᴺ Siberian Tatar –; NWˢ Kirgiz –; Fu-yü *bor* 'violet' (?); Kazak –; SE Yellow Uyghur –;
Turkic → Samoyedic:
    Kamas *bora* 'grey'; Mator *bora* 'grey-blackish horse';
Turkic ← Mongolic *boro* 'grey':
    cf. Middle Mongol: Precl.Mo; SH; HY *boro*; Muq. *bora*; LM *boro* ~ *bora*; Modern Mongol: Buryat *boro*; Khalkha *bor*; Kalmuck *borᵒ*; Dagur *bor* (E); Khamnigan *boro*;
Mongolic ← Bulghar Turkic **borŏ* < *bōz* 'grey':
    cf. Old Turkic *bōz*; NEˢ YeniseiT: –; AltaiT: Altai –; Tuba *bos* 'grey'; Qumanda *pos* 'grey', cf. *pus* 'whitish colour of horse'; Quu *pos*; Teleut *pos*; SayanT: Tuvan *bos* 'gray duck; drake'; Tofan *bos* 'mallard'; ChulymT –; NEᴺ Yakut –; NWᴺ Siberian Tatar *büz* 'white'; NWˢ Kirgiz *boz* 'light grey'; Fu-yü *bos* 'grey'; Kazak *boz* 'earthy-gray; feather grass'; light grey; SE Yellow Uyghur *poz* 'reddish color; white gray'.
Etymology: Joki LS 96; Räsänen VEWT 82a; Doerfer TMEN 2: 335–336; Ščerbak SF 196; 1997: 109; Rassadin 1971: 164; 1980: 6, 24, 38, 39, 47, 49, 60, 72; Clauson ED 388b; ESTJa 1978: 171–173; Schönig 2000: 72; SIGTJa 1997: 605–606; Helimski 1997: 220; Khabtagaeva 2009: 267; Nugteren 2011: 285

The Arin compound word consists of the Turkic words *balǥaš* 'mud; dirty, dirtiness' and *boro* 'grey'. However, the structure of the Arin compound shows an atypical combination of Yeniseian and Turkic elements. The regular word

---

1 Cf. another Old Turkic form *balčïq* 'mud', which goes back to the base **bal±* with the diminutive suffix +*čAK*.

order should be Adjective + Noun. I agree with Georg's opinion (2016: personal communication) that the Arin compound consists of two Turkic adjectives 'dirty and grey (thing)'. The Arin compound word was probably borrowed from Siberian Turkic. Both Turkic words were borrowed into Samoyedic (cf. Joki LS 81, 96; Helimski 1997: 214, 220).

As concerns the etymology of the Turkic word *balqaš* 'mud; dirty, dirtiness', the base is **bal±* with a rare deverbal noun Turkic suffix *-kAč ~ -kAš*, which is connected to the diminutive suffix *+(X)č* (ESTJa 2003: 102–105). According to Clauson (ED 333a), the Turkic word *balčïq ~ balqač* 'mud; dirty, dirtiness' displays metathesis. It is more correct to differentiate between *balčïq* and *balqaš*, both of them go back to **bal±*² with different suffixes (Róna-Tas 2016: personal communication).

Arin ***berkitak*** 'mountain' (Werner 2002/1: 122) ← Turkic *berke tag < *berke* 'big' + *taġ* 'mountain':
< *berke* 'big, great' ← Turkic *berke* 'clever, deft' ← Mongolic *berke* 'difficult, hard; burdensome, troublesome; complicated, serious; difficulty, hardship; trouble; skillful, competent, fit' ← Turkic *bärkĂ < *bärk* 'firm, stable, solid':

cf. NE^S YeniseiT: –; AltaiT: Quu *perge* 'clever, deft'; SayanT: Tuvan *berge* 'difficult'; ChulymT –; NE^N Yakut *berke* '*adverb* very, very much, strongly; fine'; Dolgan *bärkä ~ bärgä* '*adj.* strong; *adv.* very much'; NW^N Siberian Tatar *berägäy* 'fine'; NW^S Kirgiz –; Fu-yü; SE Yellow Uyghur –;

Turkic ← Mongolic *berke* 'difficult, hard; burdensome, troublesome; complicated, serious; difficulty, hardship; trouble; skillful, competent, fit':

cf. Middle Mongol: Precl.Mo. *berke*; SH *berke* 'difficult'; Ibn-Muh. *berke*; Muq. *bürke* 'strong'; HY *berke* 'difficult'; LM *berke*; Modern Mongol: Buryat *berxe*; Khalkha *berx*; Kalmuck *berkä*; Dagur *berke* (T); Khamnigan *berke ~ börke*;

Mongolic ← Bulghar Turkic *bärkĂ > *bärk* 'firm, stable':

cf. Old Turkic *bärk* 'firm, stable, solid'; NE^S YeniseiT: Khakas *pirīk* 'impenetrable'; AltaiT: –; SayanT: Tuvan *bert* 'impenetrable'; Tofan *be^crt* 'kind, good'; ChulymT *pērek* 'difficult'; NE^N Yakut *bert* 'excellent, beautiful; *particle* very, completely, entirely'; Dolgan *bär ~ bärt* 'strong; *adv.* very; *adj.* excellent, wonderful; better; great'; NW^N Siberian Tatar –; NW^S Kirgiz *berk* 'strong; very'; Fu-yü –; Kazak *berĭk* 'strong, solid, stable'; SE Yellow Uyghur *perĭk ~ perk* 'big, important', cf. *perĭk* 'strong'.

Etymology: Räsänen VEWT 71a; Clauson ED 361b; ESTJa 1978: 119; Rassadin 1980: 60, 64; Khabtagaeva 2009: 267

---

2 Cf. Hungarian *balkány* [bålkāń] 'soggy place, moor, swamp, marsh' ← West Old Turkic *balkan < **bal-* 'to become wet, marshy' *+GAn* {Turkic VN} (Róna-Tas & Berta WOT 2011: 86).

+ *taġ < tāġ 'mountain':
   cf. Old Turkic tāġ; NE^S YeniseiT: Khakas; Sagai, Koibal, Kachin; Kyzyl; Shor taġ; AltaiT: Altai; Tuba; Teleut tū; Qumanda; Quu tag; SayanT: Tuvan; Tofan daġ; ChulymT tag; NE^N Yakut; Dolgan tïa 'land; forest, tundra'; NW^N Siberian Tatar tau; NW^S Kirgiz tō; Fu-yü dah; Kazak tau̇; SE Yellow Uyghur taġ.

Etymology: Räsänen VEWT 454a; Ščerbak SF 197; Clauson ED 463a; ESTJa 1980: 117–119; SIGTJa 1997: 94

The Arin analyzed element probably belongs in the category of compound words. It consists of the Turkic words berke and taġ 'mountain'. berke functions in the Arin language as a half-affix meaning 'great, big' and also occurs in other Arin compound words (see section *Compound words*).

In this function it also occurs, a.o., in Sayan Turkic (Ragagnin 2015: personal communication).

Arin **dalaj ~ dolaj** 'sea' (Werner 2002/1: 170) ← Turkic dalay 'sea' ← Mongolic dalai 'sea' ← Turkic taluy 'sea':
   cf. Old Turkic –; NE^S YeniseiT: –; AltaiT: –; SayanT: Tuvan dalay; Tofan dalay; ChulymT –; NE^N Yakut dalay; Dolgan –; NW^N Siberian Tatar –; NW^S Kirgiz dalay 'much, many, a big number'; Fu-yü dalay 'sea'; Kazak –; SE Yellow Uyghur –;

Turkic ← Mongolic dalai 'ocean, sea, great lake; much, many, in great number of quanity; universal, great':
   cf. Middle Mongol: Precl.Mo.; SH; HY; ZY; Muq. dalai 'sea'; LM dalai; Modern Mongol: Buryat dalai; Lower Uda Buryat dalā̆; Khalkha dalai; Oirat dial. dalā̆; Kalmuck dalǟ ~ dalā; Dagur dalī (E); Khamnigan dalai;

Mongolic ← Turkic taluy 'sea':
   cf. Old Turkic taluy; NE^S YeniseiT: Khakas talay; Sagai, Koibal, Kachin talay (R); Kyzyl tala·y; Shor talay; AltaiT: Altai talay; Tuba talay; Qumanda talay; Quu talay 'a sea, a big lake'; Teleut talay; SayanT: Tuvan dalay (← Mongolic); Tofan dalay; ChulymT –; NE^N Yakut dalay; Dolgan –; NW^N Siberian Tatar talay 'much, many'; NW^S Kirgiz dalay 'much, many, a big number'; Fu-yü dalay 'sea'; Kazak talay 'some, many'; SE Yellow Uyghur taley ~ talī̆ 'lake, sea, ocean';

Turkic → Samoyedic:
   Kamas talai 'sea'; Mator talaj 'sea'.

Etymology: Joki LS 115; Kałużyński 1962: 36; Räsänen VEWT 130b; Doerfer TMEN 1: 324–326; 1985: 125; Rassadin 1971: 168; 1980: 13; Clauson ED 502a; Ščerbak 1997: 169; Helimski 1997: 350; Anikin 2000: 177; Tatarincev 2002: 70; Khabtagaeva 2009: 151; Nugteren 2011: 311

It is not clear whether the Arin word was borrowed directly from Mongolic or from Siberian Turkic dalai. There are parallel Arin forms displaying unrounded -a- and rounded -o- vowels in the first syllable, possibly due to internal Yeniseian vowel change.

Tuvan (Tatarincev 2002: 70; Khabtagaeva 2009: 151), Tofan, Yakut (Kałużyński 1962: 36) and Fu-yü forms were reborrowed from Mongolic (← Turkic). *Dalai* belongs in the 'wanderwort' category and may ultimately be of Chinese origin; for details, see Doerfer TMEN 1: 324–326; Clauson ED 502a; Ščerbak 1997: 169; Nugteren 2011: 311.

The Samoyedic forms possibly with initial consonant *t-* were borrowed from Siberian Turkic (Joki LS 115; Helimski 1997: 350), while the Tungusic[3] (SSTMJa 1: 193a; Doerfer 1985: 125) and Siberian Russian (Anikin 2000: 177) forms with initial consonant *d-* were borrowed from Mongolic.

Kott **kalšu** 'undergrowth-covered riverbank' (Werner 2002/1: 407) ← Turkic **kolčak* (cf. AltaiT: Quu dial.) < *qol* 'the upper part of a valley' +*čAK* {Turkic NN/diminutive, see Erdal 1991: 44} ← Mongolic *γol* 'river, river bed':
    cf. Old Turkic *qol* 'valley' (DTS); cf. *qōl* 'the upper part of a valley < the upper arm' (ED); NE^S YeniseiT: Khakas *xol* 'valley; dry river bed; ravine'; Sagai *qol* 'lowland' (R); Shor *qol* 'ravine, valley' (ShR), cf. 'very small river' (R); AltaiT: Quu *kolujak* 'small river'; SayanT: Tuvan *xol* 'dry river bed'; ChulymT –; NE^N Yakut –; NW^N Siberian Tatar –; NW^S Kirgiz *kol* 'river bed, river valley (*in geographic names*)'; Fu-yü –; Kazak –; SE Yellow Uyghur *qol* 'river bed';
Turkic ← Mongolic *γool* ~ *γol* 'river; river bed; valley; large lake (*rare*)':
    cf. Middle Mongol: SH *qol* 'mountain brook'; LM *γool*; Modern Mongol: Buryat *gol*; Khalkha *gol*; Kalmuck *gol*; Dagur *gol'* (E); Khamnigan *gol* (D).

Etymology: Räsänen VEWT 277a; DTS 453b; Clauson ED 614b–615a; Ščerbak SF 194; SIGTJa 2001: 90–91; Nugteren 2011: 343

The etymology of the Kott word may be connected with Altai Turkic *kolčak* 'small river', which derived from *qol* 'valley, river' and the Turkic diminutive suffix +*čAK*. My assumption may be strengthened by the change of Turkic *č* → Kott *š* in different positions and the change of Turkic rounded vowels *-o-* and *-u-* in the first syllable to unrounded vowel *-a-* (e.g. *kalôx* 'ear' ← Turkic *qulaq*, *kalkul* 'deaf' ← Turkic *qulγur* 'crop-eared'). Such changes occur in some Kott loanwords.

The etymology of the Turkic word *qol* 'valley, river' is unclear. According to Clauson, besides the meaning 'the upper part of a valley', this word has several additional metaphorical meanings in Turkic, such as 'the upper arm', 'a wing of an army', 'the central ridge of a sword or knife', or 'small hills on the flank of a mountain which abut on the plains' (ED 614b–615a). Ščerbak (1970: SF 194)

---

3 Turkic → Mongolic → Northern Tungusic: Barguzin Ewenki *dalai* 'sea, lake Baikal'; Solon *dalɛi* 'sea'.

reconstructed the Proto-Turkic form *kōl 'lowland, ravine, dry river bed; inflow', whereas Räsänen (VEWT 277a) connected the Turkic data with Mongolic.

Arin *kar* 'mountain' (Werner 2002/1: 411) ← Turkic *qïr* 'mountain':
cf. Old Turkic *qïr* 'an isolated mountain or block of mountains'; NE[S] YeniseiT: Khakas *xïr* 'mountain, mountain range, hill', cf. 'a roof of yurta' (But.); Sagai, Koibal, Kachin *qïr* 'corner, edge' (R); Kyzyl *χer ~ χər* 'high bank; small mountain, hill'; Shor *qïr* 'mountain range; edge'; AltaiT: Altai *kïr* 'mountain, mountain range; hill'; Tuba *kïr* 'mountain; edge, margin'; Qumanda *kïr* 'mountain, mountain range'; Quu *kïr* 'mountain, mountain range; edge'; Teleut *qïr* 'hill' (R); SayanT: Tuvan *kïr* 'edge; mountain range; upper surface'; Tofan *qïr* 'edge; butt of a knife; mountain range'; ChulymT *qïr* 'corner, edge' (R), cf. 'arable land, beach' (Bir.); NE[N] Yakut –; NW[N] Siberian Tatar *qïr* 'beach; earth, land'; NW[S] Kirgiz *kïr* 'mountain range, hill, edge; upper surface'; Fu-yü *gïr* 'knoll, hill, mountain ridge'; Kazak *qïr* 'hill; edge; mountain range'; SE Yellow Uyghur *qïrgïl* (? < *qïr* +*lXG* {Turkic NN, see Malov 1957: 164}) 'stone cliff, rock'.

Etymology: Doerfer TMEN 3: 567–568; Räsänen VEWT 265b; Clauson ED 641a; ESTJa 2000: 225–227; SIGTJa 1997: 95–96

The Arin word is probably of Turkic origin. The source was the Siberian Turkic form *kïr. From a phonetic perspective, the change of Turkic -*ï*- > -*a*-, as in Kott loanwords, occurred in Arin.

The Turkic word is widespread in almost all Turkic languages. The Turkic was borrowed into Mongolic[4] (Doerfer TMEN 3: 567–568) and re-borrowed into Siberian Turkic[5] (Khabtagaeva 2009: 193). From Mongolic, the word copied to Tungusic[6] (SSTMJa 1: 397; Rozycki 1994: 106).

---

4 Turkic *qïrǎ → Mongolic: cf. Middle Mongol: –; LM *kir-a* 'summit or ridge of a mountain, small mountain chain; foothills; slope; a strip (*usually of horn*) attached to the front and rear edges of the saddle'; Modern Mongol: Buryat *xyara* 'mountain range'; Khalkha *xyar* 'ridge, crest (*geog.*); ornamental trimming on a saddle-bow'; Oirat dial. *kiŕi ~ kir ~ kiŕi* 'mountain range; an edge of saddle'; Dagur *kira* (T); Khamnigan *kira*.
5 Turkic → Mongolic → Modern Turkic: Tuvan *xïra* 'a strip attached to the front and rear edges of the saddle'; Khakas *xïra* 'arable land, plowed field'; Shor; Sagai, Koibal, Kachin, Altai, Teleut, Quu *qïra* 'field, an arable field' (R); Siberian Tatar *qïra* 'arable land'.
6 Turkic → Mongolic → Tungusic: *Northern Ewenki*: Yerbogachon; *Southern Ewenki*: Podkamennyi, Sym; *Eastern Ewenki*: Zeya *kira* 'edge, side; surface; corner'; Lamut *qirγ ~ qirʼn* 'corner; mountain range; side'; Negidal *kēja* 'flint'; Oroch *kia ~ kija* 'edge'; Udihe *keæ* 'edge, beach'; Ulcha *qira* 'edge; beach; edge of a wood'; Orok *qira* 'edge; beach'; Nanai *qira* 'edge; beach; edge of a wood'; Manchu *hirγa ~ hirha* 'flint'.

Kott *kem* 'river' (Werner 2002/1: 422) ← ? Turkic **käm* 'river':

cf. Old Turkic *käm* 'Yenissei river' (R), cf. *kem* 'the name of river' (DTS); NE^S YeniseiT: –; AltaiT: –; SayanT: Tuvan *xem* 'river'; Tofan *hem* 'river'; Remaining lgs. –.

Etymology: Räsänen VEWT 250a; Rassadin 1971: 94, 188; Vásáry 1971: 469–482; Helimski 2000: 352; Anikin 2000: 281

The etymology of the word is unknown. Werner (2002/1: 422) points outlines the Turkic loanword, while Rassadin (1971: 94, 188) connects Turkic forms with Yeniseian. In any case, the Turkic and Yeniseian words are undoubtedly connected to each other. According to the authors DTS (1969: 297a), the first Old Turkic data were mentioned in the source *Inscription to Moyun Chur*, written in Runic script around 759 in the territory of Mongolia. Today the word is found only in the Sayan Turkic languages Tuvan and Tofan, and also in Siberian Russian (Anikin 2000: 281) and Samoyedic (Helimski 2000: 352) languages. Vásáry (1971) in details discussed the occurrence of the word *käm* in the different Turkic, Chinese and Finno-Ugric sources. Finally, he concludes the word was borrowed into Turkic from Samoyedic languages. Later, Helimski (2000: 306–307) confuted Vásáry's opinion about Samoyedic origin of the word. Anikin (2000: 281) regards the Turkic word as a 'substrate element'. The word belongs to the category of words of unknown etymology.

Arin *mintora* 'ice' (Werner 2002/2: 20) ← Turkic **mindir* 'hail' ← Mongolic *möndür* 'hail':

cf. NE^S YeniseiT: Khakas *mindïr*; Sagai, Koibal *mündür* (R); Kachin *mündür*; Shor *mündür*; AltaiT: Altai *möndür*; Quu *möndür*; SayanT: Tuvan –; Tofan *möndür*; ChulymT –; NE^N Yakut –; NW^N Siberian Tatar *münder* ~ *münser*; NW^S Kirgiz *möndür*; Fu-yü *mündür* 'hailstone'; Kazak –; SE Yellow Uyghur *mendor*;

Turkic ← Mongolic *möndür* 'hail, sleet':

Middle Mongol: HY; ZY; YY *mündür*; Muq. *möndür*; RH *möndür*; LM *möndür*; Modern Mongol: Buryat *münder*; Khalkha *möndör*; Oirat dial. *möndär* ~ *möndür*; Dagur *murtul* (E); Khamnigan *münder* ~ *möndör*.

Etymology: Räsänen VEWT 341b; Rassadin 1980: 28, 36, 44, 47, 48; ESTJa 2003: 79; SIGTJa 1997: 32–33; Nugteren 2011: 448

The word was borrowed from the Siberian Turkic form **mindir* 'hail' (cf. Khakas). From a phonetic perspective, the paragoge occurred in Yeniseian word. From semantic side, the lexical change 'hail' → 'ice' occurred. The disappearance of vowel harmony is regular.

The base of Mongolic word is possibly **mö*, cf. also *mölsün* 'ice' (Nugteren 2011: 448).

Kott *šurgan* 'cold weather' (Werner 2002/2: 443) ← Turkic **šūrgan* 'snowstorm, storm' ← Mongolic *siγurγan* 'snowstorm, blizzard; storm with cold rain' < *siγur-* 'to rage (*as a storm*); a blizzard or snowstorm breaks out' -*GAn* {Mongolic VN, see Poppe GWM § 149}:

cf. NE^S YeniseiT: –; AltaiT: Altai *šūrġan* 'blizzard, snowstorm'; Tuba *sïrgïn* 'strong wind'; Quu *šūrġan* 'snowstorm' (R); Teleut *sïrgïn* 'draught' (R); SayanT: Tuvan *šūrgan* 'storm, hurricane'; Tofan *šūr* 'sandstorm'; Remaining lgs. –;

Turkic ← Mongolic *šūrgan* < *siγurγan*:

Middle Mongol: –; LM *siγurγan* 'snowstorm, blizzard; storm with cold rain' < *siγur-* 'to rage (*as a storm*); a blizzard or snowstorm breaks out'; Modern Mongol: Buryat *šūrga(n)* 'storm'; Khalkha *šūrga* 'storm, blizzard'; Kalmuck *šūrγan* 'snowstorm, blizzard'; Dagur *šōroγ* (E); Khamnigan *šūrga*.

Etymology: Rassadin 1980: 24, 30; Anikin 2000: 710; SIGTJa 2001: 49;[7] Khabtagaeva 2009: 153; Nugteren 2011: 494

The Kott word was borrowed from Siberian Turkic form **šūrgan* (cf. Altai Turkic, Tuvan). Shortening of the Turkic secondary long vowel occurred.

The Turkic word has a clear Mongolic etymology (Rassadin 1980: 24, 30; SIGTJa 2001: 49; Khabtagaeva 2009: 153). The Mongolic word originated from the verb *siγur-* 'to rage (*as a storm*); a blizzard or snowstorm breaks out' and the productive deverbal Mongolic suffix -*GAn* (for the function of Mongolic suffix, see Poppe GWM § 149). The Turkic word was borrowed in the later period from a Modern Mongol variety, where the secondary vowel had already developed. The Mongolic secondary long vowel developed according to the second vowel: *igu* > *ū*. In Modern Turkic languages, the secondary long vowel developed according to the first vowel.[8]

The word was probably borrowed directly from Mongolic to Tungusic[9] (SST-MJa 2: 119a; Rozycki 1994: 195–196) and Siberian Russian (Anikin 2000: 710).

Arin *laj* 'marsh' (Werner 2002/2: 1) ← Turkic **lay* 'slime, sludge, mud' ← Persian:

cf. Old Turkic –; NE^S YeniseiT: –; AltaiT: –; SayanT –; ChulymT –; NE^N Yakut –; NW^N Siberian Tatar *lay* 'slime, sludge, mud'; NW^S Kirgiz *layka* 'slime, sludge' (?); Fu-yü –;

---

[7] Tenišev compares the Mongolic verb with the Turkic reconstructed verb **sïr-*, cf. Bashkir *härma* 'snowdrift; wet sticky snow', Tatar *säründä ~ säräntä* 'snow drift', which is not clear.

[8] E.g. Old Turkic *oġul* 'sun, boy' → Tuvan *ōl*, Old Turkic *aġïr* 'heavy' > Altai *ār*, Old Turkik *säŋir* 'a projecting part of mountain' > Altai Qumanda *sēr*, etc. (For more examples and explanation how it works in Mongolic loanwords, see Rassadin 1980: 20–21; Khabtagaeva 2009: 42–52).

[9] Mongolic → Tungusic: Southern Ewenki: Nercha *surgan* 'snowstorm'; Manchu *šurγa* 'snow blown by the wind; blowing sand'.

Kazak *lay* 'slime; dirt, clay'; SE Yellow Uyghur –; Tarachin Uyghur *lay* 'clay, dirt, mud, sludge' (R);
Turkic ← Persian *lāy* 'black viscous mud';
cf. Turkic: Yakut *lāyda* 'coastal plain near to sea' ← Russian *лайда* 'mudbank' (Vasmer 1986/2: 451) ← Uralic.

Etymology: Räsänen VEWT 314a; SSTMJa 1: 487a; Vasmer 1986/2: 451; SIGTJa 1997: 376; Anikin 2000: 349

Arin *laj* 'marsh' was probably borrowed from the Siberian Turkic form *lai* 'slime, sludge, mud', which nowadays is present in Siberian Tatar.

From an etymological aspect, the Turkic word is possibly of Persian origin (Räsänen VEWT 314a; SIGTJa 1997: 376). The Yakut form *lāyda* 'coastal plain near to sea' does not have connection with other Turkic forms, it was possibly borrowed from the Russian. In turn, the Russian *лайда* 'mudbank' is regarded as a Uralic loanword (Vasmer 1986/2: 451; Anikin 2000: 349). From the Yakut, the word was borrowed into the Northern Tungusic[10] (SSTMJa 1: 487a).

Kott *tʰantu* 'snow flurry, storm' (Werner 2002/2: 315) < *tan -tu* {Yeniseian NN/adj.} ← Turkic **tan* 'a cool breeze' < *tān*:
cf. Old Turkic *tān*; NE^S YeniseiT: Khakas *tan* 'breeze'; Sagai, Koibal, Kachin *tan* 'wind, north wind' (R); AltaiT: Altai –; Qumanda *taŋ* 'sharp wind'; Remaining lgs. –;
Turkic → Samoyedic:
Kamas *tan* 'cold, gentle winter wind; north'.

Etymology: Joki LS 308–309; Räsänen VEWT 460b; Clauson ED 510a; SIGTJa 2001: 42; Khabtagaeva 2015b: 527

The Kott word was borrowed from the Turkic *tan* 'breeze, wind' with the native Yeniseian suffix. The aspirated consonant *tʰ-* in the initial position suggests an early period of borrowing, or the difference of Kott sources. The strict difference between *t-* and *tʰ-* in the Kott sources is absent (cf. another Kott word with the aspirated initial consonant Kott *tʰategâtna* 'beside, next to').

From the Modern Turkic languages, the word is preserved only in the Yenisei Turkic and Altai Turkic dialects. The word is present in the Middle Turkic source Kāšġarī with the original long vowel *tān* 'a cold wind, which blows at dawn and sunset' (Clauson ED 510a; Räsänen VEWT 460b; SIGTJa 2001: 42). From the Turkic, the word was also borrowed into the Samoyedic (Joki LS 308–309).

---

10   Turkic: Yakut → Tungusic: *Eastern Ewenki*: Uchur, Chumikan *lāyda* 'glade, open flat area; sea shore'; Lamut *lāyda* 'sea shore, coast shallow'.

Kott *tátien* 'hill' (Werner 2002/2: 245) ← ? Turkic *tā töŋ < taġ 'mountain' + töŋ 'hill':
< *taġ* 'mountain':

cf. Old Turkic *tāġ*; NE^S YeniseiT: Khakas; Sagai; Koibal; Kachin; Kyzyl; Shor *taġ*; AltaiT: Altai; Tuba; Teleut *tū*; Qumanda; Quu *taġ*; SayanT: Tuvan; Tofan *daġ*; ChulymT *taġ*; NE^N Yakut; Dolgan *tïa* 'land; forest, tundra'; NW^N Siberian Tatar *tau*; NW^S Kirgiz *tō*; Fu-yü *dah*; Kazak *taŭ*; SE Yellow Uyghur *taġ*;

Etymology: Räsänen VEWT 454a; Ščerbak SF 197; Clauson ED 463a; ESTJa 1980: 117–119; SIGTJa 1997: 94

+ *töŋ* 'hill':

cf. Old Turkic –; NE^S YeniseiT: Khakas; Sagai; Koibal, Kachin *töŋ* 'hill'; Kyzyl *tökᵡ*; Shor *töŋ* 'mound'; AltaiT: Altai; Teleut *töŋ* 'mound, hill, elevation'; Tuba *töŋ* 'hill'; Qumanda *tön* 'mound, hill, elevation; stump'; Quu *töŋ* 'hill'; SayanT: Tuvan; Tofan *döŋ* 'hummock; hill'; ChulymT *töŋ* 'hill'; NE^N Yakut –; NW^N Siberian Tatar *tüŋ* 'elevation, small hill'; NW^S Kirgiz *döŋ* 'elevation, hill'; Fu-yü –; Kazak *döŋ* 'mound, hill, elevation'; SE Yellow Yughur –.

Etymology: Räsänen VEWT 494a; ESTJa 1980: 279–281

The etymology of the Kott word *tátien* 'hill' is unknown. I assume it originates from the Turkic combination of the words *taġ* 'mountain' and *töŋ* 'hill'. In the first syllable, the Kott vowel -*á*- probably developed from the Turkic secondary long vowel -*ā*-, while the diphtong -*ie*- in the second syllable occurred instead of the Turkic labial vowel -*ö*-.

The problematic side of my etymology is the absence of the compound word in Turkic. But the possibility of my etymology can be strengthened from a semantic point (Khabtagaeva 2015d: 137).

Kott *tipar* ~ *tîpar* 'fog' (Werner 2002/2: 265) ← Turkic *tumarïk* 'haze' < *tum* 'cold' +*Ar*- {Turkic NV, see Erdal 1991: 499} -(*X*)*K* {VN, see ED xliv, Erdal 1991: 224}:

cf. Old Turkic *tum* 'cold', cf. *tuman* 'mist, fog'; NE^S YeniseiT: –[11]; AltaiT: Altai *tumarïk* 'mist, haze', cf. *tuman* 'fog'; Tuba –;[12] Qumanda *tumarïk* 'mist, haze; dim'; Quu –[13]; Teleut *tumarïk* 'the fog; cloudy, foggy', cf. *tuman* 'fog, darkness' (R); SayanT: –[14]; ChulymT –[15]; NE^N Yakut *tumarïk* 'darkness, gloom' < *tumarïy*- 'to fog, to enter into dark-

---

11   Cf. Khakas *tuban* 'fog, mist; uncertainty in the head'; Sagai, Koibal *tuban* 'fog' (R), Shor *tuban* 'fog'.
12   Cf. Tuba *tuban* ~ *tuvan* ~ *tuman* 'fog'.
13   Cf. Quu *tuban* 'fog'.
14   Cf. Tuvan *tuman*; Tofan *tuman* 'fog'.
15   Cf. Chulym *tuman* 'fog, darkness' (R).

ness', *tumara* 'thick fog';[16] NW[N] Siberian Tatar *tumarïqla-*[17] 'to be overcast (*weather*)'; NW[S] Kirgiz *tunarïk* 'misty distance, fog; haze' < *tunar-* 'to grow dim, to get dark';[18] SE Yellow Uyghur –.

Etymology: Räsänen VEWT 498b; Doerfer TMEN 2: 567–568; Clauson ED 503a, 507a; ESTJa 1980: 295–296; Erdal 1991: 387–388; SIGTJa 1997: 33–34

The etymology of the Kott forms is unknown. I assume that they were borrowed from the Turkic form *tumarïk* 'haze'. The source of the borrowing was possibly the shortened form *tümar, where the Kott vowel *-ï-* in the first syllable was assimilated by the original Turkic *-ï-* in the last syllable. Besides this, the change of the intervocalic *VmV* > *VpV* occurred.

There are two different Turkic words, *tumarïq* 'haze' and *tuman* 'fog'. The etymology of the Turkic words is unclear. The base of both Turkic words is the form *tum* 'dark', cf. Old Uyghur *tumluġ* (< **tum+lXG*) 'dark, overcast', Tatar dial. *tumsa* 'gloomy, unfriendly' (< **tum+sA*), Turkish dial. *dumčuk* (< **tum+čXK*) 'cloudy weather' (for details, see ESTJa 1980: 295). According to Erdal (1991: 387–388), the Turkic word *tuman* is derived from the verb **tum-* and the deverbal noun suffix *-mAn*. This possibility strengthens the morphological structure of the form *tumarïk*, where the base is the reconstructed verb **tum-* with the suffix *-Ar-* and the deverbal noun suffix *-(I)K*.

Via Russian, the Turkic word was also borrowed into the Samoyedic (Joki LS 339).

Arin ***tumantolati*** 'fog' (Werner 2002/2: 265) < *tuman* + *tolatï* (?):
tuman ← Turkic *tuman 'mist, fog':

cf. Old Turkic *tuman*; NE[S] YeniseiT: Khakas *tuban*; Sagai, Koibal *tuban*, Shor *tuban*; AltaiT: Altai *tuman*; Tuba *tuban* ~ *tuvan* ~ *tuman*; Qumanda *tuban*; Quu *tuban*; Teleut *tuman*; SayanT: Tuvan *tuman*; Tofan *tuman*; ChulymT *tuman* (R); NE[N] Yakut *tuman*; Dolgan *tuman*; NW[N] Siberian Tatar –[19]; NW[S] Kirgiz *tuman*; Fu-yü –; Kazak *tüman*; SE Yellow Uyghur –;

Turkic → Russian *туман* 'fog, haze, mist' (Vasmer 1986/4: 119);
Russian → Samoyedic: Kamas *tuman* ~ *toman* 'fog'.
Etymology: Joki LS 339; Räsänen VEWT 498b; Doerfer TMEN 2: 567–568; Clauson ED 507a; ESTJa 1980: 295–296; Vasmer 1986/4: 119; SIGTJa 1997: 33–34

---

16 Cf. Yakut *tuman*, Dolgan *tuman* 'fog'.
17 < *tumarïq +*lA*- {Turkic NV, see Erdal 1991: 429}.
18 cf. Kirgiz *tuman* 'fog'; Fu-yü –; Kazak *tüman* 'fog'.
19 Cf. Siberian Tatar *tumarïqla-* 'to be overcast (*weather*)', which basically connects with Turkic *tuman* 'fog' and derived from **tum+Ar-(X)K+lA-* (for details, see Kott *tipar* ~ *tîpar* 'fog').

The etymology of the Arin word is unknown. It probably belongs among the group of compound words and consists of the Turkic *tuman* 'fog' and the unknown element **tolatï*. If the second part of the Arin word is unclear, the first compound element is obviously connected with the Turkic word *tuman*.

The base of the Turkic word is *tum* 'cold' (Clauson ED 503a), but the derivation is still unclear. See also above the Kott *tipar* ~ *tîpar* 'fog'.

From Turkic through the Siberian Russian, the word was borrowed into Samoyedic Kamas (Joki LS 339).

Kott *ušôx* ~ *ušou* 'ice' (Werner 2002/2: 376) ← Turkic **üšük* 'hard frost, frozen' < *üši-* 'to be very cold, to shiver with cold' -*K* {Turkic VN, see Erdal 1991: 224}:
    cf. Old Turkic *üšik* 'hard frost, frozen'; NE[S] YeniseiT: Khakas *üzü-* ~ *uču-* 'to be cold'; Shor *üžük* 'chill'; AltaiT: Altai *üžük* 'frost, frozen'; Qumanda *üžük* 'freezing, frostbite'; Quu *üžü-* 'to be cold'; Teleut *üžük* 'frostbitten' (R); SayanT: Tuvan *ü^cžük* 'freezing, frostbite'; Tofan *üšük* 'freezing, frostbite'; ChulymT –; NE[N] Yakut –; NW[N] Siberian Tatar *üšük* 'frostbitten' (R); NW[S] Kirgiz *üšük* 'frost, frozen'; Fu-yü –; Kazak *usīk* 'frost, frozen'; SE Yellow Yughur –.

Etymology: Räsänen VEWT 523b; Clauson ED 260a; ESTJa 1974: 644–645

The Kott forms were borrowed from the Siberian Turkic form **üšük* 'frost'. In the Kott *ušôx* form, the final consonant -*x* changed from the Turkic -*k*, which is a regular phonetic feature for Turkic loanwords in Kott (e.g. *aksax* 'lame' ← Turkic *aqsaq*, *kalôx* 'ear' ← Turkic *qulaq*, *kapax* 'forehead' ← Turkic *qapaq* 'eyelid', etc.). The disappearance of vowel harmony is also a typical phonetic feature for Turkic loanwords in Kott. In the second Kott form *ušou* instead of the Turkic -*ük* the diphthong in the final position occurred.

Kott *uruk* 'mountain valley' (Werner 2002/2: 354) ← Turkic **oruq* 'path' < *ōr-* 'to mow (*grass, etc.*), to reap (*crops*)' -*XK* {Turkic VN, see Erdal 1991: 224}:
    cf. Old Turkic *oruq*; NE[S] YeniseiT: Khakas *orġax* ~ *orax* 'path, trodden by wild animals'; Sagai *oraq* (R); Shor *oraq*; AltaiT: Altai *orïq*; Qumanda *orak*; Quu *orïk*; Teleut *oroq* (R); SayanT: Tuvan *oruk* 'road, path'; Tofan *oruq*; ChulymT *ōruq*; NE[N] Yakut *orox* 'path; a dark stripe on the back of a horse'; Dolgan *orok*; NW[N] Siberian Tatar *oraq* (R); Remaining lgs. –.

Etymology: Räsänen VEWT 364a; Rassadin 1971: 212; Clauson ED 214a; Timonina 1978: 12; ESTJa 1989: 218; SIGTJa 1997: 531–532

The Kott word was borrowed from the Siberian Turkic form **oruk*. The assimilation of the Kott initial *u-* occurred due to the second syllable, where the vowel -*u*- is found. From a semantic perspective, this represents broadening of the original meaning.

1.1.2 Names of Metals and Minerals

Kott ***altun*** ~ ***altin***, Arin ***altin*** ~ ***altinok*** 'gold' (Werner 2002/1: 27) ← Turkic **altïn* 'gold' < *altūn*:

cf. Old Turkic *altūn*; NE[S] YeniseiT: Khakas *altïn*; Kyzyl *altïn*; Shor *altïn*; AltaiT: Altai *altïn*; Tuba *altïn*; Qumanda *altïn*; Quu *altïn*; Teleut *altïn*; SayanT: Tuvan *aldïn*; Tofan *a^cltan*; ChulymT *altun*; NE[N] Yakut *altan* 'copper';[20] Dolgan *altan* 'copper'; NW[N] Siberian Tatar *altïn*; NW[S] Kirgiz *altïn*; Fu-yü *altïn*; Kazak *altïn*; SE Yellow Uyghur *altïn*;

Turkic → Samoyedic:
Kamas *altïn* 'gold'; Selkup *altïn* 'money'.

Etymology: Joki LS 64; Räsänen VEWT 18a; Clauson ED 131a; Doerfer TMEN 1: 142–143, 2: 112–114; ESTJa 1974: 142; Timonina 1978: 11; Anikin 2000: 84; Rybatzki 2006: 102–104; Nugteren 2011: 269

The Yeniseian words were clearly borrowed from Turkic. The Common Turkic word *altun* 'gold' belongs to the category of cultural words and is registered in almost all Modern Turkic languages. It was borrowed into Mongolic[21] (Rybatzki 2006: 102–104; Nugteren 2011: 269), Tungusic[22] (SSTMJa 1: 33a), Samoyedic (Joki LS 64; Filipova 1994: 45) and Siberian Russian (Anikin 2000: 84) languages. The etymology of the word is unknown. Some researchers connect it with Turkic **āl* 'red' and Chinese *ton* 'copper' (for details, see Doerfer TMEN 1: 142; Räsänen VEWT 18a; Anikin 2000: 84; Rybatzki 2006: 102–104).

Kott ***baker*** 'copper, brass', cf. *baker kumuš* 'copper money' (Werner 2002/1: 99) ← Turkic **bakïr* 'copper':

cf. Old Turkic *baqïr* 'copper; a copper coin; the wight of a copper coin'; NE[S] YeniseiT: Khakas *paġïr* (But.); Kyzyl *pāyer*; AltaiT: Altai *bakras* (< *baqïr* +(*X*)*č* {Turkic NN/diminutive, see Erdal 1991: 44}) 'copper pot'; Teleut *pakras* 'copper; a small cast-iron cover' (R); SayanT –; ChulymT *paqïr* (R); NE[N] Yakut –; NW[N] Siberian Tatar *paġïr*; NW[S] Kirgiz *bakïr* 'copper; metal bucket'; Fu-yü –; Kazak *baqïr* 'copper; metal bucket'; SE Yellow Uyghur *paqïr*;

Turkic → Samoyedic:
Kamas *bayïr* 'copper'.

---

20   Yakut ← ? Tungusic, cf. Negidal *altan* 'copper' (SSTMJa 1: 33a).
21   Turkic → Mongolic 'gold': Middle Mongol: SH; HY; Muq., Leiden *altan*; Ist. *altat* (< *altan* +*t* {Mongolic plural}) 'piece of gold money'; LM *alta(n)*; Modern Mongol: Buryat *alta(n)*; Khalkha *altan*; Oirat dial. *altän*; Dagur *alt* ~ *altā* ~ *altan* (E); Khamnigan *alta(n)*.
22   Turkic → Mongolic → Tungusic: *Southern Ewenki*: Nepa, Sym, Northern Baikal; *Eastern Ewenki*: Tungir, Aldan, Uchur, Urmi, Chumikan, Sakhalin, Barguzin *altan* 'gold; copper'; Negidal *altan* 'copper'; Oroch *akta* 'tin, zinc'; Udehe *alta* ~ *arta* 'tin, zinc'; Nanai *altã* 'tin, tin utensils' (SSTMJa 1: 33a).

Etymology: Joki LS 80; Räsänen VEWT 58b; Clauson ED 317b; Timonina 1978: 11; ESTJa 1978: 45; SIGTJa 2001: 405

The source of borrowing for this Kott word remains unclear. If the Khakas form *paġïr* may have been used with the devoiced initial consonant *p-* and with the intervocalic voiced *VġV*, while Altai Turkic forms are used with the diminutive suffix.

The etymology of the Turkic word is unknown. Some researchers originate it from Iranian (for details, see Joki LS 80; Räsänen VEWT 58b; ESTJa 1978: 45).

Kott *bolat ~ bolát*; Arin *molát*; Assan *balat* 'steel' (Werner 2002/1: 139) ← Turkic **bolat* 'steel' ← Persian:

cf. Old Turkic –; NE^S YeniseiT: Khakas *molat*; Sagai, Koibal, Kachin *molat* (R); Shor *molat*; AltaiT: Altai *bolot*; Tuba *bolot*; Qumanda *bolot ~ polot*; Quu *polot*; Teleut *pulat*; SayanT: Tuvan *bolat*; Tofan *bolat*; ChulymT *polat* (R); NE^N Yakut *bolot* 'sword'; Dolgan *bolot* 'sword'; NW^N Siberian Tatar –; NW^S Kirgiz *bolot*; Fu-yü *bolot*; Kazak *bolat*; SE Yellow Uyghur –;

Turkic → Samoyedic:

Kamas *bolat* 'steel'; Mator *bolat* 'steel';

Turkic ← Persian *pūlād* 'steel'.[23]

Etymology: Kałużyński 1962: 122; Joki LS 96; Räsänen VEWT 387a; Timonina 1978: 11; Rassadin 1980: 31, 68; Stachowski 1992: 105–119; 2006: 180; Helimski 1997: 220; Pomorska 2012: 302

The Turkic word is of Persian origin. The Yeniseian forms were borrowed from Siberian Turkic languages. Stachowski (2006: 180) refers the Yeniseian words to the category with a clear Persian etymology. The initial *m-* in the Arin form suggests a Yenisei Turkic borrowing. In the Assan form, the assimilation *-o- > -a-* occurred at the first syllable due to the vowel *-a-* in the second syllable, which was possibly stressed (cf. Kott and Arin forms).

According to some researchers, Altai (Rassadin 1980: 31), Tuvan (Tatarincev 2000/1: 241) and Yakut (Kałużyński 1962: 122; Räsänen VEWT 387a) forms are Mongolic loanwords. From Turkic, the word was borrowed into Samoyedic (Joki LS 96; Helimski 1997: 220) and Mongolic,[24] and from Mongolic to Tungusic[25] (SSTMJa 1: 93b).

---

23   Cf. also other additional meanings given by Steingass (1957: 260b) 'the finest Damascus steel, which, with that of Qūm, is esteemed the best in the East; steel generally, a sword; name of a demon and of famous warrior'.
24   Turkic ? → Mongolic: cf. LM *bolud* 'steel'; Buryat *bulad*; Khalkha *bold*; Kalmuck *bol°d*; Dagur *bolto ~ bolot* (T); Khamnigan *bolod*.
25   Mongolic → Tungusic: *Southern Ewenki*: Nercha; *Eastern Ewenki*: Barguzin *bolot* 'steel' (SSTMJa 1: 93b).

Kott *ɛkačačik* 'wax' (Werner 2002/1: 229) ← Turkic *aǧač čuk < *aǧaš* 'tree' + *čuk* 'resin':
    < *aǧač* 'tree; wood (*generally*), a piece of wood' < *üǧač* < *ï* 'vegatation' +*GAč* {Turkic NN, forming names of animals or plants: Erdal 1991: 83–84}:
    cf. Old Turkic *üǧač*; NE^S YeniseiT: Khakas *aǧas*; Sagai *aǧïs*; Koibal *aǧas ~ aǧïs*; Kyzyl *aǧas ~ āǧaš*; Shor *aǧaš*; AltaiT: Altai *aǧaš*; Tuba *agaš ~ aŋaš ~ āč*; Qumanda *agač ~ agaš*; Quu *agač ~ agaš ~ agïš*; Teleut *agaš*; SayanT: Tuvan *ïyaš*; Tofan *ńeš*; ChulymT *aǧač ~ aǧac ~ āč*; NE^N Yakut –; NW^N Siberian Tatar *aǧac ~ aǧač*; NW^S Kirgiz *jïgač*; Fu-yü *agaš ~ agïš*; Kazak *aǧaš*; SE Yellow Uyghur *yïǧaš*.

Etymology: Doerfer TMEN 1: 73–74; Räsänen VEWT 7b; Clauson ED 1a, 79b; ESTJa 1974: 71; Erdal 1991: 84; SIGTJa 2001: 104–105; Róna-Tas & Berta WOT 2011: 54–55[26]

+ *čuk* 'resin' ← Yeniseian:
    cf. Old Turkic –; NE^S YeniseiT: Khakas *čux*; Sagai *čuq*; Kyzyl *šux*; Shor *čuq*; AltaiT: –; SayanT: Tuvan *čuk*; Tofan *čuq*; Remaining lgs. –.

Etymology: Räsänen VEWT 119; Rassadin 1971: 198; Timonina 1979: 23; Stachowski 1997: 230

    The etymology of the Kott word is unknown. It probably belongs in the category of compound words. As a hypothesis, I assume it that consists of the Turkic words *aǧač* 'tree' and *čuk* 'resin' (Khabtagaeva 2015d: 130–131). The first part of Kott *ɛkača* was borrowed from Altai Turkic or Chulym Turkic, where the form *aǧač* is found. The preservation of the intervocalic *VčV* shows the early period of borrowing, usually Proto-Yeniseian -*č*- preserved in Kott (Starostin 1982: 161). The second part of the Kott word *čik* descends from Proto-Yeniseian (Vajda 2014: personal communication) and the loanword possibly belongs in the hybrid category.

    The etymology of the second part of the Kott word is unclear. Stachowski (1997: 230) connects the Yeniseian words with the Turkic *čïǧ* 'damp'. Rassadin (1971: 198) links the Siberian Turkic forms with the Ewenki *čūkse* 'resin'. The Tungusic forms (Ewenki dial. *čūkse ~ čūha ~ čūhe* 'tree sap'; Solon *sūrče* 'resin'; Lamut *čūs* 'tree sap, berry juice'; Negidal *čūxse* 'juice'; Oroch *čūkse* 'juice'; Udihe *čüöŋki* 'tree sap, juice'; Orok *sūkse ~ tūkse* 'juice') are connected with Mongolic *sigüsün* 'sap, juice; food (*usually meat*) for offerings' (SSTMJa 2: 411). According to Vajda (2014: personal communication), the Kott *čik ~ čîk*, Ket *dī·k* and Yugh *dⁱīk* 'resin' are original Yeniseian words.

---

26   Turkic: West Old Turkic *aγaččï (< *aγač* 'tree' +*čI* {Turkic NN}) 'carpenter' → Hungarian *ács* [*āč*] 'carpenter'.

Kott ***kolá*** 'copper, brass' (Werner 2002/1: 438) ← Turkic *kola 'copper, brass' ← Mongolic *γauli ~ γuuli* 'brass, copper':

> NE^S YeniseiT: Khakas *xola* 'bronze, brass'; Sagai, Koibal, Kachin *qola* 'brass' (R); Shor *qola* 'bronze, tin'; AltaiT: Altai *kolo* 'bronze, tin'; Qumanda *kola* 'copper'; Quu *kolï* 'copper'; Teleut *qūl* 'copper, brass'; SayanT: Tuvan *xola* 'copper, brass'; Tofan *qūl'i* 'brass'; ChulymT *qōla* 'silver'; NE^N Yakut –; NW^N Siberian Tatar –; NW^S Kirgiz *kolo* 'bronze'; Fu-yü –; Kazak *qola* 'bronze, tin'; SE Yellow Uyghur *qula* 'lead';

Turkic → Samoyedic:

> Kamas *kōla* 'brass, copper'; Mator *kola* 'brass';

Turkic ← Mongolic:

> Middle Mongol: Muq. *γula* 'copper'; LM *γauli ~ γuuli* 'brass, copper'; Modern Mongol: Buryat *gūli(n)* 'bronze, copper'; Khalkha *gūl'* 'brass'; Kalmuck *gūlⁱ* 'a small boiler made from copper or brass'; Dagur *gaul'* 'brass' (E); Khamnigan *gūli(n)*.

Etymology: Räsänen VEWT 277a; Rassadin 1971: 222; 1980: 36; 48; Timonina 1978: 11; ESTJa 2000: 46; Nugteren 2011: 338; Khabtagaeva 2015a: 113

Borrowing from Siberian Turkic and not directly from Mongolic is indicated by the initial voiceless consonant *k-* instead of the Mongolic *gūli*.

Mongolic origin in Turkic languages is by noted Räsänen (VEWT 277a), Rassadin (1971: 222; 1980: 36; 48) and Levitskaja (ESTJa 2000: 46). The initial consonant *k-* proves the borrowing from Turkic to Samoyedic (Joki LS 187–188; Helimski 1997: 285). The Mongolic word was also borrowed into the Ewenki dialect[27] (SSTMJa 1: 159b). The etymology of the Mongolic word is unclear. Räsänen (VEWT 277a), after Ramstedt (KWb 157a), proposes a Chinese origin.

Kott ***korkôtn ~ korogotn*** 'lead', cf. ***korkotni*** 'tin'; Assan ***korgoden*** 'tin, lead'; Pumpokol ***xórgosin*** 'tin' (Werner 2002/1: 442) ← Turkic *korgočin < *qorġušïn* 'lead':

> cf. Old Turkic *qoruġjin*; NE^S YeniseiT: Sagai *qorġajïn* (R); Kachin *qorġayïn* (R); Shor *qorġačïn*; AltaiT: Qumanda *korgočin*; Teleut *qorġožïn*; SayanT –; ChulymT *qorġuzan*; NE^N Yakut –; NW^N Siberian Tatar *qorġaš* (R); NW^S Kirgiz *korgošun*; Fu-yü –; Kazak *qorġasïn*; SE Yellow Uyghur –; Uzbek *qőrġåšin*; Uyghur *qo(r)ġušun*;

Arin ***korgoldžín*** 'tin';
Arin ***tamkorgolči*** 'tin' (Werner 2002/1: 442) < Yeniseian *tam* 'white' < *táγim* (Werner 2002/2: 249) + *korgolči*:

---

27 Mongolic → Tungusic: *Southern Ewenki*: Northern Baikal, Nercha; *Eastern Ewenki*: Barguzin *goli* 'yellow copper, brass'.

← Turkic *korgoljïn 'lead' ← Mongolic qoryoljin 'lead' ← Turkic korgočïn 'lead':
NE^S YeniseiT: Khakas xorġamjŭl; Kachin qorġanjŭl ~ qorġayïn (R); Koibal qorġayïn (R); Kyzyl χoryandžė; AltaiT: Altai qorgold'ïn; Tuba korgoldžïn; Quu korgoldžï; SayanT: Tuvan korgulčun; Tofan qorġol'čïn; ChulymT –; NE^N Yakut xorġold'un 'tin'; Dolgan korgoljūn 'tin'; NW^S Kirgiz –; Fu-yü gorgolčon; Kazak qorġasïn; SE Yellow Uyghur –; Turkic → Samoyedic:
Kamas koryōljen 'lead';
Turkic ← Mongolic qoryoljin 'lead':
Middle Mongol: Ibn-Muh. qoryalji; LM qoryoljin; Modern Mongol: Buryat –; Khalkha xorgolj; Oirat dial. xorgăldžăŋ; Kalmuck xorġaldžn; Dagur –; Khamnigan –; Mongolic ← Turkic korgočïn 'lead', see above.

Etymology: Joki LS 195; Kałużyński 1962: 61; Poppe 1969: 211; Räsänen VEWT 282; Doerfer TMEN 3: 452–454; Róna-Tas 1970: 604–606; Rassadin 1971: 221; 1980: 6, 36, 66; Clauson ED 656b; Clark 1977: 150; Timonina 1978: 11; Ščerbak 1997: 135; ESTJa 2000: 172–174; SIGTJa 2001: 408

There are two different sources for these Yeniseian words. The first group consisting of Kott, Assan and Pumpokol forms was borrowed directly from the Turkic form *korgočïn* 'lead', while the Arin form *korgoldžín* was borrowed from another Turkic form *korgoljïn*, which is a Mongolic loanword, though originally of Turkic origin. The second Arin form *tamkorgolči* is a hybrid word, where the first part *tam* is possibly of Yeniseian origin, cf. Arin *tāma ~ t'āma* 'white' < *táγim* (for details, see Werner 2002/2: 249).

The etymology of the Turkic word is unclear. Clauson (ED 656b) considers it a foreign word. Räsänen (VEWT 282) originates the Turkic forms from Mongolic. The Siberian Turkic *korgoljïn* is clearly a Turkic re-borrowing from Mongolic (see Kałużyński 1962: 61; Poppe 1969: 211; Rassadin 1971: 221; 1980: 6, 36, 66). As concerns the etymological background of Turkic word, their borrowings, and their re-borrowings, see also Doerfer (TMEN 3: 452–454), Róna-Tas (1970: 604–606), Levitskaja (ESTJa 2000: 172–174) and Tenišev (SIGTJa 2001: 408). Further, from Yakut the Turkic word was borrowed into Ewenki dialects[28] (Doerfer TMEN 3: 452; SSTMJa 1: 414b) and from Siberian Turkic to Samoyedic (Joki LS 195).

Yugh *kuʔ ~ kuʔu ~ kuʔo ~ kû*; Ket *kuʔ* 'coal, soot' (Werner 2002/1: 458) ← ? Turkic *kȫ 'coal, soot' ← Mongolic *kȫ* < *köge* 'soot; obstacle, hindrance; trouble' < *kö-GAn* {Mongolic VN, see Poppe GWM §149} ← Turkic *kȫń-* 'to catch fire, *intr.* to burn; to burn (*with anger*)' < *kö-:

---

28 Turkic → Mongolic → Turkic: Yakut → Tungusic: *Eastern Ewenki*: Aldan, Sakhalin, Tommot, Chumikan *korgoljun*; Tokko *korgoljïn*; Uchur *horgoljun*; Urmi *hergeljun* 'lead'.

cf. NE^S YeniseiT: –; AltaiT: Altai *kō* 'coal, soot'; Tuba *kō* 'coal'; Qumanda *kō* 'soot'; Teleut *kō* 'soot'; SayanT: Tuvan *xō* 'soot'; Tofan *hō* 'coal, cold peace of coal in a bonfire'; ChulymT –; NE^N –; NW^N Siberian Tatar *küö* 'soot' (R); NW^S Kirgiz *kō* 'soot'; Remaining lgs. –;

Turkic ← Mongolic **kō* < *köge* 'soot; obstacle, hindrance; trouble':
Middle Mongol: Muq. *köye*; LM *kö ~ köge ~ kögege*; Modern Mongol: Buryat *xȫ*; Khalkha *xȫ*; Oirat dial. *kȫ*; Dagur *x^{w}ō* (E); Khamnigan *kȫ*;

Mongolic ← Turkic **kȫń-* 'to catch fire, *intr.* to burn; to burn (*with anger*)' < **kö-*: cf. Old Turkic *küń-*; NE^S YeniseiT: Khakas *köyē ~ köye* 'soot' (But.) < *köy-*; Sagai, Koibal, Kachin *köy-* (R); Kyzyl *kȫy-*; Shor *köy-*; AltaiT: Altai *küy-*; Tuba *küy-*; Qumanda *küy-*; Quu *küy-*; Teleut *küy-*; SayanT –; ChulymT –; NE^N Yakut –; NW^N Siberian Tatar *köye* 'soot'; NW^S Kirgiz *küy-*; Fu-yü *güy-*; Kazak *küye* 'soot'; SE Yellow Uyghur *küy-*;

Turkic → Samoyedic:
Kamas *kös ~ küös*[29] 'coal'; Mator *köyä* 'coal'.

Etymology: Joki LS 202–203; Räsänen VEWT 286b; Rassadin 1971: 191; 1980: 57; Clauson ED 726b; ESTJa 1997: 88–89; SIGTJa 1997: 371; Helimski 1997: 284; Nugteren 2011: 423

The etymology of the Yeniseian forms is unknown. It can be the Turkic loanword (Werner 2002/1: 458), or the Turkic word can be of Yeniseian origin. According to Vajda (2016: personal communication), the Proto-Ket-Yugh reconstructed form **kupil* 'hot embers' is derived from Proto-Yeniseian **ku^ʔ* 'coal, ember' and **pil* 'mass' > Ket *kuɣul ~ ku:l* 'ember, charred, glowing log'; Yugh *kufil* 'coal'; Arin *kuburuŋ*, Assan *kuvulán* 'embers'.

I assume that the Yugh and Ket forms were borrowed from the Siberian Turkic form **kō* with the secondary long vowel, which is the Mongolic loanword (Rassadin 1971: 191; 1980: 57; SIGTJa 1997: 371), but ultimately of Turkic origin (Räsänen VEWT 286b; Clauson ED 726b; ESTJa 1997: 88–89). From the Siberian Turkic, the word was borrowed into Samoyedic (Joki LS 202–203; Helimski 1997: 284) and from Mongolic to a Manchu language[30] (SSTMJa 1: 421a; Rozycki 1994: 144).

In turn, the Turkic verb **kö- ~ *kü-* is absent in Turkic sources, but we have the Old Turkic words *köz* (<**kö-z*) 'burning embers', *kömür* (<**kö-mXr*) 'charcoal' and *küń-* 'to catch fire, to burn', which most probably came from this verb. For details of the reconstruction **kȫń-*, see ESTJa (1997: 88) and Räsänen (VEWT 307b).

---

29 Kamas ← Turkic *köz* (<**kö-z*) 'burning embers'.
30 Turkic → Mongolic → Tungusic: Manchu *ku* 'soot from cooking; frost on the grass'.

Nonetheless, the Yeniseian words belong to the group of words with uncertain etymology.

Kott *kumiš* ~ *kumuš*; Arin *kumiš*; Assan *kumís* ~ *kumus* ~ *kümüs*; Pumpokol *kümüč* 'silver' (Werner 2002/1: 450–451) ← Turkic *kümüš 'silver':

cf. Old Turkic *kümüš*; NE^S YeniseiT: Khakas *kümüs*; Sagai, Koibal *kümüs* (R); Kyzyl *kümüs*; Shor *kümüš*; AltaiT: Altai *kümüš*; Tuba *kümiš*; Qumanda *kümiš*; Quu *kümüš*; Teleut *kümüš*; SayanT: Tuvan *xümüš*; Tofan –; ChulymT *kümüš*; NE^N Yakut *kömüs* 'silver, gold'; Dolgan *kömüs*; NW^N Siberian Tatar –; NW^S Kirgiz *kümüš*; Fu-yü *gümüš*; Kazak *kümis*; SE Yellow Uyghur *kümüs* ~ *kumus* ~ *kumos* ~ *kumis*;

Turkic → Samoyedic:
Kamas *kumiš* ~ *kümüš* 'silver'; Mator *kümiš* 'silver'.

Etymology: Joki LS 209; Räsänen VEWT 308b; Clauson ED 723b; Timonina 1978: 11; ESTJa 1997: 141–142; Helimski 1997: 292; Anikin 2000: 323; SIGTJa 2001: 404

The Yeniseian words were borrowed from Turkic form *kümüš. The disappearance of vowel harmony is a regular change for Turkic loanwords in Yeniseian. The preservation of the Turkic initial consonant *k*- points to a later period of borrowing. A change of the Turkic final consonant -*š* > -*s* in Assan and -*č* in Pumpokol forms occurred.

The etymology of the Turkic word is unknown. According to Joki (LS 209) and Räsänen (VEWT 308b), it is of Chinese origin. For more details on the etymology, see ESTJa (1997: 141–142) and SIGTJa (2001: 404).

The Turkic word was borrowed into Samoyedic (Joki LS 209; Helimski 1997: 292) and Siberian Russian (Anikin 2000: 323) too.

Arin *teminkur* 'ore' (Werner 2002/2: 258) ← Turkic *temir qan 'lit. iron blood → ore' < *tämir* 'iron' + *qān* 'blood':

< *temir* 'iron':

cf. Old Turkic *tämir*; NE^S YeniseiT: Khakas *timĭr*; Sagai, Koibal, Kachin *temĭr*, Sagai *tebĭr*; Kyzyl *tēmir*; Shor *tebir*; AltaiT: Altai *temir*; Tuba *temir*; Qumanda *temir* ~ *tebir* ~ *debir*; Quu *tebir* ~ *tevir* ~ *temir*; Teleut *temir*; SayanT: Tuvan *demir*; Tofan *demir*; ChulymT *tēmir*; NE^N Yakut *timir*; Dolgan *timir*; NW^N Siberian Tatar –; NW^S Kirgiz *temir*; Fu-yü *dimir* ~ *dümür*; Kazak *temir*; SE Yellow Uyghur *temĭr* ~ *temir*;

Etymology: Räsänen VEWT 473a; Clauson ED 508b; ESTJa 1980: 188–190; SIGTJa 1997: 409

+ *qān* 'blood':

cf. Old Turkic *qān*; NE^S YeniseiT: Khakas *xan*; Sagai, Koibal, Kachin *qan*; Kyzyl *χan*; Shor *qan*; AltaiT: Altai; Tuba; Qumanda; Quu *kan*; Teleut *qan*; SayanT: Tuvan *xan*; Tofan *qan*; ChulymT *qan*; NE^N Yakut *xān*; Dolgan *kān*; NW^N Siberian Tatar *qan*; NW^S Kirgiz *kan*; Fu-yü *gan*; Kazak *qan*; SE Yellow Uyghur *qan*.

Etymology: Räsänen VEWT 230a; Clauson ED 629b; ESTJa 1997: 251

The etymology of the Arin word is unknown. As a hypothesis, I assume that the source of the Arin was probably the compound word of Turkic origin *temir kan* 'iron blood' (Khabtagaeva 2015c: 101; 2015e). An interesting fact is that a word with the meaning 'ore' is present in the Kott language with the form *šur*, and also with the meaning 'blood' (Werner 2002/2: 258). In return, the Kott word must be connected with the Common Yeniseian *sū·λ* 'blood': cf. Ket *sū·l*, Yugh *sūr*, Arin *sur* (Werner 2002/2: 219; Vajda & Werner: in preparation).

From a phonetic point of view, the Arin word of Turkic origin shows metathesis, which is a distinctive and specific feature in Yeniseian. My etymology encounters different problems. The first is the absence of this compound in the above mentioned Turkic languages; the other reasons are the phonetic and semantic changes.

The absence of the compound word *temir qan* 'iron blood → ore' in Turkic can be explained by the lack of the original Turkic word. There are two different forms for "ore" in Turkic. If the first form *pyda* is Russian,[31] the second *ken* is a Persian[32] loanword.

From a semantic perspective, there is an interesting case when a new word comes into existence. According to the Kott form *šur* with the meaning 'ore, blood', we can suppose that the Arin people created a new word "ore" from the Turkic words "iron + blood". Arin speakers were probably also fluent in the Turkic source dialect (Vajda 2015: personal communication).

1.1.3 Plants

Kott ***arba***; Arin ***arba***; Assan ***arpá*** 'barley' (Werner 2002/1: 57) ← Turkic **arba* < *arpa* 'barley':

cf. Old Turkic *arpa*; NE^S YeniseiT: Khakas *arba*; Sagai, Koibal, Kachin *arba* (R); Kyzyl *arba*; AltaiT: Altai *arba*; Tuba *arba ~ arva*; Qumanda *arba*; Quu *arba*; Teleut *arba* (R); SayanT –; ChulymT *arba* (R); NE^N Yakut –; NW^N Siberian Tatar *arba*; NW^S Kirgiz *arpa*; Fu-yü –; Kazak *arpa*; SE Yellow Uyghur –;

Turkic → Samoyedic:

Kamas *arba* 'grain, wheat'; Selkup *ārma* 'barley'.

---

31 Russian *ruda* 'ore' → Turkic: cf. Old Turkic –; NE^S YeniseiT: Khakas *ruda, timĭr ruda* 'iron ore'; Shor –; AltaiT: Altai *ruda* 'ore', *temir ruda* 'iron ore'; Tuba –; Qumanda –; Quu –; Teleut –; SayanT: Tuvan *ruda* 'ore', *demir daš* 'iron ore'; Tofan –; ChulymT –; NE^N Yakut *ruda*; Dolgan –; NW^N Siberian Tatar –; NW^S Kirgiz *ruda*; Fu-yü –; Kazak; SE Yellow Yughur –.

32 Persian *kân* 'ore' → Turkic: cf. Old Turkic *kan* 'mine; *fig.* source' (DTS); Old Uighur *kän* 'mine' (R); NE^S YeniseiT: –; AltaiT: –; SayanT –; ChulymT –; NE^N Yakut –; NW^N Siberian Tatar –; NW^S Kirgiz *ken* 'ore'; Fu-yü –; Kazak *ken* 'geol. deposit; depths of the earth, minerals; ore, mine, pit'; SE Yellow Yughur –.

Etymology: Joki LS: 69–70; Räsänen VEWT 27a; Clauson ED 198b; Doerfer TMEN 2: 24–25; ESTJa 1974: 176–177; Timonina 1986: 76; Rybatzki 2006: 142; Khabtagaeva 2009: 156; 2015b: 521; Róna-Tas & Berta WOT 2011: 77–79; Nugteren 2011: 272

For Kott and Arin, the Siberian Turkic form *arba was the source of the borrowing, while the Assan form shows the early period of borrowing.

Originally in Old Turkic, the word is found with the unvoiced cluster *arpa* (cf. also West Old Turkic). The word is widespread in almost all Turkic languages with the meaning 'barley'. It is concluded by researchers (Doerfer TMEN 2: 24–25; Clauson ED 198b) that the Turkic word was borrowed from Indo-European (for details, see Róna-Tas & Berta WOT 2011: 78). The Turkic word was borrowed into Mongolic,[33] Samoyedic (Joki LS: 69–70, Filipova 1994: 46) and Hungarian[34] (Róna-Tas & Berta WOT 2011: 77–79). In Tuvan, the re-borrowed Mongolic form *arbay* 'barley' is found (Khabtagaeva 2009: 156). From Mongolic, the word was borrowed into Manchu as *arfa* 'barley, grain' (Rozycki 1994: 20). The Samoyedic forms also show borrowing from Siberian Turkic; it seems the change -rb- > -rm- occurred in Selkup.

Kott **ariš** ~ **áriš** ~ **âreš**; Assan **ariš** 'grain, rye, barley' (Werner 2002/1: 59) ← Turkic *ariš 'rye' ← Russian *rož'*:

cf. Old Turkic –; NE^S YeniseiT: Khakas *arïs*; Sagai, Koibal, Kachin *arïs*; Kyzyl *ārẹ̄s* ~ *ārəs*; Shor *ariš*; AltaiT: Altai *ariš*; Qumanda *ariš*; Quu *ariš*; Teleut *ariš* (R); SayanT –; ChulymT *ariš* (R); NE^N Yakut *oruos*; NW^N Siberian Tatar *ariš*; NW^S Kirgiz –; Fu-yü –; Kazak *arïs*; SE Yellow Uyghur –;

Turkic → Samoyedic:
    Kamas *āriš* 'rye';
Turkic ← Russian *rož'* 'rye'.

Etymology: Joki LS 74; Timonina 1986: 76; Stachowski 2004: 192

Yeniseian words were certainly borrowed from Turkic; this is indicated by the initial vowel *a*-. The Turkic word is of Russian origin. Due to the absence of the original initial consonant *r*-,[35] the appearance of the prothetic vowel in Turkic languages is regular. Another reason to explain the borrowing from Rus-

---

33   Turkic → Mongolic: Middle Mongol: 'Phags-pa *arba*; HY *arpai*; Muq. *arbai*; Ist. *arpa* (← Turkic); LM *arbai* 'barley'; Modern Mongol: Buryat *arbai*; Khalkha *arwai*; Oirat dial. *ärwä̃*; Dagur –; Khamnigan –.
34   Turkic: West Old Turkic *arpa → Hungarian *árpa* 'barley'.
35   The words with initial *r*- usually belong to loanwords, cf. Khakas *raion* 'district' ← Russian; Kazakh *reŋq*, Turkish *renk* 'colour'← Persian; Chuvash *raštav* 'Christmas' ← Russian *roždestvo*, etc.

sian is the cultural background; the Turkic people were originally nomads and agricultural terminology came from Russian contact.

Kott *butai*; Arin *bugdaj*; Assan *bútaj* ~ *tútaj* 'wheat' (Werner 2002/1: 148) ← Turkic **būtay* < *bugday* 'wheat':
    cf. Old Turkic *buġday*; NE^S YeniseiT: Khakas *puġday*; Sagai, Koibal, Kachin *pūday* (R); Shor *puġday*; AltaiT: Altai *būday*; Tuba *būtay*; Qumanda *bugday*; Quu *pugday* ~ *pūday* ~ *pügdey* ~ *pü̆gdey*; Teleut *pūday*; SayanT –; ChulymT *puday*; NE^N Yakut –; NW^N Siberian Tatar *pitay* ~ *poytay*; NW^S Kirgiz *būday*; Fu-yü –; Kazak *biday*; SE Yellow Uyghur –;

Turkic → Samoyedic:
    Kamas *buɣdei* 'wheat'.

Etymology: Joki LS 106–108; Räsänen VEWT 86a; Clauson ED 312b; ESTJa 1978: 232–235; SIGTJa 2001: 461; Róna-Tas & Berta WOT 2011: 186–188; Nugteren 2011: 292–293

The Kott and Assan forms were borrowed from a Turkic form with the secondary long vowel **būtay*, where the long vowel was shortened and the original intervocalic *VdV* was devoiced to *VtV*. Additionally, this unvoiced consonant was influenced in Assan, where another assimilated form *tutaj* was formed. The Arin form was obviously taken from the Turkic *buġday* with the original Turkic guttural consonant *-ġ-*, which did not develop into a long vowel in some Siberian Turkic languages.

The Turkic word was borrowed into Mongolic[36] (Nugteren 2011: 292–293) and Hungarian[37] (Róna-Tas & Berta WOT 2011: 186–188). The origin of the word is unclear; it belongs to the category of cultural words.

Kott *ɛšjalikitan* 'flower, bloom' (Werner 2002/1: 257) ← Turkic **čakayaktan-* 'to cover with flowers; to blossom (*of flower buds*)', cf. Khakas *čaxayax* 'flower' +*ta-* {Khakas NV, see Baskakov & Inkiževekova-Grekul 1953: 419}; -*n-* {Khakas VV/ reflexive, see Baskakov & Inkiževekova-Grekul 1953: 421}:
    cf. Old Turkic –; NE^S YeniseiT: Khakas *čaxayaxtan-* 'to cover with flowers; to blossom (*of flower buds*)' < *čaxayax* 'flower'; Sagai *čakayak* 'flower' (R); Shor *čaqkiyekten-* 'to blossom', *čaqkiyle-* 'to bloom' < *čaqkiyek* 'flower' (ShR), cf. *čayaktan-* 'to bloom' < *čayak* 'flower' (R); AltaiT: Altai –; Qumanda *čakayak* ~ *ďakayak* 'flower'; Remaining lgs. –.

---

36   Turkic → Mongolic: LM *buyudai* ~ *buudai* 'wheat'; Modern Mongol: Buryat –; Khalkha *būdai* 'wheat; small spots, speckles'; Kalmuck *būd'ā* ~ *būdǟ* 'wheat'; Dagur –; Khamnigan –.
37   Turkic: West Old Turkic **bugday* > **buɣδay* → Hungarian **buɣzai* > *búza* [*būzå*] 'wheat'.

Etymology: –

It is clear that the Yenisei Turkic forms are connected with the Kott word. The Kott word was possibly borrowed from the Yenisei Turkic verbal form *čakayaktan-* 'to cover with flowers; to blossom *(of flower buds)*', which is derived from the noun *čakayak* 'flower' with the Turkic denominal verb suffix +*tA-* and the Turkic reflexive suffix -*n-*. A change of the original word took place in Kott. Additionally the prothesis ε- occurred and the metathesis -*kaya-* > -*jali-* took place in Yeniseian. The change of the consonant *k* > *l* is unclear.

The etymology of the Turkic word is unknown. For 'flower', the word *čäček* (Räsänen VEWT 102a; Clauson ED 400b), derived from the verb **čeč-* 'to sow, seed' (see SIGTJa 2001: 120), is widespread in Turkic languages. The Yenisei and Altai Turkic word *čakayak* 'flower' is probably connected with the Common Turkic verb *čaq-* 'to strike fire *(with a flint and steel)*', the final +*AK* is possibly the Turkic diminutive suffix.

Kott *hîta*; Yugh *kitn*; Ket *kī·tn* 'nettles, hemp' (Werner 2002/1: 437) ← Turkic **kiden* 'flax, canvas' ← Arabic:

cf. Old Turkic –; NE^S YeniseiT: Khakas *kiden* 'canvas; sailcloth; sacking, hessian; flax linen; towel'; Sagai, Koibal *kedän* 'flax, canvas' (R); Kyzyl *kèdän* 'flax, canvas'; Shor *keden* 'canvas'; AltaiT: Altai *keden* 'canvas'; Tuba *keden* 'canvas'; Qumanda *keden* 'canvas'; Quu *keden* 'canvas'; Teleut *keden* 'canvas' (R); SayanT: Tuvan *keden* 'canvas, coarse linen; sailcloth'; Tofan –; ChulymT –; NE^N Yakut –; NW^N Siberian Tatar *kitän* 'flax, canvas'; NW^S Kirgiz *kete* 'the kind of expensive material, cloth'; Fu-yü –; SE Yellow Uyghur –;

Turkic ← Arabic *kattān* 'flax, linen'; cf. *quṭn, quṭun* 'cotton'.

Etymology: Räsänen VEWT 259a; Timonina 1985: 11; SIGTJa 2001: 128

The change of the Turkic initial *k-* to *h-* in Kott is a regular phonetic feature. Semantic synecdoche probably took place in Yeniseian: 'flax, canvas' → 'nettles, hemp'.

Kott *kamagalá* 'nut' (Werner 2002/1: 407) ← Turkic **kabagalï* 'with husk, peel, shuck' < *qabaga* (cf. AltaiT) +*lXG* {Turkic NN/adj., see Erdal 1991: 121} < *qabïq* 'husk, peel, shuck, bran' < *qaβïq* 'bran':

cf. Old Turkic *qaβïq* 'bran', *käpäk* 'bran; metaph.* scurf, dandruff'; NE^S YeniseiT: Khakas *xōx* 'husk from the grain'; cf. *xubax ~ xïbax* 'chaff, husk'; Sagai *xox* 'barley husks' (KhR), Kyzyl *χaχβaš* 'bark; scab'; Shor *qabïq* 'egg shell'; AltaiT: Altai *qabïq ~ qabaga* 'egg shell, bark, peel, husk'; Tuba *kāk* 'dandruff, scabs'; Qumanda *kabïk* 'egg shell', cf. *kabaga* 'scales, husks of pine cones'; Teleut *qabïq* 'the scales of fir cones'; SayanT: Tuvan *xavïk* 'shell, corn husks'; ChulymT –; NE^N Yakut *xax* 'egg shell, potato peel, peel seed'; Yakut dial. *xax* 'a peeled outer skin of the horse'; NW^N Siberian Tatar

qabïq 'fish scales'; NW^S Kirgiz *kabïk* 'bark, egg shell'; Fu-yü –; Kazak *qabïq* 'peel, bark, shell, husk'; SE Yellow Yughur –.
Etymology: Räsänen VEWT 234b–235a; Clauson ED 583a; ESTJa 1997: 178–179; SIGTJa 2001: 107

The etymology of the Kott word is unknown. It was possibly borrowed from the Siberian Turkic form **kabagalï* 'with husk, peel, shuck', which is derived from the Common Turkic word *qabïq* 'husk, peel, shuck, bran' with productive suffix +*lXG*. The Turkic etymology fits with the semantic point 'with husk, peel, shuck' → 'nut', which shows the semantic change. From a phonetic perspective, the Altai Turkic intervocalic *VbV* changed to *VmV* in Kott.

There are two Altai Turkic forms *qabïq ~ qabaga* with the same meaning, 'egg shell, bark, peel, husk', but the final vowel -*a* in the form *kabaga* is unclear. The first form resembles a Mongolic borrowing, but the word is absent there. It seems to be an internal development in Altai Turkic. However, the form is obviously connected with the Common Turkic *qaβïq* 'bran'.

Arin ***karananuk*** 'bilberry' (Werner 2002/1: 411) ← Turkic **kara nonaġ* 'bilberry'
< *qara* 'black' + *nonaġ* 'bilberry':
< *qara* 'black':
  cf. Old Turkic *qara*; NE^S YeniseiT: Khakas *xara*; Sagai, Koibal, Kachin *qara*; Kyzyl *χara*; Shor *qara*; AltaiT: Altai; Tuba; Qumanda; Quu; Teleut *qara*; SayanT: Tuvan, Tofan *qara*; ChulymT *qara*; NE^N Yakut *xara*; Dolgan *kara ~ xara*; NW^N Siberian Tatar *qara*; NW^S Kirgiz *kara*; Fu-yü *gar*; Kazak *qara*; SE Yellow Uyghur *qara*;
Etymology: Laude-Cirtautas 1961: 17–23; Räsänen VEWT 235a; Clauson ED 643b; ESTJa 1997: 286–288; SIGTJa 1997: 680
+ *nonaġ* 'bilberry' < (?) **yomaq* < **yumaq*:
  cf. (?) Old Turkic *yumaq ~ yumġaq* 'a spherical or globular object'; NE^S YeniseiT: Khakas *nonaġ ~ noŋnïx* 'bilberry'; Sagai *nonaġ* 'bilberry'; Shor *nonġam* 'bilberry', cf. *nonam ~ ninïm* 'blueberry' (R); AltaiT: Altai –; Quu *ńunum* 'bilberry'; SayanT –; ChulymT –; NE^N Yakut –; NW^N Siberian Tatar –; NW^S Kirgiz –; Fu-yü –; Kazak –; SE Yellow Uyghur *džoma ~ džomaq* 'edible plant'.
Etymology: Räsänen VEWT 354b; Clauson ED 936a

The Arin word *karananuk* 'bilberry' is a compound word of Turkic origin. It consists of two Turkic words *qara* 'black' and *nonaġ* 'bilberry'. The Arin compound word follows the structure Adjective + Noun, which is regular for Yeniseian and Turkic (Khabtagaeva 2015d: 132).

From an etymological aspect, the first Turkic word *qara* 'black' is widespread in almost all Turkic languages. The etymology of another Turkic word *nonaġ* 'bilberry' is unknown. It is probably connected to the Old Turkic *yumaq ~ yumġaq*, 'a spherical or globular object', which is preserved as a 'berry' in some

Modern Turkic languages. From a phonetic point of view, the Turkic initial *n*-represents the Khakas phonetic feature, where the Common Turkic *y*- changes to *n*- in the words with nasal consonants[38] (Johanson 1998: 106). Judging from the second Turkic word, the Arin compound was borrowed from Yenisei Turkic.

Kott *kubúrgenaŋ* ~ *kabúrgenaŋ*; Arin *kuburgan*; Assan *kabirgina* ~ *kaburgina* 'onion' (Werner 2002/1: 447) ← Turkic **köbürgän* 'wild onion' < *köβür* +GAn {Turkic NN, see Erdal 1991: 85}:
    cf. Old Turkic *kömürgän* ~ *köβürgän*; NE[S] YeniseiT: Khakas *köbĭrgen*; Sagai, Koibal *köbürgän* (R); Shor *köbürgen*; AltaiT: Altai *köbürgen*; Quu *köbirgen*; Teleut *köbürgen*; SayanT: Tuvan Toju *kögürgün*; Tofan *kögĭrhen* ~ *kögürhen*; ChulymT –; NE[N] Yakut –; NW[N] Siberian Tatar –; NW[S] Kirgiz *köbürgön*; Remaining lgs. –;
Turkic → Samoyedic:
    Kamas *kōbörgän* 'onion'.

Etymology: Joki LS 199; Räsänen VEWT 285a; Clauson ED 691b; Rassadin 1971: 204; ESTJa 1980: 100; Timonina 1986: 176; SIGTJa 2001: 124

    The Yeniseian forms were clearly borrowed from the Siberian Turkic form **köbürgän*. The disappearance of vowel harmony is a regular phonetic change for Yeniseian loanwords. The final +*aŋ* in Kott forms *kubúrgenaŋ* ~ *kabúrgenaŋ* is a native Yeniseian plural suffix (Werner 1990: 57–58). The final additional vowel in Assan is unclear.

    The Turkic word is connected to Mongolic *kömöl*.[39]

Kott *ô* 'inedible fungus, toadstool' (Werner 2002/2: 30; 1990: 302) ← Turkic **ō* < *aġu* 'poison':
    cf. Old Turkic *aġu*; NE[S] YeniseiT: Khakas *ō*; Sagai, Koibal, Kachin *ō* (R); Shor *ō*; AltaiT: Altai *ū* (R); Quu *ō*; Teleut *ū* (R); SayanT: Tuvan *ō* 'stinking liquid, which ferret lets out for protection; poison'; Tofan *ā*; ChulymT *ua* (R); NE[N] Yakut *aba* 'poison; bitterness, bitter taste; fig. annoyance'; Dolgan –; NW[N] Siberian Tatar *aġu*; NW[S] Kirgiz *ū* 'poison; method, trick, secret'; Fu-yü –; Kazak *u*; SE Yellow Yughur –.

Etymology: Räsänen VEWT 9a; Clauson ED 78b; ESTJa 1974: 67; Tatarincev 2008: 306–307

    The etymology of the Kott word is unknown. As a hypothesis, I assume that it is connected with the Turkic word *aġu* 'poison', which developed into a

---

38 This phonetic change is peculiar not only for Khakas, but also for Shor, Tofan and Fu-yü; e.g. Old Turkic *yan*- 'to turn back' ~ Khakas, Shor *nan*-; cf. Tofan *ńan*-; Fu-yü *nan*-; Old Turkic *yaġmur* 'rain' ~ Khakas *naŋmïr*; cf. Fu-yü *namïr*; Old Turkic *yaŋï* 'new' ~ Khakas *nā*; Shor *nā* ~ *ńā*; cf. Tofan *ńā*; Fu-yü *nā*; etc.

39 Cf. Middle Mongol: –; LM *kömöl* ~ *kömöli* 'wild onion'; Modern Mongol: Buryat –; Khalkha *xömöl*; Oirat dial. *kömöl* ~ *kömül*; Dagur –; Khamnigan –.

secondary long vowel *ō* in Modern Turkic. The Kott word was possibly borrowed from one of the Yenisei Turkic varieties, where this form is present. The development of the secondary long vowel from the sequence *Vocal-Consonant-Vocal* occurred in some other Turkic loanwords in Yeniseian, e.g. Kott *kônak* 'shirt' ← Turkic **kögänäk* < *köŋläk* 'shirt', Kott *ôr* 'herd of horses' ← Turkic **ȫr* < *ögür* 'a herd'. My hypothesis confirms the lexical meaning too. The lexical change probably happened from 'poison' → 'inedible fungus, toadstool'.

Arin *ott* 'hay' (Werner 2002/2: 47) ← Turkic **ot* 'grass, vegetation; hay':
    cf. Old Turkic *ot*; NE[S] YeniseiT: Khakas *ot*; Sagai, Koibal, Kachin *ot* (R); Kyzyl *ot ~ od*; Shor *ot*; AltaiT: Altai *ot*; Quu *ot*; Teleut *ot*; SayanT: Tuvan *o^ct*; Tofan *o^ct*; ChulymT *ot*; NE[N] Yakut *ot*; Dolgan *ot*; NW[N] Siberian Tatar *ōt*; NW[S] Kirgiz *ot*; Fu-yü *ōt*; Kazak *ot*; SE Yellow Uyghur *o^ct*.
Etymology: Räsänen VEWT 366b; Rassadin 1971: 213; Clauson ED 34–35; ESTJa 1974: 481–483; SIGTJa 1997: 119–120

Arin form with unknown geminated final consonant possibly is connected with Turkic word.

Kott *pʰarpak ~ farpax* 'bark' (Werner 2002/2: 56) ← ? Turkic **parbak* 'twig of a tree; branchy (*about a tree*)' < *barmaq* 'finger':
    cf. Old Turkic –; NE[S] YeniseiT: Khakas *parbax* 'twig of a tree; branchy (*about a tree*)'; Kyzyl *parbak* 'brunched' (R); AltaiT: Tuba *parvak* 'shaggy, bushy'; Teleut *parmak* 'finger, toe' (R); SayanT –; ChulymT –; NE[N] Yakut –; NW[N] Siberian Tatar *parmaq ~ marmaq* 'finger'; NW[S] Kirgiz *barmak* 'finger'; Fu-yü –; Kazak *barmaq* 'finger'; SE Yellow Uyghur *pasïrmïq* (< *baš barmaq* 'the main finger') 'thumb (*on the hand*)'.
Etymology: Räsänen VEWT 63b; ESTJa 1978: 66–68; SIGTJa 2001: 254–255

The etymology of the Kott word is unknown. As a hypothesis, I assume it may be connected with the Yenisei Turkic *parbak* 'branchy (*about tree*)', which is etymologically related to the Common Turkic word *barmaq* 'finger'. The Kott initial *pʰ-* and *f-* originated from the Proto-Yeniseian **p-*, e.g. Proto-Yeniseian **pənʌŋ* 'sand' ~ Kott *fenaŋ/pʰenaŋ*; Proto-Yeniseian *pu* 'heart' > Ket *hūˑ*, etc. (for details, see Starostin 1982: 149).

Although the new etymology may be phonetically convenient, the lexical side is problematic; possibly semantic narrowing happened. I list this word in the category with 'unclear etymology'.

The Yenisei Turkic forms obviously relate to the Common Turkic word *barmak* 'finger'.[40] The similar lexical broadening *twig of a tree → finger* is found in

---

40   The etymology of the Turkic word is questionable. There are different hypotheses that the

Tuvan, cf. Tuvan *salā* 'finger' was borrowed from Mongolic *salaγ-a* 'branch, twig or limb of a tree, offshoot; prongs of a fork; tributary, arm of a river; bifurcation; department, branch (*as of science, office, store*)' (Khabtagaeva 2009: 165).

Arin ***tegentestek*** 'raspberry' (Werner 2002/2: 257) ← Turkic **tegen d'estek* < *tikän* 'thorn' + *yestek* 'berry':
< *tegen* 'thorn' < *tikän* < *tik-* 'to insert; to insert (*in the ground*), to sew (*insert a needle*)' -*GXn* {Turkic VN, see Erdal 1991: 327}:
    cf. Old Turkic *tikän* ~ *tikänäk* (< *tikän* +*AK* {Turkic NN/diminutive}); NE^S YeniseiT: Khakas *tīgenek* '*bot*. dog rose, blackthorn; thorn', cf. *tīgen* 'fir'; Sagai, Koibal, Kachin *tigän* 'spruce, fir'; Shor *tigen* 'fir'; AltaiT: Altai *tegenek* 'dog rose; thorn', cf. *tegen* ~ *tēgen* 'fir'; Tuba *tegen* ~ *tegenek* 'thorn'; Qumanda *tigenek* '*bot*. hip'; Quu *tegenek* '*bot*. hip', cf. *tigen* 'fir'; Teleut *tegenek* '*bot*. hip, dog rose'; SayanT: Tuvan *ten* 'thorn, needle'; Tofan *te^ch'en* 'thorn; hip, raspberry'; ChulymT *tigän* 'hip'; NE^N Yakut *tik-* 'to sew; to sting'; Dolgan *tik-* 'to sew'; NW^N Siberian Tatar –; NW^S Kirgiz *tiken* 'thorn; splinter', *tikenek* 'prickle, thorn'; Fu-yü *dĭk-* 'to put up, sew'; Kazak *tiken* 'splinter, thorn'; SE Yellow Uyghur *tiken* 'chaparral plant'.
Etymology: Räsänen VEWT 480a; Doerfer TMEN 2: 528; Clauson ED 483b, 476b; ESTJa 1980: 226–227; SIGTJa 1997: 105–106
+ *d'estek* < *čestek* < *yestek* 'berry':
    cf. Old Turkic –; NE^S YeniseiT: Khakas *čistek* 'berry'; Koibal *yestäk* 'a berry which is similar in form with strawberry, raspberry, blackberry, etc.'; Kyzyl *sestäk^χ* ~ *sestäg^χ* 'berry'; Shor *čestek* 'berry'; AltaiT: Altai *d'estek* ~ *tistek* 'berry'; SayanT: Tuvan *čestek-kat* 'strawberry' < *kat* 'berry'; ChulymT *yestäk* ~ *čästäkäi* 'wild strawberry'; Remaining lgs. –;
Turkic → Samoyedic:
    Mator *čistäk* 'strawberry'.
Etymology: SIGTJa 1997: 121; Helimski 1997: 232

    The Arin word consists of two Turkic words *tegen* 'thorn' and *d'estek* 'berry'. This compound is not attested in the Turkic dictionaries. In spite of this, the phonetic shape shows Altai Turkic influence. The first part of the compounding *tegen* with the palatal vowel -*e*- and the voiced intervocalic *VgV* is typical of all Altai Turkic varieties. The second part of the Arin compounding *testek* is also close to the Altai Turkic *d'estek* ~ *tistek* forms. From a semantic point of view,

---

    word originates from *bār* 'existence' (Räsänen VEWT 63b), from the Turkic verb *bar-* 'to go', or from the Mongolic verb *bari-* 'to keep, to hold' (for details, see Sevortjan ESTJa 1978: 66–68). On the basis of the Chuvash form, Tenišev reconstructs Proto-Turkic *parŋak (SIGTJa 2001: 254–255). The word is found from the Middle-Turkic period (for all Turkic data, see ESTJa 1978: 66–68).

the development of 'raspberry' from 'thorn' and 'berry' is clear (Khabtagaeva 2015d: 132–133).

From an etymological aspect, the first Turkic word *tegen* 'thorn', which originally was *tikän*, originated from the Common Turkic verb *tik-* 'to insert; to sew (insert a needle)' and the productive deverbal noun suffix *-GXn* (As concerns the functions, see Erdal 1991: 327). Semantically, the word is found in Modern Turkic languages as different botanical names of plants, such as 'dog rose, hip, blackthorn or fir', or somehow related to 'thorn'.

The etymology of the second Turkic word *d'estek* 'berry' is unknown. It developed from **yästäk* through **čestek*. The final *-äk* may be the diminutive suffix. The word is found only in South-Siberian Turkic languages (SIGTJa 1997: 121) and was also borrowed into Samoyedic Mator (Helimski 1997: 232).

Kott *tôteäš* ~ *toteš*, Assan *toteš* 'Siberian fir (*lat.* Abies sibirica)' (Werner 2002/2: 280) ← Turkic **tït aġas* 'larch (*lat.* Pinus Larix)', cf. Khakas *tït aġas* 'larch':
< *tït* < *tït* 'larch (*lat.* Pinus Larix)':
    cf. Old Turkic *tït*; NE[S] YeniseiT: Khakas; Sagai, Koibal, Kachin; Kyzyl; Shor *tït*; AltaiT: Altai; Qumanda; Quu; Teleut *tït*; SayanT: Tuvan *dït*; Tofan *tït*; ChulymT *tït*; NE[N] Yakut; Dolgan *tït*; NW[N] Siberian Tatar –; NW[S] Kirgiz –;[41] SE Yellow Uyghur –;
Etymology: Räsänen VEWT 7b; Rassadin 1971: 236; Clauson ED 449b
+ *aġas* 'tree':
    cf. Old Turkic *ïġač*; NE[S] YeniseiT: Khakas *aġas*; Sagai *aġïs*; Koibal *aġas* ~ *aġïs*; Kyzyl *aġas* ~ *āġaš*; Shor *agaš*; AltaiT: Altai *aġaš*; Tuba *aġaš* ~ *aŋaš* ~ *āč*; Qumanda *agač* ~ *agaš*; Quu *agač* ~ *agas* ~ *agïš*; Teleut *agaš*; SayanT: Tuvan *ïyaš*; Tofan *ńeš*; ChulymT *aġač* ~ *aġac* ~ *āč*; NE[N] Yakut –; NW[N] Siberian Tatar *aġac* ~ *aġač*; NW[S] Kirgiz *jïġač*; Fu-yü *agaš* ~ *agïš*; Kazak *aġaš*; SE Yellow Uyghur *yïġaš*.
Etymology: Räsänen VEWT 479a; Clauson ED 79b; ESTJa 1974: 71

Amalgamation probably occurred in the Yeniseian forms. In the second part of the Kott word *eäš*, the Turkic consonant *-ġ-* was dropped and influenced the first part of the compounding, which was accented (Khabtagaeva 2015d: 137).

Despite of that fact the final *-š* is peculiar to Altai Turkic, the source of borrowing should be Yenisei Turkic, where nowadays the compound word is present, cf. Khakas *tït aġas* 'larch'.[42] The change of final *-s* to *-š* is not only is

---

41   According to SIGTJa (1997: 136), the Kirgiz *tït* ~ *tut* and the Kazak *tut* forms 'mullberry' are of Persian origin.

42   The second word shows the regular Khakas feature where the the final consonant *-č* regularly changed to *-s*, e.g. Old Turkic *üč* 'three' ~ Khakas *üs*, Old Turkic *āč* 'hungry' ~ Khakas *as*, Old Turkic *küč* 'strength' ~ Khakas *küs*, etc.

specific to Kott, but also a regular change for its Turkic loanwords, cf. Turkic *abïs* 'priest' → Kott *âpeš*, Turkic *koas* 'beautiful' → Kott *koaš* ~ *koâš*, etc.

1.1.4   Wild Animals, Birds, Fishes and Insects

Kott **akāŋa ~ agaŋa** 'mallard duck (*Anas boschas*)' (Werner 2002/1: 16) ← ? Turkic *ak aŋa < *aq* 'white' + *aŋar* 'kind of duck':

< Turkic *aq* < *āq* 'white':

cf. Old Turkic *āq*; NE^S YeniseiT: Khakas *ax*; Sagai, Koibal, Kachin *aq* (R); Kyzyl *aχ*; Shor *aq*; AltaiT: Altai *ak*; Tuba *ak*; Qumanda *ak*; Quu *ak*; Teleut *aq*; SayanT: Tuvan *ak*; Tofan *aq*; ChulymT *aq*; NE^N Yakut –; NW^N Siberian Tatar *aq*; NW^S Kirgiz *ak*; Fu-yü *ah*; Kazak *aq*; SE Yellow Uyghur *aq*.

Etymology: Laude-Cirtautas 1961: 40–48; Doerfer TMEN 2: 84–85; Räsänen VEWT 12b; Rassadin 1971: 154; Clauson ED 75a; ESTJa 1974: 116

+ Turkic *aŋar* 'kind of duck':

cf. NE^S YeniseiT: –; AltaiT: Altai *aŋar* 'a water bird, smaller than a goose with reddish yellow chest' (R); *aŋïr* 'the kind of red duck (Russian *варнавка*)'; SayanT: Tuvan *aŋgïr* 'scoter'; ChulymT *aŋnan* 'kind of eagle'; NE^N Yakut *aŋïr* 'bittern (*Botaurus stellaris*)'; Yakut dial. *aŋïr* 'owl'; NW^N Siberian Tatar –; NW^S Kirgiz, Kazak *aŋgar* 'kind of duck' (R); Fu-yü –; SE Yellow Uyghur –;

Turkic ← Mongolic *aŋgir* 'a kind of yellow duck':

cf. Middle Mongol: HY *anggir*; ZY *anggir*; LM *aŋgir* 'yellow, reddish-yellow; a kind of yellow duck (*Tadorna ferruginea*)'; Modern Mongol: Buryat *angir* 'scoter; yellow, reddish-yellow'; Khalkha *angir* 'ruddy shelduck'; Oirat dial. *ängir* 'scoter'; Dagur –; Khamnigan *angir*;

Mongolic ← Turkic:

cf. Old Turkic *aŋït* 'a rather large bird predominantly red; the ruddy goose (*Anas casarca*)'; NE^S YeniseiT: Khakas *āt* 'scoter'; Shor *āt* 'wild duck'; AltaiT: –; SayanT: –; ChulymT –; NE^N Yakut *andï ~ annï* 'scoter, pochard; black duck';[43] Yakut dial. *ańńa* 'duck' (DS); NW^N Siberian Tatar –; NW^S Kirgiz –; Fu-yü –; SE Yellow Uyghur *aŋït* 'wild duck with yellow feathers'.

Etymology: Räsänen VEWT 21; Clauson ED 176a; SIGTJa 2001: 172; Tatarincev 2000: 20; Khabtagaeva 2009: 159; Nugteren 2011: 266

The etymology of the Kott word is problematic from a phonetic perspective. It might be a compound word of Turkic origin based on *aq* 'white' and another Turkic word, which designates a kind of duck *aŋar*, where the final -*r* is dropped in Kott. The word *aŋgir* may have meant a kind of yellow duck (*Tadorna ferruginea*)' in Kott, in Turkic and Mongolic languages. In Kott the name of a kind of gray, whitish duck cannot be excluded.

---

43   Yakut → Tungusic: *Eastern Ewenki*: Ayan, Uchur *anni ~ andi* 'black duck' (SSTMJa 1: 43b).

The word *aŋgir* 'a kind of yellow duck' belongs in the category of old Eurasian cultural words. Cf. Manchu *aŋgir niyehe* 'anggir duck, ruddy shelldrake, Cascara ferruginea (Pallas)', Tibetan *anggi-ra* (for details, see Róna-Tas & Berta WOT 2011: 508).

There is another solution for the etymology of Turkic origin. The Kott word might be a compound of Turkic *āq* 'white' (Clauson ED 75ab) + Turkic *aŋ* 'the name of a bird whose fat is used for medicinal purposes', which is of Chinese origin (Clauson ED 165b). The final *-a* in the Kott form could be the Yeniseian feminine suffix, or the final vowel was added by paragogue.

The Khakas word *aġïyaŋ*, 'hurruer (lat. *Circus*)—a sacred bird for the Khakas people' (But.) and the Sagai *aġaya* ~ *aġayaŋ*, 'a kind of bird' (KhR), a 'seagull' (R), which are phonetically closer to the Kott word, but from a lexical aspect this connection probably has to be rejected.

Kott ***alpaka*** ~ ***alpuga*** ~ ***alpuka*** 'flying squirrel' (Werner 2002/1: 27) ← Turkic *albaga 'sable' < *alba* 'tax, impost, tribute' +*GAn* {Turkic NN, forming nouns that designate names of animals and plants: Erdal 1991: 85–89} ← Mongolic *alban* 'compulsion, coercion; official obligation or service; tax, impost, tribute; corvée; public use':

cf. NE^S YenaiseiT: Khakas *albïga* 'sable';[44] Koibal *albaga* (R), Shor *albïga*; AltaiT: Altai *albuga*; Quu *albaga*; Teleut *albaġa* (R); Remaining lgs. –;

Turkic → Samoyedic:

Kamas *albuya* ~ *alboya* 'sable';

Turkic ← Mongolic *alban* 'compulsion, coercion; official obligation or service; tax, impost, tribute; corvée; public use':

cf. Middle Mongol: Precl.Mo. *alban*; HY *alban*; 'Phags-pa *alba*; LM *alban*; Modern Mongol: Buryat *alba(n)*; Khalkha *alban* 'official'; Kalmuck *alwa* ~ *alwn*; Dagur *alba* (T); Khamnigan *alba(n)*;

Etymology: Joki LS 61; Räsänen VEWT 16b; Timonina 1982: 163; Khabtagaeva 2015a: 117–118

The etymology of the Turkic word is unknown. The word is present only in the South Siberian languages, including Yenisei Turkic and Altai Turkic. According to Räsänen (VEWT 16b), the Turkic word consists of two words, *ala* 'colorful' and *buġa* 'bull'. Radloff (R 1: 432) derived the Teleut word *albaġa* 'mining, hunter's mining' from the Turkic verb *al-* 'to take'. Timonina (1982: 163) links the Yeniseian word component **al-* to the religious beliefs of the Yeniseian peo-

---

[44] Cf. the forms of Khakas *tabïrġan*, Sagai *pabïrġan* and Altai *babïrgan* 'flying squirrel'. By contrast, in Kott the 'sable' is *fukajaše* (Werner 1990: 250).

ples. In my opinion, the Turkic word originates from the Mongolic word *alban* 'official obligation; tax, impost, tribute' and the Turkic NN suffix +*GAn*, which forms nouns that designate the names of animals. The sable, of course, was the animal paid as tribute and tax to the Russians by Turkic and other native Siberian people.

Comparison may also be made with the Kott *alpan* 'tribute'.

Kott *bôru* ~ *boru*; Assan *boru* ~ *borü* 'wolf' (Werner 2002/1: 143) ← Turkic **börü* 'wolf':

cf. Old Turkic *böri*; NE^S YeniseiT: Khakas *pür̄*, cf. *mör̄i* (But.); Sagai, Koibal, Kachin *pörü* (R); Kyzyl *pör̄*; Shor *pörü*; AltaiT: Altai *börü*; Tuba *börü*; Qumanda *böri* ~ *börü* ~ *mör̄i* ~ *mör̄ö* ~ *möre* ~ *müre* ~ *müri* ~ *pöri*; Quu *pörü*; Teleut *pöri*; SayanT: Tuvan *börü*; Tofan *börü*; ChulymT *pör̄ä* ~ *pör̄ü* ~ *mör̄ä* ~ *mör̄ü*; NE^N Yakut *börö*; Dolgan *börö*; NW^N Siberian Tatar *pör̄ü*; NW^S Kirgiz *börü*; Fu-yü –; Kazak *böri*; SE Yellow Yughur –.

Etymology: Ščerbak 1961: 131–132; Räsänen VEWT 84a; Rassadin 1971: 165; Clauson ED 356a; Doerfer TMEN 2: 333–334; ESTJa 1978: 219–221; Timonina 1978: 12; SIGTJa 2001: 160

Due to the absence of vowel harmony in Yeniseian, the Turkic front vowels changed to the back vowels in the Yeniseian forms.

The word is present in almost all Turkic languages, but the etymology of the Turkic word is unknown. Doerfer derives it from the Persian (for details, see Doerfer TMEN 2: 333–334). From the Turkic, the word was borrowed into Mongolic[45] and re-borrowed into the Modern Turkic languages[46] (Khabtagaeva 2009: 159).

Arin *buturčinok* 'quail' (Werner 2002/1: 153) < *buturčin* -*ok* {Yeniseian suffix} ← Turkic **budurčin* < *budurčun* 'quail, Coturnyx' < *buldur* +*čIn* {? Turkic NN, see Clauson ED xlii}:

cf. Old Turkic *büldürčin* ~ *budursïn*; NE^S YeniseiT: Khakas *pudurčun* ~ *püdürčün*; Sagai *püdürčün* (R); AltaiT: –; SayanT –; ChulymT –; NE^N Yakut *bïld'ïrüt* 'Siberian snipe'; Dolgan –; NW^N Siberian Tatar *büldürcün*; NW^S Kirgiz *bulduruk* (< *buldur* +*Ak* {Turkic NN/diminutive}) 'sandgrouse'; Fu-yü –; Kazak *buldïrïq* 'grouse'; SE Yellow Yughur –.

---

45 Turkic → Mongolic 'jackal': Middle Mongol: SH *jö'eböri*; HY *čü'eberi*; LM *čögeböri*; Modern Mongol: Khalkha *cöwör*; Buryat *süben* ~ *süber*; Kalmuck *tšöwr*; Dagur –; Khamnigan –.
46 Turkic → Mongolic → Modern Turkic: NE^S YeniseiT: Shor, Sagai, Koibal, Kachin *čö pörü* 'reddish wolf' (R); AltaiT Quu *čö pörü* 'reddish wolf' (R); Teleut *čö pörü* 'wolf' (R); SayanT: Tuvan *šö-börü* 'jackal'; Tofan *šö-börü* 'jackal; one-year-old fox'; ChulymT *čö pörü* 'reddish wolf' (R); NE^N Yakut –; NW^S Kirgiz *čö* 'red wolf, jackal'; Kazak *šiböri* 'jackal'; SE Uzbek *čiyaböri* 'jackal'; Modern Uyghur *čilböri* 'jackal'.

Etymology: Doerfer TMEN 2: 312–313; Räsänen VEWT 73b–74a; Clauson ED 335b; 309a; ESTJa 1978: 305–306; SIGTJa 1997: 173

The Arin word was borrowed from the Siberian Turkic form **budurčin* with the native Yeniseian suffix -*ok*.

From an etymological point of view, the base of the Turkic word are the forms *buldur ~ bïldïr*, which are probably of onomatopoeic origin. The presence of the suffix +*čIn* assumes the Kirgiz *bulduruk* and the Kazak *buldïrïq*, where the diminutive suffix +*Ak* is found. Cf. also the Mongolic word *bilduur* 'small bird'[47] (Nugteren 2011: 282), which is possibly of Turkic origin.

Kott *d'ira ~ d'era* 'lizard' (Werner 2002/1: 223) ← ? Turkic **d'ïlan < yïlan* 'snake': cf. Old Turkic *yïlan*; NE[S] YeniseiT: Khakas *čïlan*; Sagai *čïlan* (R); Kyzyl *šïlàn ~ šlàn*; Shor *čïlan*; AltaiT: Altai *d'ïlan*; Tuba *d'ïlan*; Qumanda *d'ïlan ~ t'ïlan*; Quu *d'ïlan*; Teleut *yïlan*; SayanT: Tuvan *čïlan*; Tofan *čulan*; ChulymT –; NE[N] Yakut –; NW[N] Siberian Tatar –; NW[S] Kirgiz *jïlan*; Fu-yü *jïlan ~ jïlïn*; Kazak *žïlan*; SE Yellow Uyghur *yïlan*.

Etymology: Clauson ED 930a; Timonina 1985: 11–12; ESTJa 1989: 277; SIGTJa 2001: 180; Róna-Tas & Berta WOT 2011: 452–453

The etymology of the Kott word is unknown. Timonina (1985: 12) connects it with Turkic *yïlan* 'snake'. She explains the disappearance of the Turkic final -*n* by false analogy the Yeniseian plural suffix, which was dropped by the Kott people. The change of the initial *y*- → *d'* is typical of Kott loanwords, but the change of the intervocalic *VlV* → *VrV* is unclear because of the absence of similar examples. The word belongs in the category with uncertain etymology.

As concerns the etymology of the Turkic word, it was connected with the verb *yïl-* 'to glide, slide, creep, crawl', which is absent in Old Turkic, but is present in Tatar and some Siberian languages, cf. also the Middle Turkic *yïldam* 'quick, rapid', which probably originates from the already mentioned Turkic verb *yïl-* and the Turkic deverbal noun suffix -*dAm* (for details, see ESTJa 1989: 278–279; Róna-Tas & Berta WOT 2011: 452–453[48]).

---

47 Turkic → Mongolic: Middle Mongol: SH *bilji'ur* 'small bird, sparrow', *bildu'ur* 'lark'; Rasulid *bildūr*; LM *bilĵuuqai* 'any small bird'; Modern Mongol: Buryat *bilžūxai ~ bolžūxai ~ bulžūxai* 'small bird'; Khalkha *byalzūxai* 'a small bird' (*bilĵiu* +*KAi* {Mongolic NN/dim.}); Dagur *bellur ~ beldur* 'lark' (E); Khamnigan –.

48 Turkic: West Old Turkic **ïldam* 'tactful, well-mannered' → Hungarian *ildom* 'proper behaviour'.

Arin *džipká* 'marten' (Werner 2002/1: 225) ← Samoyedic ← Turkic *jäpkä < *yäpkä* 'wolverine':
← Samoyedic:
    cf. Mator *čibkä* 'wolverine';
Samoyedic ← Turkic:
    cf. Old Turkic –; NE^S YeniseiT: Koibal *yäkpä* (R); AltaiT: –; SayanT: Tuvan *čekpe*; Tofan *čeᶜkpe ~ čeᶜpke*; Remaining lgs. –;
cf. Mongolic 'wolverine':
    cf. Middle Mongol: –; LM *ǰegeke(n)*; Modern Mongol: Buryat *zēgen*; Khalkha *dzēx(en)*; Kalmuck *zēkn*; Dagur –; Khamnigan –;
Mongolic → Modern Turkic 'wolverine':
    cf. NE^S YeniseiT: –; AltaiT: Altai *d'ēken*; Teleut *yēken*; SayanT –; ChulymT –; NE^N Yakut *siägän*; Dolgan *hiägän*; Remaining lgs. –.

Etymology: Räsänen VEWT 195b; Rassadin 1980: 67; Helimski 1997: 231; SIGTJa 1997: 165

According to Werner (2002/1: 225), the Arin word was borrowed from Samoyedic. This seems possible, because the Mator form is closer than the Siberian Turkic forms from the phonetic side. In the Siberian Turkic forms, metathesis occurred *yäpkä > yäkpä*.

The Samoyedic Mator form was connected with the Turkic (Helimski 1997: 231). In turn, the etymology of the Turkic word is unknown, since it is present only in some Siberian Turkic languages. Tenišev (SIGTJa 1997: 165) assumes the native Turkic derivation or inner borrowing, which is close to Altai Turkic. In this way, the Teleut *yimäkkäi* 'voracious, gluttonous' and the Quu *yäbäkäi* originate from the Common Turkic noun *yämäk* 'food'.

According to Mongolic data, the Turkic word should be derived from the base *yäp with the denominal noun suffix +*KA* forming names of animals and plants, which is a variant of suffix +*GA* (for details on the function, see Erdal 1991: 83–84). In turn, the Mongolic word *ǰegeken* 'wolverine' derived from the base *ǰege and the diminutive suffix +*KAn* (for details on the suffix, see Poppe GWM §124). My assumption is strengthened by the Turco-Mongolic phonetic changes of initial *y- > ǰ-*[49] and medial *-p- > -g-*.[50] Despite the fact that the word is not widespread among Turkic languages, the base may be the Turkic verb *yē-* 'to eat' (Clauson ED 869a), which fits semantically for our etymology.

---

49   E.g. Turkic *ǰāl: cf. Old Turkic *yāš* 'fresh' → Mongolic *ǰalayu* < **ǰal+A-GUn*; Turkic **ǰorï-*: cf. Old Turkic *yorï-* 'to walk, march' → Mongolic *ǰori-* 'to move in the direction of'; etc.

50   E.g. Turkic **qapă-* 'to close': cf. Old Turkic *qap-* → Mongolic *qaγa-*; Turkic *köperüg 'bridge': cf. Old Turkic *köprüg* → Mongolic *kögerge* < **köger+GAn*; Turkic *qopur 'a stringed instrument': cf. Old Turkic *qopuz* → Mongolic *quγur*, etc.

From the Mongolic, the word was borrowed into Altai Turkic, Yakut and Dolgan languages (Rassadin 1980: 67).

Yugh *fálgi*; Ket *hál'ga* 'ruff (*fish, Gymnocephalus cernuus*)' (Werner 2002/1: 297) ← ? Turkic *palïk 'fish' < balïq:

cf. Old Turkic *balïq*; NE[S] YeniseiT: Khakas *palïx*; Sagai, Koibal, Kachin *palïq* (R); Kyzyl *pālïχ* ~ *pālï^kχ*; Shor *palïq*; AltaiT: Altai *balïq*; Tuba *balïk*; Qumanda *balïk*; Quu *palïk*; Teleut *palïq*; SayanT: Tuvan *balïk*; Tofan *balïq*; ChulymT *pālïq*; NE[N] Yakut *balïk*; Dolgan *balïk*; NW[N] Siberian Tatar *palïq*; NW[S] Kirgiz *balïk*; Fu-yü *balïh*; Kazak *balïq*; SE Yellow Yughur –.

Etymology: Doerfer TMEN 2: 96–97; Räsänen VEWT 61b; Rassadin 1971: 159; Clauson ED 335b; ESTJa 1978: 59–60; Stachowski 1997: 229; SIGTJa 1997: 177

From an etymological aspect, Vajda (2016: personal communication) regards the Yugh and Ket words as a compound word of Yeniseian origin, which goes back to Proto-Yeniseian *palgə < *pal 'bent' and *kūˑx 'mouth'. He also noted (Vajda 2014: personal communication) that it is one of the few feminine-class fish names, the others being masculine.

After Stachowski (1997: 229), Werner (2002/1: 297) connects the Yeniseian words with the Common Turkic word *balïq* 'fish'. The Turkic transferring form was with the initial devoiced consonant *p*-. This suggestion is strengthened by the regular change of original the Yenisean *p*- to *f*- in Yugh and *h*- in Ket (for details, see Starostin 1982: 149). If we accept the Turkic etymology, the Turkic word may have been borrowed in the early period. The word belongs in the category with uncertain etymology.

The Common Turkic word is widespread in almost all Turkic languages. From one of the Siberian Turkic languages the word was borrowed into Buryat as *balyūhan* 'small fry', which is probably derived from the Turkic *balïq* 'fish' and the productive Mongolic denominal noun suffix +*sUn* (Khabtagaeva 2013: 169). The Turkic word was borrowed into the Russian (Vasmer 1986/1: 119) and Persian (Doerfer TMEN 2: 96–97). The relation of the Turkic word to the Manchu *falu* 'the name of a fish similar to bream' (SSTMJa 2: 298b) is unclear.

Kott *holanka* 'weasel' (Werner 2002/1: 322) ← Turkic *qolanak 'Siberian weasel, Mustela sibirica' ← Russian *kolonok* 'weasel' ← Tungusic *holoŋgo* ~ *soloŋgo* 'weasel, Mustela sibirica' ← Mongolic *soloŋγa* 'Siberian marten; weasel':
Yeniseian ← Turkic *qolanak:

cf. Old Turkic –; NE[S] YeniseiT: Khakas *xolanax*; Sagai *xolnax*, cf. *qulunaq* (R); Koibal, Kachin *quluγaq* (R); Kyzyl *χolanaχ*; Shor *qolnaq*; AltaiT: Altai –; Quu *kolgonok*; SayanT –; ChulymT *qulanaq*; NE[N] Yakut –; NW[N] Siberian Tatar *qulunčaq* (< *qulun* +*čAK* {Turkic NN/diminutive}) (R); Remaining lgs. –;

Turkic → Samoyedic:
   Kamas *kolonok* 'Mustela sibirica';
Turkic ← Russian *kolonok* 'weasel' (Vasmer 1986/2: 295);
Russian ← Tungusic *holoŋgo* ~ *soloŋgo* 'weasel, Mustela sibirica':
   Northern Tungusic: Ewenki *soloŋō* ~ *solga* ~ *soliyā* ~ *soloŋo* ~ *sonoŋgo* ~ *honoŋgo* ~ *holoŋgo* ~ *šonoŋgō*; Solon *sōligi*; Southern Tungusic: Udehe *sölüö*; Nanai *sol'u*; Manchu *silihi* ~ *solohi*;
Tungusic ← Mongolic *soloŋya* 'Siberian marten; weasel':
   cf. Middle Mongol: SH *solangqa*; YY *solongya*; LM *solongɣ-a*; Modern Mongol: Buryat; Lower Uda Buryat *holongo*; Khalkha *solongo*; Kalmuck *solŋga*; Dagur –; Khamnigan *solongo*;
Mongolic → Turkic:
   cf. NE[S] YeniseiT: –; AltaiT: –; SayanT: Tuvan *solaŋgï* 'weasel'; Tofan –; ChulymT –; NE[N] Yakut *soloŋdo* ~ *sologdo* ~ *soloŋko* 'Siberian weasel'; Yakut dial. *solomo* ~ *soloko* ~ *soloŋgo* ~ *soloŋo* ~ *soloŋxo* ~ *holomo* ~ *holoŋuy* 'weasel'; Remaining lgs. –.

Etymology: Radloff 2: 980; Joki LS: 188; Kałużyński 1961: 95; Ščerbak 1961: 146; Räsänen VEWT 277b; SSTMJa 2: 109a; Doerfer 1985: 39–40; Vasmer 1986/2: 295; Rozycki 1994: 187; Anikin 2000: 298–299; Khabtagaeva 2009: 159

The Yeniseian word is obviously connected with Turkic or Mongolic forms, but the source of the borrowing is not clear. The phonetic shape assumes a Mongolic, and more precisely a Buryat source, where the pharyngealization[51] *s-* > *h-* is observed in the initial position. However, this may be the only case of Kott borrowing from Buryat, so that the etymology remains in question.

The Kott word most likely has connections with the Turkic *qolanak* 'Siberian weasel, Mustela sibirica', which is widespread in Siberian Turkic languages. The metathesis *ak* > *ka* took place in the final position and the change of the Turkic initial *k-* > *h-* in Kott.

The etymology of the Turkic word is also unknown. According to Radloff (R 2: 980), the Turkic word *qulanaq* is derived from *qulan* 'foal' and the Turkic diminutive suffix *+AK*. The Turkic word was borrowed from the Russian *kolonok*, as observed by Vasmer (Vasmer 1986/2: 295). In his *Etymological Dictionary of Russian*, he connects the Russian word with Tungusic. In turn, the Tungusic forms were borrowed from the Mongolic languages (SSTMJa 2: 109a; Doer-

---

51 The pharyngealization is a regular phonetic feature in Buryat, e.g. LM *sara* 'moon; month' ~ Buryat *hara* (cf. Khalkha *sar*); LM *sana-* 'to think' ~ Buryat *hana-* (cf. Khalkha *sana-*); LM *seleme* 'sword, sabre' ~ Buryat *helme* (cf. Khalkha *selem*); LM *toyosun* 'dust' ~ Buryat *tōhon* (cf. Khalkha *tōs(on)*); LM *nasun* 'age' ~ Buryat *nahan* (cf. Khalkha *nas(an)*); LM *sünesün* 'soul' ~ Buryat *hünehe(n)* (cf. Khalkha *süns*), etc.

fer 1985: 39–40; Rozycki 1994: 187). It seems that the Mongolic word spread in an early period; it is found in almost all Tungusic languages. The word belongs in the "Wanderwort" category.

Yugh *kʌčiŋej* 'magpie' (Werner 2002/1: 459) ← ? Turkic *karčïġay < *qaračqay* 'swallow' ← Mongolic *qaraɣačai* 'swallow' < *qara* 'black' +*GAčAi* {Mongolic NN, see Khabtagaeva 2001: 107}:

    NE^S YeniseiT: Khakas *xaračxai*; Sagai *qaračqay*, Kachin (R); Kyzyl *xaràšɣay*; AltaiT: –; SayanT: Tuvan *xaráčïġay*; Tofan *harāčïġay* 'zool. dipper'; ChulymT –; NE^N Yakut *xaraŋaččï* ~ *xaraġaččï* 'swallow, swift'; Dolgan –; NW^N Siberian Tatar –; NW^S Kirgiz –; Fu-yü *gargačï*; Kazak –; SE Yellow Uyghur –;

Turkic → Samoyedic:

    Kamas *karāčɣai* 'sparrow'; Mator *karačagaj* 'lark, swallow';

Turkic ← Mongolic *qaraɣačai* 'swallow':

    Middle Mongol: HY *qariyača*; ZY *qariyača*; YY *qarčā[i]*; LM *qariyačai* ~ *qaraɣačai*; Modern Mongol: Buryat *xarāsgai*; Khalkha *xarācai*; Lower Uda Buryat *karāsagae* ~ *karāsgē* ~ *krāsgē*; Oirat dial. *xarādā* ~ *xarādaē*; Dagur –; Khamnigan *xarācagai* ~ *xarādzagai*.

Etymology: Joki LS 163–164; Räsänen VEWT 235b; Rassadin 1971: 99; 1980: 35, 36, 67; ESTJa 1997: 308–309; Helimski 1997: 268; SIGTJa 2001: 175–176; Khabtagaeva 2001: 107; 2009: 160; Nugteren 2011: 405

The etymology of the Yugh word is unknown (Werner 2002/1: 459). As a hypothesis, I assume it is connected to the Turkic form *karačïġay < *qaračqay* 'swallow'. From a phonetic point of view, the internal syllable -*ra*- was dropped as in other Kott loanword **kaltum** 'bear' ← Turkic *kara yoldu* 'brown (*color of the animal*)'. In addition, the Turkic intervocalic consonant *VgV* changed to the nasal *VŋV* in the Yugh form. However, the Yugh word belongs to the category of words of uncertain etymology.

The Samoyedic forms were borrowed from the Siberian Turkic (Joki LS 163–164), while the Turkic forms are of Mongolic origin (Räsänen VEWT 235b; Rassadin 1971: 99; 1980: 35, 36, 67; ESTJa 1997: 308–309). From an etymological side, the Mongolic word is possibly derived from the adjective *qara* 'black' and the Mongolic denominal noun suffix +*GAčAi* (Khabtagaeva 2001: 107).

Kott *kalači* 'eagle' (Werner 2002/1: 405) ← ? Turkic *qal lačïn < *qal* 'strong' + *lačïn* 'falcon':

< *qal* 'strong':

    cf. Old Turkic *qal* 'wild, savage, mad'; NE^S YeniseiT: Khakas *xal* 'desperate, fearless, impenetrable; unresponsive; inexperienced'; Sagai *xal* 'powerful, brave'; cf. Sagai, Kachin *kal*; Kyzyl *qal* 'strong'; Shor *qal* 'insensitive, cruel'; AltaiT: Altai *kal* 'daring';

Teleut *qal* 'coarse'; SayanT –; ChulymT –; NE^N Yakut –; NW^N Siberian Tatar *qal* 'stupid, blunt'; Remaining lgs. –;
Etymology: Räsänen VEWT 224a; Clauson ED 614b
+ *lačïn* 'falcon':

cf. Old Turkic *lāčïn*; NE^S YeniseiT: Khakas *ïlačïn*; Sagai *lačïn*; Shor *lačïn*; AltaiT: Quu *lačïn*; SayanT –; ChulymT –; NE^N Yakut –; NW^N Siberian Tatar *ïlacïn* 'kite'; NW^S Kirgiz *ïlāčïn*; Fu-yü –; Kazak *lašïn*; SE Yellow Yughur –.

Etymology: Doerfer TMEN 4: 11–14; Räsänen VEWT 313b; Clauson ED 763b; Ščerbak 1997: 129; SIGTJa 2001: 170; ESTJa 2003: 6–8

The etymology of the Kott word is unknown. As a hypothesis, I assume that it is a compound word, though compounding is a typical feature for the Yeniseian languages. The Kott *kalači* 'eagle' is possibly connected with the Turkic combination of the words *qal* 'strong' and *lačïn* 'falcon' (Khabtagaeva 2015d: 137). Finally, amalgamation occurred in the Kott form. From a semantic point of view, the Turkic meaning 'strong falcon' fits the Kott meaning 'eagle'. Both birds belong in the same *Falconidae* family.

The etymology of the Turkic word *lačïn* 'falcon' is unknown. Clauson indicates Tocharian origin (ED 763b), while Doerfer (TMEN 4: 11–14) and Ščerbak (1997: 129) refer to the Turkic word as of unknown origin. The Turkic word was connected with the Mongolic *način* 'falcon',[52] where the change of the initial *l*- to *n*- occurred (Räsänen VEWT 313b; SIGTJa 2001: 170). There is a re-borrowing in Tuvan[53] (Khabtagaeva 2009: 63). The word belongs in the "Wanderwort" category.

Kott **kaltum** 'bear' (Werner 2002/1: 406) < *kaltu -(X)m* {Yeniseian NN/adj.} ← Turkic *kara yoldu 'brown (*colour of animal*)' < *kara* 'black' + *yoldïg* 'striped', cf. AltaiT: Quu dial. *qara yoldu* 'brown; bear' (TSSDAJa 93):
< *kara* 'black':

cf. Old Turkic *qara*; YeniseiT: Khakas *xara*; Sagai, Koibal, Kachin *qara*; Kyzyl *χara*; Shor *qara*; AltaiT: Altai; Tuba; Qumanda; Quu; Teleut *qara*; SayanT: Tuvan; Tofan *qara*; ChulymT *qara*; Yakut *xara*; Dolgan *kara ~ xara*; Siberian Tatar *qara*; Kirgiz *kara*; Fu-yü *gar*; Kazak *qara*; Yellow Uyghur *qara*;

Etymology: Räsänen VEWT 235a; Clauson ED 643b; ESTJa 1997: 286–288; SIGTJa 2001: 680

---

52 Turkic → Mongolic 'falcon': Middle Mongol: Precl.Mo. *način*; LM *način*; Modern Mongol: Buryat *našan*; Khalkha *način*; Kalmuck *natšn*; Dagur –; Khamnigan –.

53 Turkic *lačïn* 'falcon' → Mongolic *način* 'falcon' → Tuvan *načïn* 'falcon (*title given to a wrestler who wins*)'.

+ *yoldu* 'striped' < *yol* 'road, way; streak, stripe' +*lXK* {Turkic NN/adj., see Erdal 1991: 121}:

cf. Old Turkic *yōl*; YeniseiT: Khakas; Sagai *čolliġ* < *čol*; Koibal *yolliġ*; Kyzyl *šol*; Shor *čol*; AltaiT: Altai *d'ol*; cf. *yoldū* (R); Tuba *d'ol*; Qumanda *d'ol ~ t'ol ~ čol*; Quu *yoldïg* < *yol*; Teleut *yol*; SayanT: –⁵⁴; ChulymT *čol ~ yol*; Yakut *suollāx* < *suol*; Dolgan *huol*; Siberian Tatar *yulaqlï* < *yulaq* 'stripe' < *yul* 'road'; Kirgiz *žoldū* < *žol*; Fu-yü *yol*; Kazak *žol*; Yellow Uyghur *yol*.

Etymology: Räsänen VEWT 205; Clauson ED 917ab; ESTJa 1989: 217–219; SIGTJa 2001: 531

The Kott word is of unclear etymology. It was probably borrowed from the Turkic compound word *kara yoldu* 'brown ← literally with black stripes' (Khabtagaeva 2015b: 524). In the Altai Turkic Quu dialect this compound word has the meaning 'bear'. The final Kott -*m* is the Yeniseian adjective suffix. From a phonetic point of view, amalgamation and prolapse of the internal syllable -*ra*- took place, which are typical phonetic features in Altaic loanwords. These features are found in other Turkic loanwords too (cf. Kott *tôteäš* 'Siberian fir' ← Turkic *tït aġas* 'larch', or Yugh *kʌčiŋej* 'magpie' ← Turkic *karačiġay* 'swallow').

Kott *karâga* 'crow' (Werner 2002/1: 411) ← Turkic **qarġa* 'crow':

cf. Old Turkic *qarġa*; NEˢ YeniseiT: Khakas *xarġa*; Sagai, Koibal, Kachin *qarġa* (R); Kyzyl *χarγa*; Shor *qarγa*; AltaiT: Altai *qarga*; Tuba *karga*; Qumanda *karga*; Quu *karga*; Teleut *qarġā*; SayanT: Tuvan *kārgan*; Tofan *qarġan* 'crow; jackdaw'; ChulymT *qarġa*; NEᴺ Yakut –; NWᴺ Siberian Tatar *qarġa* (R); NWˢ Kirgiz *karga*; Fu-yü *garga*; Kazak *qarġa*; SE Yellow Yughur –.

Etymology: Räsänen VEWT 237b; Doerfer TMEN 3: 384–385; Rassadin 1971: 219; Clauson ED 653a; Timonina 1978: 12; ESTJa 1997: 303–304

Due to the rareness of consonant clusters, epentheses happened in the Kott form. The Kott word points to a later period of borrowing because of the preservation of the initial *k*-. *k*- usually changed to *h*- in the original Yeniseian words. Or *k* was preserved in Kott due to onomatopoeia (Vajda 2018: personal communication), since the Turkic word belongs in the group of onomatopoeic origin.

---

54   The Tuvan and Tofan word *čol* 'fate, happiness' probably is the Mongolic loanword (Rassadin 1980: 70; Khabtagaeva 2009: 127), which is of Turkic origin. Cf. Mongolic: LM *jol* 'good luck, fortune, good result, success'; Khalkha *dzol*; Buryat; Kalmuck *zol*; Dagur –; Khamnigan *dzol* ← Turkic (Räsänen VEWT 205; ESTJa 1989: 217–218; Ščerbak 1997: 124).

Arin *karasek* 'fly' (Werner 2002/1: 411) ← Turkic *qara sēk, cf. YeniseiT: Khakas *xara sēk*; Sagai Koibal, Kachin *qara sāk* 'fly'; Chulym Turkic *kara sēk* 'midge':
< *qara* 'black':

cf. Old Turkic *qara*; NE^S YeniseiT: Khakas *xara*; Sagai, Koibal, Kachin; Shor *qara*; Kyzyl *χara*; AltaiT: Altai; Tuba; Qumanda; Quu; Teleut *qara*; SayanT: Tuvan; Tofan *qara*; ChulymT *qara*; NE^N Yakut *xara*; Dolgan *kara ~ xara*; NW^N Siberian Tatar *qara*; NW^S Kirgiz *kara*; Fu-yü *gar*; Kazak *qara*; SE Yellow Uyghur *qara*.

Etymology: Laude-Cirtautas 1961: 17–23; Räsänen VEWT 235a; Clauson ED 643b; ESTJa 1997: 286–288; SIGTJa 1997: 680

+ *sēk* 'fly' < *siŋek* 'a buzzing insect' < *siŋ +*AK* {Turkic NN/diminutive, see Erdal 1991: 40}:

cf. Old Turkic *siŋäk*; NE^S YeniseiT: Khakas *sēk* 'fly'; Sagai, Koibal, Kachin *sǟk*; Shor *sēk* 'mosquito'; AltaiT: Altai *sēk* 'gadfly', cf. *sek* 'mosquito'; Qumanda *sēk* 'mosquito'; Quu *sek ~ sēk* 'mosquito, midge', cf. *sǟk* 'sandfly' (R); SayanT: Tuvan; Tofan *sēk* 'fly'; ChulymT *sēk* 'mosquito', cf. *kara sēk* 'midge'; NE^N Yakut –; NW^N Siberian Tatar –; NW^S Kirgiz –; Fu-yü *sīh* 'fly'; Kazak –; SE Yellow Uyghur *siŋgek* 'insect *in cattle*'.

Etymology: Räsänen VEWT 422b–423a; Clauson ED 838b; Erdal 1991: 445; SIGTJa 1997: 185–186; Róna-Tas & Berta WOT 2011: 822–825

The Arin word belongs in the group of compound words (Khabtagaeva 2015d: 141). This compound word also exists in Yenisei Turkic dialects. The second part *sek* of the Arin compound word assumes the later period of borrowing. This is proved by the shortened form of the Turkic secondary vowel -*ē*-, which developed from the sequence Vowel—Consonant *ŋ*—Vowel.

From an etymological aspect, this Turkic word *siŋek* 'a buzzing insect' is of onomatopoeic origin. It is derived from the base *siŋ and the Turkic diminutive suffix +*AK*. It was borrowed into Mongolic[55] (Nugteren 2011: 491) and Hungarian[56] (Róna-Tas & Berta WOT 2011: 822–825). From Mongolic, the word was re-borrowed to Tuvan[57] (Khabtagaeva 2009: 270).

Comparison may also be made with Arin *karananuk* 'bilberry', which is also a compound word and includes the Turkic *qara* 'black'.

---

55   Turkic *siŋ → Mongolic **sim+a-GUl* {Mongolic NV, VN} 'small insect, midge, gnat, mosquito': Middle Mongol: Precl.Mo. *šimuγul*; HY *šimu'ul*; Muq. *šimūl*; Rasulid *šimūl*; LM *simaγul ~ simuγul*; Modern Mongol: Khalkha; Buryat; Oirat dial. *šumūl*; Dagur *šomöl* (E); Khamnigan –.

56   Turkic: West Old Turkic *siŋuk 'a buzzing insect, mosquito' → Hungarian *szúnyog* [sūńog] 'mosquito, gnat, Culex pipens'.

57   Turkic → Mongolic → Turkic: Tuvan *šümil* 'larva; grub'.

TURKIC LOANWORDS   59

Pumpokol *kun*; Yugh *kūʰn*;⁵⁸ Southern Ket *kùn*, Central Ket *kū̇nə*, Northern Ket *kū̇ne*, Eastern Ket *kūn* 'wolverine' (Werner 2002/1: 451) ← Turkic *qunu* 'wolverine':

cf. Old Turkic –; NEˢ YeniseiT: Khakas *xunu* 'wolverine; malodorous substance emitted by wolverine'; Sagai *qunu* ~ *quna*, Kachin *quna* (R); Shor *qunučaq* (< *qunu* +*čAK* {Turkic NN/diminutive}); AltaiT: –; SayanT –; ChulymT *qunučaq*; NEᴺ Yakut –; NWᴺ Siberian Tatar *qonï* (Tum.), cf. *kunu* (R); NWˢ Kirgiz *kunu*; Remaining lgs. –;
Turkic → Samoyedic:
    Kamas *kōnu* 'bear';
Turkic ← ? Russian *kuna* 'wolverine, fur of wolverine; monetary unit, equal to 1/22 *grivnja*'.
Etymology: Joki LS 192; Räsänen VEWT 300b; Vasmer 1986/2: 417; SIGTJa 1997: 162; ESTJa 2000: 148–149; Werner 2002/1: 451

Werner (2002/1: 451) connects the Yeniseian words with the Turkic form *kunu*. If this is the case, Turkic word, the apocope change occurred.

The etymology of the Turkic word is unknown. The word is present only in some Modern Turkic languages; it is absent in Old and Middle Turkic sources. Räsänen (VEWT 300b) and Tenišev (SIGTJa 1997: 162) do not exlude Finno-Ugric or Slavic borrowing. Räsänen (VEWT 300b) and Joki (LS 192) originate the Turkic form from the Common Turkic verb *qun-* 'to steal, carry off', but the derivation is unclear.

From the Siberian Turkic, the word was borrowed into the Samoyedic Kamas (Joki LS 192).

Arin *kusku kok* 'raven' (Werner 2002/1: 455) ← Turkic **kuskun kök* 'raven' < *quzġun* 'raven' + *kök* 'blue':
< *qusqun* < *quzġun* 'raven':

cf. Old Turkic *quzġun*; NEˢ YeniseiT: Khakas *xusxun*; Sagai, Koibal, Kachin; Shor *qusqun*; AltaiT: Altai; Tuba; Qumanda; Quu; Teleut *qusqun*; SayanT: Tuvan; Tofan *qusqun*; ChulymT *qusqun*; NEᴺ Yakut –; NWᴺ Siberian Tatar –; NWˢ Kirgiz *kuzgun*; Fu-yü –; Kazak *quzġïn*; SE Yellow Uyghur *quzġun*.
Etymology: Doerfer TMEN 3: 468–469; Räsänen VEWT 305b; Rassadin 1971: 222; Clauson ED 682b; ESTJa 2000: 107–108
+ *kök* 'blue' < *kök* 'the sky; sky-coloured, blue, blue-grey':

cf. Old Turkic *kök*; NEˢ YeniseiT: Khakas; Sagai, Koibal, Kachin *kök*; Shor *kök*; Kyzyl *kökˣ*; AltaiT: Altai; Tuba; Qumanda; Quu; Teleut *kök*; SayanT: Tuvan; Tofan *kök*; ChulymT *kök*; NEᴺ Yakut *küöx*; Dolgan *küök* ~ *küöx*; NWᴺ Siberian Tatar *kük*; NWˢ Kirgiz *kök*; Fu-yü *göh*; Kazak *kök*; SE Yellow Uyghur *kök*;

---

58   The reconstruction of Old Yugh is **kuúnʼa* (Vajda & Werner: in preparation).

Turkic → Samoyedic:

cf. Koibal *kok* 'blue, green'; Kamas *kök ~ kük* 'blue, green, golden, yellow'; Mator *kök* 'blue, green'.

Etymology: Joki LS 187, 216; Laude-Cirtautas 1961: 77–83; Räsänen VEWT 287a; Rassadin 1971: 204; Clauson ED 708b; ESTJa 1980: 66–68; SIGTJa 1997: 682–683; Helimski 1997: 284

The Arin word is of unknown origin (Werner 2002/1: 455). I propose that it is a compound word, which consists of two Turkic words *quzġun* 'raven' and *kök* 'blue'. From a semantic perspective, the Turkic etymology fits, but from a morphological point of view the Turkic origin runs into a problem. The structure of the compound Noun + Adjective is atypical. This structure is not typical of Turkic languages either. However, we find Osman and Chagatay data in the non-correct structure: *quzġun siyahi* 'pitch-black raven' (Radloff 2: 1021).

Another problematic point is that the Turkic people use this bird name with the black colour and not with blue. The first part of the Yeniseian compound *kusku* was borrowed from the Siberian Turkic form *kuskun*. The devoicing of the original cluster *zg > sk* is typical of Siberian Turkic languages. In the second part of the Arin word *kok*, the change of the original Turkic velar -*ö*- > -*o*- is regular.

The Turkic word *kök* 'blue' was borrowed into Samoyedic (Joki LS 187, 216; Helimski 1997: 284), Mongolic[59] (Clauson ED 708b; Ščerbak 1997: 240; Nugteren 2011: 424–425) and Hungarian[60] (Róna-Tas & Berta WOT 2011: 519–521) languages. From the Mongolic, the Turkic word was borrowed into Tungusic[61] (SSTMJa 1: 426b; Rozycki 1994: 145).

The Arin word still has an uncertain etymology, cf. the Kott *ureäk* 'green', which is possibly also connected with the Turkic *kök* 'blue'.

Kott ***mankara ~ mangara***; Assan ***mangára ~ mankara*** 'hare, rabbit' (Werner 2002/2: 19) < *mangar -a* {Yeniseian feminine suffix, see Werner 1990: 54–55} ← Turkic *maŋar 'who is running, who is in hurry' < *maŋ-* 'gallop' *-Ar* {Turkic aorist, see Erdal 2004: 240–241}:

---

59 Turkic → Mongolic 'blue, sky blue, green, ash-coloured, dark (*of a face*)': Middle Mongol: SH; HY *kökö*; Muq. *köke*; LM *köke*; Modern Mongol: Buryat *xüxe*; Khalkha *xöx*; Kalmuck *kök*; Dagur *kuk*ʷ (E); Khamnigan *kükü ~ kökö*.
60 Turkic: West Old Turkic *kök → Hungarian *kék* [*kēk*] 'blue'.
61 Turkic → Mongolic → Tungusic: *Southern Ewenki*: Northern Baikal, Nercha; *Eastern Ewenki*: Barguzin *kuku* 'blue, green, greenish grey'; Solon *xöxö* [*wāra*] 'blue'; Manchu *kuku* 'black; blue; the kind of herb'.

cf. Old Turkic *maŋ-* 'to walk'; NE^S YeniseiT: Khakas *maŋ* 'free (*about time*)'; Sagai, Koibal, Kachin *maŋ* 'time, free time' (R); Shor *maŋ* 'gallop' (R), cf. 'free time' (ShR); AltaiT: Altai *maŋ* 'gallop, running'; Tuba *maŋ-maŋ* 'gallop'; Qumanda *maŋ* 'gallop'; Quu *maŋ* 'running, gallop'; Teleut *maŋ* 'gallop' (R); SayanT: Tuvan *maŋ* 'running; run; speed'; Tofan *maŋ* 'gallop, jump of animal; speed'; ChulymT –; NE^N Yakut *maŋïy-*[62] 'walk or run with the effort' (Pek.); NW^N Siberian Tatar *maŋ* 'measure, the quantity of volume or time; conformity'; NW^S Kirgiz *maŋ-* 'to go'; Fu-yü –; Kazak *maŋ-* 'to go'; SE Yellow Uyghur *maŋ-* 'to go';

Turkic → Samoyedic:
    Kamas *maŋna-* 'to have time, to arrive on time'.

Etymology: Joki LS 225; Räsänen VEWT 326b; Rassadin 1971: 206; Clauson ED 767a; ESTJa 2003: 31–32

The etymology of the Kott word is unknown. It may be connected with another Turkic word *maŋan* 'white', but this is questionable.[63] The element *ara* in Kott word is also unknown. Due to possibility of the taboo character of the word, I suggest as a hypothesis that Kott -*ar* could be the Turkic aorist suffix with the meaning 'who is running, who runs, who is in hurry', while the final -*a* could be the Yeniseian feminine suffix or paragogue happened, cf. similar examples in the Altai Turkic: 'legs' → *bazar* 'what, which goes' < *bas-* 'to step, to press' and the aorist suffix -*Ar* (Jaimova 1990: 140), 'hen, chicken' → *učar* 'what, which flies' < *uč-* 'to fly' and the Aorist suffix -*Ar* (Jaimova 1990: 156); etc.

The Turkic word belongs in the category of figurative words (ESTJa 2003: 31–32). The initial consonant *m-* is atypical of original Turkic words. According to Clauson (ED 766b–767a), the verb *maŋ-* is homophonous with the Turkic noun *maŋ* 'the gait of a horse; a fast gait'. The Turkic verb from Yakut was borrowed into a Northern Tungusic Lamut dialect[64] (SSTMJa 1: 530b).

Kott *mentara* 'burbot (*fish, Lota lota*)' (Werner 2002/2: 20):
cf. Turkic:
    cf. Old Turkic –; NE^S YeniseiT: Khakas *mindīr* 'burbot'; Remaining lgs. –.

---

62   < **maŋ* +(*X*)*y-* {Yakut element -*y-* in verbs, see Kharitonov 1947: 169; Ubrjatova et al. 1982: 103–107}.
63   Cf. NE YeniseiT: Khakas *maŋxan* 'pale yellow'; Sagai, Koibal, Kachin *maŋkan* 'fallow (*colour of horse*)', cf. Sagai *maġan* 'the pallor on the forehead of horses, white patches around eyes of horses (*colour of horse*)' (R); AltaiT –; SayanT: Tuvan *maŋgan* 'very white'; ChulymT –; Yakut *maŋxay-* 'to become white', *maŋan* 'white'; *maŋās* 'with white head, white-beaked (*about an animal*)'; NW Yakut –; SE – ← Mongolic: LM *mangqan* 'horse with a star on its forehead', *mangqar* 'horse or cattle with a white head or face'.
64   Turkic: Yakut → Tungusic: Lamut dial. *maŋdi-* 'to trot'.

Etymology: Räsänen VEWT 339a

The etymology of the word is unknown. Among the Yeniseian languages it is present only in Kott, and among the Turkic only in the Khakas dialect. Tatarincev (2008/4: 97–98) in his *Etymological Dictionary of Tuvan* casts doubt on the opinion of Räsänen (VEWT 339a) concerning the connection of the Tuvan *mezil* and the Khakas *mindïr* forms. The word was possibly borrowed from a third source.

Kott *pât*; Yugh *bā·tn*; Ket *bā·tn* 'lenok (*species of white salmon*), Brachymystax lenok' (Werner 2002/1: 159) ← Turkic **büŋit* < **biγit* < *büyit* 'lenok':

    cf. Old Turkic –; NE^S YeniseiT: Khakas *mindïr* 'burbot'; AltaiT: –; SayanT: Tuvan *mïyit* 'lenok'; Tofan *mīt* 'lenok'; ChulymT –; NE^N Yakut *büyit* 'lenok'; Yakut dial. *büyit* 'carp fry'; Remaining lgs. –;

cf. Samoyedic:

    Selkup *möeten* 'lenok' (Helimski 1982: 240).

Etymology: Räsänen VEWT 336b; Timonina 1979: 23; Helimski 1982: 240; SIGTJa 2001: 177; Tatarincev 2008: 209–210; Starostin, Dybo & Mudrak EDAL 2003: 1100–1101

The etymology of the Yeniseian words is probably connected to Turkic where the same lexical meaning is present. Timonina (1979: 23) links the Yeniseian forms with Tuvan *mïyit* 'lenok'. Helimski (1982: 240) suggests a Samoyedic Selkup borrowing.

The etymology of the Turkic forms is unknown. Räsänen (VEWT 336b) merely quoted the present Turkic forms, but did not give any etymological explanation. According to the authors of SIGTJa (2001: 177) and EDAL (2003: 1100–1101), the Turkic forms have the strong Proto-Altaic reconstructed form **püŋty-* and **pi̯úŋu*, 'a kind of fish' respectively.

The Khakas final consonant -*r* is problematic, but the lexical meaning and the form **mindï* seem to be connected to the reconstructed Turkic form **büŋit* through metathesis. Tatarincev's opinion may correct (2008: 209–210), he relates the Tuvan form *mīt* with the Yakut *büyit* and derives them from the reconstructed verb **büy-* ~ **mïy-* 'to be crushed, crumbled' and the deverbal noun suffix -(*I*)*t*, which forms nouns designating qualities and then the agent with the quality or process (Tatarincev 2008: 210), cf. the Old Turkic suffix -(*U*)*t*, which forms action nouns, lexemes denoting objects of transitive verbs or subjects of intransitive verbs, and a few place and instrument nouns (for details, see Erdal 1991: 308–316). In favor of the Turkic reconstruction are the Tuvan forms *mïyïr* 'scattered (*about freckles*)', *büyirgin* 'id.', *mïyïrak* 'tubers of one kind of plant', *möyürgin* 'small and spherical, round', etc. (For more details, see Tatarincev 2008: 209–210).

However, all Yeniseian, Turkic and Samoyedic forms should be connected to each other, though we do not have the reliable etymology of the word.

Arin *serga* 'louse' (Werner 2002/2: 164) ← Turkic **sirgä* < *sirkä* 'a nit':
    cf. Old Turkic *sirkä*; NE[S] YeniseiT: Khakas *sïrge*; Sagai, Koibal, Kachin *sirgä*, Koibal, Kachin [*aq*] *sirġa* (R); AltaiT: Altai *sirke*; Teleut *sirke*; SayanT: Tuvan *sirge*; Tofan *si^crhe*; ChulymT –; NE[N] Yakut –; NW[N] Siberian Tatar –; NW[S] Kirgiz *sirke* 'a nit; *fig.* the decoration in the form of raised dots'; Fu-yü –; Kazak *sirke* 'a nit; *fig.* tiny'; SE Yellow Yughur –.

Etymology: Räsänen VEWT 423b; Clauson ED 850b; Erdal 1991: 83; ESTJa 2003: 268–270; SIGTJa 1997: 182; Róna-Tas & Berta WOT 2011: 720–721

Due to the absence of vowel harmony, the final Arin vowel changed to back vowel -*a*. Another explanation may be the Koibal and Kachin form *sirġa* with back vowels.

From an etymological side, Erdal (1991: 83) considered the Turkic word formed with the suffix +*GA*, which denotes the names of small animals, insects and birds. The suffix +*GA* was devoiced due to the consonant -*r* (see also Róna-Tas & Berta WOT 2011: 720). The base of the word is **sir*, which is of unknown origin (for details on the etymology of the base, see ESTJa 2003: 269–270). The Turkic word was borrowed into Mongolic[65] and Hungarian[66] (Róna-Tas & Berta WOT 2011: 720–721) languages.

Kott *šâškana* ~ *sâškan* ~ *šaška* 'magpie' (Werner 2002/2: 437) ← Turkic **sāskan* 'magpie' < *saġïzġan* < *saġïz* +*GAn* {Turkic NN, which forms nouns that designate names of plants and animals, see Erdal 1991: 85}:
    cf. Old Turkic *saġïzġan*; NE[S] YeniseiT: Khakas *sāsxan*; Sagai *sāskan* (R); Kyzyl *sāsyaˑn*; Shor *sāsqan*, cf. *saġïsqan* (R); AltaiT: Altai *saŋïsqan*; Tuba *sagïskan*; Qumanda *sagïskan*; Quu *sagïskan* ~ *sāskan*; Teleut *saŋïsqan*; SayanT: Tuvan *sāskan*; Tofan *sāsqan*; ChulymT *sïsqan* ~ *sasqan*; NE[N] –; NW[N] Siberian Tatar *sauïsqan* ~ *saeskan*; NW[S] Kirgiz *sagïzgan* ~ *sawïzgan* 'magpie; *fig.* inconstant person'; Fu-yü –; Kazak *sawïsqan*; SE Yellow Uyghur *saqïsqan*;

Turkic → Samoyedic: Kamas *šäškin* ~ *šäškan* ~ *sāskan* 'magpie'.

Etymology: Joki LS 286; Räsänen VEWT 396b; Clauson ED 818a; ESTJa 2003: 166–169; Nugteren 2011: 484

---

65   Turkic → Mongolic: Middle Mongol: –; LM *sirke* 'a kind of flea'; Modern Mongol: Buryat *šerxe* 'louse'; Khalkha *širx* 'louse'; Kalmuck *širkˀ* 'the kind of a red louse'; Dagur –; Khamnigan –.

66   Turkic: West Old Turkic **širkä* → Hungarian *serke* [*šerke*] 'a nit'.

The Kott forms have a clear Turkic etymology. The closest form is *sâškan*, which indicates the Turkic source with secondary long vowel, cf. Yenisei Turkic and Sayan Turkic forms. The other form *šâškana* with additional final vowel shows paragogue. It may be the Yeniseian female, or the possessive suffixes. In the third form *šaška*, the final consonant *-n* is dropped.

The Turkic word derives from the base *saǵïz*, which belongs in the onomatopoeic category and the Turkic denominal noun suffix +*GAn*, which forms nouns that designate names of plants and animals (for details on function, see Erdal 1991: 85–89).

The Turkic word was borrowed into Mongolic[67] (Nugteren 2011: 484) and Samoyedic languages (Joki LS 286). The Kamas forms *šāškin ~ šāškan* were probably borrowed from Yeniseian, which proves the presence of the sibilant *š* instead of the Turkic *s* consonant. The other Samoyedic Mator form *šazgaj* was obviously borrowed from Buryat (Helimski 1991: 261; 1997: 336).

Kott *tabat*; Assan *tabát ~ tapat*; Arin *tebé* 'camel' (Werner 2002/2: 229) ← Turkic **täbä* 'camel' < *täβäy*:

cf. Old Turkic *täβäy*; NE^S YeniseiT: Khakas *tibe*; Sagai, Koibal, Kachin *tebä* (R); Shor *tö̃*; AltaiT: Altai *tö̃*; Tuba *tö̃*; Qumanda *tön*; Quu *tö̃*; Teleut *tö̃*; SayanT: Tuvan *teve*; Tofan *tebe*; ChulymT –; NE^N Yakut *taba* 'deer'; Dolgan *taba* 'deer; maral'; NW^N Siberian Tatar –; NW^S Kirgiz *tö̃* 'camel; fig. huge, big'; Fu-yü *dömö ~ dümĭ*; Kazak *tüye*; SE Yellow Uyghur *te ~ tĭ ~ če*;

Turkic: Yakut → Tungusic:

Ewenki dial. *tobo* 'deer' (SSTMJa 2: 235a).

Etymology: Doerfer TMEN 2: 669–671; 1985: 77–78; Ščerbak 1961: 103–104; 1997: 154; Räsänen VEWT 468a; Clauson ED 447b; SSTMJa 2: 235a; Timonina 1978: 9; ESTJa 1980: 313–315; Stachowski 1996: 107; SIGTJa 2001: 445–446; Nugteren 2011: 517; Róna-Tas & Berta WOT 2011: 903–906

The Yeniseian words were borrowed from the Turkic (Doerfer TMEN 2: 670; Timonina 1978: 9; Stachowski 1996: 107). The Arin form *tebé* with front vowels has the closest form to Turkic. The Kott *tabat* and Assan *tabát ~ tapat* forms are problematic. Both have back vowels and an additional final consonant *-t* of unknown origin.

The disappearance of vowel harmony is a typical phonetic feature for Turkic loanwords in Yeniseian (cf. Kott *bôru ~ boru* 'wolf' ← Turkic *börü*, Kott *urum* 'cloth, linen' ← Turkic *örüm* 'something plaited or woven', etc.).

---

67 Turkic → Mongolic *šayaǰïyai* 'magpie' < **šayaǰï* +*GAi* {Mongolic NN/diminutive, see Poppe 1964: § 123; Khabtagaeva 2001: 117}: cf. Middle Mongol: HY *saǰiqai*; LM *siyaǰïyai ~ šayaǰayai*;

The Yeniseian final consonant -*t* can be explained by assimilation due to initial *t*-. According to Stachowski (1996: 107), the Yeniseian final -*t* can be explained by the Yakut influence. There is a Yakut denominal noun suffix +*t* with a collective and plural meaning and of Mongolic origin (Kałużyński 1962: 116–117). Another coincidence for a Yakut connection is the Yakut form *taba* with back-vowels. An obstacle could be the Yakut lexical meaning 'deer' instead of the Common Turkic and Yeniseian 'camel'.

The Turkic word was borrowed into Mongolic[68] (Doerfer TMEN 2: 670; Ščerbak 1997: 154; Nugteren 2011: 517) and then from the Mongolic re-borrowed into Yakut[69] (Kałużyński 1962: 42) and further to some Ewenki dialects (SSTMJa 2: 235a; Doerfer 1985: 77–78). The Tungusic forms were also borrowed from Mongolic[70] (SSTMJa 2: 235a; Doerfer 1985: 77–78; Rozycki 1994: 206). The Turkic word is also present in Hungarian[71] (Róna-Tas & Berta WOT 2011: 903–906).

Kott ***tegteka*** 'quail' (Werner 2002/2: 257) < *tegtek* -*a* {? Yeniseian feminine suffix or possessive suffix} ← Turkic *tükteg 'with feathers' < *tüg* 'the hair of the body; feathers' +*lXG* {Turkic NN/adj., see Erdal 1991: 121}:

    cf. Old Turkic *tü̆* ~ *tüg*; NE[S] YeniseiT: Khakas *tüktīg* 'with feathers, birds'; Sagai, Koibal, Kachin *tük* (R); Kyzyl *tük*ˣ; Shor *tüktig* 'woollen, with fur' < *tük* 'wool, fur, fluff'; AltaiT: Altai *tük*; Tuba *tüktǖ* 'with hair (*about animals*)' < *tük* 'hair'; Qumanda; Quu; Teleut *tük*; SayanT: Tuvan *düktüg* < *düg* 'hair; peel of grain'; Tofan *tüktüg* < *tük*; ChulymT *tüktüg* < *tük*; NE[N] Yakut *tǖlēx* < *tǖ*; Dolgan *tǖlǟk* < *tǖ*; NW[N] Siberian Tatar *tüktü*, cf. *tüktü arï* 'bumblebee'; NW[S] Kirgiz *tüktǖ* < *tük*; Fu-yü *düh*; Kazak *tükti* < *tük*; SE Yellow Yughur –.

Etymology: Räsänen VEWT 503a; Clauson ED 433a, 476a; Doerfer TMEN 4: 277; SIGTJa 1997: 197–198

The Kott word has an unknown etymology. It possibly originates from the Turkic form *tükteg 'with feathers', derived from the noun *tüg* 'the hair of the body; feathers' and the productive Turkic suffix +*lXG*. The origin of the final vowel -*a* is questionable; it could be either the Yeniseian feminine suffix, or the

---

    Modern Mongol: Buryat *šāzgai* ~ *šāžgai*; Khalha *šādzgai*; Kalmuck *šāzᵃyā* ~ *šāzyā*; Dagur *sājiy* (E); Khamnigan *šādzagai* ~ *sādzagai*.

68 Turkic → Mongolic *temegen* < *teme +*GAn* {Mongolic NN, see Poppe 1927: 116; Szabó 1943: §157; Khabtagaeva 2001: 99}: Middle Mongol: SH *teme'en*; HY *teme'en*; Muq. *temēn*; Leiden *temēn*; LM *temege(n)* 'camel: bishop (*in chess*)'; Modern Mongol: Buryat, Khalkha *temē(n)*; Kalmuck *temēn*; Dagur *təmā* (E); Khamnigan *temē*.

69 Mongolic → Yakut *tebien* 'camel' → Tungusic: Sakhalin, Urmi Ewenki dial. *tewēn* 'camel'.

70 Turkic → Mongolic → Tungusic 'camel': *Eastern Ewenki*: Barguzin *temeyēn*; Solon *temegē*; Oroch, Nanai *teme* (← Manchu); Jurchen *tʼéh-'óh*; Manchu *temen*.

71 Turkic: West Old Turkic *teve → Hungarian *teve* 'camel'.

Yeniseian possessive suffix (Vajda 2014: personal communication). My etymology can be explained by the lexical change: 'with feathers' > 'bird' > 'quail', cf. the similar Kott loanword **kamagalá** 'nut' ← Turkic *kabagalï* 'with husk, peel, shuck'.

Kott **tokmaxon** 'locust, grasshopper' (Werner 2002/2: 272) ← ? Turkic *tomanok* 'mosquito' < *toban +AK* {Turkic NN/diminutive, see Erdal 1991: 40}:
 cf. Old Turkic –; NE[S] YeniseiT: Khakas *tubanax* 'mosquito'; Sagai *toban ~ tobanak* 'sandfly' (R), Sagai, Koibal, Kachin *tobïn* 'sandfly' (R); Kyzyl –; Shor *tobanaq* 'midge, blackfly'; AltaiT: Altai *tomonok* 'mosquito, midge'; Tuba *tomonok* 'mosquito'; Qumanda *tomonok* 'mosquito'; Quu *tobanak ~ tobonok* 'mosquito, midge'; Teleut *tomonoq* 'mosquito'; SayanT –; ChulymT –; NE[N] –; NW[N] Siberian Tatar *tomalaq* 'midge'; Remaining lgs. –.
Etymology: Räsänen VEWT 487b; Khabtagaeva 2015c: 100–101
 The etymology of the Kott word is unknown. As a hypothesis, I connect it with the Siberian Turkic form *tomanok ~ tomonok* 'mosquito'. The metathesis -*n-k* > *-k-n-* > *-x-n-* in the last syllable and distant assimilation in the first syllable possibly happened in the Kott form.
 The etymology of the Turkic word is unclear. According to Sagai, the word has the diminutive form with the suffix +*AK*. The Turkic forms underwent the *b* > *m* change, which is a typical change for some Turkic languages. (On sound shifts, see Johanson 1998: 102–103.)
 The word belongs in the group of words with uncertain etymology.

Arin **torgijan** 'lark (*bird*)' (Werner 2002/2: 277) ← Turkic *torgayaq* 'lark' < *torgay +AK* {Old Turkic and Khakas NN/diminutive, see Baskakov & Inkižekova-Grekul 1953: 403 and Erdal 1991: 40}:
 cf. Old Turkic *torïgā* 'sky-lark'; NE[S] YeniseiT: Khakas *targayax ~ torgay* 'sky-lark'; Koibal, Kachin *torgayaq* 'small bird, lark' (R); AltaiT: –; SayanT –; ChulymT *torgay ~ tōrguy* 'sky-lark'; NE[N] Yakut *tuyārar* 'sky-lark' < *tuyār-* 'to twitter'; NW[N] Siberian Tatar *turgay* 'sparrow'; NW[S] Kirgiz *torgoy* 'sky-lark'; Fu-yü –; Kazak *torgay* 'sparrow; the common name for small birds'; SE Yellow Yughur –.
Etymology: Doerfer TMEN 2: 482–483; Räsänen VEWT 490a; Clauson ED 541b; SIGTJa 1997: 176
 It is the only case where the Turkic final consonant -*k* changed to -*n* in Arin.
 The etymology of the Turkic word is unclear. From a morphological point of view, *torgayaq* is derived from the form *torgay* and the diminutive suffix +*AK* (for details on functions, see Erdal 1991: 40).
 According to Doerfer (TMEN 2: 482–483), the form *torgay* is re-borrowed from the Mongolic *torγai*, cf. the Kalmuck *torgā ~ torga* 'the name of various

small birds' (*boro torgā* 'lark', *χara torgā* 'starling', *alᵃG torgā* 'wagtail'), which can proved by Common Mongolic suffix +*Ai*, forming the names of animals, e.g. *qarčaγai* 'falcon, hawk', *noqai* 'dog', *γaqai* 'pig', etc. This suggestion is supported by Clauson (ED 541b). The reconstructed Turkic form was originally *torga 'all kinds of small birds' and was possibly borrowed into Persian *torqa* 'thrush, Turdus L.' (Doerfer TMEN 2: 482–483). The problem of this suggestion is the absence in other Mongolic languages. The word is present only in Kalmuck, which is rather possibly the Turkic loanword (SIGTJa 1997: 176).

Assan *ug* 'owl' (Werner 2002/2: 321) ← Turkic *ügü 'owl':
    cf. Old Turkic *ügi*; NE^S YeniseiT: Khakas *ügü*; Sagai *ügü* (R); Shor *ügü*; AltaiT: Altai *ükü*; Qumanda *ügü*; Teleut *ükü*; SayanT: Tuvan *ügü*; Tofan *hügü*; ChulymT *ügü*; NE^N Yakut –; NW^N Siberian Tatar *ügü* ~ *ögö*; NW^S Kirgiz *ükü*; Fu-yü –; Kazak *üki*; SE Yellow Yughur –.

Etymology: Doerfer TMEN 2: 156; Räsänen VEWT 519b; Clauson ED 101b; SIGTJa 1997: 171; Werner 2002/2: 321; Róna-Tas & Berta WOT 2011: 968–969[72]

The Assan word is connected to the Common Turkic *ügü* 'owl'. Disappearance of the vowel harmony and apocope changes occurred.

The word is of onomatopoeic origin and is present in almost all Old and Middle Turkic sources and Modern Turkic languages.

The Mongolic *uγuli* 'owl' is also regarded as a Turkic loanword[73] (Ramstedt KWb 1935: 454), where the final *-li* can relate to Mongolic non-productive suffix +*lin*, which is used with color names[74] (Khabtagaeva 2001: 140).

1.1.5 Domestic Animals

Kott *askar* ~ *askir*; Arin *askir*; Assan *askir* ~ *askir* 'stallion' (Werner 2002/1: 63) ← Turkic *asqïr 'stallion' < *azqïr* < *aδġïr*:
    cf. Old Turkic *aδġïr*; NE^S YeniseiT: Khakas *asxïr*; Sagai *aqsïr* (R); Koibal, Kachin *asqïr* (R); Shor *asqïr*; AltaiT: Altai *ayġïr*; Tuba *ayġïr*; Qumanda *ayġïr*; Quu *ayġïr*; Teleut *ayġïr* (R); SayanT: Tuvan *askïr*; Tofan *asqïr*; ChulymT *ayġïr*; NE^N Yakut *atīr*; Dolgan *atīr*; NW^N Siberian Tatar *ayġïr*; NW^S Kirgiz *ayġïr*; Fu-yü *ahsir at* 'foal'; Kazak *ayġïr*; SE Yellow Uyghur *azġïr*;

Turkic → Samoyedic:
    Kamas *askir* 'stallion';

---

72 Hungarian *ugu* in *ugufa* and *ug* 'owl' were borrowed from West Old Turkic.
73 Turkic → Mongolic 'owl': Middle Mongol: –; LM *uγuli* ~ *uuli*; Modern Mongol: Buryat *ūli*; Khalkha *ūl'*; Kalmuck *ūl'i* (KWb); Dagur –; Khamnigan *ūli*.
74 E.g. LM *čaγalin* 'plant water caltrop (*lat.* Trapa L)' < *čaγan* 'white', *noγoγalin* 'stone malachite' < *noγoγan* 'green'.

Turkic → Siberian Russian *askïr* 'stallion with a special beauty'; *aygïr* 'stallion'.
Etymology: Joki LS 75–76; Ščerbak 1961: 87–88; Doerfer TMEN 2: 185–187; Räsänen VEWT 6a; Clauson ED 47b; ESTJa 1974: 107–108; SSTMJa 1: 17a; Timonina 1978: 8; Doerfer 1985: 75; Tatarincev 2000: 149–150; Anikin 2000: 78, 100; SIGTJa 2001: 442; Nugteren 2011: 266

The Yeniseian phonetic forms demonstrate borrowing from the Yenisei Turkic, where the regular change *-δ-* > *-z-* > *-s-* is found. The unvoicing of cluster *-zg-* > *-sk-* in Yenisei Turkic can be explained by phonetic rules: the phoneme /z/ does not occur in the cluster *-zC-*, but usually only as a second consonant, while unvoiced consonants occur only with unvoiced consonants in clusters (for details, see Baskakov 1975: 33, 38). As example, Khakas *kilze* 'if (he) will come' < *kil-* 'to come' *-sA* {Turkic conditional suffix}; Khakas *alzïn* 'let (him) take' < *al-* 'to take' *-sXn* {Turkic volitional sg.3}; Khakas *aŋzā* 'gaper'; etc.

The same irregular change *-δg-* > *-zg-* > *-sk-* in Sayan Turkic (Tatarincev 2000: 149–150) as in Yenisei Turkic confirms the link between Sayan Turkic and Yenisei Turkic.

Samoyedic Kamas *askïr* was also borrowed from Yenisei Turkic (Joki LS 75–76). There are two forms in Siberian Russian originating from two different Turkic languages: *askïr* from Yenisei or Sayan Turkic, and *aygïr* from Altai Turkic (Anikin 2000: 78).

The Turkic word was borrowed into Mongolic[75] (Nugteren 2011: 266), and further from Mongolic to Tungusic[76] languages (SSTMJa 1: 17a; Doerfer 1985: 75). It seems that the Ewenki dialectal form *atir* was borrowed directly from Yakut[77] (SSTMJa 1: 17a; Doerfer 1985: 75).

Kott *atuš*; Assan *atū̄š* ~ *atīš* 'gelding' (Werner 2002/1: 80) < *at* + Yeniseian *qus* 'horse' (Werner 2002/1: 457):
at ← Turkic **at* 'horse, riding horse, gelding':
cf. Old Turkic *at*; NE^S YeniseiT: Khakas; Sagai, Koibal, Kachin; Kyzyl; Shor *at*; AltaiT: Altai; Tuba; Qumanda; Quu; Teleut *at*; SayanT: Tuvan; Tofan *a^{c}t*; ChulymT *at*; NE^N Yakut; Dolgan *at*; Yakut dial. *at* 'donkey'; NW^N Siberian Tatar –; NW^S Kirgiz *at*; Fu-yü *at*; Kazak *at*; SE Yellow Uyghur *at*.

---

75 Turkic → Mongolic 'stallion': Middle Mongol: SH; HY *ajirqa*; Muq., Leiden, Ist. *ajïrya*; LM *ajïry-a(n)*; Modern Mongol: Buryat *azarga*; Khalkha *azraga*; Oirat dial. *adži'argă*; Kalmuck *ajry*; Dagur *ad'rəy ~ ajrəy* (E); Khamnigan *adzarga*.
76 Mongolic → Tungusic 'stallion': *Southern Ewenki*: Northern Baikal, Baunt; *Eastern Ewenki*: Zeya, Tungir, Aldan, Barguzin *ajirga*; Nanai *ajïrya ~ agirkā*; Manchu *ajiryan ~ ajirhan*.
77 Yakut → Tungusic: *Eastern Ewenki*: Urmi, Sakhalin *atir* 'stallion'.

Etymology: Räsänen VEWT 30b; Doerfer TMEN 2: 4–5; Clauson ED 33a; ESTJa 1974: 197–198; SIGTJa 2001: 441; Khabtagaeva 2015b: 526–527

The etymology of the Yeniseian words is unknown. Werner assumes the compound word and puts into question the first part *at* (Werner 2002/1: 80). It probably belongs in the category of hybrid words, which consist of the Common Turkic word *at* 'horse' and the Common Yeniseian *qus* 'horse'. My assumption strengthens the same Turkic semantic meaning 'horse, riding horse, gelding' (Khabtagaeva 2015d: 138).

The change of the final Yeniseian -*s* > -*š* in Kott and Assan is a regular phonetic feature (for details of the sound shift, see Starostin 1982: 158).

Kott *bal* 'cattle' (Werner 2002/1: 99) ← Turkic *pal < *mal* 'livestock, cattle' ← Arabic:
    cf. Old Turkic *mal* 'property, wealth' (DTS); NE[S] YeniseiT: Khakas *mal* 'cattle' (KhR), cf. 'livestock, cattle, animal' (But.); Sagai, Koibal, Kachin *mal* 'property; cattle' (R); Kyzyl *mal* 'cattle'; Shor *mal* 'cattle'; AltaiT: Altai *mal* 'cattle, property'; Tuba *mal* 'cattle'; Qumanda *mal* 'cattle; means, wealth', cf. *pal* 'livestock, property'; Quu *mal* 'cattle', cf. *pal* 'cattle, property'; Teleut *mal* 'livestock; horse'; SayanT: Tuvan *mal* 'cattle, domestic animals; horse; *fig.* rude, vile man'; Tofan *mal* 'cattle, livestock, domestic animal'; ChulymT *mal* 'cattle'; NE[N] Yakut *mal* 'property, goods'; NW[N] Siberian Tatar –; NW[S] Kirgiz *mal* 'domestic animal; cattle; property, wealth'; Fu-yü *mal* 'cattle'; Kazak *mal* 'domestic animals; *fig.* person, who likes the livestock'; SE Yellow Uyghur *mal* 'livestock, cattle; domestic animals';
Turkic → Samoyedic:
    Kamas *mal* ~ *māl* 'cattle'.

Etymology: Joki LS 224; DTS 335b; Räsänen VEWT 323b; Rassadin 1971: 205–206; Timonina 1978: 9; Stachowski 1992/1993: 254; Ščerbak 1997: 169; Pomorska 2005: 143; Nugteren 2011: 439

The Turkic word is of Arabic origin (DTS 335b; Rassadin 1971: 205–206; Ščerbak 1997: 169; Stachowski 1992/1993: 254). It is present in almost all Turkic languages, but the initial consonat *m*- indicates the borrowing, this initial consonant is atypical of Turkic. The word belongs in the "Wanderwort" category. The original meaning was 'property', which broadened in Turkic to 'livestock, cattle'. From Turkic, the word was borrowed into Samoyedic (Joki LS 224) and Mongolic[78] (Nugteren 2011: 439).

---

78   Turkic → Mongolic 'domestic animal; livestock, cattle': Middle Mongol: Muq. *mal*; LM *mal*; Modern Mongol: Buryat *mal*; Khalkha *mal* 'livestock, beasts, cattle'; Kalmuck *mal* 'cattle'; Dagur *mal* (E); Khamnigan *mal*.

The Kott word was borrowed from Altai Turkic dialects, where the initial *m*- fluctuates with *p*-. This is a phonetic peculiarity of Altai Turkic, e.g. Qumanda *pultïk* < *mültïk* 'gun, rifle' (Baskakov 1972: 27). Finally the Turkic initial *p*- was voiced to *b*-, cf. another Kott word ***baktîr*** '*inf.* praise', which was borrowed from the Turkic form *paktïr-* with the Turkic causative suffix -*Xr*-, but finally originates from the Mongolic *maɣta-* 'to praise'.

See also the Arin ***pajbal*** 'cattle, cow', which consists of the Turkic words *paj* 'rich' and *bal* 'cattle'.

Kott ***boga***; Arin ***bugá***; Assan ***boka*** 'bull' (Werner 2002/1: 135) ← Turkic **buga* < *buqa* 'bull':

cf. Old Turkic *buqa*; NE^S YeniseiT: Khakas *puġa*; Sagai, Koibal, Kachin *puġa* (R); Kyzyl *puɣa*; Shor *puġa*; AltaiT: Altai *buka*; Tuba *buka*; Qumanda *puga* ~ *buga*; Quu *puga*; Teleut *puga*; SayanT: Tuvan *buga*; Tofan *bu^{c}ha*; ChulymT *puġa*; NE^N Yakut *buga*; NW^N Siberian Tatar *poġa*; NW^S Kirgiz *buka*; Fu-yü *buza*;[79] Kazak *buqa*; SE Yellow Uyghur *pïqa* ~ *puqa* ~ *bïqa*;

Turkic → Samoyedic:

Kamas *buga* ~ *buχa* 'bull'.

Etymology: Joki LS 105; Ščerbak 1961: 99; Doerfer TMEN 2: 299–300; Räsänen VEWT 87a; Clauson ED 312a; ESTJa 1978: 230–233; Timonina 1978: 8; SIGTJa 2001: 645–646

The Yeniseian forms were borrowed from the Siberian Turkic form **buga*. In Kott and Assan, the original vowel -*u*- in the first syllable was changed to -*o*-.

The Turkic word belongs in the category of onomatopoeic words. For the base, Róna-Tas and Berta reconstruct the verb **būk-* / **bū-* and the deverbal noun suffix -*GA* (Róna-Tas & Berta WOT 2011: 127–128).

The Turkic word was borrowed into Samoyedic (Joki LS 105), Mongolic[80] (Nugteren 2011: 290), Hungarian[81] (Róna-Tas & Berta WOT 2011: 127–128) and New Persian (Doerfer TMEN 2: 299–300) languages. From the Mongolic, the Turkic word was borrowed into Tungusic[82] (SSTMJa 1: 103b; Doerfer 1985: 99).

---

79   The intervocalic *VzV* in Fu-yu form is problematic, it has to be from Turkic *VδV*, e.g. Old Turkic *bäδük* 'big' ~ Fu-yu *büzïh* 'tall', Old Turkic *aδaq* 'foot' ~ Fu-yu *azïh*, etc. Probably Fu-yu *buza* 'bull' is connected to Old Turkic *buzāġu* 'calf'.

80   Turkic → Mongolic: Middle Mongol 'bull': SH; HY *buqa*; LM *buq-a*; Modern Mongol: Buryat *buxa*; Khalkha *bux*; Oirat dial. *bux* ~ *buxxă* ~ *buxa*; Dagur *baɣ* (E); Khamnigan *buxa*.

81   West Old Turkic **bika* → Hungarian *bika* 'bull'.

82   Mongolic → Tungusic: *Southern Ewenki*: Northern Baikal, Nercha; *Eastern Ewenki*: Ayan, Barguzin *buka* 'bull' (SSTMJa 1: 103b).

Kott *bušôu* ~ *bišóu* ~ *bišól*; Assan *bišol* 'calf' (Werner 2002/1: 153) < *bišo -l* {?} ←
Turkic *pïzō ~ *puzō* < *buzāģu* 'calf':

cf. Old Turkic *buzāģu*; NE^S YeniseiT: Khakas *pïzo* ~ *pïzā*; Sagai *puzā* ~ *puzū* ~ *pïzā* ~ *pïzō* (R); Shor *pïza*; AltaiT: Altai *bïza* ~ *bozu*; Tuba *bōzu*; Qumanda *pozū*; Teleut *pozū* (R); SayanT: Tuvan *bïzā*; Tofan –; ChulymT –; NE^N Yakut –; NW^N Siberian Tatar *posau*; NW^S Kirgiz *muzō*; Fu-yü *buza* 'bull'; Kazak *buzaw*; SE Yellow Yughur –;
Turkic → Samoyedic:
Kamas *buzüi* ~ *buso* 'calf'.

Etymology: Joki LS 110–112; Räsänen VEWT 74b; Clauson ED 391a; Timonina 1978: 8; ESTJa 1978: 239–242; SIGTJa 2001: 438–439; Nugteren 2011: 282; Róna-Tas & Berta WOT 2011: 151–152

The Yeniseian words were clearly borrowed from Siberian Turkic. The change of the Turkic intervocalic *VzV* through the unvoiced *VsV* to *VšV* in Yeniseian occurred due to the absence of voiced *z* as a phoneme in Yeniseian. The final diphthongs -*ôu* ~ -*óu* in Kott can be explained by the Turkic final long vowel -*ō*. The final consonant -*l* in the Kott and Assan forms is of unknown origin. There are a small number of Yeniseian words where the final -*l* occurred, mostly in the Tungusic loanwords of Ket.

The Turkic word was borrowed into Samoyedic (Joki LS 110–112), with the rhotacized form into Mongolic[83] and Hungarian[84] (Róna-Tas & Berta WOT 2011: 151–152).

Kott *koaskir* 'ram' (Werner 2002/1: 437) ← Turkic *qosqar < *qočqar* < *qočŋār* 'ram' < *qoč* +*GAr* {Turkic NN}:

cf. Old Turkic *qoč* ~ *qočŋār*; NE^S YeniseiT:[85] Khakas *xosxar* 'goat'; AltaiT: Altai *kočkor* 'ram'; Tuba; Quu; Teleut *qočqor*; SayanT: Tuvan *koškar*; Tofan[86] –; ChulymT –; NE^N Yakut –; NW^N Siberian Tatar *qōcqar* ~ *qōčqōr* ~ *qucqar*; NW^S Kirgiz *kočkor*; Fu-yü –; Kazak *qošqar*; SE Yellow Uyghur *qožģar* ~ *qužģar*.
Etymology: Joki LS 214; Ščerbak 1961: 111–112; Räsänen VEWT 274a; Doerfer TMEN 3: 539–541; 1985: 100; Clauson ED 592a; Helimski 1997: 289; ESTJa 2000:

---

83 Turkic → Mongolic: Middle Mongol: SH *bura'u*; Muq. *burū* 'three-year-old calf'; LM *biraγu(n)* 'calf in its second year'; Modern Mongol: Buryat *burū* 'calf under the age of one year (*bear, lynx, moose, red deer*)'; Khalkha *byarū* 'calf in the second year'; Oirat dial. *bürü* ~ *bürö* ~ *börü* 'calf'; Dagur –; Khamnigan *burū(n)* 'calf in the second year'.
84 Turkic: West Old Turkic *buraγu → Hungarian *borjú* [*boryū*] 'calf'.
85 Cf. Khakas *xuča*, Sagai, Shor *quča* 'ram', which is the Mongolic loanword, but ultimately of Turkic origin.
86 Tofan for 'ram' uses compound word *asqïr hoy* < *asqïr* 'stallion, male' + *hoy* 'sheep', cf. Kott *koaskir* 'ram'.

87–89; Anikin 2000: 338–339; SIGTJa 2001: 432–433; Khabtagaeva 2009: 279; 2015d: 143; Nugteren 2011: 430; Róna-Tas & Berta WOT 2011: 576–577

According to Werner (2002/1: 437), the Kott word *koaskir* 'ram' has a Yeniseian etymology. It compounds from *koy* 'sheep' and *askir* 'stallion', although both of these elements are Turkic loanwords. Vajda (2016: personal communication) also regards the Kott form as a compound word, cf. the same structure in Kott *bikaaskir* 'bull' ← Russian *bik* 'bull' and Turkic *askïr* 'stallion'; Kott *kurasaaskir* 'cock' ← Russian *kura* 'chicken' and Turkic *askïr* 'stallion'. It seems convincing; on the other hand, the Yenisei Turkic form *qoskar* also fits with our hypothesis.

The base of Turkic word is *qoč*, cf. Mongolic *quča*,[87] which was borrowed from Turkic (Doerfer TMEN 3: 539–540; Clauson ED 592a; Nugteren 2011: 430).

There are two Turkic forms *qoč* and *qočŋār*, which probably derived from *qočun and the suffix +*GAr*.[88] If the first form is clear, the second is questionable. According to Ščerbak (1961: 111) and Levitskaja (ESTJa 2000: 89), the Turkic form *qočun is connected with *qoč* morphologically similarly to other Turkic word *qōy* ~ *qōń* and *qoyun* 'sheep, ewe'.

From the West Old Turkic, the word was borrowed into Hungarian[89] (Róna-Tas & Berta WOT 2011: 576–577). The re-borrowing took place in some Modern Turkic languages as in Tuvan (Khabtagaeva 2009: 279), Khakas and Altai dialects, and Kirgiz[90] (Doerfer TMEN 3: 540). This re-borrowing was borrowed further to Samoyedic languages[91] (Joki LS 214; Helimski 1997: 289).

Through Mongolic, the Turkic word was also borrowed into Tungusic[92] (SST-MJa 1: 440–441; Doerfer 1985: 100; Rozycki 1994: 148). From the Buryat dialect, the word was borrowed into Siberian Russian (Anikin 2000: 335, 338–339, 629, 630).

---

87 Turkic *qočă 'ram' (cf. Old Turkic *qoč*) → Mongolic *quča: cf. Middle Mongol: HY; Ibn-Muh.; Muq. *quča*; LM *quča*; Modern Mongol: Buryat *xusa*; Khalkha *xuc*; Lower Uda Buryat *kusa* ~ *kusu*; Kalmuck *xutsa*; Dagur *koč* (E); Khamnigan *xuca*.

88 The suffix is unclear. According to Róna-Tas & Berta (WOT 2011: 577), it may be related to East Old Turkic suffixes +*GA*, +*GAč* and +*GAn*, which denotes living subjects (Erdal 1991: 83–90).

89 Turkic: West Old Turkic *koč 'ram' → Hungarian *kos* [koš] 'ram'.

90 Turkic *qoč* 'ram' → Mongolic *quča* 'ram' → Modern Turkic 'ram': NE^S YeniseiT: Khakas *xuča*; Koibal, Kachin *quja* (R); Sagai, Shor *quča* (R); AltaiT: Altai *kuča*; Teleut *quča* (R); NW^S Kirgiz *kuča*.

91 Turkic *qoč* 'ram' → Mongolic *quča* 'ram' → Turkic *quča* 'ram' → Samoyedic: Kamas *kuča* 'ram'; Mator *kuča* 'ram'.

92 Turkic *qoč* 'ram' → Mongolic *quča* 'ram' → Tungusic: Eweki dial. *kuča* 'ram'; Solon *xusa* 'ram'; Manchu *kūča* 'goat; ram'.

Kott *koi*; Assan *koi* ~ *kai* 'sheep' (Werner 2002/1: 437) ← Turkic *qoy < *qōń* 'sheep':
    cf. Old Turkic *qōń*; NE^S YeniseiT: Khakas *xoy*; Sagai, Koibal, Kachin *qoy* (R); Shor *qoy*; AltaiT: Altai *qoy*; Tuba *koy*; Qumanda *koy*; Quu *koy*; Teleut *qoy*; SayanT: Tuvan *xoy*; Tofan *hoy*; ChulymT *qoy*; NE^N Yakut –; NW^N Siberian Tatar *quy*; NW^S Kirgiz *koy*; Fu-yü *goy*; Kazak *qoy*; SE Yellow Uyghur *qoy*;

Turkic → Samoyedic:
    Mator *koj* 'sheep'; Selkup *koi* 'sheep'.

Etymology: Ščerbak 1961: 110; Räsänen VEWT 279b; Doerfer TMEN 3: 563–565; 1985: 37; Clauson ED 631a; Timonina 1978: 8; ESTJa 2000: 24–25; SIGTJa 2001: 431–432

The Yeniseian words were borrowed from the Turkic form *koy. The final consonant -*y* in the Yeniseian words proves a later period of borrowing; the earliest Turkic form was *qōń* with palatalized final -*ń*. The reason for the change of Turkic vowel -*o*- > -*a*- in one of the Assan forms is unclear.

The Turkic word was borrowed into Samoyedic (Helimski 1997: 283; Filipova 1994: 47) and Mongolic[93] (Nugteren 2011: 419) languages. From the Mongolic, the Turkic word was borrowed further into Tungusic[94] (SSTMJa 1: 409b; Doerfer 1985: 37; Rozycki 1994: 108).

Kott *kulun* ~ *kolun* ~ *kulún*; Arin *kulún*; Assan *kulún* 'foal' (Werner 2002/1: 448) ← Turkic *qulun 'foal':
    cf. Old Turkic *qulun*; NE^S YeniseiT: Khakas *xulun*; Sagai, Koibal, Kachin *qulun* (R); Shor *qulun*; AltaiT: Altai *qulun*; Tuba *kulun*; Qumanda *kulun* ~ *kūlin* ~ *kïlin*; Quu *kulun*; Teleut *qulun* (R); SayanT: Tuvan *kulun*; Tofan *hulun*; ChulymT *qulun* (R); NE^N Yakut *kulun*; NW^N Siberian Tatar *qolan* 'wild horse'; NW^S Kirgiz *kulun*; Fu-yü *gulun* '1-year horse'; Kazak *qulïn*; SE Yellow Uyghur *qulum* ~ *qulun* ~ *qulïm*;

Turkic → Samoyedic:
    Kamas *kuluka* 'foal' < *kulu* +*kkA* {Samoyedic NN/diminutive}; Mator *kulun* 'foal';

Turkic → Siberian Russian *kulun* 'foal'.

Etymology: Joki LS 208–209; Ščerbak 1961: 90–91; Räsänen VEWT 299a; Doerfer TMEN 3: 506–507; Clauson ED 622b; Timonina 1978: 8; ESTJa 2000: 132–133; SIGTJa 2001: 647

---

93 Turkic → Mongolic 'sheep': Middle Mongol: SH *qoni(n)*; HY *qonin*; Muq. *qonin* ~ *γonin*; LM *qoni(n)*; Modern Mongol: Buryat *xoni(n)*; Khalkha *xon'*; Kalmuck *xön*; Dagur *xon'* (E); Khamnigan *xoni(n)*.

94 Turkic → Mongolic → Tungusic: *Southern Ewenki*: Upper Lena, Northern Baikal, Baunt, Nercha; *Eastern Ewenki*: Barguzin *konin* 'sheep'; Solon *xonĩ* 'sheep'; Udehe *xuani* 'ram'; Ulcha *xonin* 'sheep, ram'; Orok *xonin* 'sheep'; Nanai *xoni*; Jurchen *huô-ni* 'sheep'; Manchu *honin* 'sheep'.

The initial *k-* in Kott points to a later period of borrowing, while in Arin to an early period. This criterion can be explained by the fact that the original Yeniseian *k-* changed to *h-* in Kott and was preserved in Arin, respectively.

The word is widespread in almost all Turkic languages (Ščerbak 1961: 90–91). Besides Yeniseian, from Siberian Turkic the word was borrowed into Samoyedic (Joki LS 208–209; Helimski 1997: 291) and Siberian Russian (Anikin 2000: 319).

Kott ***ogus***; Arin ***ogus*** 'bull' (Werner 2002/2: 32) ← Turkic **ögüs* < *öküz* < *höküz* 'ox':

cf. Old Turkic *öküz*; NE[S] YeniseiT: Khakas *ögĭs ~ öŋes ~ ügĭs* 'ox; male bear' (But.); AltaiT: Tuba *öŋüs* 'male bear'; SayanT –; ChulymT –; NE[N] Yakut *oğus* 'ox'; Dolgan *ogus*; NW[N] Siberian Tatar –; NW[S] Kirgiz *ögüz* 'ox; castrated bull'; Fu-yü –; Kazak *ögiz* 'ox'; SE Yellow Uyghur *qus* 'cow; ox, bull'.

Etymology: Ščerbak 1961: 98; Räsänen VEWT 370b; Doerfer TMEN 1: 538–540; Clauson ED 120a; ESTJa 1974: 521–523; Stachowski 1996/1:101; SIGTJa 2001: 439–440; Róna-Tas & Berta WOT 2011: 663–667; Nugteren 2011: 367

The Yeniseian words were borrowed from the Siberian Turkic voiced form **ögüs*, which developed from *öküz*. Due to the absence of vowel harmony in Yeniseian, it's disappearence is a regular change for Turkic loanwords in Yeniseian. In turn, the source of borrowing is not that obvious. The word is present in Khakas in different forms: *ögĭs ~ öŋes ~ ügĭs* with the meaning 'ox; male bear'. From the phonetic side, the back-vocalic Yakut and Dolgan forms are closer to Yeniseian than Khakas, which creates a possibility of a Yakut layer in Yeniseian. Cf. Ewenki data, which were directly borrowed from Yakut[95] (SSTMJa 2: 341a). This fact does not exclude the Tungusic impact on Yeniseian.

As concerns the etymology of the Turkic word, some researchers regard it as of foreign origin, others as native Turkic in origin, or they attribute onomatopoeic origin. For a good overview on the etymology of Turkic words, see Róna-Tas & Berta (WOT 2011: 664–665). The word is present in Mongolic[96] (Nugteren 2011: 367) and Tungusic[97] (SSTMJa 2: 341a) with the rotacized forms

---

95 Turkic: Yakut → Tungusic: *Eastern Ewenki*: Mai, Nelkan, Tokko, Uchur, Urmi, Tommot *oyus* 'ox'; Negidal *oyus* 'ox'.

96 Turkic → Mongolic 'bovine, ox': Middle Mongol: SH *hüker*; HY *hüger*; Muq. *üker*; Leiden, Ist. *hüker*; Rasulid *üker*; LM *üker*; Modern Mongol: Buryat *üxer*; Khalkha *üxer*; Kalmuck *ükr*; Dagur *xukur* (E); Khamnigan *üker ~ ökör*.

97 Turkic → Mongolic → Tungusic: *Eastern Ewenki*: Zeya, Aldan, Uchur, Barguzin *hukur*; Vitim *uku*; *Southern Ewenki*: Upper Lena, Northern Baikal, Nercha *ukur* 'cow'; Solon *uxur* 'ox'.

z > r and initial h-. The Turkic word also was loaned to Hungarian[98] (Róna-Tas & Berta WOT 2011: 663–667).

Kott **ôr** 'herd of horses' (Werner 2002/2: 46) ← Turkic *ȫr < ögür 'herd of horses':
cf. Old Turkic ögür; NE^S YeniseiT: Khakas ȫr 'herd; big family', ör 'herd of horses'; Koibal ȫr 'herd', cf. Sagai, Koibal, Kachin ür 'heap, flock, herd; society, acquaintance, clan' (R); Shor ȫr 'herd'; AltaiT: Altai ür 'herd'; Qumanda ör 'herd of horses'; Teleut ür 'herd' (R); SayanT: Tuvan ȫr 'friends'; Tofan ȫr 'friends; group, herd'; ChulymT –; NE^N Yakut üör 'herd; *fig.* gang'; Dolgan üör 'herd'; NW^N Siberian Tatar –; NW^S Kirgiz üyür 'herd; close relatives, close friends'; Fu-yü –; Kazak üyir 'herd of horses'; SE Yellow Yughur –;
Turkic → Samoyedic:
Kamas ȫr 'family, tribe'; Mator ür 'herd'.

Etymology: Joki LS 251; Räsänen VEWT 369b; Rassadin 1971: 215; Clauson ED 112a; Timonina 1978: 9

The Kott word *ôr* was borrowed from Turkic form *ȫr with secondary long vowel, which developed from the sequence -ögü- (Cf. other examples in Kott, where the similar change *ô* < *ȫ, ō* or *î* < *ī* occurred: Kott *ô* 'inedible fungus, toadstool' ← Turkic *ō* < *aɣu* 'poison'; Kott **kônak** 'shirt' ← Turkic kȫnäk < kögänäk < köŋläk 'shirt'; Kott *îri* ~ *îre* 'thread, tendon' ← Turkic sīr < siŋir 'muscle, sinew, tendon'). This feature points to a later period of borrowing. The disappearance of vowel harmony in Yeniseian form is a regular change for Turkic loanwords in Kott.

From an etymological aspect, Räsänen (VEWT 369b) connects the Turkic word with Mongolic egür 'nest, lair; "cell" as of a political party', which is problematic from semantic point. The Turkic word is present in Samoyedic with different secondary vowels, which assume different Turkic sources (Joki LS 251; Helimski 1997: 375).

Arin **pajbal** 'cattle, cow' (Werner 2002/1: 99) ← Turkic *pay 'rich' + bal 'cattle':
< pay < bāy 'rich':
cf. Old Turkic bāy; NE^S YeniseiT: Khakas pay 'rich; a rich man; abundant, plentiful; saint'; Sagai, Koibal, Kachin pay (R); Kyzyl pay ~ bay; Shor pay; AltaiT: Altai bay 'rich; a rich man; abundant, plentiful'; Tuba bay; Qumanda bay; Quu pay; Teleut pay; SayanT: Tuvan bay 'rich; a rich man; abundant, plentiful'; Tofan bay 'rich; wealth'; ChulymT pay; NE^N Yakut bāy 'wealth, property; rich, wealthy'; Dolgan bāy; NW^N Siberian Tatar pay 'husband'; NW^S Kirgiz bay 'rich; a rich man; abundant, plentiful;

---

98 Turkic: West Old Turkic *ökür 'ox' → Hungarian ökör [ökör] 'ox'.

husband; *dial.* elder brother'; Fu-yü *bay* 'rich'; Kazak *bay* 'rich; a rich man; husband'; SE Yellow Uyghur *paj ~ päy* 'rich';

Turkic → Samoyedic:

Kamas *bai* 'rich, wealthy; wealth, fortune'; Mator *baj* 'rich'.

Etymology: Joki LS 80; Doerfer TMEN 2: 59; 1985: 37; Räsänen VEWT 56a; Ščerbak SF 195; Rassadin 1971: 158; Clauson ED 384a; ESTJa 1978: 27–28; Timonina 1978: 12; Rozycki 1994: 26–27; Helimski 1997: 213; SIGTJa 2001: 668–670

+ *bal* < *mal* 'cattle':

cf. Old Turkic *mal* 'property, wealth' (DTS); NE^S YeniseiT: Khakas *mal* 'cattle' (KhR), cf. 'livestock, cattle, animal' (But.); Sagai, Koibal, Kachin *mal* 'property; cattle' (R); Kyzyl *mal* 'cattle'; Shor *mal* 'cattle'; AltaiT: Altai *mal* 'cattle, property'; Tuba *mal* 'cattle'; Qumanda *mal* 'cattle; means, wealth', cf. *pal* 'livestock, property'; Quu *mal* 'cattle', cf. *pal* 'cattle, property'; Teleut *mal* 'livestock; horse'; SayanT: Tuvan *mal* 'cattle, domestic animals; horse; *fig.* rude, vile man'; Tofan *mal* 'cattle, livestock, domestic animal'; ChulymT *mal* 'cattle'; NE^N Yakut *mal* 'property, goods'; NW^N Siberian Tatar –; NW^S Kirgiz *mal* 'domestic animal; cattle; property, wealth'; Fu-yü *mal* 'cattle'; Kazak *mal* 'domestic animals; *fig.* person, who likes the livestock'; SE Yellow Uyghur *mal* 'livestock, cattle; domestic animals'.

Turkic → Samoyedic:

Kamas *mal ~ māl* 'cattle'.

Etymology: Joki LS 224; DTS 335b; Räsänen VEWT 323b; Rassadin 1971: 205–206; Ščerbak 1997: 169; Nugteren 2011: 439

The Arin word is a compound (Werner 2002/1: 99), which consists of two Turkic loanwords *bāy* 'rich' and *mal* 'cattle'. The initial devoiced consonant *p-* in the Arin first compound *paj* assumes Yenisei Turkic influence, while the second part of the compound *bal* shows Yeniseian development. Possibly the Turkic word was loaned to Yeniseian with the form **mal* and further changed to *bal*. My hypothesis can be explained by the change in the original Yeniseian initial consonant *b-*, which regularly devoiced to *p-* in Arin (Starostin 1982: 149). If the Turkic form was borrowed with initial *b-*, it should have changed to *p-* in Arin. The change of Turkic *m-* > *b-* supposes an early period of borrowing, because of the absence of this initial nasal consonant *m-* in Yeniseian.

See also Kott ***pai*** 'rich', Arin ***bajšu*** 'wealth' and Kott ***bal*** 'cattle'.

Assan ***šar*** 'bull' (Werner 2002/2: 437) ← Turkic **šar* 'bull, ox' ← Mongolic *šar* 'ox':

cf. NE^S YeniseiT: Shor, Kachin *šar* 'ox' (R); Kyzyl *šar* 'ox'; AltaiT: Altai *čar* 'bull, ox; cow'; Tuba *čar* 'bull'; Qumanda *čar* 'ox'; Quu *čar* 'ox'; Teleut *čar* 'ox' (R); SayanT: Tuvan *šarï* 'ox'; Tofan –; ChulymT *car* 'ox' (R); NE^N Yakut –; NW^N Siberian Tatar *car* 'bull'; NW^S Kirgiz –; Fu-yü *šar* 'bull'; Kazak –; SE Yellow Uyghur –;

Turkic → Samoyedic:
Mator čārE 'bull, ram';
Turkic ← Mongolic šar 'ox':
Middle Mongol: –; LM šar ~ čar; Modern Mongol: Buryat sar 'ox, castrated bull'; Sayan Buryat: Tunka šara; Oka; Zakamna šar 'ox'; Khalkha šar 'ox'; Kalmuck tsar 'ox'; Dagur –; Khamnigan car ~ šar;
Mongolic → Siberian Russian čar 'castrated bull'.

Etymology: Ščerbak 1961: 99; Räsänen VEWT 100a; Rassadin 1971: 194; 1980: 33, 44; Stachowski 1996/1: 99; Helimski 1997: 231; Anikin 2000: 644; Werner 2002/2: 437; Khabtagaeva 2009: 159; 2015a: 116

The Assan word (Werner 2002/2: 437) was borrowed from the Siberian Turkic form šar 'ox'. The inititial consonant š- points to the Yenisei Turkic layer, while in Altai Turkic the initial č- appeared.

The Turkic forms are of Mongolic origin (Ščerbak 1961: 99; Rassadin 1980: 33, 44). From Turkic, the Mongolic word was borrowed also to Siberian Russian (Anikin 2000: 644). Helimski connects the Mator word with Mongolic jari 'steppe deer' (Helimski 1997: 231). This Mongolic word is related also to Tofan čarï 'reindeer' (Rassadin 1971: 194). The additional vowel -ï is unclear in Tuvan šarï, it may be the combination of Mongolic šar 'ox' (Khabtagaeva 2009: 159) and jari 'male reindeer'. The original Mongolic form should be *čar, because the initial sibilant š- is not typical for original Mongolic words, it developed from sibilant s with original vowel *i or *ï (for details on the development of Mongolic š-, see Poppe 1955: 122–123; Nugteren 2011: 231–232).

Kott šoška;[99] Arin šoška[100] 'pig' (Werner 2002/2: 442), cf. Kott čûčuk 'puppy' (Werner 2002/1: 167) ← Turkic *šoška < čočqa < čočuq 'pig':
cf. Old Turkic čočuq; NE^S YeniseiT: Khakas sosxa; Sagai, Koibal sosqa (R); Kyzyl šōsya ~ šošya; Shor šošqa; AltaiT: Altai čočko; Qumanda čočka ~ čočko ~ čöčkö; Quu čočka ~ šoško; Teleut čočqo (R); SayanT –; Tofan šošqa; ChulymT čočqa ~ cocqa; NE^N Yakut –; NW^N Siberian Tatar cucqï ~ čučqa; NW^S Kirgiz čočko; Fu-yü –; Kazak šošqa; SE Yellow Yughur –;
Turkic → Samoyedic:
Kamas šoška ~ šuška 'pig'; Mator šoška 'pig'; Selkup soska 'pig'.
Etymology: Joki LS 297; Räsänen VEWT 113a; Rassadin 1971: 73; Clauson ED 400b; Timonina 1978: 8; Filipova 1994: 49; Helimski 1997: 345; Anikin 2000: 679

---

99   Cf. Kott šoškaaskir 'boar' < šoška + askir 'stallion'; šoška apup 'piglet' < šoška + apup 'child'.
100 Cf. Arin šoška[ik]elja 'piglet' < šoška + akel 'son'.

The Yeniseian words were borrowed from Turkic (Timonina 1978: 8) form *šoška (cf. Shor, Kyzyl, Quu, Tofan). Another possibility is the Turkic form *soska, which changed due to the Yeniseian regular phonetic change s > š (Starostin 1982: 158–159). Interestingly, there is another Kott form čûčuk, meaning 'puppy', which may also be of Turkic origin. It was probably borrowed from another Turkic form *čočuk, which is absent in Siberian Turkic, and exists in Old Turkic (cf. also Osman čojuk 'child'). The source of borrowing of the Kott form čûčuk 'puppy' is unclear.

The Turkic word was also borrowed into Samoyedic (Joki LS 297; Filipova 1994: 49; Helimski 1997: 345) languages. The source of borrowing for Kamas and Mator is also questionable because of the consonant š. It may be the Siberian Turkic or Yeniseian form.

Arin *uške* 'he-goat' (Werner 2002/2: 376) ← Turkic *üške < äčkü 'goat':
cf. Old Turkic äčkü; NE^S YeniseiT: Khakas öskī; Sagai üskä (R); Kyzyl öškė; Shor öškü; AltaiT: Altai ečki; Qumanda ečki; Quu eške; Teleut ečki (R); SayanT: Tuvan öškü; Tofan ö^cškü; ChulymT –; NE^N Yakut –; NW^N Siberian Tatar üškä; NW^S Kirgiz ečki; Fu-yü –; Kazak eški; SE Yellow Uyghur üškö ~ ušqo.

Etymology: Räsänen VEWT 35a; Clauson ED 24b; ESTJa 1980: 34–36; SIGTJa 1997: 426; Róna-Tas & Berta WOT 2011: 518–519; Nugteren 2011: 333–334

The Arin word is connected to the Siberian Turkic form *üške (cf. Siberian Tatar), which goes back to Old Turkic äčkü 'goat'. The disappearance of vowel harmony is a regular change in Yeniseian. The change of the original cluster čk > šk is peculiar for the Yenisei Turkic, Sayan Turkic and Siberian Tatar languages.

There are two homogeneous Turkic forms äčkü and käči. The first form is typical for Siberian Turkic, Turki and some Kipchak Turkic languages, while the second form is found in the Oghuz, Volga Kipchak Turkic and Chuvash languages. From the Turkic form ečkü (> *ešge), the word was borrowed into Mongolic[101] (Nugteren 2011: 333–334) and from West Old Turkic form *käčäkä to Hungarian[102] (Róna-Tas & Berta WOT 2011: 518–519).

---

[101] Turkic → Mongolic 'kid (*young goat*)': Middle Mongol: SH ešige; LM isige(n) ~ esige; Modern Mongol: Buryat ešege(n); Khalkha išig; Kalmuck išk; Dagur –; Khamnigan išige(n) ~ isige(n) ~ ešege(n).

[102] Turkic (cf. East Old Turkic keči 'goat'): West Old Turkic *käčäkä → Hungarian kecske [kečke] 'goat'.

1.1.6   Human and Animal Body Parts

Kott **ânar ~ anar** 'hip, loin'; Pumpokol **aniŋ** 'legs, feet' (Werner 2002/1: 34):

Kott ânar ~ anar < an + Yeniseian ar 'bone';

Pumpokol aniŋ < an -iŋ {Yeniseian plural};

Yeniseian an ← Turkic *yān 'the hip; the side, flank of the body or in other contexts':

cf. Old Turkic yān 'the hip; the side, flank of the body or in other contexts'; NE^S YeniseiT: Khakas nan 'the upper part of hip; the side of cloth'; Sagai čan ~ nan 'side'; Shor čan 'side'; AltaiT: Altai d'an 'side, flank'; Tuba d'an 'side'; Qumanda d'an ~ yan 'side'; Quu ńan 'thigh, side'; Teleut yan 'side'; SayanT: Tuvan čan 'neighborhood; surrounding area'; Tofan ńan 'anat. side, the upeer part of hip; jamb; near'; ChulymT yaŋ ~ čaŋ 'side'; NE^N Yakut –; NW^N Siberian Tatar –; NW^S Kirgiz jan 'side'; Fu-yü –; Kazak žan 'side; near'; SE Yellow Uyghur yan 'side'.

Etymology: Räsänen VEWT 184b; Rassadin 1971: 208; Clauson ED 940a; Doerfer TMEN 4: 120; Timonina 1985: 13; ESTJa 1989: 113; Khabtagaeva 2015b: 526

The Kott ânar ~ anar 'hip, loin' and Pumpokol aniŋ 'legs, feet' are compound words, where one of the components is the Turkic loanword and other is a Yeniseian element. The Kott form has another Yeniseian word ar 'bone', while the Pumpokol form has the Yeniseian plural suffix -iŋ. The first component of both Yeniseian forms is Turkic word yān with the meanings 'the hip; the side, flank of the body or in other contexts' (Khabtagaeva 2015d: 138). The source of borrowing was possibly the Siberian Turkic form with the palatalized nasal consonant ń-, which disappeared due to the absence of original initial nasal consonants in Yeniseian (Starostin 2007: 163). The sporadic change of initial y- > ń- is typical for some Siberian Turkic languages (Yenisei Turkic, Tofan, Quu dialect of Altai Turkic and Fu-yü of Manchuria) due to the assimilation following nasal -n (for details on Turkic shift change, see Johanson 1998: 106[103] and Baskakov 1985: 22).

Yugh **baʔt ~ bat** 'face, forehead', cf. ā·bat ~ abbat 'my face' < ap ~ ā·p 'my' + bā^{h}t; Southern Ket **bat** 'face, forehead' (Werner 2002/1: 107) ← Turkic *bät 'the human face' < bet:

cf. Old Turkic bet 'face'; NE^S YeniseiT: –; AltaiT: Altai –; Teleut pät 'the face, the exterior, the right side of a tool, the drawing' (R); SayanT: Tuvan beti (< bet +X {poss.sg.3}) '(his) side; postpos. near, under, below'; Tofan be^{c}t 'front side'; ChulymT –; NE^N Yakut –;[104] NW^N Siberian Tatar pit 'face'; NW^S Kirgiz bet 'cheek, face; honor; muz-

---

103   E.g. Old Turkic yan- 'to turn back' ~ Tofan ńan-, Shor nan-; Old Turkic yaǧmur 'rain' ~ Khakas naŋmïr; Old Turkic yaŋāq 'cheek' ~ Khakas, Fu-yü nāh 'cheek'; Old Turkic yaŋï 'new' ~ Khakas nā, Shor ńā ~ nā; Old Turkic yumurtǧa 'egg' ~ Fu-yü nomurtga, etc.

104   The Yakut case is interesting. The authors of SIGTJa (1997: 207) connect Yakut bettex 'here,

zle; surface; page; direction'; Fu-yü –; Kazak *bet* 'face, cheek; upper layer; surface; direction; side; page; conscience, honor, shame'; SE Yellow Uyghur –;
cf. Tungusic 'face':[105]

Ewenki dial. *bāde* 'face'; Lamut *bād* 'look, appearance; structure, form, contour, outline; colour, colour of animal fur'.

Etymology: Räsänen VEWT 72a; Clauson ED 296b; ESTJa 1978: 121–122; Stachowski 1997: 230; SIGTJa 1997: 207; Werner 2002/1: 107

Werner (2002/1: 107), after Stachowski (1997: 230), connects the Yeniseian forms with Turkic *bät* 'face'. From a phonetic point of view, the disappearence of vowel harmony is typical feature for Yeniseian loanwords. The laryngealization in the Yugh form probably developed under the influence of the Yenisean word *aʔt* 'bone' (Vajda 2014: personal communication).

Ket *hɔʔq* 'excrement, filth'; Yugh *fɔʔχ* 'excrement'; Kott *fôk ~ fôx ~ pʰôk* 'feces, dirt' (Werner 2002/1: 327) ← Turkic **poq* 'excrement, dung' < *bōq*:
cf. Old Turkic *bōq* 'green mould; excrement, dung'; NE^S YeniseiT: Khakas *pox* 'child excrement', cf. *pox-söp, pox-sax* 'filth; trash'; Sagai, Koibal, Kachin, Shor *poq* 'excrement, filth, dung', cf. Sagai, Koibal *pog* 'mould' (R); AltaiT: Altai *boq* 'excrement'; Tuba *bok* 'excrement, dung'; Qumanda *bok ~ pok* 'dung'; Quu *pok* 'excrement, filth, dung'; Teleut *poq* 'excrement, filth, dung' (R); SayanT: Tuvan *bok* 'filth; trash'; Tofan *moq* 'filth; trash'; ChulymT *poq* 'excrement, filth, dung' (R); NE^N Yakut –; NW^N Siberian Tatar *poq* 'excrement, filth, dung' (R); NW^S Kirgiz *bok* 'excrement, filth, dung'; Fu-yü –; Kazak *boqta-* (< *boq+lA-* {Turkic VN}) 'to blackguard'; SE Yellow Yughur –.

Etymology: Räsänen VEWT 79a; Doerfer TMEN 2: 349; Clauson ED 311a; ESTJa 1978: 183; Timonina 1978: 12; Stachowski 1997: 232; Werner 2002/1: 327

The Yeniseian forms were borrowed from Turkic (Timonina 1978: 12; Stachowski 1997: 232; Werner 2002/1: 327) form **pōq* 'excrement, dung'. The source of borrowing should be with initial devoiced consonant **p-*. It can be explained by the regular change of original Yeniseian consonant **p-* to *f-* in Yugh *h-* to Ket and to *f- ~ pʰ-* (Starostin 1982: 149). Furthermore, the Kott form displays the Turkic original long vowel. According to these phonetic features, the Turkic word was borrowed in the early stage of borrowing.

---

close, closer, on this side; *postposition* with, from' with the Common Turkic noun *bet* 'face', while Sevortjan (1978: 124–125) connects it with another Common Turkic adverb *berü ~ bärü* 'to this side, on this side'.

105 It is not clear that the Tungusic is related to the Turkic forms. The source of borrowings is usually Yakut, where the examined word is absent.

From Turkic the word was borrowed into Mongolic[106] and Persian (Doerfer TMEN 2: 349).

Ket *kɔʔt*; Yugh *gɔʔt* 'butt, hind end' (Werner 2002/1: 445) ← Turkic *köt 'backside, buttocks':
cf. Old Turkic *köt*; NE^S YeniseiT: Khakas *köt* ~ *küt* ~ *köten*; Sagai *ködän* ~ *ködün*, Koibal *ködän* (R); Kyzyl *kōde*, *ködän*; AltaiT: Altai *köt*, *ködön* (R); Tuba *kötön*; Quu *köt* 'buttocks', cf. *kötön* 'hindgut'; Teleut *köt*, *ködön* (R); SayanT:[107] Tuvan *köt*; Tofan *köt*; ChulymT *köt*, *ködön*; NE^N Yakut –; NW^N Siberian Tatar *küt*; NW^S Kirgiz *köt*; Fuyü –; Kazak *köt*; SE Yellow Yughur *k^höt^h* ~ *k^hiot^h*;
Turkic → Samoyedic:
Kamas *köten* 'backside, buttocks'.
Etymology: Joki LS 205; Doerfer TMEN 3: 618; Räsänen VEWT 294b; Clauson ED 700b; ESTJa 1980: 84–86; Timonina 1985: 11; SIGTJa 1997: 281; Nugteren, Ragagnin & Roos 2015: 337–349

The Yeniseian words were borrowed from Turkic *köt* 'backside, buttocks' (Timonina 1985: 11; Werner 2002/1: 445). The initial voiced *g-* is unique in Yugh (Vajda 2014: personal communication). The disappearance of vowel harmony is a regular change for Yeniseian loanwords.

The Turkic word belongs to the the category of taboo words, it possibly is present in almost all Turkic languages, but not attested in dictionaries. There are two forms *köt* and *köten*, which appear side by side in Turkic languages. The second one clearly is a derived form. According to Sevortjan (ESTJa 1980: 85), it derived from the reconstructed verb **köt-* 'be round, plump' and the Turkic deverbal noun suffix *-An* (for details on the function of Turkic suffix, see Erdal 1991: 300). The etymology of Nugteren, Ragagnin and Roos (2015: 338) is correct. The ending +(A)n is the collective suffix (for details on the function of Turkic suffix, see Erdal 1991: 91), which was added to the stem *köt, because the backside was perceived as a collective 'buttocks', or the rectum was perceived as part of a collective 'entrails'. Doerfer (TMEN 3: 618) proposed that the Turkic word have developed in analogy to several terms for body parts, e.g. *tapan* 'sole', *biqin* 'hip'.

In addition to Yeniseian, the Turkic word was borrowed into Samoyedic (Joki LS 205) and New Persian (Doerfer TMEN 3: 618).

---

106 Turkic → Mongolic 'sweepings, filth, garbage, refuse, rubbish, ashes thick scum on water': Middle Mongol: –; LM *boy*; Modern Mongol: Buryat *bog*; Khalkha *bog*; Oirat dial. *bog*; Dagur –; Khamnigan *bog*.
107 The Sayan Turkic and Yellow Uyghur data are cited from the paper of Nugteren, Ragagnin and Roos (2015: 340–341).

Kott **kalôx** 'ear' (Werner 2002/1: 405) ← Turkic *qulaq 'ear' < qul +(G)AK {Turkic NN, denoting names for body parts, see Erdal 1991: 74–75}:
  cf. Old Turkic qulaq ~ qulqaq; NE^S YeniseiT: Khakas xulax; Sagai, Koibal, Kachin qulaq (R); Kyzyl χulaχ; Shor qulaq; AltaiT: Altai qulaq; Tuba kulak; Qumanda kulak; Quu kulak; Teleut qulaq (R); SayanT: Tuvan kulak; Tofan qulaq; ChulymT qulaq; NE^N Yakut kulgāx; Dolgan kulgā(k) ~ kulgak; NW^N Siberian Tatar qulaq; NW^S Kirgiz kulak; Fu-yü gulah; Kazak qulaq; SE Yellow Uyghur qolaq.
Etymology: Räsänen VEWT 298b; Clauson ED 621a; Timonina 1978: 12; Erdal 1991: 75; ESTJa 2000: 124–127, 131; SIGTJa 2001: 204–206

The Kott word was borrowed from Common Turkic *qulaq 'ear' (Timonina 1978: 12), which is widespread in almost all Turkic languages. The preservation of initial k- points to a later period of borrowing. The original Yeniseian k- changed to h- in Kott. The sprintization of Turkic final -k to -x in Kott is peculiar for Turkic loanwords in Kott (cf. aksax 'lame' ← Turkic aqsaq, Kott kapax 'forehead' ← Turkic qapaq 'eyelid'). The change of the original Turkic vowel -u- in the first syllable to -a- in Kott form is not well understood, probably due to assimilation of the Turkic vowel -a- in the the second syllable.

From the etymological point of view, the base of the Turkic word is qul 'slave' with an unproductive suffix that forms metaphorical names for body parts, cf. Old Turkic tirsgäk 'elbow' < tiz 'knee', qadïzġaq 'callosity' < qadïz 'bark of a tree', etc.

Cf. also Kott **kalkul** 'deaf'.

Kott **kankoj ~ konkoj** 'throat' (Werner 2002/1: 408):
The etymology of Kott word is unknown. I suggest two different Turkic etymologies:
(a) ? Turkic *köŋ kay 'throat singing' < kög 'melody, voice' + kai 'throat singing' (cf. Yenisei Turkic):
< kög 'melody, voice'
  cf. Old Turkic kǖg 'song, melody'; NE^S YeniseiT: Khakas kög 'fun, joy, good mood; melody, tune'; Koibal kög 'tone, sound, singing, song, melody' (R), Kyzyl köγ^x 'singing, song'; Shor kög 'melody, tone'; AltaiT: –; SayanT: Tuvan xög 'joy, amusement'; Tofan hög 'joy, good mood'; ChulymT –; NE^N Yakut –; NW^N Siberian Tatar kü 'melody, sound, voice'; NW^S Kirgiz küy 'melody formusical instrument'; Fu-yü –; Kazak küy 'melody'; SE Yellow Uyghur –;
Etymology: Räsänen VEWT 286b, 307a; Doerfer TMEN 4: 303–304; Clauson ED 709b; ESTJa 1997: 82–83; SIGTJa 2001: 613–614
+ kay 'throat singing':
  cf. NE^S YeniseiT: Khakas xay 'throat singing' (KhR); Sagai kay 'the hiss, the hissing sound, the hum; the gurgling sounds that are produced when recite the tale'

(R); Shor *qay* 'throat singing'; AltaiT: Altai *kay* 'throat singing'; Quu *kay* 'two-voice singing'; Teleut *qay* 'throat singing'; Remaining lgs. –.

Etymology: Räsänen VEWT 221a; ESTJa 1997: 205

As a hypothesis, I assume it is connected to the Turkic compound word *kögkai* 'throat singing', which consists of two Common Turkic words *kög* 'melody, voice' and *kai* 'throat singing'. My idea is strengthened by the presence of a number of Yeniseian compound words borrowed from Turkic. Because of the absence of vowel harmony, the original palatal vowels changed to the velar vowels in the first part of the Kott compound *kan ~ kon*. The assimilation probably occurred in the consonant cluster *gk* > *ŋk* > *nk*.

The etymology of the Turkic words is not obvious. The first Turkic word *kög* 'melody, voice' refers as Chinese loanword (for details, see Doerfer TMEN 4: 303–304; Clauson ED 709b; ESTJa 1997: 82–83; SIGTJa 2001: 613–614), which was borrowed into the Mongolic languages[108] (ESTJa 1997: 82–83). The etymology of second Turkic word *kay* 'throat singing' is not obvious. According to Levitskaja (ESTJa 1997: 205), the Altai Turkic and Yenisei Turkic forms connected with Old Turkic **qań-* > *qayïn- ~ qayna-* 'to boil'.

(b)   ? Turkic **kȫmey* 'throat, larynx' < **kögemey* ← Mongolic *kögemei ~ kömei* 'pharynx, throat':

cf. NE[S] YeniseiT: –; AltaiT: Teleut *kömöy* 'throat' (R); SayanT: Tuvan *xȫmey* 'type of throat singing'; Tofan –; ChulymT –; NE[N] Yakut *küömey* 'throat, larynx, pharynx'; Dolgan *küömäy* 'esophagus'; NW[N] Siberian Tatar –; NW[S] Kirgiz *kömököy* 'tongue'; Fu-yü –; Kazak *kömey* 'throat, larynx'; SE Yellow Uyghur –;

Turkic ← Mongolic:

Middle Mongol: –; LM *kögemei ~ kömei* 'fur on throat or belly of an animal; dewlap of bovines; pharynx, throat'; Modern Mongol: Buryat *xȫmei* 'fur on belly of an animal'; Khalkha *xȫmī* 'back of the mouth, pharynx; a type of double voice production or overtone singing'; Kalmuck *kömē* 'the part of a belly skin'; Dagur –; Khamnigan *kȫmegči* 'fur on belly of an animal'.

Etymology: Kałużyński 1962: 88; Räsänen VEWT 289b; Rassadin 1980: 67

My second hypothesis is connected to the Mongolic word *kögemei* 'pharynx, throat'. The Yeniseian forms *kankoj ~ konkoj* 'throat' were probably borrowed from the reconstructed Turkic form **kögemey*. I assume the metathesis of Kott *-nk-* < **-mk-* < **-meg-* < *-gem-*. The semantic meaning of the second Turkic word 'throat, larynx' is more likely.

The Kott word still belongs to the category of words of uncertain etymology.

---

108   Turkic → Mongolic: LM *kög* 'tune, music'; Modern Mongol: Buryat *xüg* 'joy, jocundity'; Khalkha *xög* 'tune, music; tuning, tone'; Kalmuck *kög* 'harmony, music'; Dagur –; Khamnigan –.

Kott *kapax* 'forehead' (Werner 2002/1: 411) ← Turkic *qabaq 'forehead' < *qapaq* 'eyelid, cover':

cf. Old Turkic *qapaq* 'eyelid'; NE^S YeniseiT: Khakas *xamax* 'forehead'; Sagai, Koibal, Kachin *qamaq* 'forehead' (R); Kyzyl *χamaχ* 'forehead'; Shor *qabaq* 'forehead'; AltaiT: Altai *qabaq* 'eyebrow, eyelid'; Tuba *kakpak* 'eyebrow'; Qumanda *kabak* 'forehead'; Quu *kabak* 'forehead'; Teleut *qamaq* 'forehead'; SayanT: Tuvan *xavaq* 'forehead; visor of a cap; hillock'; Tofan *habaq* 'eyebrow; small slope'; ChulymT *qamaq* 'forehead, temple'; NE^N Yakut *xabaġal* (< **qapaq +Al* {Yakut NN}) 'front upper part of the fireplace'; NW^N Siberian Tatar –; NW^S Kirgiz *kabak* 'eyelid; pothole'; Fuyü –; Kazak *qabaq* 'eyelid; border, edge'; SE Yellow Uyghur *qavak* 'bridge of the nose';

Turkic → Samoyedic:

Kamas *kama^c* 'high place; hill, mountain'; Mator *kamak* 'forehead'.

Etymology: Joki LS 155; Räsänen VEWT 228b; Doerfer TMEN 3: 369–370; 535; Clauson ED 582b; Timonina 1978: 12; ESTJa 1997: 161–162; SIGTJa 2001: 199–200

The Kott word was borrowed from Turkic, where the lexical meaning is 'forehead'. The original meaning is 'cover'. According to the data, the meaning 'forehead' is typical for several Siberian Turkic languages. The source for borrowing was the form *kabak with intervocalic *VbV*, which devoiced regularly in Kott loanwords, e.g. Kott *aipiš* 'old man' ← Turkic *aybiči*, Kott *êper* 'noun circle; adj. round; adv. around' ← Turkic **eber-* < *ävir-* 'to turn (*something, e.g. a wheel*)', Kott *obal* ~ *ôpal* 'sin' ← Turkic *obal*, etc. Another change, Turkic final *-k* > *-x*, is also a regular change for Kott loanwords, e.g. Kott *aksax* 'lame' ← Turkic *aqsaq*, Kott *kalôx* 'ear' ← Turkic *qulaq*, etc.

The morphological structure of the Turkic word is unclear. According to Clauson (ED 582b), it is derived from the non-productive verb *qap-* 'to close' and probably the Turkic deverbal noun suffix *-(A)k* (for details on the function of Turkic suffix, see Erdal 1991: 224). Doerfer (TMEN 3: 369–370; 535) refers to the identity of Turkic *qapaq* 'eyelid' and 'cover, lid'. There is a typical fluctuation of intervocalic *VbV* ~ *VmV* in Turkic forms.

In addition to Yeniseian, the Turkic word was borrowed into Samoyedic languages (Joki LS 155; Helimski 1997: 26).

Kott *tagaj* ~ *takai*; Assan *tógaj* ~ *tagáj* ~ *takaj* 'head' (Werner 2002/2: 230) ← Turkic *tägäy < (?) *täpäy:

cf. Old Turkic –; NE^S YeniseiT: Khakas *tigei* 'the top of a mountain; hill; the top of a head'; Kyzyl *tēgä·y* 'the top of sg.'; Shor *tegey* 'the top of a tree, a head or a mountain', cf. *tägäy* ~ *tegäy* 'a peak, a hill'; AltaiT –; SayanT: Tuvan *tey* 'hill; the top of a head; top of headgear'; Tofan *te^chek* 'the top of a head'; ChulymT *täg* 'top of the head'; Remaining lgs. –;

Turkic → Samoyedic:
Kamas *tegei* 'a top';
Cf. Turkic *töpö* 'the top (*mountain, etc.*), a man's head; a hill':
Old Turkic *töpü* ~ *töpö* 'the top (*mountain, etc.*), a man's head; a hill'; NE^S YeniseiT: –; AltaiT: Altai *töbö* 'a hill; the top of the head, the head'; Qumanda *töbe* ~ *töbö* 'the top; the top of the mountain, hill, the butt of the ax, top of the head'; Quu *tövö* 'skull; mountain'; Teleut *töbö* 'the top of mountain; the butt of the ax'; SayanT –; ChulymT –; NE^N Yakut *töbö* 'head; the top of the head, the top of sg.; the end of sg.'; Dolgan *töbö* 'the top of tree; head'; NW^N Siberian Tatar *täbä* 'hill'; NW^S Kirgiz *töbö* 'hill; the top of a head', cf. *döbö* 'hill'; Fu-yü –; Kazak *töbe* 'hill; ceiling, roof; the top of a mountain; crown of the head'; SE Yellow Uyghur – (For an etymological background, see ESTJa 1980: 197–199; SIGTJa 2001: 201).

Etymology: Joki LS 320; Doerfer TMEN 2: 450–452; Räsänen VEWT 469a

The etymology of the Yeniseian words is unknown. They probably relate to the Turkic form **tegey* 'top of a mountain; hill; top of a head' (cf. Yenisei Turkic forms). The disappearance of vowel harmony is a regular change for Turkic loanwords in Yeniseian. The Turkic origin is demonstrated by semantic analysis.

Turkic *tegey* is present only in Yenisei Turkic. The Tuvan form *tey* is the shortened form, which developed from the secondary long vowel **tēy* < **tegey*. Ölmez (2007: 273a) compares the Tuvan word with another Turkic word *töpü* 'the top (*mountain, etc.*), a man's head; a hill'. It is important to mention that Turkic *töpü* ~ *töpö* does not have a proper form in Yenisei Turkic, Sayan Turkic or Chulym Turkic, where the form *tegey* is found. From Yenisei Turkic, the word was borrowed into Samoyedic (Joki LS 320; Räsänen VEWT 469a).

The etymology of the Yenisei Turkic word *tegey* is unknown. The connection with another Turkic word *töpü* ~ *töpö* 'the top (*mountain, etc.*), a man's head; a hill' (Clauson ED 436a) is possible, but the change *VpV* > *VgV* in Yenisei Turkic is not self-evident. The original Turkic *VpV* is usually voiced or changed to *VmV* in Khakas.[109] The change *VpV* > *VgV* is typical for Mongolic loanwords. Doerfer (TMEN 2: 450–452) connects Turkic *töpö* with Mongolic **däpö* > **dege*. There is a large number of Mongolic words derived from the non-productive base **dege*,[110] but the form which perhaps connects to Turkic *tegey* is absent in Mongolic.

---

109 E.g. Old Turkic *apa* 'bear (animal)' ~ Khakas *aba*; Old Turkic *käpäk* 'bran; *metaph.* scurf, dandruff' ~ Khakas *kibek* 'shell (of nut or egg)'; Khakas *tabïġ* 'searchings' < *tap*- 'to find' -*XG* {Turkic VN}; Old Turkic *qapaq* 'a lid, eyelid' ~ Khakas *xamax* 'forehead', etc.
110 cf. LM *deger-e* (< **dege+rA*) 'top, on top of, on, at, above; high; (*with the Ablat.*) higher or better than; in addition to, besides, while, just as'; *degedüs* (< **dege+dU+s*) 'dignitaries;

A connection of the Yeniseian words with Mongolic *toloγai* 'head'[111] is also questionable. The etymology of the Turkic and Yeniseian words is still unclear.

Arin *qólpas* 'finger' (Werner 2005: 164a) ← Turkic *qol pas < *qol* 'finger (cf. Khakas)' + *baš* 'the upper part of sg.':

< *qol* 'finger' < *qōl* 'the upper arm; the forearm, hand, finger':

cf. Old Turkic *qōl* 'the upper arm; the forearm, hand; a wing of an army'; NE^S YeniseiT: Khakas *xol* 'hand, wrist; foreleg; finger'; Sagai, Koibal, Kachin *qol* 'the arm of person, the forefoot of the animals, the hand' (R); Kyzyl *χòl* ~ *χōt* 'arm, hand, forefoot'; Shor *qol* 'arm', cf. Shor *orta qol* 'the middle finger'; AltaiT: Altai *kol* 'arm, wrist;'; Tuba *kol* 'arm, the foreleg of the animals'; Qumanda *kol* 'ruka, wrist'; Quu *kol* 'arm, wrist, the foreleg of the animals'; Teleut *qol* 'arm' (R); SayanT: Tuvan *xol* 'forearm; the foreleg of the animals'; Tofan *qol* 'arm; the foreleg of the animals'; ChulymT *qol* 'arm'; NE^N Yakut *xol* 'arm; the foreleg of the animals'; Dolgan *kol* 'shoulder; the foreleg of the horse'; NW^N Siberian Tatar *qul* 'arm'; NW^S Kirgiz *kol* 'arm, wrist; the foreleg of the animals; finger; handwriting; signature'; Fu-yü *gol* 'hand'; Kazak *qol* 'army, signiture; hand; handwriting'; SE Yellow Uyghur *qol* 'side; hand'.

Etymology: Räsänen VEWT 276b; Doerfer TMEN 3: 556; Clauson ED 614b; ESTJa 2000: 37–43; SIGTJa 1997: 244–245

+ *pas* 'the upper part of sg.' < *baš* 'head, top':

cf. Old Turkic *baš* 'head; beginning'; NE^S YeniseiT: Khakas *pas* 'head; top; beginning'; Sagai, Koibal *pas*, Kachin *paš* 'head; the top of sg., upper part; leader'; cf. Sagai *pās* (R); Kyzyl *paš* 'head'; Shor *paš* 'head; the front part of sg.; source of the river, stream; upper, the top of sg.'; AltaiT: Altai *baš* 'head; the front part of sg., top; beginning'; Tuba *baš* 'head; top of sg.'; Qumanda *paš* 'head, top'; Quu *paš* 'head, top of sg.'; Teleut *paš* 'head, top of sg.'; SayanT: Tuvan *baš* 'head; the top of sg.; the end of sg.; beginning, source'; Tofan *ba^cš* 'head; top of sg.; tip; spike; bow seat; source, the upper part of a river'; ChulymT *paš* ~ *pas* 'head'; NE^N Yakut *bas* 'head; chapter of book; side; beginning, source; the front or upper part of sg.'; Dolgan *bas* 'head'; NW^N Siberian Tatar *baš* 'head'; NW^S Kirgiz *baš* 'head; the upper part of sg., the top of sg.; beginning; the end of sg.; leader'; Fu-yü *baš* 'head'; Kazak *bas* 'general, head, leader'; SE Yellow Uyghur *pas* ~ *paš* 'head; beginning, the top of sg.'.

---

ancestors; denizens of heaven, saints', *degebüri* (< **dege+l-bUri*) 'felt covering of the upper part of a yurt consisting of two semicircular pieces; roofing of a house', *degeǰi* (< *dege+ǰi*) 'the first or choicest part of food or drink offered to the deities; the first cup of tea, etc. or the first serving of food offered to the guest of honour', etc.

111   Mongolic: Middle Mongol: –; LM *toloγai*; Modern Mongol: Buryat, Khalkha *tolgoi*; Kalmuck *tolγa*; Dagur *tɔluγ*; Khamnigan *tologoi* (D). For more Mongolic data and correspondences, see Nugteren (2011: 522).

Etymology: Räsänen VEWT 64b; Doerfer TMEN 2: 246–247; Clauson ED 375a; ESTJa 1978: 85–88; SIGTJa 1997: 194

The etymology of the Arin word is unknown. I assume the word is a compound consisting of the two Turkic words *qol* 'finger' and *baš* 'the upper part of something, the top of something'. Despite the fact that this compound is absent in Siberian Turkic, both parts demonstrate the characteristics of Yenisei Turkic. If the first part has the semantic meaning 'finger', cf. Khakas *ortïn xol* 'middle finger', *ustüg xol* 'index finger' (Butanaev 1999: 187); the second part is represented by the phonetic changes: the devoicing of original Turkic initial consonant *b-* and the change of final consonant *-š* to *-s*: *baš* > *pas*.

It is an interesting fact that the Turkic compound word *qolbaš* is present in the Tatar dialects, Bashkir and Chuvash with the lexical meaning 'shoulder' (for details, see ESTJa 2000: 42; SIGTJa 1997: 245).

Yugh *χʌlčaŋ*; Ket *qʌltaŋ* 'humeral joint, humerus bone, forearm' (Werner 2002/2: 101) ← ? Turkic **qoltuq* 'armpit':

cf. Old Turkic *qoltuq*; NE^S YeniseiT: Khakas *xoltïx* 'armpit'; Sagai, Koibal, Kachin *qoltuq* 'the armpit, the space between arm and torso' (R); Shor *qoltuq* 'armpit'; AltaiT: Altai *qoltuq* 'armpit'; Tuba *koltik*; Qumanda *koltik*; Quu *koltok* 'bosom, sinus, axil'; Teleut *qoltïq* 'armpit', cf. *qoltuq* ~ *qoltïq* 'the armpit, the space between arm and torso' (R); SayanT: Tuvan *kolduk* 'armpit'; Tofan *qo^{c}ltuq* 'armpit'; ChulymT *qoltuq* 'armpit'; NE^N Yakut –; NW^N Siberian Tatar –; NW^S Kirgiz *koltuk* 'armpit'; Fu-yü –; Kazak *qoltïq* 'armpit'; SE Yellow Uyghur *qoltïq* 'armpit';

Yeniseian → Siberian Russian *kultuk* 'shoulder'.

Etymology:[112] Räsänen VEWT 276b; Doerfer TMEN 3: 557–558;[113] Clauson ED 619a; Stachowski 1997: 228; ESTJa 2000: 52–54; Anikin 2000: 318

The etymology of the Yeniseian words is unclear. It may be a native Yeniseian word or a Turkic loanword (Werner 2002/2: 101). The second syllable in the Yeniseian words is problematic (Georg 2016: personal communication). According to Vajda (2016: personal communication), the Yeniseian forms are blended with Turkic *qol* 'arm' and Yeniseian **tʲaŋ* 'head', which may be correct. For an etymological background of the Turkic word *qōl* 'the upper arm; the forearm, hand, finger', see above Arin *qólpas* 'finger'.

---

112 The etymology of Turkic word is still unclear. Clauson (ED 619a) after Doerfer (TMEN 3: 557–558, also see Räsänen VEWT 276b) derives the form *qoltuq* from the noun *qōl* 'arm'. According to ESTJa (2000: 52–54), the Turkic form cannot be connected to the word *qōl* from morphologically: the function of the Turkic diminutive suffix does not fit.

113 The Turkic word was borrowed into New Persian (Doerfer TMEN 3: 557–558).

Stachowski (1997: 228) connects the Yeniseian words with Turkic *qoltuq* 'armpit'. The connection with the Turkic word can be appropriate from a phonetic and semantic viewpoint. The change of final -*k* > -*ŋ* ~ -*n* is phonetically possible (e.g. Kott *ataŋ* ← Turkic *otïq* 'fire-steel'; Arin *torgijan* ← Turkic *torgayaq* 'lark (*bird*)', etc.). Another change of initial Turkic *q*- > *χ*- in Yugh and the preservation of *q*- Ket is a typical phonetic feature (e.g. Yugh *χan*, Ket *qaˑn* 'prince' ← Turkic *kān* < *qaġan*; Yugh *χap* ~ *χaʔp*; Ket *qap* ~ *qaʔp* 'boat' ← Turkic *kebe* < *kämi*, etc.). The change of the Turkic cluster -*lt*- > -*lč*- in Yugh occurs through palatalized *-*lt'*-. From semantic point of view, the Yeniseian and the Turkic forms relate to 'arm'.

The semantic meaning of Siberian Russian 'shoulder' proves the borrowing from Yeniseian (Vasmer 2: 411; Anikin 2000: 318).

The Yeniseain words belongs to the category of words of uncertain etymology.

Ket *iˑlʼ*, Northern Ket *iˑlʼi* 'arm' (Werner 2002/2: 434) ← Turkic *äli < *älig* 'hand, forearm; the width of a finger (*measure of length*)':

cf. Old Turkic *äl* ~ *älig* 'hand, forearm'; NE^S YeniseiT: Khakas *īlïg* 'the width of a finger (*measure of length*)'; Koibal *eliγ*, Sagai *ilig* ~ *eliγ* 'the width of a finger (*measure of length*)' (R); Shor *äliγ* 'the width of a finger (*measure of length*)' (R); AltaiT: Altai *elü* 'the width of a finger (*measure of length*)', cf. *ölü* 'vershok (*an old Russian measure of length eqv to 4.45 cm*)'; Tuba *eltek* (< *äl +*lXG*) 'gloves'; Qumanda *ilik* (< *äl +*lXG*) 'mitten'; Quu *elte* (< *äl +*lXG*) 'mitten'; Teleut *ölü* 'vershok (*an old Russian measure of length eqv to 4.45 cm*)' (R); SayanT: Tuvan *ilig* 'the width of a finger (*measure of length*)'; Tofan –; ChulymT *ällik* (< *äl +*lXG*) 'mitten'; NE^N Yakut *ilī* 'hand, forearm; the width of a finger (*measure of length*)'; Dolgan *ilī* ~ *ilīy* 'hand'; NW^N Siberian Tatar *ilü* 'the width of a finger (*measure of length*)'; NW^S Kirgiz *eli* 'the width of a finger (*measure of length*)'; Fu-yü –; Kazak –; SE Yellow Uyghur *elʼig* 'hand, forearm'.

Etymology: Räsänen VEWT 39ab; Clauson ED 140b; ESTJa 1974: 260–261, 263–264; Timonina 1985: 11; SIGTJa 1997: 251

According to Timonina (1985: 11) and Werner (2002/2: 434), the Yeniseian words are of Turkic origin. The Turkic etymology fits from the phonetic and semantic viewpoint. Apocope happened in Yeniseian, which is a typical feature for Turkic loanwords. Semantically, widening occurred. If in Turkic the word means 'hand, forearm' and in some Siberian Turkic varieties 'the width of a finger (*measure of length*)', in Yeniseian the word came to designate a more general meaning, 'arm'.

The Altai Turkic forms Tuba *eltek*, Qumanda *ilik*, Quu *elte* and Chulym *ällik* with meaning 'mitten, gloves' are derived from *äl* 'hand' and the Turkic productive denominal noun suffix +*lXG* (As concerns the function, see Erdal 1991: 121).

1.1.7   Designations of People

Kott *aibič* ~ *aipiš* 'old man' (Werner 2002/1: 18) ← Turkic *aybïčï 'fellow countryman' (cf. Altai) < *aybï* 'request; order, decree; help' +*čI* {Turkic NN, see Erdal 1991: 110} < *ay-* 'to speak; to say, declare, prescribe' -*vI*+ {Turkic VN, see Erdal 1991: 334}:

cf. Old Turkic *ay-* 'to speak; to say, declare, prescribe'; NE^S YeniseiT: Khakas –[114]; Shor *aybïla-* (< **aybï+lA-* {Turkic NV}) 'to ask, beg, call for help; to command; fight' (R); AltaiT: Altai *aybïčï* 'fellow countryman' < *aybï* 'request; order, decree; help'; Tuba *aybï* 'request, order, command' > *aybïla-* 'to ask for help'; Quu *aybïlal-* (< **aybï+lA-* {Turkic NV} -*l-* {VV/passive}) 'to be beg'; Teleut *aybï* 'entreaty, petition, petition, appeal for help' > *aybū* 'command, compulsion, help, assistance' (R); SayanT: Tuvan *aybïčï* 'messenger, courier; servant; footman' < *aybï* 'request, decree; order'; Tofan *aybï* 'order; permission'; Remaining lgs. –.

Etymology: Rassadin 1971: 152; ESTJa 1974: 99; Tatarincev 2000: 77

The Turkic word *aybüčï* derives from the verb *ay-* 'to speak, to say' (Clauson ED 266a; ESTJa 1974: 99) with Turkic deverbal noun suffix -*vI* (for details on the suffix function, see Erdal 1991: 334–337) and Turkic denominal noun suffix +*čI*, which characterises habitual or professional activities of humans. The Turkic *aybï* with meaning 'request; order, command' exists only in the South Siberian Turkic branch. According to the lexical meaning, the Kott *aibič* ~ *aipiš* 'old man' is possibly borrowed from Altai Turkic.

Kott has two forms with different final consonants -*č* and -*š*. The original borrowed form possibly was with -*č*, which later changed to -*š*. The change of Turkic *č* > *š* in all positions is regular for Kott, indicating an early period of borrowing.

Arin *argiš* 'crowd (*of people*); migration' (Werner 2002/1: 58) ← Turkic *argïš 'comrade, companion' < *arqïš*:

cf. Old Turkic *arqïš* 'a person or group of persons travelling for commercial or official purposes; travelling merchants, caravan; official envoys, mission'; NE^S YeniseiT: Khakas *arǧïs* 'comrade; engagement' (KhR), cf. 'comrade, husband, wife; henchman; invisible companion, guardian spirit' (But.); *arǧïs* 'caravan' (R); Kachin *arǧïš* 'companion' (R); Kyzyl *arɣïş* 'friend, comrade'; Shor *arǧïš* 'comrade'; AltaiT: Altai –; Tuba *arǧïš* 'comrade'; Qumanda *arǧïš* 'comrade, companion'; Quu *arǧïš* 'comrade'; Teleut *arǧïš* 'companion' (R); SayanT –; ChulymT *arǧïš* ~ *ārǧïš* ~ *arǧis* 'comrade'; NE^N Yakut *arǧïs* 'companion, comrade'; Dolgan *arǧïs* 'caravan'; Remaining lgs. –;

---

[114]   The word is absent in Khakas, but semantically the word *aybalǧï* 'slow person' (But.) probably is connected to Altai *aybïčï* 'fellow countryman'.

Yakut → Tungusic:
   Sakhalin, Tokmin, Tungir Ewenki *argis ~ argiš* 'migration'; Lamut *argin* 'distance; way' (SSTMJa 1: 50b).
Etymology: Räsänen VEWT 26b; Doerfer TMEN 2: 43–44; Clauson ED 216b; SSTMJa 1: 50b; SIGTJa 2001: 538

From phonetic point of view, the final *-š* in the Arin form shows the borrowing from Altai Turkic, but the semantic meaning is different from Turkic. In Siberian Turkic it indicates one person, while in Arin it points to 'crowd of people and migration'. According to the semantic meaning, probably the source for Arin borrowing is the Ewenki dialectal forms *argis ~ argiš* 'migration', borrowed from Yakut.

The etymology of the Turkic word is unknown. Räsänen (VEWT 26b) tentatively relates it to the noun *arqa* 'the back'. According to Clauson (ED 216b), the Turkic word derived from the verb *arqa-* 'to search, investigate', but semantically this is not clear.

Kott ***d'ônaš*** 'in a crowd' < *d'ôn -aš* {Kott comitative, see Werner 1990: 61, 63} (Werner 2002/1: 224) ← Turkic **d'on* < *jon* 'people' ← Mongolic *jon* 'people':
   cf. Old Turkic –; NE^S YeniseiT: Khakas *čon* 'the people, the public, the city's population; folk'; Sagai *čon* 'people' (R); Shor *čon* 'society, the public, the people'; AltaiT: Altai *d'on* 'people; society'; Tuba *d'on* 'population, people'; Qumanda *d'on ~ ńoŋ* 'people'; Teleut *yon* 'society, people' (R); SayanT: Tuvan *čon* 'people, population'; ChulymT *čon* 'people'; NE^N Yakut *d'on* 'people; residents, the population; relatives, family'; Dolgan *jon ~ jōn* 'people'; Yakut dial. *d'on-kihi* 'people' (DS); NW^N Siberian Tatar –; NW^S Kirgiz –; Fu-yü –; SE Yellow Uyghur *yun* 'people, society';
Turkic ← Mongolic *jon* 'people':
   Middle Mongol: –; LM *jon*; Modern Mongol: Buryat *zo(n)* 'people, population'; Dagur –; Khamnigan *dzon*.
Etymology: Räsänen VEWT 127b; Rassadin 1980: 12, 21, 37, 48; Khabtagaeva 2009: 166; 2015a: 122

The Kott word was borrowed from the Altai Turkic form *d'on* 'people' with the Yeniseian comitative suffix *+aš*.

Etymologically, the Turkic word is of Mongolic origin. The Mongolic word was borrowed as well into the Ewenki dialect.[115]

Kott ***kan***; Yugh *χan*; Ket *qaˑn* 'prince' (Werner 2002/2: 81) ← Turkic *kān < *qaġan* 'an independent ruler of a tribe or people; kagan':

---

115   Mongolic → Tungusic: *Eastern Ewenki*: Barguzin *jon* 'people' (SSTMJa 1: 264a).

cf. Old Turkic *qaġan*; NE^S YeniseiT: Khakas *xan ~ xān*; Sagai, Koibal, Kachin *qan* (R); Kyzyl *χan*; Shor *qān*; AltaiT: Altai *qān*; Tuba *kān*; Qumanda *kān*; Quu *kān ~ kan*; Teleut *qān* (R); SayanT: Tuvan *xān*; Tofan *hān*; ChulymT *qan*; NE^N Yakut *xan*; Yakut dial. *xan* 'rich person'; NW^N Siberian Tatar *qan*; NW^S Kirgiz *kan*; Fu-yü –; Kazak –; SE Yellow Uyghur *qan* 'ruler, Shamanic God';
Turkic → Samoyedic:
Kamas *kān ~ kan* 'prince, emperor'; Selkup *kān* 'prince'.
Etymology: Joki LS 157; Räsänen VEWT 219b; Doerfer TMEN 141–179; 1985: 56; Clauson ED 611a; Timonina 1978: 11; SIGTJa 2001: 321, 665–668; Nugteren 2011: 395–396
The word is widespread in almost all of the Eurasian territory. The etymology of the word is unknown; it probably has a connection with a Xiongnu title (Clauson ED 611a). For details on the etymology and its spread, see Doerfer (TMEN 141–179).
In addition to Yeniseian, from Turkic the word was borrowed into Mongolic[116] (Nugteren 2011: 395–396), Samoyedic (Joki LS 157; Filipova 1994: 47) and Siberian Russian (Anikin 2000: 253–254). From Mongolic, it was borrowed into Tungusic[117] languages (SSTMJa 1: 358b; Doerfer 1985: 56).

Kott ***najči*** 'friend' (Werner 2002/2: 24) ← Turkic *nayǰï 'friend' ← Mongolic *nayiǰi* 'friend';
Arin ***meninajči*** 'friend' (Werner 2002/2: 24) ← Mongolic *minu nayiǰi 'my friend', cf. LM *minu nayiǰi*:
Middle Mongol: –; LM *nayiǰi* 'friend'; Modern Mongol: Buryat *naiža* 'buddhist priest tutor of child in monastery'; Khalkha *naiz* 'friend; a ceremony performed by archers at the beginning and end of a match'; Oirat dial. *nādz ~ nāž* 'friend'; Kalmuck *nādž^i* 'friend, comrade'; Dagur –; Khamnigan –;
Mongolic → Turkic:
cf. NE^S YeniseiT: Khakas *nayǰï ~ nanči*; Sagai *nanǰï*, Koibal, Kachin *nanǰï* (R); Shor *nanči*; AltaiT: Altai *nadʼï*; Tuba *ńandžï*; Qumanda *nadʼï*; Quu *nayïdžï*; Teleut *nayï*; SayanT –; ChulymT *nēze* 'brother-in-law'; NE^N Yakut *ńādʼï* 'godfather, godmother'; Remaining lgs. –;
Turkic → Samoyedic:
Kamas *naije* 'friend'; Mator *nāǰǰi* 'friend'.

---

116 Turkic → Mongolic: Middle Mongol: SH *qa'an ~ qahan ~ qan*; HY *qan ~ qahan*; Muq. *xān ~ xan*; LM *qayan ~ qan*; Modern Mongol: Buryat *xān ~ xan*; Khalkha *xān ~ xan*; Kalmuck *xan*; Dagur *xān* (E); Khamnigan *xān ~ xan*.
117 Turkic → Mongolic → Tungusic: *Southern Ewenki*: Upper Lena, Northern Baikal, Nercha *kān*; *Eastern Ewenki*: Barguzin *kan*; Solon *xā*; Lamut *qaγan*; Oroch *qā*; Ulcha *qa*; Nanai *qā*; Manchu *han*.

Etymology: Joki LS 237; Kałużyński 1962: 37; Räsänen VEWT 349a; Rassadin 1980: 30; 37; 45; Khabtagaeva 2015a: 123

There are two different sources for borrowing. If the Kott word was borrowed from one of the Siberian Turkic varieties, the Arin form was borrowed directly from Western Buryat *menī naidži* with the Mongolic possessive pronoun *minu* 'my' and the Mongolic word *nayiji* 'friend'.

The Mongolic word via Turkic was borrowed into Samoyedic (Joki LS; Helimski 1997: 316).

1.1.8 Kinship Terminology

Kott ***bača*** 'brother-in-law (*sister's husband*)'; Arin ***bi-b'ača*** {Yeniseian poss. *bi-* 'my'} 'my brother-in-law' (Werner 2002/1: 97) ← Turkic **baǰa* 'brother-in-law' ← Mongolic *baǰa* 'husbands of sisters; term used by husbands of sisters in referring to each other':

cf. Old Turkic –; NE[S] YeniseiT: Khakas *paǰa*; Kyzyl *paǰa*; AltaiT: Altai *bad'a*; SayanT: Tuvan *baža*; Tofan *baǰa*; ChulymT *pača*; NE[N] Yakut *bad'a* 'sister-in-law'; NW[N] Siberian Tatar *pača ~ paca*; NW[S] Kirgiz *baǰa*; Fu-yü *baǰa*; Kazak *baža*; SE Yellow Uyghur –; Turkic ← Mongolic *baǰa* 'brother-in-law':

cf. Middle Mongol: HY *baǰa*; LM *baǰa* 'husbands of sisters; term used by husbands of sisters in referring to each other'; Modern Mongol: Buryat *baza* 'brother-in-law'; Khalkha *badz* 'brothers-in-law, husbands of sisters'; Kalmuck *baz^a* 'brother-in-law'; Dagur *badz* (E); Khamnigan *badza*.

Etymology: Doerfer TMEN 2: 232–233; Räsänen VEWT 54; ESTJa 1978: 24–25; SIGTJa 2001: 310; Khabtagaeva 2015a: 115

The Kott word was borrowed from Siberian Turkic. The change of intervocalic $VjV > V\check{c}V$ is typical for Kott loanwords, e.g. Kott *najči* 'friend' ← Turkic *nayǰï* (← Mongolic): YeniseiT *nayǰï*; Kott *šičir* 'straw' ← Turkic *čïǰïr* (← Chinese): YeniseiT *čïǰïr*; etc.

The Arin form *bi-b'ača* is used with a Yeniseian possessive marker *bi-* 'my' (Vajda 2014: personal communication).

The etymology of the Turkic word is unknown: it is present in almost all Turkic languages, but it is absent in Old Turkic. We find the word also in Mongolic languages, but it is not not clear whether it is borrowed from Turkic, or if it is an original Mongolic word which was taken into the Turkic languages. Doerfer poses a question concerning the Mongolic data, and classifies the Turkic word as a "child word" (TMEN 2: 232–233). From Mongolic, the word was borrowed into Tungusic[118] (SSTMJa 1: 63).

---

118 Mongolic → Tungusic: *Eastern Ewenki*: Barguzin *baǰa* 'brother-in-law'.

Arin *kis* 'sister-in-law' (Werner 2002/1: 479) ← Turkic **qïs* 'girl; unmarried woman; daughter' < *qïz*:
    cf. Old Turkic *qïz*; NE^S YeniseiT: Khakas *xïs*; Koibal *qïs* (R); Kyzyl *xïs*; Shor *qïs*; AltaiT: Altai *qïs*; Tuba *kïs*; Qumanda *kïs*; Quu *kïs*; Teleut *qïs* (R); SayanT: Tuvan *kïs*; Tofan *qïs*; ChulymT *qïs*; NE^N Yakut *qïs*; Dolgan *qïs*; NW^N Siberian Tatar *qïs*; NW^S Kirgiz *kïz*; Fu-yü *gïs*; Kazak *qïz*; SE Yellow Uyghur *qïz ~ qïs*.

Etymology: Räsänen VEWT 269a; Doerfer TMEN 3: 569–570; Ščerbak 1970: 194b; Rassadin 1971: 223; Clauson ED 679b; ESTJa 2000: 190–191; SIGTJa 1997: 295–296

The Arin word was clearly borrowed from the Siberian Turkic form **kïs*. The Common Turkic word is widespread in almost all the Siberian Turkic languages. In this way, the source may be any one of the Turkic languages. The Turkic initial uvular consonant *q-* is preserved in the Arin word, as in native Yeniseian words. From a lexical aspect, broadening occurred 'girl, daughter' → 'sister-in-law'.

Arin *ojakel'a* 'stepdaughter' (Werner 2002/2: 33) < *oj* 'step-' + Yeniseian *akel'a* 'daughter' < *akel* 'son' *-a* {Yeniseian feminine suffix, see Werner 1990: 54–55}: *oj* ← Turkic **ȫy* < *ögey* 'related through one parent only, step-(*father, etc.*)':
    cf. Old Turkic *ögey*; NE^S YeniseiT: Khakas; Sagai, Koibal, Kachin; Shor *ȫy*; AltaiT: Altai *öy ~ ȫy*; Qumanda *öy*; Teleut *ȫy*; SayanT –; ChulymT –; NE^N Yakut –; NW^N Siberian Tatar –; NW^S Kirgiz *ögöy*; Fu-yü –; Kazak *ögey*; SE Yellow Yughur –.

Etymology: Räsänen VEWT 369a; Doerfer TMEN 2: 159–160; Clauson ED 119b; ESTJa 1974: 495–496; SIGTJa 1997: 306

The Arin word belongs to a group of compound hybrid words. It consists of the Turkic form *ȫy* 'step-' and the native Yeniseian word *akel'a* 'daughter'. The last one is derived from the Yenisean word *akel* 'son' and the Yeniseian feminine suffix *+a*. The Arin form *oj* clearly was borrowed from the Turkic form with secondary long vowel *ȫy*, which points to a later period of borrowing. This form is characteristic for almost all Siberian Turkic variations.

Some researchers (for details, see ESTJa 1974: 495–496) connect the Turkic word with the Mongolic negation word *ügei* (For its function, see Poppe GWM § 632).

Cf. also Arin *ojakelbala* 'stepson' and Arin *ojče* 'stepmother'.

Arin *ojakelbala* 'stepson' (Werner 2002/2: 32) < *oj* 'step-' + *akel* 'son' + *bala* 'child' ← Turkic **ȫy bala* 'stepchild': cf. YeniseiT: Khakas *ȫy pala*; Shor, Sagai, Koibal, Kachin *üy pala ~ ȫy pala*; AltaiT: Altai, Teleut *ȫy pala* 'stepchild':
oj 'step-' ← Turkic **ȫy* < *ögey* 'related through one parent only, step-(*father, etc.*)':

cf. Old Turkic *ögey*; NE⁵ YeniseiT: Khakas; Sagai, Koibal, Kachin; Shor *ȫy*; AltaiT: Altai *öy* ~ *ȫy*; Qumanda *öy*; Teleut *ȫy*; SayanT –; ChulymT –; NE^N Yakut –; NW^N Siberian Tatar –; NW⁵ Kirgiz *ögöy*; Fu-yü –; Kazak *ögey*; SE Yellow Yughur –.
+ *bala* 'son' ← Turkic **bala*'child, son, boy':
cf. Old Turkic *bala*; NE⁵ YeniseiT: Khakas; Sagai, Koibal, Kachin *pala*; Kyzyl *pāla*; Shor *pala*; AltaiT: Altai *bala*; Tuba *pala* 'child, son'; Qumanda *pala* ~ *bala* 'child, boy'; Quu *pala* 'child'; Teleut *pala*; SayanT –; ChulymT *pala* 'son'; NE^N Yakut –; NW^N Siberian Tatar *pala*; NW⁵ Kirgiz *bala* 'child, son, granson'; Fu-yü *bala* 'child'; Kazak *bala* 'child, boy'; SE Yellow Uyghur *mïla* 'baby'.

Etymology: Räsänen VEWT 59b; Clauson ED 332b; ESTJa 1978: 47–49; SIGTJa 1997: 306–307

The Arin word *ojakelbala* 'stepson' belongs to a group of hybrid compound words. It consists of three parts: Turkic *ȫy* 'step-', the native Yeniseian word *akel* 'son' and Turkic *bala* 'child, son'.

I consider that the first part of the Arin word *oj* 'step-' as a half-affix of Turkic origin, cf. also Arin *ojče* 'stepmother' and Arin *ojakel'a* 'stepdaughter' (Khabtagaeva 2015d: 135).

See also Pumpokol *pʰalla* ~ *pʰala* ~ *falla* ~ *fala* 'son, boy'.

Arin *ojče* 'stepmother' (Werner 2002/2: 32) ← Turkic **ȫy ije* < *ȫy* 'step-' + *ije* 'mother': cf. YeniseiT: Khakas *ȫy ije*; Sagai, Koibal, Kachin *üy ijä* 'stepmother':
+ *ije* < *eče* 'mother':
cf. Old Turkic *eče* 'one's mother's younger sister; one's own elder sister'; NE⁵ YeniseiT: Khakas *ije* 'mother'; Sagai *ijä*; Koibal, Kachin *ijä*; Shor *üjä* 'grandmother from father's side'; AltaiT: Altai *ed'e* 'aunt; elder sister', cf. *ačï* 'father's younger brother'; Tuba *ed'e* 'aunt; elder sister; mother'; Qumanda *ed'e* 'aunt, elder sister'; Quu *edže* ~ *eže* 'elder sister, sister'; Teleut *eye* 'aunt, elder sister'; SayanT: Tuvan *ača* 'father'; Tofan *aja* 'father', cf. *iᶜhe* 'mother'; ChulymT *ēcä* 'mother'; NE^N Yakut *iye* 'mother', cf. *ehe* 'grandfather; bear'; NW^N Siberian Tatar –; NW⁵ Kirgiz *eže* 'elder sister'; Fu-yü *ije* ~ *iji* 'mother, elder sister'; Kazak *äže* 'grandmother'; SE Yellow Uyghur *ača* 'father; stepfather'.
Turkic → Samoyedic:
Kamas *ija* ~ *ijä* ~ *ja* 'mother', cf. *ugeija* 'stepmother'.

Etymology: Joki LS 136–137; 250; Räsänen VEWT 169a; Doerfer TMEN 2: 15–16; Clauson ED 20a; ESTJa 1974: 231–235; SIGTJa 1997: 299

The Arin compound word *ojče* 'stepmother' was borrowed from the Siberian Turkic compound word **ȫy ije* 'stepmother' (Cf. Yenisei Turkic). There is another compound word for 'stepmother' *öy ene* in Altai Turkic. The shortness of the Turkic secondary long vowel *ȫ* > *o* in Arin shows a later period of borrowing. From a morphological viewpoint, amalgamation occurred.

For the etymology of the first part Türkic *ȫy* < *ögey* 'step-', see Arin ***ojakel'a***
'stepdaughter'.

The Turkic word *eče* 'mother' belongs to 'child language', which is difficult to etymologize. The Turkic word *eče* 'mother' was probably borrowed into Mongolic.[119] See also the Samoyedic forms, which were borrowed from Siberian Turkic (Joki LS 136–137; 250).

Pumpokol ***pʰalla ~ pʰala ~ falla ~ fala*** 'son, boy' (Werner 2002/2: 56) ← Turkic **pala* < *bala* 'a human child, son':

cf. Old Turkic *bala*; NE^S YeniseiT: Khakas *pala*; Sagai, Koibal, Kachin *pala* (R); Kyzyl *pāla*; Shor *pala*; AltaiT: Altai *bala*; Tuba *pala*; Qumanda *pala ~ bala*; Quu *pala*; Teleut *pala*; SayanT –; ChulymT *pala*; NE^N Yakut –; NW^N Siberian Tatar *pala*; NW^S Kirgiz *bala* 'child, son, boy, grandchild'; Fu-yü *bala*; Kazak *bala*; SE Yellow Uyghur *mïla* 'baby'.

Etymology: Räsänen VEWT 59b; Clauson ED 332b; ESTJa 1978: 47–49; Stachowski 1997: 232; SIGTJa 1997: 306–307

The Pumpokol forms relate to Turkic **bala* 'child' (Stachowski 1997: 232). The source of borrowing was the Turkic form with devoiced initial consonant *p-*, which peculiar for some Siberian Turkic languages. Another reason to source the word from the Turkic form *pala* are Pumpokol initial consonants *pʰ-* and *f-*, these consonants go back to the Proto-Yenisieian initial **p-* (Starostin 1982: 149).

The Turkic word is connected to Mongolic *balčir*[120] (ESTJa 1978: 49) and Tungusic *baldi-* 'to be born'[121] (SSTMJa 1: 69).

1.1.9   Titles

Kott ***alpot*** 'chief, head' (Werner 2002/1: 27) ← Turkic **albot* 'chief, head' < **albōt* < *alpaġut* < *alp* 'warrior' *+AGUt* {Turkic NN, forming social classes mainly from titles, see Erdal 1991: 78–83}:

cf. Old Turkic *alpaġut* 'warrior'; NE^S YeniseiT: Khakas *albot ~ albut* 'head of the district; governor;' (But.); NW^N Siberian Tatar *alpaġït ~ alpavït* 'nobleman, landowner'; Remaining lgs. –;

---

119   Turkic → Mongolic 'mama (*familiar term*)': Middle Mongol: –; LM *eǰi*; Modern Mongol: Buryat *eži*; Khalkha *ēǰ*; Oirat dial. *ēdžĭ ~ ēž ~ ēdž*; Dagur –; Khamnigan *idžē*.
120   Turkic → Mongolic 'infant, baby, suckling, newborn young; inexperienced': Middle Mongol: –; LM *balčir*; Buryat *balšar*; Khalkha *balčir*; Kalmuck *balčr*; Dagur –; Khamnigan *balčir*.
121   Turkic → Mongolic → Tungusic 'to born, to be born; to give birth': Common Ewenki *baldi-*, cf. *baldi* 'origin; relative; young plant', Solon *baldi-*; Lamut *balde-*; Negidal *baldi-*; Oroch *bāgdi-*; Udihe *bagdi-*; Ulcha *baldi-*; Orok *balǰi-*; Nanai *balǰi-*; Manchu *bani-*.

< Turkic *alp* 'hero':

cf. Old Turkic *alp* 'warrior'; NE[S] YeniseiT: Khakas *alïp* 'hero'; Sagai, Koibal, Kachin, Shor *alïp* 'hero' (R); AltaiT: Altai *alïp* 'hero, athlete (*in the epic*)'; Tuba *alïp* 'hero'; Qumanda *alïp* 'hero'; Quu *alïp* 'hero'; Teleut *alïp* 'hero' (R); SayanT –; ChulymT: *alïp* 'hero' (R); NE[N] Yakut –; NW[N] Siberian Tatar –; NW[S] Kirgiz *alp* 'giant, warrior; brave'; Fu-yü –; Kazak *alïp* 'giant'; SE Yellow Uyghur –;

Turkic → Samoyedic:

Kamas *ālïp* 'hero'.

Etymology: Joki LS 63–64; Räsänen VEWT 18a; Clauson ED 128b; Doerfer TMEN 2: 110–111; ESTJa 1974: 139; Erdal 1991: 81

The Turkic word *alpaġut* 'warrior' was derived from *alp* 'warrior' with a denominal noun suffix +*AGUt* which forms social classes mainly from titles, cf. also Old Turkic *uzagut* 'expert' < *ūz* 'a skilled craftsman' (Erdal 1991: 78–83). According to Clauson (ED: xliii), the Turkic was derived with the deverbal noun suffix -*GUt*, which forms nouns describing persons. According to Róna-Tas & Berta (WOT 2011: 369), the suffix +*AGUt* in Old Turkic could also denote things consisting of multiple units like cotton.[122]

The Turkic word was borrowed into Mongolic, cf. Literary Mongolian *albaγud* 'public servant, goverment official'. The word is lacking in Modern Mongolic languages. The Mongolic word has been incorrectly connected with *alba(n)* 'compulsion, coercion; official obligation or service; tax, impost, tribute; corvée; public use' (for details, see Clauson ED 128b). In turn, the Siberian Tatar form is a re-borrowing from Mongolic (Clauson ED 128b).

The Kott word is borrowed from Yeniseian Turkic, where the secondary vowel -*ō*- was developed from the original sequence -*AGU*-. The presence of the unvoiced cluster -*lp*- characterises a typical change for Kott loanwords, while the shortness of the secondary long vowel points to a later period.

Kott *âpeš* 'priest' (Werner 2002/1: 48) ← Turkic *abïs 'priest' ← Persian:

cf. NE[S] YeniseiT: Khakas *abïs* 'priest'; Sagai, Koibal, Kachin; Shor *abïs* 'Russian chaplain' (R); Kyzyl *ābïṣ* ~ *āβîṣ* 'chaplain, priest'; AltaiT: Altai *abïs* 'priest'; Qumanda *abïs* ~ *āpïs* 'priest'; Quu *abïs* 'Russian chaplain'; Teleut *abïs* 'Russian chaplain' (R); SayanT –; ChulymT *ābïs* 'priest'; NE[N] Yakut *aġabït*[123] 'priest'; NW[N] Siberian Tatar *abïs* 'uncle';

---

122   Cf. Hungarian *gyapot* 'cotton' ← West Old Turkic *japut < *japgut, cf. East Old Turkic *yapġut* 'a stuffing or matted mass of hair or wool' < *yap* +*AGUt*.

123   < *aġa* 'father' + *bït* (< *bis < *biz*) 'we, our', cf. Modern Yakut *bihi* 'we, our'. The *-*s*(-) > -*t*(-) change is regular in Yakut, e.g. Old Turkic *asïġ* 'profit, advantage' > Yakut *atïg* 'trade, commerce', Old Turkic *isi-* 'to be hot' > Yakut *itiy-*, Old Turkic *ïsïr-* 'to bite' > Yakut *ïtïr-*, etc.

NW^S Kirgiz –; Fu-yü –; Kazak *abïz* 'priest, clever person; narrator-singer; scientist';
SE Yellow Yughur –;

cf. Old Turkic *aba* 'ancestor; grandfather; father; mother; paternal uncle; paternal aunt; elder brother; elder sister';

Turkic → Samoyedic:

Kamas *ābïs* 'clergyman; pastor; priest'; Mator *abïs* 'priest';

Turkic ← Persian *ḥāfiẓ* 'a keeper, preserver, a guardian; a commander, governor; the perserver of all things (*God*); gifted with a good memory; one who has learned by heart the whole Qur'ān' ← Arabic.

Etymology: Joki LS 56; Timonina 1978: 11; Helimski 1997: 199; Anikin 2000: 73; Werner 2002/1: 48; Pomorska 2005: 144–145

The Kott word was borrowed from Siberian Turkic *abïs* 'priest' (Timonina 1978: 11; Werner 2002/1: 48). The change of Turkic final *-s* > *-š* is a regular change in Kott, and also this is a typical feature for native Yeniseian words in Kott.

From an etymological aspect, it may be the short form of Common Turkic *aba* 'father'[124] with the 1st person plural possessive suffix *+bXz* (Helimski 1997: 199). From a semantic point of view, the original meaning 'our father' can broadened to 'Russian Orthodox priest'. According to Schönig (2015: personal communication, see also Anikin 2000: 73; Pomorska 2005: 144–145), the Turkic word is connected to the Persian word of Arabic origin *ḥāfiẓ*, which means 'a person who knows by heart the whole Qur'ān', which is probably more correct.

The Turkic word was borrowed into Samoyedic (Joki LS 56; Helimski 1997: 199) and Siberian Russian *abïz* ~ *abïs* 'angry person; person, who likes to speak' (Anikin 2000: 73).

Ket *batir*; Yugh *bádir* ~ *bátir* ~ *badir* 'hero, warrior' (Werner 2002/1: 97, 109) ← ? Turkic *bātïr < *baġatur* 'warrior, hero':

cf. Old Turkic *baġatur* 'warrior'; NE^S YeniseiT: Khakas *matïr* 'hero; bold, brave, fearless', cf. *patïr* 'warrior, hero' (But.); Sagai *matïr* 'bold, fearless' (R), AltaiT: Altai *mātïr* ~ *bātïr* 'hero, brave'; Tuba *mātïr* 'hero'; Qumanda *matïr* 'hero'; Quu *bātïr* ~ *batïr* 'hero'; Teleut *pātïr* 'hero'; SayanT: Tuvan *mādïr* hero; Tofan –[125]; ChulymT –; NE^N Yakut *bātïr* 'courageous, heroic, courageous; a brave warrior'; Dolgan *bātïr* 'wild';[126] NW^N Siberian Tatar *padïr* 'hero, strong man'; NW^S Kirgiz *bātïr* 'hero, a brave man'; Fu-yü *bātïr* 'hero'; Kazak *batïr* 'hero'; SE Yellow Uyghur *patïr* 'noble, authoritative person';

---

124 For the etymological background of the Turkic word *aba* 'father', see Clauson (ED 5ab) and Sevortjan (ESTJa 1974: 54).
125 Cf. Tofan *boġatïr* 'hero' ← Russian.
126 Cf. Dolgan *bukatür* 'hero' ← Russian.

Turkic → Samoyedic:
   Selkup *mââter* 'hero', cf. *pagatur* 'hero'.
Turkic → Mongolic 'hero; knight; heroic, brave':
   Middle Mongol: SH *ba'atur*; HY *ba'atur*; Muq. *bādur*; LM *baγatur*; Modern Mongol: Buryat, Khalkha *bātar*; Kalmuck *bātr*; Dagur *bātur* (E); Khamnigan *bātar*;
Mongolic → Tungusic *bātur* 'hero, warrior':
   cf. Northern Tungusic: Ewenki *bātur* ~ *bāter* 'warrior; strong, big; wildcat, testy (*person*); ferocious (*animal*)'; Lamut *baγtir* ~ *baγatir* ~ *baγt'r* ~ *batur* 'warrior, hero; brave'; Negidal –; Southern Amuric: Oroch *bātu* ~ *baturi* 'warrior'; Udihe –; Ulcha *bātur* ~ *baturi* 'warrior'; Orok –; Nanai *bātor* 'warrior, hero; strong'; Southern Manchuric: Jurchen –; Manchu *batoru* ~ *baturu* 'warrior, hero; brave'; Sibe –.

Etymology: Räsänen VEWT 65b; Doerfer TMEN 2: 366–377; 1985: 56; Clauson ED 313b; SSTMJa 1: 61b; ESTJa 1978: 82–85; Vasmer 1986/1: 183; Ščerbak 1997: 104–105; Helimski 1997: 63–64; Werner 2002/1: 97, 109; Nugteren 2011: 276; Róna-Tas & Berta WOT 2011: 106–107

The word belongs to the category of "Wanderwort", occurring in Turkic, Mongolic, Finno-Ugric, Persian and Russian. Werner (2002/1: 109) considers that the Yeniseian word originates from Russian.

The Yugh and Ket words were borrowed from a Siberian Turkic language or Tungusic. The Turkic secondary long vowel -*ā*- realised as -*á*- in Yugh and the original Turkic intervocalic *VtV* presented with preserved *VtV* and voiced *VdV* consonants. The source of borrowing is unclear.

The origin of the word is unknown. According to Clauson (ED 313b), the Turkic word is of Hsiung-nu origin. For the various etymological opinions of the word, see Doerfer (TMEN 2: 366–377). The word was borrowed into New Persian (Doerfer TMEN 2: 366–377), Russian (Vasmer 1986/1: 183), Samoyedic (Filipova 1994: 48, 50), Mongolic (Ščerbak 1997: 104–105; Nugteren 2011: 276), Tungusic (Doerfer 1985: 56), Hungarian[127] (Róna-Tas & Berta WOT 2011: 106–107) languages from Turkic. From Russian, the Turkic word was re-borrowed into Dolgan (Stachowski 1993: 64) and Tofan.

For some remarks on etymology of designation of *Mator*—the Samoyedic language, see Helimski (1997: 63–64).

Kott *baha* 'strong; hero' (Werner 2002/1: 98) < *beke ← Turkic *böke 'hero, strong' ← Mongolic *böke* 'strong, solid, stalwart, firm, robust, vigorous, sturdy; wrestler':

---

127   Turkic: West Old Turkic *baγatur → Hungarian *bátor* [*bātor*] 'courageous, brave, valiant'.

cf. Old Turkic *bögä ~ bökä* 'hero, strong man, warrior'[128] (DTS); NES YeniseiT: Khakas *pöke ~ möke* 'strong man, warrior' (But.); Sagai, Koibal *mökö* 'strong, powerful' (R); Shor *pökö* 'strong, brave, the strength' (R); AltaiT: Altai *bökö* 'strong, powerful'; Tuba *bökö* 'strong man'; Qumanda *pökö* 'powerful, power; manly'; Quu *pökö* 'strong, brave, strong man, power'; Teleut *pökö* 'strong, brave' (R); SayanT:[129] Tuvan *möge* 'strong man; strong'; ChulymT –; NEN Yakut *bögö* 'strong'; Dolgan *bögö* 'strong, powerful; power, athlet'; NWN Siberian Tatar *pögö* 'hero; strong man'; NWS Kirgiz *bögü ~ bökö* 'strong man'; Fu-yü –; SE Yellow Yughur –;

Turkic ← Mongolic *böke* 'strong, solid, stalwart, firm, robust, vigorous, sturdy; wrestler':

cf. Middle Mongol: Precl.Mo. *böke*; SH *bökö*; HY *bökö*; Muq. *böke*; LM *böke*; Modern Mongol: Buryat *büxe* 'strong, solid; wrestler'; Khalkha *böx* 'wrestler; firm, strong, tough, hard-wearing'; Oirat dial. *bökö* 'wrestler; strong, solid'; Dagur *buke* (E); Khamnigan *büke ~ bükü ~ böke* 'strong'.

Etymology: Räsänen VEWT 83b; Clauson ED 324b; Doerfer TMEN 2: 349–351; 1985: 101; ESTJa 1978: 211–212; Nugteren 2011: 287

The Kott word was probably borrowed from Siberian Turkic. The vowel harmony disappeared and there was a change of intervocalic $VkV > VhV$; both are typical phonetic features of Kott loanwoards. These changes point to an early period of borrowing. However, the change of Turkic vowel $ö > {}^*e > a$ in the first syllable is unclear, which may call our etymology into question.

From an etymological point of view, the Turkic word is of Mongolic origin. For the Mongolic data, see Nugteren (2011: 287). The Mongolic was borrowed into Tungusic[130] (SSTMJa 1: 105b; Doerfer 1985: 101; Rozycki 1994: 37), moreover for some Ewenki dialects the source was Yakut[131] (Doerfer 1985: 101).

Kott ***berxen*** 'warrior' (Werner 1990: 293) ← Turkic *bergen < *mergen* 'marksman; hero' ← Mongolic *mergen* 'a good marksman':

cf. NES YeniseiT: Khakas *mirgen* 'marksman; agile'; Sagai, Koibal *mergän*; Shor *märgän* 'important, strong' (R) AltaiT: Altai *mergen* 'marksman; agile, adroit'; Tuba *mergen* 'shot, rifleman'; Qumanda –; Quu *mergen* 'shot, rifleman'; Teleut *merge* 'adroit, deft'; SayanT: Tuvan *mergen* 'a good marksman; wise, genius'; Tofan *mergen* 'marks-

---

[128] Cf. Clauson's Old Turkic data: *böke* 'a big snake, it was used *metaph.* of strong warriors' (ED 324b).
[129] Cf. Tofan *bechei*, Yakut *bige* and Dolgan *bigä* 'strong, solid' forms, which perhaps belong to another Mongolic loanword: LM *beki* 'strong, firm, solid; robust, vigorous, durable'.
[130] Mongolic → Tungusic: Barguzin, Northern-Baikal Ewenki *buku* 'strong'; Solon *buxu* 'wrestler'; Manchu *buku* 'wrestler'.
[131] Mongolic → Turkic: Yakut *bögö* 'strong' → Tungusic: Sakhalin, Urmi Ewenki *buyu* 'strong'.

man; hero'; ChulymT –; NE^N Yakut *bärgän* ~ *bärkän* ~ *märgän* 'marksman, hero'; NW^N Siberian Tatar *märgän* ~ *mirgän* 'marksman'; NW^S Kirgiz *mergen* 'shot, rifleman'; Fu-yü –; SE Yellow Uyghur –;
Turkic → Samoyedic:
Kamas *mergen* 'good';
Turkic ← Mongolic *mergen* 'a good marksman; wisdom; wise, learned, sage, experienced; apt':
cf. Middle Mongol: Precl.Mo.; SH; HY; 'Phags-pa; Muq. *mergen*; LM *berke*; Modern Mongol: Buryat *merge(n)*; Khalkha *mergen*; Oirat dial. *mergen*; Dagur *mergen* (T); Khamnigan *mergen* ~ *meregen*.
Etymology: Joki LS 228; Kałużyński 1962: 41; Doerfer TMEN 1: no. 363; 1985: 80; Räsänen VEWT 335a; Rassadin 1980: 47, 51; Rozycki 1994: 158; Schönig 2000: 135; Anikin 2000: 398; Khabtagaeva 2009: 249; 2017: 117

The Kott word was borrowed from one Siberian Turkic variety. It is the only case where the Turkic consonant cluster *-rg-* changed to *-rx-* in Kott. The change of initial *m-* > *b-* is typical for some Turkic loanwords in Kott, e.g. Turkic *maktïr-* 'to praise' → Kott *baktîr-*; Turkic *mal* 'livestock, cattle; property, wealth' → Kott *bal* 'cattle'.

Etymologically, the Turkic word was borrowed from Mongolic. From Mongolic, the word was borrowed into Tungusic[132] (SSTMJa 1: 571b; Doerfer 1985: 80; Rozycki 1994: 158; Khabtagaeva 2017: 117) and New Persian (Doerfer TMEN 1: no. 363), and via Turkic to Samoyedic (Joki LS 228). Siberian Russian *mergen* 'strong man, hero' was directly borrowed from Buryat (Anikin 2000: 398).

1.1.10 Terms Pertaining to Mythology and Religion

Arin ***ajna*** 'devil' (Werner 2002/1: 21) ← Turkic *ayna 'devil, demon' ← ? Persian:
cf. NE^S YeniseiT: Khakas *ayna* 'devil'; Sagai, Koibal *ayna* 'devil, evil spirit' (R); Kyzyl *aynä*; Shor *ayna* 'devil, demon'; AltaiT: Altai –; Quu *ayna* 'demon, evil spirit'; Teleut *ayna* 'devil; evil spirit' (R); SayanT –; ChulymT *ayna* 'devil; evil spirit' (R); Remaining lgs. –;
cf. Old Turkic *ayïn-* 'to fear'.
Etymology: Räsänen VEWT 12a; Clauson ED 274b; Erdal 1991: 591; Stachowski 1996: 102; 2006: 179; Róna-Tas & Berta WOT 2011: 448–450; Nugteren 2011: 275–276; Pomorska 2012: 299–308

---

132 Mongolic → Northern Tungusic: *Eastern Ewenki*: Barguzin *mergenčī* (< *mergen +*čī* Ewenki NN) 'fine fellow, fine girl'; Solon *mergē*; Negidal *mejyen* 'tiger'; Oroch *megge* 'hero; agile'; Southern Tungusic: Udihe *merge*; Ulcha *merge* 'hero'; Orok *merge* 'hero; tiger; lucky'; Nanay *merge* 'hero'; Manchu *mergen* 'wise'.

The Arin word is obviously a Turkic loanword, but it is not clear which Turkic variation is the source for the Arin form: the word exists only in Yenisei Turkic, Altai Turkic and Chulym Turkic.

The etymology of the Turkic word is not clear. Erdal (1991: 591) on the base of the Mongolic *ayi-* ~ *ayu-* verb 'to fear, become frightened or afraid'[133] (for the Mongolic data, see Nugteren 2011: 275–276) reconstructs the Turkic verb **ayX-* (also see the reconstruction of West Old Turkic, WOT 1: 449[134]). Clauson (ED 274b) suggests the Turkic and Mongolic resemblance is accidental.

The Turkic forms are also connected with Persian *hajnā+* (Stachowski 1996: 102; 2006: 109; Pomorska 2012: 301).

Kott *alpeš* 'wonder' (Werner 2002/1: 26) ← Turkic **albïs* < *almïs* 'evil spirit' ← Mongolic *almas* 'a legendary tribe of savage people; female demon, witch (*also an invective referring to women*)':

cf. NE^S YeniseiT: –; AltaiT: Altai *albïs* 'the spirit of the disease'; Qumanda *almïs* 'one of the evil spirit'; Teleut *almïs* 'evil spirit' (R); SayanT: Tuvan *albïs* 'female demon, witch'; ChulymT –; NE^N cf. Yakut *albas* 'trick, deceit, deception, evil speech; deception, trickery, magic, enchantment' (Pek.); Yakut dial. *albas* 'epidemic disease'; NW^N Siberian Tatar –; NW^S cf. Kirgiz *albïn* 'of name of the disease; evil incantation'; Fuyü –; Kazak *albastï* (< **albïs* +*lXG* {Turkic NN}) 'witch, demon, devilry'; SE Yellow Uyghur –;

Turkic ← Mongolic *almas*:

cf. Middle Mongol: –; LM *almas* 'a legendary tribe of savage people; female demon, witch (*also an invective referring to women*)'; Modern Mongol: Buryat –; Khalkha *almas* 'abominable snowman, legendary wild man'; Kalmuck *almṣ* 'witch, female demon; devil';

cf. Mongolic *albin* 'demon, evil spirit':

Middle Mongol: –; LM *albin* 'demon, devil, evil spirit, sprite'; Modern Mongol: Khalkha *albin* 'evil, spirit'; Buryat *al'ba(n)* 'magician, wizard, witch, demon, an evil spirit; playful, smart, flirtatious (*girl*)'; Dagur –; Khamnigan *al'ban* 'charming, gentle'.

Etymology: Räsänen VEWT 18a; 16b; Doerfer TMEN 2: 109–110; Nugteren 2011: 267

The Kott word was borrowed from the Altai Turkic form **albïs*, which means 'a kind of bad spirit', while in Kott it has a positive meaning 'wonder'; possibly

---

133   Cf. Mongolic 'to fear, become frightened or afraid': Middle Mongol: Precl.Mo. *ayu-*; SH *ayu-*; HY *ayu-*; Muq. *ayi-* ~ *ai-*; Leiden *ayu-*; Ist. *ayu-*; LM *ayi-* ~ *ayu-*; Modern Mongol: Buryat, Khalkha *ai-*; Kalmuck *ǟ-*; Dagur *ai-* ~ *ay-* (E); Khamnigan *ai-*.

134   Cf. Turkic: West Old Turkic **ayï-* ~ **äyi-* 'to fear, to be afraid' → Hungarian *ijeszt* [iyest] {< **ije-Ast-*} 'to frighten', *ijed* [iyed] {< **ije-Ad-*} 'to be frightened, to take fright'.

in the course of semantic change the meaning of the word became pejorative. From a phonetic point of view, the change of final *-s* > *-š* and the unvoicing of cluster *lb* > *lp* are typical changes for Kott loanwords.

Etymologically, the word belongs to a category of European cultural words; the Turkic and Mongolic words must be of Iranian origin. The etymological background was examined in detail by Doerfer (TMEN 2: 109–110).

The relatedness of the Mongolic words *almas* and *albin* is unclear. It seems that it is a coincidence. If the fluctuation *lb* ~ *lm* is possible in Mongolic languages,[135] the final *-s* in the form *almas* cannot be the Mongolic plural suffix; it occurs only on stems ending in vowels or in the diphthong *-Ai*[136] (see Poppe GWM § 264). The fluctuation *a* ~ *i* also is problematic in Mongolic.

Kott *âsa* ~ *asa* ~ *áša*; Assan *asa* 'devil, evil spirit' (Werner 2002/1: 61) ← Turkic **aza* 'devil, demon, evil spirit' < *aða* 'danger':

cf. Old Turkic *aða* 'danger'; NE^S YeniseiT: –; AltaiT: Altai *aza* 'demon, evil spirit'; Qumanda *aze* 'spirit, smell'; Quu *aza* ~ *aze* 'devil; evil spirit, demon'; SayanT: Tuvan *aza* 'evil spirit, Satan, devil'; Tofan *aza* 'devil'; ChulymT –; NE^N Yakut –; NW^N Siberian Tatar *aza* 'evil spirit, demon'; NW^S Kirgiz *ada* 'evil spirit' (R); Fu-yü *azï* 'ghost'; SE Yellow Yughur –.

Etymology: Räsänen VEWT 5a; Rassadin 1971: 157; Clauson ED 40a; Timonina 1978: 11; Anikin 2000: 76; Vovin 2017: 799–800

The Yeniseian words clearly belong to the group of Altai Turkic loanwords. The unvoicing of original intervocalic *VzV* to *VsV* is regular for Kott loanwords (cf. Kott *bosarak* 'ruddy colored (*said of red fox fur*)', *eser* 'drunk (*adj.*)', *kasak* ~ *kasax* 'healthy, health') due to the absence original consonant **z* in Yeniseian (Starostin 2007: 148). This change points to an early layer of borrowing. Furthermore, the intervocalic *VsV* is changed to *VšV* in Kott, which is a typical change in the original Kott words and appears only in morphology, cf. as a derivation of an attributive suffix in Kott *-še* (< **-se*). E.g. *urkiše* 'soap' < *urki* 'washing', *fugaiše* 'sable' < *fugai* 'tail' (Starostin 2007: 159). The original Yeniseian intervocalic *VsV* is usually changed to *VčV* (Starostin 2007: 158–159).

In spite of the irregular form, the Altai Turkic word *aza* 'devil, demon' is probably related to Old Turkic form *aða* 'danger'. According to the phonetic rules of

---

135   E.g. LM *nilbusun* ~ *nilmusun* 'tears, mucus, spittle'; LM *čolbon* ~ *čolmon* 'morning star, Venus'; Khalkha *talbai* ~ Buryat *talmai*, cf. LM *talabai* 'square field, public square, plaza'.
136   E.g. LM *emes* 'women' < *em-e* 'woman', *üges* 'words' < *üge* 'word', *noqas* 'dogs' < *noqai* 'dog', etc.

Altai Turkic, the Old Turkic *aða* should develop to *aya; in turn, the Altai Turkic form with intervocalic *VzV* is typical for Yenisei Turkic[137] (Johanson 1998: 102).

It is important to mention that the word for 'devil, demon' in Yenisei Turkic is *ayna* (see above Arin *ajna* 'devil'), which is also irregular. The Altai Turkic form was probably borrowed from Yenisei Turkic.

For details on irregular reflexes of *d in South Siberian Turkic, see Nugteren (2012: 75–86). The Turkic word was borrowed into Mongolic with original intervocalic *VdV*.[138]

Kott *hanpen* 'pray, prayer', cf. *hanpen hit* 'praying person' (Werner 2002/1: 299) < *kanman-* < *kamna-n* {?} ← Turkic **qamna-* 'to make shamanic ritual; to make magic' < *qām* 'shaman, sorcerer, soothsayer, magician' +*lA-* {Turkic NV, see Erdal 1991: 429}:

cf. Old Turkic *qamla-*; NE[S] YeniseiT: Khakas *xamna-* 'to make shamanic ritual'; Sagai, Koibal, Kachin *qamna-*; Kyzyl *χamna-*; Shor *qamna-*; AltaiT: Altai *qamda-*; Tuba *kamna-*; Qumanda *kamda-*; Quu *kamna-*; Teleut *qamda-*; SayanT: Tuvan *xamna-*; Tofan *hamna-*; ChulymT *qamna-*; NE[N] Dolgan *kamnā-*; Yakut dial. *xamnā-*; NW[N] Siberian Tatar *qamay-* 'to predict, foretell'; NW[S] Kirgiz –; Fu-yü *gam* 'shaman'; SE Yellow Uyghur *qamna-*.

Etymology: Räsänen VEWT 228a; Clauson ED 625a, 628a; Doerfer TMEN 3: 402–406; ESTJa 1997: 240–241; Khabtagaeva 2015c: 100

The etymology of the Kott word is of unknown origin. It possibly is connected to the Turkic verbal form *qamna-* 'to make a shamanic ritual', which originally had the meaning 'to make magic', derived from the Commom Turkic word *qām* 'shaman, sorcerer, soothsayer, magician,' with the denominal verbal suffix +*lA-* (for details on the function of this suffix, see Erdal 1991: 429). The final *-n* is unexplained. In Kott, the Turkic initial *q-* changed to *h-*, as in native Yeniseian words, which points to an early layer of borrowing. Also, the metathesis *-mn-* > *-np-* occurred.

---

137 Old Turkic *adaq* 'leg, foot' ~ Khakas *azax* (cf. Yellow Uyghur *azaq*, Fu-yü *azïx*); Old Turkic *qudruq* 'tail' ~ Khakas *xuzurux* (cf. Yellow Uyghur *quzïrïq*); Old Turkic *bedük* 'large, high' ~ Khakas *pözik* (cf. Yellow Uyghur *pezik*), etc. (for more examples, see Nugteren 2012: 76).

138 Turkic → Mongolic 'evil spirit, demon, devil; object of aversion': Middle Mongol: HY *ada*; LM *ada*; Modern Mongol: Buryat *ada*; Khalkha *ad*; Kalmuck *ad*ᵃ 'madness, madness; the evil spirit of the madness'; Dagur –; Khamnigan *ada* 'evil spirit'.

Kott *komtú* 'grave' (Werner 2002/1: 439) ← Turkic *komdu 'coffin, grave' ← Mongolic *qobdu* 'case; long and narrow box, quiver':

cf. NEᔆ YeniseiT: Khakas *xomdï* 'coffin'; Koibal *kom* ~ *komda* 'coffin, grave' (R); Kyzyl *χomdị* 'box'; AltaiT: Altai –; Quu *komda* 'box'; SayanT: Tuvan *xomdu* 'a long container; coffin'; Tofan –; ChulymT –; NEᴺ Yakut *xoppo* 'basket, box, chest'; NWᴺ Siberian Tatar *qumta* 'box, bag'; NWᔆ Kirgiz –; Fu-yü –; Kazak *qobdïy* 'small box'; Karakalpak *qobdïy* 'box'; Nogai *qobda* 'box of a carpenter'; SE Yellow Uyghur –;

Turkic ← Samoyedic:

Kamas *komdu* ~ *kom* 'grave';

Turkic ← Mongolic *qobdu* 'case; long and narrow box, quiver':

cf. Middle Mongol: Muq. *qobdu* 'quiver'; LM *qobdu* 'case; long and narrow box, quiver'; Modern Mongol: Buryat *xobto* 'box, chest'; Khalkha *xowd* 'a long container'; Oirat dial. *xobdă* 'box, chest'; Dagur –; Khamnigan *xobto*.

Etymology: Joki LS 189–190; Kałużyński 1962: 58; Räsänen VEWT 279a; SSTMJa 1: 402a; Timonina 1978: 10; 1986: 71; Doerfer 1985: 111; ESTJa 2000: 6; Khabtagaeva 2015a: 119

The Turkic borrowing demonstrates the lexical meaning of the Kott word. It has the meaning 'grave', which exists only in the Khakas and Altai languages. In the Mongolic languages, it originally meant 'case; long and narrow box, quiver'. Another criterion which proves the Turkic borrowing is phonetic: the Mongolic cluster *-bd-* changed to *-md-* in Turkic and further devoiced to *-mt-* in Yeniseian.

In the Yakut form the cluster *bt* > *pp* geminated; Kałużyński (1962: 58) questions the borrowing from Buryat.

The same criteria that indicate the Turkic borrowing are characteristic for Samoyedic (Joki LS 189–190). The Mongolic word was borrowed into the Tungusic languages as well[139] (SSTMJa 1: 402a; Doerfer 1985: 111; Rozycki 1994: 141).

Kott *obal* ~ *ôpal* 'sin' (Werner 2002/2: 30) ← Turkic *obal 'sin' ← Arabic:

cf. NEᔆ YeniseiT: Khakas *obal* 'sin, the misfortune'; Sagai, Koibal, Kachin *obal* 'sin', cf. Sagai 'punishment' (R); Kyzyl –; Shor *obaġ* 'misfortune, sorrow, distress'; AltaiT: –; SayanT –; ChulymT –; NEᴺ Yakut –; NWᴺ Siberian Tatar *obal* 'sin' (R); NWᔆ Kirgiz *ubal* 'damage, sin'; Fu-yü –; Kazak *obal* 'sin, guilt'; SE Yellow Uyghur –;

Turkic → Samoyedic:

Kamas *ōbal* ~ *ōwal* 'sin, crime';

Turkic ← Arabic *wabāl* 'unhealthiness of the air or climate; evil consequences of a deed; harm, evil, curse', *wabula* 'to be unhealthy, unwholesome, noxious (climate, air)'.

---

139 Mongolic → Tungusic: *Southern Ewenki*: Nercha *kobdu* 'quiver'; Negidal *koptin* 'case; lid;

Etymology: Joki LS 243; Räsänen VEWT 356a

The Kott word was borrowed from a Yenisei Turkic source. Among Siberian Turkic languages, the word is present only in Yenisei Turkic and Siberian Tatar. In addition to the preservation of the original intervocalic *VbV*, devoicing occurred in the Kott form, which is a regular change for Turkic loanwords in Kott, e.g. Kott *âpeš ~ âpuš* 'priest' ← Turkic *abïs* 'priest', Kott *d'ipak* 'silk thread' ← Turkic *d'ibek* 'thread', Kott *êper* 'noun circle; adj. round; adv. around' ← Turkic *eber-* 'to turn (something)', etc.

According to Räsänen (VEWT 356a), the word is of Arabic origin.

1.1.11 Administrative Units

Kott *agel ~ âgel* 'tent village (*ulus*)' (Werner 2002/1: 17) ← Turkic **agïl* 'a settlement or group of tents':

cf. Old Turkic *aġïl*; NE[S] YeniseiT: Khakas *āl* 'village, town, ulus'; Sagai, Koibal, Kachin; Kyzyl; Shor *āl* 'village, group of yurts' (R); AltaiT: –; SayanT: Tuvan *āl* 'village camp; house'; Tofan *āl* 'village camp'; ChulymT *aġïl* 'village' (R); NE[N] Yakut *ïal* 'neighbor; family, home'; Dolgan *ïal* 'settlement; neighbor's house; neighbor; residents'; NW[N] Siberian Tatar *avïl* 'village'; NW[S] Kirgiz *aġïl* 'barnyard, cow barn, stables'; Fu-yü *āl* 'village'; Kazak *awïl* 'village'; SE Yellow Uyghur *aġal* 'village'.

Kott *ajel* 'tent village (*ulus*)'; Yugh *ajaŋi* 'village' (Werner 2002/1: 19) ← Turkic **ayïl* 'village, family' ← Mongolic *ayil* 'family, household; settlement, group of tents, village' ← Turkic *aġïl* 'a settlement or group of tents':

cf. NE YeniseiT: –; AltaiT: Altai *ayïl* 'house, family; yurt'; Tuba *ayïl* 'house, yurt, village'; Qumanda *ayïl* 'house, village'; Quu *ayïl* 'house, village'; Teleut *ail* 'house, village' (R); ChulymT –; NE[N] Yakut –; NW[N] Siberian Tatar *ayïl* 'village'; NW[S] Kirgiz –; Fu-yü –; SE Yellow Uyghur –;

Turkic ← Mongolic *ayil* 'family, household; settlement, group of tents, village':

cf. Middle Mongol: SH *ayil*; ZY *ai*[*l*]; YY *ayil*; LM *ayil* 'family, household; settlement, group of tents, village'; Modern Mongol: Buryat *ail*; Khalkha *ail*; Oirat dial. *ǟl*; Dagur *ail* (E); Khamnigan *ail*;

Mongolic ← Turkic *aġïl* 'a settlement or group of tents, village': see Kott *agel ~ âgel* 'tent village (*ulus*)'.

Etymology: Doerfer TMEN 2: 82–84; Räsänen VEWT 8a; Clauson ED 83b; ESTJa 1974: 83; Timonina 1978: 10; SIGTJa 2001: 492–493; Róna-Tas & Berta WOT 2011: 632–635[140]

---

pillowcase; peel, shell; eyelid'; Ulcha *koptun* 'case; cover; sheath'; Orok *kuptun* 'case; sheath'; Nanai *kopto(n)* 'case; cover; sheath'; Manchu *qobdon* 'a container for arrows or tools'.

140 Turkic: West Old Turkic **aγul > oγul > *ōl* → Hungarian *ól* 'sty, cattle pen, sheepfold'.

The original meaning of the Turkic word *aġïl* was 'an enclosure for livestock, sheepfold', which in time became widened to mean 'a settlement or group of tents, group of people living in an *aġïl*' (for details, see Róna-Tas & Berta WOT 2011: 632–635). The Turkic form *ayïl* with intervocalic *VyV* was re-borrowed from Mongolic.

There are two different sources for the Kott form. For the first Kott form *agel* ~ *âgel*, the source of borrowing may be Siberian Turkic (cf. Chulym Turkic), while for another Kott form *ajel*—the source is Altai Turkic, which is a Mongolic re-borrowing.

In the Yugh form, the Turkic final -*l* changed to nasalized -*ŋ* with the additional vowel -*i* of unknown origin. Possibly the Yugh *ajaɲi* is an assimilated form from *ayïŋa < *ayïla, where the final -*a* can be the additional vowel at the end of words (paragoge).

Arin **belkertura** 'empire'; **berketura** 'city, town' (Werner 2002/1: 121) < Arin *berke 'big, great' + *tura* 'town, village':
< *berke* ← Turkic *berke* 'clever, deft' ← Mongolic *berke* 'difficult, hard; burdensome, troublesome; complicated, serious; difficulty, hardship; trouble; skillful, competent, fit' ← Turkic *bärkĂ < *bärk* 'firm, stable, solid':

cf. NE[S] YeniseiT: –; AltaiT: Quu *perge* 'clever, deft'; SayanT: Tuvan *berge* 'difficult'; ChulymT –; NE[N] Yakut *berke* '*adverb* very, very much, strongly; fine'; Dolgan *bärkä* ~ *bärgä* '*adj.* strong; *adv.* very much'; NW[N] Siberian Tatar *berägäy* 'fine'; Remaining lgs. –;

Turkic ← Mongolic *berke* 'difficult, hard; burdensome, troublesome; complicated, serious; difficulty, hardship; trouble; skillful, competent, fit':

cf. Middle Mongol: Precl.Mo. *berke*; SH *berke* 'difficult'; HY *berke* 'difficult'; Ibn-Muh. *berke*; Муq. *bürke* 'strong'; LM *berke*; Modern Mongol: Buryat *berxe*; Khalkha *berx*; Kalmuck *berkä*; Dagur *berke* (T); Khamnigan *berke* ~ *börke*;

Mongolic ← Turkic *bärkĂ > *bärk* 'firm, stable, solid':

cf. Old Turkic *bärk*; NE[S] YeniseiT: Khakas *pirīk* 'impenetrable'; AltaiT: –; SayanT: Tuvan *bert* 'impenetrable'; Tofan *be^crt* 'kind, good'; ChulymT *pērek* 'difficult'; NE[N] Yakut *bert* 'excellent, beautiful; *particle* very, completely, entirely'; Dolgan *bär* ~ *bärt* 'strong; *adv.* very; *adj.* excellent, wonderful; better; great'; NW[N] Siberian Tatar –; NW[S] Kirgiz *berk* 'strong; very'; Fu-yü –; Kazak *berīk* 'strong, solid, stable'; SE Yellow Uyghur *perīk* ~ *perk* 'big, important', cf. *perīk* 'strong'.

Etymology: Räsänen VEWT 71a; Clauson ED 361b; ESTJa 1978: 119; Rassadin 1980: 60, 64; Khabtagaeva 2009: 267

+ *tura* 'town, village':

cf. Old Turkic *tura* 'something to shelter behind'; NE[S] YeniseiT: Khakas *tura* 'house; town', cf. 'fort, village; building; room'; Sagai, Koibal, Kachin *tura* 'house, building, city'; Shor *tura* 'town'; AltaiT: Altai *tura* 'house, building; town'; Tuba; Qumanda; Quu; Teleut *tura* 'house'; SayanT –; ChulymT *tura* 'town'; NE^N Yakut –; NW^N Siberian Tatar *tora* 'town'; NW^S Kirgiz *turak* (< *tura* +*AK* {Turkic NN/diminutive}) 'residence, dwelling'; Fu-yü –; Kazak *turaq* 'residence; site'; SE Yellow Yughur –.

Etymology: Räsänen VEWT 500; Doerfer TMEN 2: 608–611; Clauson ED 531a; Timonina 1978: 10; ESTJa 1980: 300; SIGTJa 1997: 486

There are two different Arin forms with different lexical meanings borrowed from the same Turkic compound word. The different development of the first Arin compound of *belker* and *berke* is unique. In the first Arin form, dissimilation occurred. This can be explained by the fact that Arin speakers differentiated between two similar compound words.

I would refer to the Arin partial affix *berke* 'big, great', cf. other Arin words with this compounding **berkitak** 'mountain' (< *berki* 'big, great' + Turkic *tāġ* 'mountain') and **berkuštukdu** 'strong' < *berke* 'very' + *kuštuk* 'strong, powerful' ← Turkic *küčtüg* 'strong'.

Ket *u'l's* 'country; land of gnomes' (Werner 2002/2: 342) ← Turkic **ulus* 'administrative unit, village, dynasty, people' ← Mongolic *ulus* 'people, nation; country, state; empire; dynasty' ← Turkic *uluš* 'country':

cf. NE^S YeniseiT: Khakas *ulus* 'people', cf. 'people; generation, dynasty; society; tribal group; administrative unit in Khakasia' (But.); Shor *ulus* 'people; village'; AltaiT: Altai *ulus* 'people'; Tuba *ulus* 'people'; Qumanda *ulus* 'people'; Quu *ulus* 'village, consisting of related tribes'; Teleut *ulus* 'people' (R); SayanT: Tuvan *ulus* 'people'; Tofan *ulus* 'people; relatives'; ChulymT –; NE^N Yakut *ulūs* 'ulus (*administrative unit*)'; Dolgan –; NW^N Siberian Tatar –; NW^S Kirgiz *ulut* 'nation'; Fu-yü –; Kazak *ult* 'nation, nationality'; SE Yellow Uyghur *ulus* 'people';

Turkic ← Mongolic *ulus* 'people, nation; country, state; empire; dynasty':

cf. Middle Mongol: Precl.Mo. *ulus*; SH *ulus*; HY *ulus*; YY *ulus*; Muq. *ulus*; Phags-pa *ulus*; LM *ulus*; Modern Mongol: Buryat *ulad*; Khalkha *uls*; Kalmuck *ul^us*; Dagur *olur* (E); Khamnigan *ulas*;

Mongolic ← Turkic *uluš* 'country': cf. Old Turkic *uluš*.

Etymology: Doerfer TMEN 1: 175–178; Räsänen VEWT 513a; Rassadin 1971: 237; Clauson ED 152b; ESTJa 1974: 592; Ščerbak 1997: 212; SIGTJa 1997: 494; Nugteren 2011: 531

This Ket word belongs to the mythological terminology, and is used often in fairy tales. It was probably borrowed from the Siberian Turkic form **ulus*.

From the etymological side, the word is of Turkic origin, which was borrowed into Mongolic and then re-borrowed into Turkic. The evidence of Turkic re-borrowing is the Turkic final consonant -*š*, which regularly changed to -*s* in

Mongolic[141] (e.g. Turkic *qōš* 'a pair; one of a pair' → Mongolic *qos* 'pair, double', Turkic *tūš* 'equal, equivalent, opposite' → Mongolic *tus* 'straight, upright, vertical, opposite', Turkic *yemiš* 'fruit' → Mongolic *ǰimis*, etc.)

The Mongolic loanword belongs to the category 'culture-specific words', which is very widespread in the territory of Eurasia. According to the Mongolic data, the Turkic word was borrowed into Mongolic in the early period. From Mongolic, the Turkic word was re-borrowed into Tungusic[142] (SSTMJa 2: 16a), Siberian Russian (Anikin 2000: 583) and New Persian (Doerfer TMEN 1: 175–178).

1.1.12   Food

Kott ***araka*** ~ ***arkā***; Arin ***uragā***; Assan ***araka*** 'wine, brandy' (Werner 2002/1: 57) ← Turkic *araka < *araqï* 'wine, vodka' ← Arabic:

cf. Old Turkic –; NE^S YeniseiT: Khakas *araǧa* 'alcoholic drink'; Sagai *arakï* 'milk brandy' (R); Kyzyl *ār^aγa* ~ *araγa* 'brandy'; AltaiT: Altai *arakï* 'vodka'; Tuba *aragï* 'vodka'; Qumanda *arak* ~ *arakï* 'wine'; Quu *arakï* 'vodka'; Teleut *arakï* 'milk brandy' (R); SayanT: Tuvan *araǧa* 'alcoholic drink; wine, vodka'; Tofan *araha* 'wine, vodka'; ChulymT *araǧa* 'vodka'; NE^N Yakut *arïgï* 'wine'; Dolgan *aragï* ~ *aragi* 'wine'; NW^N Siberian Tatar *araq* ~ *araqï* 'vodka'; NW^S Kirgiz *arak* 'vodka'; Fu-yü *arah* 'vodka'; Kazak *araq* 'vodka'; SE Yellow Uyghur *araqï* 'wine, vodka';

Turkic → Samoyedic:

Kamas *ara* ~ *ar(a)ga* 'strong drink, wine'; Selkup *araqa* ~ *araγa* 'vodka';

Turkic ← Arabic *ʿaraq* 'arrack, a strong colorless liquor made of raisins, milky white when diluted with water'.[143]

Etymology: Joki LS 68; Räsänen VEWT 23a; ESTJa 1974: 166; Timonina 1978: 10; Stachowski 1981: 33; 1992/1993: 253; Doerfer 1985: 37; Anikin 2000: 91, 99; Pomorska 2005: 142; Nugteren 2011: 271

The word belongs in the 'Wanderwort' category, found in numerous languages. The Yeniseian words were borrowed from Siberian Turkic dialects.

---

141   In some cases lambdacism happened, which gives the corespondence Turkic *š* and Mongolic *l* (For more details on the criterion, see Schönig 2003: 408), e.g. Mongolic *ǰalaγu* (< **ǰal+A-GUn*) 'young, youthful; youth, youthfulness' ← Turkic *ǰāl: cf. Old Turkic *yāš* 'fresh'; Mongolic *qoli-* 'to mix, mingle, blend, alloy, adulterate' ← Turkic **qolï-*: cf. Old Turkic *qoš-* 'to conjoin, unite (two things)', etc.

142   Turkic → Mongolic → Tungusic: Solon *olor* ~ *olur* 'people'.
      The word was borrowed to Dagur due to the typical phonetic feature—Daguric rotacism (For more details, see Khabtagaeva 2012: 339–340).

143   Cf. other semantic meanings in Arabic 'sweat, perspiration', *ʿariqa* 'to sweat, perspire; to make or let sweat, promote perspiration; to add water (to a drink), dilute (a drink); to take root, strike roots; to be deeply rooted; to vein, marble; to take root, strike roots'.

According to Joki (LS 68) and Filipova (1994: 46), the Samoyedic words were borrowed from Turkic also. From Turkic, the Arabic word was borrowed into Mongolic[144] (ESTJa 1974: 166; Nugteren 2011: 271), Tungusic[145] (SSTMJa 1: 48b; Doerfer 1985: 37) and Siberian Russian[146] (Anikin 2000: 91). Doerfer (1985: 37) indicates the Yakut form as a re-borrowing from Mongolic.

The second Kott form *arkā* illustrates syncope. The sporadic change of initial *a-* > *u-* is found in Arin.

Arin **čarba** 'grain' (Werner 2002/1: 163) ← Turkic *čarba 'grain, groats' < *yarma* < *yār-* 'to split, or cleave' *-mA* {Turkic VN, see Erdal 1991: 316}:
cf. Old Turkic *yarma* 'split, something split; groats (*split grain*)'; NE[S] YeniseiT: Khakas *čarba* 'grain' Sagai *čarba* 'grain' (R); AltaiT: Altai *d'arma* 'bran, barley groats'; Tuba *čarak* 'bran, fine groats; small hail; the name of the herb'; Qumanda *d'arma* 'barley groats'; Teleut *yarma* 'bran' (R); SayanT: Tuvan *čarba* 'crushed groats'; Tofan –; ChulymT –; NE[N] Yakut –; NW[N] Siberian Tatar *yarma* 'grain, barley groats'; NW[S] Kirgiz *jarma* 'large oatmeal, crushed roasted grains (*wheat, barley*); chowder from crushed roasted grains'; Fu-yü –; Kazak *žarma* 'grain'; SE Yellow Yughur –.
Etymology: Räsänen VEWT 190b; Doerfer TMEN 4: 160; Clauson ED 969a, 954b; ESTJa 1989: 137; Erdal 1991: 319; Nugteren 2011: 383

The Arin word was borrowed from the Siberian Turkic form *čarba (cf. Khakas and its dialects, Tuvan).

The original Turkic form is *yarma*, which derived from verb *yār-* 'to split, or cleave' and the deverbal noun suffix *-mA* (for details on the derivation of this word, see Erdal 1991: 319). The change of Turkic initial *y-* > *č-* is a regular phonetic feature for Yenisei Turkic and Sayan Turkic (e.g. Old Turkic *yïl* 'year' ~ Khakas, Tuvan *čïl*; Old Turkic *yāz* 'spring' ~ Khakas, Tuvan *čas*; Old Turkic *yürek* 'heart' ~ Khakas, Tuvan *čürek*, etc.). Another change of cluster *-rm-* > *-rb-* also occurred in Yenisei Turkic and Sayan Turkic languages.

The Turkic word was borrowed into Mongolic[147] (Nugteren 2011: 383).

---

144 Turkic → Mongolic: cf. Middle Mongol: –; LM *araki(n)* ~ *ariki(n)* 'alcoholic liquor; brandy, wine'; Modern Mongol: Buryat *arxi* 'vodka, wine'; Khalkha *arxi* 'spirits, drink, strong drink, alcohol'; Oirat dial. *ärkĭ* 'vodka'; Dagur *arγ'* (E); Khamnigan *araki* 'milk vodka, wine, vodka'.
145 Cf. Ewenki dialectal form, which closer to the Turkic than Mongolic forms: Podkamennyi Ewenki *araka* 'vodka, wine'.
146 Turkic → Siberian Russian *araka* 'liquor distilled from milk, kumiss'.
147 Turkic → Mongolic: Middle Mongol: –; LM *jarm-a* 'groats, grits, bran; fine meal'; Modern Mongol: Buryat –; Khalkha *dzaram* 'groats'; Oirat dial. *dzarăm* ~ *zarăm* 'bran'; Kalmuck *zarm^a* ~ *zarm* 'millet porridge, wholemeal flour'; Dagur –; Khamnigan –.

Kott *itpák* ~ *itpak* ~ *iptak*; Arin *itp'ák* ~ *itpák* ~ *itpek*; Assan *itpák* 'bread' (Werner 2002/1: 386) ← Turkic **itpäk* < *ätmäk* 'bread' < *ät-mAK* {Turkic infinitive, serving as direct object, see Erdal 2004: 279–281}:

cf. Old Turkic *ätmäk* ~ *ötmäk*; NEᔆ YeniseiT: Khakas *īpek*; Sagai, Koibal, Kachin *itpäk*; Kyzyl *ippeγx* ~ *ippeg* ~ *ippekx*; Shor *ipek*; AltaiT: Altai *ötpök*; Qumanda *iytpek*; Quu *itpek*; Teleut *ötpök*; SayanT –; ChulymT *itwäk* ~ *itpäk*; NEᴺ Yakut –; NWᴺ Siberian Tatar *itmäk* ~ *üptök*; Remainig lgs. –;

Turkic → Samoyedic:

Kamas *ippäk* ~ *itpak* ~ *itpök* 'bread'; Mator *iʔbāk* 'bread'.

Etymology: Joki LS 138; Räsänen VEWT 374b; Clauson ED 60a; ESTJa 1974: 254; Timonina 1978: 9; SIGTJa 1997: 469; Khabtagaeva 2015c: 98

It is clear that the Yeniseian forms were borrowed from the Siberian Turkic form **itpäk*, where *-tp-* appears instead of the original cluster *-tm-*. Due to the absence of vowel harmony in Yeniseian, there are Yeniseian forms with back vowels.

The Turkic word is widespread in almost all Turkic languages, but does not have a clear etymology. According to Clauson (ED 60a), it is not possible to connect the word semantically with any verb. There is another phonetic variant *äkmäk*, which is peculiar to the Oghuz and Kipchak languages of the Volga region. Probably the word was derived with the Turkic infinitive suffix *-mAk*[148] (for suffix functions, see Erdal 2004: 279–281), but the derivation of the verbal base is unclear. The word was connected with different verbs such as *äk-* 'to sow' or *ät-* 'to make, to do', but the etymology still remains uncertain.

Kott *kajax* ~ *kajag*; Arin *kaják* ~ *kajakok* 'oil, butter' (Werner 2002/1: 404) ← Turkic **qayaq* 'butter, sour cream' < *qańak* 'the skin on milk, clotted cream' < *qań-* > *qayïn-* 'to boil' *-(A)K* {Turkic VN, see Clauson ED xliv}:

cf. Old Turkic *qańaq* 'the skin on milk, clotted cream'; NEᔆ YeniseiT: Khakas *xayax* 'butter'; Sagai *xayax* 'the food prepared from clotted cream or butter' (But.), Koibal, Kachin *qayaq* 'butter' (R); Kyzyl *xaymax* 'sour cream' (But.); Shor *qaymaq* 'sour cream'; AltaiT: Altai *qaymaq* 'sour cream, cream'; Qumanda *kaymak* 'sour cream'; Teleut *qaymaq* 'sour cream' (R); SayanT –; ChulymT *qaymaq* 'cream'; NEᴺ Yakut *xayax* 'butter'; NWᴺ Siberian Tatar *qaimaq* 'boiled thick sour cream' (R); NWᔆ Kirgiz *kaymak* 'cream'; Fu-yü –; Kazak *qaymaq* 'cream, sour cream'; SE Yellow Yughur –;

Turkic → Samoyedic:

Kamas *kajaᶜ* ~ *kajak* 'butter, oil'; Mator *kajak* 'butter, oil'.

---

148   Cf. Kazak *ilmek* 'hook' < *il-* 'to catch', *toqpaq* 'mallet' < *toq-* 'to beat', etc. (for details, see Serebrennikov & Gadžieva 1986: 233–234).

Etymology: Joki LS 151; Doerfer TMEN 3: 410–412; Räsänen VEWT 231b; Clauson ED 636b; Timonina 1978: 9; ESTJa 1997: 200–201; Stachowski 1996/1: 106; Khabtagaeva 2015b: 523

The etymology of the Yeniseian words is clear (Timonina 1978: 9; Stachowski 1996/1: 106). The later period of borrowing confirms the preservation of the initial uvular consonant *q-*, while the original Yeniseian *q-* and *k-* regularly changed to *h-* in Kott. Another criterion which shows the borrowing from Siberian Turkic is the presence of intervocalic consonant *VyV* instead of original *VńV*. The Samoyedic forms also were borrowed from Siberian Turkic (Joki LS 151).

Another regular change for Turkic loanwords in Kott is the change of final *-q* to spirantized *x-*, e.g. Kott *aksax* 'lame' ← Turkic *aqsaq*, Kott *kalôx* 'ear' ← Turkic *qulaq*, Kott *kapax* 'forehead' ← Turkic *qapaq* 'eyelid', etc.

Assan *šarijag* 'butter' (Werner 2002/2: 437) ← Turkic **sarïyaġ*: cf. AltaiT: Altai *sarïyū*; SayanT: Tofan *sarïġ-čaġ* 'butter':
< *sarï* < *sarïġ* 'yellow':

cf. Old Turkic *sārïġ*; NE^S YeniseiT: Khakas; Sagai, Koibal, Kachin, Shor *sarïġ*; Kyzyl *sārï·γ^x*; AltaiT: Altai; Tuba *sarï*; Qumanda *sarï ~ sārï*; Quu *sarū ~ sarï*; Teleut *sarï* 'yellow; light bay (*colour of horse*)'; SayanT: Tuvan *sarïġ* 'yellow; light bay (*colour of horse*); white (*colour of skin*); light (*colour of hair*)'; Tofan *sarïġ*; ChulymT *sārïġ*; NE^N Yakut *araġas* (<*sārïġ +X*š* {Turkic NN/adj., which was added to colour names, see Erdal 1991: 102}) 'yellow, yellowish, straw-coloured, golden (*of colour*)', cf. *arii* 'butter'; Dolgan *arii* 'butter'; NW^N Siberian Tatar *sarï*; NW^S Kirgiz *sarï* 'yellow, red-haired, light-brown'; Fu-yü *sarih*; Kazak *sarï*; SE Yellow Uyghur *sarïġ*.

Etymology: Räsänen VEWT 403b; Clauson ED 848a; Timonina 1978: 8; ESTJa 1989: 22–23

+ *yag* < *yāġ* 'grease, fat, oil':

cf. Old Turkic *yāġ*; NE^S YeniseiT: Khakas *čaġ*; Sagai, Koibal *čaġ*; Kachin *yïġ*; Shor *čaġ*; AltaiT: Altai *d'u* 'fat', *d'ū* 'suet'; Tuba *d'ū*; Qumanda *d'u* 'fat, butter', *d'ïġ* 'fat, grease'; Quu *yïġ* 'fat, grease'; Teleut *yū* 'grease'; SayanT: Tuvan; Tofan *čaġ* 'fat'; ChulymT *čaġ* 'butter, fat'; NE^N Yakut *sia* 'fat, grease'; Dolgan *hia*; NW^N Siberian Tatar –; NW^S Kirgiz *žak-* 'to grease'; Fu-yü –; Kazak *ĵaq-* 'to grease'; SE Yellow Uyghur *yaġ* 'butter'.

Etymology: Räsänen VEWT 177b; Clauson ED 895a; ESTJa 1989: 58–59; Stachowski 1996/1: 105; SIGTJa 1997: 453

The Assan word belongs to the category of compound words. It consists of two Turkic words *sarï* 'yellow' and *yaġ* 'butter' (Timonina 1978: 8; Werner 2002/2: 437; Khabtagaeva 2015d: 131). According to its phonetic shape, it was probably borrowed in the early period. The Proto-Yeniseian initial *s-* regularly developed to *š-* in Assan. The Turkic initial *y-* also supports the hypothesis of the early period of borrowing. Turkic initial *y-* changed to *d'-* in Altai Turkic and to *č-* in Yenisei Turkic. But this change does not mirror the development of Turkic initial *y-* in the period of borrowing.

See also Kott *šar* ~ *šâr* 'isabelline (*yellowish-tan color of horses*)', which is related to Turkic *sarïġ* 'yellow'.

Kott *šera* ~ *sera* ~ *širá* ~ *sihirá*; Arin *sirá*; Assan *sir'á* 'beer' (Werner 2002/2: 438) ← Turkic *sïra 'beer' ← Persian:
    cf. Old Turkic *širä* 'grape juice, wine; cooler' (DTS); NE[S] YeniseiT: Khakas *sïra* 'beer' (But.); Sagai, Koibal, Kachin *sïra* (R); AltaiT: Altai *sïra*; Qumanda *sïra*; Quu *sïra*; Teleut *sïra*; SayanT –; ChulymT –; NE[N] Yakut –; NW[N] Siberian Tatar –; NW[S] Kirgiz *sïra*; Fu-yü –; Kazak *sïra*; SE Yellow Yughur –;
Turkic → Samoyedic:
    Kamas *sïra* 'cerevisia';
Turkic ← Persian *šīra* 'new wine; an intoxicating kind of drink; the expressed juice of any fruit except olives, syrup; oil of sesame'.
Etymology: Joki LS 270–271; Räsänen VEWT 418b; Timonina 1986: 75; Stachowski 1996: 106; ESTJa 2003: 413–414; Róna-Tas & Berta WOT 2011: 738–740

The Yeniseian forms were borrowed from the Siberian Turkic form *sïra* (Timonina 1986: 75; Stachowski 1996: 106). The change of initial *s-* > *š-* is a regular change for Turkic loanwords in Kott, while in Arin it was preserved.

The word belongs to the category of cultural-specific words which came to Turkic from the Persian language (Räsänen VEWT 418b; ESTJa 2003: 413–414). In addition to Yeniseian, the Turkic word was borrowed into Samoyedic Kamas (Joki LS 270–271) and Hungarian[149] (Róna-Tas & Berta WOT 2011: 738–740).

Kott *šut*; Assan *šut* ~ *šüt* 'milk' (Werner 2002/2: 443) ← Turkic *süt 'milk' < *sǖt*:
    cf. Old Turkic *sǖt*; NE[S] YeniseiT: Khakas *süt*; Sagai, Koibal, Kachin *süt* (R); Kyzyl *süt*; Shor *süt*; AltaiT: Altai *süt*; Tuba *süt*; Qumanda *süt*; Quu *süt*; Teleut *süt*; SayanT: Tuvan *süt*; Tofan *süt*; ChulymT *süt*; NE[N] Yakut *ǖt*; Dolgan *ǖt* ~ *üt*; NW[N] Siberian Tatar *söt*; NW[S] Kirgiz *süt*; Fu-yü *süt*; Kazak *süt*; SE Yellow Uyghur *süt* ~ *sot* ~ *söt* ~ *sut*.
Turkic → Samoyedic:
    Kamas *süt* 'milk'; Mator *süt* 'milk'.
Etymology: Joki LS 277; Räsänen VEWT 438b; Clauson ED 798b; Timonina 1978: 9; Ščerbak 1997: 150; Helimski 1997: 347; ESTJa 2003: 346–348; SIGTJa 2001: 448; Nugteren 2011: 507

---

149 West Old Turkic *sire > *šire 'beer' → Hungarian *sör* [šör], *ser* [šer] 'beer'.

The Yeniseian words were clearly borrowed from the Siberian Turkic form *süt. The change of initial s- > š- is a regular change for Turkic loanwords in Kott and Assan, as in native Yeniseian words (Starostin 1982: 158–159; Werner 2005: 141[150]). This phonetic feature points to an early layer of borrowing. Kott and Assan forms regularly lost vowel harmony; which occured due to the fact that it is absent in Yeniseian.

From Siberian Turkic, the word was borrowed into Samoyedic languages (Joki LS 277; Helimski 1997: 347). The Mongolic form sü(n) 'milk'[151] obviously connects to Turkic (Ščerbak 1997: 150; Nugteren 2011: 507). According to the Mongolic form, the base of the word should be *sü.[152]

Kott *tálgan ~ talkan*; Assan *talkán*; Yugh *tállin ~ tàli′n*; Ket *tállin ~ tàli′n* 'flour, meal' (Werner 2002/2: 233) ← Turkic *talqan* 'oat flour' < *talq-* 'to scutch' -GAn {Turkic VN, see Erdal 1991: 382}:

cf. Old Turkic *talqan* 'crushed parched grain'; NE^S YeniseiT: Khakas *talǧan* 'oat flour'; Sagai, Koibal, Kachin *talǧan* 'oat flour' (R); Shor *talqan* 'oat flour'; AltaiT: Altai *talkan* 'oat flour'; Tuba *talgan ~ talkan* 'oat flour'; Qumanda *talgan* 'oat flour'; Quu *talgan ~ talkan* 'oat flour'; Teleut *talqan* 'flour'; SayanT –; ChulymT *talgan* 'flour'; NE^N Yakut –; NW^N Siberian Tatar –; NW^S Kirgiz *talkan* 'oat flour'; Fu-yü –; Kazak *talqan* 'cereals (*wheat or millet*)'; SE Yellow Uyghur *talqan* 'oat flour';

Turkic → Samoyedic:

Mator *talkan* 'flour'.

Etymology: Doerfer TMEN 2: 546–549; 1985: 94; Räsänen VEWT 458b; Rassadin 1971: 169; Clauson ED 496b; SSTMJa 2: 157a; Timonina 1978: 9; Helimski 1997: 350; Anikin 2000: 529; SIGTJa 2001: 472; Khabtagaeva 2009: 208; Nugteren 2011: 511

Two different forms *tálgan ~ talkan* are found in Kott. They may have been borrowed from two different sources (cf. Yenisei Turkic and Altai Turkic forms), or from one Turkic dialect, where both forms existed (cf. Quu dial.). In the Yugh and Ket forms, the assimilation *lk* > *ll* occurred. The change of original vowel *-a-* in the second syllable to *-i-* is not clear.

From the etymological point of view, the Turkic word derived from the verb *talq-* 'to crush' (Clauson ED 496b) and the deverbal noun suffix -GAn.

---

150 According to the list of Assan words with initial š-, given by Werner.
151 Turkic → Mongolic 'milk': Middle Mongol: SH *sün*; Muq. *sü ~ sün*; Ist. *sün*; LM *sü(n)*; Modern Mongol: Buryat *hü(n)*; Khalkha *sü̆(n)*; Kalmuck *üsn*; Dagur *sū* (E); Khamnigan *sū̆(n) ~ sün*.
152 Kalmuck, Ordos and Eastern Yugur forms go back to reconstructed Mongolic form *üsün (Nugteren 2011: 507).

From Siberian Turkic, the word was borrowed into Samoyedic (Helimski 1997: 350) and Siberian Russian (Anikin 2000: 529). The Turkic word, via Mongolic[153] (Nugteren 2011: 511), was borrowed into the Tungusic[154] languages (SST-MJa 2: 157a; Doerfer 1985: 94). According to its lexical meaning 'flour, cake, baking', the Sayan Turkic (Tuvan and Tofan) forms were re-borrowed from Mongolic[155] (Khabtagaeva 2009: 208).

Yugh *ugur* 'soup or porridge made of grain' (Werner 2002/2: 325) ← Turkic **üg^üre* < *ügre* 'soup; noodles; broth containing noodles':

cf. Old Turkic *ügre* 'noodles; broth containing noodles'; NE^S YeniseiT: Khakas *ügre* 'soup'; Sagai, Koibal, Kachin *ügrä* 'soup, broth, soup with fine groats' (R); Kyzyl *üγrä* ~ *üg^ürä* 'soup'; Shor *ürge* 'soup'; AltaiT: Altai *üre* 'gruel from groats and milk'; Tuba *üre* 'gruel; gruel from fine grains with milk'; Qumanda *üre* 'gruel from fine grains with milk'; Quu *ürge* 'soup'; TeleutT –; SayanT –; ChulymT –; NE^N Yakut *üöre* 'soup, pottage'; Dolgan –; NW^N Siberian Tatar *ürä* 'gruel from fine grains with milk' (R); Remaining lgs. –.

Etymology: Doerfer TMEN 2: 155; Räsänen VEWT 519b; Clauson ED 112b; Timonina 1986: 77; Stachowski 1996/1: 93; 1997/2: 235; SIGTJa 1997: 458

The Yugh word was borrowed from the Siberian Turkic (Timonina 1986: 77; Stachowski 1996/1: 93; 1997/2: 235) form **üg^üre* (cf. Kyzyl), where the final vowel dropped. The disappearance of vowel harmony is a typical phonetic feature for Turkic loanwords in Yeniseian.

The Common Turkic word dates back to the Old Turkic period (Doerfer TMEN 2: 155; Räsänen VEWT 519b; Clauson ED 112b), but the base of the Turkic word is unclear. Tenišev (SIGTJa 1997: 458) derived it from the reconstructed verb **ög-* ~ **üg-* 'to heap up, accumulate' (Clauson: *ük-*), cf. *ükün* 'heap', *üküš* 'many', *ükmä* 'heaed up', etc.

1.1.13 Buildings, Constructions and Their Parts

Kott *atax* 'tent' (Werner 2002/1: 75) ← Turkic **otax* < *otaġ* 'a small temporary building, tent' < *ōt* 'fire' +*A*- {Turkic NV, see Erdal 1991: 418} 'to warm' -*G* {Turkic VN, see Erdal 1991: 172}:

---

153   Turkic → Mongolic 'powder; flour, meal; bread': Middle Mongol: Muq. *talqan*; LM *talqan*; Modern Mongol: Buryat *talxa(n)*; Sayan Buryat: Zakamna *talxan*; Oka *talxan*; Lower Uda Buryat *talka(n)*; Khalkha *talx*; Kalmuck *talxan*; Dagur –; Khamnigan *talxa(n)*.

154   Mongolic → Tungusic: *Southern Ewenki*: Podkamennyi, Sym, Tokma, Upper Lena, Northern Baikal, Nercha; *Eastern Ewenki*: Barguzin *talgan* 'flour; bread; grain'.

155   Turkic → Mongolic → Sayan Turkic: Tuvan *dalgan* 'flour; flat cake; flour from roasted barley or wheat'; Tofan *ta^clhan* 'flour, baking'.

cf. Old Turkic *otāġ*; NE^S YeniseiT: Khakas *otax* 'tent' (KhR), cf. *otax ~ odaġ* (But.); Kyzyl *ōtaγ^x ~ ōdaγ^x* 'tent, yurt, hut'; Shor *odaġ* 'tent, booth'; AltaiT: Altai *odu* 'camp, encampment; tent, where the groom brought the bride after abduction'; Tuba *otov* 'marquee'; Qumanda *odū* 'tent, camp'; Teleut *odu* 'stent, camp' (R); SayanT: Tuvan *odag* 'hearth; fire; hunting camp, camp'; Tofan *odaġ* 'hunting camp, camp, stopping place with fire'; ChulymT *otaġ* 'tent'; NE^N Yakut *otū* 'hut from hay; temporary stopping place, halt, lodging, camp'; Dolgan *otū* 'bonfire, burning pile of wood'; Yakut dial. *otū uota* 'fire diluted in the field; fire' (DS); NW^N Siberian Tatar *ōdu* 'tent'; NW^S Kirgiz *otō ~ otoq* 'small yurt camp; yurt for shepherds, yurt for newly-weds'; Fu-yü –; Kazak *otau* 'the separated family; yurt, house for young family'; SE Yellow Uyghur[156] *otaġ* 'relatives';

Turkic → Samoyedic:

Kamas *otok* 'yurt'.

Etymology: Poppe 1964a: 10; Doerfer TMEN 2: 66–69; Räsänen VEWT 366b; Rassadin 1971: 210–211; Clauson ED 46b; ESTJa 1974: 484–487; Timonina 1978: 10; 1986: 71; Ščerbak 1997: 130, 169; Anikin 2000: 432; SIGTJa 2001: 496–497

The change of Turkic final *-ġ* → *-x* in Kott is regular, e.g. Turkic *ariġ* 'clean, pure' → Kott *arix*; Turkic **qaδiġ > qaziq* 'health' → Kott *kasak ~ kasax*. The initial Turkic *o-* became delabialized in Kott, which is also a typical feature for Kott loanwords, e.g. Turkic *oyun* 'game, play, merriment' → Kott *ajaŋ*; Turkic *otiq* 'firesteel' → Kott *ataŋ*.

The etymology of the Turkic word is generally accepted (Doerfer TMEN 2: 66–69; Clauson ED 46b; ESTJa 1974: 484–487; Ščerbak 1997: 130, 169; SIGTJa 2001: 496). The base of the word is the noun *ōt* 'fire', from which the verb *ōta- ~ ota-* 'to light a fire' was derived with the productive Turkic deverbal noun suffix *-G* (for details on its function, see Erdal 1991: 172), forming the Turkic word.

The Turkic word was borrowed into Mongolic[157] (Poppe 1964a: 10; Doerfer TMEN 2: 69), from Mongolic to Tungusic[158] (SSTMJa 2: 28), Samoyedic (Joki LS 249) and Siberian Russian[159] (Anikin 2000: 432). Some Ewenki and Lamut dialects borrowed the word from Yakut directly[160] (SSTMJa 2: 28).

---

156   Cf. Yellow Uyghur *otoq* 'clan' ← Mongolic ← Turkic.
157   Turkic → Mongolic: Middle Mongol: –; LM *otoγ* 'tribe; race; clan; *hist.* lower administrative init'; Modern Mongol: Buryat *otog* 'tent; tribe, clan'; Khalkha *otog* 'a unit of an ecclesiastical estate; a group of people within a *sumun*; clan, tribe; a lodge or shelter (*for hunters, tourists, etc.*)'; Dagur –; Khamnigan *otog*.
158   Mongolic → Tungusic: *Southern Ewenki*: Upper Lena, Nercha; *Eastern Ewenki*: Barguzin *otok* 'small tent from herbs'.
159   Turkic → Mongolic: Buryat → Siberian Russian *otug* 'land owned by one owner'.
160   Yakut → Tungusic: *Eastern Ewenki*: Mai, Aldan, Uchur, Urmi, Chumikan *otū* 'camp-fire, tent, temporary stopping place'; Lamut *otū* 'fire diluted in the field'.

Kott **hagîni ~ hagîn'e ~ hagin'e** 'tent pole' (Werner 2002/1: 292) ← ? Turkic *paɣana < baǧana 'pillar, column, pole, tent-pole' ← Mongolic baɣana 'pillar, column, post, pole, tent-pole, rafter, joist' ← Turkic baqan 'torque, necklase':

cf. Old Turkic –; NE^S YeniseiT: –; AltaiT: Altai baɣana 'column, pillar', cf. baqana 'pillar, column; tower; the image of thick birch with a split top on the shaman drum'; Qumanda paɣana ~ pakana ~ paɣan 'pillar, column'; SayanT: Tuvan baɣana 'pillar, column; tent-pole, prop'; ChulymT –; NE^N Yakut baɣana ~ maɣana 'thick column, pillar, prop' (Pek.); Dolgan baɣana 'pillar'; NW^N Siberian Tatar –; NW^S Kirgiz –; Fu-yü –; Kazak baɣana 'column, pillar', cf. baqan 'tent-pole'; SE Yellow Uyghur paɣana 'small bars between two boards at the loom';

Turkic ← Mongolic baɣana 'pillar, column, post, pole, tent-pole, rafter, joist':

cf. Middle Mongol: –; LM baɣana; Modern Mongol: Buryat baxana 'post, pole'; Lower Uda Buryat bakana 'post'; Khalkha baɣana 'pillar, post, column; style (bot.)'; Oirat dial. baxăn ~ baxănă 'pillar, column, stand, tent pole'; Dagur –; Khamnigan baɣana;

Mongolic ← Turkic *bakană:

cf. Old Turkic baqan 'torque, necklase'; NE^S YeniseiT: Khakas paxan ~ maxan 'pillar, column; leg of table; tent-pole' (But.); Sagai; Shor paqqan- 'to make pillar' (R); AltaiT: Altai –; Quu paɣan 'pole for tying horses'; Teleut paqqan 'pole for tying horses', cf. paqqan- 'to make pillar' (R); SayanT –; ChulymT –; NE^N Yakut –; NW^N Siberian Tatar paɣan 'column', cf. baɣan 'pole, with which raised and propped up in the tent'; NW^S Kirgiz bakan 'tent-pole'; Fu-yü –; Kazak baqan 'pole of yurt'; SE Yellow Yughur –.

Etymology: Räsänen VEWT 58a; Clauson ED 316a; Tatarincev 1976: 26; 1: 170; ESTJa 1978: 43; Khabtagaeva 2009: 195

The etymology of the Kott word is unknown. As a hypothesis, I assume it is connected to the Siberian Turkic form paɣana ~ baɣana 'pillar, column, pole, tent-pole', which was borrowed from Mongolic baɣana 'pillar, column, post, pole, tent-pole, rafter, joist', but ultimately of Turkic origin baqan 'torque, necklace'.

The reconstructed Proto-Yeniseian initial *p- changed to f- or p^h- in Kott[161] (Vajda 2014: personal communication), which does not support my hypothesis. I assume there was an aspiration process. But the question still remains open. The Kott original initial h- goes back to Proto-Yeniseian h- (Vajda 2014: personal communication; Starostin 1982: 175).

The word belongs to the category of words of uncertain etymology.

---

161 PY *p^hača 'big' > Kott p^hača ~ p^hačâ; PY *p^hage 'bird-cherry tree (Prunus padus)' > Kott fagé ~ p^hage; PY *p^haksəm 'thin' < *p^had^j 'flat surface' + *əŋ {Yeniseian NN/adj.} > Kott fačam ~ p^hačam, cf. Ket háksem ~ háksim, Yugh fáksim; etc. (Vajda & Werner: in preparation).

Kott *kôpur* ~ *kopur* ~ *kobur* 'bridge' (Werner 2002/1: 441) ← Turkic *köpür < *köprüg* 'bridge' < *köp-* 'to swell, foam, boil over' *-(X)r-* {Turkic VV, see Erdal 1991: 537} *-(O)K* {Turkic VN, see Erdal 1991: 224}:

cf. Old Turkic *köprüg*; NE^S YeniseiT: Khakas *köbĭrgĭ* (But.); Sagai *köbür* (R); Kyzyl *kȫßᵊrüγ* ~ *kȫßrüg*; AltaiT: Altai *köpir* 'bridge, narrow and precipitous place on the mountain top' (Budagov); Tuba *kömrü* 'bridge, transition through river'; SayanT: Tuvan *kövürüg*; Tofan *keᶜprig*; ChulymT –; NE^N Yakut –; NW^N Siberian Tatar *küpre* ~ *küper* ~ *kȫprü* ~ *kümräü*; NW^S Kirgiz *köpürö*; Fu-yü –; Kazak *köpir*; SE Yellow Uyghur –;

Turkic → Samoyedic:

Kamas *kōbrüᶜ* ~ *köürü* 'bridge'; Mator *köbrük* ~ *kübrük* 'bridge'.

Etymology: Joki LS 199–200; Räsänen VEWT 292a; Clauson ED 690b; Doerfer TMEN 3: 585–587; 1985: 136; SSTMJa 1: 472b; Timonina 1978: 10; ESTJa 1997: 111–114; Helimski 1991: 261; 1997: 295

The Kott forms were borrowed from Turkic *köpür 'bridge' (Timonina 1978: 10). The disappearance of vowel harmony is a typical change for Kott loanwords, due to the absence of this phonetic peculiarity in Yeniseian.

The etymology of the Turkic word is unclear. Räsänen (VEWT 292a) suggests a Greek origin. Some researchers (Clauson ED 690b; Doerfer TMEN 3: 585–587; ESTJa 1997: 111–114) derive the Turkic word from the verb *köpür-* 'to froth, foam', which was derived from *köp-* 'to swell, foam, boil over' and the Turkic deverbal verbum suffix *-(X)r-* (for details on functions, see Erdal 1991: 537) with an inchoative function and the deverbal noun suffix *-(O)K* (for details, see Erdal 1991: 224).

The Turkic word was borrowed into Mongolic[162] (Doerfer TMEN 3: 585; Nugteren 2011: 423) and Samoyedic (Joki LS 199–200; Helimski 1997: 282) languages. The word from Buryat was possibly re-borrowed into Yakut *kürge* 'bridge' and Samoyedic Mator *kürgü* 'bridge' (Helimski 1991: 261; 1997: 295). From Mongolic, the word was borrowed into the Tungusic languages[163] languages (SSTMJa 1: 472b; Doerfer 1985: 136).

Kott *torá* 'living room', cf. *turá* 'village'; Arin *tura* 'house' (Werner 2002/2: 290) ← Turkic *tura 'house; village; town':

cf. Old Turkic *tura* 'something to shelter behind'; NE^S YeniseiT: Khakas *tura* 'house; town, stockaded town; village; building, house; room'; Sagai, Koibal, Kachin *tura*

---

162 Turkic → Mongolic: Middle Mongol: HY *ke'ürge*; Muq. *kü'ürge*; LM *kögerge* ~ *kegürge* ~ *kögürge*; Modern Mongol: Buryat *xürge*; Khalkha *xörög*; Kalmuck –; Dagur *xūruγʷ* (E); Khamnigan *kürge*.

163 Turkic → Mongolic → Tungusic: Solon *xōrgö* 'bridge'.

'house, building, town' (R); Shor *tura* 'town'; AltaiT: Altai *tura* 'house; town'; Tuba *tura* 'house'; Qumanda *tura* 'house'; Quu *tura* 'house, building; town'; Teleut *tura* 'house'; SayanT: Tuvan –; Tofan –; ChulymT *tura* 'town'; NE^N Yakut[164] –; NW^N Siberian Tatar *tora* 'town'; NW^S Kirgiz *turak* (< *tura* +AK {Turkic NN/diminutive}) 'residence, dwelling; encampment, camp'; Fu-yü –; Kazak *turaq* 'residence, stopping place'; SE Yellow Yughur –;

Turkic → Samoyedic:

Kamas *tura* 'room, house'; Mator *tura* 'town, village'.

Etymology: Joki LS 339–340; Räsänen VEWT 500b; Doerfer TMEN 2: 608–611; Clauson ED 531a; Timonina 1978: 10; ESTJa 1980: 300; SIGTJa 1997: 486; Helimski 1997: 371

The Yeniseian words clearly were borrowed from the Siberian Turkic form *tura (Timonina 1978: 10). It is remarkable that Kott has two different forms with the different meanings *torá* 'living room,' and *turá* 'village'. The sources were probably different, or they were borrowed in different periods. The fluctuation of labial vowels *o ~ u* is typical for Turkic loanwords in Kott, cf. *toi ~ tui* 'wedding'.

From an etymological point of view, probably the Turkic word *tura* 'house, town' derived from the verb *tur-* 'to stand; to stand upright; to stand still' (Radloff 3: 1446; Räsänen VEWT 500b; Doerfer TMEN 2: 608–611; ESTJa 1980: 300–301), but the final suffix -*a* is unclear.

From Turkic, the word was borrowed into Mongolic[165] and further to Tungusic[166] (SSTMJa 2: 221; Doerfer 1985: 38; Rozycki 1994: 212–213). The Turkic word was probably re-borrowed into Yakut[167] from Ewenki dialects. The Samoyedic words are borrowed from Siberian Turkic (Joki LS 339–340; Helimski 1997: 371).

---

164 ?? Cf. Yakut *durda* < *tur-dU {? Turkic VN} 'hunter termin. hiding place for hunting ducks; stronghold'.

165 Turkic → Mongolic: Middle Mongol: –; LM *tur-a* 'fortress, city, town'; Modern Mongol: Buryat *tura* 'house; building; town'; Khalkha *tur* 'citadel, the city, the fortress; town, building; shield' (BAMRS); Kalmuck –; Dagur –; Khamnigan –.

166 Turkic → Mongolic → Tungusic: *Southern Ewenki*: Podkamennyi, Sym, Nercha; *Eastern Ewenki*: Zeya, Mai, Tokko, Uchur, Urmi, Tommot *turu* 'pole, pillar'; Solon *törö* 'door jamb'; Negidal *tojo* (< *turu*) 'shaman pole; place of sacrifice'; Oroch *tū* (< *tuju < *turu) 'shaman pole'; Ulcha *tura ~ turu* 'pole'; Orok *toro ~ torro ~ turu* 'pole, pillar'; Nanai *tora* 'pole, pile of the barn'; Manchu *tura* 'pile, pillar, column'.

167 Turkic → Mongolic → Tungusic → Turkic: Yakut *turu* 'shaman tree'.

1.1.14 Household Equipment and Tools

Kott *ataŋ* 'fire-steel (*used to strike fire from a flint*)' (Werner 2002/1: 74) < *ataŋ < *ataġ < *otaġ < *otïq ← Turkic *otïk 'fire-steel' < *ottïq 'fiery' < *ōt* 'fire' +*lIK* {Turkic NN, see Erdal 1991: 139}:

cf. Old Turkic *otluġ* 'fiery'; NE[S] YeniseiT: Khakas *otïx* 'fire-steel, flint' (But.); Sagai, Kachin *ottuq* 'fire-steel' (R); Shor *otuq* 'fire-steel'; AltaiT: Altai *otïk* 'fire-steel'; Tuba *ottïk* 'fire-steel'; Qumanda *ottu* 'fiery'; Quu *ottuk* ~ *otuk* 'fire-steel'; Teleut *ottïq* 'fire-steel' (R); SayanT: Tuvan *ottuk* 'fire-steel'; Tofan *ottuq* 'fire-steel'; ChulymT *ottuq* 'fire-steel, flint'; NE[N] Yakut *uottāx* 'fiery'; Dolgan *uottāk* 'fiery'; NW[N] Siberian Tatar *ōtlu* 'fiery'; NW[S] Kirgiz *ottuk* 'fire-steel, flint'; Fu-yü *ot* 'fire'; Kazak *ottïq* 'lighter; flint; matches'; SE Yellow Uyghur *ottuq* 'flint, flintstone'.

Etymology: Räsänen VEWT 366a; Clauson ED 55b; ESTJa 1974: 484; SIGTJa 2001: 373; Khabtagaeva 2015b: 523

The etymology of the Kott word is unknown. I suppose that it might have originated from Siberian Turkic *otïk 'fire-steel'. The borrowing from Turkic *otïk* to Kott *ataŋ* can be explained by means of certain criteria which are typical for Turkic loanwords in Kott:

– The change of initial Turkic *o*- → Kott *a*-, e.g.
  – Kott *ajaŋ* 'play, game' ← Turkic *oyun*;
  – Kott *atax* 'tent' ← Turkic *otaġ*;
– The change of Turkic -*ï*- → Kott -*a*- in the non-initial syllable, explained by Yeniseian stress on the first syllable, e.g.
  – Kott *arak* 'lean (*thin*)' ← AltaiT, YeniseiT *arïk* (~ Old Turkic *aruq*);
  – Kott *askar* 'stallion' ← YeniseiT *asqïr* (~ Old Turkic *adġïr*);
  – Kott *koŋar* 'chestnut' (*said of a horse*) ← AltaiT *koŋïr* (~ Old Turkic *qoŋur*);
– The sporadical change of the final -*k* > *-*g* > -*ŋ* or -*n*, e.g.
  – Turkic *torgayaq* 'sky-lark' → Arin *torgïjan*.

There is another Turkic word *otuŋ* 'dry firewood' (cf. Khakas *odïŋ*, Altai *odïn*), which is phonetically closer than *otïq* 'flint', but semantically, this can be excluded.

The Siberian Turkic word *otïk* ~ *otuk* 'fire-steel' is connected to the Common Turkic form *ottuq* ~ *ottïk*, which derives from *ōt* 'fire' (ESTJa 1974: 484) and the extremely productive assimilated Turkic denominal nomen suffix +*lXK*/+*lXG*, which denotes characterisation by the base noun (for details on different functions and more examples, see Erdal 1991: 139–155). See as well for example Old Turkic *uluġ* 'great' < *ul* 'foundation'; Old Turkic *aðalïġ* 'dangerous' < *aða* 'danger', and so on.

It is noteworthy that there are two different suffixes in Yenisei and Altai Turkic related to the Old Turkic suffixes +*lXK* and +*lXG*. In Khakas, one of them is +*tïx*/+*tïk*, which forms nouns (Baskakov & Inkižekova-Grekul 1953: 404), e.g.

Khakas *xol* 'arm' > *xoltïx* 'armpit', Khakas *tös* 'breast, chest' > *töstïk* 'breastplate', and so on. Another is +*lIG*/+*nIG*/+*tIG*, which is used for derivational adjectives (Baskakov & Inkižekova-Grekul 1953: 407), e.g. Altai *xar* 'snow' > *xarlïğ* 'snowy', Altai *tas* 'stone' > *tastïğ* 'stony', Altai *küs* 'power' > *küstïğ* 'strong, powerful', etc.

It seems that phonetically and semantically, the first suffix is more suitable to Yenisei Turkic. Altai Turkic confirms the similar presence of two different suffixes with different functions as well. Cf. Altai nouns (Baskakov 1947: 243) and adjectives (Baskakov 1947: 245): Altai *baylïk* 'wealth' < *bay* 'rich, wealthy', Altai *jakšïlïk* 'goodness' < *jakšï* 'good, nice' and Altai *karlu* 'snowy' < *kar* 'snow', Altai *tūlu* 'mountainous' < *tū* 'mountain', and so on.

Kott ***balt*ʰ*u* ~ *baltu* ~ *báltō*; Arin ***baltó*** ~ ***balto***; Assan ***balō*** 'axe' (Werner 2002/1: 100) ← Turkic *baltu 'axe; battle axe':

cf. Old Turkic *baltu*; cf. Old Uyghur *baltō*; NE^S YeniseiT: Khakas *paltï* ~ *maltï*; Sagai, Koibal, Kachin *palta* (R); Kyzyl *palttï*; Shor *malta*; AltaiT: Altai *malta*; Tuba *palta* ~ *malta*; Qumanda *palta* ~ *malta*; Quu *palta* ~ *malta*; Teleut *palta* (R); SayanT: Tuvan *baldï*; Tofan –; ChulymT *palta*; NE^N Yakut *balta*; Dolgan *balta* 'large blacksmith hammer'; NW^N Siberian Tatar *palta*; NW^S Kirgiz *balta*; Fu-yü –; Kazak *balta*; SE Yellow Yughur –;

Turkic → Samoyedic:

Kamas *baltu* ~ *balta* 'axe'.

Etymology: Joki LS 81–82; Räsänen VEWT 61a; Clauson ED 333b; Doerfer TMEN 1: 199–200; Timonina 1978: 9; ESTJa 2003: 100–102; SIGTJa 2001: 577; Róna-Tas & Berta WOT 2011: 87–89

The Yeniseian words were borrowed from Turkic, but it is not clear which Turkic language was the source of borrowing. The transfer form possibly was *baltu with the final vowel -*u*, which changed to -*o* ~ -*ō* in Kott, Arin and Assan.

The Turkic word was subsequently borrowed into Mongolic,[168] Samoyedic (Joki LS 81–82), Siberian Russian[169] (Anikin 2000: 114) and Hungarian[170] (Róna-Tas & Berta WOT 2011: 87–89). From Yakut, the word was borrowed into the Ewenki dialects[171] (SSTMJa 1: 71). According to Róna-Tas and Berta (WOT 2011: 88–89), the Turkic word was borrowed from Persian, but ultimately it is of Arabic origin.

---

168   Turkic → Mongolic 'big hammer, sledge hammer; axe': LM *balta*; Buryat *balta*; Khalkha *balt* 'axe'; Kalmuck *baltă*; Dagur –; Khamnigan *balta*.
169   Turkic → Siberian Russian *balda* 'stick, heavy wooden mallet, wooden hammer'.
170   Turkic: West Old Turkic → Hungarian *balta* 'hatchet, axe'.
171   Yakut → Tungusic: *Southern Ewenki*: Northern Baikal, Nercha *balta* 'hammer; trap; fang'.

Yugh *bérgin* 'noun bundle, pack of things' (Werner 2002/1: 116) ← Turkic **bürken-* 'be covered, be wraped' < *bür-* 'to twist, wind round, screw together' *-k-* {Turkic VV, see ED xlvi} 'to cover' *-(X)n-* {Turkic VV/reflexive, see Erdal 1991: 583–584}:

    cf. Old Turkic *bür-*; NE^S YeniseiT: Khakas *pürgen-* 'be covered, to cover, to take cover something, to wrap up' < *pürge-* 'to cover, to wrap up' < *pür-* 'to wrap'; Sagai *pürgän-* 'to cover oneself' (R), Sagai, Koibal *pürkä-* 'to cover' (R); Shor *pürge-* 'to cover, to wrap up, to bundle'; AltaiT: Altai *bürken-* 'to be covered, to be wraped up, to take cover' < *bürke-* 'to cover, to wrap up, to take cover'; Tuba *bürke-* 'to cover'; Quu *pürkö-* 'to cover'; Teleut *pürken-* 'be covered' < *pürke-* 'to cover' < *pür-* 'to roll, wind round' (R); SayanT: Tuvan *bürge-* 'to surround; to envelope, to wrap, to wrap up; be covered with clouds; to become cloudy or rainy'; Tofan *bürhü-* 'to cover, to close (from all sides)'; ChulymT –; NE^N Yakut *bürüy-* 'to cover; to wrap; to twist, to bind'; Dolgan *bürüy-* 'to cover'; NW^N Siberian Tatar *pörgä-* 'to cover, to close'; NW^S Kirgiz *bürkön-* 'be covered; *fig.* be secretive' < *bürkö-* 'to cover, to close'; Fu-yü –; Kazak *bürke-* 'to mask, to conspire, to cover, to cover up, to hide, to wrap up'; SE Yellow Yughur –.

Etymology: Räsänen VEWT 92b; Rassadin 1971: 77; Clauson ED 355ab; ESTJa 1978: 296–298; Werner 2002/1: 116; Nugteren 2011: 294

The etymology of the Yugh word is unknown. It was probably borrowed from the Turkic reflexive verb **bürken-* 'be covered, be wraped'. The change from verb to noun occurres in some Yeniseian loanwords. The Turkic verb coordinates with the Yeniseian from the semantic view: 'to be covered' → 'bundle, pack'.

In terms of the morphological structure, the Turkic verb derived from the verb *bür-* 'to twist, wind round, screw together,' with the unproductive deverbal verbum suffix *-k-* and the reflexive suffix *-(X)n-*.

For the etymological background, and the derivation of the Turkic verb, see Räsänen (VEWT 92b), Clauson (ED 355ab) and Sevortjan (ESTJa 1978: 296–298).

The Turkic word was borrowed into Mongolic[172] and re-borrowed into Yakut[173] (Kałużyński 1962: 65[174]). Cf. also Samoyedic Kamas *bürüŋgo* 'dim, unclear' (Joki LS 112), which was borrowed from Mongolic *bürüŋgüi* 'dark'.[175]

---

172   Turkic → Mongolic *bürke-* 'to grow or become cloudy; to cover, cover up; to envelop, obscure' < *bür(i)-* 'to cover, envelop; to upholster' *-GA-* {Mongolic VV, see Poppe GWM § 225}: Middle Mongol: Precl.Mo. *bürkü-*; SH *bürgü-*; HY *bürkü-* 'to be closed'; Phags-pa *bürkhig* 'darkness'; Muq. *bürkü-*; LM *bürke-* ~ *bürkü-*; Modern Mongol: Buryat *bürxe-* 'to grow or become cloudy; *fig.* to be upset'; Khalkha *bürxe-* 'to cover; to become clouded; for eyes to become blurred'; Oirat dial. *bürkü-* 'to cover'; Dagur –; Khamnigan *bürke-* ~ *börkö-*.
173   Mongolic → Turkic: NE^N Yakut *bürküy-* 'to become cloudy or rainy (*about weather*)'.
174   Kałużyński considers the derived adjective form *bürkük* ~ *bükkük* ~ *bülkük* 'cloudy'.
175   < *bürü-ŋGXi* {Mongolic VN, see Poppe GWM § 177}.

The Turkic verb *bür-* was borrowed into Hungarian, where it took different Hungarian suffixes[176] (Róna-Tas & Berta WOT 2011: 149–151).

Kott *čogár* ~ *čukar* ~ *čukár*; Assan *čegar* ~ *čogár* 'sledge, sleigh (sledge on wooden runners steered from behind or pulled by hand, sometimes helped by a dog or two, later adapted to reindeer)' (Werner 1990: 336; 2005: 108) ← Turkic *čoġar > *sōr* 'sledge':

cf. Old Turkic –; NE[S] YeniseiT: Khakas *sōr*; Sagai, Koibal *sōr* (R); Kyzyl *şōr*; AltaiT: –; SayanT: Tofan *šeger*; ChulymT *šor* ~ *cor*; Remainig lgs. –;

Turkic → Samoyedic 'sled, sledge':

Kamas *šor* ~ *šōr*; Mator *šor* ~ *šōr*; Selkup *sour*.

Etymology: Joki LS 295–296; Räsänen VEWT 449b; 446a; Fillipova 1994: 49; Helimski 1997: 344; SIGTJa 2001: 536; Khabtagaeva 2009: 193

The Kott word belongs to the category of words of unknown etymology. As a hypothesis, I suggest it was borrowed from a Siberian Turkic variety, cf. Yenisei Turkic *sōr* or Tofan *šeger* forms. According to the phonetic features of the Turkic forms, the development of the secondary long vowel *ō* in Khakas,[177] the initial Khakas *s-*[178] and Tofan *š-*[179] consonants, the reconstructed form should be *čoġar.

According to Räsänen (VEWT 449b), the Yenisei Turkic forms are connected with Mongolic[180] *čirγ-a* 'sled, sledge, sleigh',[181] perhaps via metathesis. But it seems that it is a coincidence.

---

176 The change *u* > *o* is a Hungarian development. Cf. verbs Hungarian *borít-* [borīt] < *borīt-* 'to cover, to overturn', *borul-* [borul] < *bor-(V)l-* 'to overturn into, to get overturned, get overcast', *borogat-* [borogåt] < *bor-(O)gAt-* 'to put on (a cold compress)', *borong-* [borong] < *bor-Ong-* 'to brood, be overcast', *burkol-* [burkol] 'to cover' < *bur-(V)k+Vl-* and the nouns *ború* [borū] 'cloudiness, gloom', *burok* [burok] ~ *bürök* [bürök] < *bor-(V)k* 'cover'.

177 Mongolic: LM *aγarci* 'whey' → Khakas *ārči*; LM *kirüge* 'saw' → Khakas *kerē*; LM *toγa-* 'to respect' → Khakas *tō-*, etc. For examples and reflexes of development of Mongolic secuence VCV in Khakas, see Janiszwska (2012).

178 Old Turkic *čaq* 'exactly, precisely' ~ Khakas *sax*; Old Turkic *čïq-* 'to go out; to come out' > Khakas *six-*; Old Turkic *čerig* 'army' ~ Khakas *sïrïk*, etc. Cf. also the Mongolic loanwords with initial *č-*: LM *čida-* 'to be able' → Khakas *sïda-*; LM *čabidur* 'reddish-yellow with white mane and tail (horse)' → Khakas *sabdar*, LM *čeber* 'clean' → Khakas *siber*, etc.

179 Old Turkic *čāġ* 'time, a point in time' ~ Tofan *šaγ*; Old Turkic *čüwit* 'some kind of dye-stuff mineral, a coloured earth' ~ Tofan *šibit*; Old Turkic *čöl* 'desert' ~ Tofan *šöl*, etc. Cf. also Mongolic and Russian loanwords: LM *čögeböri* 'jackal' → Tofan *šö̂* 'one-year-old fox'; Russian *čás* 'hour' → Tofan *šās*, etc.

180 Cf. Mongolic 'sled, sledge, sleigh': cf. Middle Mongol: –; LM *čirγ-a*; Modern Mongol: Buryat *šarga*; Khalkha *čarga*; Oirat dial. *tšïrăgă* ~ *tšïrgă*; Dagur –; Khamnigan *čirga*.

181 The Mongolic word *čirγ-a* was borrowed to Tuvan *širga* 'scraper' (Tatarincev 1976: 55; Rassadin 1980: 81; Khabtagaeva 2009: 193) and Yakut *siarga* 'sledge' (Kałużyński 1962: 125).

The Samoyedic forms were clearly borrowed from Siberian Turkic *sōr* 'sledge' (Joki LS 295–296; Helimski 1997: 344; Fillipova 1994: 49).

According to Vajda (2016: personal communication), the Turkic word is of Yeniseian origin (cf. Yugh *sōl ~ soul*; Arin *šal*, Pumpokol *cel* 'snow sled'), as the hand sled is a key element in traditional Yeniseian material culture, though the Kott and Assan forms may have been re-borrowed from a Turkic source.

Kott *d'ibak ~ d'ipak* 'silk thread' (Werner 2002/1: 222) ← Turkic **d'ibek* 'thread' < *yïpäk < *yïp* 'cord, thread, string' +*AK* {Turkic NN/diminutive, see Erdal 1991: 40}:
    cf. Old Turkic *yïp*; NE^S YeniseiT: Khakas *čībek* 'silk thread'; Sagai *čībäk* 'silk, cotton', cf. *čīmäk* 'silk red thread' (R); Koibal, Kachin *yïbäk* 'silk thread' (R); Shor *čibekte-* (< *čibek* +*tA-* {Turkic NV}) 'to embroider a pattern with silk thread'; AltaiT: Altai *d'ilbek* 'strip, ribbon'; Tuba *d'ibek* 'cord'; Qumanda *čïbïk* 'rod, thin stick'; Quu *yibek* 'silk, silk thread'; Teleut *yïbäk* 'silk, silk thread' (R); SayanT: –; ChulymT *yïbäk* 'silk, silk thread' (R); NE^N Yakut –; NW^N Siberian Tatar –; NW^S Kirgiz *jibek* 'silk'; Fu-yü *yip* 'thread'; Kazak *žībek* 'silk'; SE Yellow Yughur –.

Etymology: Clauson ED 870b; ESTJa 1989: 269–270; Stachowski 1996/1: 108; Starostin, Dybo & Mudrak EDAL 2003: 890; Róna-Tas & Berta WOT 2011: 380–381.

The Kott word was obviously borrowed from the Turkic form **d'ibek*, which derived from the Common Turkic noun *yïp* 'cord, thread, string,' and the Turkic diminutive suffix +*AK*. The initial Kott consonant *d'*- points to the later period—the Altai Turkic layer of borrowing.

The Turkic word was also borrowed into Hungarian[182] (Róna-Tas & Berta WOT 2011: 380–381).

Kott *d'ôrgan* 'blanket' (Werner 2002/1: 224) ← Turkic **d'ōrgan* < *yoġurqan* 'blanket':
    cf. Old Turkic *yoġurqan*; NE^S YeniseiT: Khakas *čorġan* (KhR) ~ *čōrġan* (But.); Sagai *čōrġan* (R), Koibal, Kachin *yorġan* 'blanket, bedspread' (R); Shor *čorġan*; AltaiT: Altai *d'ūrkan* 'blanket from sheepskin'; Teleut *yūrqan* 'blanket from sheepskin'; SayanT: Tuvan *čōrġan*; Tofan *čōrhan* 'fur blanket; bearskin'; ChulymT –; NE^N Yakut *suorġan*; Dolgan *huorgan* 'bedspreads; rabbit fur pieces, which are placed under the child in the cradle'; NW^N Siberian Tatar –; NW^S Kirgiz *jūrkan ~ jūrtkan*; Fu-yü *jōrgon ~ jogorgon*; SE Yellow Uyghur –;

---

182 Turkic: West Old Turkic *jïpliγ < *yïp* +*lXG* {Turkic NN, see Erdal 1991: 121–131} → Hungarian *jïpliγ > *gyeplő* [*d'eplő*] 'rein'.

Turkic → Samoyedic:
Kamas *joryan* 'bedcover'.
Etymology: Joki LS 123; Clauson ED 907a; Timonina 1978: 10; 1986: 72; ESTJa 1989: 226

The Kott word was obviously borrowed from Siberian Turkic. The Altai Turkic layer indicates the initial consonant *d'-* which changed from Common Turkic *y-*, while the Yenisei Turkic layer points to the voiced cluster *-rg-* having changed from original *-rk-*.

From an etymological aspect, the Turkic word is of unknown origin. According to Clauson (1972: 907), the word is derived from the adjective *yoġun* 'thick' and the Turkic denominal noun suffix +*KAn*. Sevortjan and Levitskaja (ESTJa 1989: 226) suggest the derived form *yoġur-* (Clauson ED: *yuġur-*) 'to knead (dough, etc.) → to work sheepskin' and the Turkic deverbal noun suffix *-KAn*.

From Siberian Turkic, the word was borrowed into Samoyedic (Joki LS 123).

Kott *hôpetal* ~ *hôptal* 'saddle cloth; carpet' (Werner 2002/1: 325) ← Turkic **qabtal* 'side of a horse; side; saddle cloth' ← Mongolic **qabtalsun* < *qabtasun* 'board; wooden printing blocks; binding or cover of a book' < **qabta* 'flat, even' +*sUn* {Mongolic NN, see Poppe GWM § 137}:

cf. Old Turkic –; NE^S YeniseiT: –[183]; AltaiT: Altai *qaptal* 'side of the horse'; SayanT: Tuvan *kaptazïn* 'thin plates, used as the folder'; ChulymT –; NE^N Yakut *xaptal* 'math. flat', cf. *xaptahïn* 'board'; NW^N Siberian Tatar –; NW^S Kirgiz *kaptal* 'side; side of the chest; mountain side; saddle tree'; Fu-yü –; Kazak *qaptal* 'saddle tree; slope; side'; SE Yellow Uyghur –;

Turkic ← Mongolic:

cf. Middle Mongol: Precl.Mo. *qabtasun*; SH *qabtasun* ~ *qabdasun* 'board'; ZY *qabtasu* ~ *qabdasu* '(*one of the two*) side board(s) of the saddle'; LM *qabtasun* 'board; wooden printing blocks; the two wooden boards between which Mongolian and Tibetan books are preserved; binding or cover of a book; folder for letters, documents; volume; tortoise shell'; Modern Mongol: Buryat *xabtaha(n)* 'board, the board of a saddle or cart; folder (*for papers*); hardcover of a book'; Khalkha *xawtas* 'cover (*of a book*); file, folder, jacket; board cut to size for a printing-block (*xyl.*); side-board of a saddle; flap (*of the case for a book*); leaf (*of a door*); shell (*of a bivalve*)'; Oirat

---

183   Cf. Khakas *xaptal* 'women coat', Altai *qaptal* 'coat' and Teleut *qaptal* 'the long skirt, bed skirt' forms, which belong to another Turkic word *qaftan* ~ *qaptan* 'kaftan, clothing'. The etymology of word is unknown. According to the authors of the ESTJa (1997: 268–269), the word is compound from *qāb* 'a leather bag, water skin, sack' and *tōn* 'garment, clothing', and further borrowed to New Persian (see TMEN 3: 185). See also Clauson (ED 582a) and Räsänen (VEWT 234b).

dial. *xabtăs ~ xabtsă ~ xabtsăs ~ xabtsăsăŋ* 'folder, cover of a book'; Dagur *kartəs* 'board' (E); Khamnigan *xabtasu(n) ~ xabtasa(n) ~ xabtaha(n)* board, wood board of a saddle; folder (*for papers*); hardcover of a book.

Etymology: Kałużyński 1961: 82; SSTMJa 1: 377; Doerfer 1985: 25–26; ESTJa 1997: 267–268; Anikin 2000: 259; Khabtagaeva 2009: 215; Nugteren 2011: 397

It is clear that the Yeniseian word was borrowed from Turkic. This is proven not only by the phonetic form *qabtal* without the Mongolic suffix +*sUn*, but also by the special semantic meaning 'saddle cloth', which appears in Turkic languages. The regular change of Turkic initial *q-* to *h-* occurred in Kott, which points an early period of borrowing. There is another Kott form, where the epentheses appeared between the consonants *-p-* and *-t-*, which is typical for loanwords in Yeniseian, e.g. Russian *klop* 'bug' → Ket *lapa*; Russian *sklad* 'storage' → Ket, Yugh *la$^?$t*, etc.

The borrowing of Turkic forms from Mongolic was examined by Kałużyński (1961: 82), Levitskaja (ESTJa 1997: 267–268) and Khabtagaeva (2009: 215). In turn, the Turkic form *qabtal* possibly became abbreviated from the Mongolic form *qabtalsun*. The disappearance of the consonant *-l-* before *-s-* is a regular phenomenon in Mongolic languages. Cf. Literary Mongolian *čaγalsun ~ čaγasun* 'paper'; *γutulsun ~ γutusun* 'shoes'; *moyilsun ~ moyisun* 'bird-cherry'; *mölsün ~ mösün* 'ice' (for details, see Poppe 1954: 241; 1960: 86–87). The base of the Mongolic form is the non-productive form **qabta* 'something flat', cf. Literary Mongolian *qabtaγai* (< **qabta+GAi*) 'flat, even; wooden board; plane surface; flatness'; *qabtayi-* (< **qabta+yi-*) 'to be[come] flat'; *qabtaγ-a(n)* (< **qabta+GAn*) 'bag, pouch, purse; pocket', etc.

The Mongolic word was borrowed also into Tungusic[184] (SSTMJa 1: 377; Doerfer 1985: 25–26) and Siberian Russian (Anikin 2000: 259) languages.

Kott *in ~ în*; Arin *in*; Yugh *i'n*; Ket *i'n* 'needle' (Werner 2002/1: 390) ← Turkic **īnä < iŋä < ignä* 'needle':
    cf. Old Turkic *ignä*; NE^S YeniseiT: Khakas *iŋe*; Sagai, Koibal *ingä*; Kachin *iŋä*; Kyzyl *ingä*; Shor *inge*; AltaiT: Altai *iyne*; Qumanda *iyne*; Quu *iyne ~ inne*; Teleut *iyne* (TR), cf. *īnä* (R); SayanT: Tuvan *ine*; Tofan *iyne ~ inne*; ChulymT *ignä ~ iŋnä*; NE^N Yakut *inne*; Dolgan *innä* 'needle tree', cf. *iŋnä* 'needle'; Yakut dial. *inne ~ ińńe* 'arrow, arrowhead' (DS); NW^N Siberian Tatar *ignä ~ inä ~ enä*; NW^S Kirgiz *iyne* 'needle; terribly emaciated, gaunt'; Fu-yü *iŋi*; Kazak *iyne*; SE Yellow Uyghur *yiŋne*.

---

184 Mongolic → Tungusic: cf. Common Ewenki *kapta-* 'to make smooth (on the surface)' > *kaptakā-* 'to roll out the dough', *kaptama* 'flat, wide (flat objects)', etc.

Etymology: Clauson ED 110a; ESTJa 1974: 367–369; SSTMJa 1: 316; Stachowski 1996/1: 94

In the *Etymological Dictionary of Yeniseian* by Vajda and Werner (in preparation), the Yeniseian forms are regarded as inherited from Proto-Yeniseian, with the direction of borrowing between earlier forms of the Yeniseian and Turkic words still unclear. The Yeniseian forms are monosyllabic, which is typical for native Yeniseian words. According to phonetic shape, I assume a connection with the Turkic form *ignä ~ iŋä* 'needle'. The origin of the word is not clear: it may be a native Turkic or native Yeniseian word. If it is a Turkic loanword in Yeniseian, then apocope occurred. The disappearance of the final vowel is typical for some Turkic loanwords in Yeniseian.

For the etymological background of the Turkic word, see Sevortjan (ESTJa 1974: 367–369) and Clauson (ED 110a). The source of borrowing were probably Yenisei Turkic forms which underwent the metathesis -*gn*- >-*ŋ*-.

The Turkic word was borrowed into the Tungusic languages[185] (SSTMJa 1: 316).

Kott *îri ~ îre* 'thread, tendon' (Werner 2002/1: 391) ← Turkic **sīr < siŋir* 'muscle, sinew, tendon':

cf. Old Turkic *siŋir* 'muscle, sinew'; NE[S] YeniseiT: Khakas *sīr* 'tendon, sinew' (KhR); Sagai, Koibal, Kachin *sīr* 'tendon' (R); Kyzyl *sīr* 'tendon'; AltaiT: Altai *siŋir* 'tendon; bowstring; thread' (R); Teleut *siŋir* 'tendon'; SayanT: Tuvan *sīr* 'tendon, sinew'; Tofan *sīr* 'tendon, sinew'; ChulymT *sīr* 'tendon, sinew'; NE[N] Yakut *iŋīr* 'tendon, sinew'; Dolgan *iŋīr* 'tendon'; NW[N] Siberian Tatar *siŋgir ~ seŋer* 'tendon, sinew'; NW[S] Kirgiz *siŋir* 'tendon, sinew'; Fu-yü *sïyriš* (?) 'muscle'; Kazak *sïŋïr* 'tendon, sinew'; SE Yellow Yughur –.

Etymology: Räsänen VEWT 423a; Rassadin 1971: 227; Clauson ED 841a; ESTJa 2003: 267

The etymology of the Kott word is unknown. It may have a connection with the Turkic form *sīr* 'muscle, sinew, tendon', which has been documented in the Yenisei Turkic, Sayan Turkic and Chulym Turkic varieties. From a phonetic perspective, the Turkic etymology is complicated by the unexplained disappearance of the initial *s-* in Kott. This feature shows a peculiarity of Yakut and Dolgan—the languages, which most likely did not contact with Yeniseian. If the Kott word is connected to Turkic, then paragogic change occurred. There

---

185   cf. Tungusic **inmä*: Common Ewenki *inme* 'needle'; cf. Ayan, Chumikan *ilme*; Podkamennyi, Aldan, Yerbogachon, Nepa *imme*; Lamut *inme* 'needle; fir-needle'; Negidal *inme* 'needle'; Orochen *imme* 'steel needle'; Udehe *iŋme* 'needle'; Orok *xulme* 'needle'; Nanai *xurme* 'needle'; Manchu *ulme* 'needle'.

are some Yeniseian loanwords in which the additional vowel occurred regularly at the end of words. The word belongs to the category of words of uncertain etymology.

Kott **kamču** ~ **kamči**; Arin **xamčook** 'whip' (Werner 2002/1: 407) ← Turkic **kamči ~ kamču < qamčï* 'a whip' < *qam-* 'to strike down' *-čI* {Turkic VN, see ED xliii}:

cf. Old Turkic *qamčï*; NE^S YeniseiT: Khakas *xamǰï*; Sagai *qamǰï* (R); Kyzyl *χamžže*; Shor *qamčï*; AltaiT: Altai *qamčï*; Tuba *kamčï*; Qumanda *kamčï*; Quu *kamdžï* ~ *kamžï* ~ *kamčï*; Teleut *qamčï*; SayanT: Tuvan *kïmčï*; Tofan *qïmšï*; ChulymT *qamču*; NE^N Yakut *kïmnï̈*; Yakut dial. *kïmnï̈ï* 'pole to control deer'; NW^N Siberian Tatar *qamčï*; NW^S Kirgiz *kamčï*; Fu-yü –; Kazak *qamšï*; SE Yellow Yughur –;

Turkic → Samoyedic:

Kamas *kamǰu* ~ *kamd'u* 'whip'; Mator *kamǰi* 'whip'.

Etymology: Joki LS 156; Räsänen VEWT 229a; Doerfer TMEN 3: 509–511; Clauson ED 626a; Romanova, Myreeva & Baraškov 1975: 188; Timonina 1978: 9; ESTJa 1997: 247–248; Anikin 2000: 252; Róna-Tas & Berta 2011: 484–486

The Yeniseian words were clearly borrowed from the Turkic forms *qamčï* ~ *qamču*. From the phonetic point of view, the source of borrowing was the Altai Turkic or Chulym Turkic dialects. The Arin form has a native Yeniseian suffix *+ok*, which resembles the Russian diminutive suffix: e.g. Arin *kajakok* 'butter' ← Turkic *qayaq* 'butter, sour cream' (cf. Old Turkic *kańak*), Arin *altïnok* 'gold' ← Turkic *altïn* 'gold', etc. (Werner 2005: 149).

The base of the Turkic word is the Common Turkic verb *qam-* 'to strike down' and the non-productive deverbal noun suffix *-čI*.

An addition to Yeniseian, the Turkic word was borrowed into Samoyedic (Joki LS 156; Helimski 1997: 265) Siberian Russian (Anikin 2000: 252), Tungusic[186] (Doerfer TMEN 3: 510; Romanova, Myreeva & Baraškov 1975: 188), New Persian (Doerfer TMEN 3: 509–511) and Hungarian Cuman dialect[187] (Róna-Tas & Berta WOT 2011: 484–486).

Kott **kanšá**; Yugh **kàńčá**; Ket **kàńčá** 'tobacco pipe' (Werner 2002/1: 409) ← Turkic **kaŋsa < qaŋza* 'tobacco pipe' ← Mongolic *γaŋsa* 'tobacco pipe' ← Chinese:

cf. NE^S YeniseiT: Khakas *xaŋza*; Sagai, Koibal, Kachin *qaŋza* (R); Kyzyl *χan^{d}za* ~ *χanza*; Shor *qanza*; AltaiT: Altai *kaŋza*; Tuba *kaŋza*; Qumanda *kaŋza*; Quu *kaŋza*; Teleut *qaŋza*; SayanT: Tuvan *daŋza*; Tofan *daŋza*; ChulymT *qaŋza*; NE^N Yakut *xamsa*;

---

[186] Turkic: Yakut → Tungusic: *Eastern Ewenki*: Ayan, Mai, Tokko, Aldan, Uchur, Urmi, Tommot, Chumikan *kimni* 'whip'.

[187] West Old Turkic *kamčï* 'whip' → Hungarian Cuman dial. *kamcsi* [kåmči] 'whip, lash'.

Dolgan *gaŋsa* ~ *gansa* ~ *nāŋsa*; Yakut dial. *xańsa* ~ *gańsa* ~ *kańsa* ~ *lańsa* ~ *nāńsa* ~ *nāxsa* ~ *naxsa* ~ *ńāńsa* ~ *xāńsa*; NW[N] Siberian Tatar *qancá* ~ *qaŋza*; NW[S] Kirgiz *kanža*; Fu-yü –; Kazak –; SE Yellow Uyghur *qaŋza*;

Turkic → Samoyedic:

Selkup *kānsa* ~ *kant'a* ~ *kāndša* ~ *kangza* ~ *kāńďa* 'tobacco pipe';

Turkic ← Mongolic *γaŋsa* 'tobacco pipe':

cf. LM *γangsa* ~ *γansa*; Modern Mongol: Buryat *ganza* ~ *gāha(n)* ~ *dāha(n)*;[188] Sayan Buryat: Oka *dāhan* ~ *dōhan* ~ *dōhon*; Lower Uda Buryat *gāhan* ~ *dāhan*; Khalkha *gāns(an)*; Oirat dial. *gandză*; Dagur –; Khamnigan *gandza*;

Mongolic ← Chinese:

cf. Modern Chinese *guănzi* 'tube, pipe'.

Etymology: Joki LS 158; Kałużyński 1962: 122; Räsänen VEWT 232b; Rassadin 1971: 169; 1980: 21, 37, 38, 40, 68; SSTMJa 1: 139b; Timonina 1978:11; Doerfer 1985: 74; Anikin 2000: 162; Khabtagaeva 2009: 197

The Yeniseian words were possibly borrowed from Turkic form *kaŋsa, where the medial consonant -*s*- regularly changed to -*š*- in Kott (Starostin 1982: 160) and -*č*- in Yugh and Ket.

The word belongs to the category of culture-specific words, and is documented in almost all Siberian languages. From an etymological aspect, it is of Chinese origin. Through Mongolic languages, the word was borrowed into Turkic (Kałużyński 1962: 122; Räsänen VEWT 232b; Rassadin 1971: 169; 1980: 21, 37, 38, 40, 68; Khabtagaeva 2009: 197) and Tungusic,[189] and further from Yakut to the Lamut dialects[190] (SSTMJa 1: 139b; Doerfer 1985: 74). From Turkic, the Chinese word was borrowed into Samoyedic (Joki LS 158; Filipova 1994: 47; Helimski 1997: 266) and Siberian Russian (Anikin 2000: 162).

Kott *kanʰêx* ~ *kanʰêg* 'halter' (Werner 2002/1: 408) ← Turkic **kand'aga* 'saddle-thongs' ← Mongolic *γanǰuγa* 'thongs attached to a saddle for tying an object' < *γanǰu-GAn {Mongolic VN, see Poppe 1964: § 149}:

cf. NE[S] YeniseiT: Shor *xanǰïğa* 'saddle-thongs' (But.); AltaiT: Altai *kand'aga*; Quu *kanža* ~ *kanča*; Teleut *qanǰaga* (R); SayanT –; ChulymT –; NE[N] Yakut –; NW[N] Siberian Tatar *qancïğa* ~ *qanǰïğa*; NW[S] Kirgiz *qanžïğa*; Fu-yü –; Kazak *qanžïğa*; SE Yellow Uyghur –; Lobnor *ġanǰuqa*;

---

188 < *dangsan.
189 Mongolic → Tungusic: *Ewenki dial.* Ilimpeya *ganǰa*; Podkamennyi, Nepa, Tungir, Uchur, Sakhalin *ganča*; Nercha, Barguzin *gansa* 'smoking pipes with metal shank'; Nanai *γanǰa* 'smoking pipe'.
190 Yakut → Tungusic: Lamut *qansa* 'pipe'.

Turkic ← Mongolic *γanǰuγa* 'thongs attached to a saddle for tying an object':
cf. Middle Mongol: YY *ġanǰuγa*; RH *qanǰuqa*; LM *γanǰuγ-a(n)*; Modern Mongol: Buryat *ganzaga* 'saddle-thongs'; Khalkha *gandzaga* 'saddle-thongs'; Kalmuck *ganz^aγa*; Dagur *gandzuγ^w* (E); Khamnigan *gandzagu(n)* ~ *gandzaga(n)*.

Etymology: Räsänen VEWT 230b–231a; Doerfer TMEN 1: 290; SSTMJa 1: 139; Rassadin 1980: 44; 52; Rozycki 1994: 86; ESTJa 1997: 254–255; Schönig 2000: 98; Róna-Tas & Berta WOT 2011: 486–487

The Kott forms were possibly borrowed from the Turkic form **kand'aga*, where the final vowel disappeared. Apocope is a typical change for some Kott loanwords, e.g. Kott *aibič* ~ *aipiš* 'old man' ← Turkic *aybiči*, Kott *aktur* 'postp. through' ← Turkic *ötgürü*, Kott *in* ~ *în* 'needle' ← Turkic *ignä*, etc.

The Turkic word itself is of Mongolic origin. The borrowing from Turkic, and not directly from Mongolic, gifts proof of is shown by the Kott initial devoiced consonant *k-* and medial consonant *-t^h-* which devoiced from Turkic palatalized *-d'-*. The change of the Turkic final consonant *-g* is typical for some Kott loanwords, e.g. Kott *arix* 'clean' ← Turkic *arüg* 'clean, pure', Kott *atax* 'tent' ← Turkic *otaġ* 'a small temporary building, tent', etc.

In addition to Turkic (Räsänen VEWT 230b–231a; Doerfer TMEN 1: 290; Rassadin 1980: 44; 52; ESTJa 1997: 254–255; Schönig 2000: 98), the Mongolic form was borrowed into Tungusic[191] (SSTMJa 1: 139; Rozycki 1994: 86) and Hungarian Cuman dialect[192] (Róna-Tas & Berta WOT 2011: 486–487).

From an etymological point of view, it seems that the base is the Mongolic non-productive verbal form **γanǰu-* 'to attach to a saddle in order to tie an object' and the productive deverbal noun suffix *-GAn* (Poppe 1964: §149).

Kott **kaptu** ~ **káptu**; Arin **kapti** 'scissors' (Werner 2002/1: 411) ← Turkic **qïpta* 'scissors' < **qïp-* 'to cut' *-DX* {Turkic VN, see Erdal 1991: 332}:
cf. Old Turkic *kïftu*; NE^S YeniseiT: Khakas *xïptï*; Sagai, Koibal, Kachin *kïptï* (R); Kyzyl *χeptï* ~ *χîptï*; Shor *qïptï*; AltaiT: Qumanda *kïpta*; Quu *kïptï*; SayanT –; ChulymT *kïptï* (R); NE^N Yakut *kïptïy*; Dolgan *kïptïy*; Remaining lgs. –;

Turkic ← Samoyedic:
Kamas *kaptï* 'scissors'.

Etymology: Joki LS 161; Räsänen VEWT 234b; Doerfer TMEN 1: 448–451; Clauson ED 582a; SSTMJa 1: 397; Timonina 1978: 10; ESTJa 2000: 224

---

191 Mongolic → Tungusic: Barguzin Ewenki *ganǰuka-* 'to attach thongs to a saddle'; Lamut *gaŋda-* 'to bind a deer'; Manchu *γanǰuhan* ~ *γanǰurγan* ~ *γanǰurhan* ~ *γančurγan* 'saddle-thongs'.

192 Mongolic → Turkic Cuman **kanǰïka* → Hungarian Cuman dial. *kagyík* [kånd'ĩk], *kangyika* [kånd'ikå] 'saddle strap'.

The Yeniseian words were borrowed from the Turkic form *qïpta. In the Yeniseian forms, vowel metathesis occurred. Remarkably, this change happened in the Samoyedic Kamas language as well.

The Turkic word derived from the non-productive verbal form *qïp- 'to cut by scissors' (cf. Khakas xïpla-, Shor qïpla- < *qïp-lA-) and the Turkic deverbal noun suffix -DX (for details on function, see Erdal 1991: 332). The Turkic word was erroneously connected with Mongolic qayiči with the same meaning of 'scissors'.

In addition to Yeniseian (Timonina 1978: 10), the Turkic word was borrowed into Samoyedic (Joki LS 161), and from Yakut into Tungusic[193] (SSTMJa 1: 397) languages.

Kott *kep ~ qep ~ xep ~ xêp*; Assan *kep ~ xajp*; Yugh *χap ~ χaʔp*; Ket *qap ~ qaʔp* 'boat' (Werner 2002/2: 79) ← Turkic *kebe < kämi 'ship or boat':
   cf. Old Turkic kämi; NE^S YeniseiT: Khakas kime; Sagai, Koibal, Kachin kemä (R); Kyzyl kèmä ~ kēmä; Shor kebe; AltaiT: Altai keme; Tuba kebe; Qumanda keme ~ kebe; Quu kebe; Teleut keme; SayanT: Tuvan xeme; ChulymT kämä; NE^N Yakut –; NW^N Siberian Tatar kämä; NW^S Kirgiz keme; Fu-yü gimĭ; Kazak keme; SE Yellow Yughur –.

Etymology: Räsänen VEWT 251a; Clauson ED 721b; ESTJa 1980: 37–39
   The etymology of the Yeniseian words is unknown. Werner (2002/2: 79) compares them with Turkic. Apocope occurred in Yeniseian, which is a typical change for some Yeniseian loanwords (e.g. Kott *aibič ~ aipiš* 'old man' ← Turkic *aybičï*, Kott *aktur* 'postp. through' ← Turkic ötgürü, Kott *in ~ în* 'needle' ← Turkic ignä, etc.). Diphthongization occurred in the Assan form xajp due to the final Turkic -i.
   The word belongs to the category of words of uncertain etymology.

Kott *koŋoroš ~ konkorôš* 'bell' (Werner 2002/1: 441) ← Turkic *koŋraš 'a bell, one hung on an animal's neck' < *qoŋar 'bell' +AK {Turkic NN/Diminutive, see Erdal 1991: 224} +Xš {AltaiT NN/diminutive, see Baskakov OGOJa § 39}:
Yugh *χóŋirɔχ*; Ket *qóŋloq* 'bell' ← Turkic *koŋrak 'a bell, one hung on an animal's neck' < *qoŋar 'bell' +AK {Turkic NN/diminutive, see Erdal 1991: 224}:
   cf. Old Turkic qoŋrāq; NE^S YeniseiT: Khakas xoŋro ~ xoġdro; Sagai, Koibal, Kachin qoŋra- (R); Shor qoŋrā (R); AltaiT: Altai koŋïrä; Qumanda koŋara ~ koŋarak 'small bell', cf. koŋdra 'bell'; Teleut koŋïru; SayanT: Tuvan koŋurā; Tofan qoŋïra- 'to jingle,

---

193   Yakut → Tungusic 'scissors': Ewenki dial. Aldan, Yerbogachon, Zeya, Nepa, Sakhalin, Tungir, Urmi, Uchur, Chumikan kipti; Lamut kipti ~ kïptïy; Negidal kiptiy ~ xepte; Orok kipti.

tinkle, ring'; ChulymT –; NE^N Yakut –; NW^N Siberian Tatar *quŋrau ~ qïŋgïrau*; NW^S Kirgiz *koŋgurō*; Fu-yü –; Kazak *qoŋïrau*; SE Yellow Yughur –;
Turkic → Samoyedic:
Kamas *koŋgoro* 'clock, church bell; bell'; Selkup *kuŋir-* 'to rattle'.

Etymology: Joki LS 194; Räsänen VEWT 280b; Clauson ED 640a; Filipova 1994: 50; ESTJa 2000: 60–61; Róna-Tas & Berta WOT 2011: 426–428; Nugteren 2011: 419

The Yeniseian forms most likely have a connection with Turkic. Despite the fact that the word is of onomatopoeic origin, I conjecture that they were borrowed from the Altai Turkic form **koŋraš*, which itself derived from the Turkic noun *qoŋar* 'bell', with the Turkic diminutive suffix +*AK* (for details on function, see Erdal 1991: 224) and the additional Altai Turkic diminutive suffix +*Xš* (for details on function, see Baskakov OGOJa § 39).

The primary base of form is **qoŋ*, cf. Mongolic *qongqo* 'bell, hand bell'.[194] The Mongolic form was borrowed into Tuvan[195] (Khabtagaeva 2009: 101) and Literary Altai.[196] The Yakut verb *xoŋkunā-* 'to make different sounds, jingle bells, geese' was possibly borrowed from the Mongolic verb *qonggina-* 'to ring, sound resonantly' (Kałużyński 1962: 100). It is also possible that there was an unusual derivation from the "dead" form **koŋ* with the Yakut denominal verbum suffix denoting continuity of the verbal action +*GXnĀ-* (Slepcov 1972: 596), which also is of Mongolic origin (Kałużyński 1962: 100).

The Turkic word was borrowed into the Samoyedic languages (Joki LS 194; Filipova 1994: 50) and Hungarian, where metathesis occurred[197] (Róna-Tas & Berta WOT 426–428).

For the etymological background of the word, see also Räsänen (VEWT 280b), Clauson (ED 640a) and Levitskaja (ESTJa 2000: 60–61).

Kott *koskun* 'breech-band' (Werner 2002/1: 443) ← Turkic **qosqun* 'crupper' < **quδuš-GAn* {Turkic VN, see ED xliv}:
cf. Old Turkic –; NE^S YeniseiT: Khakas *xosxïn*; Sagai, Koibal, Kachin *qosqan* (R); Shor *qošqan ~ quyušqan* (R); AltaiT: Altai *quyušqan*; Tuba *kuyuškan*; Qumanda *kuyuškan*; Teleut *quyušqan* (R); SayanT –; ChulymT –; NE^N Yakut –; NW^N Siberian

---

194 Middle Mongol: HY *qongqo*; LM *qongqo* 'bell, hand-bell'; Modern Mongol: Buryat *xonxo*; Sayan Buryat: Oka *xonxo* 'groove of a saddle'; Khalkha *xonx*; Oirat dial. *xoŋxä*; Dagur –; Khamnigan *xonxo*.
195 SayanT: Tuvan *koŋga* 'signal, bell'.
196 Mongolic → Altai Turkic: *koŋko* 'the bells on the shaman belt, which belongs in the ritual clothing': cf. *qoŋo* 'small bell' (R).
197 Turkic: West Old Turkic **koŋar* > **χoŋar* → Hungarian *harang* [*hårång*] 'bell'.

Tatar *quišqan* (R); NW^S Kirgiz *kuyuškan*; Fu-yü –; Kazak *quyïsqan*; SE Yellow Uyghur *qusqon ~ qusqun*;
Turkic → Samoyedic:
Kamas *koskun* 'crupper'.

Etymology: Joki LS 197; Räsänen VEWT 297b; Doerfer TMEN 3: 477–478; Timonina 1978: 9; ESTJa 2000: 182–183

The Yeniseian word is clearly borrowed from Yenisei Turkic. The preservation of the initial consonant *k*- also indicates a later period of borrowing.

The etymology of the Turkic word is not clear. According to the reconstructions of Doerfer (TMEN 3: 477), the Proto-Turkic form could be reconstructed as **quδuš- > *quyuš*- > *qūš*- > *quš*-. The form is lacking in Old Turkic, but the base of the Turkic word, *quδ or *quδur-, is present in Old Turkic sources, cf. *quδruq* 'the tail of an animal', *quδurġun* 'crupper' (Clauson ED 604–605). For the etymology of the Turkic word, see also Räsänen (VEWT 297b) and Levitskaja (ESTJa 2000: 182).

The Turkic word with the same phonetic form was borrowed into Samoyedic (Joki LS 197).

Kott ***kûra***; Assan ***kura*** 'rope' (Werner 2002/1: 453) ← Turkic *qur 'belt, girdle':

cf. Old Turkic *qur*; NE^S YeniseiT: Khakas *xur*; Sagai, Koibal, Kachin *qur* 'belt, circle' (R); Shor *qur*; AltaiT: Altai *qur*; Tuba *kur*; Qumanda *kur*; Quu *kur*; Teleut *qur* (R); SayanT: Tuvan *kur* 'belt, girdle; wall of the cattle court'; Tofan *qur*; ChulymT *qur*; NE^N Yakut *kur*; Dolgan *kur*; NW^N Siberian Tatar *qor*; NW^S Kirgiz *kur*; Fu-yü *gur*; Kazak *qur* 'belt, used for fixing lattices of yurt'; SE Yellow Uyghur *kur*;
Yeniseian → Samoyedic:
Mator *kura* 'rope'.

Etymology: Räsänen VEWT 301b–302a; Doerfer TMEN 3: 541; Clauson ED 642a; Timonina 1978: 9; ESTJa 2000: 150–152

I propose that the Yeniseian words connect with the Turkic word *qur* 'belt, girdle'. The final vowel -*a* can be explained as a typical change for Turkic loanwords in Yeniseian, e.g. Kott *šâškana* 'magpie' ← Turkic *sāskan < *saġïzġan*; Kott *tegteka* 'quail' ← Turkic *tükteg* 'with feathers'.

The form *kura* with final vowel -*a* is present in Samoyedic Mator. According to Helimski (1997: 295), the Turkic word was borrowed from Yeniseian.

For the etymological background of the Turkic word and other derived Turkic forms, see Räsänen (VEWT 301b–302a) and Levitskaja (ESTJa 2000: 150–152).

Arin *qonda* ~ *xonta* 'bridle, rein' (Werner 2002/2: 103) ← ? Turkic **nokta* 'halter' ← Mongolic *noqto* 'halter':
   cf. NE^S YeniseiT: Khakas *noxta* 'halter'; *fig.* whiskers'; Shor, Sagai, Koibal, Kachin *noqta*, cf. Kachin *nuqta*; AltaiT: Altai *noqto*; Quu *notko*; Teleut *noqto*; SayanT: Tuvan –; Tofan *noqta*; ChulymT –; NE^N Yakut –; NW^N Siberian Tatar *nuqta*; NW^S Kirgiz *nokto*; Fu-yü *lohtï*; Kazak *noqta*; SE Yellow Uyghur *loqta* ~ *loxta*;
Turkic ← Mongolic *noqto* 'halter':
   cf. Middle Mongol: YY *noqta*; Muq. *noxta*; RH *noqta*; LM *noqto*; Modern Mongol: Buryat *nogto*; Khalkha *nogt*; Oirat dial. *nogtă* ~ *noktă* ~ *nogt* ~*noxt* ~ *nokt*; Dagur –; Khamnigan *nogto*.

Etymology: Räsänen VEWT 354b; Doerfer TMEN 1: 517–518; Rassadin 1971: 208; 1980: 21; 36; 45; Schönig 2000: 140; ESTJa 2003: 99; Nugteren 2011: 461; Khabtagaeva 2015a: 121–122; 2015c: 94

The etymology of the Arin word is unknown. It connects probably with the Siberian Turkic form *nokta* ~ *noxta* 'halter', where metathesis occurred. My suggestion is strengthened by the absence of the initial nasal consonant *n*- in native Yeniseian words. See as well Chapter *Metathesis*.

Initial *n*- is unique to Turkic. From an etymological point of view, the Turkic word was borrowed from Mongolic: it is present in almost all Turkic languages. For all data and details, see the works of Räsänen (VEWT 354b), Doerfer (TMEN 1: 517–518), Rassadin (1971: 208; 1980: 21; 36; 45), Schönig (2000: 140) and ESTJa (2003: 99).

The Mongolic word also was borrowed into Tungusic[198] (SSTMJa 1: 604a).

From an etymological point of view, Nugteren remarks that the relationship between the Mongolic and the Chinese word *lóngtou* with the same meaning is unclear (Nugteren 2011: 461). The word is present in Dagur as *lont*, which is clearly a Chinese loanword. In Middle Mongol sources the word is present, for example in the Dictionary of Mukkadimat al-Adab with the genitive case *noxtayīn* [*uyāsar*] '[the strap of] the halter,' and with derived verbal form *noxtala-ba* [*morini*] '(he) bridled [the horse]' (Poppe 1938: 259b).

Kott *tâmukol* 'tobacco tin' (Werner 2002/2: 236) < *tâmuk* 'tobacco' + Yeniseian *ol* 'container' (cf. Ket, Yugh *ɔʔl* 'cover'):
tâmuk ← Turkic **tamkï* 'tobacco' ← Persian:
   cf. Old Turkic –; NE^S YeniseiT: Khakas *tamǧï* ~ *tamkï* ~ *temki* ~ *tāxpï*; Sagai *tamqï* ~ *tämki*; Koibal, Kachin *tamqï* (R); Kyzyl *tāmkki*; Shor *tapqï*; AltaiT: Altai *tamkï* ~ *taŋkï* ~ *taŋqū*; Qumanda *tamkïla-* (< *tamqï+lA-* {Turkic NV}) 'to smoke'; Quu *takpï*; Teleut

---

198   Mongolic → Tungusic: Nercha Ewenki *nokto* 'halter'.

tamqï; SayanT: Tuvan *tapkï*; Tofan *tamhï* ~ *tamihï*; ChulymT *tämkä* ~ *tamqū* ~ *tǟmkü*; NE^N Yakut –; NW^N Siberian Tatar *tamaq*; NW^S Kirgiz *tameki*; Fu-yü –; Kazak *temeki*; SE Yellow Uyghur *tamaqï*;

Turkic ← Persian *taṃbākū* 'tobacco (*Nicotiana persica*)'.

Etymology: Räsänen VEWT 459b; Timonina 1978: 10; Stachowski 2004: 198

The Kott word belongs to the category of compound words where one of the parts is Turkic and other is native Yeniseian (Khabtagaeva 2015d: 138).

Etymologically, the Kott compound *tâmuk* was borrowed from the Turkic form *tamkï* 'tobacco', which is ultimately of Persian origin (Stachowski 2004: 198). From Turkic, the word was borrowed into Mongolic.[199] The Yakut form was most likely borrowed from Russian.[200]

From a phonetic perspective, epenthesis occurred in the consonant cluster and the final vowel was dropped in the compound *tâmuk*.

Kott ***urkan*** 'lasso' (Werner 2002/2: 353) ← Mongolic *urɣan 'a long wooden pole with a loop on the end used to catch horses, lasso pole' ← Turkic *uruq* 'rope, lasso' < *ur-* 'to put; to strike' -*XK* {Turkic VN, see Erdal 1991: 224}:

cf. Middle Mongol: SH *u'urqa* ~ *uqurqa*; LM *urɣa(n)* ~ *uɣurɣa*; Modern Mongol: Buryat *urga*; Khalkha *ūrga*; Kalmuck *ūrɣ^a*; Dagur *x^wark* ~ *wark* 'lasso' (E); Khamnigan *urga*;

Mongolic ← Turkic *uruq* 'rope, lasso':

cf. Old Turkic *uruq*; NE^S YeniseiT: Khakas *urux* ~ *ïrax* 'lasso'; Sagai, Koibal, Kachin, Sagai *uruq* (R); Kyzyl *urux* ~ *^urux*; Shor *uruq* 'loop'; AltaiT: Altai –; Teleut *ūruq* ~ *uruq* (R); SayanT: Tuvan *uruk*; Tofan –; ChulymT *uruq*; NE^N Yakut *uraġas* 'a pole, a long stick; shaft' < *uruq* + *aġas* 'tree';[201] Dolgan –; NW^N Siberian Tatar *uqruq* (R); NW^S Kirgiz –; Fu-yü *uruh* [*aġaš*]; Kazak –; SE Yellow Uyghur *uruq* 'rope; sheep intestine used in shamanic rituals';

Turkic → Samoyedic:

Kamas *uru^ʔd* 'lasso', cf. *uru^ʔ* 'yarn'.

Etymology: Joki LS 367–368; Doerfer TMEN 2: 86–89; 1985: 96; Räsänen VEWT 516b; Clauson ED 215a; ESTJa 1974: 602–603; SSTMJa 2: 352–353; Timonina 1978: 9; Ščerbak 1997: 120;[202] Nugteren 2011: 364, 536

---

199 Turkic → Mongolic 'tobacco': Middle Mongol: –; Literary Mongolian *tamaki(n)* ~ *tamiki*; Modern Mongol: Buryat; Khalkha *tamxi*; Oirat dial. *tamkă* ~ *tämkä* ~ *tamăk*; Dagur –; Khamnigan *tamaki(n)*.

200 Yakut *tabax* 'tobacco' ← Russian.

201 Cf. Old Turkic *iğač* 'tree, wood, a piece of wood'.

202 Ščerbak (1997: 120) connects the Mongolic word with another Turkic form *ïrġaq* 'hook'.

The Kott word is one of those loanwords which were borrowed directly from Mongolic and not from Siberian Turkic. The source of borrowing was the form *urgan, where the Mongolic consonant -g- in the cluster became devoiced in Kott. In turn, the Mongolic word was borrowed from Turkic *uruq* 'rope, lasso' (Räsänen VEWT 516b; ESTJa 1974: 602–603). The base of Turkic word was the verb *ur-* 'to put; to strike' with the productive deverbal noun suffix *-XK* (Clauson ED 215a).

It is important to differentiate from an other Mongolic word *uraqa* (< *huraka*)[203] 'lasso, noose, snare, trap', and which is not connected to the Mongolic word *urγa* 'a long wooden pole with a loop on the end used to catch horses'. In spite of the phonetic and semantic similarity of these Mongolic words, they are not connected to each other (Nugteren 2011: 364, 536). The first one is a native Mongolic word; the second one is a Turkic loanword.

The Mongolic word *urγa* was borrowed into Tungusic[204] (SSTMJa 2: 352–353; Doerfer 1985: 96; Rozycki 1994: 113).

1.1.15 Clothing, Cloth

Arin ***barčol badija*** 'kerchief' (Werner 2002/1: 107) ← Turkic **arčol* 'kerchief' + Russian *plat'je* 'dress':
< Turkic *arčol* 'kerchief' ← Mongolic *arčūl* < *arčiγul* 'cleaning cloth, dust rag; mop; towel' < *arči-* 'to wipe, clean, or dry by rubbing; to erase; to weed' *-GUr* {Mongolic VN, see Poppe GWM § 155}:

cf. NE[S] YeniseiT: Khakas *arčol* 'kerchief'; AltaiT: Altai *arčūl'* 'kerchief; kerchief which used by shaman during ceremony'; Tuba *arčūl* 'towel'; Teleut *arčūr* 'bag, towel, handkerchief' (R); SayanT: Tuvan *aržïl* 'kerchief, scarf; towel cloth'; Tofan –; ChulymT –; NE[N] Yakut –; NW[N] Siberian Tatar *arcuil* 'kerchief'; NW[S] Kirgiz *ārčï* ~ *ārču* 'handkerchief'; Fu-yü *ačur* ~ *ayčur* 'kerchief, handkerchief'; Kazak *aršï-* 'to clean'; SE Yellow Uyghur *ačïģïr* 'kerchief, scarf; towel cloth';

Turkic → Samoyedic:
  Mator *arčol* 'cloth';
Turkic ← Mongolic 'cleaning cloth, dust rag; mop; towel':

---

203 Cf. Middle Mongol: SH *huraqala-*; Muq. *uruqa* ~ *uruqu*; LM *uraqa(n)* ~ *uriqa(n)* 'net, snare for catching birds'; Buryat *ur'xa* 'snare, loop; trap'; Khalkha *urxi(n)* 'net, snare for catching birds'; Kalmuck *urx* 'lasso'; Dagur –; Khamnigan *urixu* 'snare, loop; trap'.
204 Mongolic → Tungusic 'a loop, a snare for catching birds or small animals': *Northern Ewenki*: Yerbogachon, Ilimpeya; *Southern Ewenki*: Podkamennyi, Nepa, Sym, Northern Baikal, *Eastern Ewenki*: Zeya, Tungir, Tokko, Aldan, Uchur, Urmi, Chumikan, Sakhalin *hurka*; cf. Nercha *orka*; Barguzin *ukurga*; Lamut *hurqa*; Oroch *xukka*; Udehe *xuka*; Ulcha *puča*; Orok *puta* ~ *putta*; Nanai *poyqa*; Manchu *hurγa* ~ *hurqa*.

cf. Middle Mongol: Precl.Mo. *arčiγur*; SH *arči-*; YY *arči'ur* 'handkerchief'; Ibn-Muh. *arčūr*; RH *arči-*; LM *arčiyul* ~ *arčiyur*; Modern Mongol: Buryat *aršūl*; Sayan Buryat *aršūl* 'silk pouch'; Khalkha *arčūr* 'cleaning cloth, dust-cloth; a hoe'; Oirat dial. *alčiur* ~ *alčur* ~ *arči* ~ *arčiǧur* 'towel, cloth'; Kalmuck *artšūl* ~ *altšūr*; Dagur –; Khamnigan *arčūl* 'rag';

Mongolic ← Turkic *artï-* 'to clean, or purify (something *Acc.*); to cleanse' < *arï-* 'to be, or become, clean, pure' -*t-* {Turkic VV/causative, see Erdal 1991: 763}:

cf. Old Turkic *arït-*; NE^S YeniseiT: Khakas *arït-*; Shor *arït-*; AltaiT: –; SayanT: Tuvan *arït-*; Tofan –; ChulymT –; NE^N Yakut –; NW^N Siberian Tatar –; NW^S Kirgiz *arït-*; Fuyü –; Kazak –; SE Yellow Yughur –.

Etymology: Räsänen VEWT 24b; Clauson ED 207b; ESTJa 1974: 184–186; Rassadin 1980: 23, 35, 38, 64; Erdal 1991: 763; Anikin 2000: 100; Khabtagaeva 2009: 204; Nugteren 2011: 272–273

The Arin hybrid is a compound word consisting of the Turkic form *arčol* 'kerchief' and the Russian word *plat'je* 'dress'. The initial *b-* in *barčol* is the Arin possesive marker of the first singular form (Vajda 2015: personal communication).

The second Arin compound is borrowed from Russian. There is another Arin compound word *kaftan badija* 'caftan', which consists of the Russian words *kaftan* 'caftan' with the above-mentioned *plat'je* 'dress'.

From an etymological aspect, the Turkic word *arčol* is a Mongolic loanword (Rassadin 1980: 23, 35, 38, 64; Khabtagaeva 2009: 204). This is a shortened form of Modern Mongol *arčūl*, which derived from Common Mongolic verb *arči-* 'to clean' and the productive Mongolic deverbal noun suffix -*GUr* which forms nouns that designate names of tools (for details on function, see Poppe GWM § 155; Szabó 1943: § 130; Khabtagaeva 2009: 285–286).

The Turkic word belongs to the category of re-borrowings. The Mongolic verb *arči-* 'to clean' was borrowed from Turkic verb *artï-* 'to clean' (Clauson ED 207b; ESTJa 1974: 184–186; Nugteren 2011: 272–273) with the Turkic causative suffix -*t-*.

The Turkic loanword *arčol* 'kerchief' was borrowed into Samoyedic (Helimski 1997: 206). Siberian Russian *arčul* 'pouch' was directly borrowed from Buryat (Anikin 2000: 100).

Yugh *bétes* ~ *bätes* 'lining of a coat' (Werner 2002/1: 118) ← Turkic **bičiš* 'cutting out, dressmaking' < *bič-* 'to cut' -*Xš* {Turkic VN, see Erdal 1991: 262}:

cf. Old Turkic *bičiš* 'the word for any piece of brocade given to a guest who attended banquets given by notables, and feasts' < *büč-* ~ *bič-* 'to cut'; NE^S YeniseiT: Khakas *pičis* 'cutting out' (But.), cf. *pïs-* 'to cut out' (KhR); Shor *piš-*; AltaiT: Altai *bičiš* 'cutting out, dressmaking' < *biči-* 'to cut, to cut out'; Qumanda *pič-*; Quu *pič-*; Teleut *pič-*;

SayanT: Tuvan *biš*-; Tofan *bi^eš*-; ChulymT *pïc*- ~ *pec*-; NE^N Yakut *büs*- 'to cut; to cut out; to kill, to bar s.o.'s way; to inoculate with'; Dolgan *bihin*- 'to cut'; NW^N Siberian Tatar *pïc*- ~ *pec*- 'to cut out'; NW^S Kirgiz *büč*- 'to cut out; to castrate; accurately determine'; Fu-yü –; Kazak *piš*- 'to cut out'; SE Yellow Uyghur *piš*- 'to cut out'.

Etymology: Rassadin 1971: 77; Clauson ED 292b, 296a; ESTJa 1978: 158–161; Werner 2002/1: 118

I connect the Yugh word with the Turkic form *bičïs 'cutting out, dressmaking'. From a semantic point of view, the Turkic lexical meaning is in accordance with the Yeniseian word: both of them indicate material created by sewing. Phonetically, the Yugh form fits with the Turkic form as well. If we accept the reconstruction of Starostin (1982: 161–162), the change in the original Yeniseian *-*č* > -*t'* is regular change in Yugh, e.g. Proto-Yeniseian *beʔč 'falling snow' ~ Yugh *bɛʔtʲ*, cf. Ket *bɛʔt*, Pumpokol *beč*.

Morphologically, the Turkic form derived from the Common Turkic verb *büč*- ~ *bič*- 'to cut' and the productive deverbal noun suffix -*Xš* which forms the object of transitive base verb (for details on different functions of suffix, see Erdal 1991: 262–275). The Yugh final consonant -*s* suggests a Yenisei Turkic influence in which the change of original Turkic final -*š* > -*s* is regular (e.g. Old Turkic *āš* 'food' ~ Khakas *as*; Old Turkic *baš* 'head' ~ Khakas *pas*; Old Turkic *kümüš* 'silver' ~ Khakas *kümüs*, etc.).

For more detail on the etymology of the Turkic verb *büč*- ~ *bič*- 'to cut,' see Clauson (ED 292b, 296a) and Sevortjan (ESTJa 1978: 158–161).

Kott ***kônak*** ~ ***kukanak*** ~ ***kononak***, Arin ***kogonek*** 'shirt' (Werner 2002/1: 440) ← Turkic *kögänäk < *köŋläk* 'shirt' < *köŋ +*lXK* {Turkic NN, see Erdal 1991: 139}:
cf. Old Turkic *köŋläk* 'shirt, i.e. the garment over the heart'; NE^S YeniseiT: Khakas *kögenek* ~ *köŋnek*; Sagai *kögänäk* ~ *kügnäk* (R); Kyzyl *köɣanäɣx*; Shor *künek*; AltaiT: Altai *künek*; Qumanda *künük* ~ *künek* ~ *küŋnek*; Quu *küŋnäk*; Teleut *künük* (R); SayanT: Tuvan *xöyleŋ*; Tofan –; ChulymT *künäk*; NE^N –; NW^N Siberian Tatar *küläk* ~ *külmäk* ~ *köyläk*; NW^S Kirgiz *köynök* 'shirt; women dress; fig. cover, husks of wheat or barley'; Fu-yü –; Kazak *köylek* 'shirt, dress'; SE Yellow Uyghur –;
Turkic → Samoyedic:
Kamas *küinäk* 'shirt'; Mator *kögenāk* 'shirt'; Selkup *kińak* 'shaggy coat with colorful border'.

Etymology: Joki LS 215; Räsänen VEWT 290–291; Doerfer TMEN 3: 614–615; Clauson ED 732a; Timonina 1978: 10–11; Filipova 1994: 47; ESTJa 1997: 89–90; Helimski 1997: 283

The Kott form *kônak* was borrowed from the Turkic form *kōnek (cf. Altai Turkic forms). It demonstrates the characteristics of the Kott vowel -*ô*- in the first syllable. It may be the particular Yeniseian development of the vowel -*ô*-

from the Turkic sequence *-ögä-* (cf. other similar examples: Kott *ô* 'inedible fungus, toadstool' ← Turkic *ō* < *aġu* 'poison'; Kott *ôr* 'herd of horses' ← Turkic *ȫr* < *ögür* 'a herd').

Another source of borrowing is present in the Arin form *kogonek* and the other two Kott forms *kukanak ~ kononak*. Here, the secondary long vowel did not develop from the original sequence of *-ögä-* as *-ogo-* (cf. Yenisei Turkic forms). The disappearance of vowel harmony in Kott and Arin is regular phonetic change for Turkic loanwords.

From an etymological point of view, the base of the Turkic word *köŋläk* 'shirt' is **köŋ*, connected with this part of the chest, cf. derived Turkic forms *köŋlä-* 'to be sunk in thought'; *köŋül* 'the mind; thought; the heart' (Clauson ED 732a). For details on this etymology, see also Räsänen (VEWT 290–291), Doerfer (TMEN 3: 614–615) and Levitskaja (ESTJa 1997: 89–90).

In addition to Yeniseian, the Turkic word was borrowed also into Samoyedic. It seems there are different sources of borrowing for the Samoyedic languages: for Kamas it is the Shor variety, whereas for Mator it is the Khakas dialects, and for Selkup, the Altai or Chulym Turkic dialects (Joki LS 215; Helimski 1997: 283; Filipova 1994: 47).

Kott **tarei ~ tarêi** 'coarse cloth' (Werner 2002/2: 243) ← Turkic **täri* 'the skin, hide (*of a human being or animal*), leather':

Old Turkic *täri*; NE YeniseiT: Khakas *tēr ~ tēri ~ tire ~ tēr*; Shor *tärä* (R); Sagai, Koibal *ter ~ terä* (R); AltaiT: Altai *tere*; Tuba *tere ~ ter*; Qumanda *tere*; Quu *tere*; Teleut *tärä* (R); SayanT: Tuvan –; Tofan *te^crhi* 'strap of a saddle'; ChulymT *tärä* (R); Yakut *tirī*; Dolgan *tirī*; NW Siberian Tatar *tärä*; Kirgiz *teri*; Fu-yü *dir*; Kazak *teri*; SE Yellow Uyghur *ter ~ terä ~ tere ~ terï*.

Etymology: Clauson ED 531a; Timonina 1978: 11; ESTJa 1980: 207–208

Timonina (1978: 11) connects the Yeniseian word with Khakas *türey* 'boot-top', which is a Turkic re-borrowing from the Mongolic languages.[205] The Kott forms are probably related to another Turkic word *täri* 'the skin, hide (*of a human being or animal*), leather'. From a phonetic perspective, diphthongization occured in the final position under of the influence of *-i-* vowel. The disappearance of vowel harmony is a regular change for Turkic loanwords in Yeniseian.

---

205 Khakas *türey* 'boot-top' ← Mongolic: LM *türei* 'bootleg, boot-top' ← Turkic: Old Turkic *tīz* 'knee' (for details on etymology, see Róna-Tas & Berta WOT 2011: 899–901).

Kott *tarup* ~ *tarûp* 'chamois leather' (Werner 2002/2: 243) ← Turkic *tup tere: cf. Altai *tup tere* 'tanned leather':
< *tup* 'tanned leather' ← Russian *dub* 'oak, oakwood':[206]

cf. Old Turkic –; NE^S YeniseiT: Sagai, Koibal *tūp* 'the leather for tanning'; Kyzyl –; AltaiT: Altai *tup [tere]* 'tanned leather (used for shaman's drum)'; Quu *tupta-* (< **tup +tA-* {Turkic NV, see Erdal 1991: 455}) 'to tan leather'; Teleut *tupta-*; SayanT –; ChulymT –; NE^N –; NW^N Siberian Tatar *tup* 'dried bark of willow (*used for tanning of leather*)'; Remaining lgs. –;

+ *täri* 'the skin, hide (*of a human being or animal*)':

cf. Old Turkic *täri*; NE^S YeniseiT: Khakas *tēr* ~ *tēri* ~ *tire*; Shor *tärä*; Sagai, Koibal *ter* ~ *terä*; AltaiT: Altai *tere*; Tuba *tere* ~ *ter*; Qumanda; Quu *tere*; Teleut *tärä*; SayanT: Tuvan –; Tofan *te^crhi* 'straps of saddle'; ChulymT *tärä*; NE^N Yakut; Dolgan *tirī*; NW^N Siberian Tatar *tärä*; NW^S Kirgiz *teri*; Fu-yü *dir*; Kazak *teri*; SE Yellow Uyghur *ter* ~ *terä* ~ *tere* ~ *terī*.

Etymology: Khabtagaeva 2015c: 98–99

The etymology of the Kott word is unknown. I propose that it is related to the Turkic compound word *tup tere* (cf. Altai *tup tere* 'tanned leather'), which consists of two Turkic words *tup* 'tanned leather' and *täri* 'the skin, hide (*of a human being or animal*'). My etymology may be proven by the lexical meaning. As is well-known, chamois leather is produced from the leather for tanning.

From a phonetic perspective, it is likely that metathesis occurred. In my analysis, metathesis occurred in certain Turkic loanwords with plosive unvoiced consonants *-p-, -t-* or *-k-*, cf. Kott *aktur* 'postp. through' ← Turkic *ötküre* < *ötgürü* 'through', Kott *häteäŋ* 'so' ← Altai Turkic *tekeneŋ* 'in vain, for no particular reason' (< *täkin* 'in vain' *+nAŋ* Ablative), Kott *iptak* 'bread' ← Turkic *itpäk* < *ätmäk* 'bread' (Khabtagaeva 2015d: 139).

See as well Kott *tarei* ~ *tarêi* 'coarse cloth'.

Kott *urum* 'cloth, linen' (Werner 2002/2: 354) ← Turkic *ürüm < *örüm* 'something plaited or woven' < *ȫr-* 'to plait' *-Xm* {Turkic VN, see Erdal 1991: 294}:

cf. Old Turkic *örüm*; NE^S YeniseiT: Khakas *ürīm* 'something plaited or woven' (KhR), cf. *örbek* 'coat; cloth made from black wool; coat made from birds' fluff' (But.); Sagai, Koibal, Kachin *ör-* 'to plait' (R); Shor *örüm* 'mesh' (R); AltaiT: Altai *örüm* 'something plaited; the part of whip'; Qumanda *ür-* 'to plait'; Quu *ör-* 'to plait'; Teleut *örüm* 'weaving'; SayanT: Tuvan *örü-* 'to plait'; Tofan *örü-* 'to plait'; ChulymT *ör-* 'to plait'; NE^N Yakut *ör-* 'to plait'; Dolgan *örǖ* ~ *örü* (< *örgü < *ör-GU {Turkic VN}) 'plait'; NW^N

---

[206] Cf. *dubil'naja koža* 'tanned leather' (Vasmer 1: 547–548).

Siberian Tatar *ürüm* 'braid' (R); NW^S Kirgiz *örüm* 'weaving; the part of whip'; Fu-yü –; Kazak *örĭm* 'weaving', cf. *örme* 'whip'; SE Yellow Uyghur *örme* 'plait, braid, pigtail'.

Etymology: Doerfer TMEN 2: 46–47; Räsänen VEWT 375b; Clauson ED 231b; ESTJa 1974: 544–546; Erdal 1991: 294; SIGTJa 1997: 394–395; Anikin 2000: 97; Nugteren 2011: 476

The Kott word was borrowed from the Siberian Turkic form *ürüm* (cf. Khakas, Siberian Tatar). It is also possible that the initial Kott vowel *u-* was assimilated under the influence of Turkic *-ü-* in the second syllable and borrowed from the form *örüm* (cf. Khakas dialects, Altai Turkic, Chulym). The disappearance of vowel harmony is a typical phonetic feature for Turkic loanwords in Kott. Lexical broadening occurred: Turkic 'something plaited or woven' → Kott 'cloth, linen'.

From an etymological view, the Turkic word *örüm* 'something plaited or woven' derived from the verb *ör-* 'to plait' and and Turkic deverbal noun suffix *-Xm* (for functions on suffix, see Erdal 1991: 294).

The Turkic derivational form *örmek* 'a plaited, knitted or woven garment' (Clauson ED 231b) was borrowed into Mongolic in the form *örmege* 'a kind of coarse fabric'[207] (Doerfer TMEN 2: 46–47; Räsänen VEWT 375b; ESTJa 1974: 545; Nugteren 2011: 476). This Turkic form is also present in Persian (Doerfer TMEN 2: 46–47) and Siberian Russian (Anikin 2000: 97).

1.1.16 Measurements

Kott *kareš ~ kariš* 'span, foot' (Werner 2002/1: 412) ← Turkic **qariš* 'a span, the distance between the tips of the outstretched thumb and little finger' < **qar-Xš* {Turkic VN, see Erdal 1991: 262}:

cf. Old Turkic *qariš*; NE^S YeniseiT: Khakas *xariṣ*; Sagai, Koibal, Kachin *qariṣ*; Kyzyl *χārʲš*; AltaiT: Altai *qariš*; Tuba *kariš*; Qumanda *kariš*; Quu *kariš*; Teleut *qariš*; SayanT: Tuvan *kariš*; Tofan *hariš*; ChulymT *qāriš*; NE^N Yakut *xariṣ*; NW^N Siberian Tatar –; NW^S Kirgiz *kariš*; Fu-yü –; Kazak *qariṣ*; SE Yellow Uyghur *qariṣ*;

Turkic → Samoyedic:

Kamas *kāreš ~ kāres* 'span'.

Etymology: Joki LS 164–165; Räsänen VEWT 238a; Rassadin 1971: 186; Clauson ED 663b; Timonina 1978: 11; ESTJa 1997: 324–326

The Kott forms were borrowed from the Turkic form **qariš*. According to the phonetic shape of the Kott forms, they belong to a later period of borrow-

---

207 Turkic → Mongolic: Middle Mongol: SH *örmege ~ örmüge* 'woollen garment'; Ibn-Muh. *örmege* 'upper garment'; LM *örmöge ~ ermüge(n)* 'coarse fabric made of hair of camel or sheep's wool, etc.'; Modern Mongol: Buryat dial. *ürmege* 'doormat'; Kalmuck *örmg* 'peasant's cloth coat; overcoat'; Dagur –; Khamnigan –.

ing. The Kott consonant š regularly changed from Proto-Yeniseian s in different positions (Starostin 1982: 159–160).

From an etymological point of view, the base of Turkic word is the reconstructed verb *qar-, cf. Old Turkic qarï (< *qar-X) 'the forearm; a cubit, the distance from the elbow to the finger tips', qarba- (< *qar-BA-) 'to grope for (*something which you cannot see*), to grasp with the hands or teeth', and so on (ESTJa 1997: 325–326). The reconstructed verb must be connected with measurement terminology. For the etymology of the Turkic word see as well Räsänen (VEWT 238a) and Clauson (ED 663b).

In addition to Yeniseian, the Turkic word was borrowed into the Samoyedic languages (Joki LS 164–165).

Arin **kemenenčak** 'week' (Werner 2002/1: 422) ← Turkic *kemineŋ čak < kemineŋ (< kem +(X)niŋ) 'measurement' + čak 'time, a point in time, a period of time': < kemineŋ < kem 'measurement' +(X)niŋ {Turkic genitive, see Tenišev 1988: 67} ← Mongolic:

cf. Old Turkic –; NE^S YeniseiT: Khakas kem 'measurement'; AltaiT: Altai kem 'time, period; measurement'; Qumanda kemner (< *kem +nAr {Turkic plural}) 'measurement'; Quu kem 'measurement, period'; Teleut kem 'measurement'; SayanT: Tuvan xemče- 'to measure' (← Mongolic kemǯi-); Tofan hem 'measurement, size, weight'; ChulymT –; NE^N Yakut kem 'unit of measure; limit; measure of time, term'; Dolgan käm 'time, season'; NW^N Siberian Tatar –; NW^S Kirgiz –; Fu-yü –; Kazak –; SE Yellow Yughur –;

Turkic ← Mongolic kem 'measure; size, proportion; limits; measure of time, term':

Middle Mongol: –; LM kem; Modern Mongol: Buryat xem; Khalkha xem; Oirat dial. kem; Dagur kem (E); Khamnigan kem.

Etymology: Räsänen VEWT 250b; Rassadin 1971: 188; Khabtagaeva 2009: 255 + čak 'time, a point in time, a period of time' ← Mongolic:

cf. Old Turkic čāġ; NE^S YeniseiT: Khakas sax 'particle just, exactly'; Sagai, Koibal sā; Kachin, Shor šak 'time'; AltaiT: Altai čak 'age, time'; Tuba čak 'measurement, time, period'; Quu čak 'time, period'; Teleut čak 'time'; SayanT: Tuvan šag 'time, period', cf. šak 'hour, time; clock'; Tofan šaġ 'time, period'; ChulymT –; NE^N Yakut sax 'time'; Dolgan haga 'size', cf. hagïna 'while'; NW^N Siberian Tatar –; NW^S Kirgiz čak 'time; period'; Fu-yü šah 'time'; Kazak šaq 'time, period'; SE Yellow Uyghur čaġ 'time';

Turkic → Samoyedic:

Kamas šaγ 'power, strength'; Mator šak 'power';

Turkic ← Mongolic čaγ 'time, period, season, age; time as general situation ot set of circumstances; tense (*gram.*); hour; clock, watch; weather, climate':

Middle Mongol: Precl.Mo. *čaɣ*; SH *čaq*; HY *čaq* ~ *čaɣ*; YY *ča[q]*; Phags-pa *č'ak*; Muq. *čaq* ~ *čaɣ*; RH *čaq*; LM *čaɣ*; Modern Mongol: Buryat *sag*; Khalkha *cag*; Kalmuck *tsag*; Dagur *čagi* (T); Khamnigan *cag*.

Etymology: Joki LS 280; Räsänen VEWT 95b; Clauson ED 403b–404a; SIGTJa 1997: 67–68; Helimski 1997: 333

The Arin word *kemenenčak* 'week' is a compound word consisting of two Turkic words *kemineŋ* 'measurement' and *čak* 'time, a point in time, a period of time'. The first part of the compound *kemineŋ* probably occurred with the Turkic genitive suffix +(*X*)*niŋ*. The structure of the Arin compound word follows native Yeniseian and Turkic morphological rules. Generally in similar structures in Turkic, the first part uses the genitive suffix, while the second part regularly includes a 3rd person possessive marker. The Yeniseian word-forming structure uses the Turkic genitive marker between the parts of the compound (Khabtagaeva 2015d: 133–134).

From a semantic perspective, the Arin word is problematic. This compound does not occur in Turkic. For this reason, the source of borrowing is unclear. Yenisei Turkic and Altai Turkic varieties for 'week' use the Russian loanword *nedelja*.

From the etymological point of view, both Turkic words are of Mongolic origin. The first one *kem* 'measurement' was borrowed from the Mongolic word *kem* 'measure; size, proportion; limits; measure of time, term' (Räsänen VEWT 250b; Rassadin 1971: 188; Khabtagaeva 2009: 255), while the second one, Turkic *čak* 'time, a point in time, a period of time' was borrowed from the Mongolic word *čaɣ* 'time, period, season, age; hour; clock, watch; weather, climate' (Räsänen VEWT 95b; Clauson ED 403b–404a; SIGTJa 1997: 67–68).

The Mongolic word *čaɣ* 'time, period' was borrowed into Samoyedic via Siberian Turkic, with a special lexical meaning (Joki LS 280; Helimski 1997: 333).

There are Tungusic languages, where the Mongolic word *kem* 'measure; size, proportion; limits' was borrowed directly[208] or via Yakut[209] (SSTMJa 1: 448a; Doerfer 1985: 102; Rozycki 1994: 137).

1.1.17 Terms Pertaining to Taxes and Finance

Kott ***alpan*** 'tribute' (Werner 2002/1: 26) ← Turkic *alban 'tribute' ← Mongolic *alban* 'compulsion, coercion; official obligation or service; tax, impost, tribute; corvée; public use' ← Turkic *al-* 'to take; to seize, collect (*a debt*), receive, accept':

---

208 Mongolic → Tungusic: Common Ewenki *kemd'ur* ~ *kemǰur* 'measure, cup'; Manchu *kemu* ~ *kemun* 'measurement; sample; rule; form'.

209 Mongolic → Turkic: Yakut → Tungusic: *Eastern Ewenki* Tokko, Uchur, Tommot *kēmej* 'measure, measurement'.

cf. NE^S YeniseiT: Khakas *alban* 'tribute' (KhR), cf. '*fig.* man, who pays a tribute' (But.); Sagai *alban* 'tribute, tax' (R), Shor *alban* 'tribute'; AltaiT: Altai *alban* 'tribute; violence, coercion'; Tuba *albïn* '*adverb* by force'; Qumanda *alman* 'tribute'; Quu *albanïg* (< *alban* +*lXG* {Turkic NN, see Erdal 1991: 121}) 'person, who pays a tribute, subject'; Teleut *albatï* (< *alban* +*tU* {Mongolic NN, see Poppe GWM §140}) 'people'; SayanT: Tuvan *alban* tribute; *adverb* necessarily; Tofan *alban* 'tribute'; ChulymT *alban* 'tribute' (R); NE^N Yakut *alban* 'harassment, extortion, begging, bigotry'; Yakut dial. *alban* 'harassment, extortion, begging, bigotry; epidemic disease'; NW^N Siberian Tatar –; NW^S Kirgiz *alman* 'tribute'; Fu-yü –; SE Yellow Uyghur *alva* 'tribute';

Turkic → Samoyedic:

Kamas *alman* 'tax';

Turkic ← Mongolic[210] **alban* 'compulsion, coercion; official obligation or service; tax, impost, tribute; corvée; public use' < **al-bAn*:

cf. Middle Mongol: Precl.Mo. *alban*; HY *alban*; 'Phags-pa *alba*; LM *alban*; Modern Mongol: Buryat *alba*(*n*); Khalkha *alban* 'official'; Kalmuck *alwa* ~ *alwn*; Dagur *alba* (T); Khamnigan *alba*(*n*);

Mongolic ← Turkic *al-* 'to take; to seize, collect (*a debt*), receive, accept; to take off (*a cap, saddle, etc.*); to marry':

cf. Old Turkic *al-*; NE^S YeniseiT: Khakas; Sagai, Koibal, Kachin; Kyzyl; Shor *al-*; AltaiT: Altai; Tuba; Qumanda; Quu; Teleut *al-*; SayanT: Tuvan; Tofan *al-*; ChulymT *al-*; NE^N Yakut; Dolgan *ïl-*; NW^N Siberian Tatar *al-*; NW^S Kirgiz; Fu-yü; Kazak *al-*; SE Yellow Uyghur *al-*.

Etymology: Kałużyński 1962: 62, 130; Doerfer TMEN 2: 110; Räsänen VEWT 16b; Rassadin 1971: 153; 1980: 12, 24, 34, 37, 48; Clauson ED 124b; ESTJa 1974: 448; Timonina 1978: 11; Tatarincev 2000: 96; Anikin 2000: 82; Khabtagaeva 2009: 169

The Kott word clearly was borrowed from Siberian Turkic: it is a Mongolic loanword, but ultimately of Turkic origin. The Mongolic word *alban* 'tribute' is possibly related to the Turkic verb *al-* 'to take; to seize, collect (*a debt*), receive, accept'. The suffix -*bAn* is non-productive in Mongolic languages, it may be connected with suffix +*GAn*, which forms numbers, cf. *ǰirɣuɣan* 'six' (< **ǰir* 'two' and **ɣu* 'three') and *doloɣan* 'seven' (< **dolo*: cf. *doloduɣar* 'seventh'). In turn, the numbers *ɣurban* 'three' and *dörben* 'four' derived with the suffix -*bAn*, which was added to verbal stems ending in consonant +*r*-: **ɣur-* < **ɣu* 'three' (cf. *ɣunan* 'three-year-old animal: bull, ox or tiger') and **dör-* < **dö* 'four' (*dönen* 'four-year-old male animal: bull, camel, or elephant').

---

210 Mongolic → Tungusic: *Ewenki dial.* Barguzin, Nercha *albatu* (< *alban* +*tu* {Mongolic NN, see Poppe GWM §140}) 'relatives'; Udihe *agba* 'government, tribute, public coffers'; Ulcha *alba* 'government, tribute, public coffers'; Nanai *albã* 'government, tribute, public coffers'; Manchu *albabun* 'tribute' (see SSTMJa 1: 30).

Some researchers (for details, see ESTJa 1974: 139) compare the Mongolic word *alban* with Turkic *alp* 'hero', which was not supported by Doerfer (TMEN 2: 110).

The devoicing of the Mongolic cluster *lb* > *lp* is a regular change in Kott.

See as well Kott *alpaka* ~ *alpuga* ~ *alpuka* 'flying squirrel'.

1.1.18   Abstract Nouns Connected with Human Life

Arin *bajšu* 'wealth' (Werner 2002/1: 99) < *baj -šu* {Yeniseian nominalizer} ← Turkic *bay 'rich; a rich man' < *bāy*:

cf. Old Turkic *bāy*; NE^S YeniseiT: Khakas *pay*; Sagai, Koibal, Kachin *pay* (R); Kyzyl *pay* ~ *bay*; Shor *pay*; AltaiT: Altai *bay*; Tuba *bay*; Qumanda *bay*; Quu *pay*; Teleut *pay*; SayanT: Tuvan *bay*; Tofan *bay*; ChulymT *pay*; NE^N Yakut *bāy*; Dolgan *bāy*; NW^N Siberian Tatar *pay*; NW^S Kirgiz *bay*; Fu-yü *bay*; Kazak *bay*; SE Yellow Uyghur *paj* ~ *päy*.

As concerns the etymology of the Turkic word, see Kott *pai* 'rich'.

Kott *d'ili* 'speech' (Werner 2002/1: 223) ← Turkic **tille-* 'to speak, say' < *til* 'the tongue; speech' +*lA-* {Turkic NV, see Erdal 1991: 429}:

cf. Old Turkic *til* 'the tongue' > *tilä-* 'to seek; to desire; to ask for'; NE^S YeniseiT: Khakas *til* > *tile-* 'to seek, to ask for', *tille-* 'to swear, slander'; Sagai, Koibal, Kachin *til* (R); Kyzyl *tiļ* ~ *teļ* ~ *tel*; Shor *til*; AltaiT: Altai *til* > *tile-* 'to ask for, desire', *tilde-* 'to communicate, speak'; Tuba; Qumanda; Quu *til*; Teleut *til*; SayanT: Tuvan *dil*; Tofan *dil* ~ *til*; ChulymT *til*; NE^N Yakut *til*; Dolgan *til*; Yakut dial. *til* 'news'; NW^N Siberian Tatar *til*; NW^S Kirgiz *til* 'language, tongue; abuse, insult; news; *mil.* language, informant'; Fu-yü *dil* 'tongue, language'; Kazak *til*; SE Yellow Uyghur *tel*.

Etymology: Clauson ED 489b, 492a; ESTJa 1980: 228–229, 231–233; SIGTJa 2001: 227–228

The etymology of the Kott word is unknown. As a hypothesis, I propose that it is connected with the Turkic verb **tille-* 'to speak, say', which derived from the noun *til* 'language, tongue' and the Turkic productive denominal verbum suffix +*lA-* (for details on function, see Erdal 1991: 429). The degemination *ll* > *l* and the change from verb to noun occurred at some point. The change of part of speech is typical for some Turkic loanwords in Kott, cf. Kott verb *kalakai* ~ *kalakei* 'to stutter' was borrowed from Turkic noun *kälägäy* 'stammerer, stutterer'. The proposed voicing and palatalization of Turkic initial *t-* > *d'-* is an atypical change which puts the Turkic etymology into question.

Kott *karei* ~ *karuj* ~ *karaul*; Assan *karei* ~ *karuj* ~ *karaul* '*noun* view, look'; Yugh *karábr* '*verb* to guard'; Ket *kalebel* '*verb* to guard, keep watch, lie in wait for' (Werner 2002/1: 412) ← Modern Turkic *karūl < *qaraul* ← Mongolic *qarayul* 'watch, sentry, guard, scout' < *qara-* 'to look at, glance, watch, observe; to regard, consider; to look after, to face' *-GUl* {Mongolic VN, see Poppe GWM §153}:

NE^S YeniseiT: Khakas *xarōl* 'guard; sight' (But.), cf. *xarol* 'front sight of gun'; Kyzyl *χarōte* 'front sight of gun'; Shor *qarol* 'front sight of gun'; AltaiT: Altai *karūl* 'guard'; Tuba *karūlčik* (< *karūl* +*čAK* {Turkic NN/diminutive}) 'guard', *karūlda-* (< *karūl* +*DA-* {Turkic NV}) 'to guard'; Quu *karūl* 'guard'; Teleut *qarūl* ~ *qaraul* 'guard, the border post' (R); SayanT: Tuvan *xarāl* 'guard; observation point'; Tofan *harāl* 'sight (*of weapons*); guard'; ChulymT –; NE^N Yakut *xarabïl* 'guard'; Dolgan *karaul* 'guard' (← ? Russian); NW^N Siberian Tatar *qaraul* 'front sight of gun'; NW^S Kirgiz *karōl* 'guard; observation point, hill; front sight of gun, sight'; Fu-yü *garōl* 'guard'; Kazak *qarawïl* 'guard; sight'; SE Yellow Uyghur –;

Turkic → Samoyedic:

Kamas *kārol* 'sight, front sight of the gun';

Turkic → Siberian Russian *karaul* 'guard; duties on protection of city' (Anikin 2000: 265–266);

Turkic ← Mongolic *qarayul* 'watch, sentry, guard, scout':

cf. Middle Mongol: Precl. Mongol *qarayūl*; SH *qara'ul* 'guard, patrol'; YY *qara-'ul* 'earth foundation built for sentinels or guards to gather intelligence'; Muq. *qara'ūl* 'watch, patrol'; LM *qarayul* 'watch, sentry, guard, scout'; Modern Mongol: Buryat *xarūl* 'guard'; Khalkha *xarūl* 'watch-post; guard, sentry, watch'; Kalmuck *xarūl* 'border guard, call, even sight on the rifle; a mast on the boat'; Dagur *xarōl* (T); Khamnigan *xarūl*.

Etymology: Joki LS 166; Räsänen VEWT 235b–236a; Kałużyński 1962: 73; Doerfer TMEN 1: 399–403; 1985: 138; Rassadin 1980: 37; Ščerbak 1997: 208; ESTJa 1997: 290–291; Schönig 2000: 152; Anikin 2000: 265–266; Khabtagaeva 2009: 170

The Yeniseian words were borrowed from the Turkic form **karūl*, where instead of the long vowel *ū*, the diphthongs *-ei*, *-ui* appeared in the Kott and Assan forms: in these cases the final consonant *-l* was dropped as well. From the semantic point of view, a lexical broadening occurred: the original military term 'guard, observation point' changed to the general meaning of 'view, look'. From a morphological perspective, the original part of speech noun changed to a verb in the Yugh and Ket languages. It is more likely that the Kott and Assan form *karaul* was borrowed via Russian.

The Turkic word is of Mongolic origin. It is widespread in almost all Turkic languages from the Middle Turkic period onward: the word belongs to military terminology (Räsänen VEWT 235b–236a; Doerfer TMEN 1: 399–403; Kałużyński 1962: 73; Rassadin 1980: 37; ESTJa 1997: 290–291; Ščerbak 1997: 208; Schönig 2000: 152; Khabtagaeva 2009: 170).

From Turkic, it was borrowed into the Samoyedic (Joki LS 166) and Russian (Anikin 2000: 265–266) languages.

The word was borrowed directly from Mongolic to the Tungusic languages[211] (SSTMJa 1: 380; Doerfer 1985: 138; Rozycki 1994: 135). There are Tungusic forms where the phonetic shape shows borrowing directly from Russian (Anikin 2000: 266) or Yakut (SSTMJa 1: 380). For borrowings of Mongolic word to different languages, see Doerfer (TMEN 1: 399–403).

The base word is the Common Mongolic verb *qara-* 'to see, to watch' and the productive deverbal noun Mongolic suffix *-GUl*, which forms nouns designating names of occupations (Poppe GWM § 153).

Kott **kasak ~ kasax** 'healthy, health' (Werner 2002/1: 413) ← Turkic **qazïq* 'health' < **qaδïǧ* < *qaδ-* 'to be hard, firm, tough' *-(X)G* {Turkic VN, see Erdal 1991: 172}:

cf. Old Turkic –; NE^S YeniseiT: Khakas *xazïx* 'healthy, health'; Sagai, Koibal *qazïq* (R); Shor *qazïq*; AltaiT: Altai *kadïk*; SayanT: Tuvan *kadïk*; Tofan *qadïq*; ChulymT –; NE^N Yakut –; NW^N Siberian Tatar –; NW^S Kirgiz –; Fu-yü –; SE Yellow Yughur –;
Turkic → Samoyedic:
Kamas *kāzïk* 'healthy'.

Etymology: Joki LS 169; Räsänen VEWT 218a; Rassadin 1971: 216; Timonina 1978: 12; Tatarincev 2004: 45–46; Ölmez 2007: 188

The Kott intervocalic unvoiced *VsV* points to a Yenisei Turkic layer of borrowing, where *VzV* occurs instead of Turkic original intervocalic *VδV*. The devoicing of intervocalic *VzV* > *VsV* is a regular change in the Kott loanwords due to the absence of consonantal *VzV* in the native Yeniseian words.

In turn, the etymology of the Turkic word is unknown. The Sayan Turkic *kadïk* and Yenisei Turkic *qazïq* forms, meaning 'health, healthy,' assume the Proto-Turkic form **qaδïǧ*,[212] which is lacking in Old Turkic. Questionable is the Altai Turkic form *kadïk*, which according to certain hypotheses should be **kayik*. Tatarincev (2004: 45–46), in his *Etymological Dictionary of Tuvan*, connects the word with Old Turkic *qaδïr* 'grim, brutal, oppressive, dangerous', which remains doubtful.

---

211 Mongolic → Tungusic: Ewenki *karulčin* 'shepherd'; Lamut *karguskis ~ kargutkis* 'guard'; Ulcha *qaryaqu* 'observation point'; Orok *qaryajtu* 'id.'; Manchu *qarun* 'observation point'.
212 The original Turkic intervocalic *VδV* is present in Yenisei Turkic as *VzV*, in Sayan Turkic as *VdV* and in Altai Turkic as *VyV*. E.g. Old Turkic *aδaq* 'leg, foot' ~ Khakas *azax*, Tuvan *adak*, Altai *ayak*; Old Turkic *qoδan* 'hare' ~ Khakas *xozan*, Tuvan *kodan*, Altai *koyon*; Old Turkic *bäδük* 'big' ~ Tuvan *bedik*, Altai *biyik*, etc.

1.1.19 Agriculture
Kott **kereunčak** 'hay-mowing' (Werner 2002/1: 422) ← Turkic *kūren čak < kūren 'hay' + čak 'time':

< kürän 'sedge, hay':
> cf. NE^S YeniseiT: Khakas köreŋ [ot] 'sedge', cf. kiren 'quinoa, goose-foot'; AltaiT: Altai köröŋ 'sedge (Carex flava)' (R); Qumanda kūreŋ 'wormwood, sagebrush'; Quu köröŋ 'sedge'; Teleut kürän 'licorice', cf. köröŋ 'sedge (Carex flava)' (R); SayanT –; ChulymT –; NE^N Yakut –; NW^N Siberian Tatar küräŋ 'hay, which mown in the swamp; hay, which consists of sedge'; Remaining lgs. –.

Etymology: Räsänen VEWT 292b; ESTJa 1997: 147–148

+ čak 'time, period' < čāġ ← Mongolic:
> cf. Old Turkic čāġ 'time, a point in time, a period of time'; NE^S YeniseiT: Khakas sax 'particle exactly', cf. saġam 'adverb now, in present moment, in present time'; Sagai, Koibal sā 'time' (R); Kachin, Shor šak 'time' (R); AltaiT: Altai čak 'century, time'; Tuba čak 'measurement, time'; Quu čak 'time, period'; Teleut čak 'time, period' (R); SayanT: Tuvan šag 'time, period', cf. šak 'hour, time; watch, clock'; Tofan šaġ 'time, period'; ChulymT –; NE^N Yakut sax 'time, period'; Dolgan haga 'as, similarly', cf. haġïna 'while, during'; NW^N Siberian Tatar –; NW^S Kirgiz čak 'time, period'; Fu-yü šah 'time'; Kazak šaq 'time, period'; SE Yellow Uyghur čaġ 'time, period'.

Turkic → Samoyedic:
> Kamas šaγ 'power, strength'; Mator šak 'power';

Turkic ← Mongolic čaγ 'time, period, season, age; time as general situation ot set of circumstances; tense (gram.); hour; clock; watch; weather, climate':
> Middle Mongol: SH; HY; Muq. čaq; LM čaγ; Modern Mongol: Buryat sag; Khalkha cag; Kalmuck tsag; Dagur čagi (T); Khamnigan cag.

Etymology: Joki LS 280; Räsänen VEWT 95b; Clauson ED 403b–404a; SIGTJa 1997: 67–68; Helimski 1997: 333

The Kott word belongs to the category of compound words. It consists of two Turkic words: kūren 'hay, sedge,' and čak 'time', which was endowed, in Yenisean, with the new lexical meaning 'time of hay-mowing' → 'hay-mowing'. This is a case where the compound word absent in Turkic, and probably had developed already in Yeniseian.

The diphthong -eu- in the second syllable of the Kott word probably developed from the Turkic long vowel -ū- in the first syllable.

The etymology of the first Turkic compound is not clear. Because of its rare spread in Turkic languages, Levitskaja (ESTJa 1997: 147–148), after Ramstedt (KWb 1935: 248a), compares the Turkic data with the Mongolic word kürmeli ~ kürümeli 'sedge, carex' (Lessing 506b). For the etymology of the second part of the Turkic compound word čak 'time, period', which is of Mongolic origin, see Räsänen (VEWT 95b), Clauson (ED 403b–404a) and Tenišev (SIGTJa 1997: 67–68).

Kott *šaban* 'plough' (Werner 2002/2: 436) ← Turkic *saban 'plough':
    cf. Old Turkic *saban*; NE^S YeniseiT: Kachin *saban* 'wood plough' (But.); Kyzyl *saban* 'ploughshare'; AltaiT: –; SayanT –; ChulymT *sabanoġ* < *saban* 'plough' +*AK* {Turkic NN/diminutive} 'pitchfork'; NE^N –; NW^N Siberian Tatar –; NW^S Kirgiz –; Fu-yü –; Kazak *saban* 'plough'; SE Yellow Yughur –.

Etymology: Räsänen VEWT 402a; Clauson ED 790a; Timonina 1986: 73; ESTJa 2003: 127–128; Anikin 2000: 469

The Kott word was borrowed from the Turkic form *saban. The change of Turkic initial consonant *s*- > *š*- in Kott is a typical phonetic feature for native Yeniseian words (Starostin 1982: 158), which points to an early period of borrowing.

The Turkic word belongs to agriculture terminology. As we know, Turkic Siberian people were nomads and it was not a typical occupation for them. It seems to have spread via areal contact in Siberia. Nowdays it is present in Yenisei Turkic dialects and in Chulym Turkic. Even though I could not locate this term in any dictionary, it may well have existed in Siberian Tatar, albeit now disappeared, cf. Literary Tatar *saban* 'plough' (TatR 459a).

The Turkic word was borrowed into Siberian Russian (Anikin 2000: 469).

Kott *šičir*; Arin *šižir* 'straw' (Werner 2002/2: 444):
    cf. Turkic *čïjïr* 'straw' ← Chinese:
        cf. NE^S YeniseiT: Khakas *sïzïr*; Sagai *čïjïr*; SE Yellow Uyghur *sïzï*; Remaining lgs. –;
Turkic → Samoyedic:
    Kamas *sïzïr* 'straw';
Turkic ← Chinese *xízi* 'straw mat' (KitR 642b).

Etymology: Joki LS 271; Roos 2000: 367

The both the Yeniseian and Samoyedic Kamas words are obviously connected to the Khakas word *sïzïr* 'straw.' Joki (LS 271) refers to it as a Turkic loanword in Kamas. But the etymology of the word is uncertain. Between the Siberian Turkic varieties it is present only in Khakas and its Sagai dialect. The word was probably borrowed from a third language. There is similar phonetic form *sïzï* with the same meaning in Yellow Uyghur. Roos (2000: 367) marks it as a Chinese loanword.

The reconstructed borrowed form might be *čïjïr (cf. Sagai). The change of initial consonant *č*- > *š*- in Kott and Arin is regular phonetic feature for native Yeniseian words (Starostin 1982: 161), which points to an early layer of borrowing.

Kott *taripan* 'field' (Werner 2005: 117) < Turkic *tarï- 'to cultivate ground' + Yeniseian *paŋ* 'earth, ground' (Werner 2002/2: 52[213]):
< *tarï*- 'to cultivate ground':
    cf. Old Turkic *tarï*-; NE[S] YeniseiT: Khakas *tarï*-; Sagai, Koibal, Kachin *tara*-; AltaiT: Altai *tarï*-; Quu *tara*-; Teleut *tarï*-; SayanT: Tuvan; Tofan *tarï*-; ChulymT *tara*-; NE[N] Yakut –; NW[N] Siberian Tatar –; NW[S] Kirgiz *tarï*-; Fu-yü *darï*- 'to plant'; Kazak *tarï* 'millet'; SE Yellow Uyghur *tarï*- ~ *taru*-;

Turkic → Samoyedic:
    Kamas *tarlïr* (← *tarlïġ < *tarï-lXG* {Turkic VN}) 'field'.

Etymology: Joki LS 314–316; Doerfer TMEN 2: 480–482; 1985: 77; Räsänen VEWT 464b; Clauson ED 532b; SSTMJa 2: 168b; ESTJa 1980: 157–159; SIGTJa 1997: 465–467; Ölmez 2007: 270b

The Kott word belongs to the category of hybrid words. It consists of a Turkic verb *tarï*- 'to cultivate ground,' and a Kott noun *paŋ* 'earth, ground' of Yeniseian origin. The Turkic component was borrowed from the form *tarï- (Khabtagaeva 2015d: 141–142). The change of Turkic back vowel -*ï*- to front -*i*- is a regular change for Turkic loanwords in Kott.

For details on Turkic etymology and data, see Räsänen (VEWT 464b), Clauson (ED 532b), Sevortjan (ESTJa 1980: 157–159) and Tenišev (SIGTJa 1997: 465–467).

The Turkic verb was borrowed into Mongolic[214] (Nugteren 2011: 512–513) and further from Mongolic to Tungusic[215] (SSTMJa 2: 168b; Doerfer 1985: 77). From Mongolic the word was re-borrowed into Tuvan[216] (Khabtagaeva 2009: 158). Cf. also Hungarian *tarló* 'plough field, arable field, stubble field,' which is of Turkic origin[217] (Róna-Tas & Berta WOT 2011: 865–866).

1.1.20   Art, Writing, Science and Entertainment

Kott *ajaŋ* 'play; game' (Werner 2002/1: 19) ← Turkic *oyïn < *oyun* 'game, play, merriment':

---

213   Cf. also Werner indicates as a half-suffix -*baŋ* in Ket and Yugh (Werner 2002/1: 102).
214   Turkic → Mongolic 'to sow, plant; to plow': cf. Precl.Mo. *tari*-; Muq. *tari*-; Leiden *tara*-; LM *tari*-; Modern Mongol: Khalkha; Buryat *tari*-; Oirat dial. *tär*-; Dagur *tar'*- (E); Khamnigan *tari*-.
215   Turkic → Mongolic → Tungusic 'to sow, plant; to plow': *Ewenki dial.* Barguzin, Nercha *tari*-; Solon *tar*-; Oroch *tariko*- ~ *tariku*-; Udehe *tali*-; Ulcha *tari*-; Nanai *tari*-; Manchu *tari*-.
216   Turkic → Mongolic: LM *tariyan* 'grain, corn, wheat; crop; field, farm' (< *tari*- 'to sow, plant; to plow' -*GAn* {Mongolic VN}) → Modern Turkic: Tuvan *tarā* 'grain, corn, wheat'.
217   Turkic: West Old Turkic *tarïlaɣ (< *tarï-lXG*) → Hungarian *tarló* [*tårlō*] 'plough field, arable field, stubble field'.

cf. Old Turkic *oyun* > *oyna-* 'to play (*a game, musical instrument*)'; NE^S YeniseiT: Khakas *oyïn* 'game, fun; joke' (KhR), cf. 'game; circle dance at the wedding' (But.); Sagai, Koibal, Kachin *oyïn* 'game, joke' (R); Shor *oyun* 'game, fun'; AltaiT: Altai *oyïn* 'game, fun'; Tuba *oyïn* 'game, festival'; Qumanda *oyïn* 'game'; Quu *oyïn* 'game, joke; playing a musical instrument, singing'; Teleut *oyïn* 'game, joke' (R); SayanT: Tuvan *oyun* 'game; joke'; Tofan *oin ~ öen* 'game'; ChulymT *oyïn* 'game, joke' (R); NE^N Yakut *ōnńū* 'game, joke, fun; recreation, fun, party; performance'; Dolgan *ōnńū* 'game'; NW^N Siberian Tatar *uyna-* 'to dance'; NW^S Kirgiz *oyun* 'game, fun, joke'; Fu-yü *ōnüm* 'play' < *ōnï-* 'to play'; Kazak *oyïn* 'game, fun, joke, mischief, interference'; SE Yellow Uyghur *oin* 'game, play'.

Etymology: Rassadin 1971: 211; Clauson ED 274a; ESTJa 1974: 435–437

The Kott word has a clear Turkic etymology. The source of borrowing may be the Yenisei Turkic or Altai Turkic form *oyïn. The changes of initial Turkic *o-* > *a-* and the final Turkic *-n* > *-ŋ* are regular in Kott.

Kott ***kat*** 'paper' (Werner 2002/1: 415) ← Turkic *qat < *qāt* < *qaġat* 'paper' ← Persian:

cf. Old Turkic *kegde* 'paper'; NE^S YeniseiT: Khakas *xat* 'letter' (But.); Koibal *keġdä* 'thick paper' (R); Shor *qaġat* 'diary', cf. *qat* 'paper'; AltaiT: Altai *kat* 'letter'; Qumanda *kat* 'letter; paper', cf. *kagat* 'paper'; Quu *kat* 'letter', cf. *kagat* 'paper'; Teleut *qat* 'letter, charter'; SayanT –; ChulymT *qat* 'letter, paper'; NE^N Yakut –; NW^N Siberian Tatar –; NW^S Kirgiz *kat* 'letter, handwriting'; Fu-yü –; SE Yellow Uyghur *kegde* 'paper';

Turkic ← Persian *kāghaz*, *kāghiz* 'paper; a letter'.[218]

Etymology: Räsänen VEWT 219b; Clauson ED 710a; Timonina 1978: 10; 1986: 72; Stachowski 2004: 196; Pomorska 2012: 302

The Kott word was borrowed from the Turkic form *qat. The preservation of initial consonant *q-* points to a later layer of borrowing; in native Yeniseian words changed to *h-*.

From an etymological point of view, the Turkic word originated from a Persian loanword (Räsänen VEWT 219b, Clauson ED 710a; Stachowski 2004: 196). The word belongs to the category of cultural-specific words.

Kott ***šašin*** 'paper' (Werner 2002/2: 437) ← Turkic *časïn (< *časïn*) 'paper' ← Mongolic *čaγasun* < *čaγarsun* 'paper':

---

[218] Cf. another semantic meaning in Persian 'a charter or patent, presented by the kings of Persia to those whom they mean to honour, and by virtue of which the governors of every district through which the holder of it travels must supply him, the moment he presents it, with carriages and every necessary to which his rank is entitled'.

cf. NE^S YeniseiT: Khakas *čazïn* ~ *čajïn*; Sagai, Koibal *sazïn*; Sagai, Beltir *čäčïn* (R); AltaiT: Altai *čāzïn* 'paper; money'; Qumanda *čazïn* 'paper, bank note'; Quu *čažïn*; SayanT: Tuvan *sāzïn*; Tofan *sāzïn* 'paper, document; letter'; ChulymT –; NE^N Yakut *jārsïn* ~ *ńārsïn* 'book' (Pek.); Fu-yü *čāsïn*; Remaining lgs. –;

Turkic → Samoyedic:

Kamas *sāzïn* ~ *sāzen* ~ *sažïn* 'paper, rubel';

Turkic ← Mongolic **čāsun* < **čaɣarsun*[219] < **ča* 'white'+GAn+r-sUn {Mongolic NN, NV, VN, see Khabtagaeva 2001: 115}:

Middle Mongol: cf. Precl.Mo. *čaɣasun*; SH; HY *ča'alsun*; Muq. *čālsun*; LM *čaɣasu(n)* ~ *čaɣalsu(n)* ~ *čaɣarsu(n)* 'paper'; Modern Mongol: Buryat *sārha(n)* 'paper'; Khalkha *cās(an)* 'paper; note (*money*); tugrig'; Kalmuck *tsāsn*; Dagur *čās* (E); Khamnigan *cārsa(n)*.

Etymology: Joki LS 262; Kałużyński 1962: 46; Räsänen VEWT 94b; Rassadin 1971: 226; 1980: 11, 13, 23, 29, 30, 37, 63; Tatarincev 1976: 84; Timonina 1986: 73; Khabtagaeva 2001: 115; 2009: 216; 2015a: 114

The Kott word was borrowed from Siberian Turkic (Timonina 1986: 73). The donor form might be **časïn* with the devoiced intervocalic consonant *VsV*, which came from the form *čazïn* with voiced intervocalic *VzV*, which is typical for Yenisei Turkic and Altai Turkic varieties. My suggestion is buttressed by the regular phonetic changes in Kott: *č-* > *š* (Starostin 1982: 161) and *VsV* > *VšV* (Starostin 1982: 159). Both changes are particular not to only Turkic loanwords, but to native Yeniseian words as well, which point to an early layer of borrowing.

The Turkic forms are obviously borrowed from Mongolic *čaɣasun* 'paper' (Kałużyński 1962: 46; Räsänen VEWT 94b; Rassadin 1971: 226; 1980: 11, 13, 23, 29, 30, 37, 63; Tatarincev 1976: 84; Khabtagaeva 2009: 216). The non-productive base of the Mongolic word is the form **ča*, which connects to the word used to designate the colour white, cf. Literary Mongolian *čayi-* (< **ča+yi-*) 'to be[come] white, turn pale; to turn grey (*of hair*); to dawn, grow light', *časun* (< **ča+sUn*) 'snow', *čaɣan* (< **ča+GAn*) 'white' (Khabtagaeva 2001: 130; 2009: 216).

The Samoyedic Mator word *sarhun* 'paper' was directly borrowed from Buryat (Helimski 1997: 335). The Kamas forms were clearly borrowed from Siberian Turkic (Joki LS 262).

Kott *toi* ~ *tui* 'wedding' (Werner 2002/2: 271) ← Turkic **toy* 'a feast; a wedding feast' < *tōy*:

---

219 The reconstruction is of Poppe (1954: 241).

cf. Old Turkic *tōy* 'a camp; a community; large gathering; a feast; a wedding feast'; NE^S YeniseiT: Khakas *toy* 'a feast; a wedding feast'; Sagai, Koibal, Kachin *toy* (R); Kyzyl *toy* ~ *tōy*; Shor *toy*; AltaiT: Altai *toy*; Tuba *toy*; Qumanda *toy*; Quu *toy*; Teleut *toy*; SayanT: Tuvan *doy*; Tofan *toy*; ChulymT *toy*; NE^N Yakut –; NW^N Siberian Tatar –; NW^S Kirgiz *toy*; Fu-yü *doy*; Kazak *toy*; SE Yellow Uyghur *toy*;
Turkic → Samoyedic:
Kamas *toi* 'wedding'; Mator *toi* 'wedding'.

Etymology: Joki LS 327–328; Räsänen VEWT 488b; Doerfer TMEN 3: 352–355; Ščerbak 1970 SF: 197; Clauson ED 566b; Timonina 1978: 11; SIGTJa 1997: 309; Helimski 1997: 364; Anikin 2000: 549

The Kott word was clearly borrowed from Turkic (Doerfer TMEN 3: 354; Timonina 1978: 11). In the Kott forms, the fluctuation *o* ~ *u* occurred.

It is unknown what the original Turkic form was. Räsänen reconstructs the form *toń (Räsänen VEWT 488b); Clauson marks with final -*y* and long vowel -*ō*- (Clauson ED 566b). According to Ščerbak (1970 SF: 197), the original vowel was short.

From Siberian Turkic, the word was borrowed into Samoyedic (Joki LS 327–328; Helimski 1997: 364), and Siberian Russian (Anikin 2000: 549). The Turkic word is present in Mongolic.[220]

1.1.21 Military Terminology

Kott *d'ida* 'spear' (Werner 2002/1: 222) ← Turkic **d'ida* 'spear' < *ǰida* ← Mongolic *ǰida* 'spear, javelin, bayonet':

cf. Old Turkic –; NE^S YeniseiT: Khakas *čïda*; Sagai *čïda* (R); Koibal, Kachin *ǰïda* (R); Shor *čïda* 'bayonet of gun; sting'; AltaiT: Altai *d'ïda*; Tuba *d'ïda*; Quu *d'ïda*; Teleut *ǰïda* (R); SayanT: Tuvan *čïda*; Tofan *čïda*; ChulymT *čïda* ~ *yida*; Remaining lgs –;

Turkic ← Mongolic *ǰida* 'spear, javelin, bayonet':
Middle Mongol: Precl.Mo. *ǰida*; SH; HY; ZY; YY *ǰida*; Muq.; Ist. *ǰida*; RH *ǰida*; LM *ǰida*; Modern Mongol: Buryat *žada*; Khalkha *ǰad*; Oirat dial. *džidīi*; Dagur *gⁱad* (← Manchu) (E); Khamnigan *džida*;

cf. Tungusic *gida* 'spear':
Northern Tungusic: Ewenki *gida*; Solon *gida*; Lamut *gid*; Negidal *gida*; Southern Tungusic: Oroch; Udihe *gida*; Ulcha; Orok; Nanai *γida*; Jurchen *kîh-tāh*; Manchu *gida*.

Etymology: Räsänen VEWT 106b; Rassadin 1971: 199; 1980: 21, 37, 45, 55, 64; SST-MJa 1: 148b–149a; Timonina 1978: 9; 1986: 73; Doerfer 1985: 24; Nugteren 2011: 387; Khabtagaeva 2015a: 116

---

220 Turkic → Mongolic: Middle Mongol: –; LM *toi* 'wedding feast, banquet'; Modern Mongol: Buryat *toi* [*bayar*] 'feast'; Khalkha *toi* 'wedding feast'; Kalmuck –; Dagur –; Khamnigan –.

The Kott word was borrowed from the Siberian Turkic form *d'ida, which points to an Altai Turkic layer of borrowing of a later period.

The Turkic forms were borrowed from Mongolic *jida* 'spear, javelin, bayonet' (Rassadin 1971: 199; 1980: 21, 37, 45, 55, 64). The word appears in almost all Middle Mongol sources and Modern Mongol languages (Nugteren 2011: 387). The etymology of the Mongolic word is not clear. Räsänen (VEWT 106b), after Ramstedt (KWb 108b), connects the Mongolic word with Tungusic Manchu *gida* 'spear'. Doerfer considers it appropriate to link the word with Chinese *giat (Doerfer 1985: 24). Rozicki (1994: 89), on a phonetical basis, refers the Manchu word to the Mongolic "pre-loan correspondence".

Kott *kaleš* ~ *kališ* 'sword' (Werner 2002/1: 405) ← Turkic *qïlïš < qïlïč 'sword':

cf. Old Turkic *qïlïč*; NE^S YeniseiT: Khakas *xïlïs*; Sagai, Koibal *qïlïs*; Kyzyl *χeliš* ~ *χiliš*; Shor *qïlïš*; AltaiT: Altai *qïlïš*; Tuba *kïlïč*; Qumanda *kïliš* ~ *kïlïč*; Quu *kïlïč* ~ *kïlïš*; Teleut *qïlïš*; SayanT: Tuvan *xïlïš* 'sword; *fig.* tusk'; ChulymT *qïlïc* (R); NE^N Yakut *kïlïs* 'knife; sabre'; NW^N Siberian Tatar –; NW^S Kirgiz *kïlïč*; Fu-yü –; Kazak *qïlïš*; SE Yellow Uyghur *qïlïš*;

Turkic → Samoyedic:

Kamas *kališ* ~ *kaleš* 'sword'.

Etymology: Joki LS 154; Räsänen VEWT 263b; Doerfer TMEN 3: 496–498; Clauson ED 618a; Timonina 1978: 9; 1986: 73; ESTJa 2000: 212–214

The Kott form is closer to the Samoyedic form. According to its phonetic shape, the Yeniseian form might have been borrowed into Kamas. The change of the Turkic vowel -*ï*- > -*a*- in the first syllable can be explained by Yeniseian stress patterns.

From an etymological point of view, the Kott form was undoubtedly borrowed from Turkic (Timonina 1986: 73). The final consonant -*š* in Kott points to the Yenisei Turkic layer (cf. Kyzyl and Shor data).

According to Levitskaja (ESTJa 2000: 212–214), the base of the Turkic word is *qïl with the meaning of 'sharp', cf. Nogay *qïlau* 'own', Yakut *qïlān* 'blade, tip', Yakut *qïlqan* 'own', etc.

The Turkic word was borrowed into Samoyedic (Joki LS 154) and New Persian (Doerfer TMEN 3: 496–498).

Arin *sulem'a* 'sabre'; Kott *pačasulema* 'sabre' (Werner 2002/2: 172) < Yeniseian *pača* 'big, large' (Werner 2002/2: 51) + *sulema*:
sulema ← Russian *sulema* 'sword, sabre' ← Turkic *seleme* 'sabre, sword' ← Mongolic *seleme* 'weapon' ← Tungusic *seleme* 'sabre, sword' < *sele* 'iron' +*mA* {NN/adj., see Vasilevič 1958: 769; Boldyrev 1987: 79}:

cf. Old Turkic –; NE^S YeniseiT: Khakas *selmey* 'sword, weapon'; AltaiT: –; SayanT: Tuvan *seleme* 'sabre, sword'; Tofan *seleme* 'sabre'; ChulymT –; NE^N Yakut –; NW^N Siberian Tatar –; NW^S Kirgiz *selebe* 'sabre, sword'; Fu-yü –; Kazak *selebe* 'large kitchen knife'; SE Yellow Uyghur –;

Turkic ← Mongolic *seleme*:

cf. Middle Mongol: –; LM *selem-e* 'sabre, sword'; Modern Mongol: Buryat *helme*; Lower Uda Buryat *helme* ~ *xelme*; Khalkha *selem*; Kalmuck *selm^ä*; Dagur *səlmī* (E); Khamnigan *selme(n)*;

Mongolic: Buryat → Samoyedic:

Mator *helme* 'sword';

Mongolic ← Tungusic *seleme*:

Northern Tungusic: Ewenki *selmi* 'metal weapon'; Solon *selem* ~ *selemen* 'sabre'; Negidal *seleme* 'metal'; Southern Tungusic: Manchu *seleme* ~ *selemu* 'sword'; Ulcha; Oroch *seleme* 'metal'.

Etymology: Räsänen VEWT 409a; Rassadin 1971: 102; SSTMJa 2: 140; Helimski 1997: 243; Anikin 2000: 510; SIGTJa 2001: 412–413; Anikin 2000: 510–511; Werner 2002/2: 172; Stachowski 2004; Khabtagaeva 2009: 192; Nugteren 2011: 486

The Kott form belongs to the category of compound hybrid words: the first part *pača* 'big, large' is of Yeniseian origin (Khabtagaeva 2015d: 139). In both Yeniseian forms the change of -*e*- > -*u*- in the first syllable occurred. As for the Yeniseian words, it has been mentioned that they are connected with Turkic (Werner 2002/2: 172).

The etymology of the word has been examined by Stachowski (2004). According to him (2004: 137), the Arin word was borrowed through Russian. This hypothesis can be explained by the presence of the vowel -*u*- instead of original -*e*- in the first syllable. This view is supported by Anikin (2000: 510–511). There is the Siberian Russian form *suleme* 'weapon', where probably the vowel -*u*- in the first syllable developed under the influence of another Russian word with a similar meaning *sulica* 'spear, lance' (Anikin 2000: 511).

From an etymological point of view, the Turkic forms were borrowed from Mongolic, while ultimately the word is of Tungusic origin. The base of the word is the Tungusic word *sele* 'iron', cf. other Tungusic derived words from this base: Northern Tungusic: Ewenki dial. *seleptin*[221] 'nail'; Negidal *selesix*[222] 'chain armor'; Southern Tungusic: Oroch *selente*[223] 'ore; solidified layer of ash in

---

221 < *sele* +*ptun* {Ewenki NN, see Vasilevič 1958: 784}.
222 < *sele* +*six* {Negidal NN, see Boldyrev 1987: 41}.
223 < *sele* +*ntA* {?}. I did not find any information about this suffix, it may connect with another Oroch denominal noun suffix +*ptA* (for details, see Boldyrev 1987: 128).

the hearth'; Ulcha, Orok *selesu*,[224] cf. Nanai *selesũ* 'chainmail, armor'; Manchu *seleŋge*[225] '*adj.* iron', etc. (For more examples, see SSTMJa 2: 140). The form *seleme* is derived from the base *sele* and the Common Tungusic denominal noun suffix +*mA*, which forms adjectival suffixes[226] (Boldyrev 1987: 79; Vasilevič 1958: 769; Avrorin 2000: 129).

The Tungusic word belongs to the category of cultural words; it is widespread in the European territory via Hungarian (for details, see Stachowski 2004: 137).

From Buryat, the word was borrowed into Samoyedic (Helimski 1997: 243).

1.2 Adjectives

1.2.1 Colour Names

Kott ***ala*** 'dappled' (Werner 2002/1: 24) ← Turkic *ala 'parti-coloured, dappled, mottled, spotted' < *āla*:

> cf. Old Turkic *āla*; NE[S] YeniseiT: Khakas *ala* 'skewbald, mottled'; Kyzyl *ala* 'colourful, spotted'; Shor *ala* 'colourful, spotted, striped' (R); AltaiT: Altai *ala* ~ *ölö* 'skewbald, mottled'; Tuba *ala* 'skewbald, mottled, striped, with large spots'; Qumanda *ala* 'skewbald, mottled'; Quu *ala* 'skewbald, mottled'; Teleut *ala* 'colourful, spotted, striped' (R); SayanT: Tuvan *ala* 'skewbald, mottled, striped'; Tofan *ala* 'skewbald, mottled'; ChulymT *ala* 'skewbald, mottled'; NE[N] Yakut *ala* 'skewbald, mottled, with white stripes'; Yakut dial. *ala* 'skewbald'; NW[N] Siberian Tatar *ala* 'skewbald, mottled, striped, with large spots'; NW[S] Kirgiz *ala* 'skewbald, mottled'; Fu-yü –; Kazak *ala* 'skewbald, mottled, not similar'; SE Yellow Uyghur *ala* 'mottled, colourful, grey-haired';

Turkic → Samoyedic:

> Kamas *ala* 'skewbald'.

Etymology: Laude-Cirtautas 1961: 70–76; Joki LS 61; Räsänen VEWT 15a; Rassadin 1971: 152; Clauson ED 126a; ESTJa 1974: 129; Doerfer TMEN 2: 95–96; SIGTJa 2001: 607; Rybatzki 2006: 93, 105; Nugteren 2011: 267; Róna-Tas & Berta WOT 2011: 59–62

The Kott word was clearly borrowed from Turkic.

It is present in almost all Turkic languages, usually used for the colour of birds, animals, plants, and so on (for details, see Laude-Cirtautas 1961: 70–76).

---

224 < *sele* +*sU* {Tungusic NN, see Boldyrev 1987: 42}.
225 < *sele* +*ŋgA* {Manchu NN/adj., see Boldyrev 1987: 146}.
226 E.g. Tungusic: Ewenki, Negidal *mōma* 'wooden' < *mō* 'wood, tree'; Oroch *ōktomo* 'herbal' < *ōkto* 'grass'; Udihe *meɲume* '*adj.* silver' < *meɲu* 'silver'; Ulcha *γiramsama* 'osseous' < *γiramsa* 'bone'; Orok *xujeme* 'corneous' < *xuje* 'horns'; Nanai *simatama* 'snowy' < *simata* 'snow'; Manchu *senggime* 'close friend, who is like a relative' < *senggi* 'blood'. In Manchu language the suffix +*mA* forms also adverbs (for details, see Avrorin 2000: 129).

Clauson (ED 126a) reconstructs the original long vowel *ā* in the first syllable (cf. Turkmen *āla* and Khalaj *hāla*). It seems that the initial *h-* in Khalaj is not original, as it is not reflected in Mongolic (cf. Middle Mongol, for details see Nugteren 2011: 267; Róna-Tas & Berta WOT 2011: 61).

The Turkic word was borrowed into Samoyedic (Joki LS 61), Mongolic[227] (Doerfer TMEN 2: 95–96; Nugteren 2011: 267), Tungusic[228] (Doerfer 1985: 75; SSTMJa 1: 27b) and Hungarian[229] (Róna-Tas & Berta WOT 2011: 59–62).

Kott ***bosarak*** 'ruddy colored (*said of red fox fur*)' (Werner 2002/1: 143) ← Turkic *bozraq < *bōz* 'grey, brown' +*rAK* {Turkic NN, forms elatives and comparatives, see Erdal 1991: 62}:

cf. NE[S] YeniseiT: Khakas *pozrax* ~ *pozïrax* 'chestnut (*of a horse*); Sunday'; Sagai *pozrak* 'fox' (R); Kachin *pozraq kün* 'Sunday' (R):
< *boz* < *bōz* 'grey':

cf. Old Turkic *bōz* 'grey'; NE[S] YeniseiT: –; AltaiT: Altai *pos* (R); Tuba *bos*; Qumanda *pos*; Quu *pos* 'grey; twilight, dawn'; Teleut *pos*; SayanT: Tuvan *bos* 'grey duck, drake'; Tofan *bos* 'mallard'; ChulymT –; NE[N] Yakut –; NW[N] Siberian Tatar *pōs*; NW[S] Kirgiz *boz* 'grey, grey (*of a horse*); dark-complexioned'; Fu-yü *bos* 'grey'; Kazak *boz* 'whitish-grey (*colour of animal fur*); white'; SE Yellow Uyghur *poz* 'reddish, whitish-grey, grey';
Turkic → Samoyedic:

Kamas *bōzrä* 'chestnut'; cf. *bōzera* 'chestnut (*of a horse*)'.

Etymology: Joki LS 100–101; Laude-Cirtautas 1961: 87; Räsänen VEWT 82a; Clauson ED 388b; ESTJa 1978: 173

The Kott word was borrowed from the Siberian Turkic form *bozrak (cf. Khakas and Sagai forms).

In Khakas it designates the chestnut colour of a horse, while in Sagai it specifies the animal known as the fox. From morphological side, the base of the Turkic word is the colour name *bōz* 'grey, brown' and Turkic denominal noun suffix +*rAK*, which forms elatives and comparatives (for details on function, see Erdal 1991: 62). This derived form was borrowed into Samoyedic as well (Joki LS 100–101).

---

227   Turkic → Mongolic 'multicoloured, parti-coloured, spotted, variegated, motley; heterogeneous, of many kinds': Middle Mongol: SH *alaq*; HY *alaq*; Muq. *ala* (← Turkic); LM *alaγ*; Modern Mongol: Buryat, Khalkha *alag*; Kalmuck *alg*; Dagur *alār* (E); Khamnigan *alag*.
228   Mongolic → Tungusic: *Ewenki dial.* Barguzin, Nepa, Uchur *alāγ* 'skewbald, mottled'.
      Cf. also Turkic: Yakut → Tungusic: *Ewenki dial.* Aldan, Zeya, Chumikan *ala* 'skewbald, mottled (*of a reindeer*)'; Lamut *ala* 'mottled'.
229   Turkic: West Old Turkic *alačï < *ala* +*č* {Turkic NN} → Hungarian *alacs* [*ålåč*] 'pied (*of an animals' coat*)'.

It is possible that in the Kott form the epenthesis change occurred in the consonant cluster -zr-. The devoicing of the Turkic sibilant consonant VzV to VsV in Kott is a regular phonetic change, due to the absence of VzV in the original Yeniseian words.

The base of the Turkic form is colour name *bōz* with original long vowel (For the etymology of the Turkic word, see Laude-Cirtautas 1961: 87; Räsänen VEWT 82a; Clauson ED 388b; ESTJa 1978: 173).

The Turkic word was borrowed into Mongolic[230] (Nugteren 2011: 285) and then re-borrowed into Modern Turkic[231] (Khabtagaeva 2009: 267).

Kott *čôgor* 'coloured' (Werner 2002/1: 166) ← Turkic **čōkur* 'variegated, multicoloured' ← Mongolic *čoqor* ~ *čooqor* 'variegated, dappled, spotted, motled; pock-marked':

cf. NE^S YeniseiT: Khakas *čoxïr* 'variegated, multicoloured'; Sagai, Koibal *soqïr* 'colourful, spotted' (R); Kachin; Shor *šokur* 'colourful, variegated; the striped squirrel' (R); Kyzyl *šōχχe·r* ~ *šōχχo·r* 'mottled'; AltaiT: Altai *čokur* 'spotted, striped; decoration'; Tuba *čokur* 'dappled (*of a horse*)'; Qumanda *čokur* ~ *čōkur* ~ *čokïr* 'spotted, striped, dappled'; Quu *čōr* 'variegated'; Teleut *čoqïr* 'variegated, multicoloured, dappled' (R); SayanT: Tuvan *šokar* 'mottled, speckled, spotted; painted, decorated with ornaments'; Tofan *sōhor* 'variegated'; ChulymT *cokur* 'colourful' (R); NE^N Yakut *čuoğur* 'variegated, multicoloured'; Dolgan *čūgur* 'multicoloured'; NW^N Siberian Tatar *čïbar* 'gray, gray dappled, spotted (*of a horse*)'; NW^S Kirgiz *čokur* 'variegated' (R); Fu-yü –; SE Yellow Uyghur *čoqur* 'spotted (*of a horse*)';

Turkic ← Mongolic *čoqor* 'variegated, dappled, spotted, motled; pockmarked':

cf. Middle Mongol: Muq. *čōqur* 'mottled'; ZY *čouqor* 'horse with white spots'; LM *čoqor* ~ *čooqor* 'variegated, dappled, spotted, motled; pockmarked'; Modern Mongol: Buryat *sōxor* 'mottled; *fig.* semi-consciousness'; Khalkha *cōxor* 'spotted, speckled; pock-marked'; Oirat dial. *tsōxăr* ~ *tsōxŏr* ~ *tsōxŭr* 'speckled, spotted (*of a horse*)'; Dagur *čōkur* (E); Khamnigan *cōxor*.

Etymology: Kałużyński 1962: 36; Räsänen VEWT 114b; Rassadin 1971: 117; 1980: 72; Timonina 1978: 8; Khabtagaeva 2001: 96; 2009: 237

---

230 Turkic **borŏ* → Mongolic *boro* 'grey, brown; dark, swarthy (*face*); plain, simple, ordinary; coarse, rough': Middle Mongol: SH; Precl.Mo, HY *boro* 'grey'; Muq. *bora*; LM *boro*; Modern Mongol: Buryat *boro*; Khalkha *bor*; Kalmuck *bor°*; Dagur *bor* (E); Khamnigan *boro*.
231 Turkic → Mongolic → Modern Turkic: NE^S YeniseiT: Khakas *pora* 'grey (*of a horse*)'; Sagai, Koibal, Shor *pora* 'whitish (*of a horse*)' (R); AltaiT: Altai *boro* 'grey'; Tuba *bor(o)* 'gray', cf. *poro* 'grey'; Qumanda *boro* 'grey, brown', cf. *poro* 'grey'; Teleut *poro* 'whitish (*of a horse*)' (R); SayanT: Tuvan *bora* 'grey (*of a horse*)'; Tofan *bora* 'grey'; ChulymT *pora* 'grey'; NE^N Yakut *boroŋ* 'dark grey'; Dolgan *boroŋ* 'grey'.

The Kott word was borrowed from the Turkic form **čōkur* 'variegated, multicoloured', which is of Mongolic origin. The phonetic shape of the Kott form proposes a borrowing from the Turkic form with the long vowel and intervocalic consonant *VkV*, which is voiced in Kott. The change of the Turkic vowel *-u-* in the second syllable to *-o-* is also peculiar to Kott loanwords. A similar change appears in the first syllable as well.

Originally, in the Mongolic languages this colour denotes the mixed or mottled colour of a horse (Khabtagaeva 2001: 96). In Kott, as in Siberian Turkic, the semantic meaning widened to mean 'colourful'.

Kott ***kaltar*** 'brown horse with white mouth' (Werner 2002/1: 406) ← Turkic **qaltar* 'bay horse with yellow markings, brown horse with white mouth' ← Mongolic *qaltar* 'variegated, spotted, blemished; have a white muzzle' < *qara* 'black' +*ltAr* {Mongolic NN/adj., see Khabtagaeva 2001: 146–147} ← Turkic *qara* 'black':

cf. NE^S YeniseiT: Khakas *xaltar* 'bay horse with yellow markings'; Sagai, Koibal, Kachin *qaltar* 'brown horse with white mouth' (R); Kyzyl *χalttar* 'brown horse with white mouth'; Shor *qaltür* 'brown horse with white mouth' (R); AltaiT: Altai *kaltar* 'bay horse with yellow markings; silver fox'; Tuba *kaltar* 'bay horse with yellow markings'; Quu *kaldar ~ kaltar* 'bay, brown (*of a horse*)'; Teleut *qaltar* 'bay' (R); SayanT: Tuvan *kaldar* 'bay (*of a horse*); with black markings (*of the domestic animals*)'; ChulymT –; NE^N Yakut –; NW^N Siberian Tatar –; NW^S Kirgiz *kaltar* 'silver fox'; Fu-yü –; SE Yellow Uyghur *qaltar ġoy* 'sheep with black hair on the forehead and around the eyes';

Turkic → Samoyedic:

Kamas *kaltar* 'brown horse with white muzzle and tail';

Turkic ← Mongolic *qaltar* 'variegated, spotted, blemished; have a white muzzle' < *qar-a* 'black, dark, obscure':

cf. Middle Mongol: Precl.Mo. *qaltar*; LM *qaltar* 'variegated, spotted, blemished; have a white muzzle'; Modern Mongol: Buryat *xaltar* 'light chestnut (*of a horse*); with red stripes on the legs and face (*of a dog*)'; Khalkha *xaltar* 'dirty, soiled, stained, spotted; brown with lighter markings (*horse, dog*)'; Kalmuck *xaltr* 'brown horse with white mouth and mane'; Dagur *kaltār* (E); Khamnigan –;

Mongolic ← Turkic *qara* 'black':

cf. Old Turkic *qara*; NE^S YeniseiT: Khakas *xara*; Sagai, Koibal, Kachin *qara* (R); Kyzyl *χara*; Shor *qara*; AltaiT: Altai; Tuba; Qumanda; Quu; Teleut *qara*; SayanT: Tuvan; Tofan *qara*; ChulymT *qara*; NE^N Yakut *xara*; Dolgan *kara ~ xara*; NW^N Siberian Tatar *qara*; NW^S Kirgiz *kara*; Fu-yü *gar*; Kazak *qara*; SE Yellow Uyghur *qara*.

Etymology: Joki LS 155; Laude-Cirtautas 1961: 106; Ščerbak 1961: 154; Clauson ED 643b; Timonina 1978: 8; ESTJa 1997: 237; Anikin 2000: 241; Khabtagaeva 2001: 146–147; 2009: 236; 2015a: 118

The Kott word was clearly borrowed from Siberian Turkic (Timonina 1978: 8). In Kott, as in Yenisei Turkic and Altai Turkic, it designates a 'brown horse with a white mouth'.

In turn, the Turkic word belongs to the category of "re-borrowings". The Turkic *qaltar* was borrowed from Mongolic *qaltar* 'variegated, spotted, blemished; having a white muzzle', which derived from the colour name *qara* 'black' with Mongolic denominal noun/adjective suffix *+ltUr/+btUr* (for details, see Khabtagaeva 2001: 146–147). Finally, the Mongolic word connects to Turkic *qara* 'black'.

For the etymological background of Mongolic *qaltar* 'bay, brown colour of horse' and their borrowings into Turkic, see Laude-Cirtautas (1961: 106), Levitskaja (ESTJa 1997: 237) and Khabtagaeva (2001: 146–147; 2009: 236).

The Mongolic word was borrowed into Ewenki as *kātala* 'blackish brown' (SSTMJa 1: 384). The Samoyedic Kamas *kaltar* 'brown horse with white muzzle and tail' (Joki LS 155) and Siberian Russian *kaltaryj* 'light chestnut' (Anikin 2000: 241), as Yeniseian, were borrowed from Siberina Turkic.

Kott **koŋar** 'chestnut colored with yellow patches' (*said of a horse*) (Werner 2002/1: 441) ← Turkic *qoŋïr 'dark chestnut (*of a horse's coat*)':
    cf. Old Turkic *qoŋur*; NE[S] YeniseiT: Khakas *xōr* 'light-chestnut'; Sagai, Koibal, Kachin *kōr*; Kyzyl *χōr* 'pale, fawn'; Shor *qōr* 'brown'; AltaiT: Altai *koŋïr* 'grayish-brown, light-chestnut'; Quu *koŋïr* 'light-chestnut'; Teleut *qoŋïr* 'light-chestnut'; SayanT: Tuvan *xōr* 'light-chestnut'; Tofan *hōr* 'reddish-brown, light-chestnut'; ChulymT –; NE[N] Yakut *xoŋor* 'light bay; brown; the kind of goose'; NW[N] Siberian Tatar *qoŋğïr* 'red'; NW[S] Kirgiz *koŋur* 'brown, dark-complexioned'; Fu-yü –; Kazak *qoŋïr* 'brown'; SE Yellow Yughur –;

Turkic → Samoyedic:
    Kamas *kōr* 'light chestnut'.

Etymology: Joki LS 194–195; Laude-Cirtautas 1961: 100–102; Doerfer TMEN 3: 1536; 1985: 37; Räsänen VEWT 280–281; Clauson ED 639b; ESTJa 2000: 62–65; Nugteren 2011: 419; Róna-Tas & Berta WOT 2011: 560–562

The Kott word clearly was borrowed from the Siberian Turkic form *koŋïr (cf. Altai Turkic). In all Yenisei Turkic forms, the secondary long vowel developed from the sequence *VŋV*. This is one of the cases where the original Turkic vowel *-ï-* in the non-initial syllable changed to *-a-* in Kott, cf. Kott *arak* 'lean (*thin*)' ← AltaiT, YeniseiT *arïk* (~ Old Turkic *aruq*); Kott *askar* 'stallion' ← YeniseiT *asqïr* (~ Old Turkic *aδğïr*). This feature can be explained by the stress on the first syllable in the Yeniseian languages.

The Turkic word belongs to the colour name of a horse. For all data and details, see Laude-Cirtautas (1961: 100–110). For details regarding the Turkic etymology, see Räsänen (VEWT 280–281), Clauson (ED 639b), Levitskaja (ESTJa 2000: 62–65) and Róna-Tas & Berta (WOT 2011: 560–562).

The Turkic word was borrowed into the Samoyedic (Joki LS 194–195), Hungarian[232] (Róna-Tas & Berta WOT 2011: 560–562) and Mongolic[233] (Nugteren 2011: 419) languages. Further, it was borrowed from Mongolic into the Tungusic languages[234] (SSTMJa 1: 411b; Doerfer 1985: 37; Rozicky 1994: 143). The lexical meaning of Siberian Russian *kangor* 'a kind of grey goose' proves that the borrowing is from Yakut (Anikin 2000: 255).

Kott *šar ~ šâr* 'isabelline (*yellowish-tan color of horses*)' (Werner 2002/2: 437) ← Turkic *sarï 'yellow; light bay (*colour of a horse*)' < *sārïğ*:
  cf. Old Turkic *sārïğ* 'yellow'; NE^S YeniseiT: Khakas *sarïğ* 'yellow; blonde'; Sagai, Koibal, Kachin *sarïğ* 'yellow' (R); Kyzyl *sārï·γ^x* 'yellow, yellowish'; Shor *sarïğ* 'yellow'; AltaiT: Altai *sarï* 'yellow; blonde, red-haired'; Tuba *sarï* 'yellow; red-haired'; Qumanda *sarï ~ sārï* 'yellow, blonde'; Quu *sarū ~ sarï* 'yellow, pale'; Teleut *sarï* 'yellow; light bay (*colour of a horse*)'; SayanT: Tuvan *sarïğ* 'yellow; light bay (*colour of a horse*)*; pale (*about skin*); blonde'; Tofan *sarïğ* 'yellow'; ChulymT *sārïğ* 'yellow'; NE^N Yakut *araģas*[235] 'yellow, yellowish, pale, goldish'; cf. *arï̄* 'butter'; Dolgan *arï̄* 'butter'; NW^N Siberian Tatar *sarï* 'yellow'; NW^S Kirgiz *sarï* 'yellow; red-haired, blonde'; Fu-yü *sarïh* 'yellow'; Kazak *sarï* 'yellow'; SE Yellow Uyghur *sarïğ* 'yellow';
Turkic → Samoyedic:
  Kamas *sār* 'grayish, yellow; isabelline (*yellowish-tan color of horses*)'; Mator *sarig* 'yellow'.

Etymology: Joki LS 261–262; Laude-Cirtautas 1961: 64–68; Doerfer TMEN 3: 220–221; Räsänen VEWT 403b; Clauson ED 848a; Timonina 1978: 8; ESTJa 1989: 22–23; Stachowski 1996: 106; Ščerbak 1997: 144; Helimski 1997: 335; Khabtagaeva 2001: 99; Nugteren 2011: 492; Róna-Tas & Berta WOT 2011: 691–695

The Kott forms were borrowed from Siberian Turkic (Timonina 1978: 8; Stachowski 1996: 106). The change of initial *s-* > *š-* in Kott is a regular phonetic feature for native Yeniseian (Starostin 1982: 158) and Turkic loanwords. The disappearance of the original Turkic final vowel (apocope) in Kott is typical for

---

232 Turkic: West Old Turkic *koŋur > *komur → Hungarian *komor* 'gloomy, grave, morose, sombre, dull-coloured; not properly castrated'.
233 Turkic → Mongolic 'fallow, yellow-bay, chestnut (*of a horse*)': Middle Mongol: SH *qongqor*; LM *qongγor*; Modern Mongol: Buryat *xongor* 'chestnut (*of a horse*)'; Khalkha *xongor* 'light bay (*horse*)'; Oirat dial. *xoŋgăr* 'light-bay, pale, light yellow'; Dagur *koŋgōr* (E); Khamnigan *xongor*.
234 Mongolic → Tungusic: Barguzin Ewenki *qongōr*, Nercha Ewenki *koŋor* 'fallow, yellow-bay, chestnut (*of a horse*)'; Manchu *qoŋoro* 'yellow-bay (*horse*)'.
235 <*sārïğ +*Xš* {Turkic NN/adj., which added to colour names, see Erdal 1991: 102}.

some Turkic loanwords, cf. Kott *aibič* ~ *aipiš* 'old man' ← Turkic *aybičï*, Kott *aktur* 'postp. through' ← Turkic *ötgürü*, Kott *in* ~ *în* 'needle' ← Turkic *ignä*, etc. The similar form without a final Turkic vowel is present in Samoyedic Kamas. The source of borrowing of the Kott word may be the Samoyedic form *sār* 'grayish, yellow', where also the long vowel appeared. The Kamas and Mator forms were borrowed from Turkic (Joki LS 261–272; Helimski 1997: 335).

The Turkic word belongs to the category of colour names and is widespread in almost all Turkic languages. For details on its distribution, derivation, lexical broadening, and frequency in the names of plants and animals, see the work of Laude-Cirtautas (1961: 64–68). From an etymological viewpoint, the Turkic word was examined by Doerfer (TMEN 3: 220–221), Räsänen (VEWT 403b), Clauson (ED 848a), Levitskaja (ESTJa 1989: 22–23) and Róna-Tas & Berta (WOT 2011: 691–695). According to his last work (Róna-Tas & Berta WOT 2011: 693), the word derives from an unattested base with the productive Turkic deverbal noun suffix -(X)G,[236] which forms adjectives. Originally the 'yellow' colour name evolved from the word for 'white'.

The Turkic word also was borrowed into Mongolic[237] (Ščerbak 1997: 144; Khabtagaeva 2001: 99; Nugteren 2011: 492) and Hungarian[238] (Róna-Tas & Berta WOT 2011: 691–695).

From the Mongolic form *sirγa* 'light bay'[239] (Nugteren 2011: 492), which is derived from *sira* 'yellow' and the non-productive suffix +GA (Khabtagaeva 2001: 148–149), the original Turkic word via Mongolic was borrowed into Tungusic[240] (SSTMJa 2: 95a; Doerfer 1985: 100; Rozycki 1994: 184).

Kott *tor* 'brown (*horse*)' (Werner 2002/2: 276) ← Turkic **torïġ* 'bay, brown (*of a horse*)' < *toruġ*:

    cf. Old Turkic *toruġ* 'bay (*of a horse*)'; NE^S YeniseiT: Khakas *torïġ* 'bay (*of a horse*)'; Sagai *tor* 'brown (*of a horse*)' (R), Koibal, Kachin *torïġ* 'bay (*of a horse*)' (R); Kyzyl *tōr* ~ *tō·rïγ** 'brown, dark brown (*of a horse*)'; AltaiT: Altai –; Quu *toro* 'skewbald'; SayanT: Tuvan *doruġ* 'bay (*of a horse*)'; Tofan *doruġ* 'bay (*of a horse*)'; ChulymT –;

---

236 E.g. *qatïġ* 'hard' < *qat-* 'to be hard', *sasïġ* 'stinking' < *sasï-* 'to stink', *tünärig* 'dark' < *tünär-* 'to be dark', etc. (Erdal 1991: 191, 201, 211).
237 Turkic → Mongolic 'yellow': Middle Mongol: SH; HY, Muq. *šira*; LM *sir-a*; Modern Mongol: Buryat *šara*; Khalkha, Kalmuck *šar*; Dagur *šar* (E); Khamnigan *šira* ~ *sira*.
238 Turkic: West Old Turkic **siarïg* > **šarug* 'yellow' → Hungarian *sárga* [*šārgå*] 'yellow'.
239 Cf. Middle Mongol SH *sirqa*; Muq. *širγa*; LM *širγa*; Modern Mongol: Buryat, Khalkha *šarga*; Kalmuck *šarγa* ~ *šarxa*; Dagur *šarəγ* (E); Khamnigan *širga* ~ *šarga*.
240 Turkic → Mongolic → Tungusic 'bay': Barguzin Ewenki *sirγa*; Lamut *hiraŋan* 'yellowish, sand colour, grayish'; Manchu *sirγa* 'bay (*colour of horse*); musk-deer'.
    Cf. Manchu → Dagur *širγā* 'bay (*colour of horse*)' (Nugteren 2011: 492).

NE^N Yakut *turaġas* (< *toruġ +*GAč* {Turkic NN, which forms nouns designate names of plants and animals) 'bay (*of a horse*)'; NW^N Siberian Tatar –; NW^S Kirgiz *toru* 'bay (*of a horse*)'; Fu-yü –; Kazak *torï* 'bay (*of a horse*)'; SE Yellow Yughur –;
Turkic → Samoyedic:
Kamas *tōr* ~ *tōra* 'brown (*of a horse*)'; Mator *toru* 'brown (*of a horse*)'.

Etymology: Joki LS 333–334; Laude-Cirtautas 1961: 106; Doerfer TMEN 2: 475–477; Räsänen VEWT 489b; Ščerbak SF 1970: 197; Rassadin 1971: 174; Clauson ED 538a; Timonina 1978: 8; ESTJa 1980: 268–269

The Kott word was borrowed from the Siberian Turkic (Timonina 1978: 8) form *tor, which nowdays is present in Yenisei Turkic dialects where the Turkic final *-Xġ* dropped.

In Old Turkic, there were two forms documented: *toruġ* ~ *torïġ*. According to the Turkmen form *dōr*, the Proto-Turkic form was reconstructed as *tōr (Räsänen VEWT 489b; Ščerbak SF 1970: 197; ESTJa 1980: 268–269). For the etymology and data, see also Laude-Cirtautas (1961: 106), Doerfer (TMEN 2: 475–477) and Clauson (ED 538a).

From Siberian Turkic, the word was borrowed as well into Samoyedic (Joki LS 333–334; Helimski 1997: 366).

Kott *ureäk* 'green' (Werner 2002/2: 352) ← Turkic *kök arak < *kȫk* 'blue' + *arax*[241] {Khakas diminutive particle for adjective forms,[242] see Baskakov & Inkiževkova-Grekul 1953: 407}, cf. Khakas *kök-arax* 'greenish':
< *kök* < *kȫk* 'blue, green':
cf. Old Turkic *kȫk* 'the sky; sky-coloured, blue, blue-grey'; NE^S YeniseiT: Khakas *kök* 'green, blue; grass'; Sagai, Koibal, Kachin; Shor *kök*; Kyzyl *kȫk*^x; AltaiT: Altai; Tuba; Qumanda; Quu; Teleut *kök*; SayanT: Tuvan; Tofan *kök*; ChulymT *kök*; NE^N Yakut *küöx*; Dolgan *küök* ~ *küöx*; NW^N Siberian Tatar *kük*; NW^S Kirgiz *kök*; Fu-yü *göh*; Kazak *kök*; SE Yellow Uyghur *kök*;
Turkic → Samoyedic:
Koibal *kok* 'blue, green'; Kamas *kük* ~ *kök* 'green, blue, yellow, golden; large pearl'; Mator *kök* 'blue, green'.

Etymology: Joki LS 187, 216; Laude-Cirtautas 1961: 77–85; Doerfer TMEN 3: 640–642; Räsänen VEWT 287a; Ščerbak SF 1970 195a; 1997: 240; Rassadin 1971: 204;

---

[241] Possibly the Khakas particle is connected with the Old Turkic suffix +*rAk*, which forms elatives and comparatives, e.g. *küčlügräk* 'stronger' < *küčlüg* 'strong' < *küč* 'power', *küčsüzräk* 'weaker' < *küčsüz* 'weak', *bäkräk* 'stronger' < *bäk* 'lord, master' etc. (for details, see Erdal 1991: 62–64).

[242] E.g. *xizïl-arax* 'reddish' < *xizïl* 'red', *xara-arax* 'blackish' < *xara* 'black', *sïlïg-arax* 'less beautiful' < *sïlïg* 'beautiful', *kičïg-arax* 'a liitle smaller, a little less' < *kičïg* 'small'.

Clauson ED 708b; SSTMJa 1: 426b; ESTJa 1980: 66–68; Rozycki 1994: 145; SIGTJa 1997: 682–683; Helimski 1997: 284; Nugteren 2011: 424–425; Róna-Tas & Berta WOT 2011: 519–521; Khabtagaeva 2015b: 525–526

The etymology of the Kott word is unknown. Semantically, the Turkic word is close to the Kott word. The Kott word is possibly the shortened form of Turkic *kök* 'blue, green' and the Yenisei Turkic diminutive particle *arax*. The vowel palatalization can be explained by the absence of synharmony in Yeniseian languages. Also the change may have happened due to influence of the first compound word. The disappearance of the Turkic first syllable *kö-* is problematic. Also, due to metathesis, initial *k-* may have been dropped (under the influence of the final consonant *-k*), and the vowel *-ö-* in the first syllable changed to the diphthong *-eä-* (Khabtagaeva 2015d: 140)

For the etymology and more data concerning Turkic colour-name, see Laude-Cirtautas (1961: 77–85), Doerfer (TMEN 3: 640–642), Räsänen (VEWT 287a), Rassadin (1971: 204), Clauson (ED 708b), Sevortjan (ESTJa 1980: 66–68) and Tenišev (SIGTJa 1997: 682–683).

The Turkic word was borrowed into the Samoyedic (Joki LS 187, 216; Helimski 1997: 284), Mongolic[243] (Clauson ED 708b; Ščerbak 1997: 240; Nugteren 2011: 424–425) and Hungarian[244] (Róna-Tas & Berta WOT 2011: 519–521) languages. From Mongolic, the Turkic word was borrowed into Tungusic[245] (SSTMJa 1: 426b; Rozycki 1994: 145).

The etymology of the Kott word remains uncertain.

1.2.2 Qualitative Adjectives

Kott *ašâme ~ ašâm ~ šam* 'bad' (Werner 2002/1: 88) < **ašam* < **ačam* < **čama* ← ? Turkic **čaman* < *jaman* (cf. AltaiT) < *yaman* 'bad, evil' < **yav-(X)n* {Turkic VN, see Erdal 1991: 300–307}:

cf. Old Turkic *yaman* 'bad, evil'; NE[S] YeniseiT: Khakas *čiben* 'ugly, scary'; AltaiT: Altai *jaman* 'evil, misery, vice; bad, ugly, evil, malicious, vicious'; Tuba *d'aman* 'bad'; Qumanda *d'aman ~ naman ~ n'aman ~ čaman* 'bad, evil; misfortune'; Quu *d'aman* 'bad'; Teleut *yaman* 'bad, evil'; SayanT –; ChulymT –; NE[N] Yakut –; NW[N] Siberian Tatar *yaman* 'bad; awful, badly'; NW[S] Kirgiz *jaman* 'bad, evil, nasty, vicious'; Fu-

---

243 Turkic → Mongolic 'blue, sky blue, green, ash-coloured, dark (*of a face*)': Middle Mongol: SH; HY *kökö*; Muq. *köke*; LM *köke*; Modern Mongol: Buryat *xüxe*; Khalkha *xöx*; Kalmuck *kök*; Dagur *kuk^w* (E); Khamnigan *kükü ~ kökö*.
244 Turkic: West Old Turkic **kök* → Hungarian *kék* [*kēk*] 'blue'.
245 Turkic → Mongolic → Tungusic: Barguzin, Nercha, Northern Baikal Ewenki *kuku* 'blue, green, greenish grey'; Solon *xöxö* [*wāra*] 'blue'; Manchu *kuku* 'black; blue; the kind of herb'.

yü –; Kazak *žaman* 'bad, evil, vicious; bad, harmful; lousy, rotten'; SE Yellow Uyghur *yaman* 'evil, bad';

cf. Turkic *yabal* < *yaval* < **yav-(X)l* {Turkic VN, see Erdal 1991: 330}:

Old Turkic –, cf. *yavlaq* 'bad, evil' < **yav*; NE^S YeniseiT: Khakas *čabal* 'mean, nasty, bad; malicious, evil'; Sagai *čabal* ~ *čebäl* 'bad, ugly, evil' (R); Koibal, Kachin *d'abal* 'bad, evil' (R); Shor *čabal* 'bad'; AltaiT –; SayanT –; ChulymT *čabal* 'harmful'; NE^N Yakut –; NW^N Siberian Tatar –; NW^S Kirgiz –; Fu-yü *yabïl* 'bad'; Kazak –; SE Yellow Yughur –.

Etymology: Räsänen VEWT 184a; Clauson ED 876–877, 937a; Doerfer TMEN 4: 311; ESTJa 1989: 47, 109–110

The etymology of the Kott word is unknown. As a hypothesis, I suppose that it was borrowed from Altai Turkic *čaman* ~ Common Turkic *yaman* 'bad'. Kott has three forms, two of them with the possibly prothetical vowel *a-*, and the third form can be shortened.

The base of the Turkic word is **yav*, from which *yavlaq* 'bad, evil' derived, as well as *yavġan* 'coarse, unsympathetic', *yavïz* 'bad' (ESTJa 1989: 47); fellow forms as *yaman* 'bad, evil', *yaġï* 'war, enemy' (Clauson ED 898a; ESTJa 1989: 47) belong to this semantic grouping as well. Clauson (ED 871a, 874b, 881b, 876b) reconstructs the verbal base, while Sevortjan and Levitskaja (ESTJa 1989: 47) obtain derivations from the nominal form.

There are two different forms: *yaman* (YeniseiT, ChulymT, Fu-yü) and *yabal* (AltaiT, Siberian Tatar, Kirgiz, Yellow Uyghur), which are clearly related to each other. The basic form must be **yab*: the change *b* > *m* in different positions is typical for Turkic languages[246] (for details, see Serebrennikov & Gadžieva 1986: 40–41; Johanson 1997: 102). The morphological background is not clear. There are two different suffixes. In spite of that fact we have the Turkic denominal nomen suffix *+Xn* with a collective meaning,[247] probably in a functional sense, the base for *yaman* was verb **yav-* with the Turkic productive deverbal noun suffix *-Xn*: this forms object nominals from transitive stems and subject nominals from intransitive stems, also known as the 'ergative.' See, for example, Old Turkic *uzun* 'long' < *uza-* 'to be or become long, or to be long drawn out', *yarïn* 'dawn, the morrow' < *yaro-* 'to be or become bright, to shine', *äsin* 'breeze, light wind' < *äs-* 'to blow', etc. (for more examples and details on the functions of this

---

[246] E.g. Old Turkic *burun* 'nose' ~ Yakut *murun*; Old Turkic *bin-* 'to ride, mount' ~ Uyghur *min-*, Tuvan *mun-*; Old Turkic *qopuz* 'a stringed instrument' ~ Yakut *xomus*, Shor *qomus* (< **qobuz*); Old Turkic *kibi* 'like' ~ Azeri *kimi*; Old Turkic *čïbun* 'a buzzing insect' ~ Kirgiz *čïmïn*, etc.

[247] E.g. Old Turkic *oġlan* 'sons, children' < *oġul* 'offspring, child, son', *ärän* 'men' < *är* 'man', *bodun* 'people' < *bod* 'tribe', etc. (Erdal 1991: 91–92).

suffix, see Erdal 1991: 300–307). For the Turkic word *yabal*, the base may be the verb **yav-* and the Turkic deverbal noun/adjective suffix -(X)l[248] (for details, see Erdal 1991: 330–332).

Nonetheless, this Kott word belongs to the group of words with unclear etymology.

Kott ***arix*** 'clean' (Werner 2002/1: 58) ← Turkic **arïğ* 'clean, pure' < *arï-* 'to be, or become clean, pure' *-G* {Turkic VN, see Erdal 1991: 172}:
  cf. Old Turkic *arïğ* 'clean, pure'; NE[S] YeniseiT: Khakas *arïğ* 'clean, bright'; Sagai, Koibal, Kachin; Kyzyl *arïğ* 'pure, holy' (R); Shor *arïğ* 'clean'; AltaiT: Altai *aru* 'clean'; Tuba *arï-* 'to become clean'; Qumanda *arï* 'clean, saint'; Quu *arïğ* 'clean, saint; completely'; Teleut *aru* 'clean'; SayanT: Tuvan *arïğ* 'neat, tidy; clean'; Tofan *arïğ* 'clean'; ChulymT –; NE[N] Yakut *ïrās*[249] 'clean, neat; *fig.* open'; Dolgan *ïras* 'clean, pure'; NW[N] Siberian Tatar –; NW[S] Kirgiz *arū* 'clean; beautiful'; Fu-yü –; Kazak *aru* 'beautiful woman'; SE Yellow Uyghur *arïğ* 'good; clean';
Turkic → Samoyedic:
  Kamas *ārïχ* ~ *ārïγ* 'pure; clean; treeless'.
Etymology: Joki LS 71–73; Doerfer TMEN 1: 129–130; Räsänen VEWT 25b; Clauson ED 213b; ESTJa 1974: 184; Timonina 1978: 12; Ščerbak 1997: 100; Starostin, Dybo & Mudrak EDAL 2003: 518; Rybatzki 2006: 148–150; Nugteren 2011: 273–274; Róna-Tas & Berta WOT 2011: 79–80

The Kott phonetic form shows a borrowing from the Yenisei Turkic group, where the Turkic deverbal noun/adjective suffix *-g* is preserved, whereas in Altai Turkic it disappeared. The change of the final velar stop consonant *-g* to *-x* is a regular change for Kott loanwords.

It seems that the Samoyedic Kamas *ārïχ* ~ *ārïγ* forms were borrowed from Yenisei Turkic as well.

The Turkic word was borrowed into both Mongolic[250] (Ščerbak 1997: 100; Rybatzki 2006: 148–150; Nugteren 2011: 273–274) and Hungarian.[251]

---

248   Cf. Old Turkic *amïl* 'calm' < **amï-* (cf. *amrïl-* 'to be at peace' < **amï-*r-Xl-* {Turkic NN/passive}, *amru* 'continuously'), *tükäl* 'complete, perfect, entire' < *tükä-* 'to come to an end, finish', *qïzïl* 'red' < **qïz-*, *osal* 'negligent' < **osa-* (cf. *osan-* 'to be negligent, listless' < **osa-n-* {Turkic NN/reflexive}), etc. (Erdal 1991: 330–332).
249   < **ārïğač* (Stachowski 1993: 261) < **ārïğ* +*Xč* {Turkic NN/diminutive, see Clauson 1972: xli}.
250   Turkic **arï-* → Mongolic **arï-GUn* {Mongolic VN/adj., see Poppe GWM § 154}: Middle Mongol: HY *ari'un*; Muq. *ari'un* ~ *ariyun*; Ist. *arūn*; LM *ariy* ~ *ariyun* 'clear, pure'; Modern Mongol: Buryat *aryūn* 'clean, clear, transparent (*water*); neat, nice, honest; saint'; Khalkha *ariun* 'pure, sacred, noble, holy; clean, pure'; Oirat dial. *ärūn* 'clean, neat; saint, honest'; Dagur *arūn* (E); Khamnigan *aryūn*.
251   Turkic: West Old Turkic **arïtan* (< **arïton* < *arït-* 'to clean, purify' *-Xn* {Turkic VN}) → Hungarian *ártány* [*ārtāń*] 'barrow'.

Kott *bêlen* 'finished' (Werner 2002/1: 121) ← Turkic *belen 'prepared, ready' ← Mongolic *belen* 'prepared, ready, in readiness, available':

cf. NE^S YeniseiT: Khakas *pilen*; Sagai, Koibal *pelän* (R); Kyzyl *pelän*; Shor *pelen*; AltaiT: Altai *belen*; Tuba *belen*; Qumanda *belen*; Quu *pelen* 'ready, comfortable, easy'; Teleut *pelen* (R); SayanT: Tuvan *belen* 'easy; prepared, ready'; Tofan *belen*; ChulymT *pälän*; NE^N Yakut *belem*; Dolgan *bälämnǟ-* ~ *bälännǟ-* (< *bälän+lA-* {Turkic NV, see Erdal 1991: 429}) 'to prepare'; NW^N Siberian Tatar *pilän*; NW^S Kirgiz *belen*; Fu-yü –; SE Yellow Uyghur *pel'en*;

Turkic → Samoyedic:

Kamas *b'elen* 'finished, ready';

Turkic ← Mongolic *belen* 'ready, prepared':

cf. Middle Mongol: Precl.Mo. *belen*; SH *belen* ~ *bölen*; Muq. *belen*; LM *belen* 'prepared, ready, in readiness, available'; Modern Mongol: Buryat *belen* 'ready, prepared; cash; not difficult, easy; fragile, durable, strong'; Khalkha *belen* 'ready'; Kalmuck *beln* 'ready, prepared'; Dagur *bələn* (E); Khamnigan *belen*.

Etymology: Kałużyński 1962: 40; Räsänen VEWT 69b; Rassadin 1971: 161; 1980: 19, 22, 40, 71; SSTMJa 1: 125; Timonina 1978: 13; Doerfer 1985: 78; Tatarincev 2000: 212; Khabtagaeva 2009: 238; Nugteren 2011: 280

The Kott word was clearly borrowed from a Siberian Turkic variety (Timonina 1978: 13). The Mongolic word is present in almost all Siberian Turkic languages (Kałużyński 1962: 40; Rassadin 1971: 161; 1980: 19, 22, 40, 71; Tatarincev 2000: 212; Khabtagaeva 2009: 238).

The Mongolic word was also borrowed into the Tungusic[252] (SSTMJa 1: 125; Doerfer 1985: 78) and Samoyedic (Joki LS 114) languages.

The base of the Mongolic word is most likely the dead form *bele, cf. Literary Mongolian *beled-* (< *bele +*d-* {Mongolic NV, see Poppe GWM § 241}) 'to prepare, make ready; to be[come] ready', *beledke-* (< *bele +*dKA-* {Mongolic NV, see Khabtagaeva 2009: 288}) 'to prepare, make ready; to supply with, equip; to prepare oneself', *beleken* (< *bele +*KAn* {Mongolic NN/diminutive}) 'ready, prepared; in readiness, handy, at hand', etc. Alternatively, the base of word may be the form *belen* with unstable final *-n*, often dropped during suffixation.

---

252 Mongolic → Tungusic: Urmi Ewenki *beline-*, Aldan, Zeya, Sakhalin, Uchur, Chumikan *belenne-* (← Mongolic *belen* +*nA-* {Tungusic NV, see Sunik 1962: 109}), *beleki-* ~ *beleke-* ~ *beletke-* (← Mongolic *beledke-* < *bele +*dKA-* {Mongolic NV, see Khabtagaeva 2009: 288}) 'to prepare'; Solon *belxê* 'ready', *belxe-* 'to prepare'; Lamut *belem* ~ *belen* 'ready'; Negidal *belixī* 'prepared, ready'; Oroch *belī-* 'to prepare'; Ulcha *belī* 'prepared, ready'; Nanai *belī* 'prepared; resources, purveyance'; Manchu *beleni* 'ready'.

Kott **bik** 'strong, heavy, solid' (Werner 2002/1: 123) ← Turkic *bik < bäk 'firm, solid, stable':

cf. Old Turkic *bäk*; NE[S] YeniseiT: Khakas *pik*; Kyzyl *ṕex*; Shor *pek*; AltaiT: Altai *bek*; Qumanda *pek* 'very, very much'; Quu *bek*; Teleut *pek*; SayanT: Tuvan *bek* 'fetters'; Tofan *be^ck*; ChulymT *päq* 'strong, powerful'; NE[N] Yakut –; NW[N] Siberian Tatar *päk*; NW[S] Kirgiz *bek* 'strong, solid; very, very much'; Fu-yü –; Kazak *bek* 'very, very much'; SE Yellow Uyghur *poq ~ piq* 'power, strength'.

Etymology: Räsänen VEWT 68a; Clauson ED 323a; ESTJa 1978: 117–120; Timonina 1978: 12

The Kott word was borrowed from a Yenisei Turkic variety, where the form with a high-unrounded vowel *-i-* is found.

The Turkic form *bäk* is usually examined together with another Turkic word *bärk* having the same meaning (Clauson ED 323a; ESTJa 1978: 117–120). Both variants were borrowed into Mongolic with, however, different lexical meanings[253] (Nugteren 2011: 287).

Also, see the etymology of Arin **berke ~ berek ~ birka** 'big, great; very', which represents a re-borrowings of this Turkic word.

Kott **êper** 'noun circle; *adj.* round; *adv.* around' (Werner 2002/1: 268) ← Turkic **ebir-* < *äβir-* 'to turn (*something, e.g. a wheel*)' < *äg-* 'to bend, bow' *-Ir-* {Turkic VV, see Erdal 1991: 535–536}:

cf. Old Turkic *äβir-*; NE[S] YeniseiT: Khakas *ibĭr-* 'to get round; to go around; surround; spin, twirl; turn out', cf. *ir-* 'to spin'; Sagai, Koibal *egir* 'bumpy, crooked, uneven', cf. *īr-* 'to spin' (R); Kyzyl *īr-* 'to spin'; Shor *īr-* 'to spin'; AltaiT: Altai *ebir-* 'to go around; surround'; Tuba *ebir-* 'to go around'; Qumanda *īr-* 'to spin'; Quu *ebir-* 'to roll, to twirl', *evir-* 'to turn out', *evir* 'around', *iyir-* 'to spin'; Teleut *īr-* 'to spin' (R); SayanT: Tuvan *ēr-* 'to turn out, to come back; to bend'; Tofan *ēr-* 'to roll, to twirl'; ChulymT *īr-* 'to spin'; NE[N] Yakut –; NW[N] Siberian Tatar *ir-* 'to spin'; NW[S] Kirgiz *iyir-* 'to spin'; Fu-yü –; Kazak *ür-* 'to twist, to gather together'; SE Yellow Yughur –.

Turkic → Samoyedic:

Kamas *erēr- ~ ērer- ~ irēr-* 'to spin, twist'.

---

253 Turkic *bäk* 'firm, stable, solid' → Mongolic *böke* 'strong, wrestler': Middle Mongol: SH; HY *bökö*; Muq. *böke*; LM *böke*; Modern Mongol: Khalkha *böx*; Buryat *büxe*; Kalmuck *bök*; Dagur *buk^w* (E); Khamnigan *büke ~ bükü ~ böke*.

Turkic *bärk* 'firm, stable, solid' → Mongolic *berke* 'difficult, hard; burdensome, troublesome; complicated, serious; difficulty, hardship; trouble; skillful, competent, fit': cf. Middle Mongol: Precl.Mo. *berke*; SH *berke* 'difficult'; Ibn-Muh. *berke*; Muq. *bürke* 'strong'; HY *berke* 'difficult'; LM *berke*; Modern Mongol: Buryat *berxe*; Khalkha *berx*; Kalmuck *berkä*; Dagur *berke* (T); Khamnigan *berke ~ börke*.

Etymology: Joki LS 126–127; Räsänen VEWT 34b; Rassadin 1971: 184; Clauson ED 14a; ESTJa 1974: 227–231; Erdal 1991: 536; Róna-Tas & Berta WOT 2011: 672–675

The phonetic shape of the Kott word shows that the source of borrowing was the Altai Turkic form *ebir-*, after which devoicing occurred in Kott. From a morphological point of view, the Turkic verb is used in Kott as a noun, adjective and adverb.

The Turkic word was borrowed into the Mongolic,[254] Samoyedic (Joki LS 126–127) and Hungarian[255] (Róna-Tas & Berta WOT 2011: 672–675) languages.

Kott *êti*; Yugh *ēˑt ~ eti*; Central Ket *ēˑt ~ ēˑti*, Northern Ket *ēˑti* 'sharp' (Werner 2002/1: 273) ← Turkic **yitī < yitig* 'sharp' < *yiti-* 'to be sharp' *-G* {Turkic VN, see Erdal 1991: 172}:

cf. Old Turkic *yitig ~ yitī*; NE^S YeniseiT: Khakas *čītíg* 'sharp, keen'; Sagai *čidíg* 'sharp, cutting' (R); Koibal, Kachin *yidig* 'sharp-edged, cutting' (R); Shor *čidig* 'sharp'; AltaiT: Altai –; Teleut *yidü* 'pointed, sharp' (R); SayanT: Tuvan *čidig* 'sharp, prickly; piercing gaze'; Tofan *čiᶜtī* 'acute; shrill, sharp; strong decoction; brave'; ChulymT *čidig* 'sharp'; NE^N Yakut *sitii* 'sharp; harsh, shrill; shrewd'; Dolgan *hitii* 'sharp; nimble, dexterous'; NW^N Siberian Tatar –; NW^S Kirgiz –; Fu-yü –; Kazak *žiti* 'sharp-eyed, sharp-sighted'; SE Yellow Yughur –.

Etymology: Räsänen VEWT 204b; Rassadin 1971: 197; Clauson ED 889a; Timonina 1979/5: 23; ESTJa 1989: 205–206

According to Vajda (2016: personal communication), the Yeniseian forms can be reconstructed to Proto-Yeniseian **etiŋ*, where the final **ŋ* is the Yenisean adjective suffix. This makes it unclear whether the word was originally Yeniseian or a very early borrowing from Turkic.

The Yeniseian words have also been regarded as of Turkic origin (Timonina 1979: 23). In this case, the Turkic initial consonant *y-* disappeared in Yeniseian. Cf. other examples with a similar change: Turkic *yiðig* 'smell, odour (*usuall unpleasant*), foul-smelling' > *yītū > yïtu* → Kott *īta* 'stinking'; Turkic *yān* 'the hip; the side, flank of the body or in other contexts' → Kott *ânar ~ anar* 'hip, loin' where *ar* is a Yeniseian word 'bone'. This change may be explained by the absence of this consonant in Yeniseian. This phonetic feature indicates an early period of borrowing.

The Turkic word is derived from the verb *yiti-* 'to be sharp', with productive the deverbal noun/adjective suffix *-G*. For the etymological background of

---

254 Turkic **epirĕ-* → Mongolic *egere-* 'to rotate, whirl, turn, revolve; to spin, twist; to surround, stand around; to gather in a pile; to entangle, mix up, confuse; to ride around a herd in order to keep it together; to recur frequently (*of illness*)': LM *egere-*; Modern Mongol: Buryat *ēre-*; Khalkha *ēre-*; Oirat dial. *ērĕ-*; Dagur *ēr-* (T); Khamnigan *ēre-*.

255 Turkic: West Old Turkic **ävir-* → Hungarian *őr* [*ör*] 'to grind, mill'.

the Turkic word, see Räsänen (VEWT 204b), Clauson (ED 889a) and Levitskaja (1989: 205–206).

Kott ***gobimojb[e]ga*** 'disgusting' (Werner 2002/1: 289) ← ? Turkic **komay* 'bad' + *ugā* 'very': cf. Khakas *uġā xomay* 'disgusting':

< *komay* 'bad' ← Mongolic *γoγomai* ~ *γoomai* 'superficial, unreliable, slapdash':

cf. Old Turkic –; NEˢ YeniseiT: Khakas *xomay* 'bad'; Sagai, Koibal, Kachin *komay* 'bad, disabled' (R); Kyzyl *χōmay* 'bad, evil'; AltaiT: Altai *kōmoy* 'bad'; Tuba *kōmoy* 'bad'; Qumanda *kōmoy* 'lean, waste, bad'; Quu *koboy* 'bad'; Teleut *komoy* 'bad, unfit, weak' (R); SayanT: Tuvan *xōmay* 'unsatisfactory, insufficient; dissatisfied'; ChulymT –; NEᴺ Yakut *kuomay* 'poor; loose' (Pek.); NWᴺ Siberian Tatar –; NWˢ Kirgiz *kōmay* 'unsociable'; Fu-yü –; SE Yellow Yughur –;

Turkic ← Mongolic 'superficial, unreliable, slapdash':

cf. LM *γoγomai* ~ *γoomai* (Kara); Modern Mongol: Buryat –; Khalkha *gōmoi*; Oirat dial. –; Dagur –; Khamnigan –.

Etymology: Räsänen VEWT 279a; Rassadin 1980: 22

+ *ugā* 'very'

cf. Old Turkic –; NEˢ YeniseiT: Khakas *ugā* 'very'; Shor *uġa* 'very' (R); AltaiT: –; SayanT: Tuvan *uvā* '*interjection expressing surprise* aj! oj! ba!'; Remaining lgs. –;

cf. Mongolic:

Buryat *ugā* 'very; too much'.

Etymology: Ölmez 2007: 285

The etymology of the Kott word is unknown. As a working hypothesis, I propose that it should be classified among the category of compound words. It consists of two words: *gobimoj* and *b[e]ga*. Hypothetically, I would connect them with the Khakas phrase *ugā xomay* 'disgusting'. The typical combination *adverb* + *adjective* probably changed to *adjective* + *adverb*. Another problematic aspect is the consonant *-b-*, of unclear origin in both compounds.

One of the compounds has stable etymology. The Turkic forms are borrowed from Mongolic *γoomai* 'superficial, unreliable, slapdash'. Another part of compound is of unknown origin.

The Kott word has an unreliable Turkic etymology.

Kott ***hagši ~ hagše*** 'good, suitable' (Werner 2002/1: 292) ← Turkic **ťakšï* (cf. Quu) < *ďakšï* < *yaqšï* 'suitable, pleasing, good looking' < *yaqïš-* 'to be suitable, becoming, proper, fit; to look well, be handsome' *-I* {Turkic VN, see Erdal 1991: 344}:

cf. Old Turkic *yaxšï*; NEˢ YeniseiT: Khakas *čaxsï* 'good, kindness; kind, good, the best'; Sagai *čaqsï* 'good, excellent' (R); Kachin *čaqšï* (R); Kyzyl *yaχsi ~ yaᵏχsi ~ yaχse ~ šaχsi* 'good'; Shor *čaqšï* 'good'; AltaiT: Altai *ďakšï* 'good'; Tuba *ďakšï* 'kindness; good, kind';

Qumanda ďakšï ~ ťakšï ~ čakšï 'good'; Quu ťakšï 'good; kindness'; Teleut yaqšï 'good'; SayanT: Tuvan –; Tofan –; ChulymT čaqšï ~ čaqsï ~ yaqšï 'good'; NE^N Yakut –; NW^N Siberian Tatar yaqšïla- (< *yaqšï +lA- {Turkic NV}) 'make up a quarrel'; NW^S Kirgiz žakšï 'good; noble'; Fu-yü jahšï 'good'; Kazak jaqsï 'good; kind'; SE Yellow Uyghur yaxšï 'good';

Turkic → Samoyedic:
Kamas yakšï 'good'; Koibal jakiš 'good'.

Etymology: Joki LS 142–143; 116; Doerfer TMEN 4: 178–179; Räsänen VEWT 180b; Clauson ED 908a, 909a; Timonina 1978: 13; ESTJa 1989: 63–64

The Kott word was borrowed from the Altai Turkic Quu dialectal form ťakšï. The change of Yeniseian initial ťi- > h- is a regular phonetic feature in Kott (Vajda 2014: personal communication). This change points to the Altai Turkic layer.

The Turkic adjective is derived from the verb yaqïš- 'to be suitable, becoming, proper, fit; to look well, be handsome' and the productive deverbal noun/adjective suffix -I. For details on South-Siberian Turkic sound shifts of original initial y-, see Schönig (1998: 405).

The Turkic adjective was borrowed into Samoyedic as well (Joki LS 142–143).

Kott **koaš ~ koâš** 'beautiful' (Werner 2002/1: 458) ← Turkic *koas < qoġas 'beautiful' ← Persian:
  cf. Old Turkic –; NE^S YeniseiT: Khakas xōs 'drawing, pattern; decoration; embroidery; fig. outline, contour; beautiful'; Sagai, Koibal kōs 'beautiful, handsome' (R); Kachin kās 'decorated, well dressed' (R); Shor kās 'decoration, drawing'; AltaiT: Altai –; Qumanda kōs 'decoration, beauty'; Quu kōs 'beautiful, prominent; decoration, embroidery, beauty'; Teleut kōs 'beautiful, handsome' (R); SayanT: Tuvan kās 'elegant, magnificent'; Tofan qās 'decoration'; ChulymT quġas ~ quwas ~ qōs 'beautiful'; NE^N Yakut –; NW^N Siberian Tatar quas 'beautiful'; NW^S Kirgiz kōz 'beautiful, elegant, art; dandyish; harmless, innocent'; Fu-yü –; Kazak –; SE Yellow Yughur –;

Turkic → Samoyedic:
Kamas kuwas 'beautiful, pretty';

Turkic ← Persian khwush, khwash 'good, sweet, excellent, beautiful, fair, charming, pleasant, delightful, agreeable, cheerful, amiable, lovely, delicate, tender, kind, gentle, humane, mild, meek, elegant; healthy, wholesome, temperate; happy, well, pleased; willingly'.

Etymology: Joki LS 214; Räsänen VEWT 295a; Rassadin 1971: 220; Timonina 1978: 12; Stachowski 1996: 98; 2006: 18; Tatarincev 2004: 21–23; Pomorska 2012: 301–302

The Kott forms were borrowed from the Turkic form *koas, which developed from qoġas. In Modern Turkic languages contains a secondary long vowel. The change of the final Kott consonant -s > -š is a regular peculiarity for native Yeniseian and Turkic loanwords in Kott.

Concerning the word's etymology, for the various hypotheses of the Turkic etymology, see Tatarincev (2004: 21–23). According to Räsänen (VEWT 295a), the Turkic word is of Persian origin. Worthy of mention as well is Stachowski's paper (2006: 18), in which he explains the Persian origin of the Yeniseian word in detail.

The word was also borrowed into Samoyedic (Joki LS 214), possibly from Siberian Turkic.

Yugh *súl'gej* 'left' (Werner 2002/2: 172) ← Turkic *sologay 'left-handed' ← Mongolic *soloγai* 'left side or hand; left-handed; awkward; wrong, faulty' < *solo +*GAi* {Mongolic NN/adj., see Poppe GWM § 123} ← Turkic *sōlŏ > *sōl* 'left':

cf. NE^S YeniseiT: Khakas *solaġay* 'left-handed'; Shor *solaġay*; AltaiT: Altai *sologoy*; Qumanda *solay* ~ *sulay*; Teleut *sologoy*; SayanT: Tuvan *solagay*; Tofan –; ChulymT –; NE^N Yakut dial. *sologoy* 'coarse, clumsy; varmint'; NW^N Siberian Tatar *sulaġay* ~ *sulamay*; NW^S Kirgiz *sologoy*; Fu-yü –; Kazak *solaqay*; SE Yellow Uyghur –;

Turkic → Samoyedic:

Kamas *solai* ~ *sologoi* 'left';

Turkic ← Mongolic *soloγai* 'left side or hand; left-handed; awkward; wrong, faulty':

Middle Mongol: –; LM *soloγai*; Modern Mongol: Buryat *halgai*, cf. West Buryat *holgoi* 'gaper'; Khalkha *solgoi*; Oirat dial. *solgā*; Dagur *solγui* (E); Khamnigan –;

Mongolic ← Turkic *sōlŏ* > *sōl* 'left':

cf. Old Turkic *sōl*; NE^S YeniseiT: Khakas *sol*; Sagai, Koibal, Kachin *sol*; Kyzyl *sōl* ~ *soŋ*; Shor *sol*; AltaiT: Altai, Tuba; Qumanda; Quu; Teleut *sol*; SayanT: Tuvan *sol*; Tofan –; ChulymT *sol*; NE^N Yakut –; NW^N Siberian Tatar –; NW^S Kirgiz *sol*; Fu-yü *sol*; Kazak *sol*; SE Yellow Uyghur *sol* ~ *söl'* ~ *sul*;

Turkic → Samoyedic:

Mator *sol* 'left hand'.

Etymology: Joki LS 272; Räsänen VEWT 427a; Doerfer TMEN 3: 302–303; Clauson ED 824a; Rassadin 1980: 13; Ščerbak 1997: 166; Helimski 1997: 343; ESTJa 2003: 299–302; Khabtagaeva 2009: 245; 2015a: 119; Nugteren 2011: 500

The Yugh word was clearly borrowed from the Siberian Turkic form *sologay. The word belongs to the category of "re-borrowings": the original Turkic word was borrowed into Mongolic, and from Mongolic it was re-borrowed into Siberian Turkic. This is evidenced by the Mongolic suffix +*GAi*, which forms adjectives designating qualities (For functions, see Poppe GWM § 123).

The Mongolic form is present in almost all Siberian Turkic languages (Doerfer TMEN 3: 302–303; Räsänen VEWT 427a; Rassadin 1980: 13; ESTJa 2003: 301;

Khabtagaeva 2009: 245). Concerning the Mongolic languages, the word is not present in Middle Mongolic; it exists as a synonym to *jegün* 'left' and in time gained additional figurative meanings such as 'awkward; wrong, faulty' (Lessing 726a; Nugteren 2011: 500).

From Siberian Turkic, the Mongolic word was borrowed into Samoyedic Kamas, where probably the intervocalic *VgV* became dropped (Joki LS 272). Another Samoyedic Mator loanword *sol* 'left hand' shows a direct Turkic borrowing (Helimski 1997: 343). The Mongolic word was borrowed into Tungusic; the source for Ewenki Nercha *salaγai* 'left' possibly was one Buryat dialect (SST-MJa 2: 57b).

For the etymology of the Turkic word, see as well Doerfer (TMEN 3: 302–303), Ščerbak (1970: 176), Clauson (ED 824a) and ESTJa (2003: 299–302).

Yugh *χoj* 'thick *(said of liquids)*', cf. *χōj uˀk* 'thick soup'; Ket *qoˑj*, cf. *qōˑj uˀk* 'thick soup', *qōˑj saˀj* 'thick tea', *qōˑj ules* 'pouring rain' (Werner 2002/2: 127) ← Turkic *qoyu < *qoyuġ* 'thick, viscid, dense' < **qoyu-(X)G* {Turkic VN, see Erdal 2001: 172}: cf. Old Turkic *qoyuġ*; NE^S YeniseiT: Khakas *χoyïġ*; Sagai *qoyïġ* (R); Sagai, Koibal, Kachin *qoyuġ* (R); Kyzyl *χōjïγ^χ*; Shor *qoyuġ*; AltaiT: Altai *qoyu*; Qumanda *koyïl-* (< **qoyu-l-* {Turkic VV}) 'to thicken'; Quu *koyïl-* (< **qoyu-l-* {Turkic VV}) 'to thicken'; Teleut *qoyu* (R); SayanT: Tuvan *χoyug* 'soft *(ground, earth)*, mild, gentle *(view)*, thock *(milk)*, fine'; Tofan *hoyuġ*; ChulymT *qōyu*; NE^N Yakut *χoyū* 'thick *(grass, forest, tea, voice)*; leaven'; Dolgan *koyū* ~ *χoyū* 'thick'; NW^N Siberian Tatar –; NW^S Kirgiz *koyū* 'thick *(tea, dust, night)*'; Fu-yü *goyuh* 'thick, dense'; Kazak *qoyu* 'thick'; SE Yellow Uyghur *qoyox* 'thick *(milk product)*'.

Etymology: Räsänen VEWT 267a; Doerfer TMEN 3: 562; Clauson ED 596a; ESTJa 2000: 32–33

The Yeniseian words are of Turkic origin (Werner 2002/2: 127); apocope occurred. The source of borrowing was the form with final vowel *koyu (cf. Altai Turkic). The disappearance of the Turkic final vowel in Yenisean is a typical phonetic feature: e.g. Kott *aktur* 'postp. through' ← Turkic *ötküre* < *ötgürü*; Kott *in* ~ *în*; Arin *in*; Yugh *iˀn*; Ket *iˀn* 'needle' ← Turkic *īnä < *ignä*, etc. The change of initial Turkic *q-* > *χ-* in Yugh and its preservation in Ket are also regular: e.g. Yugh *χan*, Ket *qaˑn* 'prince' ← Turkic *kān* < *qaġan*; Yugh *χap* ~ *χaˀp*; Ket *qap* ~ *qaˀp* 'boat' ← Turkic *kebe* < *kämi*, etc.

The disapearance of final consonant *-g* in Altai Turkic varieties is a regular change. Possibly it developed from the secondary long vowel, which shortened, e.g. Altai *sadu* 'trade' < *sat-* 'to sell', *kečü* 'crossing' < *keč-* 'to cross', etc. (Baskakov 1947: 244).

From an etymological point of view, the Yenisean adjectives go back to Turkic *qoyuġ*, derived from the reconstructed verb **qoyu-* and the Turkic productive deverbal noun suffix -(X)G which forms adjectives (for its functions, see Erdal 1991: 172). The etymology of the reconstructed verb *qoyu- is not clear. According to Clauson (ED 676a), qoy- means 'to be thick,' and goes back to *qōd- ~ qud- 'to pour out (a liquid)'. The authors of ESTJa (2000: 32–33) reconstruct *qoñu- and connect the verb with qañaq 'the skin on milk, clotted cream'.

From Turkic, the word was borrowed into Tungusic[256] (Romanova, Myreeva & Baraškov 1975: 189) and New Persian (Doerfer TMEN 3: 562).

1.2.3   Physical and Characteristic Peculiarities of Humans and Animals

Kott **aksax** 'lame' (Werner 2002/1: 22) ← Turkic *aqsaq 'lame' < aqsa- 'to limp, be lame' -K {Turkic VN, see Erdal 1991: 227}:

cf. Old Turkic aqsaq; NE^S YeniseiT: Khakas axsax; Kyzyl axşa- 'to limp'; Shor aqsaq; AltaiT: Altai aqsaq; Tuba aksak; Qumanda aksak; Quu aksak; Teleut aqsaq; ChulymT aqsaq; SayanT: Tuvan askak; Tofan aqsaq; NE^N Yakut –; NW^N Siberian Tatar –; NW^S Kirgiz aksak; Fu-yü –; Kazak aqsaq; SE Yellow Uyghur axsaq;

Turkic → Samoyedic:

Kamas axsa^c ~ aksa^c 'lame'.

Etymology: Joki LS 58; Räsänen VEWT 9b; Clauson ED 95a; ESTJa 1974: 76; Timonina 1978: 12

From the phonetic side, the Turkic final -k regularly changed to spirant -x; the Turkic cluster -ks- is regularly preserved in Kott.

The Turkic adjective was borrowed into Samoyedic also (Joki LS 58).

Kott **arak** 'lean (thin)' (Werner 2002/1: 57) ← Turkic *arïq 'tired out, exhausted, emaciated, weak for the lack of food' < ār- 'to be tired, exhausted, weak' -(X)K {Turkic VN, see Erdal 1991: 228}:

cf. Old Turkic aruq; NE^S YeniseiT: Khakas arïx 'lean, thin (about animals)'; Sagai, Kachin; Kyzyl arïq 'lean, emaciated, weak, faint' (R); Shor arïn-[257] 'to grow thin'; AltaiT: Altai arïq 'lean, thin'; Tuba arï- 'to become thin; to be tired'; Qumanda arik ~ aruq 'gaunt, emaciated'; Quu arïq 'lean, emaciated, weak, faint'; Teleut arïq 'lean, emaciated, weak, faint' (R); SayanT: Tuvan arïq ~ argan 'thin, gaunt, weak'; Tofan arïq 'thin, lean, gaunt; lean (meat)'; ChulymT arïq 'lean, emaciated, weak, faint' (R); NE^N Yakut ïr- 'to become thin; to be exhausted'; Yakut dial. aray- 'to weaken with age, to grow old' (DS); NW^N Siberian Tatar arïq 'lean, thin'; NW^S Kirgiz arik 'thin, gaunt'; Fu-yü –; Kazak arïq 'thin, lean, gaunt'; SE Yellow Uyghur –;

---

256   Turkic: Yakut → Tungusic: Tommot, Mai, Urmi Ewenki k̦oyū 'thick, strong'.
257   < ār-(X)n- {Turkic reflexive, see Erdal 1991: 588}.

Turkic → Samoyedic:
Kamas *arar*-[258] 'to dry, to lean'.
Etymology: Joki LS 69; Clauson ED 214a, 193a; ESTJa 1974: 160–162; Timonina 1978: 12; Erdal 1991: 228; Róna-Tas & Berta WOT 2011: 71–74

The Kott word was borrowed from the Siberian Turkic form **arïq*, where the change of *-ï-* > *-a-* in the second syllable is a regular change for Yeniseian loanwords. This is because of the stress on the first syllable.

For details on the morphological background of the Turkic verb *ār-* 'to be tired', see Róna-Tas and Berta (WOT 2011: 71–74).

The Turkic word was also borrowed into Samoyedic (Joki LS 69).

Arin *berke* ~ *berek* ~ *birka* 'big, great; very' (Werner 2002/1: 121);
Arin *berkutu* 'brave' (Werner 2002/1: 122) < Arin *berke* 'big, great; very' *-tu* {Yeniseian NN/adj.}:
← Turkic **berke* 'clever, deft' ← Mongolic *berke* 'difficult, hard; burdensome, troublesome; complicated, serious; difficulty, hardship; trouble; skillful, competent, fit' ← Turkic **bärkĂ* < *bärk* 'firm, stable, solid':

cf. NE[S] YeniseiT: –; AltaiT: Quu *perge* 'clever, deft'; SayanT: Tuvan *berge* 'difficult'; ChulymT –; NE[N] Yakut *berke* '*adverb* very, very much, strongly; fine'; Dolgan *bärkä* ~ *bärgä* '*adj*. strong; *adv*. very much'; NW[N] Siberian Tatar *berägäy* 'fine'; NW[S] Kirgiz –; Fu-yü; SE Yellow Uyghur –;

Turkic ← Mongolic *berke* 'difficult, hard; burdensome, troublesome; complicated, serious; difficulty, hardship; trouble; skillful, competent, fit':

cf. Middle Mongol: Precl.Mo. *berke*; SH *berke* 'difficult'; HY *berke* 'difficult'; Ibn-Muh. *berke*; Muq. *bürke* 'strong'; LM *berke*; Modern Mongol: Buryat *berxe*; Khalkha *berx*; Kalmuck *berkä*; Dagur *berke* (T); Khamnigan *berke* ~ *börke*;

Mongolic ← Turkic **bärkĂ* > *bärk* 'firm, stable':

cf. Old Turkic *bärk* 'firm, stable, solid'; NE[S] YeniseiT: Khakas *pirïk* 'impenetrable'; AltaiT: –; SayanT: Tuvan *bert* 'impenetrable'; Tofan *be^crt* 'kind, good'; ChulymT *pērek* 'difficult'; NE[N] Yakut *bert* 'excellent, beautiful; *particle* very, completely, entirely'; Dolgan *bär* ~ *bärt* 'strong; *adv*. very; *adj*. excellent, wonderful; better; great'; NW[N] Siberian Tatar –; NW[S] Kirgiz *berk* 'strong; very'; Fu-yü –; Kazak *berïk* 'strong, solid, stable'; SE Yellow Uyghur *perïk* ~ *perk* 'big, important', cf. *perïk* 'strong'.

Etymology: Räsänen VEWT 71a; Clauson ED 361b; ESTJa 1978: 119; Rassadin 1980: 60, 64; Khabtagaeva 2009: 267

The Arin forms were borrowed from Siberian Turkic **berke*. From a morphological point of view, the Arin form functions as a half-affix with the meaning

---

258 ← Turkic *arar-* < *ār-Ar-* {Turkic NN/causative, see Erdal 1991: 741}.

'big, great, very'. Cf. other Arin compound words with this half-affix: ***belkertura*** 'empire', ***berketura*** 'city, town', ***berkitak*** 'mountain', ***berkuštukdu*** 'strong' (Khabtagaeva 2015d: 134–135)

The Arin form *berkutu* 'brave' is probably used with the native Yeniseian suffix +*tu*, which forms adjectives (for details on its functions in Ket, see Georg 2007: 141). By comparison, the next example below, Arin *berkuštukdu* 'strong', has the Yenisei Turkic suffix +*tXG* (see below).

From an etymological aspect, the Siberian Turkic *berke* belongs to the category of re-borrowings. It was borrowed from the Mongolic word *berke*, which is ultimately of Turkic origin. The Mongolic borrowing into Siberian Turkic is revealed by the presence of the final vowel at the end of the word (for details on the Turko-Mongolic criterion, see Róna-Tas 1998: 72–73; Schönig 2003: 408–409; Khabtagaeva 2009: 267).

For the Turkic and Mongolic etymology, also see Räsänen (VEWT 71a), Clauson (ED 361b), Sevortjan (ESTJa 1978: 119) and Rassadin (1980: 60, 64).

Arin ***berkuštukdu*** 'strong' (Werner 2002/1: 122) < Arin *berke* 'big, great; very' + *kuštuk* 'strong' -*tu* {Yeniseian NN/adj.}:
< Arin *berke* 'big, great; very' ← Turkic;
+ Arin *kuštuk* ← Turkic *küčtüg 'strong, powerful; violent, oppressive' < *küč* 'strength' +*lXG* {Turkic NN/adj., see Erdal 1991: 121}:
    cf. Old Turkic *küčlüg* < *küč*; NE^S YeniseiT: Khakas *küstīg* 'strong; powerful; energetic' < *küs*; Sagai, Koibal *küs* (R); Kyzyl *küš* ~ *kuš*; Shor *küštig* 'strong' < *küš*; AltaiT: Altai *küč*; Tuba *küč*; Qumanda *küč*; Quu *küč*; Teleut *küčtü* 'strong' < *küč*; SayanT: Tuvan *küš*; Tofan *küš*; ChulymT *küč*; NE^N Yakut *kūs*; Dolgan *kūs* ~ *küs*; NW^N Siberian Tatar *küc*; NW^S Kirgiz *küč*; Fu-yü *güštīh* (< *küčlüg* < *küč*+*lXG*) 'strong'; Kazak *küš*; SE Yellow Uyghur *kuš*;
Turkic → Samoyedic:
    Kamas *küštü* 'strong, powerful, active'.
Etymology: Doerfer TMEN 3: 625–628; Räsänen VEWT 306ab; Ščerbak SF 195; 1997: 128; Rassadin 1971: 205; Clauson ED 693a; ESTJa 1980: 96–98; Khabtagaeva 2009: 166; Nugteren 2011: 434

The Arin word belongs to the category of compound words. It consists of two Turkic words, *berke* and *küčtüg* 'strong, powerful'. Another important change, haplology, *berkekuš > *berkuš* occurred in the Arin form.

For the etymology of the Turkic word *berke* 'clever, deft' (← Mongolic *berke* 'difficult, hard; complicated, serious, skillful, competent, fit' ← Turkic *bärkĂ < *bärk* 'firm, stable, solid'), see above in Arin ***berke*** ~ ***berek*** ~ ***birka*** 'big, great; very'.

Another Arin compound word *kuštuk* originates from the Turkic word *küč* 'power, energy' with the productive denominal noun/adjective suffix +*tXG*, which is a phonetic variant of +*LXG* (for details of function in Yenisei Turkic, see Babuškin 1975: 89–91; in Altai Turkic see Baskakov 1947: 245; and in Old Turkic see Erdal 1991: 121).

The Turkic word *küč* was borrowed into Mongolic[259] (Nugteren 2011: 434), Tungusic[260] (SSTMJa 1: 438b–439a), Samoyedic (Joki LS 219–220) and New Persian (Doerfer TMEN 3: 625–628) languages.

For the etymology of the Turkic word *küč*, see Räsänen (VEWT 306ab), Clauson (ED 693a) and Levitskaja (ESTJa 1980: 96–98).

Kott ***elor* ~ *erol*** 'sober' (Werner 2002/1: 267) ← Turkic *elür ~ *erül* 'sober' ← Mongolic *elegür* ~ *eregül* 'health; sober, abstinent':

  cf. Old Turkic –; NE^S YeniseiT: –; AltaiT: Altai *erül* 'sober', cf. *älür* (R); Teleut *erül* 'sober'; SayanT: Tuvan *elēr* 'sober'; Tofan *elēr* 'sober'; NE^N Yakut *elier* ~ *ölüör* 'healthy'; Dolgan *ölüör* 'healthy'; Yakut dial. *elier* 'healthy' (DS); Remaining lgs. –;

Turkic → Samoyedic:
  Kamas *jilör* 'sober';

Turkic ← Mongolic *elegür* ~ *eregül* 'health; healthy, sound; sober, abstinent; untouched, unploughed, virgin (*of soil*)':

  cf. Middle Mongol: Precl.Mo. *elegür* ~ *eregül*; Ibn-Muh. *elür*; Muq. *ele'ür*; LM *eregül*; Modern Mongol: Buryat *elür*; Khalkha *erül*; Oirat dial. *erül*; Dagur –; Khamnigan –.

Etymology: Joki LS 146; Kałużyński 1962: 17; Räsänen VEWT 41b; Rassadin 1971: 180; 1980: 20, 65, 72; Timonina 1978: 13; Khabtagaeva 2009: 247

The Kott forms *elor* ~ *erol* were borrowed from two different Turkic forms: *elür* ~ *erül*. The Turkic long vowel shortened, vowel harmony disappeared and the Turkic high-rounded vowel -*ü*- was changed to the low rounded vowel -*o*-. This change *u* > *o* is typical for some Kott loanwords, e.g. Kott *bogá* 'bull' ← Turkic *buqa*, Kott *torá* 'living room' ← Turkic *tura*. Abbreviation of Turkic sec-

---

259 Turkic → Mongolic 'power, force (*also military*), strength; effort; energy; validity': Middle Mongol: Precl.Mo. *küčün*; 'Phags-pa *küčün*; Muq. *küč*(*in*); Leiden *küčtü* (< *küč* +*tU* {Mongolic NN/adj.}); LM *küčü*(*n*); Modern Mongol: Buryat *xüse*(*n*); Lower Uda Buryat *küšen* ~ *küšün*; Khalkha *xüč*; Kalmuck *kütšn*; Dagur *kuč* (E); Khamnigan *küči*(*n*) ~ *köčö*(*n*).
    Cf. Turkic → Mongolic → Modern Turkic: Tuvan *küčü* 'power, might' (Khabtagaeva 2009: 166).

260 Turkic → Mongolic → Tungusic: Kachin Ewenki *kučitej* (< *küčü* +*tAi* {Mongolic NN/adj.}) 'strong'; Negidal *kusun* 'power; strong'; Udihe *kuʰi* 'power'; Ulcha *kusun* 'power'; Orok *kusun* 'power, authority'; Nanai *kusũ* 'power'; Manchu *husun* 'power, strength, force, fortness'.
    Cf. Turkic: Yakut → Tungusic: Aldan, Sakhalin, Urmi Ewenki *kuhulē-* 'to rape, violate'; Lamut *küssi* 'stronly, by force'.

ondary long vowels in Kott loanwords also is a typical change. This phonetic feature points to a later period of borrowing.

From an etymological point of view, the Turkic forms are of Mongolic origin (Kałużyński 1962: 17; Räsänen VEWT 41b; Rassadin 1971: 180; 1980: 20, 65, 72; Khabtagaeva 2009: 247). The word is present in almost all Middle and Modern Mongol languages. The metathetical forms *elegür ~ eregül* were present already in the Preclassical Mongolian period.

The etymological background of the Mongolic word is unclear. If the original base of the word was **ere*, then it must have been connected with the Mongolic noun *er-e* 'man, male; manly, daring, bold, brave, plucky,' and derived with the suffix *+GUl*, which is absent in Mongolic. In turn, there is the productive denominal noun/adjective suffix *+GUr*, which is a phonetic variant of *+GAr*[261] (Khabtagaeva 2009: 281). We do not have any information about the non-productive form **ele*.

Kott *eser ~ esirolog*; Assan *esrolagín ~ esrolokon* 'drunk' (Werner 2002/1: 268) ← Turkic **äsäriklig* < *äsär-* 'to be or become drunk, intoxicated' *-(X)K* {Turkic VN, see Erdal 1991: 228} *+lXK* {Turkic NN/adj., see Erdal 1991: 121–131}:

    cf. Old Turkic *äsür-*; NE^S YeniseiT: Khakas *izĭrĭk* 'drunk, intoxicated'; Sagai, Koibal, Kachin *ezirĭk* (R); Kyzyl *ēžirik^x*; Shor *äzirĭk* (R); AltaiT: Altai *ezirik*; Tuba *ezirik*; Qumanda *ezir-*; Quu *ezirik*; Teleut *ezirik*; SayanT: Tuvan *ezirik*; Tofan *e^csĭrik*; ChulymT *ēzerek*; NE^N Yakut *itirik*; Dolgan *itiriktä-* (< **äsäriktä-* < **äsär-(X)K+lA-*) 'to drink heavily'; NW^N Siberian Tatar *izerek*; NW^S Kirgiz *esirik* 'stupid'; Fu-yü *izir-*; Kazak *esĭriktĭk* 'intoxication; irresponsible state'; SE Yellow Uyghur *ĭser- ~ eser-*;

Turkic → Samoyedic:

    Kamas *ēzirek ~ izirek* 'intoxicated, drunk'; Mator *isir* 'drunk'.

Etymology: Joki LS 129; Räsänen VEWT 50b; Clauson ED 251a; ESTJa 1974: 309–310; Timonina 1978: 12; Khabtagaeva 2015c: 99

The Yeniseian words were borrowed from the Siberian Turkic form **äsäriklig*. The final consonant *-n* in Assan forms is possibly the native Yeniseian suffix *+Aŋ*, which forms adjectives (Details for functions, see Vajda 2004: 38). The Yeniseian forms underwent metathesis *-kl-* > *-lk-*, which is a particular feature of Altaic elements in Yeniseian.

The Turkic word derived from the verb *äsär-* 'to be or become drunk, intoxicated' with the productive deverbal noun suffix *-(X)K* and the denominal

---

[261] E.g. LM *quluyur* 'laid or pressed back ears; crop-eared' < **qul*: cf. *qulki* 'earwax, middle ear'; *bujigir* 'curly' < **bujaya*: cf. *bujïyi-* 'to curl'; *γonjoγor* 'long, stretched, thin and long, oblong, oval' < **γonja*: cf. *γonjayi-* 'to taper, have an oval or elongated shape', etc.

noun/adjective suffix +*lXK*. For other Turkic data and etymology, see Räsänen (VEWT 50b), Clauson (ED 251a) and Sevortjan (ESTJa 1974: 309–310). From Siberian Turkic, the word was borrowed into Samoyedic (Joki LS 129).

Kott **harâ** 'rapacious, voracious' (Werner 2002/1: 302) ← Turkic **qaram* 'stingy, greedy' ← Mongolic *qaram* 'jealous; stinginess; regret' < *qara-* 'to look at, glance, watch, observe; to regard, consider; to look after; to face' *-m* {Mongolic VN, see Poppe GWM § 164}:

cf. Old Turkic –; NE^S YeniseiT: Khakas *xaram* 'miser; stingy'; Sagai *qaram* 'stingy' (R); AltaiT: Altai *karam* 'envy; envious; stingy, avaricious'; Teleut *qaram* 'greedy, avaricious' (R); SayanT: Tuvan *xaram* 'stingy miser'; Tofan *haram* 'stingy, greedy'; ChulymT *qaram* 'greedy'; NE^N Yakut *xaram* 'abstinent, hoarder, miser; envy'; Remaining lgs. –;

Turkic ← Mongolic *qaram* 'jealous; stinginess; regret' < *qara-m*:

cf. SH *qaramla-*[262] 'to be greedy'; HY *qalam* ~ *qaram* 'lust'; LM *qaram* 'jealous; stinginess; regret'; Buryat *xaram* 'avarice, envy'; Lower Uda Buryat dial. *karam* 'greed'; Khalkha *xaram* 'stingy, miserly, tight, calculating; miserliness'; Kalmuck *xarm* 'envy, avarice'; Dagur –; Khamnigan *xaram*.

Etymology: Räsänen VEWT 236a; Rassadin 1971: 186, 1980: 30, 40; Anikin 2000: 611; Khabtagaeva 2009: 248

The Yeniseian word is of unknown etymology. As a hypothesis, I assume it is related to the Siberian Turkic word *qaram* 'stingy, greedy'. The lexical meaning is suggested by the borrowing from Turkic. It is probable that the Kott meaning 'rapacious, voracious' refers to a wild animal, and the Turkic meaning 'stingy, greedy' → 'voracious, greedy,' fits with our hypothesis. Possibly, the final Turkic *-m* was dropped in the Kott form. There are certain Turkic loanwords in Kott in which the suffixes disappeared in final position; this loanword probably belongs to this category. The change of initial Turkic consonant *k-* to *h-* is a regular in Kott loanwords, as in native Yeniseian words, which suggests an early period of borrowing for this Kott word.

From an etymological aspect, the Turkic forms are of Mongolic origin (Räsänen VEWT 236a; Rassadin 1971: 186, 1980: 30, 40; Khabtagaeva 2009: 248). The Mongolic noun derived from the Common Mongolic verb *qara-* 'to look at, glance, watch, observe; to regard, consider; to look after; to face' (Nugteren 2011: 404) with the productive denominal noun suffix *-m* (Poppe GWM § 164).

---

[262] < *qaram* +*lA-* {Mongolic NV, see Poppe GWM § 245}.

Ket, Yugh *īt* 'smell, aroma' ← Turkic **yīð* 'scent, odour, smell';
Yugh **itiŋsi** 'stinking' (Werner 2002/1: 385) < *it -Xŋ* {Yeniseian NN/adj.} *-si* {Yeniseian nominalizer} ← Turkic **yīð* 'scent, odour, smell';
Kott **īta** 'stinking' (Werner 1990: 294) ← Turkic **yïtu* (cf. Altai Turkic) < *yïtū* < *yiðïg* 'smell, odour (*usually, not always, unpleasant*), foul-smelling'< *yiði-* 'to have an unpleasant smell, to stink' *-G* {Turkic VN/adj., see Erdal 1991: 172} < *yīð* 'scent, odour, smell' *+I-* {Turkic NV, see Erdal 1991: 484}:

cf. Old Turkic *yiðïg*; NE⁵ YeniseiT: Khakas *čïzïg*; Sagai *čïzïq* (R); Koibal, Kachin *yïs* (R); Shor *čïzïg*; AltaiT: Altai *d'ïtu*; Tuba *d'ïttu* (< *d'ït+lXG*); Qumanda *d'ïdu*; Quu *yïttïg* (< *yït+lXG*); Teleut *yïttu* (< *yït+lXG*); SayanT: Tuvan *čïttïg* (< *čït+lXG*); Tofan *čïttïg*; ChulymT –; NEᴺ Yakut *sïttāx*; Dolgan *hït*; NWᴺ Siberian Tatar *yïs ~ is ~ yes*; NWˢ Kirgiz *žïttū*; Fu-yü –; Kazak *īs*; SE Yellow Yughur –.

Etymology: Räsänen VEWT 170a; Rassadin 1971: 200; Clauson ED 887b; ESTJa 1974: 380–382; Timonina 1979: 23

It is obvious that the Yeniseian words have a connection with the Turkic word *yïð* 'scent, odour, smell,' as well as its derived adjective form *yiðïg* 'stinking'. The origin of the word is unclear. It may be a native Yeniseian word or a Turkic loanword. If the Yeniseian forms were borrowed from Turkic, the source of borrowing could well be Altai Turkic *yïtu* or *yït* with initial *y-* and devoiced consonant *-t(-)*. The disappearance of Turkic initial *y-* is a typical change for Yeniseian loanwords. The possibility of the preservation of Turkic original long vowel **ï* in Yeniseian is should be examined.

The word belongs to the category of words of uncertain etymology.

Kott **kalakai ~ kalakei** 'verb to stutter, *adj.* stuttering' (Werner 2002/1: 405) ← Turkic **kälägäy* 'stammerer, stutterer' ← Mongolic *kelegei* 'dumb, mute; stammering, stuttering, tongue-tied' < *kelen ügei* 'without tongue' < *kelen* 'tongue; language' + *ügei* {Mongolic negative, see Poppe GWM § 632} < *kelen* 'tongue; language' < *kele-* 'to utter words, express in words; to speak, say, tell, narrate' *-n* {Mongolic VN, see Poppe GWM § 175}:

cf. Old Turkic –; NE⁵ YeniseiT: Khakas *kilegey* 'stammerer, stutterer'; Sagai, Koibal *kälägäy* (R); Shor *kelegey*; AltaiT: Altai *kelegey*; Teleut *kelegei*; SayanT –; ChulymT –; NEᴺ Yakut *keleyei*; NWᴺ Siberian Tatar –; NWˢ Kirgiz [*tili*] *kelegei* 'person, who suffers from a speech impediment'; Fu-yü –; SE Yellow Uyghur –;

Turkic ← Mongolic:

cf. Middle Mongol: –; LM *kelegei* 'dumb, mute; stammering, stuttering, tongue-tied' < *kelen ügei* 'without tongue' < *kelen* 'tongue; language' < *kele-* 'to utter words, express in words; to speak, say, tell, narrate'; Modern Mongol: Buryat *xelexei* 'tongue-tied; stutterer'; Khalkha *xelgüi* 'dumb'; Oirat dial. *kelkā* 'stutterer';

< Mongolic *kelen* 'tongue, speech, language':

Middle Mongol: SH *kele(n)*; HY, Muq. *kelen*; LM *kele(n)*; Modern Mongol: Buryat *xele(n)*; Khalkha *xel(en)*; Kalmuck *keln*; Dagur *xel'* (E); Khamnigan *kelü(n)* ~ *kölö(n)* ~ *kele(n)*.

Etymology: Räsänen VEWT 248b; Doerfer TMEN 1: 472–473; 1985: 39; SSTMJa 1: 447; Timonina 1978: 12; Rassadin 1980: 22; 72; ESTJa 1997: 30; Anikin 2000: 342; Nugteren 2011: 409; Khabtagaeva 2015a: 120–121

The Kott forms *kalakai* ~ *kalakei* 'stuttering' were clearly borrowed from the Turkic form **kälägäy* 'stammerer, stutterer'. Due to the absence of vowel harmony, the Turkic front vowels changed to back vowels. The preservation of initial *k-* in the Kott form points to a later period of borrowing, while the original Yeniseian *k-* changed to *h-* in Kott. From the morphological side, the original part of speech—adjective—becomes a verb in Yeniseian. Cf. Kott *kalakaj-â-kŋ* {-*â*- present tense, verb root -*Vk*-, and 1sg subject suffix -*ŋ*, see Werner 1990: 156–160} 'I am stuttering'; *kalakaj-âlček* {-*âlček* imperative form, see Werner 1990: 193} 'Stutter!'.

Etymologically, the Turkic forms were borrowed from the Mongolic word *kelegei* 'dumb; stammering, stuttering, tongue-tied' (Räsänen VEWT 248b; Rassadin 1980: 22; 72; ESTJa 1997: 30), which is an amalgamation of the Mongolic word *kelen* 'tongue; language' and the Mongolic negating word *ügei*. Finally, the noun *kelen* 'tongue; language' derived from the Common Mongolic verb *kele-* 'to speak, say, tell, narrate' and the deverbal noun suffix -*n* (for other Mongolic data, see Nugteren 2011: 409).

The Mongolic word was also borrowed into the Ewenki language;[263] the Lamut form was probably borrowed from Yakut[264] (SSTMJa 1: 447; Doerfer 1985: 39). Cf. also Siberian Russian *kïlegei* 'stuttering', which was directly borrowed from Buryat (Anikin 2000: 342).

Kott **kalkul** 'deaf' (Werner 2002/1: 405) ← Turkic **qulɣur* 'crop-eared' ← Mongolic *quluɣur* 'laid or pressed back (*of ears*); crop-eared' < **qul(V)* +*GUr* {Mongolic NN/adj., the phonetic variant of +*GAr*, see Poppe GWM § 150}:

cf. NE^S YeniseiT: Khakas *xulǧur* 'wretch; nasty, crappy'; AltaiT: Altai *kulugur* 'scoundrel, bastard'; Tuba *kulugur* 'wretch; mischievous, naughty'; Qumanda *kulgur* ~ *kulugïr* 'scoundrel, crappy'; Teleut *qultïr* 'sly, crafty' (TR), cf. *qulǧur* 'disabled, poor' (R); SayanT: Tuvan *kulugur* 'knave'; ChulymT –; NE^N Yakut *kulugur* 'short-eared, crop-

---

263   Mongolic → Tungusic: *Northern Ewenki*: Yerbogachon, Ilimpeya; *Southern Ewenki*: Podkamennyi, Nercha; *Eastern Ewenki*: Tokko, Aldan, Uchur, Urmi, Tommot, Chumikan, Sakhalin *keleyei* 'stutterer'.
264   Cf. Mongolic → Turkic: Yakut → Tungusic: Lamut *kelegei* 'stutterer'.

eared' (Pek.); NW^N Siberian Tatar *qulġur* 'scoundrel, shoddy; intrigues'; NW^S Kirgiz –; Fu-yü –; SE Yellow Uyghur –;
Turkic ← Mongolic:
 cf. Middle Mongol: –; LM *quluyur* 'laid or pressed back (of ears); crop-eared'; Modern Mongol: Khalkha *xulgar* 'short-eared, crop-eared, earless; convict'; Oirat *xuluyur* ~ *xuluxur* ~ *xuluyūr* 'droop-eared, blunt-eared'; Kalmuck *xuluyar* 'blunt-eared'; Dagur –; Khamnigan –;
Mongolic ← Turkic *qul, cf. *qulaq* ~ *qulqaq* 'ear':
 cf. Old Turkic *qulaq* ~ *qulqaq*; NE^S YeniseiT: Khakas *xulax*; Sagai, Koibal, Kachin *qulaq* (R); Kyzyl *χulaχ*; Shor *qulaq*; AltaiT: Altai *qulaq*; Tuba *kulak*; Qumanda *kulak*; Quu *kulak*; Teleut *qulaq* (R); SayanT: Tuvan *kulak*; Tofan *qulaq*; ChulymT *qulaq*; NE^N Yakut *kulgāx*; Dolgan *kulgā(k)* ~ *kulgak*; NW^N Siberian Tatar *qulaq*; NW^S Kirgiz *kulak*; Fu-yü *gulah*; Kazak *qulaq*; SE Yellow Uyghur *qolaq*.
Etymology: ESTJa 2000: 126; Khabtagaeva 2009: 248
 The etymology of the Kott word *kalkul* 'deaf' is unknown. It is probably related to the Siberian Turkic form *kulyur 'crop-eared'. Semantically, broadening of meaning happened in Kott. From a phonetic point of view, the final Kott -*l* assimilated due to the internal consonant -*l*-.
 The Siberian Turkic *kulġur* was borrowed from Mongolic *quluyur* 'laid or pressed back (*of ears*); crop-eared', which is possibly ultimately of Turkic origin, cf. Common Turkic *qulaq* ~ *qulqaq* 'ear'. The "dead" base of the Mongolic word is *qul, which may be connected with different Mongolic words.[265] The morphological structure of the Turkic word also supports the idea of *qul as the base of the Kott word. The Turkic word *qulaq* ~ *qulqaq* 'ear' derived from the base *qul and the Turkic denominal noun suffixes +*GAK* and +*AK*, which form names for body parts (for details, see Erdal 1991: 74–75).
 For the etymological background of the Turkic form *kulyur* 'crop-eared,' see Levitskaja (ESTJa 2000: 126) and Khabtagaeva (2009: 248).
 See also Kott *kalôx* 'ear'.

Kott **kapsagai** 'nimble, quick (*said of a person, horse or dog*)' (Werner 2002/1: 411) ← Turkic *kapčagai 'quick' ← Mongolic *γabšiγai* 'swift, expeditious; valiant; vanguard' < **γab+si-* {Mongolic NV, see Poppe GWM § 248} -*GAi* {Mongolic VN, see Poppe GWM § 148}:

---

265 E.g. LM *qulki* ~ *qulaquu* 'earwax, middle-ear', *qulayi-* (< **qul(A)+yi-*) 'to have cropped ears', Buryat *xulmagar* (<**qul+mA+GAr*) 'with laid back ears', Kalmuck *xulxa-* (<**qul+KU-*) 'die Ohren an den Kopf legen, (vom Pferd) beissen wollen, (vom Menschen) etwas zu tun beabsichtigen' (KWb), Buryat *xulmagana-* (<**qul+ma+GAnA-*), *xulmalza-* (<**qul+mA+ljA-*) 'to press the ears', etc.

cf. NE^S YeniseiT: Khakas *xapčaġay* 'fast, agile, hasty; quickly'; Koibal *kapčaġay* 'thin' (R); Shor *qapčïġay* 'fast, quick; quickly'; AltaiT: Altai *kapšaġay* 'fast, quick; quickly'; Tuba *kapčagay ~ kapčïgai* 'quick, agile' < *kapčay ~ kapšay ~ kapšāy* 'quickly'; Qumanda *kapčagay* 'quick, agile', cf. *kapčāy ~ kapčay* 'quickly'; Quu *kapžïgay ~ kapšagay ~ kapšay* 'quickly; fast, agile, nimble'; Teleut *qapšïġay* 'fast; quickly' (R); SayanT: Tuvan *kapšagay* 'clever'; ChulymT –; NE^N Yakut *xapsaġay* 'nimble, agile, clever, quick'; NW^N Siberian Tatar *qapšaġay* 'thin'; NW^S Kirgiz –; Fu-yü *ġabšïna ~ ġabšiha* 'quickly'; Kazak *qapsaġay* 'thin'; SE Yellow Uyghur –;

Turkic ← Mongolic *γabšiγai* 'quick, smart, brisk':

cf. Middle Mongol: –; LM *γabsiγai* 'swift, expeditious; valiant; vanguard; shock (*worker, troops*)'; Modern Mongol: Buryat *gabšagai* 'nimble, agile, quick; an enthusiast; agility, agility, speed'; Khalkha *gawšgai* 'quick, smart, brisk'; Kalmuck *gawš^iγǟ* 'agile, energetic, hard-working, efficient'; Oirat dial. *gawšxā* 'agile'; Dagur –; Khamnigan *gabčigai*.

Etymology: Räsänen VEWT 234a; Rassadin 1980: 30; 33; 35; 45; 47; ESTJa 1997: 270–271

The Kott word was borrowed from Turkic, which is, however, of Mongolic origin. The Turkic mediation is proven by the initial consonant *k-* as in Turkic, instead of Mongolic voiced *γ-*. This an important criterion in favor of Turkic mediation, and not direct Mongolic borrowing.

From the etymological point of view, the Mongolic word is derived from the non-productive base **γab*[266] (ESTJa 1997: 270–271), with the productive denominal verbal suffix *+si-* which forms verbs expressing attainment of a quality (Poppe GWM § 248), and the deverbal noun suffix *-GAi*, which forms adjectives designating qualities resulting from the action (Poppe GWM § 148).

The Mongolic word was borrowed into the Manchu language[267] (SSTMJa 1: 134; Rozycki 1994: 84).

Kott *keršo* 'clever' (Werner 2002/1: 422) ← Turkic **kärsü* 'clever, talanted' ← Mongolic *kersü* < *kersegüü* 'wise, circumspect, prudent; careful, circumspect, astute' < **kerse-GU* {Mongolic VN/adj., see Poppe GWM § 152}:

NE^S YeniseiT: Khakas *kirsē ~ kirse* 'talanted, clever; able, gifted'; Sagai, Koibal *kersä* 'wise, witty, eloquent' (R); Shor *kerse* 'clever, gifted'; AltaiT: Altai *kersü* 'clever, wise'; Qumanda *kersig ~ kirsig ~ kersü* 'clever, wise'; Quu *kersig* 'wise, sharp'; Teleut *kersü* 'clever'; SayanT –; ChulymT –; NE^N Yakut *körsüö* 'modest, quiet; clever, prudent'; Dol-

---

266 Cf. LM *γabi* 'as good as others, on par with others', *γabiy-a(n)* 'merit, achievement; heroism, valor; worthy service', *γabiya-* 'to refer or belong to, be included in, fall under'; Kalmuck *gawšūn* (< *γabsiyun* < **γabsi-GUn*) 'flink, hurtig, fleissig, energisch', etc.

267 Mongolic → Tungusic: Manchu *gabsian ~ gabsihan* 'quick, clever, nimble, agile'.

gan *körsüö* 'modest, sensible, quiet'; NW^N Siberian Tatar *kärsäü* 'clever'; NW^S Kirgiz *kerseyü* 'snootiness, arrogance, haughtiness'; Fu-yü –; Kazak –; SE Yellow Uyghur –;
Turkic → Samoyedic:
Kamas *kērzü* 'intelligent, clever';
Turkic ← Mongolic *kersü* < *kersegüü* 'wise, circumspect, prudent; careful, circumspect, astute':

cf. Middle Mongol: –; LM *kersegüü*; Modern Mongol: Buryat –; Khalkha *xersü* 'circumspect, cautious, careful, wide-awake'; Kalmuck *kersü* 'nimble, witty, clever'; Dagur *kərsū* (E); Khamnigan –.

Etymology: Joki LS 179; Räsänen VEWT 256b; Kałużyński 1962: 32; Timonina 1978: 12; Rassadin 1980: 52; 72; Khabtagaeva 2015a: 117

The Kott word was borrowed from the Siberian Turkic form **kersü* 'clever, talanted' (cf. Altai Turkic, Siberian Tatar). This attribution is proven by the final labial vowel *-o* in Kott form.

The Altai Turkic *kersü* and Yenisei Turkic *kerse ~ kersä* forms represent two different paths of development of the Mongolic sequence *-egü-*, which eventually became the secondary vowel *ǖ* in the Modern Mongol languages. In this way, the Altai Turkic final vowel *-ü*, which was abbreviated from Mongolic *-ǖ*, demonstrates a later period of borrowing from Mongolic. In contrast, the Yenisei Turkic form with final illabial vowel *-e* evidences an earlier period of Mongolic borrowing, due to the development of secondary long vowels according own phonetic rules.[268]

The change of Kott consonant *-š-* from *-s-* is a distinctive phonetic feature for native Yeniseian words and Turkic loanwords.

The Mongolic origin of the word is corroborated by its morphological structure. Despite the fact that the base of word **kerse-* is of unclear derivation, it is possible that the word was derived with the productive deverbal noun suffix *-GU*, which forms adjectives (for details of functions, see Poppe GWM § 152).

Through the mediation of Turkic, the Mongolic word was borrowed into Samoyedic (Joki LS 179) as well.

---

[268] The Turkic secondary long vowels developed from the sequence *Vowel-Consonant-Vowel* according to the first vowel (e.g. Old Turkic *oġul* 'boy, son' > Khakas, Tuvan *ōl*; Old Turkic *baġïr* 'liver' > Khakas *pār*, Tuvan *bār*, etc.). While in Mongolic languages the secondary vowels developed according to the second vowel (e.g. LM *arčiyul* 'scharf, kerchief' > Khalkha *arčūl*, Buryat *aršūl*; LM *mayu* 'bad' > Khalkha, Buryat *mū*, etc.). For details on the development of secondary vowels in Turkic and Mongolic languages, and Mongolic loanwords in Turkic, see Khabtagaeva 2004; Janiszevska 2012.

Kott **kolča** 'slow (*a person, horse, reindeer, etc.*)' (Werner 2002/1: 438) ← Turkic **kö̆lje* 'slow, slowly' < *köŋül* 'the mind; thought; the heart' +*CA* {Khakas NN/adv., see Baskakov 1975: 109} < **köŋ*:
 YeniseiT: Khakas *kö̆lje* 'slow, quiet; slowly, quietly, slowly, gently'; Kyzyl *kö̆l^dža* ~ *kö̆l^dža* 'quiet; slowly'; Shor *kö̆če* 'softly, slowly';
< *kö̆l* < *köŋül*:
 cf. Old Turkic *köŋül*; NE^S YeniseiT: Khakas *kö̆l* 'mood; feeling; love'; Sagai, Koibal *kö̆lüg* (< *kö̆l* +*lXG* {Turkic NN/adj.}) 'with sense' (R); Shor *köŋnü* 'desire, will, mood'; AltaiT: Altai *kün* 'strong desire, love, attention, mood, will'; Tuba *kȫn* ~ *kün* 'desire'; Qumanda *küŋne* 'desire'; Quu *kün* 'desire, will; jealousy, envy'; Teleut *küni* 'desire'; SayanT: Tuvan *xȫn* 'mood, desire'; Tofan *hö̆l* 'desire; mood, consent; soul'; ChulymT –; NE^N Yakut *köŋül* 'freedom, will, independence; will, desire; permission, permit'; Dolgan *köŋül* 'freedom'; NW^N Siberian Tatar *küŋel* 'soul, heart'; NW^S Kirgiz *köŋül* ~ *kȫn* 'heart, sympathy'; Fu-yü –; Kazak *köŋil* 'desire, attention, mood'; SE Yellow Uyghur *köŋul* ~ *koŋil* ~ *künel* 'heart'.

Etymology: Räsänen VEWT 291a; Clauson ED 731b; Timonina 1978: 13; ESTJa 1980: 75–77; SIGTJa 2001: 274

The Kott word *kolča* was borrowed from the Yenisei Turkic form **kö̆lje* with the same meaning of 'slow'. The Turkic secondary vowel shortened, and vowel harmony disappeared.

From the morphological point of view, the Yenisei Turkic form derived from noun *kö̆l* 'mood; feeling; love' and the productive denominal noun suffix +*čA* / +*jA* which forms adverbs[269] (for details on function, see Baskakov 1975: 109). Generally in Turkic languages, the word has a range of lexical meanings connected to different kinds of emotions. The base of word *köŋül* 'the mind; thought; the heart' is the non-productive form **köŋ*, cf. Old Turkic *köŋlä-* 'to be sunk in thought'; AltaiT: Altai *köŋül-* 'to be overcome with emotion'; Teleut *köŋül-* 'to be overcome with emotion, to be touched', are derived from **köŋ* and Turkic denominal verbum suffix +*lA-*.

The Turkic word was borrowed into the Ewenki dialects via Yakut[270] (SST-MJa 1: 434).

Kott **kul'uk** 'bold, boldness' (Werner 2002/1: 450) ← Turkic **külük* 'clever, wise, famous' < *külüg* < *kü* 'rumour, fame, reputation' +*lXG* {Turkic NN/adj., see Erdal 1991: 139}:

---

269 E.g. Khakas *istinje* 'convenient, with' < *istin* {poss.sg.3} < *istīg* 'usual; comfortable; nice, cute' < *istī* 'convenience', *aġirinja* 'silently' < *aġ(i̇)rin* 'slowly, quietly, gradually', *čalbaġinja* 'flat' < *čalbaġï* {+*i̇* poss.sg.3} 'width of the street', etc.
270 Yakut → Tungusic: Sakhalin, Urmi, Chumikan Ewenki *kuŋul* 'will, desire; pamperedness'.

cf. Old Turkic külüg 'famous'; NE^S YeniseiT: Khakas külük 'wisdom; smart, wise; nimble, agile; daring'; Sagai, Koibal külük 'hero' (R); Kyzyl külük^χ 'intelligent, educated; clever'; Shor külük 'smart, wise, clever, agile, daring'; AltaiT: Altai külük 'athlete, heart of oak; nimble, agile'; Tuba külük 'hero'; Qumanda külük 'athlete, heart of oak, clever'; Quu külük 'athlete, hero'; Teleut külük 'heart of oak; clever, agile, lively, desperate'; SayanT –; ChulymT –; NE^N Yakut –; NW^N Siberian Tatar külük 'famous'; NW^S Kirgiz –; Fu-yü –; Kazak –; SE Yellow Uyghur –;

Turkic → Samoyedic:
Kamas külük 'nimble, quick, quick; diligent, hard-working'.

Etymology: Joki LS 216–217; Räsänen VEWT 306a; Doerfer TMEN 3: 653–654; Clauson ED 717b; ESTJa 1997: 140; Khabtagaeva 2015b: 522

The Kott word was borrowed from Siberian Turkic *külük 'clever, wise, hero'. The disappearence of vowel harmony is a regular feature for Yeniseian loanwords. The palatalization of the Kott sound cluster Vl/V is an expected change in the environment of Turkic palatal vowels. The preservation of Turkic initial consonant k- points to a later period of borrowing.

From the etymological side, the Turkic word was derived from the noun kü 'rumour, fame, reputation,' and the Turkic productive denominal noun suffix +lXG, which forms adjectives (Erdal 1991: 139).

The Turkic word was borrowed into Samoyedic as well (Joki LS 216–217). Semantic widening happened in Mongolic; in Turkic, the word gained the specific meaning 'a strong and swift horse,' related to horse terminology[271] (Doerfer TMEN 3: 653–654). From Mongolic, the word was borrowed into Manchu[272] (Rozycki 1994: 145).

Kott **kuštu** 'very strong' (Werner 2002/1: 458) < kuš -tu {Yeniseian NN/adj.} ← Turkic *küč < kǖč 'strength, power, energy':

cf. Old Turkic kǖč; NE^S YeniseiT: Khakas küs; Sagai, Koibal küs (R); Kyzyl küš ~ kuš; Shor küš; AltaiT: Altai küč; Tuba küč; Qumanda küč; Quu küč; Teleut küč; SayanT: Tuvan küš; Tofan küš; ChulymT küč; NE^N Yakut kǖs; Dolgan kǖs ~ küs; NW^N Siberian Tatar küc; NW^S Kirgiz küč; Fu-yü güštīh (< küčlüg < kǖč+lXG) 'strong'; Kazak küš; SE Yellow Uyghur kuš;

Turkic → Samoyedic:
Kamas küštü 'strong, powerful, vigorous'; Mator küštü 'strong, powerful'.

Etymology: Joki LS 220; Räsänen VEWT 306ab; Ščerbak SF 195; Clauson ED 693a; ESTJa 1980: 96; Nugteren 2011: 434

---

271 Turkic → Mongolic: Middle Mongol: –; LM külüg ~ kölüg 'a strong and swift horse'; Modern Mongol: Buryat xüleg; Khalkha xölög; Oirat dial. kölög; Dagur kulug (T); Khamnigan külüg.
272 Turkic → Mongolic → Tungusic: Manchu kuluk 'enduring horse'.

The Kott word was borrowed from Turkic *küč 'strength, power, energy' and it has its own Yeniseian derivation. It may well originate from the Yeniseian suffix -tu, a productive denominal noun suffix which forms adjectives (for details on functions, see Werner 2002/2: 290; Georg 2007: 141–142). But the possible connection to the Turkic adjective form küčtig 'strong, powerful; violent' (cf. Khakas küstĭg ~ Old Turkic küčlüg) with the assimilated productive suffix +lXG (for details on function, see Erdal 1991: 139) should by no means be excluded.

There are similar forms with the suffix +tü in Samoyedic languages (Joki LS 220; Helimski 1997: 296). In these cases, the source of borrowing is unclear. They may have been borrowed from Yeniseian or directly from Turkic.

The Turkic word was borrowed into the Mongolic languages[273] as well (Clauson ED 693a; Ščerbak 1997: 128; Nugteren 2011: 434).

Kott **munkan ~ munxan** 'poor' (Werner 2002/2: 22) ← Turkic *muŋkan 'unfortunate; cripple' < munǧan 'mentally disturbed' < buŋ- 'to be mentally deranged or disturbed; being senile, feeble-minded, losing control of oneself, going fighting mad' -GAn {Turkic VN/adj., habitual action, see Erdal 1991: 382}:

cf. Old Turkic munǧan 'mentally disturbed'; NE^S YeniseiT: Khakas munu- 'to age, to grow old'; Sagai, Koibal, Kachin muŋ 'the ill-health, the malady' (R); AltaiT: Altai muŋkan 'unfortunate; cripple'; SayanT: Tuvan mönü- 'to age, to grow old'; Tofan –; ChulymT –; NE^N Yakut mun- 'to stray'; Dolgan mun- 'to be embarrassed'; Reamining lgs. –;

Turkic → Samoyedic:
Kamas mukan 'difficult, laborious, arduous; poor'.

Etymology: Joki LS 232; Räsänen VEWT 343a; 344b; 349a; Clauson ED 347a; 769a; ESTJa 2003: 83–86; Róna-Tas & Berta WOT 2011: 620–622

It is probable that the Yeniseian word was borrowed from the Siberian Turkic form *muŋkan 'unfortunate; cripple' (cf. Altai Turkic), which is connected with Old Turkic munǧan 'mentally disturbed'. There are two different forms in Kott: in one, the cluster -nk- changed to -nx-, which can explained by the typical phonetic change of $k > x$ in different positions for Turkic loanwords in Yeniseian.

The Turkic form munǧan derived from the verb buŋ- 'to be mentally deranged or disturbed; to be senile, feeble-minded, to lose control of oneself, to

---

273 Turkic → Mongolic 'power, force (also military); strength; effort; energy; validity': Middle Mongol: Precl.Mo. küčün; 'Phags-pa küčün; Muq. küč(in); Leiden küčtü (< küč +tU {Mongolic NN/adj.}); LM küčü(n); Modern Mongol: Buryat xüse(n); Lower Uda Buryat küšen ~ küšün; Khalkha xüč; Kalmuck kütšn; Dagur kuč (E); Khamnigan küči(n) ~ köčö(n).

go fighting mad' and the Turkic deverbal noun suffix -*GAn*, forming adjectives which denoting habitual actions (for details on function, see Erdal 1991: 382). The Turkic word was borrowed into the Mongolic languages.[274]

Kott *pai* 'rich' (Werner 2002/1: 99) ← Turkic *baγ 'rich; a rich man' < *bāy*:
    cf. Old Turkic *bāy*; NE^S YeniseiT: Khakas *pay* 'rich; a rich man; abundant, plentiful; saint'; Sagai, Koibal, Kachin *pay* (R); Kyzyl *pay* ~ *bay*; Shor *pay*; AltaiT: Altai *bay* 'rich; a rich man; abundant, plentiful'; Tuba *bay*; Qumanda *bay*; Quu *pay*; Teleut *pay*; SayanT: Tuvan *bay* 'rich; a rich man; abundant, plentiful'; Tofan *bay* 'rich; wealth'; ChulymT *pay*; NE^N Yakut *bāy* 'wealth, property; rich, wealthy'; Dolgan *bāy*; NW^N Siberian Tatar *pay* 'husband'; NW^S Kirgiz *bay* 'rich; a rich man; abundant, plentiful; husband; dial. elder brother'; Fu-yü *bay* 'rich'; Kazak *bay* 'rich; a rich man; husband'; SE Yellow Uyghur *paj* ~ *päy* 'rich';
Turkic → Samoyedic:
    Kamas *bai* 'rich, wealthy; wealth, fortune'; Mator *baj* 'rich'.
Etymology: Joki LS 80; Doerfer TMEN 2: 59; 1985: 37; Räsänen VEWT 56a; Ščerbak SF 195; Rassadin 1971: 158; Clauson ED 384a; ESTJa 1978: 27–28; Timonina 1978: 12; Rozycki 1994: 26–27; Helimski 1997: 213; SIGTJa 2001: 668–670; Nugteren 2011: 279

The Kott word was clearly borrowed from Turkic (Timonina 1978: 12). The devoicing of the Turkic initial labial consonant *b*- is a regular change in Kott, not only in loanwords, but in native Yeniseian words too, which points to an early period of Turkic borrowings. This phonetic change can also be explained via a Yenisei Turkic influence.

If we compare the Kott word *pai* 'rich' with Arin *bajšu* 'wealth'—which both go back to the same Turkic word *bāy*—the different fate of the Turkic initial consonant *b*- demonstrates the different period or the source of borrowing for Yeniseian words. The original Yeniseian *b*- in both the Kott and Arin languages is devoiced, e.g. Proto-Yeniseian *bej 'wind' ~ Kott *pēi*, Arin *paj*; Proto-Yeniseian *bis 'evening' ~ Kott *pīš*, Arin *pis* (Starostin 1982: 149). In this way, the Kott word was most likely borrowed in the early period, whereas the Arin word was borrowed in the later period.

For the etymological background of the Turkic word, see the works of Doerfer (TMEN 2: 59), Räsänen (VEWT 56a), Clauson (ED 384a), Sevortjan (ESTJa 1978: 27–28) and Tenisev (SIGTJa 2001: 668–670).

The Turkic word also was borrowed into Samoyedic (Joki LS 80; Helimski 1997: 213) and Mongolic[275] (Doerfer TMEN 2: 59; Nugteren 2011: 279). The Tun-

---

274 Turkic *buŋ*- → Mongolic *muna-, cf. LM *muna*- ~ *munu*- 'to become weak or feeble-minded'.
275 Turkic → Mongolic 'richness, prosperity, abundance; rich, wealthy, well-to-do': Middle

gusic loanwords were borrowed via two paths: from Mongolic[276] and directly from Yakut[277] (SSTMJa 1: 65b; Doerfer 1985: 37; Rozycki 1994: 26–27). From Mongolic, the Turkic word was re-borrowed into Tuvan[278] (Khabtagaeva 2009: 173).

Kott *šugur* 'one-eyed' (Werner 2002/2: 442) ← Turkic *sogor 'blind' ← Mongolic *soqor* 'blind' < *soqo +*r* {Mongolic NN, see Khabtagaeva 2009: 283}:

    cf. NE[S] YeniseiT: Kyzyl *sōger*; Shor *sogïr* (R); AltaiT: Altai *sokor*; Qumanda *sokor* ~ *sogïr*; Quu *sogïr*; Teleut *sogïr*; SayanT: Tuvan *sogur*; Tofan *soġur*; ChulymT –; NE[N] Yakut *soxxor* 'crooked, one-eyed, blind'; NW[N] Siberian Tatar *soġïr* (R); NW[S] Kirgiz *sokur*; Fu-yü –; Kazak *soqïr*; SE Yellow Yughur –;

Turkic → Samoyedic:

    Kamas *sïγïr* 'one-eyed; crooked'; Mator *sogor* 'one-eyed';

Turkic ← Mongolic *soqor* 'blind':

    Middle Mongol: Precl.Mo. *soqar*; SH *soqor*; ZY *suqur*; Leiden *soqar*; Ibn-Muh. *soγur*; Muq. *soqar*; Ist. *soqar*; LM *soqor*; Modern Mongol: Buryat *hoxor*; West Buryat; Khalkha *soxor*; Oirat dial. *soxăr*; Dagur *soγur* (E); Khamnigan *soxor*.

Etymology: Joki LS 269; Kałużyński 1962: 67; Räsänen VEWT 426b; Rassadin 1980: 72; Doerfer 1985: 128; Helimski 1997: 342; Schönig 2000: 169; Anikin 2000: 213; Khabtagaeva 2009: 245; Nugteren 2011: 500; Khabtagaeva 2015a: 117

The Kott word was borrowed from the Siberian Turkic form *sogïr ~ *sogor*. The change of initial *s*- > *š*- is a regular phonetic feature for Turkic loanwords in Kott and native Yeniseian words (Starostin 1982: 158).

The Turkic forms are of Mongolic origin (Kałużyński 1962: 67; Rassadin 1980: 72; Khabtagaeva 2009: 245). It may be an early loanword in Turkic, cf. West Oghuz Turkic *soqur* 'blind' (Schönig 2000: 169).

From the morphological side, the Mongolic word derived from the dead base *soqo[279] with the denominal noun sufix +*r* (Khabtagaeva 2009: 283). The word is present in almost all Middle Mongol and Modern Mongol languages (Nugteren 2011: 500).

Through Siberian Turkic, the Mongolic word was borrowed into the Samoyedic languages (Joki LS 269; Helimski 1997: 342). The Siberian Russian words

---

    Mongol: Precl. Mongol *bayan*; SH *baiyan*, HY, Muq. *bayan*; LM *bayan*; Buryat, Khalkha *bayan*; Kalmuck *bayn*; Dagur *bayin* (E); Khamnigan *bayan*.

276 Turkic → Mongolic → Tungusic 'wealth; a rich man; rich': Common Ewenki; Negidal *bayan*; Oroch, Udehe, Ulcha, Orok *bayan*; Manchu *bayan* 'rich, rich man'.

277 Turkic: Yakut → Tungusic: Podkamennyi, Ilimpi Ewenki *bay* 'wealth; a rich man; rich'.

278 Mongolic: LM *bayatan* 'rich people' < *bayan* 'rich' +*tAn* {Mongolic NN forming collective nouns, see Poppe GWM §139} → Tuvan *bayāt(an)* 'rich man'.

279 Cf. LM *soqoyi*- (< **soqo+yi*-) 'to be[come] blind'; *soqola*- (< **soqo+lA*-) 'to [make] blind'; *soqora*- (< **soqo+rA*-) 'to become blind; to be extinguished, go out (*as fire, light*)'.

zokor and *sokor*, a 'kind of rodent animal,' were most likely borrowed through Siberian Turkic (Anikin 2000: 213–214; 502). The Mongolic word, via Yakut, was borrowed into certain Ewenki dialects[280] (Doerfer 1985: 128).

Arin *tok* 'full, satiated' (Werner 2002/2: 272) ← Turkic **tok* 'full, satiated' < *to-* 'to close, block' *-K* {Turkic VN, see Erdal 1991: 248}:

cf. Old Turkic *toq*; NE^S YeniseiT: Khakas *tox*; Kyzyl *toχ*; Shor *toq*; AltaiT: Altai *toq*; Qumanda *tok*; Quu *tok*; Teleut *toq* (R); SayanT: Tuvan –; Tofan *to^{c}q*; ChulymT *toq*; NE^N Yakut –; NW^N Siberian Tatar –; NW^S Kirgiz *tok* 'satiated; *fig.* prosperous'; Fu-yü –; Kazak *toq*; SE Yellow Yughur –.

Etymology: Räsänen VEWT 484b; Rassadin 1971: 234–235; Clauson ED 464b; ESTJa 1980: 252–253; Erdal 1991: 248; Stachowski 2004: 199

The Arin word is clearly of Turkic origin. The phonetic shape and lexixal meaning fit with the Yeniseian data.

From an etymological point of view, the Common Turkic word derived from the verb *to-*, 'to close, to block' and the productive deverbal noun suffix *-K*.

Kott *turkatu* 'quick, rapid' (cf. *bonturkantu* 'shy' < *bon* 'not' + *turkatu*) (Werner 2002/2: 290) < *turkan* 'quick' *-tu* {Yeniseian NN/adj.} ← Turkic **türgen* 'quick, rapid' ← Mongolic *türgen* 'quick, swift, rapid, speedy; hurried; soon' < **türge-n* {Mongolic VN/adj., see Poppe GWM §175; Khabtagaeva 2009: 287}:

cf. NE^S YeniseiT: Khakas *türgün* 'quick, hurried' (But.); Shor –; AltaiT: Altai *türgen* 'quick, rapid; quickly, soon'; Tuba *türgen* 'quick, rapid; quickly, hurried'; Qumanda *türgen* 'quick, hurried'; Teleut *türgän* 'hurry, fast' (R); SayanT: Tuvan *dürgen* 'quick, rapid; speed'; *fig.* irascible, hotheaded; Tofan *türgen* 'quick, rapid'; ChulymT –; NE^N Yakut *türgän* 'speed; quick, fast'; Dolgan *türgän* 'quick'; NW^N Siberian Tatar –; NW^S Kirgiz *dürgü-* 'to run in fear'; Fu-yü –; Kazak –; SE Yellow Uyghur *türgen* 'quickly';

Turkic ← Mongolic *türgen* 'quick, swift, rapid, speedy; hurried; soon':

Middle Mongol: Precl.Mo. *türgen*; SH *türgen* ~ *türgün*; Muq. *türgen*; HY *türgen*; LM *türgen*; Modern Mongol: Buryat *türgen*; Khalkha *türgen*; Kalmuck *türgn*; Dagur *turγun* (E); Khamnigan *türgen*.

Etymology: Kałużyński 1962: 20, 28; Räsänen VEWT 506a; Rassadin 1971: 104; 1980: 71; SSTMJa 2: 219; Tatarincev 1976: 37; 2: 299; Doerfer 1985: 82; Schönig 2000: 183; Khabtagaeva 2009: 242; Nugteren 2011: 528; Khabtagaeva 2015a: 122

The Kott word was borrowed from the Siberian Turkic form **türgen*. The final syllable *-tu* is the native denominal noun Yeniseian suffix, which forms adjec-

---

[280] Mongolic → Turkic: Yakut → Tungusic: Eastern Ewenki: Zeya, Tungir, Ayan, Mai, Nelkan, Tokko, Aldan, Uchur, Urmi, Tommot, Chumikan, Sakhalin, Barguzin *sokor* 'with sick eyes'.

tives. Due to the absense of vowel harmony in Yeniseian, the borrowed Turkic form *türgen changed to turkan in Kott. The Turkic consonant cluster -rg- is devoiced in Kott.

From an etymological aspect, the Turkic form is of Mongolic origin (Kałużyński 1962: 20, 28; Räsänen VEWT 506a; Rassadin 1971: 104; 1980: 71; Tatarincev 1976: 37; 2: 299; Schönig 2000: 183; Khabtagaeva 2009: 242).

The Mongolic word is present in almost all Middle Mongol sources and in Modern Mongol languages (Nugteren 2011: 528). The Mongolic word derived from the dead base *türge±[281] with the productive deverbal noun suffix -n, which forms adjectives[282] (Poppe GWM § 175; Khabtagaeva 2009: 287).

The Mongolic word also was borrowed into the Tungusic languages[283] (SST-MJa 2: 219; Doerfer 1985: 82; Rozycki 1994: 213).

1.3 Adverbs

Kott *arai* 'hardly, with' (Werner 2002/1: 57) ← Turkic *aray* 'slowly, gently, with difficulty, hardly' ← Mongolic *arai* 'just a little too …; not quite …; hardly, scarcely, barely, with difficulty' ← Turkic *$\bar{a}r$ +Ai {Mongolic NN, see Ramstedt 1957: 182–183}, cf. Old Turkic $\bar{a}z$ 'few, scanty, a little':

cf. NE^S YeniseiT: Khakas *aray*; Sagai, Koibal *aray* (R); Kyzyl *ärïy*; Shor *arïy*; AltaiT: Altai *aray*; Tuba *aray*; Qumanda *aray*; Quu *arïy*; Teleut *aray* (R); SayanT: Tuvan *aray*; Tofan *aray*; ChulymT –; NE^N Yakut *arïy*; Dolgan *aray*; NW^N Siberian Tatar *aray* (R); NW^S Kirgiz –; Fu-yü –; SE Yellow Uyghur –;

Turkic → Samoyedic:

Kamas *ärïy* 'little, very little'; Selkup *areí* 'hardly';

Turkic ← Mongolic *arai* 'just a little too …; not quite …; hardly, scarcely, barely, with difficulty':

cf. Middle Mongol: –; LM *arai*; Modern Mongol: Buryat *arai*; Khalkha *arai* 'rather, somewhat, a bit'; Oirat dial. *ärǟ*; Dagur *arān* (E); Khamnigan *arai ~ ari*;

Mongolic ← Turkic *$\bar{a}r$+Ai {Mongolic NN, see Ramstedt 1957: 182–183}:

---

281 Cf. LM *türged-* 'to be rash; to be too quick; to fly into a temper' (< *türge +d- {NV}); *türgedke-* 'to accelerate, speed up; to urge, incite' (< *türge +dKA- {NV}); *türgele-* 'to speed up; to hurry, hasten' (< *türge +lA- {NV}); *türgedügün* 'rash, hasty' (< *türge +dA- {NV} -GUn {VN}), etc.

282 LM *dolgin* 'hot-tempered, quick-tempered, passionate; imprudent' < *dolgi-* 'to wave, undulate; to splash out; to be restless'; *singgen* 'fluid' < *singge-* 'to be absorbed'; etc.

283 Mongolic → Tungusic: *Southern Ewenki*: Nercha; *Eastern Ewenki*: Zeya, Ayan, Mai, Tokko, Aldan, Uchur, Urmi, Chumikan, Sakhalin *turgen* 'quick, rapid; vigorous, energetic'; Lamut *turgun* 'quick, fleet-footed'; Negidal *tujgen* (< *turgen) 'quick, clever'; Oroch *tuggen* (< *tujgen < * turgen) 'quick'; Udihe *tuge* (< *tuggen < *tujgen < * turgen) 'quick'; Ulcha *turgen*; Nanai *turge*; Manchu *turgen* 'quick; fast; urgent; serious illness'.

cf. Old Turkic *āz* 'few, scanty, a little'; NE^S YeniseiT: Khakas *as*; AltaiT: Altai *as*; SayanT: Tuvan *as*; NW^S Kirgiz *az*; Kazak *az*; SE Yellow Uyghur *az*.

Etymology: Räsänen VEWT 23a; Rassadin 1971: 155; 1980: 35; Clauson ED 277a; ESTJa 1974: 93–94; SSTMJa 1: 48a; Doerfer 1985: 44; Tatarincev 2000: 70, 127; Khabtagaeva 2009: 267; 2015a: 114–115

The Kott word was borrowed from the Siberian Turkic form **aray*. The Turkic borrowing is in accord with phonetic and semantic patterns.

In turn, the Turkic forms were borrowed from Mongolic (Rassadin 1971: 155; 1980: 35; Khabtagaeva 2009: 267), but are ultimately of Turkic origin. The Mongolic rhotacized form *arai* 'just a little' originates from Turkic *āz* 'few, scanty, a little' (ESTJa 1974: 93–94) with the denominal noun suffix +*Ai*[284] (Ramstedt 1957: 182–183; Khabtagaeva 2009: 279).

In addition to Siberian Turkic and Kott, Mongolic *arai* was borrowed into Samoyedic (Joki LS 73; Filipova 1994: 46). From Mongolic, the word *arai* was directly borrowed into Tungusic[285] (SSTMJa 1: 48a; Doerfer 1985: 44).

Kott *häteäŋôk* 'just as'; *häteäŋ* 'so' (Werner 2002/1: 307) ← Turkic **tegeneŋ* 'in vain, for no particular reason' (cf. Altai) < *tegin* 'just, so, in vain' +*nAŋ* {Turkic ablative, see Erdal 2004: 374}:

cf. Old Turkic *täkin* ~ *täkün* 'in vain' (DTS) < *täk* 'only' (ED); NE^S YeniseiT: Khakas *tikke* 'in vain' < *tik* 'free, gratuitous'; Shor *tegen* 'just, so, in vain'; AltaiT: Altai *teginneŋ tegin* 'for no reason' < *tegin* 'in vain'; Tuba *tegin* 'simple, peaceful'; Qumanda *tegin* 'simple, usually'; Quu *tegin* 'for no reason, for nothing'; Teleut *täginäŋ tägin* 'for no reason' < *tägin* 'without purpose, intention, success, cause, in vain; without rank, dignity, honor; without particular feature' (R); SayanT –; ChulymT –; NE^N Yakut –; NW^N Siberian Tatar *tigen* 'free'; NW^S Kirgiz *tegin* 'free; in vain'; Fu-yü –; Kazak *tekke* 'free; in vain'; SE Yellow Yughur –.

Etymology: Räsänen VEWT 470a; Clauson ED 475ab; Khabtagaeva 2015c: 96–97

The etymology of the Yeniseian word is unknown. As a hypothesis, I connect it with the Common Turkic adverb *tegeneŋ* 'in vain, for no particular reason', itself derived from the word *tegin* 'just, so, in vain,' with the Turkic ablative suffix +*nAŋ*. If we accept the hypothesis, the Kott form underwent metathesis.

---

[284] The suffix is used in Mongolic words of Turkic origin. E.g. Mongolic: cf. LM *türei* (< **tirei*) 'bootleg, boot top' ← Turkic **tīr* (cf. Old Turkic *tīz* 'knee'); Mongolic: cf. LM *taulai* 'hare' ← Turkic **tabïš* (cf. Old Turkic *taβïšğan*); etc.

[285] Mongolic → Tungusic: *Southern Ewenki*: Northern Baikal, Baunt; *Eastern Ewenki*: Aldan, Uchur, Urmi, Chumikan, Barguzin *arai* 'just a little; once, suddenly; slowly, gradually, a little bit'.

The etymology of Turkic word is unclear. Turkic *tägin* 'in vain' is connected to the form *täk* 'only, just' (Räsänen VEWT 470a). For the etymology and distribution of Turkic *täk* 'only,' see Clauson (ED 475a).

The Kott word belongs to the category of words of uncertain etymology.

Kott *tʰategâtna* 'beside, next to' (Werner 2002/2: 316) ← Turkic **ta tiginde* 'there'
< *ta* {Turkic strengthening-differential particle} + *tiginde* 'there':
< *ta* {Turkic strengthening-differential particle}:
    cf. Old Turkic *ta* (DTS); NE^S YeniseiT: Khakas *tā* ~ *tē* ~ *dā* ~ *dē*; Sagai, Koibal, Kachin; Shor *tā* (R); Kyzyl –; AltaiT: Altai *ta* '*negative reply* I do not know'; Tuba *ta* '*conj*. and, with' (B.); Qumanda *tā* 'strengthening particle; *conj*. and, also, who knows'; Quu *tā* 'an exclamation of doubt'; Teleut *ta* 'negative particle'; SayanT: Tuvan *ta* '*particle* who knows'; Tofan *ta* 'strengthening particle'; ChulymT *tā* 'an exclamation of doubt' (R); NE^N Yakut –; NW^N Siberian Tatar *tā* 'more'; NW^S Kirgiz *da* '*conj*. and, also; strengthening particle'; Fu-yü *da* 'also'; Kazak *da* ~ *de* ~ *ta* ~ *te* '*conj*. and'; SE Yellow Uyghur *ta* 'and'.

Etymology: Räsänen VEWT 457a; Ščerbak SF 197; ESTJa 1980: 109–110; SIGTJa 1988: 511–513

+ *tiginde* 'there' < *tigi* 'he, she, it' +(*n*)*dA* {Turkic locative, see Tenišev 1988: 35} ← Mongolic *tegün* 'stem of the demonstrative pronoun *tere*':
    cf. Old Turkic –; NE^S YeniseiT: Khakas *tigide*; Sagai, Koibal, Kachin *tigĭdä* (R); Kyzyl –; Shor *tigi* 'that'; AltaiT: Altai *tu* 'that'; Teleut *tiginde* 'there'; SayanT: Tuvan *dŏ̄* ~ *dū* ~ *dü* 'that'; Tofan *tē* 'that'; ChulymT *tegdä* 'that'; NE^N Yakut –; NW^N Siberian Tatar –; NW^S Kirgiz *tigine* 'there'; Fu-yü –; Kazak –; SE Yellow Yughur –;

Turkic ← Mongolic *tegün* 'stem of the demonstrative pronoun *tere*':
    cf. LM *tegün* 'stem of the demonstrative pronoun *tere*'; Modern Mongol: Buryat –; Khalkha *tǖn* 'oblique stem of *ter*, *tǖnd* to him, her, or it, *tǖnī* his, her'; Kalmuck; Oirat dial. *tǖnä* ~ *tennä* (< *tegün-ü* 'his'); Dagur –; Khamnigan –.

Etymology: Räsänen VEWT 479b; Baskakov 1975b: 148–152; Ščerbak 1977: 130–131; Tatarincev 2002: 237–239

The origin of the Kott word is unknown. As a hypothesis, I propose it was borrowed from the Turkic compound word *ta tiginde* 'there', which consists of the Turkic strengthening-differential particle *ta* and Turkic adverb *tiginde* 'there'. Even though I could not locate this compound word *ta tiginde* in any dictionary, it may well have existed in Siberian Turkic. It is possible that the lexical change 'there' → 'next to, beside' occurred.

The base of the adverb is the personal pronoun *tigi* 'he, she, it' with the locative case suffix +*dA*. Most likely, etymologically speaking, the Turkic pronoun is connected to the Mongolic stem of the demonstrative pronoun *tere* 'he, she, it' *tegün* 'his, her'.

For the etymological background of the Turkic adverb, see Ščerbak (1977: 130–131) and Tatarincev (2002: 237–239).

Kott *una ôjaŋ* 'therefore' (Werner 2002/2: 346) ← Turkic *onoŋ učun 'therefore': cf. Altai *onoŋ učun* 'therefore'[286] < *onoŋ* 'after it, then' + *učun* 'because of':
< *onoŋ* 'after it, then' < *ol* 'this' +*nXŋ* {AltaiT ablative, see Tenišev 1988: 67}:
  cf. Old Turkic *anïn* (< *ol* +*In* {instrumental case}) 'therefore, thereby'; NE^S YeniseiT: Khakas *annaŋ* 'after it, thence'; Kyzyl –; Shor *anaŋ* 'there; then'; AltaiT: Altai *onoŋ* 'from this, then'; Tuba *onoŋ* 'then', cf. *anïŋ učun* 'because of'; Teleut *anaŋ* 'then, afterwards'; SayanT: Tuvan *ōn ~ ōŋ* 'thence, from there'; Tofan *ān* 'later, a little later; however, because'; ChulymT *andïn* 'from him', cf. *andïnaq* 'therefore'; NE^N Yakut *onon* 'thus, therefore; however, because'; Dolgan *onton* 'where? why? herefore, it, so, then, in these circumstances; and, on the other hand'; NW^N Siberian Tatar *anan ~ annarï* 'then, after then'; NW^S Kirgiz *anan* 'then, later, after', cf. *an učun* 'because, for the reason'; Fu-yü –; Kazak *anadan* 'from there'; SE Yellow Uyghur *andan* 'from him'.
Etymology: Räsänen VEWT 19b; 169a, Clauson ED 187a

+ *učun* < *üčün* 'because of, for the sake of, for; because, in order to':
  cf. Old Turkic *üčün*; NE^S YeniseiT: Khakas *üčün*; Sagai *üǰün* (R); Sagai, Koibal *üzün* (R); Kyzyl *üžün*; Shor *üčün*; AltaiT: Altai *učun*; Tuba *učun*; Qumanda *učun*; Quu *udžun ~ učun ~ üžün*; Teleut *učun*; SayanT: Tuvan *užun*; Tofan –; ChulymT *üčün*; NE^N Yakut *ihin*; Dolgan *ihin*; NW^N Siberian Tatar –; NW^S Kirgiz *üčün*; Fu-yü –; Kazak *üšin*; SE Yellow Yughur –.
Etymology: Räsänen VEWT 509b; Clauson ED 28b; ESTJa 1974: 642–643; Serebrennikov & Gadžieva 1986: 243–244

The etymology of Kott word *una ôjaŋ* 'therefore' is unknown. I suggest it originates from the Turkic collocation *onoŋ učun*, nowadays present in Altaic Turkic. Most likely the disappearance of the Turkic final consonant *-ŋ* in the first Kott form *una*, and its appearance in the second Kott form *ôjaŋ*, is due to the combination of Turkic final nasal consonants. My hypothesis is reinforced by the similarity of the lexical meaning.

The Turkic compound adverb *onoŋ učun* 'therefore' consists of the Altai Turkic adverb *onoŋ* 'after it, then' and the postposition *učun* 'because of'. The adverb *onoŋ* is derived from the pronoun *ol* 'he, she, it' with the ablative suffix. This is a good example of the differing development of adverbs in Turkic lan-

---

286 Cf. also Khakas *annaŋar* (< *annaŋ* + *andar* 'there, in the direction') 'however, because; further from'; Shor *anaŋ āra* (< *anaŋ* + *āra* 'further, there; about; because') 'therefore, due to this'.

guages, formed as they are by the addition of a case suffix. Cf. Old Turkic *anïn* 'therefore, thereby', which is formed from the pronoun *ol* with the instrumental case *+In*.

From an etymological aspect, the Turkic postposition *üčün* 'because of, for the sake of, for; because, in order to' is connected to the Turkic word *ūč* 'extremity, end, tip,' derived with the instrumental case suffix *+In* (for details, see Sevorjan ESTJa 1974: 642–643).

Kott *uŋo* ~ *uŋôjaŋ* 'why' (Werner 2002/2: 351) ← Turkic **noġa učun*: cf. AltaiT: Altai, Teleut *neniŋ učun*; Khakas *noġa*; Old Turkic *nägü üčün* 'why?':
< *noġa* < *nägü* 'why' < *nā̆* 'what?' *+GU* {NN, see Clauson xl}:

cf. Old Turkic *nägü*; NE^S YeniseiT: Khakas *noġa* 'why'; Sagai, Koibal, Kachin *noġa* 'where?', *noniŋ üjün* 'why?'; Kyzyl –; Shor *nōġa*; AltaiT: Altai *neniŋ* (< *ne* 'what' *+nIŋ* {AltaiT ablative}); Tuba; Teleut *neniŋ*; SayanT –; ChulymT *noġa*; NE^N Yakut –; NW^N Siberian Tatar *ni*; NW^S Kirgiz *nege*; Fu-yü *nʸem* 'what?'; Kazak *nege*; SE Yellow Uyghur *nege*;

Etymology: Räsänen VEWT 352a; Clauson ED 774ab, 776b; ESTJa 2003: 96–99
+ *učun* 'because of, for the sake of, for; because, in order to':

cf. Old Turkic *üčün*; NE^S YeniseiT: Khakas *üčün*; Sagai *üjün*; Sagai, Koibal *üzün*; Kyzyl *üžün*; Shor *üčün*; AltaiT: Altai; Tuba; Qumanda; Teleut *učun*; Quu *udžun* ~ *učun* ~ *üžün*; SayanT: Tuvan *užun*; Tofan –; ChulymT *üčün*; NE^N Yakut; Dolgan *ihin*; NW^N Siberian Tatar –; NW^S Kirgiz *üčün*; Fu-yü –; Kazak *üšin*; SE Yellow Yughur –.

Etymology: Räsänen VEWT 509b; Clauson ED 28b; ESTJa 1974: 642–643; Serebrennikov & Gadžieva 1986: 243–244

The etymology of the Kott word is unknown. As a hypothesis, I propose that Kott *uŋôjaŋ* 'why' is a compound word consisting of the two words *uŋo* and *ôjaŋ*. The second word was most likely borrowed from the Turkic postosition *učun* (< *üčün*) 'because', which can be found in another Kott adverbial form, **una ôjaŋ** 'therefore'. The first part of the compound, *uŋo*, however, is questionable. Most likely it is connected with the Turkic interrogative pronoun *nägü* 'why'. The source for the Kott form *uŋo* may be the Siberian Turkic form *noġa*, cf. the Yenisei Turkic and Chulym Turkic forms. It is possible that the prosthesis *u-* occurred in the Kott form due to the absence of initial nasal consonants in native Yeniseian words. My hypothesis is strengthened by the continuity of the lexical meaning (Khabtagaeva 2015d: 140).

From an etymological aspect, the Turkic interrogative pronoun *nägü* 'why' derived from the pronoun *nā̆* 'what?' and the non-productive denominal noun suffix *+GU* (Clauson ED 776b). The pronoun *nā̆* is one of the few Turkic words with initial *n-* belonging to native Turkic words. Generally, Turkic words with initial *n-* are loanwords.

For the etymology of the second Turkic word *učun* (< *üčün*), see Kott **una** *ôjaŋ* 'therefore'.

1.4 Numerals

Arin **yus** 'hundred' (Werner 2002/1: 398) ← Turkic **yüs* < *yūz* 'a hundred':

cf. Old Turkic *yūz*; NE[S] YeniseiT: Khakas *čüs*; Sagai *čüs* (R), Koibal, Kachin *yüs* (R); Shor *čüs*; AltaiT: Altai *d'üs*; Tuba *d'üs*; Qumanda *čüs*; Quu *yüs*; Teleut *yüs*; SayanT: Tuvan *čüs*; Tofan *čüs*; ChulymT *yus* ~ *čus*; NE[N] Yakut *sǖs* 'hundred; rouble'; Dolgan *hǖs* ~ *sǖs*; NW[N] Siberian Tatar *yüs* (R); NW[S] Kirgiz *jüz*; Fu-yü –; Kazak *žüz*; SE Yellow Uyghur *yüz*;

Turkic → Samoyedic:

Kamas *d'üs* 'hundred'; Mator *čüs* 'hundred'.

Etymology: Joki LS 124; Räsänen VEWT 213b; Clauson ED 983a; Doerfer TMEN 4: 221–222; ESTJa 1989: 260; Stachowski 1996: 103; Helimski 1997: 237

The Arin word was borrowed from the Siberian Turkic (Stachowski 1996: 103) form **yüs* (cf. Koibal and Kachin dialects, Quu and Teleut dialects, Chulym Turkic, Siberian Tatar). The disappearance of vowel harmony is regular for Turkic loanwords in Yeniseian due to its absence in Yeniseian languages. Word-initial *y*- is typically found only in loanwords in Yeniseian. In this way, the preservation of Turkic initial *y*- points to a later layer of borrowing, i.e. a borrowing from a Siberian Turkic variety.

The Turkic numeral also was borrowed into Samoyedic (Joki LS 124; Helimski 1997: 237).

For etymological background, and more data, see Räsänen (VEWT 213b), Clauson (ED 983a) and Levitskaja (ESTJa 1989: 260).

Kott **min** 'a thousand' (Werner 2005: 114) ← Turkic **miŋ* < *biŋ* 'a thousand':

cf. Old Turkic *biŋ*; NE[S] YeniseiT: Khakas *muŋ*; Sagai, Koibal, Kachin *muŋ* (R); Kyzyl *mùn* ~ *mūn*; Shor *muŋ*; AltaiT: Altai *muŋ*; Tuba *muŋ*; Qumanda *muŋ*; Quu *muŋ*; Teleut *muŋ* (R); SayanT: Tuvan *muŋ*; Tofan –; ChulymT *miŋ*; NE[N] Yakut[287] *muŋ* 'limit, boundary; extreme degree of something'; Dolgan *muŋ* 'edge, end, limit'; NW[N] Siberian Tatar *miŋ*; NW[S] Kirgiz *miŋ*; Fu-yü –; Kazak *miŋ*; SE Yellow Uyghur *miŋ*;

Turkic → Samoyedic:

Kamas *miŋ* 'a thousand'.

Etymology: Joki LS 230; Räsänen VEWT 76ab; Doerfer TMEN 4: 31–34; 1985: 77; Ščerbak SF 195; Clauson ED 346b; SSTMJa 1: 537b; ESTJa 2003: 67–69; Nugteren 2011: 444

---

[287] 'Thousand' in Yakut is the Russian loanword *tïhïünča*.

The Kott word was borrowed from a Siberian Turkic form with the unrounded vowel -i- (cf. Chulym Turkic). In Siberian Turkic, the original Turkic vowel -i- usually occurs as -u-.

Due to the Mongolic forms, the original Turkic form was *büŋ*, which in several Turkic languages changed to *müŋ*. From an etymological point of view, certain researchers have traced the origin of the numeral to Chinese. For details, see Räsänen (VEWT 76ab), Doerfer (TMEN 4: 31–34), Clauson (ED 346b) and Levitskaja (ESTJa 2003: 67–69).

In addition to Yeniseian and Samoyedic (Joki LS 230), the word was borrowed into Mongolic[288] (ESTJa 2003: 67–69; Nugteren 2011: 444) as well from Turkic, and further to Tungusic[289] (SSTMJa 1: 537b; Doerfer 1985: 77) languages.

1.5 Verbs

Kott *baktîr* 'inf. praise' (Werner 2002/1: 99) ← Turkic **paktïr-* < *makta- -Xr-* {Turkic VV/causative, see Erdal 2001: 709–710} ← Mongolic *maγta-* 'to praise, eulogize, laud, extol, glorify':

cf. Old Turkic –; NE^S YeniseiT: Khakas *maxta-* 'to praise, encourage'; Sagai, Koibal, Kachin *maqta-* 'to praise' (R); Kyzyl *maxta-* 'to praise'; Shor *paqta-* 'to praise'; AltaiT: Altai *makta-* 'to praise'; Qumanda *makta- ~ pakta-* 'to praise'; Quu *makta- ~ pakta-* 'to praise'; Teleut *maqta-* 'to praise'; SayanT: Tuvan *makta-* 'to praise, encourage'; Tofan *maqta-* 'to praise, encourage'; ChulymT *maqta-* 'to praise'; NE^N Yakut *maxtay-*[290] 'to praise'; NW^N Siberian Tatar *maqtančïq ~ maqtancaq* (< *maqta-nč {Turkic VN} +*AK* {Turkic NN/diminutive}) 'bouncer'; NW^S Kirgiz *makta-* 'to praise'; Fu-yü –; Kazak *maqta-* 'to praise'; SE Yellow Uyghur *paqta-* 'to pray to the gods';

Turkic → Samoyedic:
Kamas *makta-* 'to praise, to brag about sg., to talk big fib';

Turkic ← Mongolic:
Middle Mongol: Precl.Mo. *maγta-*; HY *maqta-*; Muq. *maqta-*; LM *maγta-* 'to praise, eulogize, laud, extol, glorify'; Modern Mongol: Buryat *magta-* 'to praise'; Khalkha *magta-* 'to praise'; Oirat dial. *maktă-*; Dagur –; Khamnigan *magta-*.

Etymology: Kałużyński 1962: 73; Räsänen VEWT 321a; Schönig 2000: 134; ESTJa 2003: 11–13; Khabtagaeva 2009: 256; 2015a: 113; Nugteren 2011: 438

---

288 Turkic → Mongolic 'thousand': Middle Mongol: SH *minqa(n)*; HY *minγan*; Muq. *minqan*; LM *mingγan*; Modern Mongol: Buryat, Khalkha *myanga(n)*; Kalmuck *miŋγn*; Dagur *m'aŋgə* (E); Khamnigan *minga(n)*.

289 Turkic → Mongolic → Tungusic 'thousand': Nercha Ewenki *miŋan*; Solon *miŋā*; Negidal *miŋgan*; Oroch, Udihe, Ulcha, Orok, Nanai *miŋa*; Jurchen *ming-kān*; Manchu *miŋγan*.

290 < **maǵta-y-* {additional final sound in Yakut verbs, cf. Old Turkic *ači-* 'to be bitter' ~ Yakut *ahïy-*, Old Turkic *isi-* 'to be hot' ~ Yakut *itiy-*, Old Turkic *udï-* 'to sleep' ~ Yakut *utuy-*}.

The Kott verb was clearly borrowed from the Siberian Turkic form with initial *p-* (cf. Qumanda, Shor), which became voiced to *bakta-*. Furthermore, the evidence of Turkic borrowing is found in the Turkic causative suffix *-Xr-*.

From the etymological side, this Turkic word is of Mongolic origin (Kałużyński 1962: 73; Räsänen VEWT 321a; Schönig 2000: 134; ESTJa 2003: 11–13; Khabtagaeva 2009: 256).

The Mongolic word is present in both Western and Eastern Middle Mongol sources, and in almost all Modern Mongol languages (Nugteren 2011: 438).

The Mongolic word was possibly borrowed into Samoyedic (Joki LS 223) from Siberian Turkic.

Kott ***kačei*** 'to read' (Werner 2002/1: 404) ← Turkic **kiči-* < *qičir-* 'to read':
 cf. Old Turkic –; NE^S YeniseiT: –; AltaiT: Altai *qičir-* 'to call, invite; read'; Tuba *qičir-* 'to cry, shout, invite; read', cf. *qišir-* 'to read'; Qumanda *qičir-* 'to call, cry, shout; read'; Quu *kičir-* 'to cry, shout'; Teleut *qičir-* (R); Remaining lgs. –.

Etymology: Räsänen VEWT 261a; Rassadin 1971: 223

The etymology of the Kott word is unknown. As a hypothesis I connect it with Altai Turkic forms. Because of the final diphthong in the Kott form, the Turkic reconstructed borrowed form should be **kiči-*.

The etymology of the Altai Turkic verb *kičir-* is unknown. There are three possible variants concerning the etymology:

a)   The Turkic verb *čaqir-* 'to call out, shout', in which metathesis occurred:

 cf. Old Turkic *čaqir-*; NE^S YeniseiT: Khakas *saγira-* 'to chirr, chatter (*about magpie*)'; AltaiT: –; SayanT –; ChulymT –; NE^N Yakut –; NW^N Siberian Tatar –; NW^S Kirgiz *čakir-* 'to call, invite'; Fu-yü; Kazak *šaqir-* 'to call, invite'; SE Yellow Uyghur –.

Etymology: Clauson ED 410a

b)   The Altai Turkic verb may have been borrowed from the Mongolic verb *qaškir-* 'to shout, scream, yell, howl':

 cf. NE AltaiT: Altai *qišqir-* 'to shout, to yell'; SayanT: Tuvan *kiškir-* 'to scream, to yell'; Tofan *qišqir-* 'to shout'; SE Yellow Uyghur *qišqir-* 'to shout'

← Mongolic *qaškir-* < **qaš +kirA-*[291] {Mongolic NV, see Poppe GWM § 259}:
 Middle Mongol –; LM *qaškir- ~ qaskir-*; Modern Mongol: Buryat *xašxar-*; Khalkha *xašgar-* 'to shout, to yell'; Oirat dial. *xǟškär-*; Kalmuck *xäškr-*; Dagur –; Khamnigan *xašgira- ~ xatkira-*.

---

291   E.g. LM *barkira-* 'to roar, to bellow, to cry' < **bar +kirA-*; *urkira-* 'to roar, bellow; to growl' < **ur +kirA-*, etc.

c) The word may be connected with another Turkic word *qïqïr-* 'to shout':
Cf. Old Turkic *qïqïr-* 'to shout' < *qïqï* 'outcry, shouting'; NE^S YeniseiT: Khakas *xïġïr-* 'to call, to invite; to read' < *xïyġï* 'shout'; Koibal *qï:ġïr-* 'to scream, to shout, to talk loudly' (R), Shor *qïyġïr-* 'to shout, to speak loudly, to call; to invite' (R); AltaiT: Altai *qïyġïr-* 'to shout, to call; to read aloud' < *qïyġï* 'cry, exclamation, buzzword'; Teleut *qïyġïr-* 'to shout, to speak loudly; to call; to invite' < *qïyġï* 'scream' < *qïy* 'scream' (R); SayanT: Tuvan *kïyġïr-* 'to call, to yell; to read' < *kïyġï* 'scream, calling'; Tofan *qïġïr-* 'to call, to invite; to read'; ChulymT –; NE^N Yakut –; NW^N Siberian Tatar *qïyġïr-* 'to shout, to speak loudly; to call; to invite' (R); NW^S Kirgiz *kïykïr-* 'to sout, to call'; Fu-yü –; Kazak –; SE Yellow Uyghur *qaqïr-* ~ *qaqar-* 'to call, to invite'.

Etymology: Clauson ED 612a, 609b
The etymology of Kott word still remains uncertain.

Kott ***kuštap parak*** 'I take away' (Werner 2002/1: 458) ← Turkic **kučaktap bar-* 'to take away' < *kučakta-* 'to embrace, take in one's arms' *-(X)p* {Turkic converb, see Erdal 2004: 309} + *bar-* 'to go' *-Ak* (?):
← Turkic *kučakta-* 'to embrace, take in one's arms' < *quč-* 'to embrace' *-AK+* 'the bosom, lap, an armful' {Turkic VN, see Erdal 1991: 224} *+lA-* {Turkic NV, see Erdal 1991: 429}:
cf. Old Turkic *qučaqla-*; NE^S YeniseiT: Khakas *xujaxta-*; Sagai *qučaqta-* (R); Shor *qučaqta-*; AltaiT: Altai *kučakta-*; Tuba *kučakta-*; Qumanda *kuštan-* < *qučaqtan-* < *qučaqta-n-* {Turkic VV/reflexive} 'to hug, to take in one's arms'; Quu *kudžakta-*; Teleut *qučaqta-* 'to hug'; SayanT: Tuvan *kužakta-*; Tofan *qujaqta-*; ChulymT *qučaq* 'armful'; NE^N292 Yakut *kūs-* 'to bow from all sides; to hug'; Dolgan *kūs-* 'to embrace; to hug; to take in one's arms'; NW^N Siberian Tatar *qočaqla-* 'to hug'; NW^S Kirgiz *kučakta-*; Fu-yü *gujahtïr-* < *qučaqtïr-* < *qučaqta-(X)r-* {Turkic VV/causative} 'to embrace'; Kazak *qušaqta-*; SE Yellow Uyghur *qučaqta-* 'to hug; to carry a child in the bosom'.

Etymology: Räsänen VEWT 295b–296a; Doerfer TMEN 3: 420; Clauson ED 591ab; ESTJa 2000: 105–110

bar- 'to go':
cf. Old Turkic *bar-*; NE^S YeniseiT: Khakas *par-*; Sagai, Koibal, Kachin *par-* (R); Kyzyl *par-* ~ *pār-*; Shor *par-*; AltaiT: Altai, Tuba, Qumanda, Quu *bar-*; Teleut *par-* (R); SayanT: Tuvan, Tofan *bar-*; ChulymT *par-*; NE^N Yakut, Dolgan *bar-*; NW^N Siberian Tatar –; NW^S Kirgiz *bar-*; Fu-yü *bar-*; Kazak *bar-*; SE Yellow Uyghur *par-*.

Etymology: Räsänen VEWT 62a; Ščerbak SF 195; Clauson ED 354a; ESTJa 1978: 64–65

---

292 The Yakut and Dolgan forms *kūs-* 'to bow from all sides; to hug' suggest the Proto-Turkic **kūč* form with original long vowel (Ščerbak SF 194).

Werner (2002/1: 458) connects the Kott phrase with two Kott words *kuštu* 'very strong, violent' and *forak* 'I take'. It is more likely though that the Kott phrase is of Turkic origin consisting of two Turkic verbs *kučakta-* 'to take in arms' and *bar-* 'to go'.

As is usual in Turkic, the first main verb connects the auxiliary verb with form *-(X)p*, and has an actional meaning (for details on the Turkic construction, see Erdal 2004: 249–250, 254). Most likely, the final *-ak* in Kott developed from the verbal element *-aŋ*, which refers to the present-tense first-person singular form (Werner 1990: 173–174). This is in accord with the lexical meaning. It is also possible that metathesis occurred: the syllable *-ak-* in first compound element was dropped and moved to the second compound element: Turkic *kučaktap bar* → Kott *kuš tap parak*.

Kott ***xoxutajut*** 'to offend, to hurt' (Werner 2002/2: 385) ← Turkic **kokïylat*- (cf. AltaiT) < *qoqïyla-* 'to lead to despair' < *qoqïy* 'a cry of despair' +*lA*- {Turkic NV, see Erdal 1991: 429} *-(X)t-* {Turkic VV/passive, see Erdal 2004: 229} ← Mongolic *qoki* 'scarce, scanty; unfortunate; loss, failure, harm':

cf. NE^S YeniseiT: Khakas *xoxay* ~ *xōxay* 'a cry of despair'; Shor *qoqqïylan-* 'to moan, whine' (R); AltaiT: Altai *qoqïylat-* 'to lead to despair' < *qoqïyla-* 'to emit cries of despair; to sigh' < *qoqïy* 'a cry of despair'; Qumanda *kokïyla-* < *kokïy*; Teleut *qoqqïyla-* < *qoqqïy* (R); SayanT: Tuvan *koguy* 'own fault'; Tofan –; ChulymT –; NE^N Yakut –; NW^N Siberian Tatar –; NW^S Kirgiz *kokuylat-* 'to lead to despair' < *kokuyla-* 'to emit cries of despair' < *kokuy* '(*a cry of despair*) oh-oh! Help!'; Fu-yü –; Kazak –; SE Yellow Yughur –;

Turkic ← Mongolic *qoki* 'scarce, scanty; unfortunate; loss, failure, harm':

cf. Middle Mongol: –; LM *qoki*, cf. *qokida-* ~ *qokira-* 'to be damaged, hurt; to suffer a loss; to perish, be ruined, devasted; to become dry and hard; to wither'; Modern Mongol: Buryat *xoxi* 'loss, failure'; Khalkha *xox'* 'loss, misfortune; fault; alone, all alone; quite, altogether'; Oirat dial. *xokă* 'loss, failure; poor, alone, loonely'; Dagur *kokil-* (E); Khamnigan *xoki*.

Etymology: Tatarincev 2004: 167; Khabtagaeva 2009: 178

The Kott verb was borrowed from the Siberian Turkic form **kokïylat-* 'to lead to despair'. From a phonetic perspective, it is possible that long-distance regressive assimilation occurred. This is one of those cases where initial *k-* changes to *x-* in Kott. In native Yeniseian words, the initial *k-* regularly changes to *h-* in Kott.[293] In this way, the change of Turkic initial *q-* > *x-* occurred in early the period of borrowing.

---

[293] E.g. Proto-Yeniseian **qaŋo* 'better, more' > Kott *haŋo*; Proto-Yeniseian **qabaʔŋ* 'a long time'

From an etymological point of view, the Turkic verb is of Mongolic origin. The base is the Mongolic noun *qoki* 'scarce, scanty; unfortunate; loss, failure, harm' (Tatarincev 2004: 167; Khabtagaeva 2009: 178). The Turkic verb *koküylat-* is derived from the noun *qoqïy* 'a cry of despair', with the denominal verbum suffix +*lA*- and the deverbal verbum suffix -(*X*)*t*-, forming passive verbs. The Turkic mediation of the original Mongolic word in the Kott form is evidenced by the presence of the Turkic Passive form -(*X*)*t*-.

Arin *bičisagnibašu* 'I want, I would like' (Werner 2002/1: 123) < *biči- (?) *sagni*- (← Turkic) -*bašu* (?):
sagni- ← Turkic **saġïn-* 'to think' < *sā-* 'to count' -(*X*)*k-* {Turkic VV, see Erdal 1991: 645–651} 'to think' -*Xn-* {Turkic VV/reflexive, see Erdal 1991: 583}:
cf. Old Turkic *saqïn-* 'to think'; NE[S] YeniseiT: Khakas *saġïn-* 'to think; to dream, to desire, to mean; to take care of; to miss, to be sad'; Sagai, Koibal, Kachin *saġïn-* 'to think, to remember' (R); Kyzyl *ṣāɣîn-* 'to think'; Shor *saġïn-* 'to miss'; AltaiT: Altai *saġïš* (< *saq-Xš* {Turkic VN}) 'mind, thought'; Tuba *saġïš* 'mind, consciousness, thought, mood, feeling'; Qumanda *saġïš* 'mind, thought, reason, memory, spirit, mood'; Quu *saġïn-* 'to think, to consider; to miss', cf. *saġïš* 'consciousness, mind, intelligence, memory'; Teleut *saġïn-* 'to yearn, to long', cf. *saġïš* 'mind, thought, memory; sadness, melancholy' (R); SayanT: Tuvan *saġïn-* 'to remember; to miss'; Tofan *saġïn-* 'to think; to remember; to be sad; to dream'; ChulymT *saġïn-* 'to think'; NE[N] Yakut *aġïn-* 'to remember, to mention to remind; to miss'; Dolgan *aġïn-* 'to remember, to yearn'; NW[N] Siberian Tatar –; NW[S] Kirgiz *saġïn-* 'to miss'; Fu-yü –; Kazak *saġïn-* 'to be bored, to earn'; SE Yellow Uyghur *saqïn-* 'to think, to suppose; to be sad';
Turkic → Samoyedic:
Kamas *sāɣïš ~ sāgaš* 'memory, mind; worry'.
Etymology: Joki LS 260; Clauson ED 804b; Erdal 1991: 612; ESTJa 2003: 144, 158

The etymology and structure of the Arin phrase *bičisagnibašu* 'I want, I would like' is unclear and to date unknown. I propose the element *sagni-* is of Turkic origin. Cf. the Turkic verb *saġïn-* 'to think, to desire', which accords with the Arin verb from the lexical aspect.

The Turkic verb *saġïn-* is widespread in Siberian Turkic with various meanings: 'to think; to dream, to desire, to mean; to take care of; to miss, to be sad,

---

(< *qaʔ 'big' + *baʔŋ 'place') > Kott *hâpag ~ hâpax*; Proto-Yeniseian **qam(ə)* 'vessel, cup' > Kott *ham*, etc. (Vajda & Werner: in preparation).

to remember, to yearn'. This is a reflexive verb derived from the verb *sāq-* 'to think', which is itself probably the emphatical and intensive form originating from the verb *sā-* 'to count' (Clauson ED 804b; ESTJa 2003: 158).

It is likely that the Kamas *sāγïš ~ sāgaš* 'memory, mind; worry' (Joki LS 260) was borrowed from the Altai Turkic form *saǧïš* 'mind, thought', derived from the verb *saq-* 'to think' with the deverbal noun suffix *-Xš* (for functions of this suffix, see Erdal 1991: 262).

Yugh *sáŋa* '*inf.* to feel, guess, imagine, understand, remember, keep in mind, find out, test, examine' (Werner 2002/2: 158) ← Turkic **sana-* 'to think, desire, feel, miss' ← Mongolic *sana-* 'to think, reflect, ponder; to hold an opinion; to intend, plan; to remember, keep in mind; to recall; to long for' ← Turkic *sana-* 'to count' < *sān* 'number' +*A-* {NV, see Erdal 1991: 308} < *sā-* 'to count' -*n* {Turkic VN, see Erdal 1991: 308}:

cf. NE[S] YeniseiT: Shor *sana-* 'to wish'; AltaiT: Altai *sana-* 'to think, dream, wish; take care, miss'; Tuba *sana-* 'to think, wish, dream'; Qumanda *sana-* 'to think, wish, decide'; Quu *sana-* 'to think, deside, wish'; Teleut *sanan-* < **sana-n-* {Turkic VV/reflexive} 'to think'; SayanT: Tuvan *sanal* (< *sana-l* {Mongolic VN, see Poppe GWM § 159}) 'proposal; speech'; Tofan *sana-* 'to read'; ChulymT *sana-* 'to read'; NE[N] Yakut *sanā-* 'to think; wish, desire'; Dolgan *hanā-* 'think; plan projects; celebrate'; NW[N] Siberian Tatar –; NW[S] Kirgiz *sana-* 'to think; miss'; Fu-yü –; Kazak *sana* (< **sanā* < *sana-GAn* {Mongolic VN, see Poppe GWM § 149}.) 'consciousness, thought'; SE Yellow Uyghur –;

Turkic ← Mongolic *sana-* 'to think, reflect, ponder; to hold an opinion; to intend, plan; to remember, keep in mind; to recall; to long for':

Middle Mongol: Precl.Mo. *sana-*; HY *sana-*; LM *sana-*; Modern Mongol: Buryat *hana-*; Khalkha *sana-*; Kalmuck *san^a-*; Dagur *sanə-* (E); Khamnigan *sana-*;

Mongolic ← Turkic *sana-* 'to count' < *sān* 'number' < *sā-* 'to count' -*n* {Turkic VN, see Erdal 1991: 306} +*A-* {Turkic NV, see Erdal 1991: 423}:

cf. Old Turkic *sana-*; NE[S] YeniseiT: Khakas *sana-*; Sagai, Koibal, Kachin *san* 'number' (R); Kyzyl *sāna-*; Shor *sana-*; AltaiT: –; SayanT: Tuvan *sana-*; Tofan *sana-*; ChulymT *sana-*; NE[N] Yakut –; NW[N] Siberian Tatar –; NW[S] Kirgiz *sana-*; Fu-yü *sani-* 'to reckon'; Kazak *sana-*; SE Yellow Uyghur *sana-*.

Etymology: Kałużyński 1962: 48; Doerfer TMEN 2: 231–233; Räsänen VEWT 400a; Clauson ED 835a, 831a, 781b; SSTMJa 2: 61a; Rassadin 1980: 23, 46, 68; Erdal 1991: 306, 423; Stachowski 1993: 95; Ščerbak 1997: 144; ESTJa 2003: 187–188; Khabtagaeva 2009: 271; 2015a: 120; Róna-Tas & Berta WOT 2011: 771–773; Nugteren 2011: 482

According to the Yugh word's lexical meaning, the Yugh verb was borrowed from the Siberian Turkic *sana-* 'to think', which is a Mongolic loanword. Phonetically, the Turkic nasal consonant *VnV* appears to have changed to *VŋV* in Yugh, though this is not a regular development.

The Siberian Turkic word belongs to the category of "re-borrowings" (Kałużyński 1962: 48; Rassadin 1980: 23, 46, 68; Stachowski 1993: 95; Khabtagaeva 2009: 271), ultimately of Turkic origin (Räsänen VEWT 400a; Clauson ED 835a, 831a, 781b; Ščerbak 1997: 144; ESTJa 2003: 187–188; Róna-Tas & Berta WOT 2011: 771–773). The original Turkic lexical meaning 'to count' derived from verb *sā-* 'to count,' with the Turkic deverbal noun suffix *-n* (Erdal 1991: 306), and the Turkic denominal verbum suffix *+A-* (Erdal 1991: 423).

Via Mongolic and Yakut, the Turkic word was borrowed into Northern Tungusic[294] (SSTMJa 2: 61a). From Turkic, the word was also borrowed into New Persian (Doerfer TMEN 2: 231–233) and Hungarian[295] (Róna-Tas & Berta WOT 2011: 771–773).

Yugh ***utčij ~ uččij*** 'to put out (*fire*)' (Werner 2002/2: 328) < *uč -ij* {Yugh action nominal suffix} ← ? Turkic **üč-* < *öč-* '*of a fire* to go out, be extinguished':
  cf. Old Turkic *öč-* '*of a fire* to go out, be extinguished'; NE^S YeniseiT: Khakas *us-* 'to go out (*fire*)'; Sagai, Koibal, Kachin *ös-* 'to go out'; Shor *öč-* 'to go out, disappear', cf. *öš-* 'go out (*of a fire*)' (R); AltaiT: Altai *öč-* 'to go out'; Tuba *öč-*; Qumanda *öč-* 'to go out, to die'; Quu *öč-* 'to go out (*of a fire*)'; Teleut *üč-* (R); SayanT: Tuvan *öš-*; Tofan *ö^cš-*; ChulymT –; NE^N Yakut *ös-* 'to go out (*of a fire, eyes*); *fig.* to be depressed'; Dolgan –; NW^N Siberian Tatar *üč-* 'to go out (*of a fire*)'; NW^S Kirgiz *öč-* 'to out (*of a fire*); to be destroyed'; Fu-yü *öš-* 'to go out (*fire*)'; Kazak *öš-* 'to go out (*of a fire*); to be erased, to keep quiet; to die'; SE Yellow Yughur –.

Etymology: Räsänen VEWT 368a; Rassadin 1971: 215; Clauson ED 19b; ESTJa 1974: 559–560

The etymology of the Yugh word is unknown (Werner 2002/2: 328). The final *-ij* is probably an allomorph of the Yeniseian action nominal suffix. As a hypothesis, I propose that the Yugh verb may be connected with the Turkic verb *öč-* 'to go out (of a fire).' The problematic aspect of my proposed etymology is that the Turkic verb is intransitive, whereas the Yugh verb is transitive. From a semantic perspective, however, the Turkic meaning is in accord with the Yugh form. From a phonetic perspective, the initial vowel *ü-*, instead of Common Turkic initial *ö-*, is present, which may point to a Teleut or Siberian Tatar influence.

---

[294] Turkic → Mongolic → Turkic: Yakut → Tungusic: Sakhalin, Urmi Ewenki *sanā* 'thought, intention', *sanā-* 'to think, to remember, to intend'.

[295] Turkic: West Old Turkic **sān-* 'to think' → Hungarian *szán-* [sān] 'to wish, to intend something for somebody/something, to devote'.

Yugh *χĭlčaχan* ~ *χʌlčakŋ* 'verb to tickle' (Werner 2002/2: 398) < *qʌlčak -(V)ŋ* {Yugh action nominal suffix: Werner 2005: 74–75}
qʌlčak ← Turkic **qïlčïq* (cf. Khakas) 'tickle' < **qïčïlïq* < *qïč +I-* {Turkic NV, see Erdal 1991: 474} *-(X)l-* {Turkic VV, see Erdal 1991: 651} *-XK* {Turkic VN, see Erdal 1991: 224}:
  cf. Old Turkic *qïčï* 'tickle' < **qïč-* 'to irritate, tickle'; NE^S YeniseiT: Khakas *xïlčïx*, cf. *xïčï-* 'to scratch yourself, to itch'; Sagai *qïljïq* 'tickle'; Shor *qïčï-* 'to itch'; AltaiT: Altai *qïčïq* 'tickle' < *qïčï-*, cf. *qïlčïq* (R); Tuba *kïčïn-* (< **qïčï-n-* {Turkic VV/reflexive}) 'to itch, to feel itchy'; Qumanda *kïčit* (< **qïčï-t* {Turkic VN}) 'itching, scratching'; Quu *kïdžï-* 'to itch'; Teleut *qïlčïq* 'tickle', *qïčï-* 'to itch'; SayanT: Tuvan *kïžï-* 'to itch'; Tofan *kïjï-* 'to itch'; ChulymT *qïjï-* 'to itch' (R); NE^N Yakut *kïhïy-* 'to scratch; to itch; fig. to be irritated'; Dolgan –; NW^N Siberian Tatar *qïdzï-* 'to scratch'; NW^S Kirgiz *qïčïq* 'tickle, sensitivity to tickling; nicety', cf. *qïčïš-* (< **qïčï-š-* {Turkic VV/cooperative}) 'to itch'; Fu-yü –; Kazak *qïš-* 'to itch'; SE Yellow Uyghur *qïtïs-* 'to itch'.
Etymology: Räsänen VEWT 260b; Rassadin 1971: 203; Clauson ED 591b; ESTJa 1980: 42–43; 2000: 186–187

The Yugh verb is of unknown origin (Werner 2002/2: 398). The base is *qʌlčak* with the action nominal suffix *-(V)ŋ*. It is probable that Yugh *qʌlčak* goes back to the Turkic noun *qïlčïq* 'tickle', which is typical for some Yenisei Turkic and Altai Turkic varieties. From a phonetic perspective, the spirantization of initial *q-* > *χ-* is a regular change in native Yenisean words and Turkic loanwords. A later period of borrowing is possibly shown by the preservation of the consonant cluster *-lč-*. According to Yugh phonetic rules, Proto-Yeniseian *-č-* goes back to *-t'-* (Starostin 1982: 161).

The base of the Yugh verb *qʌlčak* can be traced back to the Turkic form *qïlčïq*, itself a metathesized form of **qïčïlïq*. It is derived from the base *qïč* (ESTJa 1980: 42; 2000: 187) with the Turkic denominal verbum suffix *+I-*, the deverbal verbum suffix *-(X)l-*, forming passive verbs, and the deverbal noun suffix *-(X)K*. According to its phonetic shape, the word belongs to the category of onomatopoetic words.

The Turkic verb was borrowed into Mongolic[296] (ESTJa 1980: 43).

1.6   Postpositions

Kott **aktur** ~ **atkur** 'through' (Werner 2002/1: 77) ← Turkic **ötküre* < *ötgürü* 'through' < *öt-* 'to cross, penetrate into something' *-GXr-* 'to cause to pass

---

296   Turkic *qïčï-* → Mongolic 'tickle': cf. Middle Mongol: –; LM *gejige*; Modern Mongol: Buryat *gežegi* 'ticklish'; Khalkha *gijig* 'tickle, ticklishness'; Kalmuck *gidžŋn^ɔ-* 'to tickle'; Dagur –; Khamnigan *gičigē ~ gičige ~ gidzagai*.

through' {Turkic VV/causative, see Erdal 1991: 751, 756} -*A* {Turkic converb, see Erdal 2004: 333–335}:

cf. Old Turkic *ötgürü* 'postp. because of'; NE^S YeniseiT: Khakas *ötīre* 'through'; Sagai, Koibal, Kachin *üt-*; Shor *öttire*; AltaiT: Altai *ötküre* 'through, by, past'; Tuba *ötküre* 'through'; Qumanda *ötküre*; Quu *ötire* ~ *ötrö* ~ *ötüre*; Teleut *ötküre*; SayanT: Tuvan *öttür* 'through; all, the whole of'; Tofan *ö^ctkürü* 'through'; ChulymT –;[297] NE^N Yakut *ötörü* 'through'; Dolgan –; NW^N Siberian Tatar –; NW^S Kirgiz *ötkör-* 'to conduct; to make pass'; Fu-yü –; Kazak *ötker-* 'to let pass'; SE Yellow Yughur –.

Etymology: Räsänen VEWT 376a; Rassadin 1971: 215; Clauson ED 52b, 54a; ESTJa 1974: 554–555; Erdal 1991: 751, 756; 2004: 333; Khabtagaeva 2015c: 95

The Kott word has a clear Turkic etymology. The Turkic postposition is derived from the verb *öt-* 'to cross, to penetrate into something' with the causative and converb suffixes (for details on derivation, see Erdal 1991: 751, 756; 2004: 333).

Different phonetic changes occurred in the Kott form. Because of the absence of synharmony in Yeniseian, it disappeared in Kott. In addition, due to the metathesis of the cluster *-tk-* > *-kt-*, the final Turkic vowel is dropped. Morphologically, it is a postposition in Kott, as in Turkic languages.

Yugh ***unče*** 'because' (Werner 2002/2: 347) ← Turkic *üčün 'because of, for the sake of, for; because, in order to':

cf. Old Turkic *üčün*; NE^S YeniseiT: Khakas *üčün*; Sagai *üjün*; Sagai, Koibal *üzün*; Kyzyl *üžün*; Shor *üčün*; AltaiT: Altai; Tuba; Qumanda *učun*; Quu *udžun* ~ *učun* ~ *üžün*; Teleut *učun*; SayanT: Tuvan *užun*; Tofan –; ChulymT *üčün*; NE^N Yakut; Dolgan *ihin*; NW^N Siberian Tatar –; NW^S Kirgiz *üčün*; Fu-yü –; Kazak *üšin*; SE Yellow Yughur –.

Etymology: Räsänen VEWT 169a, 509b; Clauson ED 28b; ESTJa 1974: 642–643; Khabtagaeva 2015c: 102

The etymology of the Yugh word is unknown (Werner 2002/2: 347). It very possibly is connected to the Turkic postposition *üčün* 'because'. From a phonetic perspective, vowel harmony disappeared and the metathesis of consonants occurred.

The etymology of the Turkic word is unclear. Räsänen (VEWT 169a, 509b) derived the Turkic postposition from the noun *ič* 'inside, inner.' Sevortjan has listed some earlier proposed etymologies in which the Turkic postposition

---

297 Chulym has the strange form *ažïra* 'through', which fits semantically, but is problematic from a phonetic perspective. Possibly Chulym *ažïra* changed from *atïra < *ötire < *ötüre < *ötgüre, but it is not regular. Probably the Chulym word was borrowed from another source.

was connected to the Turkic nouns ūč 'end', ōč 'malice, spite, revenge', and so on (for details, see ESTJa 1974: 642–643).

1.7   Interjections

Kott *hára* '*interjection of impatience* come on already!' (Werner 2002/1: 302) ← Turkic **qara-* 'to look, to watch; to peer, to pay attention, to observe; to wait' {Turkic imperative sg.2, see Erdal 2004: 234–235} ← Mongolic *qara-* 'to look at':

cf. Old Turkic *qara-* 'to look at'; NE[S] YeniseiT: Khakas *xara-* 'to stare; to observe anything; to pay attention; to look for someone, to watch'; Sagai, Koibal, Kachin *kara-* 'to look into the distance, to see' (R); AltaiT: Altai *kara-* 'to look, to watch; to peer, to pay attention, to observe; to wait'; Tuba *kara-* 'to watch, to guard, to wait'; Qumanda *kara-* 'to wait'; Quu *kara-* 'to wait'; Teleut *qara-* 'to look, to watch' (R); SayanT: Tuvan *xara-* 'to see; to survey'; Tofan *hara-* 'to aim; to watch, to watch from a top; to graze cattle'; ChulymT –; NE[N] Yakut *xaray-* 'to guard, to protect, to care about someone, something'; Dolgan *karay-* 'to care; to bury'; NW[N] Siberian Tatar *qara-* 'to look into the distance'; NW[S] Kirgiz *kara-* 'to look; to inspect; to pay attention; to care about anyone; to wait'; Fu-yü –; Kazak *qara-* 'to look around, to inspect; to consider, to look'; SE Yellow Uyghur *qara-* 'to look';

Turkic ← Mongolic *qara-*:

cf. Middle Mongol: Precl.Mo. *qara-*; SH *qara-* 'to see'; HY *qara-* 'to watch'; Muq. *qara-* 'to look at'; LM *qara-* 'to look at, glance, watch, observe; to regard, consider; to look after; to face'; Modern Mongol: Buryat *xara-* 'to look, to see; to look after, to care for anyone; to read; to inspect, to observe'; Khalkha *xara-* 'to look, to look at, to face; to look after, to care for; to look out for'; Kalmuck *xar^a-* 'to inspect'; Dagur –; Khamnigan *xara-*.

Etymology: Doerfer TMEN 3: 434–436; 1985: 51; Räsänen VEWT 235b; Rassadin 1971: 186; Clauson ED 645b; SSTMJa 1: 380; ESTJa 1997: 288–289; Schönig 2000: 152–153; Khabtagaeva 2009: 170; Nugteren 2011: 404

The etymology of the Kott word is connected to the Turkic imperative form *qara!* with the lexical meaning 'look! pay attention! see! etc.' → come on!. The phonetic change of initial Turkic *q-* to *h-* in Kott is a regular feature.

The Turkic word is ultimately of Mongolic origin, which is a widespread phenomenon in Modern Turkic languages (Clauson ED 645b; ESTJa 1997: 288–289).

The Mongolic word was borrowed as well into the Tungusic languages[298] (SSTMJa 1: 380; Doerfer 1985: 51). The Yakut final additional *-y* in Ewenki and

---

298 Mongolic → Tungusic: Nanai *qaryaču-* 'to watch'; Orok *qarya-* 'to watch, to look, to observe'; Nanai *qaryači-* 'to look at'; Manchu *qara-* 'to look, to watch'.

Lamut verbs[299] points to a borrowing from Yakut and not directly from Mongolic (For criteria, see Khabtagaeva 2011: 102).

2 Phonetic Features

2.1 *Turkic Vowels and Consonants in Yeniseian*

In this chapter I consider Turkic vowels and consonants in Yeniseian languages in the table form for convenience and transparency for reader. Examples are given for every phonetic change.

Common Turkic displays a symmetrical basic set of eight vowel phonemes, which can be classified with respect to the features front vs. back, unrounded vs. rounded, and high vs. low:

	front		back	
	unrounded	rounded	unrounded	rounded
high	i	ü	ï	u
low	e	ö	a	o

The consonant system of Common Turkic has seventeen phonemes including labials, alveolars, palatals and velars. Voiced and voiceless stops form a phonemic contrast:

	voiceless stops	voiced stops	nasals	sibilants	liquids
labials	p	b	m		
alveolars	t	d	n	s z	l
palatals	č	y ǰ	ń	š	
velars	k q	g ġ	ŋ		r

---

[299] Mongolic → Yakut → Tungusic: Aldan, Sakhalin, Urmi, Uchur, Chumikan Ewenki *karaj-* 'to take care; to protect; to save'; Lamut *karay-* 'to guard'.

2.1.1 Kott
2.1.1.1 Turkic Vowel Phonemes in Kott

Turkic	Kott	Examples
\multicolumn{3}{l}{Low unrounded vowels}		
a	a-	Turkic *altūn* > *altïn* 'gold' → Kott *altun* ~ *altin*;
		Turkic *aybïčï* 'fellow countryman' → Kott *aibič* ~ *aipiš* 'old man';
		Turkic *arïg* 'clean, pure' → Kott *arix*;
	-a¹-	Turkic *baqïr* 'copper' → Kott *baker*;
		Turkic *tān* > *tan* 'a cool breeze' → Kott *tʰantu* {-*tu* Yeniseian NN} 'snow flurry, storm';
	-a²- ~ -á²-	Turkic *bolat* 'steel' → Kott *bolat* ~ *bolát*;
	-a²-	Turkic *šūrgan* 'snowstorm, storm' → Kott *šurgan* 'cold weather';
		Turkic *tumarïk* 'haze' → Kott *tipar* ~ *típar* 'fog';
	-a	Turkic *arpa* 'barley' → Kott *arba*;
	-á	Turkic *kola* 'copper, brass' → Kott *kolá*;
	-ô¹-	Turkic *qabtal* 'saddle cloth' → Kott *hôpetal* ~ *hôptal*;
	-ô²-	Turkic *qulaq* 'ear' → Kott *kalôx*;
	-e²-	Turkic *qamla-* > *kamna-* 'to make magic' → Kott *hanpen* 'pray, prayer' {-*n* Yeniseian VN/adj.};
ä	e-	Turkic *elūr* ~ *erūl* 'sober' → Kott *elor* ~ *erol*;
e		Turkic *ävir-* > *ebir-* 'to turn (e.g. a wheel)' → Kott *êper* 'noun circle; adj. round; adv. around';
		Turkic *äsūr-* > *äsäriklig* 'drunk' → Kott *eser* ~ *esirolog*;
	-e¹-	Turkic *kärsū* 'clever, talented' → Kott *keršo* 'clever';
		Turkic *mergen* 'marksman; hero' → Kott *berxen* 'warrior';
	-e²-	Turkic *belen* 'prepared, ready' → Kott *bêlen* 'finished';
		Turkic *mergen* 'marksman; hero' → Kott *berxen* 'warrior';
	-a²-, -á²-	Turkic *ätmäk* 'bread' → Kott *itpák* ~ *itpak* ~ *iptak*;
	-a²-	Turkic *yip* > *d'ibek* 'thread' → Kott *d'ibak* ~ *d'ipak*;
		Turkic *täβäy* > *täbä* 'camel' → Kott *tabat*;
	-a	Turkic *bökä* > *böke* 'hero, strong' → Kott *baha*;
	i-	Turkic *ätmäk* 'bread' → Kott *itpák* ~ *itpak* ~ *iptak*;
	-i¹-	Turkic *bäk* 'firm, solid, stable' → Kott *bik*;

(cont.)

Turkic	Kott	Examples
Low rounded vowels		
o	o- ~ ô-	Turkic *obal* 'sin' → Kott *obal* ~ *ôpal*;
	-o¹-	Turkic *kola* 'copper, brass' → Kott *kolá*;
		Turkic *bolat* 'steel' → Kott *bolat* ~ *bolát*;
		Turkic *qorġušïn* > *korgočin* 'lead' → Kott *korkôtn* ~ *korogotn* 'lead', cf. *korkotnɨ* 'tin';
		Turkic *qōń* > *qoy* 'sheep' → Kott *koi*;
	a-	Turkic *oyun* 'game, play, merriment' → Kott *ajaŋ*;
		Turkic *otāġ* > *otaġ* 'a small temporary building, tent' → Kott *atax*;
		Turkic *otüq* 'fire-steel' → Kott *ataŋ*;
	-a¹-	Turkic *kolčak* 'the upper part of a valley' → Kott *kalšu* 'riverbank';
	u-	Turkic *oruq* 'path' → Kott *uruk* 'mountain valley';
		Turkic *onoŋ učun* 'therefore' → Kott *una ôjaŋ*;
	-u¹-	Turkic *sogur* 'blind' → Kott *šugur* 'one-eyed';
	-o¹- ~ -u¹-	Turkic *tōy* > *toy* 'a wedding feast' → Kott *toi* ~ *tui*;
ö	o-	Turkic *öküz* 'ox' → Kott *ogus* 'bull';
	a-	Turkic *ötgürü* 'through' → Kott *aktur*;
	-a¹-	Turkic *bökä* > *böke* 'hero, strong' → Kott *baha*;
	u-	Turkic *örüm* 'something plaited or woven' → Kott *urum* 'cloth, linen';
	-u¹-	Turkic *köβürgän* > *köbürgän* 'wild onion' → Kott *kubúrgenaŋ*;
High unrounded vowels		
ï	-i²-	Turkic *aðġïr* 'stallion' → Kott *askɨr*;
		Turkic *arïš* 'rye' → Kott *ariš* ~ *áriš*;
	-i¹-	Turkic *bïŋ* > *büŋ* 'a thousand' → Kott *min*;
		Turkic **yïpaq* > *d'ïbek* 'thread' → Kott *d'ibak* ~ *d'ipak*;
		Turkic *jïda* > *d'ïda* 'spear' → Kott *d'ida*;
	-i²-	Turkic *aybïčï* 'fellow countryman' → Kott *aibič* ~ *aipiš* 'old man';
		Turkic *čazïn* 'paper' → Kott *šašin*;
		Turkic *tarï-* 'to cultivate ground' → Kott *taripan* 'field' (cf. *pan*: Yeniseian *baŋ* 'earth, ground');

(cont.)

Turkic	Kott	Examples
	-i	Turkic *qamčï* 'a whip' → Kott *kamči*;
		Turkic *nayjï* 'friend' → Kott *najči*;
	-a¹-	Turkic *qïlïč* 'sword' → Kott *kaleš ~ kališ*;
		Turkic *qïčïr-* 'to read' → Kott *kačei*;
	-a²-	Turkic *arïq* 'tired out, exhausted' → Kott *arak* 'lean (thin)';
		Turkic *otïq* 'fire-steel' → Kott *ataŋ*;
		Turkic *qoŋïr* 'dark chestnut (of a horse)' → Kott *koŋar*;
	-a	Turkic *arakï* 'wine, vodka' → Kott *araka*;
	-e²-	Turkic *abïs* 'priest' → Kott *âpeš*;
		Turkic *albïs* 'evil spirit' → Kott *alpeš* 'wonder';
		Turkic *baqïr* 'copper' → Kott *baker*;
		Turkic *qarïš* 'a span' → Kott *kareš ~ kariš*;
	-e	Turkic *yaxšï > yaqšï* 'suitable' → Kott *hagše* 'good, suitable';
	-e¹- ~ -i¹-	Turkic *sïra* 'beer' → Kott *šera ~ sera ~ širá*;
	-ô¹- ~ -o¹-	Turkic *tït aġas* 'larch' → Kott *tôteäš ~ toteš*;
	-u²-	Turkic *qoqïylat-* 'to lead to despair' → Kott *xoxutajut* 'to offend, hurt';
	-u	Turkic *qamčï* 'a whip' → Kott *kamču*;
i	-ï¹-	Turkic *kiden* 'flax, canvas' → Kott *hîta* 'nettles, hemp';
	-i	Turkic *yitig > yitī* 'sharp' → Kott *êti*;
	-e²-	Turkic *ävir- > äbir-* 'to turn (sg.)' → Kott *êper* 'circle; round; around';

High rounded vowels

u	-u¹-	Turkic *tura* 'house; village; town' → Kott *turá* 'village';
	-û¹-	Turkic *qur* 'belt, girdle' → Kott *kûra* 'rope';
	-u²-	Turkic *oruq* 'path' → Kott *uruk* 'mountain valley';
		Turkic *qosqun* 'crupper' → Kott *koskun* 'breech-band';
	-o¹-	Turkic *buqa* 'bull' → Kott *boga*;
		Turkic *tura* 'house; village; town' → Kott *torá* 'living room', cf. *turá* 'village';
	-o²-	Turkic *čokur* 'variegated, multicoloured' → Kott *čôgor* 'coloured';
	-ō	Turkic *baltu* 'axe' → Kott *báltō*;

(cont.)

Turkic	Kott	Examples
	-*i¹*- ~ -*î¹*-	Turkic *tumarïk* 'haze, fog' → Kott *tipar* ~ *tîpar* 'fog';
	-*a¹*-	Turkic *qulaq* 'ear' → Kott *kalôx*;
		Turkic *qulġur* 'crop-eared' → Kott *kalkul* 'deaf';
ü	*u*-	Turkic *üšik* > *üšük* 'hard frost, frozen; frostbitten' → Kott *ušôx* ~ *ušou* 'ice';
	-*u¹*-	Turkic *kǖlük* > *külük* 'clever, wise, famous' → Kott *kuľuk* 'bold, boldness';
		Turkic *kümüš* 'silver' → Kott *kumiš*;
		Turkic *kǖč* > *küč* 'strength, power, energy' → Kott *kuštu* 'very strong' {-*tu* Yeniseian NN/adj.};
		Turkic *sǖt* > *süt* 'milk' → Kott *šut*;
	-*u²*-	Turkic *öküz* 'ox' → Kott *ogus*;
		Turkic *köprüg* > *köpür* 'bridge' → Kott *kôpur* ~ *kopur* ~ *kobur*;
	-*u*	Turkic *böri* > *börü* 'wolf' → Kott *bôru* ~ *boru*;
	ô-	Turkic *onoŋ učun* 'therefore' → Kott *una ôjaŋ*;
	-*ô²*-	Turkic *üšük* 'hard frost, frozen' → Kott *ušôx* 'ice';
	-*o*	Turkic *kärsü* 'clever, talanted' → Kott *keršo*;
	-*e¹*-	Turkic *tükteg* 'with feathers' → Kott *tegteka* 'quail';
	-*i²*-	Turkic *kümüš* 'silver' → Kott *kumiš*.

2.1.1.2   *Turkic Consonant Phonemes in Kott*

Turkic	Kott	Examples
Voiceless stops		
p	VpV	Turkic *qapaq* 'eyelid; forehead' → Kott *kapax* 'forehead';
	VpV ~ VbV	Turkic *köprüg* > *köpür* 'bridge' → Kott *kôpur* ~ *kopur* ~ *kobur*;
		Turkic **yïpak* > *d'ibek* 'thread' → Kott *d'ibak* ~ *d'ipak*;

(cont.)

Turkic	Kott	Examples
t	tʰ-[300]	Turkic *tān > tan* 'a cool breeze' → Kott *tʰantu* 'snow flurry, storm';
		Turkic *ta tiginde* 'there' → Kott *tʰategâtna* 'beside, next to';
	t-	Turkic *talqan* 'oat flour' → Kott *tálgan ~ talkan* 'flour, meal';
		Turkic *toruġ > torüġ > tor* 'bay, brown (*of a horse*)' → Kott *tor*;
		Turkic *tura* 'house; village; town' → Kott *torá ~ tura* 'living room', *turá* 'village';
		Turkic *türgen* 'quick, rapid' → Kott *turkatu* {-*tu* Yeniseian NN/adj.};
		Turkic *tamkï* 'tobacco' → Kott *tâmukol* 'tobacco tin' (+ Yeniseian *ol* 'container');
	VtV	Turkic *yitig > yitī <* 'sharp' → Kott *êti*;
		Turkic *otāġ > otaġ* 'a small temporary building, tent' → Kott *atax*;
		Turkic *otiq* 'fire-steel' → Kott *ataŋ*;
	-t	Turkic *alpaġut > albot* 'head of the district; governor' → Kott *alpot*;
		Turkic *bolat* 'steel' → Kott *bolat ~ bolát*;
		Turkic *qaġat > qāt > qat* 'paper' → Kott *kat*;
		Turkic *sūt > süt* 'milk' → Kott *šut*;
k	k-	Turkic *küč > küč* 'strength, power, energy' → Kott *kuštu* 'very strong' {-*tu* Yeniseian NN/adj.};
		Turkic *kümüš* 'silver' → Kott *kumiš ~ kumuš*;

---

[300] There are two cases with initial *t*-, where aspiration occurred in Kott. The problematic side of this phonetic statement is that we do not know the exact difference between *t*- and *tʰ*- in the Kott sources. Starostin reconstructs Proto-Yeniseian initial **t*- without aspiration (Starostin 1982: 151). Werner (1990b: 235–236) reconstructs the aspirated consonant *tʰ*- in Proto-Yeniseian, which was preserved in Kott, while in Ket, Arin and Yugh is generally transcribed as simple *t*-, e.g. Kott *tʰapui* 'staff' (cf. Yugh *tāfa*, Northern Ket *tāˑ*) < Proto-Yeniseian **tʰapʰa*; Kott *tʰêg ~ tʰêx* 'belt' (cf. Ket *tiˀ* 'rope, string') < Proto-Yeniseian **tʰeg*; Kott *tʰip* 'iron' (cf. Arin *tep ~ ten*, Assan *tip*) < Proto-Yeniseian **tʰep* 'iron', etc. This phonetic feature assumes an early period of borrowing or the difference of the Kott sources.

(cont.)

Turkic	Kott	Examples
	-k	Turkic *ätmäk* > *itpäk* 'bread' → Kott *itpák* ~ *itpak* ~ *iptak*; Turkic *bäk* 'firm, solid, stable' → Kott *bik*; Turkic *köŋläk* > *kögänäk* 'shirt' → Kott *kônak* ~ *kukanak* ~ *kononak*; Turkic **yïpäk* > *dʹibek* 'thread' → Kott *dʹibak* ~ *dʹipak*;
	h-	Turkic *kiden* 'coarse linen, canvas' → Kott *hîta* 'nettles, hemp';
	VhV	Turkic *bökä* > *böke* 'hero, strong' → Kott *baha*;
	VgV	Turkic *öküz* 'ox' → Kott *ogus*;
	k- ~ q- ~ x-	Turkic *kämi* > *kebe* 'ship or boat' → Kott *kep* ~ *qep* ~ *xep* ~ *xêp*;
	-x	Turkic *üšik* > *üšük* 'hard frost, frozen' → Kott *ušôx* 'ice';
q	k-[301]	Turkic *qolčak* 'the upper part of a valley' → Kott *kalšu* 'undergrowth-covered riverbank'; Turkic *qulun* 'foal' → Kott *kulun* ~ *kolun* ~ *kulún*; Turkic *qur* 'belt, girdle' → Kott *kûra* 'rope';
	VkV	(Arabic →) Turkic *arakï* 'wine, vodka' → Kott *araka*; Turkic *baqïr* 'copper' → Kott *baker*;
	-k	Turkic *oruq* 'path' → Kott *uruk* 'mountain valley';
	h-[302]	Turkic *qamla-* > *qamna-* 'to make magic' → Kott *hanpen* 'pray, prayer, praying' {-*n* Yeniseian VN/adj.}; (Mongolic →) Turkic *qabtal* 'saddle cloth' → Kott *hôpetal* ~ *hôptal*; Turkic *qaram* 'stingy, greedy' → Kott *harâ* 'rapacious, voracious'; Turkic *qara-* 'look, watch; wait!' {Turkic imperative sg.2} → Kott *hâra* 'interjection of impatience come on already!'; Turkic *qolanak* 'Siberian weasel' → Kott *holanka*;

---

[301] The preservation of initial Turkic *q-* points to a later period of borrowing.
[302] The Turkic initial *q-* changed to *h-* in Kott as in original Yeniseian words. This feature points to an early period of borrowing: e.g. Kott *hatam* 'cough; saliva' < Proto-Yeniseian **qaqtəm* 'noun cough'; Kott *hatačei* 'inf. to kindle' < Proto-Yeniseian **qatatʲej* < **qat* 'fire' + **tʲej* 'rub'; Kott *hîma* 'grandmother' < Proto-Yeniseian **qima ~ qema* < **qax* 'big, great' + **ama* 'mother', etc. (Vajda & Werner: in preparation; Werner 1990b: 25; 231).

TURKIC LOANWORDS 213

(cont.)

Turkic	Kott	Examples
	x-[303]	Turkic *qokïylat-* 'to lead to despair' → Kott *xoxutajut* 'to offend, hurt';
	-x	Turkic *aqsaq* 'lame' → Kott *aksax*;
		Turkic *qańaq* > *qayaq* 'butter, sour cream' → Kott *kajax* 'oil, butter';
		Turkic *qulaq* 'ear' → Kott *kalôx*;
		Turkic *qapaq* 'eyelid' > *qabaq* 'forehead' → Kott *kapax* 'forehead';
	g-[304]	Turkic *komay* 'bad' + **ugā* 'very' (cf. Khakas *uġā xomay* 'disgusting') → ? Kott *gobimojb[e]ga* 'disgusting';
	VgV	Turkic *buqa* 'bull' → Kott *boga*;
		Turkic *čokur* 'variegated, multicoloured' → Kott *čôgor* 'coloured';
	-g	Turkic *qańaq* > *qayaq* 'butter, sour cream' → Kott *kajag* 'oil, butter';
	-ŋ	Turkic *otüq* 'fire-steel' → Kott *ataŋ*;

Voiced stops

b	b-[305]	Turkic *baqïr* 'copper' → Kott *baker*;
		Turkic *baltu* 'axe' → Kott *balt^hu* ~ *baltu* ~ *báltō*;
		Turkic *bäk* > *bik* 'firm, solid, stable' → Kott *bik*;
		Turkic *buqa* 'bull' → Kott *boga*;
		Turkic *böri* > *börü* 'wolf' → Kott *bôru* ~ *boru*;
	VbV	Turkic *saban* 'plough' → Kott *šaban*;
	p-[306]	Turkic *bāy* > *bay* 'rich; a rich man' → Kott *pai*;
		Turkic *kučaktap bar-* 'to take away' → Kott *kuštap parak* 'I take away';
		Turkic *bōq* 'excrement, dung' → Kott *p^hôk* 'feces, dirt';

---

303 There are some cases where the initial *q-* changed to *x-* in Kott. This change is possibly the variant of *h-* which was occurred in another different Yeniseian source.
304 The problematic side of this change is the uncertainty of the Turkic etymology.
305 The Kott cases, where the Turkic initial *b-* is preserved, belong to the later period of borrowing.
306 There are only two cases in Kott, where the Turkic initial consonant *b-* devoiced. This fea-

(cont.)

Turkic	Kott	Examples
f- < *p-		Turkic bōq > *poq 'excrement, dung' → Kott fôk ~ fôx 'feces, dirt';
	VpV	Turkic abïs 'priest' → Kott âpeš ~ âpuš;
	VbV ~ VpV	Turkic obal 'sin' → Kott obal ~ ôpal;
	h-[307]	Turkic baġana 'tent-pole' → Kott hagîni ~ hagîn'e ~ hagin'e;
	m-[308]	Turkic biŋ > bïŋ 'a thousand' → Kott min;
d	VdV	Turkic d'ïda 'spear' → Kott d'ida;
	VtV	Turkic buġday > būday 'wheat' → Kott butai;
		Turkic kiden 'flax, canvas' → Kott hîta 'nettles, hemp';
δ[309]	*-z- > -s-	Turkic aðġïr > azqïr > asqïr 'stallion' → Kott askar ~ askïr;
	(Yenisei	Turkic *qaðïġ > qazïq 'health' → Kott kasak ~ kasax;
	Turkic)	Turkic *quðuš-GAn {Turkic VN} > qosqun 'crupper' → Kott koskun 'breech-band';

ture characterizes the regular change in original Yeniseian words (Werner 1990b: 21, 25, 233; Vajda 2013: personal communication), which points to an early period of borrowing, e.g. Kott paŋ 'earth, place, ground, land, region' < Proto-Yeniseian *baʔŋ; Kott pʰatap 'palm' < Proto-Yeniseian *batqop < *baʔt 'out-facing part' + *qaʔp 'center portion of flat area of the body'; Kott pej 'wind' < Proto-Yeniseian *bej 'wind', etc.

This phonetic feature is peculiar for Khakas dialects and some Altai Turkic varieties also (e.g. Old Turkic baġïr 'the liver' ~ Yenisei Turkic: Khakas, Shor pār; Altai Turkic: Quu pār; Qumanda pagïr; Old Turkic bēš 'five' ~ Yenisei Turkic: Khakas pis; Shor peš; Altai Turkic: Quu peš; Qumanda piš ~ peš; Teleut peš; Old Turkic biläk 'the wrist' ~ Yenisei Turkic: Khakas pïlek; Shor pilek; Altai Turkic: Quu pilek 'elbow'; Teleut pilek 'forearm'; etc.). In this way, the change b- > p- designates the Common Yenisei Turkic—Altai Turkic layer too.

307   There is only one case where the Turkic initial b- changed to h- via *p-.
308   The change of initial b- > m- in the Turkic languages is a typical feature in words with nasal consonants, e.g. Old Turkic burun 'nose' ~ Yakut murun; Old Turkic bin- 'to mount, ride a horse' ~ Modern Uyghur min-, Tuvan mun-; Old Turkic biŋ 'thousand' ~ Tuvan muŋ, etc. There are some cases where the change b- > m- happened, which is not inevitably conditioned by another nasal consonant. E.g. Old Turkic baqïr 'copper' ~ Tuvan makïr; Old Turkic būz 'ice' ~ Modern Uyghur muz, etc. E.g. Old Turkic bän 'I, me' in almost all Modern Turkic languages is män, except for Turkish and Chuvash (Johanson 1998: 102–103).
   The Kott loanwords with initial m- usually were borrowed from Siberian Turkic, where the b- > m- change already happened. In this way, the Kott loanwords with initial m- belong to the later period of borrowing.
309   The Turkic -δ- regularly changed to -z- in Yenisei Turkic, but to -y- in Altai Turkic, e.g. Old

(cont.)

Turkic	Kott	Examples
	VsV ~ VšV	Turkic *aða* 'danger' > *aza* 'demon, evil spirit' → Kott *âsa* ~ *asa* ~ *áša*;
	VtV < *VdV	Turkic *yiðig* 'smell, odour' → Kott *īta* 'stinking';
g	VgV ~ VkV	Turkic *tägäy* 'the top of a mountain or a head' → Kott *tagaj* ~ *takai* 'head';
	VkV	Turkic *kälägäy* 'stammerer, stutterer' → Kott *kalakai* ~ *kalakei* 'verb to stutter, adj. stuttering';
ġ	VgV	Turkic *aġïl* 'a settlement or group of tents, village' → Kott *agel* ~ *âgel*;
		Turkic *kabagalï* 'with husk, peel, shuck' → Kott *kamagalá* 'nut';
		Turkic *kapčagai* 'quick' → Kott *kapsagai* 'nimble, quick';
		Turkic *sogur* 'blind' → Kott *šugur* 'one-eyed';
	VkV	Turkic *albaġa* 'sable' → Kott *alpaka* ~ *alpuka* 'flying squirrel';
	-x	Turkic *ariġ* 'clean, pure' → Kott *arix*;
		Turkic *otāġ* > *otaġ* 'a small temporary building, tent' → Kott *atax*;
		Turkic *kand'aga* 'saddle-thongs' → Kott *kant^{h}êx* 'halter';
		Turkic **qaðiġ* > *qazïq* 'health' → Kott *kasak* ~ *kasax*;

Nasals

n[310]	VnV	Turkic *köŋläk* > *kögänäk* 'shirt' → Kott *kônak* ~ *kukanak* ~ *kononak*;

Turkic *aðaq* 'leg, foot' ~ Khakas *azax* (cf. Yellow Uyghur *azaq*, Fu-yü *azïx*); Altai *ayaq*; Old Turkic *quðruq* 'tail' ~ Khakas *xuzurux* (cf. Yellow Uyghur *quzïrïq*), Altai *quyruq*; Old Turkic *beðük* 'large, high' ~ Khakas *pözik* (cf. Yellow Uyghur *pezik*), Altai *biyik*, etc.

The Turkic loanwords in Yeniseian with medial -s- or -š- through -z- were borrowed from Yenisei Turkic, while the loanwords with -y- were borrowed from Altai Turkic.

310 The Turkic *n* is an atypical consonant in initial position, it usually occurred in intervocalic and final positions. It is questionable that the Turkic interrogative pronoun *nä̃* 'what?' whether is the original Turkic word. The words with initial *n-* are usually loanwords in Turkic.

(cont.)

Turkic	Kott	Examples
	-n	Turkic *altūn* > *altïn* 'gold' → Kott *altun* ~ *altïn*; Turkic *yoġurqan* > *d'ōrgan* 'blanket' → Kott *d'ôrgan*; Turkic *qaġan* > *kān* 'an independent ruler of a tribe or people; kagan' → Kott *kan* 'prince'; Turkic *qulun* 'foal' → Kott *kulun* ~ *kolun* ~ *kulún*; Turkic *šūrgan* 'snowstorm, storm' → Kott *šurgan* 'cold weather'; Turkic *talqan* 'oat flour' → Kott *tálgan* ~ *talkan* 'flour, meal';
	-ŋ	Turkic *oyun* 'game, play, merriment' → Kott *ajaŋ*; Turkic *onoŋ učun* 'therefore' → Kott *una ôjaŋ*;
	-ø	Turkic *kiden* 'flax, canvas' → Kott *hîta* 'nettles, hemp';
ŋ	VŋV	Turkic *qoŋur* > *qoŋïr* 'dark chestnut (*of a horse*)' → Kott *koŋar*; Turkic *koŋraš* 'a bell' → Kott *koŋoroš* ~ *konkorôš*;
	-n	Turkic *biŋ* > *büŋ* 'a thousand' → Kott *min*;
ń[311]	-j-	Turkic *qańaq* 'the skin on milk' → Kott *kajax* ~ *kajag* 'oil, butter';
	-i	Turkic *qōń* 'sheep' → Kott *koi*;
m	m-[312]	Turkic *maŋar* 'who is running, who is in hurry' (< *maŋ-*) → Kott *mankara* ~ *mangara* 'hare, rabbit'; Turkic *munġan* 'mentally disturbed' → Kott *munkan* ~ *munxan* 'poor';

---

[311] The Turkic nasal consonant *ń* occurred in Kott in intervocalic and final positions. It changed to *y* in both Kott cases as in Altai and Yenisei Turkic, which points to a later period of borrowing.

[312] Initial *m-* is atypical in Turkic. The words with this labial consonant are usually loanwords or onomatopoeic words. There are some Turkic forms with initial *m-* in the words with nasal consonants which changed from the original consonant *b-* (e.g. Old Turkic *burun* 'the nose' ~ Yakut *murun*; Old Turkic *bin-* 'to mount, or ride (*a horse*)' ~ Uyghur *min-*; Old Turkic *bän* 'me, I' ~ Turkmen *men*, etc.) or changed sporadically (e.g. Old Turkic *bašaq* 'a small head; an arrow-head; ear of corn' ~ Tuvan *mažak* 'ear of corn'; Old Turkic *baqïr* 'copper' ~ Tuvan *makïr* 'very white, pure white'; Old Turkic *baġatur* 'brave; hero' ~ Tuvan *mādïr*, etc.). For more details, see Johanson 1998: 102–103 and Khabtagaeva 2009: 53.

(cont.)

Turkic	Kott	Examples
	VmV	Turkic *kümüš* 'silver' → Kott *kumiš ~ kumuš*;
	-m	Turkic *örüm* 'something plaited or woven' → Kott *urum* 'cloth, linen';
		Turkic *käm* 'river' → ? Kott *kem*;
*p- > b-		Turkic *maktür-* 'to praise' → Kott *baktîr*;
		Turkic *mal > pal* 'livestock, cattle; property, wealth' → Kott *bal* 'cattle';
		Turkic *mergen* 'marksman; hero' → Kott *berxen* 'warrior';
	VpV	Turkic *tumarïk* 'haze' (< *tuman*) → Kott *tipar ~ tîpar* 'fog';

Affricates

č	č-[313]	Turkic *čokur* 'variegated, multicoloured' → Kott *čôgor*;
		Turkic *čočuq* 'pig; child' → Kott *čûčuk* 'puppy';
	VčV	Turkic *čočuq* 'pig; child' → Kott *čûčuk* 'puppy';
		Turkic *qičir-* 'to read' → Kott *kačei* 'to read';
	š-[314]	Turkic *čazïn* 'paper' → Kott *šašin*;
		Turkic *čočuq > čočqa* 'pig; child' → Kott *šoška*;
		Turkic *čijir* 'straw' → Kott *šičir*;
	-š	Turkic *qilič* 'sword' → Kott *kaleš ~ kališ*;
		Turkic *küč > küč* 'strength, power, energy' → Kott *kuštu* 'very strong' {*-tu* Yeniseian NN/adj.};
	-č ~ -š	Turkic *aybiči* 'fellow countryman' → Kott *aibič ~ aipiš* 'old man';
	VjV	Turkic *onoŋ učun* 'therefore' → Kott *una ôjaŋ*;

---

[313] The preservation of Turkic *č-* in initial position points to a later period of borrowing, while in an early period it changed to *š-* as in the native Kott words.

[314] The original Yeniseian consonant **č-* (< **tʲ-*, Werner 1990b: 236; Vajda 2014: personal communication) in Kott is realizes as *š-* (Vajda & Werner: in preparation; Starostin 1982: 161; Werner 1990b: 236), e.g. Kott *šâk ~ šâx ~ šâg* 'ice-crust' < Proto-Yeniseian **tʲəʔx* 'crust'; Kott *šiŋeäŋ* 'rock' < Proto-Yeniseian **tʲəŋaːn ~ *tʲəŋaːŋ*; Kott *šîgi* 'swan' < Proto-Yeniseian **tʲigə*, etc. This feature points to an early period of borrowing.

(cont.)

Turkic	Kott	Examples
Sibilants		
s	VsV	Turkic *äsäriklig* 'drunk, intoxicated' (< *äsür-*) → Kott *eser* ~ *esirolog*;
	š-[315]	Turkic *saban* 'plough' → Kott *šaban*;
		Turkic *sārïġ* > *sarï* 'yellow, light bay (colour of horses)' → Kott *šar* ~ *šâr*;
		Turkic *sogur* 'blind' → Kott *šugur* 'one-eyed';
		Turkic *sǖt* > *süt* 'milk' → Kott *šut*;
	-*š*	Turkic *abïs* 'priest' → Kott *âpeš*;
		Turkic *albïs* 'evil spirit' → Kott *alpeš* 'wonder';
		Turkic *koas* 'beautiful' → Kott *koaš* ~ *koâš*;
		Turkic *tït aġas* 'larch' → Kott *tôteäš* ~ *toteš*;
	š- ~ *s-*	Turkic *saġïzġan* > *sāskan* 'magpie' → Kott *šâškana* ~ *šaška* ~ *sâškan*;
		Turkic *sïra* 'beer' → Kott *šera* ~ *širá* ~ *sera* ~ *sihirá*;
	ø-[316]	Turkic *siŋir* > *sīr* 'muscle, sinew, tendon' → Kott *îri* ~ *îre* 'thread, tendon';
z	VsV[317]	Turkic *bozraq* 'brownish' (< *bōz*) → Kott *bosarak* 'ruddy colored';
	-*s*[318]	Turkic *öküz* 'ox' → Kott *ogus* 'bull';
	VsV > *VšV*	Turkic *buzāġu* > *puzō* 'calf' → Kott *bušôu* ~ *bišóu* ~ *bišól*;
		Turkic *čazïn* 'paper' → Kott *šašin*;

---

[315] The original Yeniseian *s-* in initial position regularly changed to *š-* in Kott (Werner 1990b: 25, 236; Vajda & Werner: in preparation), e.g. Kott *šal* 'sharp edge' < Proto-Yeniseian **saʔλ*; Kott *šâŋpi* 'to test' < Proto-Yeniseian **saŋbetʲ* 'inf. to test' < **saŋ* 'test' + **bedʲ* 'to make'; Kott *šága* ~ *šagá* squirrel < Proto-Yeniseian **saʔq* ~ **saga*, etc. This phonetic feature is typical for almost all Turkic loanwords in Kott, which points to an early period of borrowing.

[316] There is only one unclear case in Kott *îri* ~ *îre* 'thread, tendon' where the Turkic *s-* dropped in the initial position. This phonetic feature is typical for Yakut also.

[317] The Turkic sibilant *z* regularly devoiced to *s* in Kott, it can be explained by the absence of consonant *z* in the original Yeniseian words.

[318] The final Turkic consonant *-z* unvoiced in Yeniseian as in the intervocalic position. This change is also peculiar for Altai and Yenisei Turkic.

(cont.)

Turkic	Kott	Examples
š	š-	Turkic šürgan 'snowstorm, storm' → Kott šurgan 'cold weather';
	VšV	Turkic üšik > üšük 'hard frost, frozen' → Kott ušôx ~ ušou 'ice';
	-š	Turkic ariš 'rye' → Kott ariš ~ áriš ~ âreš;
		Turkic qariš 'span' → Kott kareš ~ kariš;
		Turkic kümüš 'silver' → Kott kumiš ~ kumuš;

The labial fricative and the palatal consonant

β	VbV	Turkic köβürgän 'wild onion' → Kott kubúrgenaŋ ~ kabúrgenaŋ;
		Turkic täβäy > täbä 'camel' → Kott tabat;
	*VbV > VpV	Turkic äβir- 'to turn' → Kott êper 'circle; round; around';
	*VbV > VmV	Turkic kabagalï 'with husk, peel, shuck' → Kott kamagalá 'nut';
y[319]	ø-[320]	Turkic yitig > yitī 'sharp' → Kott êti;
		Turkic yiðig 'smell, odour (usuall unpleasant), foul-smelling' > yitū > yitu → Kott īta 'stinking';
		Turkic yān 'the hip; the side, flank of the body or in other contexts' → Kott ânar ~ anar 'hip, loin' (+ Yeniseian ar 'bone');
	d'-[321]	Turkic yoġurqan 'blanket' → Kott d'ôrgan;
		Turkic yip+AK > d'ibek 'thread' → Kott d'ibak ~ d'ipak;
	*t'- > h-[322]	Turkic yaxšï > yaqšï > t'akšï 'suitable, pleasing' → Kott hagši ~ hagše 'good, suitable';
	VjV	Turkic oyun 'game, play, merriment' → Kott ajaŋ;
		Turkic ayïl 'village, family' → Kott ajel 'tent village';

---

319 The initial y- is absent in native Yeniseian words. The preservation of Turkic initial y- in Yeniseian points to the later period.

320 The disappearence of initial Turkic y- in Kott may be explained by the absence of this consonant in Yeniseian.

321 The change of Turkic initial y- > d'- in Kott points to the later period, i.e. the Altai Turkic layer of borrowing.

322 There is one case where the original Turkic initial y- changed to h- in Kott, possibly through another, intermediate sound change. This change points to Altai Turkic as the source of borrowing.

(cont.)

Turkic	Kott	Examples
	-i	Turkic *aray* 'slowly, gently, with difficulty, hardly' → Kott *arai* 'hardly, with'; Turkic *bāy* 'rich; a rich man' → Kott *pai*; Turkic *tägäy* 'the top of a mountain; hill; the top of a head' → Kott *tagaj* ~ *takai* 'head';
Liquids		
l[323]	VlV	Turkic *āla* 'parti-coloured, dappled, spotted' → Kott *ala*; Turkic *bolat* 'steel' → Kott *bolat* ~ *bolát*; Turkic *qola* 'copper, brass' → Kott *kolá*; Turkic *qolanak* 'weasel' → Kott *holanka*; Turkic *qulaq* 'ear' → Kott *kalôx*;
	-l	Turkic *agïl* 'a settlement or group of tents' → Kott *agel* ~ *âgel* 'tent village'; Turkic *erǖl* 'sober' → Kott *erol*; Turkic *qabtal* 'side of the horse; side; saddle cloth' → Kott *hôpetal* ~ *hôptal*; Turkic *obal* 'sin' → Kott *obal* ~ *ôpal*;
	Vl'V	Turkic *kǖlük* 'clever, wise, famous' → Kott *kul'uk* 'bold, boldness';
r	VrV	Turkic *aray* 'slowly, with difficulty, hardly' → Kott *arai*; Turkic *ariš* 'rye' → Kott *ariš* ~ *áriš* ~ *âreš*; Turkic *böri* > *börü* 'wolf' → Kott *bôru* ~ *boru*; Turkic *tura* 'house; village; town' → Kott *torá* ~ *tura* 'living room', *turá* 'village'; Turkic *oruq* 'path' → Kott *uruk* 'mountain valley';

---

323   The initial *l-* is atypical consonant for original Turkic words, and words with initial *l-* are usually loanwords or onomatopoeic words.

(cont.)

Turkic	Kott	Examples
	-r	Turkic *aðǵïr* > *azqïr* > *asqïr* 'stallion' → Kott *askar* ~ *askɨr*;
		Turkic *baqïr* 'copper' → Kott *baker*;
		Turkic *qočŋār* > *qočqar* > *qosqar* 'ram' → Kott *koaskɨr*;
		Turkic *köprüg* > *köpür* 'bridge' → Kott *kôpur* ~ *kopur* ~ *kobur*;
		Turkic *ögür* > *ȫr* 'herd of horses' > Kott *ôr*.

2.1.2 Assan
2.1.2.1 *Turkic Vowel Phonemes in Assan*

Turkic	Assan	Examples
Low unrounded vowels		
a	*a-*	Turkic *aðǵïr* 'stallion' → Assan *askir* ~ *askɨr*;
		Turkic *arïš* 'rye' → Assan *ariš*;
	-a¹-	Turkic *šar* 'bull, ox' → Assan *šar* 'bull';
	-a²-	Turkic *arakï* 'wine, vodka' → Assan *araka*;
		Turkic *bolat* 'steel' → Assan *balat*;
		Turkic *buǵday* 'wheat' → Assan *bútaj*;
	-a	Turkic *buqa* 'bull' → Assan *boka*;
	-á	Turkic *arpa* 'barley' → Assan *arpá*;
ä (e)	*e-*	Turkic *äsür-* > *äsäriklig* 'drunk, intoxicated' → Assan *esrolagín* ~ *esrolokon*;
	-a¹- ~ -ó¹-	Turkic *tägäy* 'the top of a head' → Assan *tagáj* ~ *takaj* ~ *tógaj* 'head';
	-a²- ~ -á²-	Turkic *täβäy* > *täbä* 'camel' → Assan *tabát* ~ *tapat*;
	-á²-	Turkic *ätmäk* 'bread' → Assan *itpák*;
	i-	Turkic *ätmäk* 'bread' → Assan *itpák*;
	-i³-	Turkic *köβürgän* > *köbürgän* 'wild onion' → Assan *kabirgina* ~ *kaburgina*;

(cont.)

Turkic	Assan	Examples
Low rounded vowels		
o	-o¹-	Turkic *qorġušïn* 'lead' → Assan *korgoden*;
	-a¹-	Turkic *bolat* 'steel' → Assan *balat*;
		Turkic *qōń* > *qoy* 'sheep' → Assan *kai*;
ö	-o¹-	Turkic *böri* > *börü* 'wolf' → Assan *boru*;
	-a¹-	Turkic *köβürgän* > *köbürgän* 'wild onion' → Assan *kabïrgina* ~ *kaburgina*;
High unrounded vowels		
ï	-ï²-	Turkic *arïš* 'rye' → Assan *arïš*;
	-ï²- ~ -ɨ²-	Turkic *aδġïr* > *azqïr* > *asqïr* 'stallion' → Assan *askir* ~ *askïr*;
	-i¹-	Turkic *sïra* 'beer' → Assan *sir'á*;
	-i²-	Turkic *sarï yaġ* 'butter' → Assan *šarijag*;
	-o¹-	Turkic *tït aġas* 'larch' → Assan *toteš*;
	-a	Turkic *arakï* 'wine, vodka' → Assan *araka*;
High rounded vowels		
u	-u¹-	Turkic *qur* 'belt, girdle' → Assan *kura* 'rope';
	-ú²-	Turkic *qulun* 'foal' → Assan *kulún*;
	-o¹-	Turkic *buqa* 'bull' → Assan *boka*;
	-ō	Turkic *baltu* 'axe' → Assan *balō*;
ü	-ü¹- ~ -u¹-	Turkic *kümüš* 'silver' → Assan *kümüs* ~ *kumís* ~ *kumus*;
		Turkic *sǖt* > *süt* 'milk' → Assan *šüt* ~ *šut*;
	-ü ~ -u	Turkic *böri* > *börü* 'wolf' → Assan *borü* ~ *boru*;
	u-	Turkic *ǖgi* > *ügü* 'owl' → Assan *ug*;
	-u²-	Turkic *köβürgän* > *köbürgän* 'wild onion' → Assan *kaburgina*;
	-ï²-	Turkic *köβürgän* > *köbürgän* 'wild onion' → Assan *kabïrgina*.

2.1.2.2 Turkic Consonant Phonemes in Assan

Turkic	Assan	Examples
Voiceless stops		
p	-	There are no attested loans with this sound.
t	t-	Turkic *talqan* 'oat flour' → Assan *talkán* 'flour, meal'; Turkic *tägäy* 'the top of a mountain; hill; the top of a head' → Assan *tógaj* ~ *tagáj* ~ *takaj* 'head'; Turkic *tït aġas* 'larch' → Assan *toteš*;
	-t	Turkic *bolat* 'steel' → Assan *balat*; Turkic *sǖt* > *süt* 'milk' → Assan *šut* ~ *šüt*;
k	k-	Turkic *köβürgän* > *köbürgän* 'wild onion' → Assan *kabïrgina* ~ *kaburgina*; Turkic *kümüš* 'silver' → Assan *kumís* ~ *kumus* ~ *kümüs*;
	-k	Turkic *ätmäk* 'bread' → Assan *itpák*;
	k- ~ x-	Turkic *kämi* 'ship or boat' → Assan *kep* ~ *xajp*;
q	k-	Turkic *qorġušïn* > *korgočïn* 'lead' → Assan *korgoden*; Turkic *qulun* 'foal' → Assan *kulún*; Turkic *qur* 'belt, girdle' → Assan *kura* 'rope';
	VkV	Turkic *arakï* 'wine, vodka' → Assan *araka*; Turkic *buqa* 'bull' → Assan *boka*;
Voiced stops		
b	b-	Turkic *bolat* 'steel' → Assan *balat*; Turkic *böri* > *börü* 'wolf' → Assan *boru* ~ *borü*; Turkic *buzāġu* > *bïzō* 'calf' → Assan *bišol*; Turkic *buqa* > *buga* 'bull' → Assan *boka*;
	b- ~ t-	Turkic *buġday* > *būday* 'wheat' → Assan *bútaj* ~ *tútaj*;
d	VtV	Turkic *buġday* > *būday* 'wheat' → Assan *bútaj* ~ *tútaj*;

(cont.)

Turkic	Assan	Examples
δ	*-z- > -s- (Yenisei Turkic)	Turkic *aða* 'danger' > *aza* 'demon, evil spirit' → Assan *asa*; Turkic *aðġïr* > *azqïr* > *asqïr* 'stallion' → Assan *askir* ~ *askir*;
g	VgV ~ VkV	Turkic *tägäy* 'the top of a mountain or a head' → Assan *tógaj* ~ *tagáj* ~ *takaj* 'head';
ġ	-g	Turkic *sarïyaġ* 'butter' → Assan *šarijag*;
Nasals		
n	-n	Turkic *qorġušïn* > *korgočïn* 'lead' → Assan *korgoden*; Turkic *qulun* 'foal' → Assan *kulún*; Turkic *talqan* 'oat flour' → Assan *talkán* 'flour, meal';
ŋ	-	There are no attested loans with this sound.
ń	-i[324]	Turkic *qōń* > *koy* 'sheep' → Assan *koi* ~ *kai*;
m	m- VmV	Turkic *maŋ-* > *maŋar* 'who is running' → Assan *mangára* ~ *mankara* 'hare, rabbit'; Turkic *kümüš* 'silver' → Assan *kumís* ~ *kumus* ~ *kümüs*;
Affricates		
č	-	There are no attested loans with this sound.
Sibilants		
s	š-[325]	Turkic *sarïyaġ* 'butter' → Assan *šarijag*; Turkic *süt* > *süt* 'milk' → Assan *šut* ~ *šüt*;

---

324   The Turkic nasal consonant *-ń* in final position changed to *-y* in Assan loanwords as in Altai and Yenisei Turkic, which points to a later period of borrowing.

325   The original Yeniseian *s-* in the initial position regularly changed to *š-* in Assan (Werner 1990b: 25; 2005: 141), e.g. Assan *šagá* ~ *šaha* 'squirrel' < Proto-Yeniseian *saʔq* ~ *saga*; Assan

(cont.)

Turkic	Assan	Examples
	s-[326]	Turkic *sïra* 'beer' → Assan *sir'á*;
	-š	Turkic *tït aġas* 'larch' → Assan *toteš*;
z	*VsV > VšV	Turkic *buzāġu > bïzō* 'calf' → Assan *bišol*;
š	š-	Turkic *šar* 'bull, ox' → Assan *šar* 'bull';
	-š	Turkic *ariš* 'rye' → Assan *ariš*;
	-s	Turkic *kümüš* 'silver' → Assan *kumís ~ kumus ~ kümüs*;

The labial fricative and the palatal consonant

β	VbV	Turkic *köβürgän* 'wild onion' → Assan *kabïrgina ~ kaburgina*;
	VpV	Turkic *täβäy* 'camel' → Assan *tapat ~ tabát*;
y	VjV	Turkic *sarï yaġ* 'butter' → Assan *šarijag*;
	-j	Turkic *buġday* 'wheat' → Assan *bútaj ~ tútaj*;
		Turkic *tägäy* 'the top of a mountain; hill; the top of a head' → Assan *tógaj ~ tagáj ~ takaj* 'head';

Liquids

l	VlV	Turkic *bolat* 'steel' → Assan *balat*;
		Turkic *qulun* 'foal' → Assan *kulún*;
	-l	Turkic *qaraul* 'guard; sight' → Assan *karaul* 'view, look';

šéga 'year' < Proto-Yeniseian **suɡə*; Assan *šúxa ~ šuga* 'back, backwards' < Proto-Yeniseian **sugej < *sug* 'back' + **ej* {directional NN/adv.}, etc. (Vajda & Werner: in preparation). The Turkic loanwords with initial *s-* are regularly changed to *š-* in Assan, which points to an early period of borrowing.

326   The Turkic loanwords in Assan where the initial *s-* is preserved belong to the later period of borrowing.

(cont.)

Turkic	Assan	Examples
r	VrV	Turkic *arakï* 'wine, vodka' → Assan *araka*;
		Turkic *ariš* 'rye' → Assan *ariš*;
		Turkic *böri* > *börü* 'wolf' → Assan *boru* ~ *borü*;
		Turkic *qur* 'belt, girdle' → Assan *kura* 'rope';
		Turkic *sarïyaġ* 'butter' → Assan *šarijag*;
	-r	Turkic *aðġïr* → Assan *askir* ~ *askïr*;
		Turkic *šar* 'bull, ox' → Assan *šar* 'bull';
	Vr'V	Turkic *sïra* 'beer' → Assan *sir'á*.

2.1.3 Arin
2.1.3.1 Turkic Vowel Phonemes in Arin

Turkic	Arin	Examples

Low unrounded vowels

a	a-	Turkic *arpa* 'barley' → Arin *arba*;
		Turkic *arqïš* 'comrade, companion' → Arin *argiš* 'crowd (of people); migration';
		Turkic *aðġïr* > *azqïr* > *asqïr* 'stallion' → Arin *askir*;
	-a¹-	Turkic *baltu* 'axe' → Arin *baltó* ~ *balto*;
		Turkic *bāy* > *bay* 'rich; a rich man' → Arin *bajšu* 'wealth' {-*šu* Yeniseian nmlz.};
		Turkic *lay* 'slime, sludge, mud' → Arin *laj* 'marsh';
	-á²-	Turkic *balgaš boro* 'dirty' → Arin *balgaš bore*;
		Turkic *qańaq* 'butter, sour cream' → Arin *kaják* 'oil, butter';
		Turkic *tuman* 'mist, fog' → Arin *tumantolati* 'fog' (+ Yeniseian *tolati*);
	-a	Turkic *arpa* 'barley' → Arin *arba*;
	-á	Turkic *buqa* 'bull' → Arin *bugá*;
	-ï²-	Turkic *torgayaq* 'sky-lark' → Arin *torgïjan*;
	u-	Turkic *arakï* 'wine, vodka' → Arin *uragā*;
	-o¹-	Turkic *dalay* 'sea' → Arin *dolaj*;

(*cont.*)

Turkic	Arin	Examples
ä (*e*)	-*e*²-	Turkic *tikän yestek* 'thorned berry' → Arin *tegentestek* 'raspberry';
	-*é*	Turkic *täβäy* > *täbä* 'camel' → Arin *tebé*;
	-*á*²-	Turkic *ätmäk* 'bread' → Arin *itp'ák* ~ *itpák*;
	-*a*	Turkic *sirkä* 'nit' → Arin *serga* 'louse';
		Turkic *berke* 'clever, deft' → Arin *birka* 'big, great; very';
	i-	Turkic *ätmäk* 'bread' → Arin *itp'ák* ~ *itpák* ~ *itpek*;
	-*i*¹-	Turkic *berke* 'clever, deft' → Arin *birka* 'big, great; very';
	u-	Turkic *äčkü* 'goat' → Arin *uške* 'he-goat';

Low rounded vowels

o	*o*-	Turkic *ot* 'grass, vegetation; hay' → Arin *ott* 'hay';
	-*o*¹-	Turkic *toq* 'full, satiated' → Arin *tok*;
		Turkic *bolat* 'steel' → Arin *molát*;
		Turkic *qorgolǰin* 'lead' → Arin *korgoldžín* 'tin';
		Turkic *torgayaq* 'sky-lark' → Arin *torgijan* 'lark';
	-*a*¹-	Turkic *kara nonaġ* 'bilberry' → Arin *karananuk*;
ö	*o*-	Turkic *öküz* 'ox' → Arin *ogus* 'bull';
	-*u*¹-	Turkic *köβürgän* > *köbürgän* 'wild onion' → Arin *kuburgan*;

High unrounded vowels

ï	-*i*¹-	Turkic *qïz* 'girl; daughter' → Arin *kis* 'sister-in-law';
		Turkic *sïra* 'beer' → Arin *sirá*;
	-*i*²-	Turkic *aðġïr* 'stallion' → Arin *askir*;
	-*i*³-	Turkic *korgolǰin* 'lead' → Arin *korgoldžín* 'tin';
	-*a*¹-	Turkic *qïr* 'mountain' → Arin *kar*;
	-*ā*	Turkic *arakï* 'wine, vodka' → Arin *uragā*;
i	-*e*¹-	Turkic *sirkä* 'nit' → Arin *serga* 'louse';
		Turkic *tikän yestek* 'thorned berry' → Arin *tegentestek* 'raspberry';

(*cont.*)

Turkic	Arin	Examples
High rounded vowels		
u	-*u¹*-	Turkic *buqa* 'bull' → Arin *bugá*;
		Turkic *tuman* 'mist, fog' → Arin *tumantolati* 'fog' (+ ? Yeniseian *tolati*);
		Turkic *tura* 'house; village; town' → Arin *tura* 'house';
	-*u²*-	Turkic *budurčun* 'quail' → Arin *buturčinok*;
	-*ú²*-	Turkic *qulun* 'foal' → Arin *kulún*;
	-*o* ~ -*ó*	Turkic *baltu* 'axe' → Arin *baltó* ~ *balto*;
ü	-*u¹*-	Turkic *yüz* 'a hundred' → Arin *yus*;
		Turkic *kümüš* 'silver' → Arin *kumiš*;
	-*u²*-	Turkic *öküz* 'ox' → Arin *ogus*;
		Turkic *köbürgän* 'wild onion' → Arin *kuburgan*;
	-*i²*-	Turkic *kümüš* 'silver' → Arin *kumiš*.

2.1.3.2 *Turkic Consonant Phonemes in Arin*

Turkic	Arin	Examples
Voiceless stops		
p	-	There are no attested loans with this sound.
t	t-	Turkic *tikän yestek* 'thorned berry' → Arin *tegentestek* 'raspberry';
		Turkic *toq* 'full, satiated' → Arin *tok*;
		Turkic *torġayaq* 'sky-lark' → Arin *torgijan*;
		Turkic *tura* 'house; village; town' → Arin *tura* 'house';
	VtV	Turkic *berke* 'big' + *tag* 'mountain' → Arin *berkitak* 'mountain';
	-t	Turkic *bolat* 'steel' → Arin *molát*;
	-tt	Turkic *ot* 'grass, vegetation; hay' → Arin *ott* 'hay';

(cont.)

Turkic	Arin	Examples
k	k-	Turkic *kümüš* 'silver' → Arin *kumiš*;
	-k	Turkic *qara sēk* 'fly' → Arin *karasek*;
		Turkic *köŋläk* > *kögänäk* 'shirt' → Arin *kogonek*;
	VgV	Turkic *öküz* 'ox' → Arin *ogus* 'bull';
		Turkic *tikän yestek* 'thorned berry' → Arin *tegentestek* 'raspberry';
q	k-[327]	Turkic *qïr* 'mountain' → Arin *kar*;
		Turkic *qïz* > *qis* 'girl; daughter' → Arin *kis* 'sister-in-law';
		Turkic *qorgoljïn* 'lead' → Arin *korgoldžín* 'tin';
		Turkic *qulun* 'foal' → Arin *kulún*;
	-k	Turkic *qańaq* > *qayaq* 'butter, sour cream' → Arin *kaják* 'oil, butter';
		Turkic *toq* 'full, satiated' → Arin *tok*;
	x-[328]	Turkic *qamčï* 'a whip' → Arin *xamčook* {-*ok* Yeniseian suffix/diminutive};
	VgV	Turkic *arakï* 'wine, vodka' → Arin *uragá*;
		Turkic *baqa qulaqï* 'mussel' → Arin *bagakulak*;
		Turkic *buqa* 'bull' → Arin *bugá*;
	-n	Turkic *torgayaq* 'sky-lark' → Arin *torgijan*;

---

[327] The Turkic initial velar consonant *q*- was preserved in most Arin cases as in native Yeniseian words (Werner 1990b: 25, 231; Vajda & Werner: in preparation). This change indicates an early period of borrowing, e.g.: Arin *qaj* 'fur coat' < Proto-Yeniseian *$qa^ʔd$; Arin *qʲagaŋ* ~ *qiágaŋ* 'hair' < Proto-Yeniseian *qax^w 'hair, fur' + *$əŋ$ {plural}; Arin *qip* ~ *kibä* 'he-bear' (taboo) < Proto-Yeniseian *$qibə$ 'grandfather' < *$qaxŋ$ 'great, big' + *$obə$ 'father'; Arin *qut* ~ *kūt* 'wolf' < Proto-Yeniseian *$qū·t^he$, etc.

[328] There are some cases where initial *q*- changed to *x*- in Arin as in some native Yeniseian words (Vajda & Werner: in preparation), e.g. Arin *xatu* 'he' < Proto-Yeniseian *$qadu$ < *qa 'that' + *du {sg.3 masc. pred. suff.}; Arin *xin* 'shoulder' < Proto-Yeniseian *qen, etc.

(cont.)

Turkic	Arin	Examples
Voiced stops		
b	b-[329]	Turkic *baqa qulaqï* 'mussel' → Arin *bagakulak*; Turkic *bāy* > *bay* 'rich; a rich man' → Arin *bajšu* 'wealth' {*-šu* Yeniseian nmlz.}; Turkic *buġday* 'wheat' → Arin *bugdaj*; Turkic *buqa* 'bull' → Arin *bugá*; Turkic *budurčun* 'quail' → Arin *buturčinok* {*-ok* Yeniseian NN/diminutive};
	p-[330]	Turkic *bay* 'rich' + *bal* 'cattle' → Arin *pajbal* 'cattle, cow';
	m-	Turkic *bolat* 'steel' → Arin *molát*;
d	d-	Turkic *dalay* 'sea' → Arin *dalaj* ~ *dolaj*;
	VtV	Turkic *budurčun* 'quail' → Arin *buturčinok* {*-ok* Yeniseian NN/diminutive};
δ	-s- < *-z- (Yenisei Turkic)	Turkic *aðġïr* > *azqïr* > *asqïr* 'stallion' → Arin *askïr*;
g	-	There are no attested loans with this sound.
ġ	-k	Turkic **berke* 'big' + *taġ* 'mountain' → Arin *berkitak*; Turkic *kara nonaġ* 'bilberry' → Arin *karananuk*;

---

[329] The Turkic initial *b-* is regularly preserved in Arin, which points to the later period of borrowing. The original Yeniseian initial **b-* is regularly devoiced in Arin (Starostin 1982: 149; Werner 1990b: 25, 233; Vajda & Werner: in preparation), e.g. Arin *pis* 'evening' < Proto-Yeniseian **bīs*; Arin *ponʲa* ~ *punä* 'duck' < Proto-Yeniseian **bəʔn*; Arin *paj* 'wind' < Proto-Yeniseian **bej* 'wind'; etc.

[330] There is an interesting compound word in Arin where the Turkic consonant *b-* is devoiced in the first part, but preserved in the second part. It can be explained by the different periods of borrowing. The Arin form with initial *p-* belongs in the early period; due to the fact initial *p-* was regularly preserved in the native Arin words. The second Arin form *bajšu* 'wealth' with initial *b-* was borrowed in the later period.

(cont.)

Turkic	Arin	Examples
Nasals		
n	VnV	Turkic *ayna* 'devil, demon, evil spirit' → Arin *ajna*;
		Turkic *kara nonaġ* 'bilberry' → Arin *karananuk*;
		Turkic *kemineŋ čak* 'measure of time' → Arin *kemenenčak* 'week';
		Turkic *köŋläk > kögänäk* 'shirt' → Arin *kogonek*;
	-n	Turkic *altūn > altïn* 'gold' → Arin *altin*;
		Turkic *korgoljïn* 'lead' → Arin *korgoldžín* 'tin';
		Turkic *köbürgän* 'wild onion' → Arin *kuburgan*;
		Turkic *qulun* 'foal' → Arin *kulún*;
ŋ	-	There are no attested loans with this sound.
ń	VjV[331]	Turkic *qańaq* 'the skin on milk' → Arin *kaják* 'oil, butter';
m	m-	Turkic *mindir* 'hail' → Arin *mintora* 'ice';
	VmV	Turkic *kümüš* 'silver' → Arin *kumiš*;
		Turkic *kemineŋ čak* → Arin *kemenenčak* 'week';
		Turkic *tuman* 'mist, fog' → Arin *tumantolati* 'fog' (+ Yeniseian *tolati*);
Affricates		
č	š-	Turkic *čočuq > čočqa* 'pig' → Arin *šoška*;
		Turkic *čïjïr* 'straw' → Arin *šižir*;

---

[331] The Turkic final nasal consonant *VńV* changed to *VyV* as in Altai and Yenisei Turkic, which points to a later period of borrowing.

Turkic	Arin	Examples
Sibilants		
s	s-[332]	Turkic *sirkä* 'nit' → Arin *serga* 'louse'; Turkic *seleme* 'sabre, sword' → Arin *sulem'a*; Turkic *sïra* 'beer' → Arin *sirá*;
z	-s[333]	Turkic *yüz* 'a hundred' → Arin *jus*; Turkic *qïz* > *qïs* 'girl; daughter' → Arin *kis* 'sister-in-law'; Turkic *öküz* > *ögüs* 'ox' → Arin *ogus* 'bull';
š	-š -s	Turkic *arqiš* 'comrade, companion' → Arin *argiš* 'crowd; migration'; Turkic *kümüš* 'silver' → Arin *kumiš*; Turkic *qol* 'the upper arm; the forearm, hand, finger' + *baš* 'the upper part of sg.' > *qolbaš* → Arin *qólpas* 'finger';
The labial fricative and the palatal consonant		
β	VbV	Turkic *köβürgän* 'wild onion' → Arin *kuburgan* 'onion'; Turkic *täβäy* > *täbä* 'camel' → Arin *tebé*;
y	j-[334] VjV -j	Turkic *yüz* 'a hundred' → Arin *yus* [*jus*]; Turkic *ayna* 'devil, demon, evil spirit' → Arin *ajna*; Turkic *torġayaq* 'sky-lark' → Arin *torgijan*; Turkic *ögey* > *öy* 'step-(father, etc.)' → Arin *ojakel'a* 'stepdaughter' (+ Yeniseian *akel'a* 'daughter'); Turkic *buġday* 'wheat' → Arin *bugdaj*; Turkic *lay* 'slime, sludge, mud' → Arin *laj* 'marsh';

---

[332] The original Yeniseian s- in initial position usually preserved in Arin (Werner 1990b: 23, 25, 234; Vajda & Werner: in preparation), e.g. Arin *sava* 'squirrel' < Proto-Yeniseian *saʔq ~ *saga.

[333] The Turkic final consonant -z regularly devoiced in Arin, as in Altai Turkic and Yenisei Turkic varieties.

[334] The preservation of the Turkic initial y- in Arin points to the later period, due to the absence of this consonant in native Yeniseian words.

(cont.)

Turkic	Arin	Examples
	č-[335]	Turkic *yarma* 'grain, groats' → Arin *čarba* 'grain';
	d'- > *t'- > t-[336]	Turkic *tikän yestek* 'thorned berry' > *tegen d'estek* → Arin *tegen-testek* 'raspberry';
Liquids		
l	*l-*	Turkic *lay* 'slime, sludge, mud' → Arin *laj* 'marsh';
	V*l*V	Turkic *bolat* 'steel' → Arin *molát*;
		Turkic *baqa qulaqï* 'mussel' → Arin *bagakulak*;
		Turkic *dalay* 'sea' → Arin *dalaj ~ dolaj*;
		Turkic *qulun* 'foal' → Arin *kulún*;
	-*l*	Turkic *arčol* 'kerchief' → Arin *barčol* [*badija*] 'kerchief';
		Turkic *bāy* 'rich' + *mal* 'cattle' > **pay bal* → Arin *pajbal* 'cattle, cow';
r	V*r*V	Turkic *arakï* 'wine, vodka' → Arin *uragā*;
		Turkic *balgaš boro* 'dirty' → Arin *balgaš bore*;
		Turkic *sïra* 'beer' → Arin *sïrá*;
		Turkic *tura* 'house; village; town' → Arin *tura* 'house';
	-*r*	Turkic *aðğïr* > *azqïr* > *asqïr* 'stallion' → Arin *askïr*;
		Turkic *qïr* 'mountain' → Arin *kar*.

---

335 The change of the Turkic initial *y-* > *č-* in Arin points to the later period, i.e. Yenisei Turkic or Sayan Turkic layers of borrowing.

336 The change of initial Turkic *y-* > *d'-* is a typical feature for Altai Turkic varieties, which points to a later period of borrowing in Arin.

2.1.4 Pumpokol

2.1.4.1 Turkic Vowel Phonemes in Pumpokol

Turkic	Pumpokol	Examples
Low unrounded vowels		
a	-a	Turkic *bala* 'a human child, son' → Pumpokol *pʰalla* ~ *pʰala* ~ *falla* ~ *fala*;
Low rounded vowels		
o	-ó¹-	Turkic *qorġušïn* 'lead' → Pumpokol *xórgosin* 'tin';
High unrounded vowels		
ï	-i³-	Turkic *qorġušïn* 'lead' → Pumpokol *xórgosin* 'tin';
High rounded vowels		
u	-u¹- -o²-	Turkic *qunu* 'wolverine' → Pumpokol *kun*; Turkic *qorġušïn* 'lead' → Pumpokol *xórgosin* 'tin';
ü	-ü¹- -ü²-	Turkic *kümüš* 'silver' → Pumpokol *kümüč*.

2.1.4.2 Turkic Consonant Phonemes in Pumpokol

Turkic	Pumpokol	Examples
Voiceless stops		
p	-	There are no attested loans with this sound.
t	-	There are no attested loans with this sound.

(cont.)

Turkic	Pumpokol	Examples
k	k-	Turkic *kümüš* 'silver' → Pumpokol *kümüč*;
q	k- x-	Turkic *qunu* 'wolverine' → Pumpokol *kun*; Turkic *qorġušin* 'lead' → Pumpokol *xórgosin* 'tin';
Voiced stops		
b	pʰ- ~ f-[337]	Turkic *bala* > *pala* 'child, son' → Pumpokol *pʰalla* ~ *pʰala* ~ *falla* ~ *fala* 'son, boy';
δ	-	There are no attested loans with this sound.
g	-	There are no attested loans with this sound.
ġ	-	There are no attested loans with this sound.
Nasals		
n	-n	Turkic *qorġušin* 'lead' → Pumpokol *xórgosin* 'tin';
ŋ	-	There are no attested loans with this sound.
ń	-	There are no attested loans with this sound.
m	VmV	Turkic *kümüš* 'silver' → Pumpokol *kümüč*;

---

[337] The initial Pumpokol consonants *pʰ-* and *f-* go back to Proto-Yeniseian initial **p-* (Starostin 1982: 149; Werner 1990b: 233), e.g. Pumpokol *pínniŋ* ~ *fenug* 'sand' < Proto-Yeniseian **pənəŋ* < **pən* 'small'; Pumpokol *pfu* 'heart' < Proto-Yeniseian **pu*; Pumpokol *fídam* 'low' < Proto-Yeniseian **pitəm* < **puut* 'down' + **əŋ* {NN/adjective}, etc.

The Pumpokol loanwords with initial *pʰ-* and *f-* were possibly borrowed from a Turkic source with initial *p-*, which originally changed from Common-Turkic **b-*.

(cont.)

Turkic	Pumpokol	Examples
Affricates		
č	-	There are no attested loans with this sound.
Sibilants		
s	-	There are no attested loans with this sound.
z	-	There are no attested loans with this sound.
š	-č	Turkic *kümüš* 'silver' → Pumpokol *kümüč*;
The labial fricative and the palatal consonant		
β	-	There are no attested loans with this sound.
y	ø-	Turkic *yān* 'the hip; the side, flank of the body or in other contexts' → Pumpokol *aniŋ* 'legs, feet' {-*iŋ* Yeniseian plural};
Liquids		
l	VlV ~ VllV	Turkic *bala* 'child, son' → Pumpokol *pʰalla ~ pʰala ~ falla ~ fala*
r	-	There are no attested loans with this sound.

2.1.5 Yugh
2.1.5.1 *Turkic Vowel Phonemes in Yugh*

Turkic	Yugh	Examples
Low unrounded vowels		
a	a- -á¹-	Turkic *ayïl* 'village, family' → Yugh *ajaŋi* 'village'; Turkic *balïq > palïk* 'fish' → Yugh *fálgi* 'ruff (*fish*)';

(cont.)

Turkic	Yugh	Examples
	-a²-	Turkic *sana-* 'to think, desire, feel, miss' → Yugh *sáŋa*;
	-á	Turkic *qaŋza* 'tobacco pipe' → Yugh *kàńčá*;
	-ʌ¹-	Turkic *qaračiġay* 'swallow' → Yugh *kʌčiŋej* 'magpie';
	-i²-	Turkic *talqan* 'oat flour' → Yugh *tállin* ~ *tàlin* 'flour, meal';
	-e³-	Turkic *sologay* 'left-handed' → Yugh *súl'gej* 'left';
ä (e)	-a¹-	Turkic *bet* 'the human face' → Yugh *baʔt* ~ *bat* 'face, forehead';
	-i²-	Turkic *bürken-* 'to be covered,' → Yugh *bérgin* 'noun bundle, pack of things';

Low rounded vowels

o	-o¹-	Turkic *qoyuġ* 'thick, viscid, dense' → Yugh *χoj* 'thick';
	-ɔ¹-	Turkic *bōq > poq* 'excrement, dung' → Yugh *fɔʔχ*;
	-ʌ¹-	Turkic *qoltuq* 'armpit' → Yugh *χʌlčaŋ* 'forearm';
	-ú¹-	Turkic *sologay* 'left-handed' → Yugh *súl'gej* 'left';
ö	-ɔ¹-	Turkic *köt* 'backside, buttocks' → Yugh *gɔʔt*;

High unrounded vowels

ï	ī¹-	Turkic *yïð* 'scent, odour, smell' → Yugh *īt* 'smell, aroma';
	-ʌ́¹- ~ -ʌ¹-	Turkic *qïlčïq* 'tickle' → Yugh *χʌ́lčaχan* ~ *χʌlčakŋ* 'to tickle';
	-é¹- ~ -ä¹-	Turkic *bïčïs* 'cutting out, dressmaking' → Yugh *bétes* ~ *bätes* 'lining of a coat';
	-a²-	Turkic *ayïl* 'village, family' → Yugh *ajaŋi* 'village';
	-e²-	Turkic *bïčïs* 'cutting out, dressmaking' → Yugh *bétes* ~ *bätes* 'lining of a coat';
i	-i¹-	Turkic *kiden* 'flax, canvas' → Yugh *kitn* 'nettles, hemp';
	-i	Turkic *yitig > yitī* 'sharp' → Yugh *eti*;

(cont.)

Turkic	Yugh	Examples
High rounded vowels		
u	-ū¹-	Turkic *qunu* 'wolverine' → Yugh *kū ʰn*;
ü	u-	Turkic *ügre* 'soup; noodles' → Yugh *ugur* 'soup or porridge made of grain'; Turkic *üčün* 'because of' → Yugh *unče*;
	-é¹-	Turkic *bürken-* 'to be covered, to be wraped' → Yugh *bérgin* '*noun* bundle'.

2.1.5.2 Turkic Consonant Phonemes in Yugh

Turkic	Yugh	Examples
Voiceless stops		
p	-	There are no attested loans with this sound.
t	t-	Turkic *talqan* 'oat flour' → Yugh *tállin* ~ *tàli ́n* 'flour, meal';
	VtV	Turkic *yitig* > *yitī* 'sharp' → Yugh *eti*;
	-t	Turkic *bät* 'the human face' → Yugh *baʔt* ~ *bat* 'face, forehead'; Turkic *köt* 'backside, buttocks' → Yugh *gɔʔt* 'butt, hind end';
k	k-	Turkic *kiden* 'flax, canvas' → Yugh *kitn* 'nettles, hemp'; Turkic *kȫ* 'coal, soot' → Yugh *kuʔ* ~ *kuʔu* ~ *kuʔo* ~ *kû*;
	g-	Turkic *köt* 'backside, buttocks' → Yugh *gɔʔt*;
	χ-	Turkic *kämi* 'ship or boat' → Yugh *χap* ~ *χaʔp*;
q	k-	Turkic *qaŋza* 'tobacco pipe' → Yugh *kàńčá*; Turkic *qarčiɣay* 'swallow' → Yugh *kʌčiŋej* 'magpie'; Turkic *qunu* 'wolverine' → Yugh *kū ʰn*;

(cont.)

Turkic	Yugh	Examples
	χ-[338]	Turkic *qaġan* > *qān* 'an independent ruler of a tribe or people; kagan' → Yugh χ*an*;
		Turkic *qoyuġ* > *qoyu* 'thick, viscid, dense' → Yugh χ*oj* 'thick (*said of liquids*)';
		Turkic *qoltuq* 'armpit' → Yugh χʌ*lčaŋ* 'humeral joint, humerus bone, forearm';
		Turkic *qoŋrak* 'bell' → Yugh χɔ́*ŋirɔχ*;
	-χ	Turkic *bōq* 'excrement, dung' → Yugh *fɔʔχ*;
		Turkic *qoŋraq* 'bell' → Yugh χɔ́*ŋirɔχ*;

Voiced stops

b	b-	Turkic *bet* 'the human face' → Yugh *baʔt ~ bat* 'face, forehead';
		Turkic *bürken-* 'be covered, be wraped' → Yugh *bérgin* 'noun bundle, pack of things';
		Turkic *bičïs* 'cutting out, dressmaking' → Yugh *bétes ~ bätes* 'lining of a coat';
	f-[339]	Turkic *bōq* > *poq* 'excrement, dung' → Yugh *fɔʔχ*;
		Turkic *baliq* > *palïk* 'fish' → Yugh *fálgi* 'ruff (*fish*)';
d	-t-	Arabic → Turkic *kiden* 'flax, canvas' → Yugh *kitn* 'nettles, hemp';
ð	-t < *-d	Turkic *yïð* 'scent, odour, smell' → Yugh *ï·t* 'smell, aroma';

---

338 The Proto-Yeniseian *q-* in initial position changed to χ- in Yugh (Starostin 1982: 169–170; Werner 1990b: 25, 231; Vajda & Werner: in preparation), e.g. Yugh χɔ*duŋ ~* χ*ou* 'die, kill, hunt' < Proto-Yeniseian **qodəŋ* 'inf. die, kill, be sick, dead, death' < **qaxʷ* 'die, kill' + **əŋʷ* (inf.); Yugh χā· 'word, speech, language' < Proto-Yeniseian **qaʔg*; Yugh χɔ́*baŋ* 'noun sandbank, ford; adj. shallow' < Proto-Yeniseian **qobaŋ* 'dry or shallow place in a river' < **qō* 'dry' + **baʔŋ* 'place', etc.

339 The Turkic loanwords with original initial **b-*, via Turkic **p-*, were borrowed to Yugh with initial *f-*. It may be explained by the change of the original Proto-Yeniseian initial **p-*, which occurred in a similar way (Starostin 1982: 149; Werner 1990b: 25, 233), e.g. Yugh *fā* 'once, time, often' < Proto-Yeniseian **pa*; Yugh *fa:ʰti* 'thick, dense (*forest, crowd*)' < Proto-Yeniseian **pa:tə*; Yugh *fʌnʲa ~ fənʲa, fʌnʲnʲa ~ fənʲnʲa* 'little, small' < Proto-Yeniseian **pəna ~ *pənʲa*, etc.

(cont.)

Turkic	Yugh	Examples
g	-	There are no attested loans with this sound.
ġ	VŋV	Turkic *karačiġay* 'swallow' → Yugh *kʌčiŋej* 'magpie';
Nasals		
n	-n	Turkic *bürken-* 'to be covered, to be wraped' → Yugh *bérgin* '*noun* bundle, pack of things'; Turkic *kiden* 'flax, canvas' → Yugh *kitn* 'nettles, hemp'; Turkic *qaġan* > *kān* 'an independent ruler of a tribe or people; kagan' → Yugh *χan* 'prince'; Turkic *talqan* 'oat flour' → Yugh *tállin* ~ *tàli´n* 'flour, meal';
	VŋV	Turkic *sana-* 'to think, desire, feel, miss' → Yugh *sáŋa*;
ŋ	VŋV	Turkic *qoŋaraq* 'a bell, one hung on an animal's neck' → Yugh *χóŋirɔχ*;
	-ń-	Turkic *qaŋza* 'tobacco pipe' → Yugh *kàńčá*;
ń	-	There are no attested loans with this sound.
m	-	There are no attested loans with this sound.
Affricates		
č	VčV	Turkic *qaračiġay* 'swallow' → Yugh *kʌčiŋej* 'magpie';
	VtV[340]	Turkic *bičïs* 'cutting out, dressmaking' → Yugh *bétes* ~ *bätes* 'lining of a coat';

---

340 According to Starostin's reconstruction (1982: 161–162), the change of original Yeniseian *-č > -tʼ* is a regular development in Yugh, e.g. Yugh *bɛʔtʼ* 'falling snow' < Proto-Yeniseian *beʔč*. This change points to an early period of borrowing.

(cont.)

Turkic	Yugh	Examples
Sibilants		
s	s-[341]	Turkic *sana-* 'to think, desire, feel, miss' → Yugh *sáŋa*; Turkic *sologay* 'left-handed' → Yugh *súl'gej* 'left';
z	-	There are no attested loans with this sound.
š	-s	Turkic *bičïs* 'cutting out, dressmaking' → Yugh *bétes ~ bätes* 'lining of a coat';
The labial fricative and the palatal consonant		
β	-	There are no attested loans with this sound.
y	VjV	Turkic *ayïl* 'village, family' → Yugh *ajaŋi* 'village';
	-j	Turkic *sologay* 'left-handed' → Yugh *súl'gej* 'left'; Turkic *qaračigay* 'swallow' → Yugh *kʌčiŋej* 'magpie'; Turkic *qoyuġ > qoyu* 'thick, viscid, dense' → Yugh *χoj* 'thick (*said of liquids*)';
	ø-	Turkic *yitig > yitī* 'sharp' → Yugh *ē·t ~ eti*; Turkic *yïð > yït* 'scent, odour, smell' → Yugh *ī·t* 'smell, aroma';
Liquids		
l	-l'-	Turkic *sologay* 'left-handed' → Yugh *súl'gej* 'left';
	-ŋV	Turkic *ayïl* 'village, family' → Yugh *ajaŋi* 'village';
	-r	Turkic *qarabil* 'guard' → Yugh *karábr* 'to guard (*verb*)'.
r	-	There are no attested loans with this sound.

---

[341] The original Yeniseian s- in initial position regularly preserved in Yugh (Werner 1990b: 25, 234; Vajda & Werner: in preparation), e.g. Yugh *saʔr* 'sharp edge' < Proto-Yeniseian **saʔʎ*; Yugh *saŋbetʲ* 'to test' < Proto-Yeniseian **saŋbetʲ* '*inf*. to test'; Yugh *saʔχ* 'squirrel' < Proto-Yeniseian **saʔq ~ *saga*, etc.

2.1.6 Ket
2.1.6.1 *Turkic Vowel Phonemes in Ket*

Turkic	Ket	Examples
Low unrounded vowels		
a	-á¹-	Turkic *balïq* > *palïk* 'fish' → Ket *hál'ga* 'ruff (*fish*)';
	-á	Turkic *qaŋza* 'tobacco pipe' → Ket *kàńčá*;
	-i-	Turkic *talqan* 'oat flour' → Ket *tállin* ~ *tàlin* 'flour, meal';
ä (e)	-a¹-	Turkic *bet* 'the human face' → Southern Ket *bat* 'face, forehead';
	i-	Turkic *älig* 'hand, forearm' → Ket *i·l'*, Northern Ket *i·l'i* 'arm';
Low rounded vowels		
o	-o¹-	Turkic *qoyuġ* 'thick, viscid, dense' → Ket *qo·j* 'thick';
	-ɔ¹-	Turkic *bōq* > *poq* 'excrement, dung' → Ket *hɔʔq*;
	-ʌ¹-	Turkic *qoltuq* 'armpit' → Ket *qʌltaŋ* 'forearm';
ö	-ɔ¹-	Turkic *köt* 'backside, buttocks' → Ket *kɔʔt* 'butt, hind end';
High unrounded vowels		
ï/ï̄	ī¹-	Turkic *yïð* 'scent, odour, smell' → Ket *īt* 'smell, aroma';
i	-ī¹-	Turkic *kiden* 'flax, canvas' → Ket *kī·tn* 'nettles, hemp';
	-i	Turkic *yitig* > *yitī* 'sharp' → Ket *ē·ti*;
High rounded vowels		
u	u-	Turkic *ulus* 'village, people' → Ket *u·l's* 'country; land of gnomes';
	-ù¹- ~ -ū¹-	Turkic *qunu* 'wolverine' → Southern Ket *kùn*, Central Ket *kŭnə*, Northern Ket *kŭne*, Eastern Ket *kūn*.

2.1.6.2 Turkic Consonant Phonemes in Ket

Turkic	Ket	Examples
Voiceless stops		
p	-	There are no attested loans with this sound.
t	t-	Turkic *talqan* 'oat flour' → Ket *tállin* ~ *tàli´n* 'flour, meal';
	VtV	Turkic *yitig* > *yitī* 'sharp' → Ket *ē·ti*;
	-t	Turkic *bet* 'the human face' → Southern Ket *bat* 'face, forehead';
		Turkic *köt* 'backside, buttocks' → Ket *kɔˀt* 'butt, hind end';
k	k-	Turkic *köt* 'backside, buttocks' → Ket *kɔˀt* 'butt, hind end';
		Turkic *kȫ* 'coal, soot' → Ket *kuˀ*;
	q-	Turkic *kämi* 'ship or boat' → Ket *qap* ~ *qaˀp*;
q	q-[342]	Turkic *qaġan* > *kān* 'an independent ruler of a tribe or people; kagan' → Ket *qa·n* 'prince';
		Turkic *qoyuġ* > *qoyu* 'thick, viscid, dense' → Ket *qo·j* 'thick (*said of liquids*)';
		Turkic *qoŋrak* 'a bell' → Ket *qɔ́ŋloq*;
		Turkic *qoltuq* 'armpit' → Ket *qʌltaŋ* 'humeral joint, humerus bone, forearm';
	-q	Turkic *bōq* 'excrement, dung' → Ket *hɔˀq*;
		Turkic *qoŋraq* 'bell' → Ket *qɔ́ŋloq*;
	k-	Turkic *qaŋza* 'tobacco pipe' → Ket *kàńčá*;
		Turkic *qunu* 'wolverine' → Southern Ket *kùn*, Central Ket *kū̃nə*, Northern Ket *kū̃ne*, Eastern Ket *kūn*;

---

[342] The original Yeniseian initial consonant *q-* is preserved in Ket (Starostin 1982: 169–170; Werner 1990b: 15, 231), e.g. Southern Ket *qɔraŋ* ~ *qo:*, Central Ket *qɔdeŋ* ~ *qō* 'inf. die, kill, be sick, dead, death' < Proto-Yeniseian **qodəŋ* < **qaxʷ* 'die, kill' + **əŋʷ* (inf.); Ket *qaˀ* ~ *qā·* 'word, speech, language' < Proto-Yeniseian **qaˀg*; Ket *qɔ̄baŋ* 'noun ford' < Proto-Yeniseian **qobaŋ* 'dry or shallow place in a river' < **qō* 'dry' + **baˀŋ* 'place' (Vajda & Werner: in preparation), etc. This change indicates an early period of borrowing.

(*cont.*)

Turkic	Ket	Examples
Voiced stops		
b	*b-* *h-*343	Turkic *bet* 'the human face' → Ket *bat* 'face, forehead'; Turkic *balïq* > *palïk* 'fish' → Ket *hál'ga* 'ruff (*fish*)'; Turkic *bōq* > *poq* 'excrement, dung' → Ket *hɔˀq*;
d	*-t-*	Turkic *kiden* 'flax, canvas' → Ket *kī·tn* 'nettles, hemp';
ð	*-t* < **-d*	Turkic *yïð* 'scent, odour, smell' → Ket *ī·t* 'smell, aroma';
g	-	There are no attested loans with this sound.
ġ	-	There are no attested loans with this sound.
Nasals		
n	*VnV* *-n*	Turkic *qunu* 'wolverine' → Ket *kūnə*; Turkic *kiden* 'flax, canvas' → Ket *kī·tn* 'nettles, hemp'; Turkic *qaġan* > *kān* 'an independent ruler of a tribe or people; kagan' → Ket *qa·n* 'prince'; Turkic *talqan* 'oat flour' → Ket *tállin* ~ *tàlíˊn* 'flour, meal';
ŋ	*-ŋ-* *-ń-*	Turkic *koŋrak* 'a bell' → Ket *qóŋloq*; Turkic *qaŋza* 'tobacco pipe' → Ket *kàńčá*;
ń	-	There are no attested loans with this sound.
m	-	There are no attested loans with this sound.

---

343 The Turkic loanwords with original initial **b-*, via Turkic forms with initial **p-*, were possibly borrowed to Ket with initial *h-*. The original Yeniseian initial **p-* regularly changed to *h-* in Ket (Starostin 1982: 149; Werner 1990b: 233), e.g. Ket *hā·* 'once, time, often' < Proto-Yeniseian *pa; Southern Ket *hat*, Northern Ket, Central Ket *hà:te* 'thick, dense (*forest, crowd*)' < Proto-Yeniseian **pa:tə*; Ket *hána* 'little, small' < Proto-Yeniseian *pəna / *pənʲa (Vajda & Werner: in preparation), etc.

(*cont.*)

Turkic	Ket	Examples
Affricates		
č	-	There are no attested loans with this sound.
Sibilants		
s	-s'	Turkic *ulus* 'administrative unit' → Ket *u·l's'* 'country; land of gnomes';
z	-	There are no attested loans with this sound.
š	-	There are no attested loans with this sound.
The labial fricative and the palatal consonant		
β	-	There are no attested loans with this sound.
y	-j ø-	Turkic *qoyuġ* 'thick, viscid, dense' → Ket *qo·j* 'thick (*liquids*)'; Turkic *yitig* > *yitī* 'sharp' → Ket *ē·t ~ ē·ti*; Turkic *yïð* > *yït* 'scent, odour, smell' → Ket *ī·t* 'smell, aroma';
Liquids		
l	-l Vl'V, -l'	Turkic *qaraul* 'guard; sight' → Ket *kalebel* 'to guard, keep watch, lie in wait for (*verb*)'; Turkic *älig* 'hand, forearm' → Ket *i·l'*, Northern Ket *i·l'i* 'arm'; Turkic *ulus* 'administrative unit, village, dynasty, people' → Ket *u·l's'* 'country; land of gnomes';
r	-l-	Turkic *qaraul* 'guard; sight' → Ket *kalebel* 'to guard, keep watch, lie in wait for (*verb*)'; Turkic *koŋrak* 'bell' → Ket *qɔ́ŋloq*.

2.2 Long Vowels

2.2.1 Turkic Original Long Vowels

2.2.1.1 The Preservation of Original Long Vowels? '

Kott *īta* 'stinking'; Ket *īˑt*, Yugh *īˑt* 'smell, aroma' ← Turkic *yït* (cf. Altai Turkic) < *yïð* 'scent, odour, smell';
Kott *pʰôk* 'feces, dirt' ← Turkic *bōq* 'excrement, dung';

2.2.1.2 Shortening of Original Long Vowels

It seems that in the most cases the Turkic original long vowel not reflected in Yeniseian. It proves the later period of borrowing:

Kott *ala* 'dappled' ← Turkic *ala* 'parti-coloured, dappled, mottled, spotted' < *āla*;
Yugh *fɔˀχ* 'excrement'; Ket *hɔˀq* 'excrement, filth' ← Turkic *poq* 'excrement, dung' < *bōq*;
Arin *yus* [*jus*] 'hundred' ← Turkic *yüs* < *yǖz*;
Arin *kis* 'sister-in-law' ← Turkic *qïs* 'girl; unmarried woman; daughter' < *q̄ïz*;
Kott *kuštu* 'very strong' < *kuš -tu* {Yeniseian NN/adj.} ← Turkic *küč* 'strength, power, energy' < *kǖč*;
Kott *pai* 'rich' ← Turkic *bay* < *bāy*;
Kott *šut* 'milk' ← Turkic *süt* < *sǖt*;
Kott *toi* ~ *tui* 'wedding' ← Turkic *toy* 'a feast; a wedding feast' < *tōy*.

2.2.2 Turkic Secondary Long Vowels

2.2.2.1 The Development of Secondary Long Vowels

There are some Yeniseian loanwords where the secondary long vowels developed from the *Vowel-Consonant-Vowel* pattern as in Modern Turkic. This feature points to a later period of borrowing, e.g.

Modern Turkic *ō* → Yeniseian *ô*

Kott *čôgor* 'coloured' ← Turkic *čōkur* 'variegated, multicoloured' ← Mongolic *čoqor* ~ *čooqor* 'variegated, dappled, spotted, motled; pockmarked';
Kott *d'ôrgan* 'blanket' ← Turkic *d'ōrgan* < *yoġurqan*;
Kott *ô* 'inedible fungus, toadstool' ← Turkic *ō* < *aġu* 'poison';

Modern Turkic ȫ → Yeniseian ô

> Kott ôr 'herd of horses' ← Turkic ȫr < ögür;
> Kott kônak 'shirt' ← Turkic könäk < kögänäk < köŋläk;

Modern Turkic ī → Yeniseian î

> Kott îri ~ îre 'thread, tendon' ← Turkic sīr < siŋir 'muscle, sinew, tendon'.

2.2.2.2 Shortening of Secondary Long Vowels

There are also some Yeniseian loanwords where Turkic secondary long vowels are shortened. This phonetic feature points a later period of borrowing, e.g.

Modern Turkic ā → Yeniseian a

> Ket batir; Yugh bádir ~ bátir ~ badir 'hero, warrior' ← Turkic bātïr < baġatur;
> Kott kan; Yugh χan; Ket qaˑn 'prince' ← Turkic kān < qaġan 'an independent ruler of a tribe or people; kagan';
> Kott šâškana ~ sâškan ~ šaška 'magpie' ← Turkic sāskan < saġïzġan;

Modern Turkic ē → Yeniseian e

> Arin karasek 'fly' ← Turkic qara sēk[344] < qara 'black' + sēk 'fly' < siŋek 'a buzzing insect';

Modern Turkic ō → Yeniseian o

> Kott alpot 'chief, head' ← Turkic albot < albōt < alpaġut;

Modern Turkic ȫ → Yeniseian o

> Kott kolča 'slow' ← Turkic kȫlje 'slow, slowly' < kȫl 'mood; feeling' +CA {Khakas NN/adv.} < köŋül 'the mind; thought; the heart';
> Arin ojakel'a 'stepdaughter' (< oj 'step-' + Yeniseian akel'a 'daughter') ← Turkic ȫy < ögey 'step-(father, etc.)';

---

344 Cf. YeniseiT: Khakas xara sēk; Sagai Koibal, Kachin qara säk 'fly'; Chulym Turkic kara sēk 'midge'.

Modern Turkic ū → Yeniseian u

> Kott *butai*; Assan *bútaj* ~ *tútaj* 'wheat' ← Turkic *būtay* < *buġday*;
> Kott *šurgan* 'cold weather' ← Turkic *šūrgan* 'snowstorm, storm' ← Mongolic *siγurγan* 'snowstorm, blizzard; storm with cold rain';

Modern Turkic ǖ → Yeniseian o

> Kott *elor* ~ *erol* 'sober' ← Turkic *elǖr* ~ *erǖl* 'sober' ← Mongolic *elegür* ~ *eregül* 'health; sober, abstinent';
> Kott *keršo* 'clever' ← Turkic *kärsǖ* 'clever, talanted' ← Mongolic *kersegüü* 'wise, circumspect, prudent; careful, circumspect, astute'.

2.2.2.3   *Diphthongization of Secondary Long Vowels*
Modern Turkic ō → Yeniseian óu ~ ôu

> Kott *bušôu* ~ *bišóu* 'calf' ← Turkic *pïzō* ~ *puzō* < *buzāġu*;

Modern Turkic ȫ → Yeniseian uʔo

> Yugh *kuʔo* 'coal, soot' ← Turkic *kȫ* ← Mongolic *kȫ* < *köge* 'soot; obstacle, hindrance; trouble' ← Turkic **kö-*, cf. *kȫń-* 'to catch fire, *intr*. to burn; to burn (*with anger*)';

Modern Turkic ū → Yeniseian uj ~ ei

> Kott *karei* ~ *karuj*; Assan *karei* ~ *karuj* 'view, look (*noun*)' ← Modern Turkic *karūl* 'guard; sight' < *qaraul* ← Mongolic *qaraγul* 'watch, sentry, guard, scout'.

2.2.2.4   *The Preservation of Vowel—Consonant* g—*Vowel Pattern*
There is an interesting case where the pattern *VGV* preserved Yeniseian, while in Yenisei Turkic and Altai Turkic it developed to secondary long vowel. The Kott form indicates the period of borrowing when the long vowel had not developed yet:

> Kott *agel* ~ *âgel* 'tent village (*ulus*)' ← Turkic *aġïl* 'a settlement or group of tents, village'.

There is Arin case where the pattern *VgV* preserved, whereas the secondary long vowel developed in Kott:

Arin *kogonek* 'shirt', cf. Kott *kônak* ← Turkic *kögänäk* < *köŋläk*.

2.3 Consonant Clusters
2.3.1 Kott
2.3.1.1 Preservation

Turkic *-pt-*

> Kott *kaptu* ~ *káptu* 'scissors' ← Turkic *qïpta*;

Turkic *-rg-*

> Kott *kubúrgenaŋ* ~ *kabúrgenaŋ* 'onion' ← Turkic *köβürgän* 'wild onion';
> Kott *šurgan* 'cold weather' ← Turkic *šūrgan* 'snowstorm, storm' ← Mongolic *siɣurɣan* 'snowstorm, blizzard; storm with cold rain';

Turkic *-kt-*

> Kott *baktîr* 'to praise' ← Turkic *paktïr-* {*-Xr-* Turkic VV/causative} < *pakta-* 'to praise' ← Mongolic *maɣta-* 'to praise, eulogize, laud, extol, glorify';

Turkic *-ks-*

> Kott *aksax* 'lame' ← Turkic *aqsaq*;

Turkic *-lk-*

> Kott *talkan* 'flour, meal' ← Turkic *talqan* 'oat flour';

Turkic *-lt-*

> Kott *altun* ~ *altin* 'gold' ← Turkic *altïn* < *altūn*;
> Kott *baltʰu* ~ *baltu* ~ *báltō*; Arin *baltó* ~ *balto* 'axe' ← Turkic *baltu* 'axe; battle axe';
> Kott *kaltar* 'brown horse with white mouth' ← Turkic *qaltar* 'bay horse with yellow markings, brown horse with white mouth' ← Mongolic *qaltar* 'variegated, spotted, blemished; have a white muzzle';

Turkic -*mč*-

> Kott *kamču* ~ *kamči* 'whip' ← Turkic *qamčï.*

2.3.1.2   *Voicing*
Turkic -*rk*- → Kott -*rg*-

> Kott *dôrgan* 'blanket' ← Turkic *dōrgan* < *yoġurqan*;

Turkic -*lk*- → Kott -*lg*-

> Kott *tálgan* 'flour, meal' ← Turkic *talqan* 'oat flour';

Turkic -*rp*- → Kott -*rb*-

> Kott *arba* 'barley' ← Turkic *arpa*;

Turkic -*kt*- → Kott -*gt*-

> Kott *tegteka* 'quail' ← Turkic *tükteg* 'with feathers';

Turkic -*kš*- → Kott -*gš*-

> Kott *hagši* ~ *hagše* 'good, suitable' ← Turkic *ťakšï* < *ďakšï* < *yaxšï* 'suitable, pleasing, good looking'.

2.3.1.3   *Devoicing*
Turkic -*bt*- → Kott -*pt*-

> Kott *hôptal* 'saddle cloth; carpet' ← Turkic *qabtal* 'side of the horse; side; saddle cloth' ← Mongolic *qabtalsun* < *qabtasun* 'board; wooden printing blocks; binding or cover of a book';

Turkic -*lb*- → Kott -*lp*-

> Kott *alpan* 'tribute' ← Turkic *alban* 'tribute' ← Mongolic *alban* 'compulsion, coercion; tax, impost, tribute';
> Kott *alpeš* 'wonder' ← Turkic *albïs* 'evil spirit' ← Mongolic *almas* 'female demon, witch';
> Kott *alpot* 'chief, head' ← Turkic *albot* 'chief; head of the district; governor' < *albōt* < *alpaġut* 'warrior';

Kott *alpaka* ~ *alpuga* ~ *alpuka* 'flying squirrel' ← Turkic *albaga* 'sable' ← Mongolic;

Turkic *-lg-* → Kott *-lk-*

Kott *kalkul* 'deaf' ← Turkic *qułyur* 'crop-eared' ← Mongolic *quluγur* 'crop-eared' ← Turkic;

Turkic *-md-* → Kott *-mt-*

Kott *komtú* 'grave' ← Turkic *komda* 'coffin, grave; box' ← Mongolic *qobdu* 'case; long and narrow box, quiver';

Turkic *-rg-* → Kott *-rk-*

Kott *korkôtn* ~ *korogotn* 'lead', cf. *korkotni* 'tin' ← Turkic *korgočïn* < *qorġušïn* 'lead';
Kott *turkatu* 'quick, rapid' < *turkan* 'quick' *-tu* {Yeniseian NN/adj.} ← Turkic *türgen* 'quick, rapid' ← Mongolic *türgen* 'quick, swift, rapid, speedy; hurried'.

2.3.1.4   *Changing*
Turkic *-pč-* → Kott *-ps-*

Kott *kapsagai* 'nimble, quick (*said of a person, horse or dog*)' ← Turkic *kapčagai* 'quick' ← Mongolic *γabšïyai* 'swift, expeditious; valiant; vanguard';

Turkic *-rg-* → Kott *-rx-*

Kott *berxen* 'warrior' ← Turkic *mergen* 'marksman; hero';

Turkic *-rs-* → Kott *-rš-*

Kott *keršo* 'clever' ← Turkic *kärsü* 'clever, talented' ← Mongolic *kersǖ* < *kersegüü* 'wise, circumspect, prudent; careful, circumspect, astute';

Turkic -*zg*- > -*sk*- → Kott -*šk*-

> Kott *šâškana ~ sâškan ~ šaška* 'magpie' ← Turkic *sāskan* 'magpie' < *saġ-ïzġan*;

Turkic -*čk*- → Kott -*sk*-

> Kott *koaskir* 'ram' ← Turkic *qosqar* < *qočqar* < *qočŋār*;

Turkic -*čk*- → Kott -*šk*-

> Kott *šoška* 'pig' ← Turkic *čočqa* < *čočuq*;

Turkic -*lč*- → Kott -*lš*-

> Kott *kalšu* 'undergrowth-covered riverbank' ← Turkic *kolčak* < *qol* 'the upper part of a valley' +*čAK* {Turkic NN/diminutive} ← Mongolic *γol* 'river, river bed';

Turkic -*lj̆*- → Kott -*lč*-

> Kott *kolča* 'slow (*a person, horse, reindeer, etc.*)' ← Turkic *kȫlǰe* 'slow, slowly' < *kȫl* 'mood; feeling' +*CA* {Khakas NN/adv.} < *köŋül* 'the mind; thought; the heart';

Turkic -*mn*- → Kott *-*nm*- > -*np*-

> Kott *hanpen* 'pray, prayer, praying' < *kanma-n* {Yeniseian VN/adj.} ← Turkic *kamna-* 'to make magic';

Turkic -*ŋz*- > -*ŋs*- → Kott -*nš*-

> Kott *kanšá* 'tobacco pipe' ← Turkic *qaŋza* ← Mongolic *γaŋsa* ← Chinese;

Turkic -*ŋ*- → Kott -*nk*- ~ - *nx*-

> Kott *munkan ~ munxan* 'poor' ← Turkic *muŋkan* 'unfortunate; cripple' (cf. Altai Turkic) < *munġan* 'mentally disturbed' < *buŋ-* 'to be mentally deranged or disturbed' -*GAn* {Turkic VN/adj., habitual action}.

2.3.2   Assan
2.3.2.1   *Preservation*
Turkic -*lk*-

> Assan *talkán* 'flour, meal' ← Turkic *talqan* 'oat flour';

Turkic -*rg*-

> Assan *kabïrgina* ~ *kaburgina* 'onion' ← Turkic *köβürgän* 'wild onion';
> Assan *korgoden* 'tin, lead' ← Turkic *korgočïn* < *qorġušïn* 'lead';

Turkic -*rp*-

> Assan *arpá* 'barley' ← Turkic *arpa* 'barley'.

2.3.2.2   *Compensatory Lengthening*
There is one Assan case where the secondary long vowel developed from Turkic consonant cluster -*lt*-. It is not a regular change, it may have been borrowed from Turkic form with long vowel **baltō* and the consonant -*t*- dropped, the reason is unclear:
> Assan *balō* 'axe' ← Turkic *baltu*.

2.3.3   Arin
2.3.3.1   *Preservation*
Turkic -*pt*-

> Arin *kaptï* 'scissors' ← Turkic *qïpta*;

Turkic -*rk*-

> Arin *berke* ~ *birka* 'big, great; very' ← Turkic *berke* 'clever, deft' ← Mongolic *berke* ← Bulgar Turkic *bärkĕ*: cf. Old Turkic *bärk*;

Turkic -*rg*-

> Arin *korgoldžín* 'tin' ← Turkic *korgoljïn* 'lead' ← Mongolic *qoryoljïn* 'lead' ← Turkic *korgočïn* 'lead';
> Arin *kuburgan* 'onion' ← Turkic *köβürgän* 'wild onion';
> Arin *torgïjan* 'lark (*bird*)' ← Turkic *torgayaq* 'sky-lark';

Turkic -rč̣-

>Arin *barčol badija* 'kerchief' ← Turkic *arčol* 'kerchief' + Russian *plat'je* 'dress';
>Arin *buturčinok* 'quail' < *buturčin -ok* {Yeniseian NN/diminutive} ← Turkic *budurčun*;

Turkic -ġd-

>Arin *buġdaj* 'wheat' ← Turkic *buġday*;

Turkic -lt-

>Arin *altin* 'gold' ← Turkic *altïn* < *altūn*;
>Arin *baltó ~ balto* 'axe' ← Turkic *baltu*;

Turkic -st-

>Arin *tegentestek* 'raspberry' ← Turkic *tikän yestek* 'thorned berry';

Turkic -mč-

>Arin *xamčook* 'whip' ← Turkic *qamčï*.

2.3.3.2 *Voicing*
Turkic -rp- → Arin -rb-

>Arin *arba* 'barley' ← Turkic *arpa*;

Turkic -rk- → Arin -rg-

>Arin *argiš* 'crowd (*of people*); migration' ← Turkic *argiš* 'comrade, companion' < *arqïš*;
>Arin *serga* 'louse' ← Turkic *sirgä* < *sirkä* 'nit'.

2.3.3.3 *Devoicing*
Turkic -lb- → Arin -lp-

>Arin *qólpas* 'finger' ← Turkic *qol pas* < *qol* 'the upper arm; the forearm, hand, finger' + *baš* 'the upper part of sg.';

Turkic -nd- → Arin -nt-

> Arin *mintora* 'ice' ← Turkic *mindir* 'hail' ← Mongolic *möndür* 'hail';

Turkic -zg- → Arin -sk-

> Arin *kusku kok* 'raven' ← Turkic *kuskun kök* 'raven' < *quzġun* 'raven' + *kök* 'blue'.

2.3.3.4 *Changing*
Turkic -čk- → Arin -šk-

> Arin *šoška* 'pig' ← Turkic *čočqa* < *čočuq*;
> Arin *uške* 'he-goat' ← Turkic *üške* < *äčkü* 'goat';

Turkic -čt- → Arin -št-

> Arin *berkuštukdu* 'strong' < *berke* 'big, great; very' + *kuštuk* 'strong' -*tu* {Yeniseian NN/adj.} ← Turkic *berke* 'clever, deft' + *küčtüg* 'strong, powerful; violent, oppressive';

Turkic -lǰ- → Arin -ldž-

> Arin *korgoldžín* 'tin' ← Turkic *korgolǰïn* 'lead' ← Mongolic *qoryolǰin* ← Turkic *korgočïn*;

Turkic -rm- → Arin -rb-

> Arin *čarba* 'grain' ← Turkic *čarba* 'grain, groats' < *yarma*.

2.3.4 Pumpokol
2.3.4.1 *Preservation*
Turkic -rg-

> Pumpokol *xórgosin* 'tin' ← Turkic *korgočïn* < *qorġušïn* 'lead'.

2.3.5 Yugh
2.3.5.1 Preservation
Turkic -lč-

The preservation of Turkic cluster -lč- in Yugh indicates the later period of borrowing. According to Yugh phonetic rules, the Proto-Yeniseian *č goes back to t' (Starostin 1982: 161; Werner 2005: 62):

> Yugh χʌ́lčaχan ~ χʌlčakŋ 'verb to tickle' < qʌlčak -(V)ŋ {Yugh infinitive suffix} ← Turkic qïlčïq 'tickle'.

2.3.5.2 Voicing
Turkic -rk- → Yugh -rg-

> Yugh bérgin 'noun bundle, pack of things' ← Turkic bürken- 'be covered, be wraped'.

2.3.5.3 Changing
Turkic -lk- → Yugh -ll-:

> Yugh tállin 'flour, meal' ← Turkic talqan 'oat flour';

Turkic -ŋz- > -ŋs- → Yugh -ńč-

> Yugh kàńčá 'tobacco pipe' ← Turkic qaŋza ← Mongolic γaŋsa ← Chinese.

2.3.6 Ket
2.3.6.1 Changing
Turkic -lk- → Ket -ll-

> Ket tállin 'flour, meal' ← Turkic talqan 'oat flour';

Turkic -ŋz- > -ŋs- → Ket -ńč-

> Ket kàńčá 'tobacco pipe' ← Turkic qaŋza ← Mongolic γaŋsa ← Chinese.

CHAPTER 3

Tungusic Loanwords

1 Etymology

In this chapter I analyze the etymology of Tungusic loanwords in Yeniseian from a semantic perspective. The main bulk of the lexical items are referenced from he *Ewenki-Russian dictionary* of Vasilevič (1958) which lists even dialectal forms, and the *Comparative Tungusic dictionary* (= SSTMJa) edited by Cincius (1975; 1979). Morphologically, most loanwords are nouns. In addition, there are a small number of verbs, adverbs and particles.

1.1 *Nouns*

1.1.1 Inanimate Nature

Yugh *ajā𝜒n ~ ajā𝜒in* 'ford, sandbank' (Werner 2002/1: 19) < **ajā* + Yeniseian *qiʼń* 'flow, current' (Werner 2002/2: 154):

*ajā ← Northern Tungusic: Ewenki *ajān* 'old bed of river; channel; bay, cove' ← Turkic: Yakut *ayān* 'old bed of river'; cf. Old Turkic *sāy* 'a dry stony riverbed' +*An* {Turkic NN, see Erdal 1991: 91; Stachowski 1993: 48}:

   Northern Ewenki: Yerbogachon; *Southern Ewenki*: Podkamennyi, Nepa, North-Baikal; *Eastern Ewenki*: Zeya, Aldan, Khingan, Uchur, Urmi, Sakhalin *ajan ~ ajān*;
   Cf. Northern Tungusic: Lamut *ajān*; Remaining lgs. –;

Tungusic ← Turkic:
   NE[N] Yakut *ayān* 'old bed of river' < *say* 'riverbed' +*An* {Turkic NN}; Dolgan –; cf. Old Turkic *say* 'an area of (*level*) ground covered with stones; stony desert'; NE[S] YeniseiT: Khakas *say* 'sandbank'; Sagai, Koibal, Kachin; Shor *say* 'small, shallow (*on the river*); rift, dry river bed, covered with pebbles'; AltaiT: Altai *say* 'pebbles, sandbank; stone'; Teleut *say* 'pebbles'; SayanT: Tuvan *say* 'pebbles, sandbank'; Tofan *say* 'pebbles'; ChulymT *say* 'small, shallow (*about a river*); rift, dry river bed, covered with pebbles'; NW[N] Siberian Tatar *say* 'sandbank, not deep (*about a river*)'; NW[S] Kirgiz *say* 'riverbed'; Fu-yü *say* 'riverbed'; Kazak *say* 'ravine'; SE Yellow Yughur –.

Etymology: Räsänen VEWT 394b; Rassadin 1971: 225; Clauson ED 858a; SSTMJa 1: 21a; Stachowski 1993: 48; SIGTJa 1997: 93; ESTJa 2003: 150–152; Anikin 2000: 104

The Yugh word is a hybrid compound word. If the second part is clearly a native Yeniseian word *qiʼń* 'flow, current' (Werner 2002/2: 154), the first part is connected to the Ewenki dialectal form *ajān* 'old bed of river; channel; bay, cove', which was borrowed from Yakut (SSTMJa 1: 21a).

The Yakut form *ayān* goes back to Turkic *sāy* 'dry riverbad, pebbles, sandbank, etc.' with the Turkic denominal noun suffix +(*A*)*n* (Stachowski 1993: 48), which forms nouns with a collective meaning[1] (Erdal 1991: 91). Due to Yakut phonetic rules, the Turkic initial *s-* disappeared[2] and the Turkic original long vowel *ā* preserved.[3]

For additional etymological and semantic background on the Turkic word, see Räsänen (VEWT 394b), Clauson (ED 858a), Tenišev (SIGTJa 1997: 93) and ESTJa (2003: 150–152).

From Yakut, the word was borrowed into Siberian Russian (Anikin 2000: 104). The Turkic word was also borrowed into Mongolic[4] and from Mongolic, re-borrowed into Tuvan[5] (Khabtagaeva 2009: 270).

Northern Ket *aʁidɛ* 'marsh, tundra'; Central Ket *ajgiddɛ*, Southern Ket *ajgitdɛ* 'wooded tundra, pine bog' < *ajgi / *aʁi + Yeniseian *deʔ* 'lake' (Werner 2002/1: 85):

*ajgi / *aʁi ← Northern Tungusic: Ewenki *aɣī* 'taiga, tundra, marsh' < *aɣī-* 'to walk in the snow':

Northern Ewenki: Yerbogachon, Ilimpeya; *Southern Ewenki*: Podkamennyi, Nepa; *Eastern Ewenki*: Zeya, Aldan, Tungir, Uchur, Urmi, Chumikan, Sakhalin, Barguzin *aɣī* 'taiga', cf. Podkamennyi 'forest on the plain', Barguzin 'the open desert place, steppe', Aldan 'field', Tungir 'tundra, marsh'; cf. *aɣī-* 'to walk in the snow; to bypass; get the beast';

cf. Northern Tungusic: Lamut *āju-* ~ *āwi-* 'to walk in the snow; to go on the sand, water'; Negidal *awī-* 'to walk in the snow (*without road, without skis*)'; Southern Tungusic: Udihe *ai-* 'to go through deep snow'; Ulcha *ajī-* ~ *u-* 'to walk in the snow (*without road, without skis*)'; Orok *āwi-* 'to walk in the snow (*without road, without skis*)'; Nanai *aoi-* 'to go through deep snow', *āi-* 'to walk in the snow

---

1 E.g. Old Turkic *ärän* 'men' < *är* 'man'; *toran* 'system of nets' < *tōr* 'a net for catching bird or fish', *boδun* 'people' < *bōδ* 'tribe', etc.
2 E.g. Old Turkic *sǖt* 'milk' ~ Yakut *üt*; Old Turkic *sän* 'you' ~ Yakut *en*; Old Turkic *sarïɣ* 'yellow' ~ Yakut *arï* 'butter'; Old Turkic *suɣ* 'water' ~ Yakut *ū*; etc.
3 The list of Yakut examples with the reconstructed Turkic original long vowels can be found in the work of Ščerbak (1970: 50–52), e.g. Old Turkic *āč* 'hungry' ~ Yakut *ās*; Old Turkic *qīz* 'girl' ~ Yakut *kīs*; Old Turkic *tūz* 'salt' ~ Yakut *tūs*; Old Turkic *tǖn* 'night' ~ Yakut *tün*; etc. The original long vowels *ǟ*, *ō* and *ȫ* reflected as diphthongs in Yakut, e.g. Old Turkic *bǟr-* 'to give' ~ Yakut *biär-*; Old Turkic *ōt* 'fire' ~ Yakut *uot*; Old Turkic *kȫl* 'lake' ~ Yakut *küöl*; etc.
4 Turkic → Mongolic *sayir* 'dry bed of a stream; shallow place in river; pebble; callus' < **sayi+r* {Mongolic NN, see Khabtagaeva 2009: 283}: Middle Mongol: –; LM *sayir*; Modern Mongol: Buryat –; Khalkha *sair*; Oirat dial. *sǟr*; Dagur –; Khamnigan –.
5 Turkic → Mongolic → Turkic: Tuvan *sayïr* 'shallow place in river; pebble'.

(*without road, without skis*)'; Oroch –; Jurchen –; Manchu *ajli-* 'to go away from a straight road'; Sibe –.
Etymology: SSTMJa 1: 13a; Khabtagaeva 2017: 79

The Ket dialectal forms belong to a group of compound hybrid words. They consist of the Common Tungusic form *aγī* 'taiga, tundra, marsh' and the native Yeniseian word *deʔ* 'lake'. The diphthongization of vowel *a-* in the first syllable of Cental and Southern Ket forms can be explained by the long vowel *ī* in the Ewenki forms. The reason for the gemination of consonant *-d-* in Central and Southern Ket is unclear.

Central Ket *aqtul* 'spring (*water coming out of the ground*)' (Werner 2002/1: 55) < *aqtu -l {?}:
*aqtu ← Northern Tungusic: Ewenki *jūktu* 'spring, brook' < *jū-* 'to get out; to leave' *-ktA* {Ewenki VN, see Vasilevič 1958: 764}:
    Northern Ewenki: Yerbogachon, Ilimpeya *jūktu*; *Southern Ewenki*: Podkamennyi *jūkte*; *Eastern Ewenki*: Tungir, Uchur, Urmi, Sakhalin, Chulman *jūktu*; cf. Aldan, Chumikan *ńūkte* 'spring, brook';
    cf. Northern Tungusic: Lamut *ńȫ- ~ jō- ~ ńu-*; Negidal *jū- ~ ńū-*; Southern Tungusic: Oroch *ńū-*; Udihe *ńū-*; Ulcha *ńie- ~ ńē-*; Orok *nē-*; Nanai *ńie- ~ ńē- ~ ńiu-*; Remaining lgs. –;
Tungusic → Turkic:
NE^N Yakut *d'ukta* 'spring, brook'.
Etymology: Cincius 1949: 308; SSTMJa 1: 348b–349a; Khabtagaeva 2017d: 82

The Ket word was probably borrowed from the Northern Ewenki dialectal form *jūktu, where the final vowel *-u* is found. From a phonetic side, the Tungusic initial consonant *j-* dropped as in some other loanwords (see *Aphaeresis*). The final consonant *-l* is of unknown origin.

The Tungusic word derived from the verb *jū-* 'to get out; to leave' and the productive deverbal noun suffix *-ktA*, which forms nouns designating results of action (for details on functions, see Vasilevič 1958: 764). The borrowing from Ewenki is evident from the presence of the suffix, which is absent in other Tungusic forms.

The Ewenki word was borrowed into Yakut (Romanova, Myreeva & Baraškov 1975: 164).

Ket *daŋtakan*; Northern Ket *deŋtiyin ~ däŋtiyin* 'marsh' (Werner 2002/1: 184) ← Northern Tungusic: Ewenki *detkēn* 'marsh' < *det* 'tundra, marsh, mossy glade' *+kĀn* {Ewenki NN/diminutive, see Vasilevič 1958: 759}:
    Northern Ewenki: Yerbogachon; *Southern Ewenki*: Podkamennyi, Nepa, Sym; *Eastern Ewenki*: Zeya, Urmi, Chumikan, Sakhalin *detkēn* 'tundra, marsh, mossy glade';

cf. also Northern Tungusic: Lamut *det*; Negidal *det* ~ *detkēn*; Southern Tungusic: Oroch *detu*; Udihe –; Ulcha *detu*; Orok *detu*; Nanai *detu*; Remaining lgs. –.
Etymology: SSTMJa 1: 238b; Khabtagaeva 2017d: 82

The etymology of the Ket words is unknown (Werner 2002/1: 184). They are possibly connected with the Ewenki word *detkēn* 'marsh'. From a phonetic perspective, internal -*ŋ*- was inserted as occurs before the dental consonant -*t*- in some Ket loanwords. There are three different Ket forms with velar and palatal vowels.

The Ewenki word is derived from *det* 'tundra, marsh, mossy glade' and the Tungusic diminutive suffix +*kĀn* (for details on functions, see Boldyrev 1987: 5–6). It is an interesting fact that Southern Tungusic languages of the Amuric group have a form *detu* with the final vowel -*u* and without diminutive suffix.

Ket *dɔgbən* 'area between two riverbends' (Vajda & Werner: in preparation) ← Northern Tungusic: Ewenki *dāgwūn* 'crossing, ford across a river' < *dāɣ*- 'to cross, to pass river' -*wūn* {Ewenki VN, see Vasilevič 1958: 748}:
   Podkamennyi Ewenki *dāgwūn* 'crossing, ford across a river';
   Northern Ewenki: Yerbogachon, Ilimpeya; *Southern Ewenki*: Podkamennyi, Nepa, Sym, Upper Lena *dāɣ*- 'to cross, to pass river';
   cf. Northern Tungusic: Lamut *daw*-; Negidal *daw*-; Southern Tungusic: Oroch *dau*-; Udihe *dau*-; Ulcha *dau*-; Orok *dāu*-; Nanai *dā*-; Jurchen –; Manchu *dō*-; Sibe *dō*- 'to land'.
Etymology: SSTMJa 1: 187; Khabtagaeva 2017: 76

The Ket word was borrowed from the Podkamennyi Ewenki dialectal form *dāgwūn*. Despite the fact that the verb *dāɣ*- 'to cross, pass river' is present in several Ewenki dialects, the noun *dāgwūn* exists only in the Podkamennyi Ewenki dialect. This noun derived with the Ewenki deverbal noun suffix -*wūn*, which forms nouns designating abstract nouns, processes, names of tools, animals, etc. It is a 'highly' productive not only in Ewenki (for details on functions and more examples, see Vasilevič 1958: 748 and Boldyrev 1987: 11–13), but also in almost all Tungusic languages (On correspondences, see Benzing 1955: 63; Boldyrev 1987: 18–24).

Ket *hágdaŋ* 'snowstorm' (Werner 2002/1: 333) < *hág* -*d*- {? epenthetic consonant} -*aŋ* {? Ket collective suffix} ← Northern Tungusic: Ewenki *higin* 'snowstorm, whirlwind, storm':
   Northern Ewenki: Yerbogachon, Ilimpeya; *Southern Ewenki*: Podkamennyi, Nepa, Tokma; *Eastern Ewenki*: Zeya, Tungir, Aldan, Uchur, Urmi *hiɣin* 'vortex; storm, hurricane; rain with the wind; the wind howl, snowstorm; rainwater';

cf. *Eastern Ewenki*: Zeya, Tungir, Aldan, Uchur, Chumikan, Sakhalin *huɣun* 'snowstorm, the wind howl, blizzards, wind';

cf. Northern Tungusic: Lamut –; Negidal *xiɣin ~ xijin* 'vortex; storm, hurricane'; Southern Tungusic: Oroch –; Udihe *sī* 'storm'; Ulcha *piwsun* 'a gust of hurricane'; Orok *sī* 'storm'; Nanai *piugi-* 'to howl (*about wind*)'; Remaining lgs. –.

Etymology: SSTMJa 2: 322, 337

The Ket word possibly relates to the Ewenki dialectal form *hiɣin* 'snowstorm'. The Tungusic borrowing is in accord from a semantic perspective, though the reason for the change of *-in* > *-daŋ* in the final syllable is unclear.

Despite the fact that the Ewenki words are examined separately (SSTMJa 2: 322, 337), the forms *hiɣin* and *huɣun* are probably related to each other. The base of the Ewenki words goes back to Proto-Tungusic form with initial *p-* consonant (for details on the change of Tungusic **p-* in Tungusic languages, see Benzing 1955: 32–33). According to their phonetic shape, the words belong to the category of onomatoepic words.

Central Ket *kʌdaŋ ~ kʌdəŋ* 'marshy place' (Werner 2002/1: 459) < **kʌda -ŋ* {Ket collective suffix}:

*kʌda ← Northern Tungusic: Ewenki *kuta* 'marsh':

Southern Ewenki: Podkamennyi, Nepa, Kachug, Nercha; *Eastern Ewenki*: Urmi, Chumikan, Sakhalin *kuta* 'marsh, bog, clay', cf. Podkamennyi, Nepa, Sakhalin, Urmi *kuta-* 'to get bogged down in the swamp';

cf. Northern Tungusic: Lamut *kuta* 'bog, swamp'; Negidal *kota* 'bog, swamp'; Southern Tungusic: –.

Etymology: SSTMJa 1: 439b; Romanova, Myreeva & Baraškov 1975: 164; Khabtagaeva 2017d: 80

The lexical meaning of the Ket word corresponds to the hypothesis that it is borrowed from Ewenki. The final *-ŋ* in the Ket form could be the Yeniseian plural suffix used in the function of 'collective' meaning.

The Tungusic word was also borrowed into Yakut: *kuta* 'bog, peat' (SSTMJa 1: 439b; Romanova, Myreeva & Baraškov 1975: 164).

Ket *qɔ́lan* 'ashes' (Werner 2002/2: 98) ← ? Northern Tungusic: Ewenki *huleptēn* 'ashes':

Northern Ewenki: Yerbogachon, Ilimpeya; *Southern Ewenki*: Podkamennyi, Tokma, Northern Baikal; *Eastern Ewenki*: Zeya, Aldan, Uchur, Urmi, Sakhalin, Barguzin *huleptēn*;

cf. Northern Tungusic: Lamut *hultēn ~ hultán*; Negidal *xulēptēn*; Southern Tungusic: Oroch *xulepte*; Udihe *xulepten*; Ulcha *punekten ~ puńekte*; Orok *punekten*; Nanai *puńektẽ ~ fuńekte*; Jurchen *fûh-léh-kîh*; Manchu *fuleŋgi* 'ashes; grey (*colour*)'; Sibe *fuleŋgi*.

Etymology: SSTMJa 2: 347a

As a hypothesis, I assume that the Ket word is related to the Ewenki word. Possibly, the loss of the Ewenki internal *-ptē* or final *-ptēn* syllables occurred in the Ket form due to polysyllabic Tungusic word. This is typical for Yeniseian, usually the polysyllabic loanwords simplified, e.g. Ket *enčil* 'little owl that catches rats' ← Ewenki *intilgun* 'owl'; Ket *tə·qtə ~ tə·qt* 'wagtail' ← Ewenki *tïgdevkī* 'lark'; Northern Ket *ti:l* 'gadfly', Ket *til* 'horsefly, reindeerfly' ← Ewenki *dilkēn* 'fly', etc. Besides of this, the initial Tungusic *h-* changed to *q-* in Ket.

For details regarding the Tungusic etymology, see SSTMJa (2: 347a). The Ewenki word derived from the base *hule* and the productive Tungusic suffix ±*ptun ~* ±*ptin*, which forms nouns equally from verbs and nouns (for details on functions, see Boldyrev 1987: 123–133).

According to other Tungusic data, Ewenki *hule* goes back to the reconstructed Proto-Tungusic **pule ~ *pune*, which may connect with Mongolic *hünesün*[6] 'ashes' (for Mongolic correspondences, see Nugteren 2011: 369).

The Ket word belongs to the category of words of uncertain etymology.

Central Ket *tamtul* 'marsh lake' (Werner 2002/2: 235) < **tamt* + Yeniseian *u·l* 'water' (Werner 2002/2: 378):

*tamt ← ? Northern Tungusic: Ewenki *amut* 'marsh lake':

> *Northern Ewenki*: Yerbogachon, Ilimpeya; *Southern Ewenki*: Podkamennyi, Nepa, Sym, Tokma, Northern Baikal; *Eastern Ewenki*: Vitim, Uchur, Urmi, Chumikan, Barguzin *āmut*;
>
> cf. Northern Tungusic: Lamut –; Negidal *amut* 'lake'; Southern Tungusic: Oroch *amu* 'lake'; Udihe –; Ulcha –; Orok –; Nanai *amoã* 'small lake; puddle'; Jurchen *wôh-móh* 'lake'; Manchu *omo* 'lake, marsh lake'; Sibe *om*.

Etymology: SSTMJa 1: 40b

I assume that the Ket word is a hybrid compound word where the second part *u·l* is a native Yeniseian word 'water' (Werner 2002/2: 235). I propose that the first part of word *tamt* is an assimilated form of Tungusic *amut*.

The word belongs to the category of words of uncertain etymology.

Ket *toqtis* 'slope of a riverbank or hill' (Vajda & Werner: in preparation) < **tokti* *-s* {Ket nominalizer}

*tokti ← Northern Tungusic: Common Ewenki *tuktï-* 'to go up a slope or mountain':

---

[6] Mongolic *hünesün* 'ashes' < *hüne+sUn* {Mongolic NN, see Poppe GWM §137}. Cf. Middle Mongol: SH *hünesü*; Muq. *hünesü*; LM *ünesü(n)*; Modern Mongol: Buryat *ünehe(n)*; Khalkha *üns(en)*; Kalmuck *ümsn*; Dagur *xuns* (E); Khamnigan *ünüse(n) ~ ünese(n)*.

cf. Northern Tungusic: Lamut *töt-* ~ *tüöt-*; Negidal *tukti-*; Southern Tungusic: Oroch *tukti-*; Udihe *tukti-*; Ulcha *tō-*; Orok *tōqpo-* ~ *tōpqo-*; Nanai *tō-*; Jurchen –; Manchu *tuk'e-*; Sibe *tuqi-*.

Etymology: SSTMJa 2: 209b

The Ket word was borrowed from the Common Ewenki verb *tuktï-* 'to go up a slope or mountain'. Through the Yeniseian nominalizer -s the Tungusic verb changed to noun in Ket. This is one of the important functions of the nominalizer in Ket (for details, see Georg 2007: 122–124).

The Tungusic verb is widespread in almost all Tungusic languages.

Southern Ket *tōˑj*; Northern Ket *tōˑji*; Yugh *tōˑj* 'river arm' (Werner 2002/2: 283) ← Northern Tungusic: Ewenki *togoi* 'bend of a river' ← Siberian Turkic *toqoy* 'river arm' ← Mongolic *toqoi* 'elbow, cubit; bend of a river, bay, port, harbor':

Southern Ewenki: Tokma; *Eastern Ewenki*: Aldan, May, Uchur, Urmi, Sakhalin *togoi* 'bend of a river';

cf. *Southern Ewenki*: Podkamennyi *toyočī* 'winding (*about the river*)';

Northern Ewenki: Yerbogachon, *Southern Ewenki*: Sym *toyor-* 'to wind (*about the river*)';

Remaning Tungusic languages –;

Tungusic ← Siberian Turkic 'river arm':

NE^S YeniseiT: –; AltaiT: Altai *tokoy*; Quu *toqoy*; Teleut *toqoy*; SayanT: Tuvan *dugay*; ChulymT –; NE^N Yakut *toġoy*; NW^N Siberian Tatar *toġay* (R); NW^S Kirgiz *tokoy* 'forest near a river'; Fu-yü *toho* 'elbow'; Kazak *toġay* 'forest'; SE Uyghur *toqay* 'forest undergrowth';

Turkic ← Mongolic *toqoi* 'elbow, cubit; bend of a river, bay, port, harbor':

Middle Mongol: HY *toqai*; Muq. *toqai*; Leiden *toqai*; Ist. *toqai*; Literary Mogolian *toqoi* ~ *toqai*; Modern Mongol: Buryat *toxoi*; Khalkha *toxoi*; Oirat dial. *toxa*; Dagur –; Khamnigan *toxoi*.

Etymology: Räsänen VEWT 485a; Romanova, Myreeva & Baraškov 1975: 201; SSTMJa 2: 190b; Doerfer 1985: 69; SIGTJa 1997: 95, 110; Anikin 2000: 558; Khabtagaeva 2009: 222; Nugteren 2011: 522

The source of borrowing is not obvious. The Yeniseian words may have been borrowed from Ewenki or directly from Turkic. The borrowed form was **togoi*, where -ogo- was developed to the secondary long vowel -ō- in Yeniseian.

Etymologically, the word is of Mongolic origin. The Ewenki forms were borrowed through Yakut mediation (SSTMJa 2: 190b; Doerfer 1985: 69; Romanova, Myreeva & Baraškov 1975: 201). The Yakut mediation is proven by the intervocalic *VgV*, which was regularly voiced in Mongolic loanwords[7] and native

---

7 E.g. Tommot, Tokko, Uchur, May, Urmi Ewenki *bögö* ~ *bügü* 'strong, solid' ← Yakut *bögö* 'id.'

Turkic words[8] (for details on the change, see Khabtagaeva 2011: 99–100). The Mongolic word is widespread in almost all Siberian Turkic languages (Räsänen VEWT 485a; SIGTJa 1997: 95, 110; Anikin 2000: 558; Khabtagaeva 2009: 222).

From a morphological perspective, the non-productive base of the Mongolic word is *toqo, cf. Buryat *toxonog* (< *toqa +nA-G) 'elbow'; Buryat *toxonobšo* (< *toqa +nA-bči) 'bolster'; Buryat *toxonoglo-* (< *toqa +nA-G+lA-) 'to lean on somebody's elbow', etc. (Khabtagaeva 2009: 152).

Ket *úl'ba* 'moss on tree trunks' (Werner 2002/2: 335) ← ? Northern Tungusic: Ewenki *lālbuka* 'moss' < *ńalbukā* < *lalbu +kĀ* {Ewenki NN, see Vasilevič 1958: 758}:

> *Northern Ewenki*: Yerbogachon, Ilimpeya; *Southern Ewenki*: Podkamennyi, Nepa, Sym, Upper Lena, Nercha; *Eastern Ewenki*: Ayan, Zeya, May, Totti, Uchur, Urmi, Sakhalin *lālbukā*; cf. Yerbogachon *ńalbuka* 'moss in the swamp; green moss; turf; grass for drying dishes';
>
> cf. Southern Tungusic: Oroch *nāpka ~ nabo ~ nabua ~ nabuxa* 'moss'; Remaining lgs. –;

Tungusic → Turkic:

NE^N Yakut *nalbakā ~ nalbïkta* 'moss'.

Etymology: SSTMJa 1: 489

As a hypothesis, I assume that the Ket word was borrowed from the Ewenki dialectal form **lālbuka* or **ńalbuka* where the initial consonant disappeared. Besides this, regressive assimilation of vowel *-u-* and palatalization of *-l-* occurred in the Ket form. Due to the polysyllabic Ewenki form, the final suffix *+kĀ* also dropped in Ket. The Tungusic etymology fits from a semantic perspective.

The Ewenki word *lālbukā ~ ńalbuka* was derived from the base *lālbu ~ ńalbu* with the productive denominal noun suffix *+kĀ*, which forms nouns the meaning of which is usually the same as that of the primary word (for details on functions, see Vasilevič 1958: 758). The primary base of the Tungusic word is **lālbi ~ *lalbu*, which may have proven by the Ewenki dialectal forms with different suffixes.[9] Phonetically, the fluctuation *l- ~ ń- ~ j- ~ ǰ-* is typical for Ewenki

---

← Mongolic *böke* 'strong, solid, stalwart, firm, robust, vigorous, sturdy'; Uchur Ewenki *čōgur* 'variegated, spotted' ← Yakut *čuogur* 'id.' ← Mongolic *čoqor ~ čooqor* 'variegated, dappled, spotted, motled; pock-marked'; Tokko Ewenki *mugur* 'blind gut, caecum; blunt' ← Yakut *mugur ~ muǰur* 'blunt' ← Mongolic *muqur* 'blunt, blunted; cropped'; etc.

8 E.g. Old Turkic *säkiz* 'eight' ~ Yakut *aġïs*; Old Turkic *öküz* 'ox' ~ Yakut *oġus*; Old Turkic *yaqa* 'the edge, or border' ~ Yakut *saġa*; etc.

9 E.g. Ewenki dial. *lālbikta ~ lēlbikte* (< **lālbi +ktA* {Ewenki NN, see Vasilevič 1958: 764}) 'moss',

dialecs (Cincius 1949: 213), e.g. Ewenki dial. *jū-* ~ *ǰū-* ~ *ńū-* ~ *lū-* 'go out', *jantakī* ~ *ńantakī* ~ *ǰantakī* 'volwerine', *ńēke* ~ *jeke* 'perch, redfish', *ńuŋun* ~ *juɣun* 'six', etc. (for more details and examples, see Vasilevič 1948: 335–336).

The Ewenki word was borrowed into Yakut as well (SSTMJa 1: 489; DSJaJa 1976: 173).

The Ket word belongs to the category of words of uncertain etymology.

1.1.2   Wild Animals, Birds and Insects

Yugh *číčik* 'wagtail' (Werner 2002/1: 165) ← Northern Tungusic: Ewenki *čičakūn* 'wagtail' < **čiča +kūn* {Tungusic NN, see Vasilevič 1958: 765}:

    Southern Ewenki: Podkamennyi *čičakān* 'sparrow', *čičakūn* 'wagtail'; *čičakūtkān* 'small bird'; cf. *Northern Ewenki*: Yerbogachon; *Southern Ewenki*: Nepa *čičakūn* 'wagtail';

    cf. Northern Tungusic: Negidal *čičaxin* ~ *čičakin* 'wagtail'; Southern Tungusic: Oroch *čičoku* 'wagtail'; Ulcha *čičo* ~ *čiče* 'wagtail'; Nanai *čičō* 'wagtail; small bird'; Manchu *čečike* 'small bird'; Sibe *čiškə* ~ *čiškə* 'sparrow, little bird';

cf. Turkic *čičak* 'small bird' < (?) **čibičiq* < **čibï +čAK* {Turkic NN/diminutuve, see Erdal 1991: 44}:

    cf. Old Turkic –; NE^S YeniseiT: –; AltaiT: –; SayanT: Tuvan –; Tofan *šïǰek* 'small bird'; ChulymT –; NE^N Yakut *čīčāx* 'small bird', *silgi čīčāga* 'wagtail'; Dolgan *čīčāk* 'small bird'; NW^N Siberian Tatar –; NW^S Kirgiz *čïmčik* 'small bird'; Fu-yü –; Kazak *šïbïšïq* 'canary-bird; small bird'; SE Yellow Uyghur –;

cf. Mongolic *čegčegei* 'linnet, wagtail' < **čegče +GAi* {Mongolic NN/diminutive, see Poppe GWM § 123; Khabtagaeva 2009: 280}:

    Middle Mongol: –; LM *čegčegei* 'linnet'; Modern Mongol: Buryat *xüxe sesegī* (< **köke* 'blue' + *čečegei*) 'tit'; Khalkha *cegcgī* 'wagtail' (BAMRS); Kalmuck –; Oirat dial. –; Dagur –; Khamnigan *cēceceldei* 'tit'.

Etymology: Rassadin 1971: 94; SSTMJa 2: 401, 422a; Stachowski 1993: 77; SIGTJa 1997: 176–177

The Yugh word is connected to the Podkamennyi Ewenki dialectal form *čičakūn* 'wagtail'. Phonetically, the final Ewenki *-ūn* disappeared in Yugh. From a semantic point of view, the Tungusic lexical meaning is in accordance with the Yeniseian word. It is not clear the connection with Northern Ket *titipka* and Kott *čičipa* 'wagtail' which are clearly somehow related to the Yugh word.

According to its phonetic shape, the word belongs to the category of ideophonic words and is present in Mongolic and Turkic (Rassadin 1971: 94; SIGTJa

---

    lālbukāɣ ~ *lālbukīɣ* (< **lālbu +kĀ* {Ewenki NN, see Vasilevič 1958: 758}) 'the place with moss', *lālbukādā-* (< **lālbu +kĀ +dĀ-* { Ewenki NN, NV see Vasilevič 1958: 758, 753}) 'to collect moss', etc.

1997: 176–177) languages as well. It is remarkable that both language families use the word with the diminutive suffix.

Ket *enčil* 'little owl that catches rats (*species unidentified*)' (Werner 2002/1: 267) ← Northern Tungusic: Ewenki *intilgun* 'owl' < **inti* 'kind of bird' +*l*- {Ewenki NV, see Vasilevič 1958: 765} -*wun* {Ewenki VN, see Vasilevič 1958: 748; Boldyrev 1987: 11–19}:

> *Northern Ewenki*: Yerbogachon; *Southern Ewenki*: Podkamennyi, Nepa; *Eastern Ewenki*: Olekma, Sakhalin, Barguzin *intilgun* 'owl';
>
> cf. Southern Tungusic: Manchu *intu* [*čečike*] 'a kind of small bird with red feathers'; Remaining lgs. –.

Etymology: SSTMJa 1: 318a

The Ket word is clearly connected to the Ewenki dialectal word *intilgun* 'owl'. The new etymology can be strengthened by the same semantic meaning and the regular phonetic change *ti* > *či*. Due to the absence of polysyllabic words in Ket, the Ewenki suffix +*lgUn* disappeared, as in some other loanwords.

The base of the Tungusic word is *inti* ~ *intu* 'a kind of bird', cf. Manchu form. The authors of SSTMJa (1: 318a) consider the Ewenki and Manchu forms separately.

Ket *qúmlej* ~ *qúmilej*; Yugh *χúmiljej* ~ *χómuljej*, *χúmal* ~ *χúmil* 'butterfly' (Werner 2002/2: 130) ← ? Northern Tungusic: Ewenki *kumalāndō* 'black butterfly with a white border around the edges of the wings' < *kumalān* 'rug made of the reindeer skin' < **kuma* +*lĀn* {Ewenki NN, see Vasilevič 1958: 766} +*dō* {Ewenki NN, which forms names of insects, see Vasilevič 1958: 754}:

> *Eastern Ewenki*: Tommot *kumalāndō*;
>
> cf. Northern Tungusic: Lamut *qūmnan* 'embroidered cover of bag'; Negidal *komalan* 'rug made of the reindeer skin'; Southern Tungusic: Oroch *kumala* 'fur rug'; Orok *qumala* 'small rug'; Remaining lgs. –.

Etymology: SSTMJa 1: 430a

As a hypothesis, I connect the Yeniseian words with the Tommot Ewenki dialectal form *kumalāndō* 'black butterfly with a white border around the edges of the wings'. The Tungusic etymology fits from the phonetic and semantic viewpoint. Because of the Ewenki polysyllabic word, the Yeniseian forms are shortened, as in other some borrowings. The change of initial *k*- > *χ*- in Yugh and its preservation in Ket indicate an early period of borrowing; this change is also typical for the native Yeniseian words. Due to the previous vowel -*i*- the diphthongization in the final position of the Yeniseian forms is occurred. The problematic side of a new etymology is the rareness in Ewenki, the etymology of the Yeniseian words still remains uncertain.

The Ewenki word *kumalāndō* 'butterfly' derived from the noun *kumalān* 'rug made of the reindeer skin' with the Ewenki productive denominal noun suffix +*dō*, which forms names of insects[10] (details on function, see Vasilevič 1958: 754). The lexical change from a 'rug' to 'butterfly' is interesting. This change may be explained by the similar colour of butterfly and rug's material made from the fur of reindeer. The base of the Tungusic noun *kumalān* is **kum(a)*, cf. *kumle-* 'to clasp, to enfold', *kumule-* 'to cover', *kumma* 'clothes', etc. (For more Tungusic data and correspondences, see SSTMJa 1: 430–431).

Ket *ôgə* 'cave, nest, den' (Werner 2002/2: 32) ← Northern Tungusic: Ewenki *hugi* 'nest':

Northern Ewenki: Yerbogachon, Ilimpeya; *Southern Ewenki*: Podkamennyi, Nepa; *Eastern Ewenki*: Barguzin *hugi* ~ *hugī* 'nest (of eagle or crow)';

cf. Northern Tungusic: Solon *ubī* ~ *ūvī* 'nest'; Lamut *hevi* ~ *evi* 'nest'; Negidal *xūyī* 'nest'; Southern Tungusic: Udihe *xui* 'nest, den'; Manchu *feje* 'cave, nest, den'; Remaining lgs. –.

Etymology: Cincius 1949: 328; SSTMJa 2: 337

The etymology of the Ket word is connected to the Ewenki dialectal word *hugi* 'nest'. The disappearance of the initial consonant *h*- is a typical phonetic feature in the original Ket words (Starostin 1982: 175). In this way, the loanword may be borrowed in the early period.

Ket *tə·qtə* ~ *tə·qt* 'wagtail (*several species of birds of the genus Motacilla*)' (Werner 2002/2: 305) ← Northern Tungusic: Ewenki *tügdewkī* 'lark' < *tügde-* 'to rain' -*wkī* {Ewenki VN, see Vasilevič 1958: 747}; cf. *tügde* 'rain':

Northern Ewenki: Ilimpeya *tügdewkī* 'lark';

cf. Northern Tungusic: Lamut *tīd* 'rainy, cloudy'; Negidal *tigde*; Southern Tungusic: Oroch *tigde*; Udihe *tigde*; Ulcha *tugde*, cf. *tugdeku-* 'to herald rain (*about birds*)'; Orok *tugde* ~ *tugje*; Nanai *tugde* ~ *tigde*; Remaining lgs. –.

Etymology: SSTMJa 2: 175b

The Ket forms may be connected to the Ilempeya Ewenki word *tügdewkī* 'lark'. Despite the fact that the Ewenki and Ket words designate the various names of birds, both of them belong to the same class *Aves* and order *Passeriformes*. I assume that the Ewenki suffix has been dropped in Ket, as in some Tungusic loanwords. From a phonetic perspective, the devoicing of the Tungusic cluster -*gd*- > -*qt*- and the change of Tungusic vowel -*i*- > -*ə*- in Ket occurred.

---

10 E.g. Ewenki *loredō* 'butterfly' (< *lure, cf. *lurekī* 'night fly'), *koŋnodō* 'black butterfly' (< *koŋno, cf. *koŋnomo* 'black', *koŋnoki-* 'to paint in black colour'), etc.

Etymologically, the Ewenki word was derived from the verb *tügde-* 'to rain' and the productive deverbal noun suffix *-wkī* forming nouns, which indicate agent names of actions, e.g. *bejukte-* 'to hunt' > *bejuktewkī* 'hunter', *kapči-* 'to squeeze, to grip' > *kapčiwkī* 'lobster', etc. (Vasilevič 1958: 747). According to superstition us signs, the lark is one of the birds heralding rain.

Northern Ket *tīl* 'gadfly'; Ket *til* 'horsefly, reindeerfly' (Vajda & Werner: in preparation) ← Northern Tungusic: Common Ewenki *dilkēn* 'fly' < *dil +kĀn* {Ewenki NN/diminutive, see Vasilevič 1958: 759}:

> Common Ewenki *dilkēn ~ delkēn* 'fly';
> cf. Northern Tungusic: Lamut *dileken ~ dilken ~ deliken*; Negidal *dirkēn ~ dilken*; Southern Tungusic: Oroch *giluwe ~ giluɣe*; Udihe –; Ulcha *gilekte*; Orok *ǰīl'o*; Nanai *ǰilekū*; Jurchen –; Manchu *derhuwe*; Sibe –.

Etymology: SSTMJa 1: 207a

The Ket forms were borrowed from the Ewenki form *dilkēn* 'fly', where the Ewenki diminutive suffix *+kĀn* has been dropped. The initial Tungusic **d-* is usually preserved in Ket, its devoicing may be occurred due to the following vowel *-i-*.

The word is present in almost all Tungusic languages (SSTMJa 1: 207a).

Ket ***ullen ~ úlen***; Yugh ***úl'an*** 'pochard (diving duck, *Aythya ferina*)' (Werner 2002/2: 341), cf. 'smew (diving duck, *Mergellus albellus*, Russian *lutok, nyrok*)' (Donner 1955: 97; Vajda & Werner: in preparation) ← Northern Tungusic: Ewenki *ulanmukī* 'pochard' < *ula-* 'to get wet' *-n* {Ewenki VN, see Vasilevič 1958: 777} *+mukī* {Ewenki NN, see Vasilevič 1958: 776}:

> Northern Ewenki: Yerbogachon *ulanmukī* 'pochard (*Russian* утка-нырок)' (Vasilevič);
> cf. Northern Tungusic: Lamut *ul- ~ ula-*; Negidal *ola- ~ ulla-*; Southern Tungusic: Oroch –; Udihe *ula-*; Ulcha –; Orok *ula-*; Nanai *ularikō* 'dial. wet'; Jurchen –; Manchu *ulɣa-*; Sibe –.

Etymology: SSTMJa 2: 257–258

The etymology of the Yeniseian words is uncertain. Werner connects them with the native Yeniseian word *u·l* 'water'[11] and puts under question the element *-en* (Werner 2002/2: 341). According to Vajda (2016: personal communication), it cannot be connected with the Yeniseian *ul* 'water' since that would give Yugh **uran* and not *ulan*. Possibly, the Yeniseian forms are related to the

---

11 cf. Yeniseian **Huλ* 'water': Ket *ū·l*; Yugh *ūr*; Pumpokol *ul*; Arin *kul ~ kūl*; Assan *ul*, Kott *ul*.

Yerbogachon Ewenki word *ulanmukī* with the same lexical meaning 'pochard'. The Ewenki suffix +*mukī* disappeared in Yeniseian due to the polysyllabic structure of the Ewenki word.

The suffix +*mukī* is productive in Ewenki, it forms the names of animals, e.g. *ōranmukī* 'a kind of duck' < *ōran* 'rapids', *solonmukī* 'small bug', etc. (Vasilevič 1958: 776). From an etymological point of view, the Ewenki word derived from a Common Tungusic verb *ula-* 'to get wet' which is present in almost all Tungusic languages. In turn, it is not be excluded the possiblity to connect the Tungusic verb with a native Yeniseian word **Huλ* 'water'.

1.1.3 Human and Animal Body Parts

Ket *boksel* 'bosom, lap' (Vajda & Werner: in preparation) < **bokse* + Yeniseian **al* 'half; side' (Werner 2002/1: 24; Vajda 2016: personal communication):
*bokse ← ? Northern Tungusic: Common Ewenki *buksu* 'buttocks' ← Mongolic *bögse* 'backside, posterior part, rear, rump, buttock':

Common Ewenki *buksu* 'buttocks';

cf. Southern Tungusic: Manchu *buqsu* 'buttocks; hind leg'; Remaining lgs. –;

Tungusic ← Mongolic *bögse* 'backside, posterior part, rear, rump, buttock':

cf. Middle Mongol: SH *bökse*; Muq. *bökse*; LM *bögse(n)*; Modern Mongol: Buryat *bügse*; Khalkha *bögs*; Oirat dial. *bökäs*; Kalmuck *bögs*; Dagur *burs* 'hindquarters of an animal'; Khamnigan *bügsü ~ bügse*;

Mongolic → Turkic:

cf. Old Turkic *böksäg* 'the upper part of the chest; a woman's breast'; NW[N] Siberian Tatar *pöksü* 'bottom part of body'; NW[S] Kirgiz *böksö* 'side; torso'; Kazak *bökse* 'buttocks'; Remaining lgs. –.

Etymology: Räsänen VEWT 83b; Clauson ED 329a; SSTMJa 1: 104b; ESTJa 2: 213–214; Doerfer 1985: 130; Nugteren 2011: 287

According to Vajda (2016: personal communication), the Ket word has a stable Yeniseian etymology: it derives from **paxʷ(ad)* (odd **paxʷ > paps ~ boks*) 'pelvis' + **al* 'side, half'. As a hypothesis, I assume that the Ket word is a hybrid word, where the second part *el* may be related to the Yeniseian word *al*, while the first part is temptingly connected to Common Ewenki *buksu* 'buttocks'.

Etymologically, the Tungusic word is of Mongolic origin (SSTMJa 1: 104b), which was also borrowed into some Middle- and Modern Turkic languages (Räsänen VEWT 83b; Clauson ED 329a).

The Mongolic word is present from the Middle Mongol period: in the eastern (Secret History) and western (*Mukaddimat al-Adab*) sources and in almost all Modern Mongol languages (Nugteren 2011: 287). Sevortjan (ESTJa 2: 214) gives Ramstedt's (KWb 55b) convergence with a Mongolic verb *bökeyi- ~ bököyi-* 'to bend down, bow, bow one's head, salute by bowing, stoop, incline; to lean'. The non-productive base of the Mongolic verb is *bökе± or *bög±.[12] From a morphological point of view, the suffix +sA is unclear, it is not attested in Mongolic languages.

The Ket word belongs to the category of words of uncertain etymology.

Ket *qäpil* 'stomach' (Werner 2002/2: 69) ← Northern Tungusic *kebel* 'stomach'
← Mongolic *kebeli* 'belly, stomach; paunch, womb':
   Ewenki –;
   cf. Northern Tungusic: Lamut *kēbel* ~ *kābäl* ~ *kēbel* ~ *kebel* 'stomach (of squirrel or calf); cheese, curd (*from reindeer's milk*)'; Southern Tungusic: Jurchen *hefuli*; Manchu *hefali* ~ *hefeli* 'belly; inside, at the heart'; Remaining lgs. –;
Tungusic ← Mongolic *kebeli* ~ *kegeli* 'belly, stomach; paunch, womb':
   Middle Mongol: SH *ke'eli*; HY *ke'eli*; Muq. *kēli*; Ist. *kehli*; Leiden *kēli* ~ *keili*; RH *keheli*; LM *kebeli* 'belly, stomach; paunch, womb', cf. *kegeli* 'womb, pregnancy, embryo, belly'; Modern Mongol: Buryat *xēli*; Khalkha *xewlī*; Oirat dial. *kewěl*; Kalmuck *kēl*; Dagur *kēl'*; Khamnigan *kēli* ~ *kȫli*;
Mongolic → Modern Turkic:
   NE^N Yakut *kiäli* 'belly, womb'.

Etymology: Kałużyński 1962: 29; SSTMJa 1: 387b; Rassadin 1980: 67; Doerfer 1985: 93; Rozycki 1994: 104; Nugteren 2011: 408; Róna-Tas & Berta 2011: 516–518

The Ket word was possibly borrowed from the Tungusic form *kebel* 'stomach'. However, the word is absent in Ewenki, which puts the Tungusic borrowing into question. If the Ket word was borrowed from Tungusic, it is one of the rare cases where Lamut may be the source of borrowing. Phonetically, a direct borrowing from Mongolic *kebeli* is also possible. In this way, the word was borrowed in the early period before the secondary long vowel has not developed yet.

In turn, the Tungusic forms were borrowed from Mongolic (Doerfer 1985: 93; Rozycki 1994: 104). The word is present in the Middle Mongol sources and almost all Modern languages (Nugteren 2011: 408). From Mongolic, the word was borrowed into Yakut (Kałużyński 1962: 29; Rassadin 1980: 67).

There is a Hungarian word *kebel* 'bosom, breast' (Róna-Tas & Berta 2011: 516–518), which has been connected to the Mongolic word *kebeli* 'belly'. Either as a

---

12   Cf. also *böküger* (< *böke +GXr {Mongolic NN/adj., see Khabtagaeva 2009: 281}) 'bent, inclined forward', *bökülje-* (< *böke -ljA- {Mongolic VV, see Poppe GWM § 239}) 'to bend or bow repeatedly', *bögtüyi-* ~ *bökütüyi-* (< *böke -tA- {Mongolic VV, see Poppe GWM § 231} ±yi- {MongolicNV/VV, see Khabtagaeva 2009: 290}) 'to bend, stoop over, bow; to be stooped, bent, curved', etc.

direct loanword or as a word of Turkic origin which disappeared from the Turkic languages, but was preserved in Mongolic.

1.1.4   Designations of People

Ket *beʔj* 'friend' (Werner 2002/1: 156) ← Northern Tungusic: Ewenki *beye* 'man, person, body' ← Mongolic *beye* 'body, physique, organism; health':

cf. Northern Ket *bejetil* 'cannibal' (Werner 2002/1: 154) < *bejeti -l* {?} ← Northern Tungusic: Ewenki *beyetī* 'cannibal' < *beye* 'man, person, body' +*tī* {Ewenki NN, see Vasilevič 1958: 793}:

Northern Ewenki: Yerbogachon, Ilimpeya; *Southern Ewenki*: Podkamennyi, Nepa, Sym, Kachug, Upper Lena, Nercha; *Eastern Ewenki*: Zeya, Tungir, Ayan, Uchur, Urmi, Chumikan, Sakhalin, Barguzin *beye* 'human; man; male; husband; personality; body; appeal to a man or woman; generation';

Northern Ewenki: Yerbogachon, Ilimpeya; *Southern Ewenki*: Podkamennyi *bejetī* 'cannibal';

cf. Northern Tungusic: Lamut *bej* 'human; man; person, personality'; Negidal *beje* 'human; man; person; body; self'; Southern Tungusic: Oroch *beje* 'body; self; similar'; Udihe *beje* 'body; self; present, real'; Ulcha *beje* 'body; self'; Orok *beje* 'body; trunk, stem'; Nanai *beje* 'body; corpus; shape; self, personal'; Jurchen *péi-yè* 'body'; Manchu *beje* 'body; life; personality, individual, own'; Sibe *bəy* 'body, self';

Tungusic ← Mongolic *beye* 'body, physique, organism; health':

Middle Mongol: SH *beye ~ be'e*; HY *beye*; Muq. *beye*; Leiden *biye*; LM *beye(n)*; Modern Mongol: Buryat *beye*; Khalkha *biye*; Kalmuck *biy*; Dagur *bəy* (E); Khamnigan *beye ~ biye*.

Etymology: SSTMJa 1: 122a; Werner 2002/1: 156; Nugteren 2011: 281; Khabtagaeva 2017: 78–79

The Ket words were clearly borrowed from Tungusic (Werner 2002/1: 156). Both of them go back to the Ewenki form *beye* 'man, person, body'. The Northern Ket form *bejetil* 'cannibal' was borrowed from one of the Ewenki dialects (Yerbogachon, Ilimpeya or Podkamennyi) where the word with the same lexical meaning is found. The word was derived with the Ewenki productive denominal noun suffix +*tī* which forms nouns with the meaning of owning an object (for details on the function, see Vasilevič 1958: 793; Boldyrev 1987: 6). The Ket form has the element -*l* of unknown origin. From a phonetic perspective, in the Ket form *beʔj* 'friend' the Tungusic final vowel -*e* disappeared.

Etymologically, the Tungusic word is of Mongolic origin (SSTMJa 1: 122a). In Mongolic the word originally means 'body' which changed to 'person, man' in Tungusic. The Mongolic word in Ket is used with the positive and negative semantic meanings as 'friend' and 'cannibal'.

Ket *bōŋ* 'dead person', *boŋnij* 'cemetery; grave' < *boŋ-nij* {?}; Yugh *boŋsi* 'dead person' < *boŋ* -*si* {Yeniseian nominalizer} (Werner 2002/1: 145–146)
*boŋ ← Northern Tungusic: Ewenki *bunī* 'dead person; cemetery, grave' < *bu-* 'to die' -*nī* {Ewenki VN, see Vasilevič 1958: 782}:

Common Ewenki *bunī* 'death; dead corpse; burial place, grave; hell, ghost; dead person';

cf. Northern Tungusic: Lamut *buni* 'dead person; long-lived people'; Negidal *bunī* 'death; afterworld'; Southern Tungusic: Oroch *buńi* 'afterworld'; Udihe *bunige* ~ *buniŋe* 'afterworld'; Ulcha *bu-* 'to die'; Orok *bu-* 'to die'; Nanai *bu-* 'to die'; Jurchen *pùh-čḕ-hēi*; Manchu *bude-* ~ *buče-* 'to die'; Sibe –.

Etymology: SSTMJa 1: 98–99

The Yeniseian words were borrowed from the Common Tungusic form *bunī* 'dead person; cemetery, grave'. Ket has two different words with different lexical meanings going back to the same Tungusic word. The first Ket word *bōŋ* 'dead person' presents the changes of apocope and *-n-* > *-ŋ-*, while the second word *boŋnij* 'cemetery; grave' shows gemination of the consonant *-n-* and diphthongization of the final vowel *-i*. This fact assumes the different periods or the different sources of borrowing. The Yugh word *boŋsi* 'dead person' is used with the Yeniseian nominalizer *-si*.

From an etymological point of view, the Tungusic noun was derived from the verb *bu-* 'to die' and the Ewenki productive deverbal noun suffix *-nī* which forms nouns designating state, condition or natural phenomenon, e.g. *d'uganī* 'summer' < *d'uga-* 'to be (*about summer*)', *binī* 'life' < *bi-* 'to be', etc. (for details, see Vasilevič 1958: 782).

Ket *qitet* 'grandchild of father's sister or mother's brother' (Werner 2002/2: 152) < *qite -kit {Ket diminutive half-suffix, see Georg 2007: 130–131}
*qite ← Northern Tungusic: Ewenki *hute* 'child, son or daughter':

Common Ewenki *hute* 'child';

cf. Northern Tungusic: Lamut *hut* ~ *ut* 'child; grandchild; younger brother or sister; nephew or niece; descendant; young'; Negidal *xute* 'child'; Southern Tungusic: Oroch *xī* 'children, descendants'; Udihe *site* 'child'; Ulcha *pikte* 'child'; Orok *putte* ~ *pute* 'child'; Nanai *pikte* ~ *fikte* ~ *fute* 'child'; Jurchen –; Manchu *fusen* 'offspring; sprouts (*cereals, vegetables*); breeding (*animals*); brood'; Sibe –.

Etymology: Cincius 1949: 329; SSTMJa 2: 357

As a hypothesis, I propose that the Ket word is of Tungusic origin. From a phonetic viewpoint, the initial Ewenki *h-* changed to *q-* in Ket. The origin of the final dental consonant *-t* in the Ket form is unclear. It probably occurred due to the previous *-t-* or it may have developed from the Ket diminutive half-suffix *-kit*, which usually uses in a designation for human and animal children (for details on the function, see Georg 2007: 130–131).

The Tungusic word is widespread in almost all Tungusic languages. According to Tungusic data, the reconstructed Proto-Tungusic form is *pute. For details on its distribution, derivation, lexical broadening, see SSTMJa (2: 357).
The Ket word belongs to the category of words of uncertain etymology.

Ket *sūliŋ* [dɛˀŋ] 'people coming to meet each other' (Werner 2002/2: 175) ← Northern Tungusic: Ewenki *suglān* 'meeting' ← Turkic: Yakut *sugulān* 'the place of meetings, gatherings' ← Mongolic *čuɣlaɣan* 'assembly, gathering, meeting; wrapper' < *čuɣla-* 'to gather, assemble; to wrap' *-GAn* {Mongolic VN, forming nouns designating results of actions or abstract ideas, see Poppe GWM § 106}:
Northern Ewenki: Yerbogachon, Ilimpeya *huglan*; *Southern Ewenki*: Podkamennyi, Nepa; *Eastern Ewenki*: Tungir, Aldan *suglān*; cf. Nercha; Barguzin *čuglan* 'meeting'; cf. Northern Tungusic: –; Southern Tungusic: Manchu *čulyan* 'meeting' < *čulya-* 'to hold an assembly'; Remaining lgs. –;
Tungusic: Ewenki ← Turkic:
Yakut *sugulān* 'the place of meetings, gatherings';
Turkic ← Mongolic *suglān* < *čuɣlaɣan* 'assembly, gathering, meeting; wrapper' < *čuɣla-* 'to gather, assemble; to wrap':
Middle Mongol: SH *čula-*; LM *čuɣlaɣ-a(n)* 'assembly, gathering, meeting; wrapper'; cf. *čiyulyan* 'gathering, throng, society; assembly, meeting; league, confederacy'; Modern Mongol: Buryat *suglā(n)* 'meeting'; Khalkha *cuglā(n)*; Kalmuck *tsūlyan*; Dagur –; Khamnigan *cuglān*.
Etymology: Kałużyński 1962: 25; SSTMJa 2: 119b; Doerfer 1985: 235; Rozycki 1994: 51; Nugteren 2011: 308

The Ket word was borrowed from the Podkamennyi Ewenki dialect. It is proven by the initial consonant *s-*. In addition, the secondary long vowel *-ū-* developed from *-ug-*, which is a peculiar characteristic of some loanwords in Ket.

The Ewenki word was borrowed from Yakut (SSTMJa 2: 119b; Doerfer 1985: 235), which can be explained by the initial consonant *s-*. In turn, the Yakut word is of Mongolic origin (Kałużyński 1962: 25). The Mongolic initial *č-* regularly changed to *s-* in Yakut, e.g. Mongolic *čola* 'rank; title; nickname' → Yakut *solo*, Mongolic *čile-* 'to be tired' → Yakut *sïlay-*, Mongolic *čime-* 'to decorate' → Yakut *simē-* ~ *simie-*, etc. (Rassadin 1980: 79–81). The Mongolic word was also borrowed into Manchu (Rozycki 1994: 51).

1.1.5   Terms Pertaining to Mythology and Religion
Ket *kɔɣón* 'myth. forbidden jewelry in a snake's nest; copper pendant of shaman's costume' (Werner 2002/1: 445) ← ? Northern Tungusic: Ewenki **kulitkōn*

'the image of snake in the shaman's costume' < *kulin* 'snake' +*tkĀn* {Ewenki NN/diminutive, see Vasilevič 1958: 791; Boldyrev 1987: 163–167; Nedjalkov 1997: 297}:

cf. Barguzin, Sakhalin Ewenki *kulitkān* 'the image of snake in the shaman's costume' < *kulin* 'snake':

Northern Ewenki: Yerbogachon, Ilimpeya; *Southern Ewenki*: Podkamennyi, Nepa, Tokma, Nercha, Northern Baikal; *Eastern Ewenki*: Aldan, Uchur, Urmi, Chumikan, Sakhalin, Barguzin *kulin*; Upper Lena *kolin*;

cf. Northern Tungusic: Lamut *qulin ~ quličān ~ qolisān ~ kuličan ~ quličān* 'mosquito'; Negidal *kolixān ~ kulikān* 'worm, bug'; Southern Tungusic: Oroch *kulæ* 'worm (*common name for worms, snakes, caterpillars*)'; Udihe *kuliga* 'id.'; Ulcha *qoli* 'kind of aquatic insect', *qula* 'worm'; Orok *qola ~ qolia ~ qoliya* 'insect, worm'; Nanai *qolã* 'worm; caterpillar; insect'; Remaining lgs. –.

Etymology: SSTMJa 1: 428b; Khabtagaeva 2017d: 80

As a hypothesis I assume the Ket word is connected to the Ewenki dialectal forms **kulitkōn ~ *kulitkān* 'the image of snake in the shaman's costume' which today present in Barguzin and Sakhalin Ewenki. My idea is strengthened by the lexical meaning of the Ket word '*myth*. forbidden jewelry in a snake's nest; copper pendant of shaman's costume'. From a phonetic perspective, the internal syllable *-lit-* dropped in Ket due to the monosyllabic structure of Yeniseian words, which is a typical feature for some Altaic loanwords in Yeniseian. See also the Chapter *Typical features of Altaic loanwords in Yeniseian*.

The Ket word belongs to the category of words of uncertain etymology.

Southern Ket *qùt ~ qùr* 'the great "first" person; shaman's main spirit helper'; Northern Ket *qū̀re*, Central Ket *qū̀de* 'make magic (*said of a shaman*)' (Werner 2002/2: 139) ← ? Northern Tungusic: Ewenki *kutu* 'happiness, good luck, success' ← Turkic *qut* 'soul; spirit':

Podkamennyi Ewenki *kuta ~ kutu*;

Northern Ewenki: Yerbogachon, Ilimpeya; *Southern Ewenki*: Nepa, Sym, Upper Lena, Nercha; *Eastern Ewenki*: Aldan, Uchur, Sakhalin, Barguzin *kutu* 'happiness, good luck; well-being';

cf. Northern Tungusic: –; Southern Tungusic: Jurchen *hūh-t'ūh-rh* 'happiness'; Manchu *huturi* 'happiness, good luck; well-being; benefaction';

Tungusic ← Turkic *qut* 'soul; spirit':

cf. Old Turkic *qut* 'the favour of heaven; good fortune; happiness; spirit, soul, strength' (DTS); NE^S YeniseiT: Khakas *xut* 'soul, spirit, strength'; Shor *qut* 'soul'; AltaiT: Altai *kut* 'soul, strength; embryo'; Tuba –; Qumanda –; Quu *kut* 'soul'; Teleut *qut* 'soul; means, remedy'; SayanT: Tuvan *kut* 'soul; life-giving power'; Tofan –; ChulymT *qutu* 'spul'; NE^N Yakut *kut* 'soul'; Dolgan *kut* 'soul'; NW^N Siberian Tatar *qot* 'the kind of rite'; NW^S Kirgiz *kut*; Fu-yü *got* 'soul'; Kazak *qut* 'happiness'; SE Yellow Yughur –;

Turkic → Mongolic *qutuɣ* 'sanctity, holy rank; dignity, distinction; happiness, bliss; benediction'< **qutŭ* +G {Mongolic NN, see Khabtagaeva 2009: 280}:
    cf. Middle Mongol: SH *qutuq*; 'Phags-pa *quduq*; Ibn-Muh. *qutuɣtu*; Muq. *qutuqtu*; LM *qutuɣ*; Modern Mongol: Buryat –; Khalkha *xutag* 'sanctity, holiness, happiness, felicity, blessing'; Kalmuck *xut^ug* 'happiness, holiness'; Dagur –; Khamnigan –.

Etymology: Doerfer TMEN 3: 551–554; 1985: 136; Räsänen VEWT 305a; Clauson ED 594; SSTMJa 1: 440a; Ščerbak 1997: 143; ESTJa 2000: 175–177; Anikin 2000: 337; Khabtagaeva 2009: 269

The form of borrowing probably was **qudu* with with voiced consonant *VdV* in intervocalic position. The intervocalic consonant *VdV* regularly changed to *VrV* in the Ket dialects (Werner 1990: 35). The final vowel in Northern and Central Ket dialects could be the vocative form (Georg 2007: 117). The source of borrowing is unclear. The Ket forms may have been borrowed from Tungusic or directly from Turkic.

Originally, the Turkic word was borrowed into Tungusic (SSTMJa 1: 440a; Ščerbak 1997: 143) and Mongolic (Doerfer TMEN 3: 551–554; ESTJa 2000: 175–177) languages. From Mongolic, the word was re-borrowed into Tuvan (Khabtagaeva 2009: 269).

1.1.6 Hunting Terminology

Ket *áʁses* 'bear trap' (Werner 2002/1: 56) < **áʁse* -s {Ket nominalizer}:

*áʁse ← ? Northern Tungusic: Ewenki *amākākse* 'bear's skin; bear's flesh' < *amā* 'father; *taboo* bear' +*kā* {Ewenki NN, see Vasilevič 1958: 758} +*kse* {Ewenki NN/adj., see Vasilevič 1958: 763}:
    Podkamennyi, Upper Lena, Tokmin Ewenki *amākākse* 'bear's skin; bear's flesh' < Common Ewenki *amākā* 'grandfather (*father's or mother's father*); uncle (*older brother of father or mother*); ancestor; bear; sky, God' < *amā* 'father';
    cf. Northern Tungusic: Lamut *amā* 'father; grandfather (*father's or mother's father*)'; Negidal *amaj* 'father'; Southern Tungusic: Oroch *ama* 'father'; Udihe *amin-* 'father's'; Ulcha *ama* 'father'; Orok *ama ~ amma* 'father', cf. *amaqa* 'grandfather; bear'; Nanai *ama* 'father'; Jurchen *'á-mîn* 'father'; Manchu *ama* 'father'; Sibe *ama* 'father'.

Etymology: SSTMJa 1: 34b–35a; Khabtagaeva 2017d: 81

The Ket word probably contains a Yeniseian nominalizer *-s*. As a hypothesis, I assume that it is connected with the Podkamennyi Ewenki form *amākākse* 'bear's skin; bear's flesh', which was derived from the Common Tungusic word *amā* 'father' with the Ewenki diminutive suffix +*kā* (Vasilevič 1958: 758) and the Ewenki productive denominal noun suffix +*kse* forming the adjective forms

(Vasilevič 1958: 763). It is an interesting case that the Tungusic taboo word 'bear' goes back to the original meaning 'father'. From a phonetic perspective, the loss of the internal syllables occurred in the Ket form, which is typical for some Altaic loanwords.

The Ket word belongs to the category of words of uncertain etymology.

Ket *húktɛŋ* ~ *huktɛn* 'taboo bear eyes' (Werner 2002/1: 328) < **huktɛ -ŋ* {Ket plural}:
*huktɛ ← Northern Tungusic: Ewenki *hugdï* 'rapacious, predatory' < *hug* 'bear, predator' +*dï* {Ewenki NN/adj., see Vasilevič 1958: 755}:

    Podkamennyi Ewenki *hugdï* 'rapacious, predatory'; cf. *Northern Ewenki*: Yerbogachon; *Southern Ewenki*: Podkamennyi, Nepa, Upper Lena; *Eastern Ewenki*: Aldan, Uchur, Chumikan *hug* ~ *hūg* 'bear; hungry';

    cf. Northern Tungusic: Lamut *hukečen* 'bear'; Negidal *xūγēčēn* ~ *xūxēčēn*; Southern Tungusic: –.

Etymology: SSTMJa 2: 337a

The etymology of Ket word 'bear eyes' may be connected to the Podkamennyi Ewenki adjective *hugdï* 'rapacious, predatory bear' with the Ket plural suffix -*ŋ* (for details, see Georg 2007: 92–93).

The word also belongs to a group of taboo words in Tungusic.

Ket *tʌnsʼuk* 'taboo designation of a bear stomach' (Werner 2002/2: 298) ← Northern Tungusic: Ewenki *tuŋsuku* 'a bear head, a "funeral" of bear':

    Eastern Ewenki: Uchur, Urmi, Chumikan *tuŋsuku* 'a bear head, a "funeral" of bear; a funeral of people on the tree (*ancient way of burial*)';

    cf. Northern Tungusic: Negidal *texseke* 'a forehead of bear'; Remaining lgs. –.

Etymology: SSTMJa 2: 216b

The Ket word is obviously related to the Ewenki word, possibly, the semantic change happened: "head" → "stomach". From a phonetic point of view, the Tungusic vowel -*u*- in the first syllable regularly changed to -*ʌ*- and the final Ewenki consonant is dropped in Ket.

The Ewenki word belongs to the group of taboos. The base of word is **tuŋ* 'head', cf. Ewenki dial. *tuŋkulbu-* (< **tuŋ* +*kU-lbU-* {Ewenki NV, VV, see Vasilevič 1958: 767}) 'to bend, to incline a head down', *tuŋkin-* (< **tuŋ* +*kIn-* {Ewenki NV, see Vasilevič 1958: 762}) 'to bend, to incline a head down', *tuŋulkēn* (< **tuŋ* +*lkĀn* {Ewenki NN, see Vasilevič 1958: 768}) 'crown, skull'. The derivation of Ewenki *tuŋsuku* is uncertain.

1.1.7   Harness and Means of Conveyance

Ket *aluk ~ álək ~ áləq ~ álok ~ áloq* 'dog harness' (Werner 2002/1: 27) ← Northern Tungusic: Ewenki *alaγ* 'strap' < **hala* 'harness' +γ {Ewenki NN, see Boldyrev 1987: 181–182}:

> *Northern Ewenki*: Yerbogachon; *Southern Ewenki*: Podkamennyi, Nepa; *Eastern Ewenki*: Zeya, Tungir, Aldan *alaγ* 'strap in reindeer harness';
> cf. Ewenki dial.: Ilimpeya, Sakhalin, Urmi, Chumikan *ala*; Uchur *aliγ ~ alik*;
> Northern Tungusic: Lamut *al ~ alak ~ ālik* 'strap in reindeer harness; dogharness'; Negidal *ala ~ alan* 'dogharness'; Southern Tungusic: Oroch *ala* 'dogharness'; Udihe *ala* 'dogharness'; Ulcha *hala* 'dogharness; gun belt'; Orok *hali* 'harness'; Nanai *hala* 'dogharness'; Jurchen –; Manchu *alami-* 'carry on the back'; Sibe –;

Tungusic → Turkic:
> Yakut *ālik* 'belt of dog harness' (Slepcov); Yakut dial. *ala* 'reindeer harness' (Romanova, Myreeva & Baraškov 1975: 166).

Etymology: SSTMJa 1: 28b

The Ket word was clearly borrowed from Ewenki (Werner 2002/1: 27). From a phonetic perspective, the Tungusic vowel *-a-* in the second syllable—possibly due to an accent in the first syllable—changed to *ə ~ o ~ u* in Ket; and the Ewenki final consonant *-g* devoiced in Ket.

Etymologically, the Tungusic word derived from the noun *ala* 'harness' and the Common Tungusic productive denominal noun suffix +γ, which forms nouns with the collective or the same meaning (for details on functions, see Boldyrev 1987: 181–185).

The Tungusic word was borrowed into Literary Yakut and the Yakut dialects (Romanova, Myreeva & Baraškov 1975: 166).

Ket *imejaŋ* 'reindeer harness neck-rope' (Vajda & Werner: in preparation) < **ime -j-* {linking consonant} + *aŋ* 'rope' (Werner 2002/1: 39):
*ime ← Northern Tungusic **imme*: Podkamennyi *immer*, Nepa *immen* 'halter (*occipital strap, reindeer halter straps*); halter belt, over the eyes of a deer, across the forehead':

> Southern Ewenki: Podkamennyi *immer*, Nepa *immen*, Upper Lena *inman ~ inmar*; Eastern Ewenki: Uchur, Chumikan, Tommot *itmar*, Sakhalin *inman ~ inmar*;
> cf. Northern Tungusic: Lamut *inmer ~ inmar ~ inmor*; Remaining lgs.: –.

Etymology: SSTMJa 1: 316a

The Ket word belongs to a group of compound hybrid words, which consists of the Ewenki base **imme* 'halter' and a native Yeniseian word *àŋ* 'rope'. The source of borrowing was the Podkamennyi or Nepa dialects, where the palatal vowel *-e-* is found. The Ewenki intervocalic geminate *VmmV* simplified and the final consonant (*-n* or *-r*) merged to a second part of the compound word. The appearance of consonant -*j*- before Yeniseian -*aŋ* can explained as a linking consonant between vowels.

The etymological background of the Tungusic word is uncertain. The word is present only in Ewenki and Lamut. The morpohological structure of the Tungusic word is also unclear.

Central Ket, Northern Ket *lačako* ~ *lúčkɔ* 'reindeer saddle'; Central Ket *lɔčik* 'child's saddle' (Werner 2002/2: 1) ← Northern Tungusic: Ewenki *ločoko* 'saddle':

> *Northern Ewenki*: Yerbogachon, Ilimpeya; *Southern Ewenki*: Podkamennyi, Nepa, Northern Baikal; *Eastern Ewenki*: Barguzin *ločoko*, cf. Nercha *lačako* 'saddle for transportation the packs; the wooden base of saddle';
> Remaining lgs. –.

Etymology: SSTMJa 1: 506a

The Ket word is considered to be a Tungusic loanword (Werner 2002/2: 1). The etymology of the Ewenki word is not clear. Among Tungusic languages, the word is present only in the Ewenki dialects.

Central Ket *naroboks*, Northern Ket *naravoks* 'long steering pole of a reindeer team' (Werner 2002/2: 26) < **nara -b-* {epenthetic consonant, Vajda 2014: personal communication} -*oks* {Ket half-affix with meaning 'wooden object'} (Werner 2002/1: 34; Georg 2007: 133):

*nara ← Northern Tungusic: Ewenki *nara* 'castrated reindeer bull, reindeer':

> *Northern Ewenki*: Yerbogachon *nara* 'reindeer'; *Southern Ewenki*: Podkamennyi *nārā* 'castrated reindeer bull', Sym *nara* 'reindeer';
> cf. Remaining lgs. –.

Etymology: SSTMJa 1: 585a

The Ket word belongs to the category of hybrid compound words, where the first part connects to the Ewenki word *nara* 'reindeer', while the second part -*oks* is the Ket half-affix, which forms words designating wood and wooden objects (for details on functions, see Georg 2007: 133).

In turn, the etymology of the Ewenki word is uncertain. Among Tungusic languages, the word is present only in Ewenki and may be the loanword.

Northern Ket *ɔmɔyin* 'reindeer saddle' (Vajda & Werner: in preparation) ← Northern Tungusic: Ewenki *emegen* 'saddle; reindeer saddle' ← Mongolic *emegel* 'saddle':

> *Northern Ewenki*: Yerbogachon, Ilimpeya; *Southern Ewenki*: Podkamennyi, Upper Lena, Nercha; *Eastern Ewenki*: Zeya, Ayan, Aldan, Uchur, Urmi, Tokko, Tommot, Sakhalin, Barguzin *emegen*;

cf. Northern Tungusic: Lamut *emgun ~ ömgun ~ umgun*; Southern Tungusic: Orok *emēn ~ emeγen*; Jurchen *'ēn-kô-mài*; Manchu *eŋgemu*; Sibe *eŋemu*; Remaining lgs. –;
Tungusic ← Mongolic *emegel* 'saddle':
Middle Mongol: Precl.Mo. *emegēl*; SH *eme'el*; YY *eme'el*; ZY *emēl*; Muq. *emel*; Ist. *yeme'el*; RH *emēl*; LM *emegel*; Modern Mongol: Buryat *emēl*; Khalkha *emēl*; Oirat dial. *emā̆l' ~ emā̆l*; Dagur *ämā̆l*; Khamnigan *emēl ~ emō̆l ~ ömō̆l*.

Etymology: SSTMJa 2: 452b; Derfer 1985: 21; Rozycki 1994: 70; Nugteren 2011: 329

The Ket word was clearly borrowed from Ewenki. It can be strengthened by phonetic and semantic comparisons. Phonetically, the Ewenki vowel -*e*- in different positions rounded to -*ɔ*- and changed to -*i*-.

From an etymological point of view, the Tungusic word is of Mongolic origin (SSTMJa 2: 452b; Doerfer 1985: 21; Rozycki 1994: 70). The Ket final consonant -*n* proves that the borrowing is from Tungusic.

Southern Ket *sū·ŋ* 'team of dogs' (Vajda & Werner: in preparation) < **sū -ŋ* {Ket collective suffix}:
*sū ← Northern Tungusic: Podkamennyi Ewenki *suna* 'team of dogs; belt, which is tied to hunting dogs (*in team of dogs*)':
Northern Ewenki: Yerbogachon, Ilimpeya *huna*; Southern Ewenki: Podkamennyi; Eastern Ewenki: Zeya, Aldan, Uchur, Urmi, Chumikan, Sakhalin *suna*;
cf. Northern Tungusic: Lamut *hūŋkan*; Negidal –; Southern Tungusic: Oroch –; Udihe –; Ulcha *suna* 'shaman's belt'; Orok *suna* 'team of dogs'; Nanai *sona* 'belt; shaman's belt'; Jurchen –; Manchu *suna ~ sūna* 'team of dogs'; Sibe –.

Etymology: SSTMJa 2: 127a

The Ket word is clearly connected to Ewenki *suna*. The final nasal -*ŋ* is probably the Ket collective suffix. Possibly, the Ket vowel *ū* was lengthened to compensate for the loss of the Ewenki segment -*na*.

Semantic widening occurred in Tungusic; besides the original meaning 'belt' (cf. Ulcha, Nanai),[13] the word gained the meaning 'belt which is tied to hunting dogs' related to harness terminology and further 'team of dogs'. The last meaning was borrowed into Ket.

Northern Ket *učik* 'saddle for a reindeer' (Vajda & Werner: in preparation) ← Northern Tungusic: Podkamennyi Ewenki *ūčak* 'reindeer' < *uγ(u)-* 'to sit to ride a reindeer' -*čA*- {Ewenki VV, see Vasilevič 1958: 796} -*k* {Ewenki VN, see Vasilevič 1958: 757–758}:

---

13 Cf. the Common Tungusic verb *sūn-* 'to strech (*about leather*)' (SSTMJa 2: 126b).

Northern Ewenki: Yerbogachon; *Southern Ewenki*: Podkamennyi, Northern Baikal, Nercha; *Eastern Ewenki*: Aldan, Uchur, Chumikan *ūčak* 'reindeer';

cf. Northern Tungusic: Lamut *ūčiq* ~ *ūčaq*; Negidal *okčax* ~ *okčāk*; Southern Tungusic: Oroch *ū-* 'to sit, to ride'; Ulcha *ū-* 'to sit (*transport*)'; Orok *ū-*; Nanai *ō-*; Remaining lgs. –.

Etymology: SSTMJa 2: 243b

The Ket word was obviously borrowed from Ewenki. The original lexical meaning 'reindeer' acquired in Ket the special meaning of 'saddle for a reindeer'.

From an etymological point of view, the Ewenki word derived from the Common Tungusic verb *uγ(u)-* ~ *ū-* 'to sit to ride a reindeer' with the Northern Tungusic productive deverbal verbum suffix *-čA-*[14] and the productive deverbal noun suffix *-k*.

1.1.8 Food

Ket *kútgit* 'dish of intestines' (Werner 2002/1: 456) < *kútgi -t* {?} ← Northern Tungusic: Ewenki *gudige* 'stomach of animals' ← Mongolic *güjege* 'stomach of animals; rumen used as container for butter, kumiss':

Northern Ewenki: Yerbogachon, Ilimpeya; *Southern Ewenki*: Podkamennyi, Nercha; *Eastern Ewenki*: Barguzin *gudiyē*;

cf. Northern Tungusic: *Eastern Ewenki*: Zeya, Tokko, Uchur, Urmi, Tommot, Chumikan, Sakhalin *gudī*; *Southern Ewenki*: Northern Baikal *gūdexe*; Lamut *gudi*; Negidal *gudi*; Southern Tungusic: Oroch –; Udihe *gudie*; Ulcha –; Orok –; Nanai *gūjẽ*; Jurchen –; Manchu *guwejihe*; Sibe *gujuge*;

Tungusic ← Mongolic *güjege* 'stomach of animals; rumen used as container for butter, kumiss':

Middle Mongol: YY *güje[e]* 'belly, stomach'; Muq. *güjēn*; RH *güjēn*; LM *güjege*; Modern Mongol: Buryat *güzē(n)*; Khalkha *güdzē*; Kalmuck *güzän*; Dagur *gujē* (E); Khamnigan *güdzē(n)* ~ *güdzō(n)* ~ *güdžō(n)*.

Etymology: SSTMJa 1: 167a; Doerfer 1985: 22; Nugteren 2011: 346

The Ket word was possibly borrowed from the Ewenki form **gudige*. The devoicing of initial Tungusic *g-* > *k-* is a characteristic phonetic feature for Ket loanwords, which points to an early period of borrowing. In addition, a syncope occurred. The origin of the Ket final consonant *-t* is uncertain, it may have happened as the result of assimilation.

---

14 The Northern Tungusic suffix *-čA-* forms intransitive verbs from transitive, e.g. Ewenki *nī-* 'to open' > *niče-* 'to be opened', *bē-* 'to put baby in the cradle' > *bēče-* 'to lie in the cradle' (for details, see Vasilevič 1958: 796). In this way, Ewenki *uγu-* 'to sit on or ride a reindeer' > *uγuča-* ~ *ūkča-* 'to ride reindeer'.

Etymologically, the Tungusic word is of Mongolic origin (SSTMJa 1: 167a; Doerfer 1985: 22).

Ket *qʌbdal* 'slice of bear bacon fat' (Werner 2002/2: 141) ← Northern Tungusic: Podkamennyi Ewenki *hepete tile* 'bear bacon fat' < *hepete* 'bear' + *tile* 'bear bacon fat':
< *hepete* 'bear':
   Southern Ewenki: Podkamennyi *hepete*;
   cf. Remaining lgs. –;
Etymology: SSTMJa 2: 368a
+ *tile* 'bear bacon fat':
   Northern Ewenki: Yerbogachon; Southern Ewenki: Podkamennyi *tile* 'bear bacon fat, bear';
   Northern Ewenki: Yerbogachon, Ilimpeya; Southern Ewenki: Podkamennyi, Sym; Eastern Ewenki: Zeya, Aldan, Uchur *tile-* 'to eat bear meat';
   cf. Remaining lgs. –;
Etymology: SSTMJa 2: 181b

As a working hypothesis, I suggest that the Ket word was borrowed from the Podkamennyi Ewenki compound word *hepete tile* 'bear bacon fat'. Possibly, amalgamation occurred and the original final vowel dropped. The initial Ewenki *h-* changed to *q-* in Ket, which is a typical feature for Tungusic loanwords.

In turn, the etymologies of the Tungusic words are unknown, since they exist only in a few Ewenki dialects.

1.1.9   House, Household Equipment and Tools

Ket *dankijaj* 'rucksack' (Vajda & Werner: in preparation) < *dankij + Yeniseian *aj* 'sack' (Werner 2002/1: 18):
*dankij ← Northern Tungusic: Ewenki *daŋanī* 'name of bone (*shoulder bone, hip bone, shin bone*)':
   Southern Ewenki: Podkamennyi *daŋańā ~ daŋanī ~ daɣańa*;
   cf. Northern Tungusic: Southern Ewenki: Sym, Upper Lena, Northern Baikal; Eastern Ewenki: Uchur, *daɣańa*; Northern Ewenki: Yerbogachon; Eastern Ewenki: Tungir *daŋajā*; Southern Ewenki: Sym; Eastern Ewenki: Zeya *daŋanī*; Southern Ewenki: Nepa; Eastern Ewenki: Zeya *daŋańā*; Negidal *daɣańa* 'hip bone'; Southern Tungusic: Orok *dāna* 'name of bone (*shoulder bone, hip bone, shin bone*); thigh; shoulder (*upper arm until elbow*)'; Remaining lgs. –.
Etymology: SSTMJa 1: 188b; Khabtagaeva 2017: 79

The Ket word belongs to a group of hybrid compound words, which consists of the Ewenki word *daŋanī* 'name of shoulder bone' and the Yeniseian word *aj* 'sack'.

Ket *hɔttɔn* 'left or the right area in a tent'; Northern Ket *hɔ́ttɔn* 'middle place in a tent' (Werner 2002/1: 327) ← Northern Tungusic: Ewenki *horan* < *haran* 'house; the place for tent; floor; hearth area in the middle of Tungusic house':

> *Northern Ewenki*: Yerbogachon, Ilimpeya; *Southern Ewenki*: Podkamennyi *horan*; cf. Northern Tungusic: *Eastern Ewenki*: Zeya, Tungir, Aldan, Uchur, Urmi, Sakhalin, Barguzin *haran* ~ *harān*; Lamut *harān* ~ *arān*; Negidal *xajān*; Southern Tungusic: Oroch *xān* (< **xajan* < **xaran*); Remaining lgs. –.

Etymology: SSTMJa 2: 317

The Ket word is clearly related to the Ewenki form *horan* with the rounded vowel *-o-* peculiar for the Podkamennyi, Yerbogachon and Ilimpeya dialects, but the change of Tungusic intervocalic *VrV* > *VtV* is unclear. The Tungusic etymology fits from the a semantic perspective.

Originally, the Ewenki form goes back to *haran* with unrounded vowels.

Ket *il't* ~ *íl'tə* 'roof of a dugout' (Werner 2002/1: 361) ← ? Northern Tungusic **eltin*: Ewenki *elben* 'roof of *chum*—Tungusic house' < *elbe-* (> **elbi-* ~ **elti-*) 'to cover *chum*' *-n* {Ewenki VN, see Vasilevič 1958: 777; Boldyrev 1987: 138}:

> *Southern Ewenki*: Podkamennyi, Nepa, Sym, Upper Lena, Northern Baikal; *Eastern Ewenki*: Zeya, Aldan, Uchur, Chumikan *elben*; Urmi *ilben*, Tokko *elbeptun*, Tungir *elwun* 'roof for *chum*—Tungusic house' < *Southern Ewenki*: Podkamennyi, Nepa, Sym, Kachug, Upper Lena, Northern Baikal; Eastern Ewenki: Zeya, Tungir, Aldan, Uchur, Sakhalin *elbe-*, cf. Urmi *ilbe-* 'to cover *chum*';
> cf. Northern Tungusic: Lamut *elbe-* ~ *älbä-* ~ *ölbö-* ~ *ölbe-* ~ *elbi-* ~ *elti-*; Negidal *elbe-*; Southern Tungusic: Oroch *ebbe-*; Udihe *egbe-*; Ulcha *elbene* 'covering (*for fish or meat*)'; Orok –; Nanai *elbẽ* 'roof'; Jurchen –; Manchu *elbe-*; Sibe –.

Etymology: SSTMJa 2: 445

I assume the Ket forms are linked to the reconstructed Northern Tungusic form **eltin*, which is absent in Ewenki. There are different Ewenki dialectal forms *elbene* ~ *elwun* ~ *elbun* ~ *ilben* ~ *ellun* with the same meaning 'roof of *chum*' and derived from the verb *elbe-* 'to cover house' with a highly productive Tungusic deverbal noun suffix *-n* (for details on functions, see Boldyrev 1987: 138). For a reconstruction **elti* help the different Lamut forms *elbe-* ~ *älbä-* ~ *ölbö-* ~ *ölbe-* ~ *elbi-* ~ *elti-* 'to cover *chum*' where the assimilated *lb* > *lt* clusters are found (SSTMJa 2: 445).

The disappearance of the final Tungusic *-n* in the Ket forms may have occurred when the sound was reanalyzed as the Ket plural suffix *-n*.

The word belongs to the category of words of uncertain etymology.

Kott ***kaltapen*** 'wedge for splitting wood' (Werner 2002/1: 406) < *kalta -p-* {?} + Yeniseian *e·n* 'wedge' (Werner 2002/1: 272):

kalta ← Tungusic: Ewenki *kalta-* 'to crack, to break up in two parts; to split in half':

Southern Ewenki: Podkamennyi; *Eastern Ewenki*: Zeya, Tokko, Aldan, Uchur, Tommot, Sakhalin *kalta-*;

cf. Northern Tungusic: Lamut *kalta- ~ kalti-*; Negidal *kalta-*; Southern Tungusic: Oroch *kākta-*; Udihe *kaktaga-* 'to be splitted'; Ulcha *qalta* 'half; crack; side; country'; Orok *qalta ~ qaltā* 'half; crack'; Nanai *qaltā-* 'to crack, to split'; Remaining lgs. –.

Etymology: SSTMJa 1: 367b

According to Werner (2002/1: 406), the final part *eˑn* of the Kott word is clearly of Yeniseian origin, but the first part is uncertain. The Kott word possibly belongs to the category of hybrid compound words, which consists of the Tungusic verb *kalta-* 'to split' and the native Yeniseian word *eˑn* 'wedge'. The problematic side of the Tungusic etymology is the absence of Tungusic loanwords in Kott. In the most cases, Turkic elements are typical for Kott. From a semantic and phonetic perspective, however, the Tungusic meaning is in accord with the Kott word. The consonant -*p*- in the Kott form is of unknown origin.

The Common Tungusic verb *kalta-* 'to crack, to break up in two parts; to split in half' is widespread in almost all the Tungusic languages.

Southern Ket *käˑr* 'clothes rack made of bird-cherry (*Prunus padus*) wood' (Werner 2002/1: 418) ← Northern Tungusic: Ewenki *karje* 'root of bird-cherry':

Yerbogachon *karje*; *Northern Ewenki*: Ilimpeya; *Southern Ewenki*: Podkamennyi, Sym *kar*;

cf. Upper Lena *karjen*; Uchur, Urmi *kari*;

cf. Remaining lgs. –.

Etymology: SSTMJa 1: 379a

The Ket word clearly is connected to the Ewenki word. From a semantic perspective, broadening occurred in Ket: 'root of bird-cherry' → 'rack made of bird-cherry wood'. Phonetically, the palatalization of the Ewenki vowel -*a*- > -*ä*- in Ket can be explained by the following vowel -*je*, which dropped word-finally in Ket. The disappearance of the final vowel in the Southern Ket dialect is a regular phonetic feature, e.g. Southern Ket *bāk*, cf. Central *bāke* 'block of wood'; Southern Ket *ēj*, cf. Central Ket *ējə*, Northern Ket *ēji* 'tongue'; Southern Ket *qād*, cf. Central and Northern Ket *qāde* 'wool', etc. (for details and more examples, see Georg 2007: 53–56).

In turn, the etymology of the Ewenki word is unknown. Among Tungusic languages, the word is present only in Ewenki. Authors of SSTMJa (1: 379) link it with the Yakut word *xarï* 'forearm' (cf. Old Turkic *qarï*), which is not be sustained from a semantic point of view.

Ket ***kɔjel*** ~ ***kɔ́jil*** 'pan' (Werner 2002/1: 438) < *kɔje + Yeniseian *εˀl* 'cup' (Werner 2002/1: 256):
*kɔje ← Northern Tungusic: Ewenki *kaja* 'pan' ← Mongolic *kayiba* 'large kettle; frying pan':
> *Northern Ewenki*: Ilimpeya; *Southern Ewenki*: Podkamennyi *kāja* 'pan';
> cf. Remaining lgs. –;

Tungusic ← Mongolic *kayiba* 'large kettle; frying pan':
> Middle Mongol: –; LM *qayiba* ~ *qayibi* ~ *qayibu*; Modern Mongol: Buryat –; Khalkha *xaiw* 'a broad-rimmed pot or pan'; Kalmuck –; Dagur –; Khamnigan –.

Etymology: SSTMJa 1: 361b

Werner (2002/1: 438), after Helimski (1982: 22), connects the Ket word with Selkup *kɔjɔl* ~ *kɔjal* 'pan'.

I suppose that it might have been the hybrid compound word, which consists of Ewenki *kaja* 'pan' and a native Yeniseian word *εˀl* 'cup' (Werner 2002/1: 256). It is also possible that the final -*l* is another example of this sound appearing at the end of Ewenki loans into Ket (see chapter *Word-final -l of unknown origin in Altaic loanwords*), and Selkup then borrowed it from Ket.

From an etymological aspect, the Ewenki word was borrowed from Mongolic (SSTMJa 1: 361b), but the etymology of the Mongolic word is uncertain. Among Mongolic languages, it is present only in Literary Mongolian and Khalkha. Possibly, the base of the word is *qayi which is connected to *qayira-* 'to fry, grill, roast; to single with a hot iron; to cauterize, to scorch' and *qayil-* 'to thaw, to fuse, to melt'. The origin of the Mongolic suffixes +*bA* /+*bi* / +*bU* is also unclear.

Ket ***kolij*** 'covered storeroom' (Werner 2002/1: 439) < *kol + Yeniseian *iˀ* 'storage shed' (Werner 2002/1: 389):
*kol ← Northern Tungusic: Ewenki *kolbo* 'storage shed' ← Mongolic *qolbo-* 'to unite, combine, connect, incorporate; to link to; to unite in marriage' ← Turkic *kolbŏ-*: cf. Old Turkic *qoš-* 'to conjoin, unite (*two things*)':
> *Southern Ewenki*: Podkamennyi *kolbo* 'storage shed (*platform on piles, with a roof*); storeroom, barn';
> cf. *Eastern Ewenki*: Zeya, Tungir, Tokko, Aldan, Uchur, Urmi, Tommot, Chumikan, Sakhalin, Barguzin *kolbo* 'storage shed (*platform on piles, with a roof*); storeroom, barn', *kolbo-* 'to put products on storage shed';
> Southern Tungusic: Manchu *holbo-* 'to connect, to join; to pair, to mate, to get married, to implicate'; Sibe *holbo-* ~ *holbu-* 'id.'; Remaining lgs. –;

Tungusic ← Mongolic *qolbo-* 'to unite, combine, connect, incorporate; to link to; to unite in marriage':
   Middle Mongol: Precl.Mo. *qolba-*; SH *qolba'ara- ~ qolbara-* (< *qolba-rA-*) *'intr.* to unite'; Muq. *qolba-*; LM *qolbo- ~ qolba-*; Modern Mongol: Buryat *xolbo-*; Khalkha *xolbo-*; Oirat dial. *xolwă- ~ xolbă-*; Dagur *xolb-* (E); Khamnigan *xolbo-*;
Mongolic → Modern Turkic:
   cf. NE^S YeniseiT: –; AltaiT: Altai *kolbo-* 'to bind several objects into one, put in a bunch'; SayanT: Tuvan *xolbā* 'connection'; ChulymT –; NE^N Yakut *xolbū* 'connection'; Dolgan *kolbō-* 'to connect'; Remaining lgs. –;
Mongolic ← Turkic:
   cf. Old Turkic *qoš-*; NE^S YeniseiT: Khakas *xos-*; AltaiT: Altai *koš-*; SayanT: Tuvan *koš-*; Tofan *qo*^{cš}*-*; ChulymT *qoš-*; NE^N –; NW^N Siberian Tatar *quš-*; NW^S Kirgiz *koš-*; Fu-yü –; Kazak *qos-*; SE Yellow Yughur –.
Etymology: Kałużyński 1961: 17; Räsänen VEWT 278a; Clauson ED 670b; SSTMJa 1: 406; Rassadin 1980: 65; Doerfer 1985: 61; Stachowski 1993: 150; Rozycki 1994: 107; Ščerbak 1997: 136; Helimski & Anikin 2007: 158; Nugteren 2011: 418

The Ket word belongs to category of hybrid compound words. It consists of two parts, Tungusic **kol* and Yeniseian *i*ˀ 'storage shed' (Werner 2002/1: 389). The first part **kol* is connected to the Podkamennyi Ewenki word *kolba* 'storage shed', where the final syllable disappeared.

From an etymological aspect, the Ewenki word is a Mongolic loanword (SST-MJa 1: 415; Doerfer 1985: 61), which is ultimately of Turkic origin (Clauson ED 670b; Ščerbak 1997: 136). Among Tungusic languages, the word was borrowed into Manchu and Sibe from Mongolic (Rozycki 1994: 107). The Mongolic verb was re-borrowed into some Siberian Turkic languages (Kałużyński 1961: 17; Räsänen VEWT 278a; Rassadin 1980: 65; Stachowski 1993: 150). Anikin and Helimski (2007: 158) erroneously connect the Ket word with other Tungusic form *korigan* 'fence, barn'.

Northern Ket *kɔlɔmɔ ~ gɔ́lɔmɔ* 'a kind of winter dwelling covered with sod' (Werner 2002/1: 439) ← Northern Tungusic: Ewenki *golomo* 'a kind of winter dwelling' < *golo* 'a log, a beam' +*mA* {Ewenki NN, see Vasilevič 1958: 769}:
   Northern Ewenki: Yerbogachon, Ilimpeya; *Southern Ewenki*: Podkamennyi, Tokma; *Eastern Ewenki*: Ayan *golomo* 'a kind of winter dwelling' < Yerbogachon, Ilimpeya; Podkamennyi, Nepa, Sym, Northern Baikal; Tungir, Aldan, Uchur, Urmi, Chumikan, Sakhalin *golo* 'a log, a beam';
   cf. Northern Tungusic: Lamut *goloma* < *gol* 'firewood'; Negidal *golo* 'log, beam'; Southern Tungusic: Oroch *golo*; Udihe *golo* 'half-rotten log'; Ulcha *goloŋqo* 'firewood, stack'; Orok *golo* 'log'; Nanai *γoloŋqo* 'firewood, stack'; Jurchen –; Manchu *γoldon ~ γolton* 'charred ends of wood, charred stump'; Sibe –;

Tungusic → Modern Turkic:
   cf. NE^N Yakut *golomo* 'tent, summer tent made of birch bark', cf. *kalïman ~ kuluma* 'temporary winter dwelling'; Dolgan *golomo ~ xolomo* 'dugout; a kind of winter tent, which covered with soil or snow';

Tungusic → Siberian Russian:
   golomo 'old type of dwelling'.

Etymology: SSTMJa 1: 159b; Romanova, Myreeva & Baraškov 1975: 165; Stachowski 1993: 86; Anikin 2000: 167; Khabtagaeva 2017: 76

The Northern Ket word has clear Tungusic etymology. It was borrowed from the Ewenki form *golomo*, which derived from the Common Tungusic word *golo* 'log, beam' and the Ewenki productive suffix +*mA* (for details on the functions, see Vasilevič 1958: 769; Boldyrev 1987: 75–77; Nedjalkov 1997: 297).

The devoicing of the Tungusic initial *g*- is a regular change in Ket, which points to an early period of borrowing. The initial *g*- is typical only for loanwords in Ket.

In addition to Yeniseian, the word was borrowed into Yakut and Dolgan from Tungusic as well (SSTMJa 1: 159b; Romanova, Myreeva & Baraškov 1975: 165; Stachowski 1993: 86), and further to Siberian Russian (Anikin 2000: 167).

Ket *layun ~ laún*; Yugh *lagún* 'barrel' (Werner 2002/2: 4) ← ? Northern Tungusic: Ewenki *lagun* 'barrel' ← Russian *lagun* 'wooden barrel for liquid' (cf. Turkic *lāġūn* 'a hollow object like a grain measure used for drinking milk or water'):
   Podkamennyi Ewenki *lagun* 'barrel (*big wooden tub for fish, berries, wild onion*)';
   cf. Remaining lgs. –;

Tungusic ← Russian *lagun* 'wooden barrel for liquid';
cf. Turkic:
   cf. Old Turkic *lāġūn* 'a hollow object like a grain measure used for drinking milk or water'.

Etymology: Clauson ED 764a; SSTMJa 1: 486b

The Ket word has a clear Russian etymology. The source of borrowing may be Podkamennyi Ewenki or directly from Russian. The word belongs to the category of "Wanderwort", present also in Turkic. Clauson (ED 764a) considers that the Turkic word originates from Assyrian. Vasmer (1986/2: 446) traces the Russian word back to Greek. In turn, the Tungusic word was borrowed from Russian (SSTMJa 1: 486b).

Ket *saŋɔl* 'chimney of a dug-out', cf. Central Ket *sɔnal* 'smoke hole of a dug-out' (Vajda & Werner: in preparation) < *saŋɔ / *sɔna -*l* {?}
*saŋɔ / *sɔna ← Northern Tungusic: Ewenki *sōna* 'smoke hole of a dug-out; chimney of a dug-out':

Southern Ewenki: Podkamennyi, Nepa, Tokma, Baunt; *Eastern Ewenki*: Zeya, Tungir, Ayan, Aldan, Uchur, Urmi *sōna*;

Eastern Ewenki: Barguzin *sōŋa*; *Northern Ewenki*: Yerbogachon, Ilimpeya *hōna*;

cf. Northern Tungusic: Lamut *hōnan ~ hōnān* 'smoke hole of a dug-out; rafter'; Negidal *sōna* 'id.'; Southern Tungusic: Oroch *sōno* 'smoke hole of a dug-out'; Udihe –; Ulcha *sōn* 'roof rafter'; Orok *sōno* 'smoke hole of a dug-out; rafter'; Nanai *sõ* 'roof rafter; pole'; Jurchen –; Manchu *son* 'pole'; Sibe –;

Tungusic → Turkic:

NE^N Yakut *suona* 'chimney of a dug-out'.

Etymology: SSTMJa 2: 110; Khabtagaeva 2017d: 83

The Ket forms are clearly connected with Podkamennyi Ewenki. There are two different phonetic forms in Ket where a vowel metathesis occurred. In one case, the *-n- > -ŋ-* change occurred. The Ket final consonant *-l* is of unknown origin.

The Ewenki word was also borrowed into Yakut where the Ewenki long vowel *-ō-* presented as a diphthong *-uo-* (Romanova, Myreeva & Baraškov 1975: 175).

Ket *tál'ma* 'vessel of birch bark for berries' (Werner 2002/2: 233) ← Northern Tungusic: Ewenki *talmī* 'vessel of birch bark (carried on back)' < *talu* 'birchbark' +*mī* {Ewenki NN, see Vasilevič 1958: 773}:

Northern Ewenki: Yerbogachon, Ilimpeya; *Southern Ewenki*: Podkamennyi, Sym *talmī* 'vessel of birch bark for berries';

cf. *Northern Ewenki*: Yerbogachon, Ilimpeya; *Southern Ewenki*: Podkamennyi, Nepa, Sym, Northern Baikal, Nercha; *Eastern Ewenki*: Zeya, Tungir, Ayan, Tokko, Aldan, Uchur, Urmi, Chumikan, Sakhalin *talu* 'birchbark';

Northern Tungusic 'birchbark': Lamut –; Negidal *talu*; Southern Tungusic: Oroch *talu*; Udihe *taluga*; Ulcha *talu*; Orok *talu*; Nanai *talo*; Jurchen –; Manchu *tolhon*; Sibe –.

Etymology: SSTMJa 2: 158

The Ket word obviously was borrowed from the Ewenki form *talmī* with the same lexical meaning. The Ewenki consonant *-l-* palatalized in Ket under of the influence of *-ī* vowel.

1.1.10   Clothing

Northern Ket *dɔktɔraŋ* 'socks made from reindeer hide' (Werner 2002/1: 195) ← Northern Tungusic: Ewenki *doktokōn* 'fur shoes, worn on boots' < *doqto* 'fur or cotton stockings' +*KĀn* {Ewenki NN/diminutive, see Vasilevič 1958: 759}:

Podkamennyi Ewenki *doktokōn ~ dektekēn* 'fur shoes, worn on boots';

cf. *Northern Ewenki*: Ilimpeya; *Southern Ewenki*: Podkamennyi, Tokma; *Eastern Ewenki*: Zeya, Tokko, Uchur, Urmi, Tommot, Chumikan *dokton ~ dekten* 'fur stockings';

Northern Tungusic: Lamut *dōten* 'fur stockings'; Negidal *dokton* 'stockings (*fur, cloth, cotton*)'; Southern Tungusic: Oroch *dokton* 'fur or leather stockings'; Udihe *dokti* 'fur stockings'; Ulcha *doqto* 'fur or cotton stockings'; Orok *doqto* 'fur or cotton stockings'; Nanai *doqto* 'fur or cotton stockings'; Remaining lgs. –.

Etymology: SSTMJa 1: 213a; Khabtagaeva 2017d: 80

The Ket word is obviously connected to the Common Tungusic word *doqto* 'fur stockings', which is present in almost all Tungusic languages. The Podkamennyi Ewenki borrowing is demonstrated by the presence of the diminutive suffix +*KĀn* (for details on functions and examples, see Vasilevič 1958: 759; Boldyrev 1987: 5–6), which is absent in other Tungusic forms.

The origin of the Ket final -*aŋ* is unclear, it may be the Yeniseian plural suffix or the Tungusic diminutive suffix. The Ket unrounded vowel -*a*- is in favor of Yeniseian solution, but the change of the Tungusic consonant *n* > *ŋ* in different positions is typical for Ket loanwords. The change of *VkV* > *VrV* is also uncertain.

Ket *hitaj* 'size (*of clothes*)' (Werner 2002/1: 346) ← Northern Tungusic: Ewenki *hegdï* 'size; big; many':

Northern Ewenki: Yerbogachon, Ilimpeya; *Southern Ewenki*: Podkamennyi, Nepa, Kachug, Upper Lena, Nercha; *Eastern Ewenki*: Zeya, Tungir, Aldan, Uchur, Urmi, Chumikan, Sakhalin, Barguzin *hegdï* 'quantity, size; big, tall';

cf. Northern Tungusic: Lamut *egde ~ ēgdi ~ egǰe* 'most of; big; more'; Negidal *egdi* 'a lot of'; Southern Tungusic: Oroch *egdi* 'a lot of, many'; Udihe *egdi* 'many'; Ulcha *egdi* 'many, a lot of'; Orok *eǰi* 'a lot of'; Nanai *eǰi* 'a lot of, many'; Remaining lgs. –.

Etymology: SSTMJa 2: 359

The Ket word was possibly borrowed from the Ewenki form *hegdï* with the same lexical meaning. The diphtongization of the final vowel -*ï* in Ket is a regular phonetic feature in Tungusic loanwords. The Tungusic cluster -*gd*- simplified and devoiced to -*t*- in Ket.

The Tungusic word is widespread in Northern Tungusic and Southern Amuric with various meanings. According to other Tungusic forms, the initial *h*- is protethical in Ewenki.

Northern Ket *kulgum ~ hulgum*, Central Ket *hilgum* 'type of men's winter boots' (Werner 2002/1: 450) < **kulgu -um* {? < Ket plural -*əŋ*} ← Northern Tungusic: Ewenki *kelkē* 'fur shoes':

Eastern Ewenki: Tokko, Uchur, Tommot *kelkē* 'child's winter shoes; fur boots (*worn over shoes*)';

cf. Remaining lgs. –.

Etymology: SSTMJa 1: 446b

According to Werner (2002/1: 450), the Ket forms are borrowed from Ewenki. From a semantic perspective, the Tungusic lexical meaning is in accordance with the Ket word. Phonetically, the atypical change of vowels -*e*- > -*u*- happened. The origin of the Ket final -*m* is unclear: it may be the assimilated Ket plural suffix -*ŋ*, but the absence of similar examples does not support our hypothesis. The alternation of initial consonants *h*- ~ *k*- also suggests borrowing (Vajda: personal communication 2016).

The etymology of the Ewenki word is also problematic, it is present only in Ewenki dialects of Yakutia (SSTMJa 1: 446b). Cf. another Ewenki word *kelpeke* 'winter clothes of child', which is probably connected with *kelkē* 'child's winter shoes; fur boots (*worn over shoes*)'.

The etymology of the Ket word remains uncertain.

1.1.11   Names of Illness, Disease

Ket *doʔk* 'smallpox; pock marks' (Vajda & Werner: in preparation) ← Northern Tungusic: Ewenki *jūdek* 'smallpox' < *jūd'ēk* < *jū*- 'to get out; to leave' -*jĀk* {Ewenki VN, see Vasilievič 1958: 756}:

Southern Ewenki: Podkamennyi *jūdek* 'smallpox' (Boldyrev), cf. *jūd'ēk* 'exit, exanthema, rush, smallpox' (SSTMJa) < *jū*- 'to get out; to leave';

cf. Northern Tungusic: Lamut *ńō̆*- ~ *jō*- ~ *ńu*- ~ *ńū*-; Negidal *jū*- ~ *ńū*-; Southern Tungusic: Oroch *ńū*-; Udihe *ńū*-; Ulcha *ńie*- ~ *ńē*-; Orok *nē*-; Nanai *ńie*- ~ *ńē*- ~ *ńiu*-; Remaining lgs. –.

Etymology: SSTMJa 1: 348b–349a

The Ket word was borrowed from the Podkamennyi Ewenki dialectal form *jūdek* where the intervocalic consonant *VdV* developed from palatalized *Vd'V*. The Ewenki borrowing also shows the same meaning and the disappearance of the Ewenki initial syllable *jV*-, which is a typical phonetic feature for some Tungusic loanwords, cf. Ket *enna* 'really?' ← Ewenki *yēŋan*, Central Ket *aqtul* 'spring (*water coming out of the ground*)' ← Ewenki *jūkte* 'spring, brook', etc.

The fluctuation *j* ~ *d'* is characteristic not only for Ewenki dialects (Vasilevič 1948: 335), but for some Tungusic languages too (Cincius 1949: 211–212). The Ewenki form *jūjēk* derived from the Common Tungusic verb *jū*- 'to get out; to leave' and the Ewenki productive deverbal noun suffix -*jAk* which forms nouns that designate abstract ideas or process (for details on functions, see Vasilievič 1958: 753).

1.1.12   Monetary Units
Central Ket, Northern Ket **ulla ~ úlle** 'ruble, the monetary unit in Russia' (Donner 1955: 97) ← Northern Tungusic: Ewenki *ulukī* 'squirrel' < **ulu-kī* {Ewenki VN, see Vasilevič 1958: 761}:

Common Ewenki *ulukī*;

cf. Northern Tungusic: Lamut *öliki ~ úlikí ~ uliki ~ ul'ki*; Negidal *ölöxī ~ ölukī ~ eluxi*; Southern Tungusic: Oroch *oloki*; Udihe *oloxi*; Ulcha *xolo*; Orok *xolo ~ xulu*; Nanai *xulu ~ uluki*; Jurchen –; Manchu *ulhu*.

Etymology: SSTMJa 2: 263–264; Khabtagaeva 2017d: 85

As a hypothesis, I propose that the Ket forms may be connected with the Common Ewenki word *uluki* 'squirrel'. My assumption can be confirmed by the fact that the price of squirrel furs in the early 20th century was one ruble (Dolgikh 1934: 91). It is a well-known fact that Tungusic, Turkic and other native Siberian people paid fur animals like squirrel and sable as tribute and tax to the Russians.

Analogically, the Common Turkic word *täyiŋ* 'squirrel' with the lexical meaning 'squirrel, sable, lizard' also has an additional meaning of 'a small coin'. Clauson (ED 1972: 569a) it explained by the fact that squirrel skins were used as currency in early Russia during the period when coins were scarce.

From a phonetic perspective, the Ewenki final suffix *-kī* disappeared in Ket as in other borrowed names of animals. This suffix *-kī* is productive in Tungusic, it forms not only the names of animals, but also names of body parts, and human characteristics[15] (Vasilevič 1958: 761; Boldyrev 1987: 46–53). The base of the Tungusic word is **ulu-*, which connects to squirrel, cf. Ewenki *ulumēn* 'a dog used to hunt squirrel', *ulumī-* 'to hunt squirrel', Lamut *ulmijēk* 'the place, where earlier hunted squirrel', Nanai *xulukse* 'squirrel fir', etc.

1.1.13   Abstract Nouns
Ket *sē·tal ~ sē·til* 'height' (Vajda & Werner: in preparation) ← Northern Tungusic: Ewenki *sigdilē* 'distance between objects, interval':

Southern Ewenki: Podkamennyi, Nepa, Nercha; *Eastern Ewenki*: Zeya, Tungir, Tokko, Aldan, Uchur, Urmi, Tommot, Chumikan, Sakhalin *sigdilē*;

cf. Northern Tungusic: Lamut *hidlá ~ hitle ~ hi'le*; Negidal *sigle ~ sille*; Southern Tungusic: Ulcha *siduen* (← Manchu) 'pole for drying nets'; Nanai *sidū* 'beam, crossbar on

---

15   E.g. Ewenki *tuksakī* 'hare' < *tuksa-* 'to run', *arpukī* 'fin' < *arpu-* 'to swing, to wave', *ŋēlekī* 'coward' < *ŋēle-* 'to fear, to be afraid', Lamut *ŋēlekī* 'wolf' < *ŋēle-* 'to fear, to be afraid', *turākī* 'crow' < *tur-* 'to open a mouth', Oroch *sulaki* 'fox', *ŋāčaki* 'heron', etc. For more examples and suffix function in other Tungusic languages see Boldyrev (1987: 46–53).

the ceiling, on the platform'; Manchu *sīdu* ~ *sīden* 'distance; middle, center; space (*between heaven and earth*)'; Remaining lgs. –.

Etymology: SSTMJa 2: 76

The Ket forms are related to the Podkamennyi Ewenki form *sigdilē* 'distance between objects, interval'. The Ket secondary vowel -*ē*- possibly developed from the Ewenki syllable -*ig*-, which is typical for some Tungusic loanwords. The Tungusic etymology fits from a phonetic and semantic perspective.

Ket *úl'l'ɔŋ* ~ *úl'ɔŋ* 'echo' (Werner 2002/2: 341) < *úl'l'ɔ* -*ŋ* {Ket collective suffix}: *úl'l'ɔ* ← Northern Tungusic: Ewenki *ūlta* 'echo':
    Northern Ewenki: Yerbogachon, Ilimpeya; *Southern Ewenki*: Podkamennyi, Baunt, Nepa, Sym, Northern Baikal; *Eastern Ewenki*: Tungir, Urmi, Sakhalin *ūlta*; cf. *ūlta*- 'to be heard echo';
    cf. Northern Tungusic: Lamut *ūldon*; Negidal *olbun*- 'to echo'; Southern Tungusic: Ulcha *holdi*- 'to echo'; Orok *hulbun*- 'to echo'; Nanai *hōlǰi*- 'to echo'; Remaining lgs. –.

Etymology: SSTMJa 2: 263a

Probably, the Ket word was borrowed from the Podkamennyi Ewenki form *ūlta*. The Tungusic origin strengthents the same lexical meaning. From a phonetic perspective, the Tungusic cluster -*lt*- may be assimilated and palatalized. This change is unclear due to the fact the cluster *lt* is typical for Ket. But there are some Ket cases where the assimilation of clusters happened, e.g. *beˀl* 'immoral' + *qīm* 'woman' > *béllim* 'prostitute'; *bəʔn* 'duck' + *hīs* 'tail' > *bánnis* 'duck's tail', *kəən* 'fox' + *qūk* 'hole' > *kə́nnuk* 'earth of fox' (Georg 2007: 85). The Ket final -*ŋ* is possibly the Yeniseian collective suffix.

1.2 Adverbs

Ket *enna* 'really?' (Vajda & Werner: in preparation) ← Northern Tungusic: Ewenki *jēŋan* 'really?' < *jē* 'what; how; really?' +*ŋĀn* {Ewenki NN, see Vasilevič 1958: 778}, cf. Common Tungusic *jē*- 'quest. verb what to do?':
    Common Ewenki *jēŋan* 'as mean, really?';
    cf. Northern Tungusic: Lamut *ā̃*- ~ *ē*- ~ *iä*- 'quest. verb what to do?'; Negidal *ē*- 'id.'; Southern Tungusic: Oroch *ja*- ~ *je*- 'quest. verb what to do?'; Udihe *ja*- ~ *je*- 'id.'; Manchu *ja* 'what, who; which, which kind?'; Sibe *ya* 'id.'; Remaining lgs. –.

Etymology: SSTMJa 1: 286; Khabtagaeva 2017d: 81

The Ket adverb was certainly borrowed from the Common Ewenki word *jēŋan* with the same lexical meaning. The Ewenki initial consonant *j*- regularly disappeared as in other cases.

The base of the Common Tungusic word is the interrogative pronoun *jē* and the Ewenki denominal noun suffix +*ŋĀn*, which forms nouns with the same meaning (Vasilevič 1958: 778). Etymologically, the Tungusic word is probably connected with the Mongolic interrogative pronoun *yaɣun* 'What? What kind of? Which?'.

Ket *kat sim* 'like' (Werner 2002/1: 415) ← Northern Tungusic: Ewenki *-gAčin* 'as if, similar': denominal nomen suffix, which denotes the standard of comparison (for details on the functions, see Vasilevič 1958: 750; Boldyrev 1987: 6; Nedjalkov 1997: 285), e.g.
- *birgačin* 'like a river' < *bira* 'river';
- *targačin* 'such as ...' < *tar* 'that';
- *ergečin* 'such as ...' < *er* 'this';
- *muringačin* 'as a horse' < *murin* 'horse'.

Ket *kʌndaŋ* 'good (*said of a dog*)' (Werner 2002/1: 466) < **kʌn -daŋ* {?} ← ? Northern Tungusic: Ewenki *kēńe-* 'to approve, to praise, to flatter':
Common Ewenki *kēńe-*;
cf. Northern Tungusic: Negidal *kēn'e-* 'to praise; to be proud; to put the evil eye'; Southern Tungusic: Oroch *kenexi* 'voice'; Udihe *keni-* 'to curse'; Orok *kene-* 'to boast of'; Remaining lgs. –.

Etymology: SSTMJa 1: 449b

The etymology of the Ket word is unknown. As a hypothesis I assume it is connected to the Common Ewenki verb. The origin of the Ket final syllable *daŋ* is unclear.

Northern Ket *ɔkɔŋɔ* 'adverb from memory, by heart' (Werner 2002/2: 33) < **ɔkɔn -kɔ* {Ket locative suffix}:
*ɔkɔn ← Northern Tungusic: Ewenki *ōkin* 'when':
Common Ewenki *ōkīn-dā* 'constantly, always'; *ōkīdalā* 'how long'; *ōkija* 'long ago'; *ōkīlā-dā* 'at any time'; *ōkīmaka* 'forever, evermore';
cf. Northern Tungusic: Lamut *ōqta ~ ōqan-da ~ ōq-ta* 'once; always; *in negation* never' < *ōq* 'when'; Negidal *ōxïn-dā* 'always; *in negation* never' < *ōxïn ~ ōkïn* 'when'; Remaining lgs. –.

Etymology: SSTMJa 2: 10a

The Ket adverb is possibly of Tungusic origin. The change of the nasal consonant *-n- > -ŋ-* may be explained by the merge of the Ewenki loanword with the Ket locative suffix *-ko*, which denotes not only the location, but also has a temporal function (for details on the functions, see Georg 2007: 112–113). Cf. the similar example: Ewenki *bān* 'refusal' → Ket *báŋa* 'under no circumstance, never'.

The base of the Tungusic word is *ōq* 'when' (cf. Lamut). In Ewenki, the base is *ōkin* from which derived different temporal adverbs. Among Tungusic languages, the adverb is present only in Northern Tungusic (SSTMJa 2: 10a).

1.3 Verbs

The Ket verbal system is highly complicated and it is not typical for Ket to borrow verbal forms (for details on the Ket verbal system, see Vajda 2004). However, there are some verbs of Tungusic origin found as incorporated nominal elements inside of Yeniseian polysynthetic verb structures:

Ket *alepqaj* '*inf*. flare up, fly into a rage' (Werner 2002/1: 25) < **alepq -aj* {Ket action nominal suffix}

*alepqa ← Northern Tungusic: Ewenki *alipkī-* 'to be angry' < *ali-* 'to be angry, to anger, make angry' *-pkī-* {Ewenki VV, see Vasilevič 1958: 784, 747}:

> Southern Ewenki: Podkamennyi, Sym *ali-* 'to be angry, to anger, make angry';
> cf. Northern Tungusic: Lamut *alel-* ~ *ālil-* 'to be angry'; Negidal *ali-* 'to be angry, hate'; Remaining lgs. –.

Etymology: SSTMJa 1: 32ab; Khabtagaeva 2017d: 84

The Ket verb was clearly borrowed from Tungusic with the native Yeniseian action nominal suffix.

In turn, the origin of the Tungusic word is unclear. Among Tungusic languages, it is present only in Northern Tungusic. From a morphological perspective, the Ewenki verb *alipkī-* 'to be angry' was derived from the verb *ali-* 'to be angry, to anger, make angry' and the Ewenki non-productive deverbal verbum suffix *-pkī-* (for details on origin and functions, see Vasilevič 1958: 784, 747 and Boldyrev 1987: 50).

Ket *ígäj* ~ *ígij* 'to make noise, sound' (Werner 2002/1: 351) < **íg -Vj* {Ket action nominal suffix}

*íg ← Northern Tungusic: Ewenki *īg* 'sound' < *ī-* 'to be heard, to sound' *-g* {Ewenki VN, see Vasilevič 1958: 749}:

> Common Ewenki *īg* 'sound, noise, whisper, roar; lapping';
> cf. Northern Tungusic: Lamut *īg* ~ *īw* ~ *ig* 'sound, noise; news; rumor, gossip; rustle; sonorous, ringing'; Negidal *īg* 'sound, noise, rustle'; Southern Tungusic: Udihe *igdi* 'voice; loud'; Ulcha *ujsi-* 'to make noise (*of the boat*)'; Orok *ui* ~ *uji* ~ *ujsi* 'noice'; Nanai *hujsi-* 'to sound, to make noice'; Remaining lgs. –.

Etymology: SSTMJa 1: 293b

The Ket verbs are obviously connected with the Common Tungusic noun. The final *-äj* and *-ij* in the Ket forms are the action nominal suffixes (Georg 2007: 311–312).

The Tungusic word is of onomatopoeic origin. It derived from the verb *ī-* 'to be heard, to sound' and the Ewenki non-productive deverbal noun suffix *-g* (for details on functions, see Vasilevič 1958: 749).

Yugh **namčej** '*inf.* to press, press together one's lips; to clench one's teeth; to press to one's breast; to put the tail between the legs (*said of dogs*)' (Werner 2002/2: 24) < *namč -ej {Yeniseian action nominal suffix}:
*namč ← ? Northern Tungusic: Ewenki *namuwčā* '*adj.* folded up, rolled up, packed' < *namū-* 'to fold; to roll up, to pack':
> *Southern Ewenki*: Podkamennyi, Nepa *namuwčā* < *namū-* 'to fold (*bedlinen, clothing*); to roll up (*paper, textiles, leather*)'; cf. Podkamennyi *nama-* 'id.';
>> cf. Ulcha *namo-*; Orok *namulitči-* 'to fold (*paper, textiles*)'; Nanai *namï-* 'to tuck in, to bend under'; Remaining lgs. –.

Etymology: SSTMJa 1: 582a

The base of the Yugh verb is probably connected with Common Tungusic verb **namV-*. The final diphtong *-ej* is a Yugh action nominal suffix. The internal consonant *-č-* is unclear, it may be refered to the Ewenki passive participle suffix *-wčā* (for details on the functions, see Vasilevič 1958: 749).

Ket **ulan-mukŋ** 'morphemes in verbs referring to dogs gnawing bones' (Werner 2002/2: 329) < *ulan-mu + Yeniseian verb base *-qoŋ* 'to gnaw' (Vajda 2016: personal communication):
*ulan-mu ← Northern Tungusic: Ewenki *ulme-* 'to gnaw bones', cf. *ulle* 'meat':
> Common Ewenki *ulme-* 'to gnaw bones';
>> cf. Northern Tungusic: Lamut *ulme-* 'to gnaw bones', cf. *ulre ~ ulde ~ uldu ~ ulle* 'meat; body, organism'; Negidal *ulle-* 'to slaughter animal for meat', cf. *ule* 'meat'; Southern Tungusic: Oroch *ukte ~ utte* 'meat'; Udihe *ulehe* 'meat; muscles; skin of human'; Ulcha *ulse* 'meat'; Orok *ul'ise* 'meat'; Nanai *ulikse ~ ule* 'meat; muscles'; Remaining lgs. –.

Etymology: SSTMJa 2: 262

The root of the Ket word is *mukŋ*, while the incorporate is *ulan* (Georg 2016: personal communication). This is a unique example of Tungusic loanword which merged with a Ket verb base. The Ket word is related to the Common Ewenki verb *ulme-* 'to gnaw bones'.

The Common Tungusic word *ulle* 'meat' is present in almost all Tungusic languages, expect the Manchuric group. For more derivations and correspondences, see SSTMJa (2: 262).

Ket **ut-qo** morphemes in the taboo replacement verb '*submit*', used when a bear is killed by a hunter, *lit.* 'the bear submits to a hunter' (Werner 2002/2: 367) < *ut* + Yeniseian verb base *-qo* 'to kill' (Werner 2002/2: 123; Vajda 2014: personal communication):
*ut ← Northern Tungusic: Ewenki *utu* 'old, weak, helpless, defenceless, unprotected' ← Mongolic *ötege* 'taboo bear' < *öte +*GA(n)* {Mongolic NN, see Khabtagaeva 2009: 280}:

Northern Ewenki: Yerbogachon; *Southern Ewenki*: Podkamennyi *utu*;
cf. Lamut *ute* 'old (*about dog*)'; Remaining lgs. –;
Tungusic ← Mongolic *ötege* 'taboo bear' < *öte +*GA*(*n*) {Mongolic NN, see Khabtagaeva 2009: 280}:
Middle Mongol: Precl.Mo. *ötegü ~ ötögü*; SH *ötögü* 'old person'; HY *ötögü* 'old person', *ötögö* 'bear'; YY *ötüge* 'bear'; Muq. *ötege* 'bear', *ötegü* 'old man'; Leiden *ö(t)ege* 'bear', *ötegü* 'old man'; RH *ötege* 'bear'; LM *ötege*; Modern Mongol: Buryat *ütȫ* 'grandmother'; Khalkha *ötög*; Kalmuck *ötög⁀ ~ ötkö* 'old person, bear'; Dagur *ətə̄γʷ* 'old woman'; Khamnigan *ütel- ~ ütöl-* 'to grow old'.
Etymology: SSTMJa 2: 294b; Nugteren 2011: 478
The first part of the Ket verb is connected to the Ewenki dialectal word. Due to the Ket word belonging to the category of taboo words, the borrowing of only one of the elements is possible.

From an etymological point of view, the Tungusic words are of Mongolic origin. The Mongolic word *ötege* 'taboo bear' is present in almost all Middle Mongol sources and Modern languages (Nugteren 2011: 478). The non-productive base of the Mongolic word is *öte, cf. *ötegü* (< *öte +*GU* {Mongolic NN/adj., see Poppe GWM §152}) 'old man, senior', *ötel-* (< *öte +*lA-* {Mongolic NV, see Poppe GWM §245}) 'to age, grow old', *ötelül* (< *öte +*lA-* {Mongolic NV, see Poppe GWM §245} -*l* {Mongolic VN, see Poppe GWM §159}) 'the state of being old, aging, senility', etc.

The Tungusic borrowing, and not Mongolic, proves the initial vowel *u-* in Ket. Possibly, the taboo lexical meaning was already added in Ket.

1.4 Particles

Ket *āna ~ ána* 'intensive negative particle (not) even, (don't) even' (Werner 2002/1: 34) ← Northern Tungusic: cf. Lamut *ana* 'intensive negative particle (not) even, (don't) even':
Ewenki –;
cf. Northern Tungusic: Lamut *ān ~ āŋ ~ jān* 'not having someone or something; without someone or something'; Southern Tungusic: Oroch *ana* 'not, missing'; Ulcha *ana* 'not'; Orok *ana ~ anā ~ anaγa* 'not having someone or something; not, missing'; Nanai *anā* 'not, missing'; Remaining lgs. –.
Etymology: SSTMJa 1: 41a; Khabtagaeva 2017d: 85
The source of borrowing in Ket is usually Ewenki, but this is one of the rare cases where the Tungusic word is absent in Ewenki and present in almost all other Tungusic languages. The Ket particle was borrowed from Northern Tungusic, though absent in the recorded Ewenki.

Kẹt *báɲa* 'under no circumstance, never' (Werner 2002/1: 102) < *bán -ka {Ket locative suffix}:
*bán ← Northern Tungusic: Ewenki *bān* 'refusal, repudiation; failure' < *bā-* 'to be unable, to resist, to refuse' *-n* {Ewenki VN, see Vasilevič 1958: 777}:
  Common Ewenki *bān* 'refusal, repudiation; failure' (Boldyrev);
  cf. Northern Tungusic: Lamut *bā-* 'to be lazy, to sit back'; Southern Tungusic: Oroch *bāki* 'lazy'; Orok *baja* ~ *bāju* 'lazy, idler, loafer'; Nanai *bāqi* 'lazy, loafer'; Remaining lgs. –.
Etymology: SSTMJa 1: 60b–61a; Khabtagaeva 2017d: 84

The Ket adverb is possibly used with the locative suffix *-ka* (Vajda 2016: personal communication) which denotes not only location, but also has a temporal function (for details on the functions, see Georg 2007: 112–113). The base of the adverb *bán* is connected with the Common Ewenki noun *bān* 'refusal, repudiation; failure', which derived from the verb *bā-* 'to be unable, to resist, to refuse' and the Ewenki productive deverbal noun suffix *-n*, which forms nouns designating results of actions (details on the functions, see Vasilevič 1958: 777; Boldyrev 1987: 137–138).

Ket *hiˑlʹ* 'intensive particle' (Werner 2002/1: 349) ← Northern Tungusic: Ewenki *hila* 'well!; well ... then! come on!':
  Southern Ewenki: Podkamennyi *hila*;
  cf. Northern Tungusic: Lamut *hilakan* 'even if, if only'; Remaining lgs. –.
Etymology: SSTMJa 2: 323b

The Ket intensive particle was borrowed from Podkamennyi Ewenki. From a phonetic perspective, due to the stress in the Ket first syllable, the Ewenki vowel disappeared and the previous consonant palatalized in Ket.

The etymology of the Tungusic word is unclear. The particle is present only in Ewenki and Lamut.

1.5 Interjections

Ket *qiˑlʹa*; Yugh *χiˑlʹa* 'quickly!' (Werner 2002/2: 154) ← Northern Tungusic: Ewenki *helin* 'hurry, rush; quickly':
  Southern Ewenki: Podkamennyi, Nepa *helin* 'rush; no time', cf. *helinǯi* 'quickly (*about action*)';
  cf. Northern Tungusic: Lamut *helūŋe* 'rush, urgent, hurried; hurry'; Negidal *xenindu-* [*kexadu*] 'I am in hurry!'; Southern Tungusic: Udihe *xeli* 'hurry'; Orok *pelin-* 'to rush'; Nanai *penin-* ~ *xeline-* ~ *fenin-* 'to hurry'; Remaining lgs. –.
Etymology: SSTMJa 2: 364

The Yeniseian words were possibly borrowed from the Southern Ewenki form *helin* 'hurry, quickly'. The Tungusic initial *h-* regularly changed to *q-* in

Ket. Due to the Tungusic vowel *-i-* the palatalization of the Ket consonant *-l-* is occurred.

An interesting fact that the Tungusic word is used as noun, verb, adverb and interjection.

Ket *úkta* 'slowly', cf. Southern Ket *úkta índɛt!* 'read slowly!' (Werner 2002/2: 328) ← Northern Tungusic: Ewenki *udakta* 'let me be slow' < *uda-* 'to be slow, to delay' *-ktA* {Ewenki sg.1 optative, see Boldyrev 2000: 454} ← Mongolic *uda-* 'to tarry, hesitate, delay; to be late or delayed; to last':
> Northern Ewenki: Ilimpeya; Southern Ewenki: Podkamennyi, Nepa, Sym; Eastern Ewenki: Zeya, Tungir, Ayan, Tokko, Aldan, Uchur, Urmi, Tommot, Sakhalin *uda-* 'to delay, to be late';
> cf. Northern Tungusic: Lamut *uda* 'slow, dreary; melancholy', cf. *udij-* ~ *udït-* 'to delay, to be late' (← Yakut); Remaining lgs. –;

Tungusic ← Mongolic *uda-* 'to tarry, hesitate, delay; to be late or delayed; to last': Middle Mongol: Precl.Mo. *uda-*; SH *uda-*; Muq. *uda-*; LM *uda-*; Modern Mongol: Buryat *uda-*; Khalkha *uda-*; Kalmuck *ud^a-*; Dagur –; Khamnigan *uda-*;

Etymology: Kałużyński 1962: 69; SSTMJa 2: 248; Romanova, Myreeva & Baraškov 1975: 204; Doerfer 1985: 67; Nugteren 2011: 529

The Ket interjection is obviously of Tungusic origin. It was borrowed from the Ewenki first singular optative form *udakta* 'let me be slow'. The loss of internal syllable occurred in the Ket form, which is typical for Tungusic loanwords in Ket.

From an etymological perspective, the Tungusic word is of Mongolic origin (Doerfer 1985: 67). The base of word is the Mongolic verb *uda-* 'to tarry, hesitate, delay; to be late or delayed; to last' which is present in almost all Mongolic languages (Nugteren 2011: 529).

The Mongolic verb was borrowed into Yakut (Kałużyński 1962: 69), and further was re-borrowed into some Ewenki dialects (Doerfer 1985: 67), which is proveen by the Yakut phonetic features and suffixes. Cf. Uchur Ewenki dial. *utalïy-* 'to delay' was borrowed from Yakut *utalïy-* 'to delay, to be slow' (Romanova, Myreeva & Baraškov 1975: 204) where the original Mongolic intervocalic *VdV* devoiced and derived with the Yakut deverbal verbum suffix *-lïy-*.

2   Phonetic Features

2.1   *The Northern Tungusic Vowels and Consonants in Ket and Yugh*

Common Ewenki displays the following symmetrical basic set of eleven vowels, which can be classified with respect to the features front vs back, high vs low, short vs long (for details, see Lebedeva at al. 1979: 13–14; Nedjalkov 1997: 309):

	front		central		back	
	V	V̄	V	V̄	V	V̄
high	i	ī			u	ū
mid		jē	e	ē	o	ō
low	a	ā				

The consonant system of Ewenki has eighteen phonemes including labials, dentals, palatals, alveolars and velars. Voiced consonants constrast phonemically with voiceless consonants (for details, see Lebedeva et al. 1979: 15–16; Nedjalkov 1997: 309–318):

		labials	dentals	palatals	alveolars	velars
plosives	voiceless	p	t	č		k
	voiced	b	d	ď (or ǰ)		g
fricatives	voiceless				s	h
	voiced	v		j		
sonants	nasals	m	n	ń		ŋ
	liquids		l			
	trills		r			

2.1.1 Northern Tungusic Vowels in Ket and Yugh Loanwords

Northern Tungusic	Ket and Yugh	Examples
Short vowels		
a	Ket, Yugh *a-*	Ewenki *ayān* 'old bed of river; channel; bay, cove' → Yugh *ajāχin* 'ford' (cf. *χin*: Yeniseian *qiˑń* 'flow, current'); Ewenki *alipkī-* 'to be angry' → Ket *alepqaj* 'inf. flare up, fly into a rage' {*-aj* Ket action nominal suffix};

(cont.)

Northern Tungusic	Ket and Yugh	Examples
	Ket á-, ā-	Northern Tungusic *ana* 'negative particle (not) even, (don't) even' → Ket *āna* ~ *ána*; Ewenki *alaɣ* 'strap' → Ket *aluk* ~ *álək* ~ *áləq* ~ *álok* ~ *áloq* 'dogharness';
	Ket -á¹-	Ewenki *talmī* 'vessel of birch bark' → Ket *táĺma*;
	Ket, Yugh -a¹-	Ewenki *daŋajā* 'name of shoulder bone' → Ket *dankijaj* 'rucksack' (cf. Yeniseian *aj* 'sack'); Ewenki *nara* 'reindeer' → Ket *naroboks* 'long steering pole of a reindeer team' {Ket -*b*- epenthetic consonant, half-affix -*oks*}; Ewenki *namuwčā* 'adj. folded up, rolled up, packed', *namč → Yugh *namčej* 'inf. to press, press together one's lips' {-*ej* Yeniseian action nominal suffix}
	Ket -a	Ewenki *udakta* 'let me be slowly' → Ket *úkta* 'slowly';
	Ket -ä¹-	Ewenki *karje* 'root of bird-cherry' → Southern Ket *käˑr* 'rack made of bird-cherry wood';
	Ket -ɔ¹-, -ɔ́-¹	Ewenki *kaja* 'pan' → Ket *kɔjel* ~ *kɔ́jil* (cf. Yeniseian *ɛˀl* 'cup');
	Ket -o²-	Ewenki *nara* 'reindeer' → Ket *naroboks* 'long steering pole of a reindeer team' {Ket -*b*- epenthetic consonant, half-affix -*oks*};
	Ket -i²-	Ewenki *ūčak* 'reindeer' → Ket *učik* 'saddle for a reindeer';
	Ket -ɔ²-	Ewenki *ūlta* 'echo' → Ket *úĺĺɔŋ* ~ *úĺɔŋ* {-*ŋ* Ket collective suffix};
o	Ket -o¹-	Ewenki *kolbo* 'storage shed' → Ket *kolij* 'covered storeroom' (cf. Yeniseian *iˀ* 'storage shed');
	Ket -a¹-, -ú¹-, -ɔ¹-	Ewenki *ločoko* 'saddle' → Ket *lačako* ~ *lúčkɔ* 'reindeer saddle', *lɔčik* 'child's saddle';
	Ket -ɔ¹,²-	Ewenki *doktokōn* 'fur shoes, worn on boots' → Northern Ket *dɔktɔraŋ* 'socks made from reindeer hide';
	Ket -ɔ¹,²-, -ɔ́¹-, -ɔ	Ewenki *golomo* 'winter dwelling' → Northern Ket *kɔlɔmɔ* ~ *gɔ́lɔmɔ*;

(cont.)

Northern Tungusic	Ket and Yugh	Examples
e	Ket -e¹-	Ewenki *beye* 'man, body' → Ket *beʔj* 'friend';
	Ket -e²-	Ewenki *immen* 'halter' → Ket *imejaŋ* 'reindeer harness neck-rope' (cf. Yeniseian -*j*- linking consonant, *aŋ* 'rope');
	Ket -ə	Ewenki *tügdewkī* 'lark' → Ket *tə·qtə* 'wagtail';
	Ket, Yugh -i¹-	Ewenki *helin* 'quickly' → Ket *qi·l'a*; Yugh *χi·l'a*; Ewenki *kelkē* 'fur shoes' → CKet *hilgum*; Ewenki *hegdï* 'size; big; many' → Ket *hitaj* 'size (*of clothes*)';
	Ket -i²-	Ewenki *gudige* 'stomach of animals' → Ket *kútgit* 'dish of intestines';
	Ket -i³-	Ewenki *emegen* 'saddle' → NKet *ɔmɔyin*;
	Ket -i²-	Northern Tungusic *kebel* 'stomach' → Ket *qäpil*;
	Ket -o²-	Ewenki *jūdek* 'smallpox' → Ket *doʔk*;
	Ket ɔ-, -ɔ¹-	Ewenki *emegen* 'saddle' → NKet *ɔmɔyin*;
	Ket -u¹-	Ewenki *kelkē* 'fur shoes' → NKet *kulgum ~ hulgum*;
i	Yugh -i¹-	Ewenki *čičakūn* 'wagtail, small bird' → Yugh *čičik* 'wagtail';
	Ket *i*-	Ewenki *immen* 'halter' → Ket *imejaŋ* 'reindeer harness neck-rope' (cf. Yeniseian -*j*- linking consonant, *aŋ* 'rope');
	Ket -i¹-	Ewenki *dilkēn* 'fly' → Ket *til* 'horsefly, reindeerfly'; Ewenki *hila* 'well!; well ... then! come on!' → Ket *hi·l'* 'intensive particle';
	Ket -i²-	Ewenki *gudige* 'stomach of animals' → Ket *kútgit* 'dish of intestines';
	Ket *e*-	Ewenki *intilgun* 'owl' → Ket *enčil*;
	Ket -e²-	Ket *alipkī*- 'to be angry' → Ket *alepqaj* 'inf. flare up, fly into a rage' {-*aj* Ket action nominal suffix};
	Ket -ə	Ewenki *hugi* 'nest' → Ket *ôgə* 'cave, nest, den';
ï	Ket -ɛ²-	Ewenki *hugdï* 'rapacious' → Ket *húktɛŋ* 'bear eyes' {-*ŋ* Ket plural};
	Ket -ə¹-	Ewenki *tügdewkī* 'lark' → Ket *tə·qtə* 'wagtail';

(cont.)

Northern Tungusic	Ket and Yugh	Examples
	Ket -aj	Ewenki *hegdï* 'size; big; many' → Ket *hitaj* 'size (*of clothes*)';
u	Ket u-	Ewenki *ulme-* 'to gnaw bones' → Ket *ulan-mukŋ* 'morphemes in verbs referring to dogs gnawing bones' (cf. Yeniseian verb base *-qoŋ* 'to gnaw');
		Ewenki *utu* 'old, weak, bear' → Ket *ut-qo* morphemes in the taboo replacement verb '*submit*', used when a bear is killed by a hunter, *lit.* 'the bear submits to a hunter' (cf. Yeniseian verb base *-qo* 'to kill');
	Ket -u²-	Ewenki *tuŋsuku* 'a bear head, a "funeral" of bear' → Ket *tʌns'uk* '*taboo* designation of a bear stomach';
	Ket u- ~ ú- Yugh ú-	Ewenki *ulukī* 'squirrel' → Ket *ulla ~ úlle* 'ruble, the monetary unit in Russia';
		Ewenki *ulanmukī* 'pochard' → Ket *ullen ~ úlen*; Yugh *úlʲan*;
	Ket -ú¹-	Ewenki *gudige* 'stomach of animals' → Ket *kútgit* 'dish of intestines';
		Ewenki *hugdï* 'rapacious' → Ket *húktɛŋ* 'bear eyes' {-*ŋ* Ket plural};
	Ket, Yugh -o¹-	Ewenki *bunī* 'dead person; cemetery, grave' → Ket *boŋnij* 'cemetery; grave'; Yugh *boŋsi* 'dead person' {-*si* nominalizer};
		Ewenki *hugi* 'nest' → Ket *ogə* 'cave, nest, den';
		Ewenki *tuktī-* 'to go up a slope or mountain' → Ket *toqtis* 'slope of a riverbank or hill' {-*s* Ket nominalizer};
	Ket -ō¹-	Ewenki *bunī* → Ket *bō·ŋ* 'dead person';
	Ket -ʌ¹-	Ewenki *kuta* 'marsh' → CKet *kʌdaŋ* {-*ŋ* Ket collective suffix};
		Ewenki *tuŋsuku* 'a bear head, a "funeral" of bear' → Ket *tʌns'uk* '*taboo* designation of a bear stomach';

(cont.)

Northern Tungusic	Ket and Yugh	Examples
Long vowels		
ā	Ket á-	Ewenki *amākākse* 'bear's skin; bear's flesh' → Ket *áʁses* 'bear trap' {-*s* Ket nominalizer};
	Ket -á¹-	Ewenki *bān* 'refusal' → Ket *báŋa* 'never' {-*ka* Ket locative suffix};
	Yugh -ā²-	Ewenki *ayān* 'old bed of river; channel; bay, cove' → Yugh *ajāχin* 'ford' (cf. Yeniseian *qi·ń* 'flow, current');
	Ket -ɔ¹-	Ewenki *dāgwūn* 'ford across a river' → Ket *dɔgbən* 'area between two riverbends';
ō	Ket ɔ-	Ewenki *ōkin* 'always' → NKet *ɔkɔŋɔ* 'by heart';
	Ket -a³-	Ewenki *doktokōn* 'fur shoes, worn on boots' → NKet *dɔktɔraŋ* 'socks made from reindeer hide';
ē	Ket -e¹-	Ewenki *jēŋan* 'really?' → Ket *enna*;
	Ket -i²-	Ewenki *detkēn* 'marsh' → NKet *deŋtiɣin ~ däŋtiɣin*;
	Ket -u²-	Ewenki *kelkē* 'fur shoes' → NKet *kulgum ~ hulgum* {-*m* < -*ŋ* Ket plural};
ī	Ket -i³-	Ewenki *bejetī* 'cannibal' → NKet *bejetil* {? -*l*};
ū	Ket -ə²-	Ewenki *dāgwūn* 'ford across a river' → Ket *dɔgbən* 'area between two riverbends'.

2.1.2   Northern Tungusic Consonants in Ket and Yugh Loanwords

Northern Tungusic	Yeniseian	Examples
Labial consonants		
b	Ket, Yugh b-	Ewenki *bān* 'refusal' → Ket *báŋa* 'never' {-*ka* Ket locative suffix};
		Ewenki *beye* 'man, person, body' → Ket *beʔj* 'friend';
		Ewenki *bunī* 'dead person; cemetery, grave' → Ket *bōˑŋ* 'dead person', *boŋnij* 'cemetery; grave'; Yugh *boŋsi* 'dead person' {-*si* Yeniseian nominalizer};
	Ket *VpV*	Tungusic *kebel* 'stomach' → Ket *qäpil*;
m	Ket *VmV*	Ewenki *golomo* 'winter dwelling' → NKet *kɔlɔmɔ* ~ *gɔ́lɔmɔ*;
		Ewenki *emegen* 'saddle; reindeer saddle' → NKet *ɔmɔyin*;
Dental and alveolar consonants		
t	Ket *t-*	Ewenki *talmī* 'vessel of birch bark' → Ket *tál'ma*;
		Ewenki *tuŋsuku* 'a bear head, a "funeral" of bear' → Ket *tʌns'uk* 'taboo designation of a bear stomach';
		Ewenki *tigdewkī* 'lark' → Ket *təˑqtə* ~ *təˑqt* 'wagtail';
	Ket *VtV*	Ewenki *bejetī* 'cannibal' → NKet *bejetil*;
		Ewenki *hute* 'child, son or daughter' → Ket *qitet* 'grandchild of father's sister or mother's brother' {-*kit* Ket diminutive half-suffix};
	Ket *VdV*	Ewenki *kuta* 'marsh' → CKet *kʌdaŋ* {-*ŋ* Ket collective suffix};
	CKet *VdV*, NKet *VrV*[16]	Ewenki *kutu* 'happiness, good luck' → CKet *qū̆de*, NKet *qūre* 'to make magic (*shaman*)';[17]

---

16 The change of consonant *VdV* > *VrV* is a typical phonetic feature in Ket dialects (Werner 1990b: 35), e.g. 'I lie down': Central Ket *taditn*, Southern Ket *tär'ētn*, Northern Ket *tar'etn*; 'root': Central Ket *tīde*, Southern Ket *tir'*, Northern Ket *tīr'i*; 'I know': Central Ket *itpadam*, Southern Ket *itpar'em*, Northern Ket *itpar'am*, etc.

17 The Tungusic word of Turkic origin was possibly borrowed in an early period. Firstly, the *VtV* was voiced to *VdV* and then changed to *VrV*.

(cont.)

Northern Tungusic	Yeniseian	Examples
	Ket -či-	Ewenki *intilgun* 'owl' → Ket *enčil*;
d	Ket d-	Ewenki *dāgwūn* 'ford across a river' → Ket *dɔgbən*; Ewenki *daŋajā* 'name of shoulder bone' → Ket *dankijaj* 'rucksack' (cf. Yeniseian *aj* 'sack'); Ewenki *detkēn* 'marsh' → Ket *daŋtakan*; NKet *deŋtiɣin* ~ *däŋtiɣin*; Ewenki *doktokōn* 'fur shoes, worn on boots' → NKet *dɔktɔraŋ* 'socks made from reindeer hide';
	Ket t-	Ewenki *dilkēn* 'fly' → Ket *til* 'horsefly';
	Ket VtV	Ewenki *sigdilē* 'distance between objects, interval' → Ket *sēˑtal* ~ *sēˑtil* 'height';
s	Ket s-	Ewenki *sōna* ~ *sōŋa* 'chimney' → Ket *saŋɔl* 'chimney of a dug-out', cf. CKet *sɔnal* 'smoke hole of a dug-out' {-*l* ?}; Ewenki *sigdilē* 'distance between objects, interval' → Ket *sēˑtal* ~ *sēˑtil* 'height'; Ewenki *suglān* 'meeting' → Ket *sūliŋ* [*dɛʔŋ*] 'people coming to meet each other'; Ewenki *suna* 'team of dogs' → SKet *sūˑŋ* {-*ŋ* Ket collective suffix};
n	Ket n-	Ewenki *nara* 'reindeer' → Ket *naroboks* 'pole of a reindeer team' {-*b* epenthetic consonant; -*oks* Ket half-affix};
	Ket VnV	Tungusic *ana* 'negative particle (not) even' → Ket *āna* ~ *ána*;
	Ket -n	Ewenki *detkēn* 'marsh' → Ket *daŋtakan*; NKet *deŋtiɣin* ~ *däŋtiɣin*; Ewenki *kulitkān* 'the image of snake in the shaman's costume' → Ket *kɔyɔ́n* 'myth. forbidden jewelry in a snake's nest; copper pendant of shaman's costume'; Ewenki *emegen* 'saddle; reindeer saddle' → NKet *ɔmɔyin* 'reindeer saddle';

Northern Tungusic	Yeniseian	Examples
	Ket -ŋ	Ewenki *doktokōn* 'fur shoes, worn on boots' → Northern Ket *dɔktɔraŋ* 'socks made from reindeer hide'; Ewenki *suglān* 'meeting' → Ket *sūliŋ*;
	Ket -Vŋ	Ewenki *bunī* 'dead person; cemetery, grave' → Ket *bō·ŋ* 'dead person';
	Ket -m	Ewenki *-gАčin* 'as if, similar' → Ket *kat sim* 'like';
	Ket, Yugh -ø	Ewenki *jēŋan* 'really?' → Ket *enna*; Ewenki *helin* 'quickly' → Ket *qi·l'a*; Yugh *χi·l'a*;
l	Ket *l-*	Ewenki *ločoko* 'saddle' → Ket *lačako*;
	Ket *VlV*	Ewenki *alipkī-* 'to be angry' → Ket *alepqaj* 'inf. flare up, fly into a rage' {*-aj* Ket action nominal suffix}; Ewenki *alaɣ* 'strap in reindeer harness' → Ket *aluk ~ álək ~ áləq ~ álok ~ áloq* 'dogharness'; Ewenki *golomo* 'winter dwelling' → NKet *kɔlɔmɔ ~ gólɔmɔ*;
	Ket *VllV*	Ewenki *ulukī* 'squirrel' → Ket *ulla ~ úlle* 'ruble, the monetary unit in Russia';
	Ket, Yugh *-l'-*	Ewenki *helin* 'quickly' → Ket *qi·l'a*; Yugh *χi·l'a*; Ewenki *hila* 'well!; well ... then! come on!' → Ket *hi·l'* 'intensive particle'; Ewenki *eltin* 'roof of a house' → Ket *il't ~ íl'tə* 'roof of a dugout'; Ewenki *talmī* 'adj. birchbark' → Ket *tál'ma* 'vessel of birch bark for berries';
	Ket *-l*	Tungusic *kebel* 'stomach' → Ket *qäpil*; Ewenki *sigdilē* 'distance between objects, interval' → Ket *sē·tal ~ sē·til* 'height';
r	Ket *VrV*	Ewenki *nara* 'reindeer' → Ket *naroboks* 'pole of a reindeer team'{Ket *-b-* epenthetic consonant, half-affix *-oks*};
	Ket *VttV*	Ewenki *horan* 'the middle place in house' → Ket *hɔttɔn*;

(*cont.*)

Northern Tungusic	Yeniseian	Examples
Palatal consonants		
č	Yugh č-, VčV	Ewenki čičakūn 'wagtail' → Yugh číčik;
	Ket VčV	Ewenki ločoko 'saddle' → Ket lačako 'reindeer saddle'; Central Ket bčik 'child's saddle'; Ewenki ūčak 'reindeer' → NKet učik 'saddle for a reindeer';
d'	Ket VdV < *Vd'V	Ewenki jūd'ek 'smallpox' → Ket doʔk 'smallpox; pox-marks';
j	Ket ø-[18]	Ewenki jēŋan 'really?' → Ket enna; Ewenki jūkte 'spring, brook' → CKet aqtul {-l?}; Ewenki jūdek 'smallpox' → Ket doʔk;
	Ket, Yugh VjV	Ewenki ajān 'old bed of river; channel; bay, cove' → Yugh ajāχn ~ ajāχin 'ford, sandbank' (cf. Yeniseian qi·ń 'flow, current'); Ewenki bejetī 'cannibal' → NKet bejetil {-l?}; Ewenki kaja 'pan' → Ket kɔjel ~ kɔ́jil 'pan' (cf. Yeniseian εʔl 'cup');
	Ket, Yugh -j	Ewenki togoj 'bend of a river' → SKet tō·j, Yugh tō·j 'river arm';
Velar consonants		
k	Ket k-	Ewenki kari 'root of bird-cherry' → SKet kä·r 'rack'; Ewenki kolbo 'storage shed' → Ket kolij 'covered storeroom' (cf. Yeniseian iʔ 'storage shed'); Ewenki kuta 'marsh' → CKet kʌdaŋ ~ kʌdəŋ 'marshy place' {-ŋ Yeniseian collective suffix};

---

18   An important typical phonetic feature for Tungusic loanwords in Yeniseian is aphaeresis. The Tungusic initial consonant j(V)- regularly disappeared in Ket loanwords.

(cont.)

Northern Tungusic	Yeniseian	Examples
	Ket q-	Tungusic *kebel* 'stomach' → Ket *qäpil*;
		Ewenki *kutu* 'happiness, good luck, success' → SKet *qùt* ~ *qùr* 'the great "first" person; shaman's main spirit helper'; NKet *qū̃re*, CKet *qū̃de* 'make magic (*said of a shaman*)';
	Ket *h*-	Ewenki *kelkē* 'fur shoes' → Ket *hulgum*;
	Ket *VkV*	Ewenki *ločoko* 'saddle' → Ket *lačako*;
		Ewenki *ōkin* 'when' → NKet *ɔkɔŋɔ* '*adverb* from memory, by heart' {-*kɔ* Ket locative suffix};
	Ket *VrV*	Ewenki *doktokōn* 'fur shoes, stockings' → NKet *dɔktɔraŋ*;
	Ket -*k*	Ewenki *jūdek* 'smallpox' → Ket *doʔk*;
		Ewenki *ūčak* 'reindeer' → NKet *učik* 'saddle for a reindeer';
g	Ket *k*-[19]	Ewenki *-gAčin* 'as if, similar' → Ket *kat sim* 'like';
		Ewenki *golomo* 'a kind of winter dwelling' → NKet *kɔlɔmɔ* 'a kind of winter dwelling covered with sod';
		Ewenki *gudige* 'stomach of animals' → Ket *kútgit*;
	Ket *VgV*	Ewenki *īg* 'sound' → Ket *ígäj* ~ *ígij* 'to noice, to sound' {-*ij* Yeniseian action nominal form};
		Ewenki *hugi* 'nest' → Ket *ôgə* 'cave, nest, den';
	Ket *VʁV*, *VgV*	Ewenki *ayī* 'taiga, tundra, marsh' → NKet *aʁidɛ*; CKet *ajgiddɛ*, SKet *ajgitdɛ* (cf. Yeniseian *deʔ* 'lake');
	Ket *VγV*	Ewenki *emegen* 'saddle' → NKet *ɔmɔyin*;
	Ket -*k* ~ -*q*	Ewenki *alaγ* 'strap' → Ket *aluk* ~ *áləq* ~ *álok* ~ *áloq* 'dogharness';

---

19 The devoicing of Tungusic initial *g*- is regular change in Ket, which reflects an early period of borrowing. The initial *g*- is typical only for loanwords in Ket.

(cont.)

Northern Tungusic	Yeniseian	Examples
NT *h-* ~ Proto-T **p-*[20]	Ket *h-*[21]	Ewenki *haran* > *horan* 'house; the place for tent; floor; the place of hearth in the middle of Tungusic house' > Ket *hɔttɔn* 'left or the right area in a tent'; NKet *hɔ́ttɔn* 'middle place in a tent'; Ewenki *hegdï* 'size; big; many' → Ket *hitaj* 'size *(of clothes)*'; Ewenki *hila* 'intensive particle' → Ket *hi·ĺ*;
	Ket *q-*	Ewenki *helin* 'quickly' → Ket *qi·ĺa*; Ewenki *hepete tile* 'bear bacon fat' → Ket *qʌbdal* 'slice of bear bacon fat'; Ewenki *hute* 'child, son or daughter' → Ket *qitet* 'grandchild of father's sister or mother's brother';
	Yugh *χ-*	Ewenki *helin* 'quickly' → Yugh *χi·ĺa*;
	Ket *ø-*[22]	Ewenki *hugi* 'nest' → Ket *ôgə* 'cave, nest, den'.

2.2 The Development of Secondary Long Vowels from VCV Sequence

There are Tungusic loanwords in Ket, where the secondary long vowels developed from the sequence *Vocal—Consonant—Vocal*:

Ket *sē·tal* ~ *sē·til* 'height' ← Northern Tungusic: Ewenki *sigdilē* 'distance between objects, interval';

Ket *sūliŋ* [*dɛˀŋ*] 'people coming to meet each other' ← Northern Tungusic: Ewenki *suglān* 'meeting';

Southern Ket *tō·j*; Northern Ket *tō·ji*; Yugh *tō·j* 'river arm' ← Northern Tungusic: Ewenki *togoi* 'bend of a river'.

---

20 The original Tungusic *p-* in initial position developed in Northern Tungusic to *h-*, in Southern Amuric group to *x-* (Oroch, Udihe), in Ulcha, Orok, Nanai it usually preserved and changed to *f-* in Manchu (Cincius 1949: 154–155; Benzing 1955: 32–33).
    In the most cases, the Ket loanwords with initial *h-* were borrowed from Northern Tungusic, i.e. Ewenki. But some cases, as following example, show the early period of borowing. As in native words, the Ket initial *h-* and Yugh *f-* go back to **p-* (Starostin 1982: 149).
21 The preservation of Tungusic initial *h-* points to the later period of borrowing.
22 The Tungusic initial *h-* disappeared in Ket as in original Yeniseian words (Starostin 1982: 175), which points this feature to the early period of borrowing.

2.3 Consonant Clusters
2.3.1 Preservation
-kt-

> Northern Tungusic: Ewenki *doktokōn* 'fur shoes, worn on boots' → Northern Ket *dɔktɔraŋ* 'socks made from reindeer hide';
> Northern Tungusic: Ewenki *udakta* 'let me be slowly' → Ket *úkta* 'slowly', cf. Southern Ket *úkta índɛt!* 'read slowly!';

-kt- > -qt-

> Northern Tungusic: Ewenki *jūkte* 'spring, brook' → Central Ket *aqtul* 'spring (*water coming out of the ground*)';
> Northern Tungusic: Ewenki *tuktī-* 'to go up a slope or mountain' → Ket *toqtis* 'slope of a riverbank or hill' < *tokti -s {Yeniseian nominalizer};

-pk- > -pq-

> Northern Tungusic: Ewenki *alipkī-* 'to be angry' → Ket *alepqaj* '*inf.* flare up, fly into a rage' < *alepq -aj {Ket action nominal suffix};

-lt-

> Northern Tungusic: Ewenki *kalta-* 'to crack, to break in two parts; to split in half' → Kott *kaltapen* 'wedge for splitting wood' < *kalta -p {?} + Yeniseian *eˑn* 'wedge'.

2.3.2 Voicing
-ks- → *-ʁs-*

> Northern Tungusic: Ewenki *amākākse* 'bear's skin; bear's flesh' → Ket *áʁses* 'bear trap' < *áʁse -s {Ket nominalizer};

-lk- → *-lg-*

> Northern Tungusic: Ewenki *kelkē* 'fur shoes' → Northern Ket *hulgum* ~ *kulgum* 'type of men's winter boots' < *kulgu -um* {? < *-əŋ* Ket plural}.

2.3.3 Devoicing
-gd- → *-kt-, -qt-*

> Northern Tungusic: Ewenki *hugdï* 'rapacious, predatory' → Ket *húktɛŋ* ~ *huktɛn* 'taboo bear eyes' < *huktɛ -ŋ* {Ket plural};
> Northern Tungusic: Ewenki *tïgdewkī* 'lark' → Ket *təˑqtə* ~ *təˑqt* 'wagtail (*several species of birds of the genus Motacilla*)';

-ŋ- > *-ng-* → *-nk-*

> Northern Tungusic: Ewenki *daŋanī* 'name of shoulder bone' → Ket *dankịjaj* 'rucksack' < **dankịj* + Yeniseian *aj* 'sack'.

2.3.4 Changing
-lt- → *-l'l'-*

> Northern Tungusic: Ewenki *ūlta* 'echo' → Ket *úl'l'ɔŋ* 'echo';

-ŋs- → *-ns'-*

> Northern Tungusic: Ewenki *tuŋsuku* 'a bear head, a "funeral" of bear' → Ket *tʌns'uk* 'taboo designation of a bear stomach'.

CHAPTER 4

Mongolic Loanwords

Mongolic loanwords in Yeniseian comprise three different groups. Two of them contain loanwords mediated through Turkic and Tungusic languages. The third group is the smallest and the most uncertain group: there are insufficient criteria to posit a direct influence on Yeniseian of Mongolic.

1   Turkic Elements of Mongolic Origin in Yeniseian

There are Mongolic loanwords in Yeniseian, which have linguistic criteria peculiar to loanwords borrowed via Turkic and not directly from Mongolic languages. They display typical characteristics of Siberian Turkic languages. Two layers may be distinguished: Yenisei Turkic and Altai Turkic.

1.1   *Phonetic Considerations*
1.1.1   Criteria
1.1.1.1   *Shortening of Secondary Long Vowels*

There are some cases where Turkic mediation is revealed by the shortness of Mongolic secondary vowels:

Kott *keršo* 'clever' ← Altai Turkic *kärsü* 'clever, talanted' ← Mongolic *kersǖ* < *kersegüü* 'wise, circumspect, prudent; careful, circumspect, astute' < **kerse-GU* {Mongolic VN/adj., see Poppe GWM §152}:
    NE^S YeniseiT: Khakas *kirsē* ~ *kirse*; Sagai, Koibal *kersǟ*; Shor *kerse*; AltaiT: Altai *kersǖ*; Qumanda *kersig* ~ *kirsig* ~ *kersü*; Quu *kersig*; Teleut *kersü*;
Turkic ← Mongolic:
    cf. Middle Mongol: –; LM *kersegüü*; Modern Mongol: Khalkha *xersǖ*; Kalmuck *kersǖ*; Dagur *kərsū*.

Kott *šašïn* 'paper' ← Turkic **časïn* 'paper' ← Mongolic **čāsun* < *čaγasun* 'paper' < *čaγarsun* < **ča* 'white' +*GAn*+*r*-*sUn* {Mongolic NN, NV, VN, see Khabtagaeva 2001: 115}:
    cf. NE^S YeniseiT: Khakas *čazïn* ~ *čajïn*; Sagai, Koibal *sazïn*; Sagai, Beltir *čā́čïn*; AltaiT: Altai *čāzïn*; Qumanda *čazïn*; Quu *čažïn*;
Turkic ← Mongolic:
    Middle Mongol *čālsun*; LM *čaγasu(n)* ~ *čaγalsun* ~ *čaγarsun*; Modern Mongol: Buryat *sārha(n)*; Khalkha *cās(an)*; Kalmuck *tsāsn*; Dagur *čās*; Khamnigan *cārsa(n)*.

1.1.1.2   *Mongolic* m-

Initial *m-* is atypical for Turkic, usually initial *b-* changes to *m-* in Turkic languages (for details, see the chapter *Turkic m-*). The Turkic initial *m-* sporadically changed to *p-* in Altai Turkic (Baskakov 1972: 26, 27). There are some cases where the Mongolic *m-* changed to *b-* in Altai (Rassadin 1980: 28), e.g.

> Old Turkic *mal* (← Arabic) 'cattle, livestock' > Qumanda *pal*,
> Turkic *mïltïk* 'gun' > Qumanda *pultik*, etc.
> Mongolic: LM *mayiqan* 'tent' → Altai *baikan*.

The change *m-* > *p-* occurred in the Shor variety of Yenisei Turkic, e.g.

> Mongolic: LM *mergen* 'a good marksman; wisdom; wise, learned, sage, experienced' → Shor *pergen* 'a good marksman' (Rassadin 1980: 47).

From a phonetic perspective, the Kott verb *baktîr-* 'to praise' is a loanword from the Qumanda dialect of the Altai Turkic group or the Shor variety of Yenisei Turkic, where the original Mongolic initial *m-* changed to *p-*. As an example, Mongolic *mayta-* changed to *paqta-*. Moreover, in Kott it was voiced to *bakta-*. Further evidence of Turkic borrowing is the Turkic causative suffix *-Xr-*:

Kott *baktîr* 'inf. praise' ← Turkic *paktïr-* < *makta-Xr-* {Turkic VV/causative, see Erdal 2001: 709–710} ← Mongolic *mayta-* 'to praise, eulogize, laud, extol, glorify':
   cf. NE^S YeniseiT: Khakas, Kyzyl *maxta-*; Sagai, Koibal, Kachin *maqta-*; Shor *paqta-*; AltaiT: Altai *makta-*; Qumanda, Quu *makta-* ~ *pakta-*; Teleut *maqta-*; ChulymT *maqta-*; NW^N Siberian Tatar *maqta-*;
Turkic ← Mongolic:
   Middle Mongol *maqta-*; LM *mayta-*; Modern Mongol: Buryat, Khalkha *magta-*; Oirat dial. *maktă-*; Khamnigan *magta-*.

1.1.1.3   *Mongolic* g-

The initial consonant *g-* is also atypical for Turkic. The Mongolic initial *g-* and *γ-* regularly devoiced or spirantized in Siberian Turkic languages, e.g.

> Altai *kakay* 'pig' ← Mongolic: LM *γaqai*;
> Altai *kereči* 'witness' ← Mongolic: LM *gereči*, etc. (Rassadin 1980: 29);
> Khakas *kijege* 'braid, pigtail' ← Mongolic: LM *gejege*;
> Khakas *xom* 'sorrow' ← Mongolic: LM *γom* (Rassadin 1980: 40);
> Shor *kenetīn* 'suddenly' ← Mongolic: LM *genedteyin*;

Shor *kaŋza* 'pipe' ← Mongolic: LM *γangsa*, etc. (Rassadin 1980: 47);
Tuvan *xamčïk* 'epidemic' ← Mongolic: LM *γamšiγ*;
Tuvan *kudumču* 'street, lane' ← Mongolic: LM *γudumǰi*, etc. (Khabtagaeva 2009: 85).

Borrowing from Turkic, and not directly from Mongolic languages, is indicated by the initial voiceless consonant *k-* in the Yeniseian words instead of the Mongolic initial *g-* or *γ-*, e.g.

Kott *kolá* 'copper, brass' ← Turkic *kola* 'copper, brass' ← Mongolic *γauli ~ γuuli* 'brass, copper':
   NE^S YeniseiT: Khakas *xola*; Sagai, Koibal, Kachin *qola*; Shor *qola*; AltaiT: Altai *kolo*; Qumanda *kola*; Quu *koli*; Teleut *qūl*; SayanT: Tuvan *xola*; Tofan *qūl'i*; ChulymT *qōla*;
Turkic ← Mongolic:
   Middle Mongol *γula*; LM *γauli ~ γuuli*; Modern Mongol: Buryat *gūli(n)*; Khalkha *gūl'*; Kalmuck *gūl'*; Dagur *gaul'*; Khamnigan *gūli(n)*.

Kott *kant^{h}êx ~ kant^{h}êg* 'halter' ← Altai Turkic *kand'aga* 'saddle-thongs' ← Mongolic *γanǰuγa* 'thongs attached to a saddle for tying an object' < *γanǰu-GAn* {Mongolic VN, see Poppe 1964: §149}:
   cf. NE^S YeniseiT: Shor *xanǰïġa*; AltaiT: Altai *kand'aga*; Quu *kanža ~ kanča*; Teleut *qanǰaga*; NW^N Siberian Tatar *qancïġa ~ qanǰïġa*;
Turkic ← Mongolic:
   cf. Middle Mongol *ǰanǰuγa, qanǰuqa*; LM *γanǰuγ-a(n)*; Modern Mongol: Buryat *ganzaga*; Khalkha *gandzaga*; Kalmuck *ganz^{a}γa*; Dagur *gandzuγ^w*; Khamnigan *gandzagu(n) ~ gandzaga(n)*.

Kott *kanšá*; Yugh *kàńčá*; Ket *kàńčá* 'tobacco pipe' ← Turkic *kaŋsa < qaŋza* 'tobacco pipe' ← Mongolic *γaŋsa* 'tobacco pipe' ← Chinese:
   cf. NE^S YeniseiT: Khakas *xaŋza*; Sagai, Koibal, Kachin *qaŋza*; Kyzyl *χan^{d}za ~ χanza*; Shor *qanza*; AltaiT: Altai *kaŋza*; Tuba *kaŋza*; Qumanda *kaŋza*; Quu *kaŋza*; Teleut *qaŋza*; ChulymT *qaŋza*; NW^N Siberian Tatar *qancá ~ qaŋza*;
Turkic ← Mongolic:
   cf. Middle Mongol: –; LM *γangsa ~ γansa*; Modern Mongol: Buryat *ganza ~ gāha(n) ~ dāha(n)*; Khalkha *gāns(an)*; Oirat dial. *gandzā*; Khamnigan *gandza*.

Kott *kapsagai* 'nimble, quick (*said of a person, horse or dog*)' ← Turkic *kapčagai* 'quick' ← Mongolic *γabšiγai* 'swift, expeditious; valiant; vanguard' < *γab+si-* {Mongolic NV, see Poppe GWM §248} *-GAi* {Mongolic VN, see Poppe GWM §148}:

cf. NE^S YeniseiT: Khakas *xapčaǧay*; Koibal *kapčaǧay*; Shor *qapčïǧay*; AltaiT: Altai *kapšaǧay*; Tuba *kapčaǧay ~ kapčïǧai*; Qumanda *kapčaǧay*; Quu *kapžïǧay ~ kapšaǧay*; Teleut *qapšïǧay*; NW^N Siberian Tatar *qapšaǧay*;
Turkic ← Mongolic:
cf. Middle Mongol: –; LM *γabsiγai*; Modern Mongol: Buryat *gabšagai*; Khalkha *gawš-gai*; Kalmuck *gawšⁱγā*; Oirat dial. *gawšxā*; Khamnigan *gabčigai*.

1.1.1.4   *Mongolic n-*
Mongolic initial *n-* is also atypical for Turkic. The Turkic words with initial *n-* are usually loanwords, e.g.

Turkish *nar* 'pomegranate' ← Persian;
Turkmen *noqta*, Azeri *noxta*, Kazak, Karakalpak, Nogay *noqta*; Kirgiz
    noqto, Uzbek *noxta*; Tatar, Bashkir *nuqta*, Chuvash *năxta* ← Mongolic:
    LM *noγto* 'halter'; etc.

Kott *najči* 'friend' ← Turkic *nayǰï* ← Mongolic *nayiǰi*:
cf. NE^S YeniseiT: Khakas *nayǰï ~ nanči*; Sagai *nanǰï*, Koibal, Kachin *nanǰï*; Shor *nanči*; AltaiT: Altai *nadʼï*; Tuba *ńanǰži*; Qumanda *nadʼï*; Quu *nayidži*; Teleut *nayï*; ChulymT *nēze*;
Turkic ← Mongolic:
cf. Middle Mongol: –; LM *nayiǰi*; Modern Mongol: Buryat *naiža*; Khalkha *naiz*; Oirat dial. *nǟdz ~ nǟž*; Kalmuck *nǟdžⁱ*.

1.1.2   Re-borrowings
Some Yeniseian words are Turkic loanwords borrowed from Mongolic, but of ultimately Turkic origin. We have clear phonetic and morphological criteria to identify them, as the presence of vowels at the end of words, rotacism, lambdacism and the Mongolic suffixes.

1.1.2.1   *Rotacism*
Kott *arai* 'hardly, with' ← Turkic *aray* 'slowly, gently, with difficulty, hardly' ← Mongolic *arai* 'just a little too …; not quite …; hardly, scarcely, barely, with difficulty' ← Turkic **ār > āz* 'few, scanty, a little' +*Ai* {Mongolic NN, see Ramstedt 1957: 182–183}:
cf. NE^S YeniseiT: Khakas, Sagai, Koibal *aray*; Kyzyl *ārïy*; Shor *arïy*; AltaiT: Altai, Tuba, Qumanda, Teleut *aray*; Quu *arïy*; SayanT: Tuvan, Tofan *aray*; NW^N Siberian Tatar *aray*;
Turkic ← Mongolic:
cf. Middle Mongol: –; LM *arai*; Modern Mongol: Buryat, Khalkha *arai*; Oirat dial. *ärā*; Dagur *arān*; Khamnigan *arai ~ arï*;

Mongolic ← Turkic:
cf. Old Turkic *āz*; NE^S YeniseiT: Khakas *as*; AltaiT: Altai *as*; SayanT: Tuvan *as*.

1.1.2.2   *Turkic* VgV → *Mongolic* VyV

Kott *ajel* 'tent village'; Yugh *ajaɲi* 'village' ← Turkic *ayïl* 'village, family' ← Mongolic *ayil* 'family, household; settlement, group of tents, village' ← Turkic *aġïl* 'a settlement or group of tents':

cf. NE^S YeniseiT: –; AltaiT: Altai, Tuba, Qumanda, Quu *ayïl* 'house, village'; Teleut *ail* 'house, village'; NW^N Siberian Tatar *ayïl* 'village';

Turkic ← Mongolic:
cf. Middle Mongol *ayil*; LM *ayil*; Modern Mongol: Buryat, Khalkha *ail*; Oirat dial. *äl*; Dagur, Khamnigan *ail*;

Mongolic ← Turkic:
cf. Old Turkic *aġïl*; NE^S YeniseiT: Khakas, Sagai, Koibal, Kachin; Kyzyl, Shor *āl*; AltaiT: –; SayanT: Tuvan, Tofan *āl*; ChulymT *aġïl*; NW^N Siberian Tatar *avïl*.

1.2   *Morphological Considerations*

Below, three examples are presented, which belong to the category of "re-borrowings":

– The Kott word *alpaka* ~ *alpuga* ~ *alpuka*, meaning 'flying squirrel', which is the Turkic loanword *albïga* ~ *albuga* ~ *albaga* 'sable', is present in both Yenisei Turkic and Altai Turkic. The Turkic word originates from the Mongolic word *alban* 'official obligation; tax, impost, tribute' and the Turkic NN suffix +*GAn*, which forms nouns that designate the names of animals:

Kott *alpaka* ~ *alpuga* ~ *alpuka* 'flying squirrel' ← Turkic *albaga* 'sable' < *alba(n)+GAn* {Turkic NN forming nouns that designate names of animals and plants: Erdal 1991: 85–89} ← Mongolic *alban* 'compulsion, coercion; official obligation or service; tax, impost, tribute; corvée; public use':

cf. NE^S YeniseiT: Khakas, Shor *albïga*; Koibal *albaga*; AltaiT: Altai *albuga*; Quu, Teleut *albaga*;

Turkic ← Mongolic:
cf. Middle Mongol *alban*; LM *alban*; Modern Mongol: Buryat, Khalkha *alban*; Kalmuck *alwa*~ *alwn*; Dagur *alba*; Khamnigan *alba(n)*.

– The Mongolic word *kaltar* is used to denote a colour of horses, meaning 'variegated, spotted, blemished; having a white muzzle'. It is borrowed from the Turkic *qara* 'black' with Mongolic NN +*ltUr*/+*btUr*. It is a re-borrowing in Siberian Turkic languages. The evidence of Turkic borrowing in Kott is furnished not only by the phonetic form, but also by the semantic meaning. In Kott, as in Yenisei Turkic and Altai Turkic, the meaning is a 'brown horse with a white mouth':

Kott *kaltar* 'brown horse with white mouth' ← Turkic *qaltar* 'bay horse with yellow markings, brown horse with white mouth' ← Mongolic *qaltar* 'variegated, spotted, blemished; have a white muzzle' < *qara* 'black' +*ltAr* {Mongolic NN/adj., see Khabtagaeva 2001: 146–147} ← Turkic *qara* 'black':
 cf. NE^S YeniseiT: Khakas *xaltar* 'bay horse with yellow markings'; Sagai, Koibal, Kachin *qaltar* 'brown horse with white mouth'; Kyzyl *χalttar* 'brown horse with white mouth'; Shor *qaltïr* 'brown horse with white mouth'; AltaiT: Altai *kaltar* 'bay horse with yellow markings; silver fox'; Tuba *kaltar* 'bay horse with yellow markings'; Quu *kaldar ~ kaltar* 'bay, brown (*of a horse*)'; Teleut *qaltar* 'bay'; SayanT: Tuvan *kaldar* 'bay (*of a horse*); with black markings (*of the domestic animals*)';
Turkic ← Mongolic:
 cf. Middle Mongol *qaltar*; LM *qaltar*; Modern Mongol: Buryat *xaltar* 'light chestnut (*of a horse*); with red stripes on the legs and face (*of a dog*)'; Khalkha *xaltar* 'dirty, soiled, stained, spotted; brown with lighter markings (*horse, dog*)'; Kalmuck *xaltr* 'brown horse with white mouth and mane'; Dagur *kaltār*;
Mongolic ← Turkic:
 cf. Old Turkic *qara*; NE^S YeniseiT: Khakas *xara*; Sagai, Koibal, Kachin *qara*; Kyzyl *χara*; Shor *qara*; AltaiT: Altai; Tuba; Qumanda; Quu; Teleut *qara*; SayanT: Tuvan; Tofan *qara*; ChulymT *qara*; NW^N Siberian Tatar *qara*.

– In this case the Mongolic NN suffix +*GAi* demonstrates the Mongolic source of the Yeniseian form. The Yugh *súl'gej* 'left' was borrowed from Altai or Yenisei Turkic. In turn, the Mongolic word *soloγai* 'left-handed' was borrowed from Turkic *sōl* 'left':

Yugh *súl'gej* 'left' ← Turkic *sologay* 'left-handed' ← Mongolic *soloγai* 'left side or hand; left-handed; awkward; wrong, faulty' < **solo* +*GAi* {Mongolic NN/adj., see Poppe GWM § 123} ← Turkic **sōlŏ* > *sōl* 'left':
 cf. NE^S YeniseiT: Khakas, Shor *solaġay*; AltaiT: Altai *sologoy*; Qumanda *solay ~ sulay*; Teleut *sologoy*; SayanT: Tuvan *solagay*; NW^N Siberian Tatar *sulaġay ~ sulamay*;
Turkic ← Mongolic:
 Middle Mongol: –; LM *soloγai*; Modern Mongol: Buryat *halgai*, cf. West Buryat *holgoi* 'gaper'; Khalkha *solgoi*; Oirat dial. *solgā*; Dagur *solγui*;
Mongolic ← Turkic *sōlŏ* > *sōl* 'left':
 cf. Old Turkic *sōl*; NE^S YeniseiT: Khakas, Sagai, Koibal, Kachin, Shor *sol*; Kyzyl *sōl ~ soŋ*; AltaiT: Altai; Tuba; Qumanda; Quu; Teleut *sol*; SayanT: Tuvan *sol*; ChulymT *sol*.

1.2.1   Change of the Original Word Class
There are a few loanwords in Yeniseian where the original word class changed. This feature is peculiar to Yeniseian languages.

– The Kott verb *kalakai ~ kalakei* 'to stutter'[1] was borrowed from the Turkic form *kälägäi* 'stutterer'. The Yeniseian word occurs as an adjective too. The Mongolic origin can be explained morphologically, since it is derived from the Mongolic noun *kelen* 'tongue; language' and the Mongolic negative word *ügei*, literally 'without a tongue, without language':

Kott *kalakai ~ kalakei* '**verb** to stutter, *adj.* stuttering' ← Turkic *kälägäy* '**noun** stutterer' ← Mongolic *kelegei* 'dumb, mute; stammering, stuttering, tongue-tied' < *kelen ügei* 'without tongue' < *kelen* 'tongue; language' + *ügei* {Mongolic negative, see Poppe GWM § 632} < *kelen* 'tongue; language' < *kele-* 'to utter words, express in words; to speak, say, tell, narrate' *-n* {Mongolic VN, see Poppe GWM § 175}:
    cf. Old Turkic –; NE[S] YeniseiT: Khakas *kilegey* 'stammerer, stutterer'; Sagai, Koibal *kälägäy*; Shor *kelegey*; AltaiT: Altai, Teleut *kelegei*;
Turkic ← Mongolic:
    cf. Middle Mongol: –; LM *kelegei*; Modern Mongol: Buryat *xelexei*; Khalkha *xelgüi*; Oirat dial. *kelkä*.

1.3   *Semantic Considerations*
The lexical meaning proves the Turkic borrowing of some Mongolic words:

– The Turkic loanword in Kott *komtú* has the meaning 'grave', which exists only in the Khakas and Altai languages. In Mongolic languages, it originally meant 'case; long and narrow box, quiver':

Kott *komtú* '**grave**' ← Turkic **komdu* < *komda* '**coffin, grave**' ← Mongolic *qobdu* '**case**; long and narrow **box, quiver**':
    cf. NE[S] YeniseiT: Khakas *xomdï*; Koibal *kom ~ komda*; Kyzyl *χomdị*; AltaiT: Quu *komda*; SayanT: Tuvan *xomdu*; NW[N] Siberian Tatar *qumta*;
Turkic ← Mongolic:
    cf. Middle Mongol *qobdu*; LM *qobdu*; Modern Mongol: Buryat, Khamnigan *xobto*; Khalkha *xowd*; Oirat dial. *xobdă*.

---

[1] Cf. Kott *kalakaj-â-kŋ* {*-â-* present tense, *-kŋ-* sg.1, see Werner 1990: 156–160} 'I am stuttering'; *kalakaj-âlček* {*-âlček* imperative form, see Werner 1990: 193} 'Stutter!'.

– From a semantic perspective, the Yugh verb *sáŋa*, with the meaning 'to feel, imagine, understand, keep in mind, examine', must be a Mongolic loanword. In Mongolic we find the verb *sana-* with the same meanings. In turn, the Mongolic word is of Turkic origin, with the meaning 'to count'.

Yugh *sáŋa* 'inf. **to feel, guess,** imagine, understand, remember, keep in mind, find out, test, examine' ← Turkic *sana-* '**to think**, desire, feel, miss' ← Mongolic *sana-* '**to think**, reflect, ponder; to hold an opinion; to intend, plan; to remember, keep in mind; to recall; to long for' ← Turkic *sana-* '**to count**' < *sān* 'number' +*A-* {NV, see Erdal 1991: 308} < *sā-* 'to count' *-n* {Turkic VN, see Erdal 1991: 308}:
  cf. NE^S YeniseiT: Shor *sana-* 'to wish'; AltaiT: Altai *sana-* 'to think, dream, wish; take care, miss'; Tuba *sana-* 'to think, wish, dream'; Qumanda *sana-* 'to think, wish, decide'; Quu *sana-* 'to think, deside, wish'; Teleut *sanan-*[2] 'to think'; SayanT: Tuvan *sanal*[3] 'proposal; speech'; Tofan *sana-* 'to read'; ChulymT *sana-* 'to read';
Turkic ← Mongolic:
  Middle Mongol *sana-*; LM *sana-*; Modern Mongol: Buryat *hana-*; Khalkha, Khamnigan *sana-*; Kalmuck *san^a-*; Dagur *sanə-*;
Mongolic ← Turkic:
  cf. Old Turkic *sana-*; NE^S YeniseiT: Khakas *sana-*; Sagai, Koibal, Kachin *san* 'number'; Kyzyl *sāna-*; Shor *sana-*; SayanT: Tuvan, Tofan *sana-*; ChulymT *sana-*.

1.4 Loanwords with Yeniseian Suffixes

The next two Mongolic loanwords examined here were used in the Kott language with productive Yeniseian suffixes:

Kott *dʼônaš* 'in a crowd' < *dʼôn -aš* {Kott comitative} ← Turkic *dʼon* 'people' ← Mongolic *ǰon* 'people':
  cf. NE^S YeniseiT: Khakas, Sagai, Shor *čon*; AltaiT: Altai, Tuba *dʼon*; Qumanda *dʼon* ~ *ńoŋ*; Teleut *yon*; SayanT: Tuvan *čon*; ChulymT *čon*;
Turkic ← Mongolic:
  cf. Middle Mongol: –; LM *ǰon*; Modern Mongol: Buryat *zo(n)*; Khamnigan *dzon*.

Kott *turkatu* 'quick, rapid' < *turka -tu* {Yeniseian NN/adj.} ← Turkic *türgen* 'quick, rapid' ← Mongolic *türgen* 'quick, swift, rapid, speedy; hurried; soon':
  cf. NE^S YeniseiT: Khakas *türgün*; AltaiT: Altai, Tuba, Qumanda, Teleut *türgen*; SayanT: Tuvan *dürgen*; Tofan *türgen*;

---

2 < **sana-n-* {Turkic VV/reflexive}.
3 < *sana-l* {Mongolic VN, see Poppe GWM §159}.

Turkic ← Mongolic:
Middle Mongol *türgen* ~ *türgün*; LM *türgen*; Modern Mongol: Buryat, Khalkha, Khamnigan *türgen*; Kalmuck *türgn*; Dagur *turɣun*.

2   Tungusic Elements of Mongolic Origin in Yeniseian

There are Mongolic loanwords in Yeniseian which exhibit linguistic criteria peculiar to loanwords borrowed via Tungusic and not directly from Mongolic languages. They display features typical of the Ewenki language.

2.1   *Phonetic Considerations*
2.1.1   Criteria
2.1.1.1   *The Mongolic Consonant* č-

The Mongolic word under examination here was possibly borrowed into Ket through the mediation of Yakut and Ewenki. This is proven by the change of the Mongolic initial č- > s- in Yakut[4] and further in the Ewenki dialects:[5]

Ket *sūliŋ* [*dɛʔŋ*] 'people coming to meet each other' ← Northern Tungusic: Ewenki *suglān* 'meeting' ← Turkic: Yakut *sugulān* 'the place of meetings, gatherings' ← Mongolic *čuɣlaɣan* 'assembly, gathering, meeting; wrapper' < *čuɣla-* 'to gather, assemble; to wrap' -*GAn* {Mongolic VN, see Poppe GWM § 106}:
  Northern Ewenki: Yerbogachon, Ilimpeya *huglan*; *Southern Ewenki*: Podkamennyi, Nepa *suglān*;
Ewenki ← Turkic:
  Yakut *sugulān* 'the place of meetings, gatherings';
Turkic ← Mongolic:
  Middle Mongol *čula-*; LM *čuɣlaɣ-a(n)*; Modern Mongol: Buryat *suglā(n)*; Khalkha *cuglā(n)*; Kalmuck *tsūlɣan*; Khamnigan *cuglān*.

2.1.1.2   *The Development of a Secondary Long Vowel in Ket*
The Ket forms were clearly borrowed from Ewenki. This may be proven by the development of the secondary long vowel from sequence *Vowel—Consonant g—Vowel*. This is a typical feature for Yeniseian loanwords and generally for

---
4   According to Yakut phonetic rules, Turkic č- regularly changed to s-, e.g. Old Turkic *čärig* 'army' ~ Yakut *särī* 'war; battle; army'; Old Turkic *čāġ* 'time, a point in time, a period of time' ~ Yakut *sax*; etc.
5   Ewenki *siär* 'rule, custom' ← Yakut *siär* 'id.' ← Mongolic: cf. LM *čeger* 'taboo, prohibition; abstinence; quarantine (*due to epidemics*)'; Ewenki *simē-* 'to decorate' ← Yakut *simā-* 'id.' ← Mongolic: cf. LM *čime-* 'to adorn, decorate, bedeck, dress up'; etc. (For more examples and details, see Khabtagaeva 2011: 97–98).

Modern Turkic and Modern Mongol languages. The Tungusic word *togoi* 'bend of a river' was borrowed or via Yakut, or directly from Mongolic. The original Mongolic form *toqoi* is with the devoiced consonant *VqV*, which regularly spirantized in Modern Mongolic:

Southern Ket *tōˑj*; Northern Ket *tōˑji*; Yugh *tōˑj* 'river arm' (Werner 2002/2: 283) ← Northern Tungusic: Ewenki *togoi* 'bend of a river' ← Siberian Turkic *toǵoy* 'river arm' ← Mongolic *toqoi* 'elbow, cubit; bend of a river, bay, port, harbor':
  Southern Ewenki: Podkamennyi *toγočī* 'winding (*about the river*)'; *Northern Ewenki*: Yerbogachon, *Southern Ewenki*: Sym *toγor-* 'to wind (*about the river*)';
Tungusic ← Siberian Turkic:
  NE^S AltaiT: Altai *tokoy*; Quu *toqoy*; Teleut *toqoy*; SayanT: Tuvan *dugay*; NE^N Yakut *toǵoy*; NW^N Siberian Tatar *toǵay*;
Turkic ← Mongolic *toqoi*:
  Middle Mongol *toqai*; LM *toqoi* ~ *toqai*; Modern Mongol: Buryat, Khalkha *toxoi*; Oirat dial. *toxa*;

2.1.1.3 The Mongolic Final Consonat -l

The Ket final consonant -*n* is one piece of evidence for the Tungusic and not direct Mongolic borrowings. The Mongolic loanwords in Tungusic, where the final -*l* regularly changed to -*n*, were explained by Doerfer (1985: 21) as a 'difference' from the Tungusic plural suffix -*l*:

Northern Ket *ɔmɔγuun* 'reindeer saddle' ← Northern Tungusic: Ewenki *emegen* 'saddle; reindeer saddle' ← Mongolic *emegel* 'saddle':
  Northern Ewenki: Yerbogachon, Ilimpeya; *Southern Ewenki*: Podkamennyi *emegen*;
Tungusic ← Mongolic:
  Middle Mongol *eme'el* ~ *emēl*; LM *emegel*; Modern Mongol: Buryat, Khalkha *emēl*; Oirat dial. *emǟlʻ* ~ *emǟl*; Dagur *ämǟl*; Khamnigan *emēl* ~ *emȫl* ~ *ömȫl*.

2.1.1.4 The Mongolic Consonant -ǰ-

The Mongolic affricate -ǰ- in some Northern Tungusic loanwords changed to -*d(i)*-, e.g.

Common Ewenki *edī* 'husband', Lamut *edi* 'husband, man', Negidal *edī* 'husband, man; friend' ← Mongolic *eǰin*: LM *eǰen* 'lord, master, ruler, owner' ← Turkic: cf. Old Turkic *äyä* ~ *iyä* ~ *iδi* 'master, owner, the Lord' (SSTMJa 2: 437–438);
Ewenki dial. *kadal* ~ *kadar* 'bridle' ← Mongolic *kadal* cf. Dagur *xadal*: LM *qaǰaγar* (Doerfer 1985: 57);

Barguzin Ewenki *gunadin* 'three-year-old cow' ← Mongolic **gunaǰin*: LM *γunaǰin* (Khabtagaeva 2010/2011: 251), etc.

The next Ket word of Mongolic origin was clearly borrowed from Ewenki. Further, the Tungusic intervocalic *VdV* devoiced in Ket:

Ket *kútgit* 'dish of intestines' < *kútgi -t* {?} ← Northern Tungusic: Ewenki *gudige* 'stomach of animals' ← Mongolic **güǰige*: LM *güǰege* 'stomach of animals; rumen used as container for butter, kumiss':
  Northern Ewenki: Yerbogachon, Ilimpeya; Southern Ewenki: Podkamennyi *gudiγē*;
  Tungusic ← Mongolic:
  Middle Mongol *güǰēn*; LM *güǰege*; Modern Mongol: Buryat *güzē(n)*; Khalkha *güdzē*; Kalmuck *güzän*; Dagur *guǰē*; Khamnigan *güdzē(n) ~ güdzō̄(n) ~ güdžō̄(n)*.

2.2 Morphological Considerations
2.2.1 Ewenki Suffixes

– The Tungusic mediation of the Ket word is proven by the Ewenki productive denominal noun suffix *+tī*, which forms names of animals based on what they eat[6] (Vasilevič 1958: 793; Nedjalkov 1997: 297):

Northern Ket *bejetil* 'cannibal' < *bejeti -l* {?} ← Northern Tungusic: Ewenki *beyetī* 'cannibal' < *beye* 'man, person, body' *+tī* {Ewenki NN}:
  Northern Ewenki: Yerbogachon, Ilimpeya; Southern Ewenki: Podkamennyi *beyetī*;
  Tungusic ← Mongolic:
  Middle Mongol *beye ~ biye*; LM *beye(n)*; Modern Mongol: Buryat *beye*; Khalkha *biye*; Kalmuck *biy*; Dagur *bəy*; Khamnigan *beye ~ biye*.

– The Tungusic mediation of the Ket compound is demonstrated by the Ewenki optative suffix *-ktA* of first person in singular form (Nedjalkov 1997: 19; Boldyrev 2000: 454):

Ket *úkta* 'slowly!', cf. Southern Ket *úkta índɛt!* 'read slowly!' ← Northern Tungusic: Ewenki *udakta* 'let me be slow' < *uda-* 'to be slow, to delay' *-ktA* {Ewenki sg.1 optative} ← Mongolic *uda-* 'to tarry, hesitate, delay; to be late or delayed; to last':
  Common Ewenki *uda-*;

---

6 Ewenki *sēktakān* 'willow' > *sēktakātï* 'elk'; *mō* 'tree' > *mōtï* 'elk'; *ollo* 'fish' > *ollotï* 'seagull', etc.

Tungusic ← Mongolic:
Middle Mongol *uda-*; LM *uda-*; Modern Mongol: Buryat, Khalkha, Khamnigan *uda-*; Kalmuck *ud^a-*.

2.3 Semantic Considerations

The Tungusic borrowing may be proven by the lexical meaning also. There are some Tungusic words of Mongolic origin where the original lexical meaning is broadened or narrowed:

- The Ket word with meaning 'friend' was clearly borrowed from Ewenki *beye* 'man, person, body'. Originally, in Mongolic it means 'body, physique, organism; health':

Ket *be⸱j* '**friend**' ← Northern Tungusic: Ewenki *beye* '**man, person**, body' ← Mongolic *beye* '**body, physique**, organism; health' (For data, see above Northern Ket *bejetil* 'cannibal').

- The following Ket word is a compound, where the first part was borrowed from Ewenki. This is shown by the special Tungusic lexical meaning 'storage shed' which developed to 'covered storeroom' in Ket. In turn, the Tungusic word borrowed from Mongolic verb *qolbo-* 'to unite, combine, connect, etc.', which is ultimately of Turkic origin:

Ket *kolij* '**covered storeroom**' < *kol* + Yeniseian *i⸱* 'storage shed':
*kol ← Northern Tungusic: Ewenki *kolbo* '**storage shed**' ← Mongolic *qolbo-* 'to unite, combine, connect, incorporate; to link to; to unite in marriage' ← Turkic **qolă-*, cf. Old Turkic *qoš-* 'to conjoin, unite (*two things*)':
Southern Ewenki: Podkamennyi *kolbo* 'storage shed (*platform on piles, with a roof*); storeroom, barn';
Tungusic ← Mongolic:
Middle Mongol *qolba-*; LM *qolbo- ~ qolba-*; Modern Mongol: Buryat, Khalkha, Khamnigan *xolbo-*; Oirat dial. *xolwă- ~ xolbă-*; Dagur *xolb-*.

3 Direct Mongolic Loanwords?

In some cases, it is difficult to decide whether the Mongolic words borrowed by Yeniseian came directly from Mongolic or via Turkic or Tungusic mediation.

3.1 Kott

Kott *saran* 'wild lily-bulb' (Werner 2002/2: 160) ← Mongolic **sarana* 'Lilium martagon, a lily with an edible bulb':

cf. Middle Mongol: –; LM *sarana*; Western Buryat *harāna*; Khalkha *sarāna*; Remaining lgs. –;

Mongolic → Turkic:

NW[N] Tatar *sarana* 'lily'; Siberian Tatar –; Bashkir *harïna* 'lily'; Chuvash *sarana* 'lily, a kind of the bulbs' (← Tatar);

cf. Turkic *sarġay* 'Lilium martagon' (?) < *sarïġ* 'yellow' + *ay*:

cf. Old Turkic –; NE[S] YeniseiT: Khakas *sarġay*; Sagai, Koibal *sarġay* (R); Shor *sarġay*; AltaiT: Altai *sarġay*; Qumanda *sarġay*; Quu *sarġay*; Teleut *sarġay*; SayanT: Tuvan *ay*; Tofan *ay*; NE[N] Yakut *sardaŋa ~ sardaġa ~ sardāna*; NW[N] Siberian Tatar *sarġay*; Remaining lgs. –.

Etymology: Räsänen VEWT 403a; Vasmer 1986/3: 560; Anikin 2000: 484; Dmitrieva 2001: 103–104

The Kott word *saran* 'wild lily-bulb' was directly borrowed from Mongolic *sarana* or Siberian Russian *sarana* 'forest purple flower, similar to a lily' (Anikin 2000: 484). This form is absent in Siberian Turkic. From a phonetic perspective, apocope occurred in the Kott form.

According to the Sayan Turkic form *ay*, the Turkic word *sarġay* 'Lilium martagon' could originally be a compound word which consists of *sarïġ* 'yellow' and *ay* 'moon'. According to Dmitrieva (2001: 103–104), the Mongolic word is of Turkic origin. The base is Turkic **sarï(ġ)* 'yellow', which was derived with Mongolic suffix +*GAnA*, forming the names of plants and animals (for details on suffix, see Poppe GWM § 119; Khabtagaeva 2009: 280). In this way, the secondary long vowel in Buryat and Khalkha forms is explainable. The Turkic languages of Volga region as Tatar, Bashkir and Chuvash re-borrowed the Mongolic word *sarana*.

Anikin (2000: 484) after Vasmer (1986/3: 560), consider Russian *sarana* as a Tatar loanword. The Chuvash form was probably borrowed from Tatar.

3.2 Arin

Arin *meninajči* < **meni* + *najči* 'friend' (Werner 2002/2: 24) ← Mongolic **minu nayiji* 'my friend':

LM *nayiji* 'friend'; Modern Mongol: Buryat *naiža* 'buddhist priest tutor of child in monastery'; Khalkha *naiz* 'friend; a ceremony performed by archers at the beginning and end of a match'; Oirat dial. *nǟdz ~ nǟž* 'friend'; Kalmuck *nǟdž[i]* 'friend, comrade'; Dagur –; Khamnigan –;

Mongolic → Turkic:

cf. NE[S] YeniseiT: Khakas *nayǰï ~ nanči*; Sagai *nanǰï*, Koibal, Kachin *nanǰï* (R); Shor nanči; AltaiT: Altai nadʼï; Tuba ńandži; Qumanda nadʼï; Quu nayïdži; Teleut nayï; ChulymT nēze 'brother-in-law'; NE^N Yakut ńādʼï 'godfather, godmother'; Remaining lgs. –.

Etymology: –

From a morphological perspective, the Arin word menïnajči 'friend' consists of the Mongolic possessive pronoun minu 'my' and the Mongolic word nayiǰi 'friend'. Despite the existence of Turkic forms, the Arin word was probably borrowed directly from Western Buryat.

Arin *oo* 'woods' (Werner 2002/2: 44) ← Mongolic *oi 'woods, forest, grove' < *hoi*:
cf. Middle Mongol: Precl.Mo. *oi*; SH *hoi*; HY *hoi*; YY *oi*; LM *oi*; Modern Mongol: Buryat *oi*; Khalkha *oi*; Oirat dial. *ȫ*; Dagur –; Khamnigan *oi*;

Mongolic → Turkic:
NE^N Yakut *oy* 'small forest in the open field; forest' (Pek.);

Mongolic ← Turkic *oy* < *ōy* 'hole, cavity; valley':
cf. Old Turkic *ōy* 'hole, cavity; valley'; NE^S YeniseiT: Khakas *oy* 'lowland valley; cavity, hollow; deepening'; Sagai, Koibal, Kachin *oy* 'the hole, the pit, the valley, the deepening' (R); Shor *oyas* 'edge of a wood'; AltaiT: Altai *oy* 'lowland, cavity, hollow'; Tuba *oyduk*[7] 'hole'; Qumanda *oydïk* 'lowland, cavity, hollow'; Teleut *oydïk* 'hole, pit, hollow'; SayanT: Tuvan *oy* 'lowland, hollow'; Tofan *oy* 'spring (*water*)'; ChulymT *oy* 'hollow'; NE^N Yakut –; Dolgan –; NW^N Siberian Tatar *uy* 'lowland'; NW^S Kirgiz *oy* 'lowland, cavity, hollow'; Fu-yü –; Kazak *oy* 'lowland, cavity, hollow'; SE Yellow Uyghur *oy* 'valley, steppe, land'.

Etymology: Kałużyński 1962: 36; Doerfer TMEN 1: 546; 541; Räsänen VEWT 358b; Clauson ED 265b; ESTJa 1974: 425–428; SSTMJa 2: 330; SIGTJa 1997: 98; Nugteren 2011: 358; Khabtagaeva 2015a: 123

The Arin word was borrowed directly from Mongolic, because the Turkic languages possess the same phonetic form, though with a different meaning.

Arin *tʼugal* 'calf' (Werner 2002/2: 314) ← Mongolic *tugal (cf. Buryat) < *tuɣul* 'calf less than a year old; calf in the first year':
cf. Middle Mongol: Precl.Mo. *tuɣūl*; SH *tuqul*; HY; ZY *tuqul*; YY *toqol*; Muq. *tuɣul*; LM *tuɣul*; Modern Mongol: Buryat *tugal*; Khalkha *tugal*; Kalmuck *tuɣ^ul*; Dagur *tokul'* (E); Khamnigan *tugal ~ tugul*;

Mongolic → Turkic:
NE^S SayanT: Tofan *tuɣul* 'calf of cattle less than a year old'; NE^N Yakut *tugut* 'calf of reindeer less than a year old'; Dolgan *tugut ~ tubut* 'calf of reindeer'; NW^S Fu-yü *duhul* 'calf';

---

7 < *oy +*lXG* {Turkic NN}.

cf. Turkic *toqlï* 'a lamb of a few months':

cf. Old Turkic *toqlï*; NE^S YeniseiT: –; AltaiT: –; SayanT: Tuvan *togdu*; ChulymT –; NE^N –; NW^N Siberian Tatar *tuqlï*; NW^S Kirgiz *toktu*; Fu-yü –; Kazak *toqtï*; SE Yellow Uyghur *toqtï*.

Etymology: Kałużyński 1961: 117; Doerfer TMEN 2: 524–525; Rassadin 1971: 235; Clauson ED 469a; Stachowski 1993: 229; Anikin 2000: 560; SIGTJa 2001: 434; Nugteren 2011: 524

The etymology of the Arin word is unknown (Werner 2002/2: 314). The vowel -*a*- in the non-initial position and the lexical meaning suggest direct borrowing from Buryat. The reason for the palatalization of the Arin initial consonant *t'*- is unclear.

The Common Mongolic word is present in almost all Middle Mongol sources and Modern non-archaic and archaic languages (Nugteren 2011: 524). The Mongolic word is present also in some Siberian Turkic languages. Phonetically, the Tofan form *tuɣul* 'calf of cattle less than a year old' shows the early period of borrowing (Rassadin 1971: 235). The Yakut and Dolgan forms were borrowed from the Mongolic form **tuɣud* with the Mongolic plural suffix +*d* (for details on functions, see Poppe GWM § 265), and the semantic change occurred (Kałużyński 1961: 117; Stachowski 1993: 229). From Yakut, the word was borrowed further into Siberian Russian (Anikin 2000: 560). The Mongolic word was borrowed into Fu-yü with voiced consonant *d*-.

The Mongolic word clearly is connected with the Turkic word *toqlï*, which means 'a lamb a few months old' (Doerfer TMEN 2: 524–525; Clauson ED 469a). From Cuman, Turkic the word was borrowed into Hungarian.[8] The etymological background of the Hungarian word was discussed by Róna-Tas & Berta (WOT 2011: 915), where they exclude the Turkic-Mongolic connection and do not accept the Mongolic influence of the Yakut and Dolgan forms.

3.3   Yugh

Yugh *usn-č-tuj* 'let down one's hair' (Werner 2002/2: 357) < **usn* 'hair' -*č* {?} + *tújuŋ* 'to hang' (Werner 2002/2: 284):

*usn ← Mongolic *üsün* 'hair, fur' < *hüsün*:

Middle Mongol: Precl.Mo. *üsün*; SH *hüsu(n)*; HY *hüsün*; YY *hüsü*; Muq. *üsün*; Leiden *hüsün*, Ist. *hüsün*; RH *hüsün*; LM *üsü(n)*; Modern Mongol: Buryat *ühe(n)*; Khalkha *üs*; Oirat dial. *üs^ü ŋ ~ üs*; Kalmuck *üsn*; Dagur *xus* (E); Khamnigan *üse(n) ~ ösö(n)*.

Etymology: Nugteren 2011: 371

The Yugh word belongs to the category of words of uncertain etymology.

---

8   Turkic: Cuman **toklu* → Hungarian *toklyó* [*tokyō*] 'one-year-old lamb'.

3.4 Ket

Ket *bilʲda* ~ *bilʲdɛ*; Yugh *bilʲlʲa* ~ *bildʲa* 'all' (Werner 2002/1: 159) ← Mongolic **bulta* < *bultu* 'all, whole, without exception; entire[ly], complete[ly]':

Middle Mongol: –; LM *bultu*; Modern Mongol: Buryat *bulta* ~ *bultan*; Khalkha *bult*; Kalmuck *bultᵘ*; Dagur *bolto* (T); Khamnigan *bultu* ~ *bulta*;

Mongolic → Tungusic 'quite, entirely, completely':

cf. Northern Tungusic: Solon Ewenki *bultu* 'entirely, completely; all at once'; Southern Tungusic: Udihe *bultai* 'entirely, completely, for ever'; Ulcha *bulti* 'entirely, completely; for ever; all, any, anyone'; Orok *bulta* ~ *bultai* ~ *bultay* ~ *bultey* 'entirely, completely; for ever; all at once, suddenly'; Remaining lgs. –.

Etymology: SSTMJa 1: 108b

The etymology of the Yeniseian words is unknown. Probably, they connect with the Mongolic pronoun *bultu* 'all, whole'. The Mongolic etymology fits from the phonetic and semantic viewpoint.

The Tungusic borrowing exludes the lexical meaning of the Tungusic forms and the lack of the Ewenki data.

Ket *nikkor* 'sorcerer (*in shaman's speech*)' (Vajda & Werner: in preparation) ← Mongolic **nökör* 'friend, comrade, companion; husband':

cf. Middle Mongol: Precl.Mo. *nökür*; SH *nökör*; HY *nökör*; Muq. *nöker* ~ *nökör*; LM *nökör*; Modern Mongol: Buryat *nüxer*; Khalkha *nöxör*; Oirat dial. *nökär*; Kalmuck *nökr*; Dagur *nuɣur* (E); Khamnigan *nüker* ~ *neker*.

Etymology: Nugteren 2011: 463

The Ket word is probably connected with the Mongolic word *nökör* 'friend, comrade, companion; husband'. The problematic side of the etymology is the absence of any other direct Mongolic borrowings into Ket.

In the Ket form the gemination of consonant -*k*- occurred and the change of vowel *ö* > *i* happened in the first syllable.

CHAPTER 5

Typical Features of Altaic Loanwords in Yeniseian

1   Phonetic Peculiarities

1.1   *Disappearance of Vowel Harmony*
Due to absence of the vowel harmony in Yeniseian, the Turkic and Tungusic front vowels regularly became back vowels in the Yeniseian loanwords.

1.1.1   Disappearance of Vowel Harmony in Turkic Loanwords
Kott

> Kott *aktur* 'postp. through' ← Turkic *ötküre* < *ötgürü*;
> Kott *baha* 'strong; hero' < *beke* ← Turkic *böke* 'hero, strong' ← Mongolic *böke* 'strong, solid, stalwart, firm, robust, vigorous, sturdy; wrestler';
> Kott *bôru* ~ *boru*; Assan *boru* ~ *borü* 'wolf' ← Turkic *böri*;
> Kott *kalakai* ~ *kalakei* 'verb to stutter, *adj.* stuttering' ← Turkic *kälägäy* 'stammerer, stutterer' ← Mongolic *kelegei* 'dumb, mute; stammering, stuttering, tongue-tied';
> Kott *kolča* 'slow (*a person, horse, reindeer, etc.*)' ← Turkic *kȫlǰe* 'slow, slowly';
> Kott *kumiš* ~ *kumuš*; Arin *kumiš*; Assan *kumís* ~ *kumus* 'silver' ← Turkic *kümüš*;
> Kott *ogus*; Arin *ogus* 'bull' ← Turkic *ögüs* < *oküz* 'ox';
> Kott *tabat*; Assan *tabát* ~ *tapat* 'camel' ← Turkic *täbä* < *täβäy*;
> Kott *turkatu* 'quick, rapid' < *turkan -tu* {Yeniseian NN/adj.} ← Turkic *türgen* 'quick, rapid' ← Mongolic *türgen* 'quick, swift, rapid, speedy; hurried; soon';
> Kott *urum* 'cloth, linen' ← Turkic *ürüm* < *örüm* 'something plaited or woven';

Yugh and Ket

> Yugh *baʔt* ~ *bat* 'face, forehead' ← Turkic *bät* 'the human face' < *bet*;
> Yugh *χap* ~ *χaʔp*; Ket *qap* ~ *qaʔp* 'boat' ← Turkic *kebe* < *kämi* 'ship or boat';
> Yugh *ugur* 'soup or porridge made of grain' ← Turkic *ügre* 'soup; noodles; broth containing noodles';

Yugh *unče* 'because' ← Turkic *üčün* 'because of, for the sake of, for; because, in order to';

Arin

Arin *uške* 'he-goat' ← Turkic *üške* < *äčkü* 'goat'.

1.1.2 Disappearance of Vowel Harmony in Tungusic Loanwords

Ket *daŋtakan* 'marsh' ← Ewenki *detkēn* 'marsh' < *det* 'tundra, marsh, mossy glade' +*kĀn* {Ewenki NN/diminutive}.

1.2 *Diphthongization*

There are some Yeniseian cases where the diphthong appeared in different positions of words. Possibly, it occurred under the influence of the vowels -*i*- or -*ï*- in the following or previous syllable.

1.2.1 Diphthongization in Turkic Loanwords

Assan *xajp* 'boat' ← Turkic *kebe* < *kämi* 'ship or boat';
Kott *tarei* ~ *tarêi* 'coarse cloth' ← Turkic *täri* 'the skin, hide (*of a human being or animal*)'.

1.2.2 Diphthongization in Tungusic Loanwords

Central Ket *ajgiddɛ*; Southern Ket *ajgitdɛ* 'wooded tundra, pine bog' < *agij* ← Ewenki *aγī* 'taiga, tundra, marsh' + Yeniseian *deʔ* 'lake';
Ket *alepqaj* '*inf.* flare up, fly into a rage' ← Ewenki *alipkī-* 'to be angry' < *ali-* 'to be angry, to anger, make angry' -*pkī-* {Ewenki VV};
Ket *boŋnij* 'cemetery; grave' ← Ewenki *bunī* 'dead person; cemetery, grave' < *bu-* 'to die' -*nī* {Ewenki VN}.

1.3 *Prothesis in Turkic Loanwords*

Kott *ɛšjalikitan* 'flower, bloom' ← Turkic *čakayaktan-* 'to cover with flowers; to blossom (*of flower buds*)', cf. Khakas *čaxayax* 'flower' +*ta-* {Khakas NV}; -*n-* {Khakas VV/reflexive}.

1.4 Apocope

There are some Turkic and Tungusic loanwords in Yeniseian where the final vowel regularly dropped.

1.4.1 Apocope in Turkic Loanwords

Kott *aibič* ~ *aipiš* 'old man' ← Turkic *aybičï* 'fellow countryman';
Kott *aktur* 'postp. through' ← Turkic *ötküre* < *ötgürü*;
Kott *in* ~ *în*; Arin *in*; Yugh *iˀn*; Ket *iˀn* 'needle' ← Turkic *īnä* < *ignä*;
Kott *kantʰêx* ~ *kantʰêg* 'halter' ← Turkic *kandʼaga* 'saddle-thongs' ← Mongolic *γanǰuγa* 'thongs attached to a saddle for tying an object';
Kott *kep* ~ *qep* ~ *xep* ~ *xêp*; Assan *kep* ~ *xajp*; Yugh *χap* ~ *χaˀp*; Ket *qap* ~ *qaˀp* 'boat' ← Turkic *kebe* < *kämi* 'ship or boat';
Pumpokol *kun*; Yugh *kūʰn*; Southern Ket *kùn*, Central Ket *kū̀nə*, Northern Ket *kū̀ne*, Eastern Ket *kūn* 'wolverine' ← Turkic *kunu*;
Kott *šar* ~ *šâr* 'yellowish-tan colour of horses' ← Turkic *sarï* < *sārïġ* 'yellow, light bay (*colour of horses*)';
Assan *ug* 'owl' ← Turkic *ügü* < *ṻgi*;
Yugh *χoj*, Ket *qoːj* 'thick (*said of liquids*)' ← Turkic *qoyu* < *qoyuġ* 'thick, viscid, dense';
Ket *iˑlʼ* 'arm' ← Turkic *äli* < *älig* 'hand, forearm; the width of a finger (*measure of length*)'.

1.4.2 Apocope in Tungusic Loanwords

Ket *beˀj* 'friend' ← Ewenki *beye* 'man, person, body' ← Mongolic *beye* 'body, physique, organism; health';
Ket *bōŋ* 'dead person', *boŋnij* 'cemetery; grave' ← Ewenki *bunī* 'dead person; cemetery, grave' < *bu-* 'to die' -*nī* {Ewenki VN};
Yugh *číčik* 'wagtail' ← Ewenki *čičakūn* 'wagtail, small bird';
Ket *hiˑlʼ* 'intensive particle' ← Ewenki *hila* 'well!; well ... then! come on!';
Central Ket *lɔčik* 'child's saddle' ← Ewenki *ločoko* 'saddle';
Southern Ket *qùt* ~ *qùr* 'the great "first" person; shaman's main spirit helper'; cf. Northern Ket *qū̀re*, Central Ket *qū̀de* 'make magic (*said of a shaman*)' ← Ewenki *kutu* 'happiness, good luck, success' ← Turkic *qut* 'soul; spirit';
Ket *sēˑtal* ~ *sēˑtil* 'height' ← Ewenki *sigdilē* 'distance between objects, interval';
Ket *tʌnsʼuk* 'taboo designation of a bear stomach' ← Ewenki *tuŋsuku* 'a bear head, a "funeral" of bear'.

1.5   *Paragoge*

An additional vowel appeared at the end of words in some Yeniseian loanwords. The origin is unknown, and a connection with the Yeniseian feminine or the possessive suffixes is not excluded.

1.5.1   Paragoge in Turkic Loanwords

Yugh *ajaŋi* 'village' ← Turkic *ayïl* 'village, family' ← Mongolic *ayil* 'family, household; settlement, group of tents, village' ← Turkic *aġïl* 'a settlement or group of tents';
Kott *îri* ~ *îre* 'thread, tendon' ← Turkic *sīr* < *siŋir* 'muscle, sinew, tendon';
Assan *kabirgina* ~ *kaburgina* 'onion' ← Turkic *köβürgän* 'wild onion';
Kott *šâškana* 'magpie' ← Turkic *sāskan* < *saġïzġan*;
Kott *tegteka* 'quail' ← Turkic *tükteg* 'with feathers' < *tüg* 'the hair of the body; feathers';
Kott *kûra*; Assan *kura* 'rope' ← Turkic *qur* 'belt, girdle';
Arin *mintora* 'ice' ← Turkic *mindir* 'hail' ← Mongolic *möndür* 'hail'.

1.5.2   Paragoge in Tungusic Loanwords

Ket *báŋa* 'under no circumstance, never' ← Ewenki *bān* 'refusal, repudiation; failure';
Northern Ket *ɔkɔŋɔ* 'adverb from memory, by heart' ← Ewenki *ōkin* 'when'.

1.6   *Epentheses in Turkic Loanwords*

Kott *bosarak* 'ruddy colored (*said of red fox fur*)' ← Turkic *bozraq* < *bōz* 'grey, brown' +*rAK* {Turkic NN};
Kott *karâga* 'crow' ← Turkic *qarġa*;
Kott *hôpetal* 'saddle cloth; carpet' ← Turkic *qabtal* 'side of the horse; side; saddle cloth' ← Mongolic *qabtalsun* < *qabtasun* 'board; wooden printing blocks; binding or cover of a book' < *qabta* 'flat, even' +*sUn* {Mongolic NN};
Kott *tâmukol* 'tobacco tin' < *tâmuk* + Yeniseian *ol* 'container' ← Turkic *tamkï* 'tobacco'.

1.7 Gemination

1.7.1 Gemination in Turkic Loanwords

-l- → *-ll-*

> Pumpokol *pʰalla ~ falla*, cf. *pʰala ~ fala* 'son, boy' ← Turkic *pala < bala* 'a human child, son';

-t → *-tt*

> Arin *ott* 'hay' ← Turkic *ot* 'grass, vegetation; hay'.

1.7.2 Gemination in Mongolic Loanwords

-k- → *-kk-*

> Ket *nikkor* 'sorcerer (*in shaman's speech*)' ← Mongolic *nökör* 'friend, comrade, companion; husband'.

1.7.3 Gemination in Tungusic Loanwords

-d- → *-dd-* or *-td-*

> Central Ket *ajgiddɛ*; Southern Ket *ajgitdɛ* 'wooded tundra, pine bog' < *agij* ← Ewenki *aγī* 'taiga, tundra, marsh' + Yeniseian *deʔ* 'lake';

-n- → *-ŋn-*

> Ket *boŋnij* 'cemetery; grave' ← Ewenki *bunī* 'dead person; cemetery, grave' < *bu-* 'to die' *-nī* {Ewenki VN};

-ŋVn- → *-nn-*

> Ket *enna* 'really?' ← Ewenki *jēŋan* 'really?' < *jē* 'what; how; really?' *+ŋĀn* {Ewenki NN};

-r- → *-tt-*

> Ket *hɔttɔn* 'left or the right area in a tent'; Northern Ket *hɔ́ttɔn* 'middle place in a tent' ← Ewenki *horan < haran* 'house; the place for tent; floor; the place of hearth in the middle of Tungusic house';

-l- → -ll-

Ket *ullen*, cf. *úlen*; Yugh *úlʲan* 'pochard (diving duck, *Aythya ferina*)' ← Ewenki *ulanmukī* 'pochard';
Central Ket, Northern Ket *ulla* ~ *úlle* 'ruble, the monetary unit in Russia' ← Ewenki *ulukī* 'squirrel'.

1.8 Syncope
There are some Yeniseian loanwords which omit the original Altaic medial vowel.

1.8.1 Turkic Loanwords

Kott *arkā* 'wine, brandy' ← Turkic *arakï* 'wine, vodka';
Assan *esrolagín* ~ *esrolokon* 'drunk' ← Turkic *äsäriklig* 'drunk, intoxicated';
Yugh *kitn*; Ket *kīˑtn* 'nettles, hemp' ← Turkic *kiden* 'flax, canvas';
Yugh *súlʲgej* 'left' ← Turkic *sologay* 'left-handed' ← Mongolic *soloɣai* 'left side or hand; left-handed; awkward; wrong, faulty' ← Turkic *sōl* 'left';
Ket *uˑlʲsʲ* 'country; land of gnomes' ← Turkic *ulus* 'administrative unit, village, dynasty, people' ← Mongolic *ulus* 'people, nation; country, state; empire; dynasty' ← Turkic *uluš* 'country'.

1.8.2 Tungusic Loanwords

Ket *kútgit* 'dish of intestines' ← Ewenki *gudige* 'stomach of animals' ← Mongolic *güǰege* 'stomach of animals';
Central Ket, Northern Ket *lúčkɔ* 'reindeer saddle' ← Ewenki *ločoko* 'saddle'.

1.9 The Loss of Internal Syllables
Usually the Yeniseian words are monosyllabic, the loss of syllable(s) in internal position is typical of polysyllabic loanwords, e.g. Russian *nedelʲa* 'week' in Ket is *nela*; Russian *samovar* in Ket is *sambar*, etc. (see Vajda 2009: 486). This change is also typical for Altaic loanwords.

1.9.1 Turkic Loanwords

Arin **berkuštukdu** 'strong' < *berke* 'big, great; very' + *kuštuk* 'strong' -*tu* {Yeniseian NN/adj.} ← Turkic **berke küčtüg** < *berke* 'big, great; very' + *küčtüg* 'strong, powerful; violent, oppressive';

Kott **kaltum** 'bear' < *kaltu -(X)m* {Yeniseian NN/adj.} ← Turkic **kara yoldu** 'brown (*colour of animal*)' < *kara* 'black' + *yoldïg* 'striped' (cf. AltaiT: Quu dial. *qara yoldu* 'brown, bear');

Yugh **kʌčiŋej** 'magpie' ← Turkic **karačigay** < *qaračqay* 'swallow' ← Mongolic *qaraɣačai* 'swallow';

Kott **kuštap parak** 'I take away' ← Turkic **kučaktap bar-** 'to take away' < *kučakta-* 'to embrace, take in one's arms' *-(X)p* {Turkic converb} + *bar-* 'to go' *-Ak* (?).

1.9.2   Tungusic Loanwords

Ket **áʙses** 'bear trap' < *áʙse -s* {Yeniseian nominalizer} ← Ewenki *amākākse* 'bear's skin; bear's flesh' < *amākā* 'grandfather; uncle; ancestor; bear; sky, God' < *amā* 'father; *taboo* bear' *+kā* {Ewenki NN} *+kse* {Ewenki NN/adj.};

Ket **kɔɣón** '*myth*. forbidden jewelry in a snake's nest; copper pendant of shaman's costume' ← Ewenki **kulitkān** 'the image of snake in the shaman's costume' < *kulīn* 'snake' *+tkĀn* {Ewenki NN/diminutive};

Ket **úkta** 'slowly', cf. Southern Ket *úkta índɛt!* 'read slowly!' ← Ewenki **udakta** 'let me be slow' < *uda-* 'to be slow, to delay' *-ktA* {Ewenki sg.1 optative} ← Mongolic *uda-* 'to tarry, hesitate, delay; to be late or delayed; to last'.

1.10   *Word-Final -l of Unknown Origin in Altaic Loanwords*

During my research I found several Turkic and Tungusic loanwords with a final consonant *-l* of unknown origin. According to Yeniseian forms, it would appear to be a Yeniseian peculiarity, but we do not have any information about this feature. It occurs mainly in Tungusic loanwords in Ket.

1.10.1   Turkic Loanwords

Kott *bišól*; Assan *bišol* 'calf' < *bišo -l* ← Turkic *pïzō ~ puzō* < *buzāɣu* 'calf'.

1.10.2   Tungusic Loanwords

Central Ket *aqtul* 'spring (*water coming out of the ground*)' < *aqtu -l* ← Tungusic: Ewenki *jūkte* 'spring, brook';

Northern Ket *bejetil* 'cannibal' < *bejeti -l* ← Tungusic: Ewenki *bejetī* 'cannibal' < *beje* 'man, person, body' ← Mongolic;

Ket *boksel* 'bosom, lap' < *bokse -l* ← Tungusic: Ewenki *buksu* 'buttocks' ← Mongolic;
Ket *saŋɔl* 'chimney of a dug-out', cf. Central Ket *sɔnal* 'smoke hole of a dug-out' < *sona -l* ← Tungusic: Ewenki *sōna ~ sōŋa* 'chimney'.

1.11 The Final -t of Unknown Origin in Altaic Loanwords

There are some loanwords in Yeniseian where the final consonant -*t* occurred in the final position in the words with a dental consonant. The origin is uncertain, probably it appeared due to assimilation.

1.11.1 Turkic Loanwords

Kott *tabat*; Assan *tabát ~ tapat* 'camel' ← Turkic *täbä* < *täβäy*;

1.11.2 Tungusic Loanwords

Ket *kútgit* 'dish of intestines' ← Ewenki *gudige* 'stomach of animals' ← Mongolic *güjege* 'stomach of animals';
Ket *qitet* 'grandchild of father's sister or mother's brother'[1] ← Ewenki *hute* 'child, son or daughter'.

1.12 *Metathesis*

Metathesis is an important characteristic feature in the Yeniseian languages. Because it is not typical for Altaic languages, it is important to pay attention to this characteristic property during the research of different loanwords in Yeniseian. According to the examples examined, metathesis happened in Altaic loanwords with nasal and plosive consonants, while in the original Yeniseian words it usually occurred with the labial and velar consonants.

1.12.1 Metathesis in Yeniseian

Metathesis is a sporadic phonetic feature in Yeniseian. Vajda (2013) cited examples from nominal and verbal morphology to explain this specific distinction in Modern Ket. Usually it happens in words with labial consonants and or the

---

[1] The etymology of Ket word is uncertain. It has two possibilities. The word may belong to a group of compound hybrid words where amalgamation occurred, in which case it consists of the Tungusic word *hute* 'child' and the Yeniseian half-suffix -*kit* with diminutive meaning. Or the Ket word belongs to the previously examined category of words with an unknown final consonant -*t*.

velar nasal consonant -ŋ-, which expresses plural agreement in adjectival modifiers or redundant plural agreement in a subset of verbs, e.g.

Ket *dabatomnet* < Yeniseian *da-ba-t-on-wet 'she understood him';
Ket *daatpines* < Yeniseian *da-a-t-in-wes 'she drew him', etc.

Through comparison with Kott, where the metathesis did not occur, it seems that it can be viewed as evidence of innovation in Ket (Vajda 2014: personal communication).

The *Etymological Dictionary of Yeniseian languages* (Vajda & Werner: in preparation) lists many examples where metathesis can be found, e.g.

With labial -*p*- and velar -*k*- consonants:

Ket *qopqun ~ qoqpun* 'cuckoo bird' (onomat.);
Central Ket, Northern Ket *dápqul* 'heap' (cf. Southern Ket *dáqpul*; Yugh *dʲáχpuul*) < Yeniseian *dʲaq 'put down' + *pəl 'accumulation';
Southern Ket *qapqat ~ qaqpɛt ~ qaqpat* '*inf.* to enter (*a dwelling*)' < Yeniseian *qapə 'inside' (cf. Yugh *χāˑp*, Ket *qāˑ* 'home, at home') + *qodʲ 'walk';
Central Ket, Northern Ket *sápqul* 'heel' (cf. Southern Ket *saqpul*, Yugh *sáχpuul*) < Yeniseian *sax 'base' + *būˑl 'foot, leg';
Central Ket, Northern Ket *tópqul* 'snow piled on a branch' (cf. Southern Ket *tóqpul*, Yugh *tóχpuul*) < Yeniseian *tʰīˑk 'fallen snow' + *pəl 'accumulation';

With labial -*p*-/-*m*-, velar -*k*- and liquid -*l*-:

Ket *qolap*, Yugh *χolap* 'half, side' < Yeniseian *qop 'flat surface' + *al 'half';
Ket, Yugh *bólba* mushroom < Yeniseian *baʔŋ 'earth' + *pəl 'growth';
Pumpokol *kómulsi* 'green' < Yeniseian *qəl 'bile' + *wes 'like' + *əŋ {adj. suff.} + *si {nominalizer};
Yugh *igl ~ igel* 'postp. (located) near' (cf. Ket *ilga ~ ilka*) < Yeniseian *ul 'near' + *kej (loc. suff.); etc.

1.12.2 Metathesis in Altaic Loanwords

The Altaic loanwords where metathesis occurred are divided into two groups: loanwords with plosive unvoiced consonants and loanwords with nasal consonants.

1.12.2.1 *Metathesis with Plosive Unvoiced Consonants* -p-, -t- *or* -k-

Kott *aktur 'postp*. through' ← Turkic *ötküre* < *ötgürü* 'through';
Kott *iptak* 'bread'[2] ← Turkic *itpäk* < *ätmäk* 'bread';
Kott *tarup ~ tarûp* 'chamois leather' ← Turkic *tup tere*: cf. Altai *tup tere* 'tanned leather';
Assan *esrolokon* 'drunk' < *eserekli -Aŋ* {Yeniseian NN/adj.} ← Turkic *äsäriklig* 'intoxicated, drunk' < *äsür-* 'to get drunk' *-(X)K* {Turkic VN/adj.} *+lXK* {Turkic NN/adj.}.

1.12.2.2 *Metathesis with Nasal Consonants* -m-, -n- *or* -ŋ-

Kott *hanpen* 'pray, prayer, praying' < *kanma -n* {Yeniseian VN/adj.} ← Turkic *qamna-* 'to make magic' < *qām* 'shaman, sorcerer, soothsayer, magician' *+lA-* {Turkic NV};
Arin *teminkur* 'ore' ← Turkic *temir qan* '*lit*. iron blood → ore' < *tämir* 'iron' + *qān* 'blood';
Yugh *unče* 'because' ← Turkic *üčün* 'because of, for the sake of, for; because, in order to'.

2 **Morphological Peculiarities**

2.1 *Yeniseian Suffixes in Altaic Loanwords*

2.1.1 Arin suffix *-ok*

Some Arin words of Turkic origin have Yeniseian suffix *-ok* which resembles the Russian diminutive suffix and typical mostly for loanwords (Werner 2005: 149):

Arin *buturčinok* 'quail' < *buturčin -ok* ← Turkic *budurčun* < *budursïn* 'quail, Coturnyx';
Arin *xamčook* 'whip' < *qamčï -ok* ← Turkic *qamčï* 'a whip';
Arin *kajakok* 'oil, butter' < *kajak -ok* ← Turkic *qayaq* 'butter, sour cream' < *qańaq* 'the skin on milk, clotted cream';
Arin *altinok* 'gold' < *altïn -ok* ← Turkic *altïn* 'gold' < *altūn*.

2.1.2 Yeniseian Plural Suffix *-ŋ /-n*

Some Altaic loanwords are used with the Yeniseian plural suffix *-(V)ŋ* or *-(V)n* (for details on functions, see Werner 1990: 57–58; Porotova 2004: 129–134; Georg

---

[2] Cf. other Yeniseian forms without metathesis: Kott *itpák ~ itpak*; Arin *itp'ák ~ itpák ~ itpek*; Assan *itpák* 'bread'.

2007: 92–102). Besides a plurality function, the suffix derives words with a collective meaning.

2.1.2.1   *Turkic Loanwords*

Kott *kubúrgenaŋ* ~ *kabúrgenaŋ* 'onion' < *kubúrgen -aŋ* ← Turkic *köβürgän* 'wild onion';
Pumpokol *aniŋ* 'legs, feet' < *an -iŋ* ← Turkic *yān* 'the hip; the side, flank of the body or in other contexts'.

2.1.2.2   *Tungusic Loanwords*

Ket *húktɛŋ* ~ *huktɛn* 'taboo bear eyes' < *huktɛ -ŋ* ← Ewenki *hugdï* 'rapacious, predatory' < *hug* 'bear, predator' +*dï* {Ewenki NN/adj.}.

2.1.3   Yeniseian Nominalizer *-s*
One of the productive suffixes in Yeniseian is the nominalizer *-s* (Ket *-s*, Yugh *-si*, Kott *-še*, Arin *-šu*) which forms nouns from words belonging to other part of speech (Georg 2007: 122–125; Vajda 2014: personal communication), e.g.

From adjectival roots:

Ket *ēt* 'sharp' → *ēts* 'something sharp, a sharp one';

From inflected nouns and pronouns:

Ket *ām* 'mother' > *ámdi* 'mother's' → *ámdis* 'which belongs to mother';
Ket *ū(k)* 'you' > *ūk* 'yours' → *úkis* 'which belongs to you';

From verbal roots:

Ket *kī* 'to fly away' → *kīs* 'a bird, which is flying away or has flown away';
Ket *bèd* 'to do, make' → *bèds* 'something which is done, made';
Ket *dɔldaq* 'he lived' → *dɔldaqs* 'one who lived';
Ket *dbanbun* 'they repeatedly give me something' → *dbanbuns* 'those who repeatedly give me something'; etc.

2.1.3.1   *Turkic Loanwords*

    Arin *bajšu* 'wealth' < *baj -šu* ← Turkic *bay* 'rich; a rich man'< *bāy*.

2.1.3.2   *Tungusic Loanwords*

    Ket *áʁses* 'bear trap' < *áʁse -s* ← Tungusic: Ewenki *amākākse* 'bear's skin; bear's flesh' < *amākā* 'grandfather; uncle; ancestor; bear; sky, God' < *amā* 'father; *taboo* bear' +*kā* {Ewenki NN} +*kse* {Ewenki NN/adj.};
Yugh *boŋsi* 'dead person' < *boŋ -si* ← Tungusic: Ewenki *bunī* 'dead person; cemetery, grave' < *bu-* 'to die' -*nī* {Ewenki VN};
Ket *toqtis* 'slope of a riverbank or hill' < *tokti -s* ← Tungusic: Ewenki *tuktï-* 'to go up a slope or mountain'.

2.1.4   Yeniseian Adjective-Forming Suffix -*Xŋ* in Turkic Loanwords
There are some Turkic loanwords in Yeniseian derived with Yeniseian non-productive denominal noun suffix -*Xŋ*, which forms adjectives (e.g. Ket *qà* ~ *qàŋ* 'big', *bɔ'l* ~ *bɔlaŋ* 'fat', *ugdɛ* ~ *ugdɛŋ* 'long', *hilaŋ* 'sweet' < *hi'l* 'birch sap', etc. For details, see Vajda 2004: 38).

    Assan *esrolokon* 'drunk' < *eserekli -Aŋ* ← Turkic *äsäriklig* 'intoxicated, drunk' < *äsür-* 'to get drunk' -*(X)K* {Turkic VN/Adj.} +*lXK* {Turkic NN/adj.};
Yugh *itiŋ* 'stinking' < *ī't* 'smell, aroma' -*Xŋ* ← Turkic *yï∂* 'scent, odour, smell';
Kott *hanpen* 'pray, prayer', cf. *hanpen hit* 'praying person' < *kanma -n* ← Turkic *kamna-* < *qamla-* 'to make magic' < *qām* 'shaman, sorcerer, soothsayer, magician' +*lA-* {Turkic NV}.

2.1.5   Yeniseian Adjective-Forming Suffix -*tu* in Turkic Loanwords
Some Altaic loanwords are used with the Yeniseian suffix -*tu*, which usually forms adjectives. According to Georg (2007: 141–142), the Yeniseian denominal adjectives with this suffix may be rendered as 'having sg., endowed with sg.', e.g. Ket *kūl* 'beard' → *kúltu* 'bearded', *ūl* 'water' → *últu* 'wet', *du'* 'smoke' → *dútu* 'smoky', etc.

    Arin *berkuštukdu* 'strong' < *berke* 'big, great; very' + *kuštuk* 'strong' -*tu* ← Turkic *berke* 'clever, deft' (← Mongolic ← Turkic) + *küčtüg* 'strong, powerful; violent, oppressive' (< *küč* 'strength' +*lXG* {Turkic NN/adj.});

Arin *berkutu* 'brave' < *berke* 'big, great; very' *-tu* ← Turkic *berke* ← Mongolic *berke* ← Turkic;

Kott *kuštu* 'very strong' < *kuš -tu* ← Turkic *küč* < *kǖč* 'strength, power, energy';

Kott *tʰantu* 'snow flurry, storm' < *tan -tu* ← Turkic *tan* 'a cool breeze' < *tān*;

Kott *turkatu* 'quick, rapid' < *turkan* 'quick' *-tu* ← Turkic *türgen* 'quick, rapid' ← Mongolic.

2.1.6 Yeniseian Adjective-Forming Suffix *-m*

There is one Kott word with unknown final *-m*. I assume it can be connected with a non-productive Yeniseian element *-(V)m*, discussed by Georg (2007: 142). According to him, it is clearly derivative and etymologically identical with the impersonal predicative concord suffix *-am* (Georg 2007: 316–317), e.g.

Ket *súlem* 'red', cf. *sūl* 'blood';
Ket *qɔ́lam* 'bitter', cf. *qəəl* 'gall';
Ket *tákim* 'white', cf. *tīk* 'snow', etc.

The Kott loanword under examination belongs to the category of taboo words; possibly, the meaning 'bear' was earned after Turkic meaning 'brown':

Kott *kaltum* 'bear' < *kaltu -m* ← Turkic *kara yoldu* 'brown (*colour of animal*)' < *kara* 'black' + *yoldïg* 'striped' cf. AltaiT: Quu dial. *qara yoldu* 'brown' (TSSDAJa 93).

2.1.7 Yeniseian Action Nominal (Infinitive) Suffixes or Elements in Verbs

There are a small number of infinitive verbs of Altaic origin in Yeniseian. Some of them, as native Yeniseian words, contain an incremental element *-aj ~ -ij ~ -j* which is not present in the corresponding incorporate (for details, see Georg 2007: 311–312) and some have the action nominal suffix *-ŋ* (Werner 2005: 74–75; Vajda 2014: personal comminication). Yeniseian action nominals (usually called "infinitives" in earlier descriptions) are a type of modifier like adjectives, they can be preposed to nouns, e.g. Ket *bagdeŋ kɛ't* 'person who drags or is dragged', cf. *bagd-eŋ* 'to pull, drag' (Vajda 2014: personal communication).

2.1.7.1 Turkic Loanwords

Yugh χáɫčaχ**an** ~ χʌlčak**ŋ** 'verb to tickle' < qʌlčak -(V)ŋ ← Turkic *qïlčïq* 'tickle' < *qïčïlïq* < *qïč* +*I*- {Turkic NV} -(X)l- {Turkic VV} -XK {Turkic VN};
Yugh *utčij* ~ *uččij* 'to put out (*fire*)' (transitive verb) < *uč -ij* ← Turkic *üč-* < *öč-* '*fire* to go out, be extinguished' (intransitive verb).

2.1.7.2 Tungusic Loanwords

Ket *ígäj* ~ *ígɨj* 'to noice, to sound' < *íg -Aj* ← Tungusic: Ewenki *īg* 'sound';
Yugh *namčej* '*inf.* to press, press together one's lips; to clench one's teeth; to press to one's breast; to put the tail between the legs (*said of dogs*)' < *namč- ej* ← Tungusic: Ewenki *nam-* 'to fold; to roll up, to pack'.

2.2 The Loss of Altaic Suffixes

There is a number of Turkic and Tungusic loanwords where the suffixes dropped, which may be explained by the monosyllabic structure of Yeniseian words.

2.2.1 Turkic Loanwords

Kott *eser* 'drunk' ← Turkic *äsärik* 'drunk, intoxicated' < *äsür-* 'to be or become drunk, intoxicated' -(X)K {Turkic VN};
Yugh *ēˑt*; Central Ket *ēˑt* 'sharp' ← Turkic *yitī* < *yitig* 'sharp' < *yiti-* 'to be sharp' -G {Turkic VN};
Kott *tipar* ~ *tîpar* 'fog' ← Turkic *tumarïk* 'haze' < *tum* 'cold' +*Ar-* {Turkic NV} -(X)K {Turkic VN}.

2.2.2 Tungusic Loanwords

There are some names of plants, birds and insects where the Tungusic suffix dropped. It may have happened due to the polysyllabic nature of the original Tungusic words, which is not typical of Yeniseian, e.g.

Ket *enčil* 'little owl that catches rats (*species unidentified*)' ← Ewenki *intilgun* 'owl' < *inti* 'kind of bird' +*l*- {Ewenki NV} -*wun* {Ewenki VN};
Ket *qúmlej* ~ *qúmilej*; Yugh *χúmilʲej*, *χúmal* ~ *χúmil* 'butterfly' ← Ewenki *kumalāndō* 'black butterfly with a white border around the edges of the wings' < *kumalān* 'rug made of the reindeer skin' <

*kuma +lĀn {Ewenki NN} +dō {Ewenki NN suffix, which forms names of insects};

Ket *tɔˑqtə ~ tɔˑqt* 'wagtail (*several species of birds of the genus Motacilla*)' ← Ewenki *tïgdewkī* 'lark' < *tïgde-* 'to rain' *-wkī* {Ewenki VN};

Northern Ket *tīl* 'gadfly'; Ket *til* 'horsefly, reindeerfly' ← Ewenki *dilkēn* 'fly' < *dil* +*kĀn* {Ewenki NN/diminutive};

Ket *úl'ba* 'moss on tree trunks' ← Ewenki *jalbuka* 'moss' < *ńalbukā* < *lalbi* +*kĀ* {Ewenki NN};

Ket *ullen ~ úlen*; Yugh *úlʲan* 'pochard (diving duck, *Aythya ferina*)' ← Ewenki *ulanmukī* 'pochard' < *ula-* 'to get wet' *-n* {Ewenki VN} +*mukī* {Ewenki NN};

Central Ket, Northern Ket *ulla ~ úlle* 'ruble, the monetary unit in Russia' ← Ewenki *ulukī* 'squirrel' < *ulu-kī* {Ewenki VN};

In the case below the verbal suffix dropped:

Ket *toˑk* 'axe' ← Ewenki *tokto-* 'to chop with an axe' < *tok +*tA-* {Tungusic NV}.

2.3 Change of the Original Word Classes
2.3.1 Turkic Loanwords
2.3.1.1 Noun → Verb

Yugh *karábr* 'verb to guard'; Ket *kalebel* 'verb to guard, to keep watch, to lie in wait for' ← Turkic *qaraul* 'noun guard' ← Mongolic *qarayul* 'noun watch, sentry, guard, scout' < *qara-* 'verb to look at, glance, watch, observe; to regard, consider; to look after, to face' *-GUl* {Mongolic VN}.

2.3.1.2 Adjective → Verb

Kott *kalakai ~ kalakei* 'verb to stutter' ← Turkic *kälägäy* 'noun stutterer, adjective stuttering' ← Mongolic *kelegei* 'adjective dumb, mute; stammering, stuttering, tongue-tied' < *kelen ügei* 'without tongue' < *kelen* 'tongue; language' + *ügei* {Mongolic negative} < *kelen* 'tongue; language' < *kele-* 'to utter words, express in words; to speak, say, tell, narrate' *-n* {Mongolic VN}.

2.3.1.3 Verb → Noun

Kott *ešjalikitan* 'flower, bloom' ← Turkic *čakayaktan-* 'to cover with flowers; to blossom (*of flower buds*)', cf. Khakas *čaxayax* 'flower' +*ta*- {Khakas NV}; -*n*- {Khakas VV/reflexive};

Yugh *bérgin* '*noun* bundle, pack of things' ← Turkic *bürken-* 'to be covered, to be wraped' < *bür-* 'to twist, wind round, screw together' -*k*- {Turkic VV} 'to cover' -(*X*)*n*- {Turkic VV/reflexive};

Kott *d'ili* 'speech' ← Turkic *tille-* 'to speak, say' < *til* 'the tongue; speech' +*lA*- {Turkic NV}.

2.3.1.4 Verb → Noun/Adjective/Adverb

Kott *êper* '*noun* circle; *adj.* round; *adv.* around' ← Turkic *ebir-* < *äβir-* 'to turn (*something, e.g. a wheel*)' < *äg-* 'to bend, bow' -*Ir*- {Turkic VV}.

2.3.1.5 Verb → Interjection

Kott *hâra* '*interjection of impatience* come on already!' ← Turkic *qara-* {Turkic sg.2 imperative } ← Mongolic *qara-* 'to look at'.

2.3.2 Tungusic Loanwords
2.3.2.1 Noun → Adverb

Ket *báŋa* 'under no circumstance, never' < *bán-ka* {Ket locative} ← Ewenki *bān* 'refusal, repudiation; failure' < *bā-* 'to be unable, to resist, to refuse' -*n* {Ewenki VN}.

3 Compound Words

3.1 Compound Words in Yeniseian

The Yeniseian lexicon can be divided into three basic morphosyntactic classes: nouns, modifiers and finite verbs.

Nouns are morphologically of three types. Many basic nouns are non-derived monosyllables such as *kɛˀt* 'person,' *āˑm* 'mother,' *tīˑk* 'snow,' *sēˑs* 'river', etc. Suffixal derivation is atypical of Yeniseian. A small number of derivative morphemes may be distinguished, the most important of which is the frequent nominalizer -*s*, which converts other parts of speech into substantive nouns. The third morphological type of nouns is root compounding. There is no reduplication in either inflection or derivation.

Yeniseian is a strongly synthetic language family in terms of its morphosyntax but its stem-building processes are based primarily on root compounding rather than affixation (Vajda 2015: 510).

The derived noun stems contain nominal affixes originated from noun roots (for details and more examples, see Werner 1976; 1998: 6–11; 53–58; Georg 2007: 129–134; Vajda 2015: 510–511), cf.

- The Ket suffix -*kit*, originated from Yeniseian word *kʌ'd* 'offspring', derives nouns denoting immature trees, fish, or animals: e.g. *bɛskit* 'baby rabbit' < *bɛ's* 'rabbit', *qurgit* 'immature pike' < *qùr* 'pike (fish)'; *uːlgit* 'aspen sapling' < *uːl* 'aspen';
- The Ket suffix -*aj* with meaning 'container': *dáqaj* 'eagle's nest' < *dàq* 'eagle'; *qámnaj* 'quiver' < *qámn* 'arrows';
- The Ket singular suffix -*dis*, originated from Yeniseian word *dē·s* 'eye', derives count nouns denoting a small, individuated portion of a larger pourable mass: e.g. *imdis* 'single pine nut' < *īm* 'pine nuts'; *qondis* 'glass bead' < *qō·n* 'beads'; etc.

There is not an exact term to underscore the transitional nature between compounded root and derivational affix. Werner and Vajda call them 'half-affixes' (Werner 1976; 1998: 53, Vajda 2015: 511), while Georg calls them 'semi-suffixes' or 'heads in compounds' (Georg 2007: 129).

The predominant noun-forming technique of Yeniseian is compounding. Yeniseian nominal compounds usually consist of two elements, the first of which may be referred to as the determiner and the second one as the semantic 'head'. Most common is the compounding of a head with a determiner, which is a noun itself. Adjectival and verbal roots may also function as determiners in nominal compounds (for details and more examples, see Georg 2007: 125). E.g.

Noun + Noun:

> *ísal* 'fish soup' < *īs* 'fish' + *āl* 'soup';
> *kúbkul* 'moustache' < *kūb* 'front end' + *kūl* 'beard';
> *mámul* 'milk' < *maʔm* 'breast' + *ūl* 'water';

Adjective + Noun:

> *kíboŋ* 'body, corpse' < *kiʔ* 'new' + *bōŋ* 'dead person';

Verb + Noun:

qiked 'merchant' < *qi* 'to sell' + *keʔd* 'human';
táŋsel 'leading reindeer' < *tàŋ* 'to pull' + *sèl* 'reindeer', etc.

The second type of Yeniseian nominal compounds is characterized by the presence of a petrified genitive formant -*d*- between both parts (Georg 2007: 126–127). Vajda calls it a lexicalized possessive construction (Vajda 2015: 511). E.g.

baʔŋ 'earth' + *iʔl* 'spirit' > *báŋdil* 'earth spirit';
békin 'hand' + *təqol* 'ring' > *békinttəqol* 'bracelet';
bəʔn 'duck' + *hīs* 'tail' > *bəndis* 'duck-tail';
daan 'grass' + *ūl* 'handle' > *dándul* 'blade of grass'; etc.

According to Georg (2007: 126), the presence or absence of this marker may be indicative of the relative age of the formation, the compounds with genitive link being younger.

3.2 Turkic Compound Words in Yeniseian
In my material, Turkic compound words are found only in Arin, Kott and Assan.

3.2.1 Nominal Compounds with Determiner and Semantic 'Head'
The Turkic compounds follow the Yeniseian structure; they have a determiner and semantic 'head'. E.g.

Kott *ɛkačačik* 'wax' ← Turkic *aġač čuk* < *aġač* 'tree' + *čuk* 'resin' (← Yeniseian);
Assan *šarijag* 'butter' ← Turkic *sarï yaġ*: cf. AltaiT: Altai *sarï yū*; SayanT: Tofan *sarïġ-čaġ* 'butter' < *sarï* (< *sarïġ* 'yellow') + *yag* (< *yāġ* 'grease, fat, oil').

3.2.2 Compounds with Clear Source of Borrowing
Most compounds belong to the category of loanwords with a clear source of borrowing. As an example see the next two Arin compounds *karananuk* 'bilberry' and *tegentestek* 'raspberry'. If the first one was clearly borrowed from Yenisei Turkic, while the second one was borrowed from Altai Turkic:

Arin **karananuk** 'bilberry' ← Turkic *kara nonaġ* 'bilberry' < *qara* 'black' + *nonaġ* 'bilberry' < (?) **yomaq* < **yumaq*;

Arin *tegentestek* 'raspberry' ← Turkic *tegen d'estek* < *tegen* 'thorn' (< **tikän* < **tik-* 'to insert; to insert (*in the ground*), to sew (*insert a needle*)' -GXn {Turkic VN}) + *d'estek* (< *čestek* < *yestek* 'berry').

3.2.3 Genitive-Linked Compounds

There are some borrowed compounds are developed according to a Yeniseian structure where the genitive marker between compound parts can be found. In similar structures in Turkic, the first part generally uses genitive, while the second part regularly contains a 3rd person possessive marker: e.g. Altai *d'erdiŋ üsti* 'land surface'; *attïŋ beli* 'the horse's back'; Khakas *inektiŋ südi* 'cow's milk'; *xakas tili* 'Khakas language' (Baskakov 1947: 297; Baskakov & Grekul 1975: 282).

The source of borrowing of the next Arin data is unclear. This compound does not exist in Turkic. Yenisei Turkic and Altai Turkic use the Russian loanword *nedel'a* to mean "week":

Arin *kemenenčak* 'week' ← Turkic *kemineŋ čak* < *kemineŋ* (< *kem* 'measurement' +(*X*)*niŋ* {Turkic genitive} ← Mongolic *kem* 'measure; size, proportion; limits; measure of time, term') + *čak* 'time, a point in time, a period of time' (← Mongolic *čaɣ* 'time, period, season, age; time as general situation or set of circumstances; tense (*gram.*); hour; clock, watch; weather, climate').

3.2.4 'Half-Affixes' of Turkic Origin

There is another group of Yeniseian compound words, where the Turkic loanword appears as a 'half-affix'. In this way the Turkic word *berke* 'strong, stable' appears in Arin compound words as a half-affix meaning 'big, great, very':

Arin *berke* ~ *berek* ~ *birka* 'big, great; very' ← Turkic *berke* 'very, strong' ← Mongolic *berke* 'difficult, hard; complicated, serious; skillful, competent, fit' ← Turkic *bärk* 'firm, stable, solid'.

There are two Arin examples with this half-affix, borrowed from the same Turkic compound word *berke tura* 'big, great town':

Arin *belkertura* 'empire' and
Arin *berketura* 'city, town'

< Arin *berke* 'big, great' + Turkic *tura* 'town, village'.

Arin ***berkitak*** 'mountain' < Arin *berke* 'big, great' + Turkic *tāġ* 'mountain';
Arin ***berkuštukdu*** 'strong' < Arin *berke* 'very' + *kuštuk* 'strong, powerful' ← Turkic *küčtüg* 'strong' (< **küč* 'strength, power' +*lXG* {Turkic NN/Adj.}) -*tu* {Yeniseian NN/adj.}.

Another Yeniseian half-affix of Turkic origin is *ȫy* 'step-', which derives Arin compound words of kinship terminology:

> Arin ***oj-*** 'step-' ← Turkic *ȫy* < *ögey* 'related through one parent only, step- (*father*, etc.)'.

There are three words indicating marital connections with Siberian Turkic people. If the first Arin word *ojče* 'stepmother' clearly was borrowed from Yenisei Turkic, while other two appear with Yeniseian words *akel* 'son' and *akel'a* 'daughter' with Yeniseian feminine suffix:

> Arin ***ojče*** 'stepmother' < Arin *oj* 'step-' + Turkic *ije* 'mother': cf. YeniseiT: Khakas *ȫy ije*; Sagai, Koibal, Kachin *ǖy ijä* 'stepmother'.

The Arin compound word possibly was borrowed from Yenisei Turkic; in Altai Turkic we have another compound *öy ene* 'stepmother'.

> Arin ***ojakelbala*** 'stepson' < Arin *oj* 'step-' + Arin *akel* 'son' + Turkic *bala* 'child': cf. YeniseiT: Khakas *ȫy pala*; Shor, Sagai, Koibal, Kachin *ǖy pala* ~ *ȫy pala*; AltaiT: Altai, Teleut *ȫy pala* 'stepchild';
> Arin ***ojakel'a*** 'stepdaughter' < Arin *oj* 'step-' + Yeniseian *akel'a* 'daughter' < *akel* -*a* {Yeniseian feminine suffix}.

It is important to remark that the half-affixes of Turkic origin follow the Turkic word order, the half-affix in the first syllable, while in Yeniseian the half-affix is in second syllable, compare some Ket words as *ammas* 'stepmother', *hunnas* 'stepdaughter' and *oppas* 'stepfather' with Yeniseian half-affix **pas*, which denotes a non-consanguinal relationship.

3.2.5   Amalgamations
This special group includes assimilated amalgamations:

> Kott ***tôteäš*** ~ ***toteš***, Assan ***toteš*** 'Siberian fir (*lat.* Abies sibirica)' ← Turkic *tït aġas*, cf. YeniseiT: Khakas *tït aġas*; Kyzyl *tït aġaš* 'larch';

Possibly Kott *tôteäš* 'Siberian fir' originated from Turkic compound *tït aġas* 'larch'. In the second part of Yeniseian word *eäš* the Turkic consonant -*ġ*- dropped and possibly took influence on the first part of compounding, which was pitched.

> Kott *kalači* 'eagle' ← Turkic *qal lačïn* < *qal* 'strong' + *lačïn* 'falcon';
> Kott *tátien* 'hill' ← Turkic *tā töŋ* < *taġ* 'mountain' + *töŋ* 'hill'.

3.2.6   Hybrid Compounds

The next group consists of hybrid words, where one part is of Turkic origin, while the other part is of Yeniseian origin:

> Kott *ânar ~ anar* 'hip, loin' < *an* + Yeniseian *ar* 'bone': *an* ← Turkic *yān* 'the hip; the side, flank of the body or in other contexts';
> Kott *atuš* 'gelding' < *at* + Yeniseian *uš* 'horse': *at* ← Turkic *at* 'horse, riding horse, gelding';
> Kott *tâmukol* 'tobacco tin' < *tâmuk* + Yeniseian *ol* 'container': *tâmuk* ← Turkic *tamkï* 'tobacco';
> Kott *pačasulema* 'sabre' < Yeniseian *pača* 'big, large' + *sulema* ← Turkic *seleme* 'sabre, sword' ← Mongolic *seleme* 'sabre, sword' ← Tungusic: Ewenki *seleme* 'sabre, sword' < *sele* 'iron' +*mA* {NN/adj.}.

3.2.7   Metathesis

In some cases it is difficult to recognize the source of borrowing or the etymology of a word. Certain Yeniseian words sporadically exhibit metathesized forms, which is a distinctive feature of Yeniseian languages, e.g.

> Kott *tarup ~ tarûp* 'chamois leather' ← Turkic *tup tere* (cf. Altai *tup tere* 'tanned leather') < *tup* 'tanned leather' (← Russian) + *täri* 'the skin, hide (*of a human being or animal*)';
> Kott *uŋôjaŋ* 'why' ← Turkic *noġa učun* (cf. AltaiT: Altai, Teleut *neniŋ učun*; Khakas *noġa*; Old Turkic *nägü üčün* 'why?') < *noġa* < *nägü* 'why' < *nā* 'what?' +*GU* {NN} + *učun* 'because of, for the sake of, for; because, in order to';
> Kott *ureäk* 'green, greenery' ← Turkic *kök arak* < *kök* 'blue' + *arax* {Khakas diminutive particle for adjective forms}.

3.2.8   Types of Combinations of Different Word-Classes

From a typological point of view, the borrowed Turkic compound words follow the Yeniseian structure, which is similar in Turkic: Noun + noun, adjective + noun and verb + noun.

Noun + noun:

> Arin **ba[g]akulak** 'mussel' ← Turkic *baġa qulaq*, cf. Khakas *paġa xulaġï*[3] 'mussel' < *baġa* (< *baqa* 'frog') + *qulaq* 'ear';
> Arin **qólpas** 'finger' ← Turkic *qol pas* < *qol* 'finger' (< *qōl* 'the upper arm; the forearm, hand, finger') + *pas* 'the upper part of sg.' (< *baš* 'head, top');

Adjective + noun:

> Arin **karasek** 'fly' ← Turkic *qara sēk*, cf. YeniseiT: Khakas *xara sēk*; Sagai Koibal, Kachin *qara sǟk* 'fly' < *qara* 'black' + *sēk* 'fly' < *siŋek* 'a buzzing insect' < **siŋ* +*AK* {Turkic NN/diminutive};
> Arin **pajbal** 'cattle, cow' ← Turkic *pay bal* < *pay* 'rich' (< *bāy*) + *bal* 'cattle' (< *mal*);
> Arin **tamkorgolči** 'tin' < Yeniseian *tam* 'white' (< *táɣim*) + *korgolči* ← Turkic *korgoljïn* 'lead' ← Mongolic *qorɣoljin* 'lead' ← Turkic *korgočin* 'lead';

Verb + noun:

> Kott **taripan** 'field' < *tari* + Yeniseian *baŋ* 'earth, ground': *tari* ← Turkic *tarï-* 'to cultivate ground'.

3.3 Tungusic Compound Words in Yeniseian

Most Tungusic compound words in Yeniseian belong in the group of hybrid compounds, where one part is of Tungusic origin, while another part is a native Yeniseian word. As original Yeniseian compounds, the hybrid words consist of two elements: the determiner and the semantic head. In most cases the determiner is of Tungusic origin and the "head" is a native Yeniseian word or half-affix. An interesting fact is the lack of genitive-linked compounds, which is typical of Yeniseian. In all cases the structure regularly follows the typical order as in native Yeniseian compound words: noun + noun, adjective + noun and verb + noun. There is only one case where amalgamation and metathesis occurred.

---

[3] The Khakas form *xulaġï* is used accordig to Turkic rules with possessive marker of 3rd person +*X*.

3.3.1 Hybrid Compounds with Yeniseian Semantic Head

Usually the hybrid compounds consist of a Tungusic determiner and Yenisiean 'head', e.g.

> Yugh *ajāχn ~ ajāχin* 'ford, sandbank' < *ajā* + Yeniseian *qiˑń* 'flow, current':
> *ajā* ← Northern Tungusic: Ewenki *ajān* 'old bed of river; channel; bay, cove' ← Turkic: Yakut *ayān* 'old bed of river' < Common Turkic *say* 'riverbed' +*An* {Turkic NN};

> Northern Ket *aʁidɛ* 'marsh, tundra'; Central Ket *ajgiddɛ*, Southern Ket *ajgitdɛ* 'wooded tundra, pine bog' < *agij* + Yeniseian *deˀ* 'lake':
> *agij* ← Northern Tungusic: Ewenki *aγī* 'taiga, tundra, marsh' (< *aγī-* 'to walk in the snow');

> Central Ket *tamtul* 'marsh lake' < *tamt* + Yeniseian *uˑl* 'water':
> *tamt* ← ? Northern Tungusic: Ewenki *amut* 'marsh lake, lake, sea'.

3.3.2 Hybrid Compounds with Yeniseian Half-Affixes

3.3.2.1 *Yeniseian* -aj *'Container'*

The half-affix originates from *àj* 'sack' (for details and examples, see Georg 2007: 129; Werner 2002/1: 18):

> Ket *dankijaj* 'rucksack' < *dankij* + Yeniseian -*aj* 'sack, container':
> *dankij* ← Northern Tungusic: Ewenki *daŋanī* 'name of shoulder bone'.

3.3.2.2 *Yeniseian* -oks *'Wooden Object'*

The half-affix originates from *ōks* 'tree' (for details and examples, see Georg 2007: 133; Werner 2002/1: 34):

> Central Ket *naroboks*, Northern Ket *naravoks* 'long steering pole of a reindeer team' < *nara* +*b* {epenthetic consonant, Vajda 2014: personal communication} + Yeniseian -*oks*:
> *nara* ← Northern Tungusic: Ewenki *nara* 'castrated reindeer bull, reindeer'.

3.3.2.3 *Yeniseian Diminutive* -kit

The half-affix originates from *keˀd* 'human' (for details and examples, see Georg 2007: 130–131):

Ket *qitet* 'grandchild of father's sister or mother's brother' < *qite* + *-kit*: *qite* ← ? Northern Tungusic: Ewenki *hute* 'child, son or daughter'.

3.3.3 The Structure of Compounds

3.3.3.1 Noun + Noun

Ket *imejaŋ* 'reindeer harness neck-rope' < *ime -j-* {linking consonant} + Yeniseian *aŋ* 'rope':
ime ← Northern Tungusic: Ewenki *immen* 'halter (*occipital strap, reindeer halter straps*); halter belt, over the eyes of a deer, across the forehead';
Ket *kolij* 'covered storeroom' < *kol* + Yeniseian *iʔ* 'storage shed':
kol ← Northern Tungusic: Ewenki *kolbo* 'storage shed' ← Mongolic ← Turkic;
Ket *kɔjel ~ kɔ́jil* 'pan' < *kɔje* + Yeniseian *ɛʔl* 'cup';
kɔje ← Northern Tungusic: Ewenki *kaja* 'pan' ← Mongolic *kayiba* 'large kettle; frying pan';

3.3.3.2 Verb + Noun

Kott *kaltapen* 'wedge for splitting wood' < *kalta- -p* {? VN} + Yeniseian *eˑn* 'wedge':
kalta ← Northern Tungusic: Ewenki *kalta-* 'to crack, to break up in two parts; to split in half'.

3.3.4 Amalgamations

Ket *qʌbdal* 'slice of bear bacon fat' ← Northern Tungusic: Ewenki *hepete tïle* 'bear bacon fat' < *hepete* 'bear'+ *tïle* 'bear bacon fat'.

4 Semantic Peculiarities

4.1 Change in Semantics

The meaning of loanwords taken from Altaic languages is usually preserved. There appear some cases in which a change or broadening of meaning has occurred.

4.1.1 Metaphor
4.1.1.1 *Turkic Loanwords*
Turkic '*with husk, peel*' > Yeniseian '*nut (name of fruit)*':

> Kott **kamagalá** 'nut' ← Turkic *kabagalï* 'with husk, peel, shuck' (< *qabaga* (cf. AltaiT) +*lXG* {Turkic NN/adj.} < *qabïq* 'husk, peel, shuck, bran' < *qaβïq* 'bran');

Turkic '*with feathers*' > Yeniseian '*quail (name of bird)*':

> Kott **tegteka** 'quail' ← Turkic *tükteg* 'with feathers' (< *tüg* 'the hair of the body; feathers' +*lXG* {Turkic NN/adj.});

Turkic '*thorny berry*' > Yeniseian '*raspberry*':

> Arin **tegentestek** 'raspberry' ← Turkic *tegen d'estek* < *tikän* 'thorn' (*tik-* 'to insert; to insert (*in the ground*), to sew (*insert a needle*)' -*GXn* {Turkic VN}) + *yestek* 'berry'.

4.1.1.2 *Tungusic Loanwords*
Tungusic '*squirrel*' > Yeniseian '*price of squirrel fur > money > ruble*':

> Central Ket, Northern Ket **ulla** ~ **úlle** 'ruble, the monetary unit in Russia' ← Northern Tungusic: Ewenki *ulukī* 'squirrel' < *ulu-kī* {Ewenki VN}.

4.1.2 Synecdoche
4.1.2.1 *Turkic Loanwords*
Turkic '*fish*' > Yeniseian '*ruff (kind of fish)*':

> Yugh **fálgi**; Ket **hál'ga** 'ruff (*fish, ɢymnocephalus cernuus*)' ← Turkic *palïk* 'fish' < *balïq*;

Turkic '*flax, canvas*' > Yeniseian '*nettles, hemp*':

> Kott **hîta**; Yugh **kitn**; Ket **kī·tn** 'nettles, hemp' ← Turkic *kiden* 'flax, canvas';

Turkic '*crupper*' > Yeniseian '*breech-band*':

> Kott **koskun** 'breech-band' ← Turkic *qosqun* 'crupper' < *quδuš-GAn* {Turkic VN};

Turkic *'clever, wise, hero, agile'* > Yeniseian *'bold, boldness'*:

> Kott **kuľuk** 'bold, boldness' ← Turkic *külük* 'clever, wise, famous' < *külüg* < *kü* 'rumour, fame, reputation' +*lXG* {Turkic NN/adj.};

Turkic *'belt, girdle'* > Yeniseian *'rope'*:

> Kott **kûra**; Assan **kura** 'rope' ← Turkic *qur* 'belt, girdle';

Turkic *'unfortunate; cripple; mentally disturbed'* > Yeniseian *'poor'*:

> Kott **munkan ~ munxan** 'poor' ← Turkic *muŋkan* 'unfortunate; cripple' cf. Altai Turkic < *muŋġan* 'mentally disturbed' < *buŋ-* 'to be mentally deranged or disturbed; being senile, feeble-minded, losing control of oneself, going fighting mad' *-GAn* {Turkic VN/Adj., habitual action};

Turkic *'blind'* > Yeniseian *'one-eyed'*:

> Kott **šugur** 'one-eyed' ← Turkic *soɣur* 'blind' ← Mongolic *soqor* 'blind';

Turkic *'there'* > Yeniseian *'beside, next to'*:

> Kott **tʰategâtna** 'beside, next to' ← Turkic *ta tiginde* 'there' < *ta* {Turkic strengthening-differential particle} + *tiginde* 'there' (< *tigi* 'he, she, it' +(*n*)*dA* {Turkic locative} ← Mongolic *tegün* 'stem of the demonstrative pronoun *tere*');

Turkic *'tanned leather'* > Yeniseian *'chamois leather'*:

> Kott **tarup ~ tarûp** 'chamois leather' ← Turkic *tup tere*: cf. Altai *tup tere* 'tanned leather';

Turkic *'to lead to despair'* > Yeniseian *'to offend, hurt'*:

> Kott **xoxutajut** 'to offend, hurt' ← Turkic *kokïylat-* (< *qoqïyla-* 'to lead to despair' < *qoqïy* 'a cry of despair' +*lA-* {Turkic NV} -(*X*)*t-* {Turkic VV/passive} ← Mongolic *qoki* 'scarce, scanty; unfortunate; loss, failure, harm').

4.1.2.2   Tungusic Loanwords

Tungusic *'root of bird-cherry'* > Yeniseian *'clothes rack made of bird-cherry wood'*:

> Southern Ket *kä·r* 'clothes rack made of bird-cherry (*Prunus padus*) wood' ← Tungusic: Ewenki *karje* 'root of bird-cherry';

Tungusic *'belt, which is tied to hunting dogs'* > Yeniseian *'team of dogs'*:

> Southern Ket *sū·ŋ* 'team of dogs' < **sū -ŋ* {Ket collective suffix} ← Northern Tungusic: Ewenki *suna* 'belt, which is tied to hunting dogs (*in team of dogs*)';

Tungusic *'reindeer'* > Yeniseian *'saddle for a reindeer'*:

> Northern Ket *učik* 'saddle for a reindeer' ← Northern Tungusic: Ewenki *ūčak* 'reindeer' (< *uɣ(u)*- 'to sit to ride' *-čA-* {Tungusic VV} *-k* {Tungusic VN}).

4.1.3   Widening
4.1.3.1   Turkic Loanwords

Turkic *'fellow country man; person, who gives request, order, help'* > Yeniseian *'old man'*:

> Kott *aibič ~ aipiš* 'old man' ← Turkic *aybïčï* 'fellow countryman' (< *aybï* 'request; order, decree; help');

Turkic *'tired out, exhausted, emaciated, weak for the lack of food'* > Yeniseian *'lean (thin)'*:

> Kott *arak* 'lean (*thin*)' ← Turkic *arïq* 'tired out, exhausted, emaciated, weak for the lack of food' (< *ār-* 'to be tired, exhausted, weak' *-(X)K* {Turkic VN});

Turkic *'comrade, companion'* > Yeniseian *'crowd (of people); migration'*:

> Arin *argiš* 'crowd (*of people*); migration' ← Turkic *argiš* 'comrade, companion' < *arqïš*;

Turkic '*hand, forearm*' > Yeniseian '*arm*':

> Ket *i·l'*, Northern Ket *i·l'i* 'arm' ← Turkic *äli* < *älig* 'hand, forearm; the width of a finger (*measure of length*)';

Turkic '*stingy, greedy*' > Yeniseian '*rapacious, voracious*':

> Kott **harâ** 'rapacious, voracious' ← Turkic *qaram* 'stingy, greedy' ← Mongolic *qaram* 'jealous; stinginess; regret' < *qara-* 'to look at, glance, watch, observe; to regard, consider; to look after; to face' *-m* {Mongolic VN};

Turkic '*to look, to watch; to peer, to pay attention, to observe; to wait*' > Yeniseian '*interjection come on already!*':

> Kott **hâra** 'interjection of impatience come on already!' ← Turkic *qara-* 'to look, to watch; to peer, to pay attention, to observe; to wait' {Turkic sg.2 imperative } ← Mongolic *qara-* 'to look at';

Turkic '*crop-eared*' > Yeniseian '*deaf*':

> Kott **kalkul** 'deaf' ← Turkic *qulɣur* 'crop-eared' ← Mongolic *quluɣur* 'laid or pressed back (*of ears*); crop-eared' < **qul(V) +GUr* {Mongolic NN/adj., the phonetic variant of *+GAr*};

Turkic '*guard; sight*' > Yeniseian '*view, look*':

> Kott **karei ~ karuj ~ karaul**; Assan **karei ~ karuj ~ karaul** 'view, look' ← Modern Turkic *karūl* 'guard; sight' < *qaraul* ← Mongolic *qaraɣul* 'watch, sentry, guard, scout';

Turkic '*girl; unmarried woman; daughter*' > Yeniseian '*sister-in-law*':

> Arin **kis** 'sister-in-law' ← Turkic *qïs* 'girl; unmarried woman; daughter' < *qïːz*;

Turkic '*to count*' > Mongolic '*to think, reflect, ponder; to hold an opinion; to intend, plan; to remember, keep in mind; to recall; to long for*' > Turkic '*to think, desire, feel, miss*' > Yeniseian '*to feel, guess, imagine, understand, remember, keep in mind, find out, test, examine*':

Yugh *sáŋa* 'to feel, guess, imagine, understand, remember, keep in mind, find out, test, examine' ← Turkic *sana-* 'to think, desire, feel, miss' ← Mongolic *sana-* 'to think, reflect, ponder; to hold an opinion; to intend, plan; to remember, keep in mind; to recall; to long for' ← Turkic *sana-* 'to count';

Turkic *'snowstorm, storm'* > Yeniseian *'cold weather'*:

> Kott *šurgan* 'cold weather' ← Turkic *šūrgan* 'snowstorm, storm' ← Mongolic *siɣurɣan* 'snowstorm, blizzard; storm with cold rain' (< *siɣur-* 'to rage (*as a storm*); a blizzard or snowstorm breaks out' *-GAn* {Mongolic VN});

Turkic *'leather'* > Yeniseian *'coarse cloth'*:

> Kott *tarei ~ tarêi* 'coarse cloth' ← Turkic *täri* 'the skin, hide (*of a human being or animal*), leather';

Turkic *'path'* > Yeniseian *'mountain valley'*:

> Kott *uruk* 'mountain valley' ← Turkic *oruq* 'path' (< *ōr-* 'to mow (*grass, etc.*), to reap (*crops*)' *-XK* {Turkic VN}).

4.1.3.2 *Tungusic Loanwords*
Tungusic *'constantly, always'* > Yeniseian *'from memory, by heart'*:

> Northern Ket *ɔkɔŋɔ* '*adverb* from memory, by heart' ← Northern Tungusic: Ewenki *ōkin* 'when'.

4.1.4 Narrowing
4.1.4.1 *Turkic Loanwords*
Turkic *'measure of time'* > Yeniseian *'week'*:

> Arin **kemenenčak** 'week' ← Turkic *kemineŋ čak*
> < *kemineŋ* (< *kem* 'measurement' *+(X)niŋ* {Turkic genitive} ← Mongolic *kem* 'measure; size, proportion; limits; measure of time, term');
> + *čak* 'time, a point in time, a period of time' (← Mongolic *čaɣ* 'time, period, season, age; time as general situation ot set of circumstances');

Turkic '*hail*' > Yeniseian '*ice*':

> Arin **mintora** 'ice' ← Turkic *mindir* 'hail' (← Mongolic *möndür* 'hail');

Turkic '*poison*' > Yeniseian '*inedible fungus, toadstool*':

> Kott **ô** 'inedible fungus, toadstool' ← Turkic *ō* < *aġu* 'poison';

Turkic '*village, dynasty, people*' > Yeniseian '*country; land of gnomes*':

> Ket **u·l's** 'country; land of gnomes' ← Turkic *ulus* 'administrative unit, village, dynasty, people' (← Mongolic *ulus* 'people, nation; country, state; empire; dynasty' ← Turkic *uluš* 'country');

Turkic '*something plaited or woven*' > Yeniseian '*cloth, linen*':

> Kott **urum** 'cloth, linen' ← Turkic *örüm* 'something plaited or woven' (< *ör-* 'to plait' -*Xm* {Turkic VN});

Turkic '*hard frost, frozen*' > Yeniseian '*ice*':

> Kott **ušôx ~ ušou** 'ice' ← Turkic *üšük* 'hard frost, frozen' (< *üši-* 'to be very cold, to shiver with cold' -*K* {Turkic VN}).

4.1.4.2   *Tungusic Loanwords*

Tungusic '*to fold; to roll up, to pack*' > Yeniseian '*to press, press together one's lips; to clench one's teeth; to press to one's breast; to put the tail between the legs (said of dogs)*':

> Yugh **namčej** '*inf.* to press, press together one's lips; to clench one's teeth; to press to one's breast; to put the tail between the legs (*said of dogs*)' < **namč -ej* {Yeniseian action nominal form}:
> *nam-* ← Northern Tungusic: Ewenki *nam-* 'to fold; to roll up, to pack'.

4.1.5   Amelioration

4.1.5.1   *Turkic Loanwords*

Turkic '*evil spirit*' > Yeniseian '*wonder*':

> Kott **alpeš** 'wonder' ← Turkic *albïs* 'evil spirit' ← Mongolic *almas* 'a legendary tribe of savage people; female demon, witch (*also an invective referring to women*)'.

4.1.6 Taboo Words

There are some loanwords belonging to the taboo category, most of them dealing with hunting, especially bear hunting:

4.1.6.1 *Turkic Loanwords*
Turkic '*brown*' > Yeniseian '*bear*':

> Kott ***kaltum*** 'bear' < *kaltu -m* {Yeniseian NN/adj.} ← Turkic *kara yoldu* 'brown (*colour of animal*)' < *kara* 'black' + *yoldïg* 'striped' cf. AltaiT: Quu dial. *qara yoldu* 'brown' (TSSDAJa 93);

Turkic '*who is running*' > Yeniseian '*hare, rabbit*':

> Kott ***mankara*** ~ ***mangara***; Assan ***mangára*** ~ ***mankara*** 'hare, rabbit' < *mangar -a* {Yeniseian feminine suffix} ← Turkic *maŋar* 'who is running, who is in hurry' < *maŋ* 'gallop' +*Ar* {Turkic aorist}.

4.1.6.2 *Tungusic Loanwords*
Tungusic '*bear's skin; bear's flesh*' > Yeniseian '*bear trap*':

> Ket ***ábses*** 'bear trap' < *ábse -s* {Yeniseian nominalizer} ← Northern Tungusic: Ewenki *amākākse* 'bear's skin; bear's flesh' < *amākā* 'grandfather; uncle; ancestor; bear; sky, God' < *amā* 'father; *taboo* bear' +*kā* {Ewenki NN} +*kse* {Ewenki NN/adj.};

Tungusic '*rapacious, predatory*' > Yeniseian '*bear eyes*':

> Ket ***húktɛŋ*** ~ ***huktɛn*** 'taboo bear eyes' < *huktɛ -ŋ* {Ket plural} ← Northern Tungusic: Ewenki *hugdï* 'rapacious, predatory' < *hug* 'bear, predator' +*dï* {Ewenki NN/adj.};

Tungusic '*a bear head, a "funeral" of bear*' > Yeniseian '*a bear stomach*':

> Ket ***tʌnsʼuk*** 'designation of a bear stomach' ← Northern Tungusic: Ewenki *tuŋsuku* 'a bear head, a "funeral" of bear';

Tungusic '*old, weak, helpless, defenceless, unprotected*' > Yeniseian '*a bear, when it is killed by a hunter*':

Ket ***ut-qo*** morphemes in the taboo replacement verb '*submit*', used when a bear is killed by a hunter, *lit.* 'the bear submits to a hunter' < *ut* + Yeniseian verb base *-qo* 'to kill':

ut ← Northern Tungusic: Ewenki *utu* 'old, weak, helpless, defenceless, unprotected' ← Mongolic *ötege* 'taboo bear' < **öte +GA(n)* {Mongolic NN}.

4.1.7 Yeniseian New Words Created through Compounding

There are some compound loanwords lacking in Turkic, but in Yenisean formed new words, usually from distinct nouns:

4.1.7.1 Turkic Loanwords

Kott ***ɛkačačik*** 'wax' ← Turkic *aġač čuk* < *aġač* 'tree' + *čuk* 'resin' ← Yeniseian;

Kott ***kalači*** 'eagle' ← Turkic *qal lačïn* < *qal* 'strong' + *lačïn* 'falcon';

Arin ***kemenenčak*** 'week' ← Turkic *keminëŋ čak* < *keminëŋ* (< *kem* 'measurement' *+(X)nïŋ* {Turkic genitive} ← Mongolic *kem* 'measure; size, proportion; limits; measure of time, term') + *čak* 'time, a point in time, a period of time' (← Mongolic *čaɣ* 'time, period, season, age; time as general situation ot set of circumstances');

Kott ***kereunčak*** 'hay-mowing' ← Turkic *kürən čak* < *kürən* 'sedge, hay' + *čak* 'time, period' (← Mongolic *čaɣ* 'time, period, season, age; time as general situation ot set of circumstances');

Kott ***tátien*** 'hill' ← Turkic *tā töŋ* < *taġ* 'mountain' + *töŋ* 'hill'.

CHAPTER 6

False Etymologies or Coincidences

During my research I found some words in Yeniseian which at first glance look like Altaic loanwords, but in fact have a Yeniseian etymology. They in fact represent native Yeniseian words rather than actual loanwords.

1   Turkic Words

Kott *abičijak* 'I am angry' (Werner 2002/1: 13):
cf. Turkic *ačinčak* 'angry' < *ačin-* 'to feel pain, grief, anger, or compassion; to grudge; to be pitied' < *ači-* 'to be bitter, to be sour; to be painful, to feel pain, to feel the pain of others, to feel compassion' *-n-* {Turkic NN/reflexive, see Erdal 1991: 584} *-čAk* {Altai VN/adj., see Baskakov 1947: 246}:

cf. Old Turkic *ačin-* 'to feel pain, grief, anger, or compassion; to grudge; to be pitied'; NE^S YeniseiT: Khakas *ačinjax* 'compassionate' < *ačin-* 'to regret, spare'; Sagai *ačin-* 'to be sad, sorrow, to feel pain, to be angry' (R); Shor *ajïnjak* 'compassionate, merciful' (R); AltaiT: Altai *ačinčak* 'angry; pity; touchy' < *ačin-* 'to be angry'; Tuba *ačingan* (< *ačin-GAn* {Turkic VN, see Erdal 1991: 382}) 'anger' < *ačin-* 'to spare'; Qumanda *ačin-* 'to get angry'; Quu *ačinčak* 'compassionate'; Teleut *ačin-* 'to be sad, sorrow, to feel pain, to be angry' (R); SayanT: Tuvan *ažinčak* 'short-tempered, unbalanced; angry' < *ažin-* 'to be angry'; Tofan *ajïn'jïg̈* 'bothersome; irritating'; ChulymT –; NE^N Yakut *ahïnïgas* 'compassionate, responsive'; Dolgan *ahïn-* 'to be pity'; Yakut dial. *aģïn-* 'to suffer before to give birth (*of a cow*)'; NW^N Siberian Tatar *ačučan* 'angry'; NW^S Kirgiz *ačin-* 'to suffer, to get angry'; Fu-yü –; Kazak *ašïn-* 'to feel pain; offense'; SE Yellow Uyghur *ači-* 'to get angry' **Etymology:** Räsänen VEWT 4a; Clauson ED 29a; ESTJa 1974: 91; Erdal 1991: 584

Originally, as a working hypothesis, I assumed that the source of the Kott expression *abičijak* 'I am angry' is the Altai Turkic form *ačinčak* 'angry' with the Turkic reflexive suffix *-n-* and Turkic deverbal noun adjective suffix *-čAk*. During etymologization, I claimed that the Turkic medial *-n-* disappeared in the Kott form, whereas the sound combination *-bi-* in the second syllable is the Yeniseian possessive suffix of the singular subject of first person, where the denasalization occurred.

Georg (2016: personal communication) drew my attention on another Kott word *haipičáŋ* 'angry' (Castrén 1858: 207a).

Vajda (2016: personal communication) proposed the Yenisean etymology for the Kott word, and also noted that the 1sg possessive *-b-* occurs only in Ket-Yugh-Arin, and never in Kott. He reconstructs Proto-Yeniseian compound word **qəjbes* (being) angry, (being) fierce; adj. 'angry, ill-tempered, evil' < **qəj ~ *qoj* < **qəl* 'bile' + **wes* 'resemble' + **əŋ* {anom/adj.}, Ket *qəjbes*, Yugh *χəjbes* '(be) angry, mean'. Kott *abičijak* 'I get angry' goes back to *habičij-ak-ŋ*, cf. *hapič* 'anger', *haipičáŋ* 'furious, evil', *haipičáŋ* {anom *-aŋ*} 'be irritated', *haipičaŋaiči* 'to get angry': *haipičaŋaja âttaŋ* 'I get angry'.

The opinions seem to be convincing.

Ket ***baŋos ~ baŋgos ~ baŋguˑs***; Yugh ***báŋguˑs*** 'earth spirit' < Yeniseian *baʔŋ* 'earth' + *kūs* 'spirit' (Werner 2002/2: 105):

cf. Turkic *maŋgïs ~ moŋgus ~ muŋus* 'devil; monster':

NE^S YeniseiT: Shor *möŋüs* 'bad'; AltaiT: Altai *moŋgus* 'huge'; Tuba *muŋus* 'devil'; Quu *moŋus* 'strong, brave, skilful; hero, warrior; evil, wicked'; Teleut *maŋgïs* 'locust'; SayanT: Tuvan *maŋgïs* 'monster'; NE^N Yakut *maŋïs* 'insatiable, greedy'; Dolgan *moŋus* 'monster'; NW^N Siberian Tatar –; NW^S Kirgiz –; Fu-yu –; SE Yellow Uyghur *maŋgïs* 'devil (*lives on the moon*)';

Turkic ← Mongolic *maŋγus* 'fabulous, usually many-headed monster, a kind of ogre':

cf. Middle Mongol: MNT *manggus ~ mangqus*; LM *mangγus*; Modern Mongol: Buryat *mangad*; Khalkha *mangas*; Kalmuck *maŋys* (for more Mongolic correspondences, see Nugteren 2011: 441).

From a phonetic and semantic points of view, the Ket and Yugh words are close to Siberian Turkic forms. However, the Yeniseian words have a native Yeniseian etymology; it is a Yeniseian compound of *baʔŋ* 'earth' and *kūs* 'spirit'.

In turn, the Turkic words are of Mongolic origin.

Arin ***bikašeb*** 'middle of the foot (metatarsals)' (Werner 2002/1: 159)

cf. Turkic **bakačaq < baqayaq < baqańaq < baqay ~ baqań* 'tibia, name of several bones above the hoof' +*AK* {Turkic NN/diminutive, see Erdal 1991: 76} < **baqa* 'ankle' < **baqqa* 'joint' < *ba-* 'to tie, join together' *-(O)k* {Turkic VN, see Erdal 1991: 224} +*KA* {Turkic NN/diminutive suffix}:

cf. Old Turkic *baqāyaq ~ baqāńaq* '*the frog* in a horse's hoof', cf. *baqāčuq* 'the muscle of the forearm'; NE^S YeniseiT: Khakas *paġayax ~ maxayax* 'ankle', cf. *maxpayax ~ paxpayax ~ paġayax* 'ankle; leather slippers dressing until the ankles; socks' (But.); Sagai *maxpayax* 'ankle'; AltaiT: Altai –; Quu *paqpayaq* 'bend of the hand'; Teleut *päkäyäk* 'wrist' (R), cf. *päktäk* 'ankle'; SayanT: Tuvan –[1]; Tofan –; ChulymT *paqa*

---

[1] Cf. *makpalčïk* 'knuckle bone (*as used in games*)'.

'pastern'; NE^N Yakut *begečček* 'wrist'; NW^N Siberian Tatar *pağayaq* 'shin'; NW^S Kirgiz *bakay* 'pastern', cf. *bagalčak* 'space between the hoof and ankle of a horse, shin'; Fu-yü –; Kazak *baqayšaq* < *baqay* 'pastern'; SE Yellow Uyghur *baqalčäq* 'shin' (**Etymology**: Räsänen VEWT 58a–b; Clauson ED 316b, 312b; SSTMJa 1: 67; ESTJa 1978: 43–45; SIGTJa 1997: 286–287; Róna-Tas & Berta 2011: 145–146).

Originally, I proposed that the Arin word belongs to a group of hybrid compound words where the first part **bikaš* connects to the Turkic form **bakačak* < *bakayak*. More likely, the first two syllables of this form could also be interpreted as the Arin-Yugh-Ket 1sg possessive prefix *bi-* 'my' followed by the native Yeniseian root *kaš* 'foot' (cf. Ket and Yugh *ki's* 'foot, leg', Ket *kassat* 'heel') (Vajda 2018: personal communication).

Kott *pêj* 'wind' (Werner 2002/1: 122), cf. Ket *bēˑj*; Yugh *bēj*; Arin *paj*; Assan *pej* ~ *bej*; Pumpokol *baj* ~ *boi*:
cf. Turkic *key* 'air':
 cf. NE^S YeniseiT: Khakas *kī*; Sagai *kī* (R); AltaiT: Altai *key*; Qumanda *key* ~ *kiy*; Quu *key*; Teleut *käy* (R); SayanT: Tuvan *xey*; Tofan *hey*; Remaining lgs. –;
Turkic ← Mongolic *kei* 'air, wind, atmosphere, gas; empty, idle; in vain':
 Middle Mongol: Precl.Mo.; MNT; HY; 'Phags-pa; Ibn-Muh.; Muq.; Ist. *kei*; ZY *ke(i)*; LM *kei*; Modern Mongol: Buryat *xī*; Khalkha *xī*; Oirat dial. *kī* ~ *kxī* (As concerns the etymology of the Mongolic word and its borrowings to Turkic languages, see Räsänen VEWT 247b; Rassadin 1971: 187; 1980: 22; Khabtagaeva 2009: 153).

From a semantic perspective, the Yeniseian word at first glance appears to be connected to Turkic *kei* 'air, wind', which may have developed through **hey* < **pej*. But the Kott word has a stable Yeniseian etymology.

Kott *čik* ~ *čîk*, Ket *dīˑk*, Yugh *dʲīk* 'resin' (Werner 2002/1: 193) < Yeniseian **dʲīˑk* 'resin':
cf. Turkic *čuk* 'resin':
 cf. Old Turkic –; NE^S YeniseiT: Khakas *čux*; Sagai *čuq*; Kyzyl *šux*; Shor *čuq*; AltaiT: –; SayanT: Tuvan *čuk*; Tofan *čuq*; Remaining lgs. –;
cf. Tungusic *čūkse* 'resin, tree sap, juice':
 Northern Tungusic: Northern Ewenki: Yerbogachon; Southern Ewenki: Podkamennyi, Nepa *čūksa*; Sym *čūha*; Eastern Ewenki: Zeya, Aldan, Tokma *čūhe* 'tree sap'; Solon *sūrče* 'resin'; Lamut *čūs* 'tree sap, berry juice'; Negidal *čūxse* 'juice'; Southern Tungusic: Oroch *čūkse* 'juice'; Udihe *čüöŋki* 'tree sap, juice'; Orok *sūkse* ~ *tūkse* 'juice'; Remaining lgs. –.

The etymology of the Turkic word is unclear. Stachowski (1997: 230) connects the Yeniseian words with Turkic *čüg* 'damp'. Rassadin (1971: 198) originates the Siberian Turkic forms from Ewenki *čūkse* 'resin'. The Tungusic forms are connected with Mongolic *sigüsün* 'sap, juice; food (*usually meat*) for offerings' (SSTMJa 2: 411). According to Vajda (2014: personal communication), the Yeniseian words are native. Cf. Kott *ɛkačačik* 'wax'.

Kott *dôt* 'to go to sleep' (Werner 2002/1: 224) < Yeniseian: cf. *dʲ-gat* ~ *dʲ-ôt* ~ *dʲ-atam*: Kott morphemes in verbs meaning 'sleep, be lying down'
< **-dʲ* ~ **j-* {Yeniseian prefix shape found in certain non-past forms of a handful of basic Kott verbs, probably an amalgam of thematic consonant and following conjugation marker}, e.g. *dʲ-ax* 'become', *dʲ-čagar* 'say', *dʲ-čakŋ* 'go downriver', *dʲ-čen* 'weep', *dʲ-fel* 'grow, mature', *dʲ-ga* 'leave', etc. (Vajda 2014: personal communication):
cf. Turkic *d'at-* < *yat-* 'to lie down':
   cf. Old Turkic *yat-*; NE[S] YeniseiT: Khakas *čat-*; Sagai *čat-*; Koibal, Kachin *yat-* (R); Kyzyl *šat-*; Shor *čat-*; AltaiT: Altai *d'at-*; Tuba *d'at-*; Qumanda *čad-*; Quu *d'at-*; Teleut *yat-*; SayanT: Tuvan *čït-*; Tofan *čïᶜt-*; ChulymT *čat-* ~ *yat-*; NE[N] Yakut *sït-*; Dolgan *hït-*; NW[N] Siberian Tatar –; NW[S] Kirgiz *žat-*; Fu-yü –; Kazak *žat-*; SE Yellow Uyghur *yat-* (for etymology on Turkic verb, see Räsänen VEWT 192b; Clauson ED 884a; ESTJa 1989: 156–158).

The Kott word has a clear Yeniseian etymology. The word contains a Yeniseian prefix that is also present in other Kott verbs.

Assan *haj*; Pumpokol *xaj*; Yugh *χaʔj*; Ket *qaʔj* 'high riverbank, forested upland, mountain' (Werner 2002/2: 78):
cf. Turkic *qaya* 'a rock, a sharp upstanding rock or rocky cliff; a mountain':
   cf. Old Turkic *qaya*; NE[S] YeniseiT: Khakas *xaya*; Sagai, Koibal, Kachin *qaya* (R); Shor *qaya*; AltaiT: Altai *kaya*; Tuba *kaya*; Qumanda *kaya*; Quu *kaya*; Teleut *qaya* (R); SayanT: Tuvan *xaya*; Tofan *haya*; ChulymT *qaya* 'stone'; NE[N] Yakut *xaya* 'mountain'; Dolgan *kaya*; NW[N] Siberian Tatar –; NW[S] Kirgiz *kïya* 'hillside'; Fu-yü –; Kazak –; SE Yellow Uyghur *qaya* (for details on the etymology[2] of Turkic word, see Räsä-

---

[2] The connection between the Turkic word and the Mongolic *qada* 'rock, mountain' (for details, see ESTJa 1997: 198–199) is unclear. Doerfer exludes it and claims that the original Turkic form should be **qaya* (TMEN 3: 566); cf. the Sayan Turkic and Yakut forms, where the original -δ- regularly changed into -d- and -t-, respectively. The analyzed data may confirm Doerfer's opinion.

From the Mongolic *qada* (Nugteren 2011: 398), the word was borrowed to Tungusic (SSTMJa 1: 360; Doerfer 1985: 18; Rozycki 1994: 96) and further from Tungusic to Yakut (Doerfer TMEN 1: 393–394; 1985: 18; ESTJa 1997: 199).

nen VEWT 221ab; Doerfer TMEN 1: 269; 3: 1591; 1985: 18; Rassadin 1971: 185; Clauson ED 674b; SSTMJa 1: 360; Rozycki 1994: 96; ESTJa 1997: 198–199; SIGTJa 1997: 96–97; Werner 2002/2: 78; Nugteren 2011: 398).

The Yeniseian words were connected with a Turkic word by Werner (2002/2: 78). The Turkic etymology fits from the phonetic and semantic viewpoint.[3] However, the Yeniseian words have a reliable etymology. According to Vajda (2016: personal communication), the Proto-Yeniseian form *qaʔj 'high riverbank, hill' is a compound word and goes back to *qax 'big' + *ŋ {adj.pl.} + *dʲi 'slope'. The Yeniseian etymology is strengthened by plural forms in Ket qaʔj > qaŋnʲeŋ ~ qaŋnʲiŋ and Yugh χaʔj > χaŋnʲiŋ.

Kott *hônaŋ* 'recently' (Werner 2002/1: 325):
cf. Turkic onaŋ ~ anaŋ 'since' < ol 'that; he, she, it' +nAŋ {Khakas ablative, see Baskakov & Inkižekova-Grekul 1953: 443; Altai ablative, see Baskakov 1947: 271}, (cf. Old Turkic ablative +dXn, see Erdal 2004: 174–175):

cf. Old Turkic andan ~ andïn[4] 'thence, thereafter'; NE^S YeniseiT: Khakas annaŋ 'from, thence'; Sagai, Koibal, Kachin anaŋ ~ andaŋ 'thence' (R); Shor anaŋ 'thence; then'; AltaiT: Altai onoŋ 'then, since'; Tuba andaŋ ~ andïŋ 'then, after'; Qumanda anaŋ 'after, then'; Teleut anaŋ 'after'; SayanT: Tuvan ōn 'thence'; ChulymT andïn 'thence'; NE^N Yakut onton 'then, after'; Dolgan onton 'why? therefore, well, then; and, as well; and, on the other hand'; NW^N Siberian Tatar anan ~ anaŋ 'then, after'; NW^S Kirgiz anan 'then, after'; Fu-yü –; SE Yellow Uyghur andan 'thence' (Regarding the etymology of the Turkic word, see Clauson ED 177b; ESTJa 1974: 444–445).

During my investigation I connected the Kott word with the Altai Turkic or Yenisei Turkic adverb onoŋ ~ anaŋ 'then, since'. The problematic side of my etymology was the origin of the initial prothetic h- in the Kott form. According to Vajda (2016: personal communication), the Kott word goes back to Yeniseian *kun 'previous' and Yeniseian suffix *aŋ, which forms adjectives and adverbs.

---

3 The regular change of Common-Yeniseian *q- in initial position shows that the Turkic word was borrowed in the early period. Proto-Yeniseian *q- was preserved in Ket, but changed to χ- in Pumpokol and Yugh (Vajda 2014: personal communication; see also Starostin 1982: 169–170). Additionally, several cases of apocope—a typical phenomenon for Turkic loanwords—occurred in Yeniseian words.

4 The formation of the Turkic adverb andan ~ andïn 'thence, thereafter,' from the pronoun ol 'he, she, it' with the ablative case was examined by Clauson (ED 177b). For details on the derivation of Khakas adverbs with the ablative case, see Patačkova (1975: 105).

Arin *-kul* 'water' < Yeniseian **Hū·λ* 'water' (Werner 2002/1: 448):
cf. Turkic *kȫl* 'pool, lake':

cf. Old Turkic *kȫl*; NE^S YeniseiT: Khakas *köl*; Shor *köl*; AltaiT: Altai *köl*; SayanT: Tuvan *xöl*; Tofan *höl*; ChulymT *köl*; NE^N Yakut *küöl*; Dolgan *küöl* ~ *kȫl*; NW^N Siberian Tatar *kül*; NW^S Kirgiz *köl*; Fu-yü *göl*; Kazak *köl*; SE Yellow Uyghur *k^cöl* (for etymology on Turkic word, see Clauson ED 715a; ESTJa 1997: 95–96).

From a phonetic and a semantic viewpoint, the Arin form looks like a borrowing from Turkic. But it has a stable native Yeniseian etymology, which goes back to Proto-Yeniseian **Huλ* 'water' (Vajda 2014: personal communication), cf. Ket *ū·l*, Yugh *ūr*, Assan *ul*, Kott *ul*, Yugh *ur*, Pumpokol *ul*, Kott *ûl* ~ *ul*. The Arin component 'river' is present in many Siberian toponyms: *Am-ul, Aška-ul, Kos-ul, Yun-kul, Ači-kul, Karma- kul*, etc.

Kott *xalpen*; Arin ***kilph'an*** 'spoon' (Werner 2002/2: 383):
cf. Turkic *qalbaq* 'spoon' ← Mongolic *qalbaγa* 'spoon' ← Turkic **qalbă-*: Old Turkic *qaši-* 'to stratch':

cf. NE^S YeniseiT: Khakas *xalbaġas* (< *qalbaq* + *ās* 'mouth') 'a kind of duck'; Shor, Sagai *qalbaġas* 'a wide beak of duck' (R); AltaiT: Altai *kalbak* 'spoon'; Tuba *kalbak* 'spoon'; Qumanda *kalbak* 'wide'; Teleut *qalbaq* 'spoon'; SayanT: Tuvan *xalbaga* 'ladle'; Tofan –; ChulymT –; NE^N Yakut *xalbïga* 'small spoon'; NW^N Siberian Tatar –; NW^S Kirgiz –; Fu-yü –; Kazak *qalbaq* 'spoon'; SE Yellow Uyghur –;

Turkic ← Mongolic *qalbaγa* 'spoon' < *qalba-GAn* {Mongolic VN, see Poppe 1964: § 149}:

cf. Middle Mongol: Precl.Mo. *qalbuγ-a*; SH; HY; ZY *qalbuqa*; Muq. *qalbuγa*; LM *qalbaγ-a(n)* ~ *qalbuγ-a* 'spoon; the knob on a flag staff; bobber (*in fishing*); spoonbill (*bird*)'; Modern Mongol: Buryat *xalbaga* 'spoon'; Sayan Buryat: Tunka; Oka *xalbaga* 'paddle'; Lower Uda Buryat *kalbaga* 'ladle'; Khalkha *xalbaga* 'spoon; a tool for clearing out a camel's foot'; Oirat dial. *xalwăgă* ~ *xalbăg* 'spoon'; Dagur *xalbeγ* 'hoe blade' (E); Khamnigan *xalbaga*;

Mongolic ← Turkic **qalbă-* > *qaši-* 'to scratch':

cf. Old Turkic *qašuq* 'spoon'; NE^S YeniseiT: Khakas *xazïx*; Sagai, Koibal *kazik* (R); Shor *qažïq*; AltaiT: Altai –; Teleut *qažïq* (R); SayanT: Tuvan –; Tofan *qa^chiq*; ChulymT *qažuq* ~ *qāžuq*; NE^N Yakut –; NW^N Siberian Tatar *qažïq*; NW^S Kirgiz *kašïk*; Fu-yü –; Kazak *qasïq*; SE Yellow Yughur – (for details on the etymology, see Kałużyński 1962: 76; Räsänen VEWT 241a; Clauson ED 671b; ESTJa 1997: 353–354; Rassadin 1980: 11, 69; Ščerbak 1997: 135–136; Khabtagaeva 2009: 201; Nugteren 2011: 402).

Werner (2002/2: 383) after Stachowski (1996: 96), originated the Yeniseian words from Turkic *qalbaq* 'spoon'.[5] The Kott form *xalben* and Arin *kilph'an* may changed from the nasalized form **qalban* < **qalbaŋ*, which is originally was **kalbak*, cf. Altai Turkic forms.[6] Compare also the Kott word *ataŋ* 'fire-steel' borrowed from Turkic *otïq* 'fire-steel', where a similar change occurred.

According to Vajda (2016: personal communication), the Yeniseian **kilpen* 'spoon' is derived from **kil* 'bent' + **pen* 'utensil with cupped end', cf.

Yeniseian **egpiʔn* 'metal ladle; scoop' < **eg* 'iron' + **piʔn* 'ladle' > Ket *eɣin* ~ *eyin*; Yugh *eifin*;

Yeniseian **padbedpin* 'spoon for mixing dough' < **pad* 'flat' + **bed* 'press' + **piʔn* 'spoon' > Ket *happa tiʔn* ~ *habbatn* ~ *habätin* ~ *habetin*;

Yeniseian **paleb* 'beater for soft dough' < **pal* 'turning' + **piʔn* 'spoon' > Ket *halep*.

2 Tungusic Words

Southern Ket *däкɔ* ~ *déкɔ* 'block of ice' (Werner 2002/1: 183):
cf. Northern Tungusic: Ewenki **dˊuke* < *ǯuke* 'ice':
  Ewenki dialects (*Northern Ewenki*: Yerbogachon, Ilimpeya; *Southern Ewenki*: Podkamennyi, Nepa, Sym, Tokma, Upper Lena, Nercha; *Eastern Ewenki*: Tungir, Aldan, Uchur, Urmi, Chumikan, Barguzin) *ǯuke* 'block of ice; ice';
  cf. also Northern Tungusic: Lamut *ǯök* ~ *ǯuk*; Negidal *ǯuxe* ~ *ǯuke*; Southern Tungusic: Oroch *ǯuke*; Udihe *ǯuge*; Ulcha *ǯū* ~ *ǯue*; Orok *duve* ~ *dūkke* ~ *duke* ~ *ǯuɣe*; Nanai *ǯuke*; Jurchen *ču-hēi*; Manchu *ǯuhe*; Sibe – (for the etymological background and the derivation of the Tungusic word, see SSTMJa 1: 271b–272a and Cincius 1949: 305).

---

5 The Siberian Turkic form *kalbak* was re-borrowed from Mongolic *qalbaɣa* (Kałużyński 1962: 76; Rassadin 1980: 11, 69; Khabtagaeva 2009: 201), which is ultimately of Turkic origin (Räsänen VEWT 241a; Clauson ED 671b; Ščerbak 1997: 135–136; ESTJa 1997: 353–354; Nugteren 2011: 402).

6 There is another Turkic word for 'spoon' *qalaq* ~ *qalǧaq* (cf. Khakas *xalǧax* ~ *xallax* 'stirrer; a chute for preparing moonshine; a stick for playing *lapta*; a wooden clapper for a of shaman'), which is not to be connected to the Turkic form *qašuq* 'spoon' and Mongolic *qalbuɣa* (for details, see ESTJa 1997: 231–232).

According to Werner (2002/1: 183), the Ket word consists of two Yeniseian words *dɛˀ* 'lake' and *qo* 'ice'. Despite the fact that the Ket word is close phonetically (Ewenki *d-* shows up as *d-* in Ket), the word belongs to the 'coincidence' category.

Ket *ɔnéŋ* 'ebb' (Werner 2002/2: 40):
cf. Northern Tungusic: Ewenki *ŋenē* 'movement, motion' < *ŋene-* 'to move' *-Ā* {Ewenki VN, see Vasilevič 1958: 749}:
> Ewenki *ŋenē* 'passing, departing, leaving; movement, motion, travel, going, speed, passanger' < *ŋene-* ~ *gene-* ~ *mene-* ~ *nene-* ~ *ŋono-* 'to move, to go, to travel, to fly; to run (*about time*); to continue do *sg.*; to flow (*about ship*)';
> cf. Northern Tungusic: Lamut *ŋen-* ~ *ŋön-* ~ *ŋän-* 'to move, to go, to disappear'; Negidal *gunu-* ~ *munu-* ~ *ŋunu-* ~ *ŋune-* 'to come back'; Southern Tungusic: Oroch *ŋei-* 'to go'; Udihe *ŋein-* ~ *ŋeni-* ~ *ŋeńi-* 'to go, to come back'; Ulcha *ŋene-* 'to go'; Orok *ŋenne-* ~ *ŋene-* 'to move, to go'; Nanai *ene-* 'to move, to go, to go back'; Jurchen *kôh-niēh-hēi* 'to go away'; Manchu *gene-* 'to go'; Sibe *gən(ə)-* 'to go there' (For etymological background, see SSTMJa 1: 669b–671b).

During my work I connected the Ket word *ɔnéŋ* 'ebb' with the Ewenki noun *ŋenē* 'movement, motion'. The appearance of prothetical *ɔ-* in the initial position of Ket word was explained by absence of the initial nasal consonant *ŋ-* in Yeniseian. The change of original vowel *e* > *ɔ* is also typical for some Tungusic loanwords in Ket (e.g. Northern Ket *ɔmɔyin* 'reindeer saddle' ← Tungusic: Ewenki *emegen*).

However, the semantic meaning of the Ewenki word is not the same, since the 'movement, motion' is not specifically connected to water as in Yeniseian. According to Vajda (2016: personal communication), the Ket word *onéŋ* 'ebb' is etymologically derived from Yeniseian **an* 'wave' and plural suffix **eŋ*. The Yeniseian root **an* ~ **en* is present in words meaning 'wave': Kott *en* ~ *ên* (pl. *ênaŋ*) 'wave'; Ket *anbok* ~ *anbək* (pl. *anbokŋ*), *ânbakŋ* 'big wave' (*an* 'water' + **bəg* 'pull').

Ket **kudab** 'wrinkle' (Werner 2002/1: 447, 454):
cf. Northern Tungusic: Ewenki *kotï-* 'to wrinkle a face':
> *Southern Ewenki*: Podkamennyi; *Eastern Ewenki*: Uchur *kotï-* 'to wrinkle a face' (Vasilevič); cf. Podkamennyi, Ilimpeya *kotïra-*, Kachin, Tokko, Tommot, Uchur *kotoro-* 'to crease, wrinkle (*about clothes during drying*)' < *kotï-rA-* {Ewenki VV, see Vasilevič 1958: 785)};
> cf. Northern Tungusic: Lamut *qotïn-* ~ *kotän-* ~ *kotīn-* 'to dry (*about clothes*)'; Remaining lgs. – (SSTMJa 1: 417b).

Despite the fact that the Ket word is close to the Ewenki verb both phonologically and semantically, the word is of Yeniseian origin. This is proven by the Southern Ket form *kurep*, which corresponds to with the Central Ket form *kudep*. According to Vajda (2016: personal communication), the Ket word etymologically is a compound and goes back to **kud* 'bend, roll, furrow' + **ep* 'skin, surface'.

Ket *dib* ~ *ip* 'edge of sg.; hem of a dress' (Vajda & Werner: in preparation):
cf. Northern Tungusic: Ewenki *japqa* ~ *d'apka* < *ǰapqa*[7] 'edge, border':
> Common Ewenki *d'apka* 'shore, shoreline, the boundary (*between land and water*); foot of a mountain; board, the edge of something' (Boldyrev);
>
> cf. Northern Tungusic: Lamut *japqa* 'crack; seam; edge, border'; Negidal *ǰapqa* 'space, crack'; Southern Tungusic: Oroch *ǰappa* 'flap'; Udihe *ǰakpa-* 'to put on each other'; Ulcha *ǰaqpa* 'branch, fork'; Orok *daqpa* ~ *dapqa* ~ *ǰapqa* 'space, crack'; Nanai *ǰaqpa* 'space'; Jurchen –; Manchu *ǰaqa-* 'to cut out grooves in beam'; Sibe – (SSTMJa 1: 250b).

At first glance, the Ket forms seem connected with the Common Ewenki word *ǰapqa* 'edge, border', where the Ewenki final syllable dropped in Ket as in other loanwords. But the original Yenisean form is *ip* and another form *dip* refers to the possessive third-person singular form (Georg 2016: personal communication; Vajda 2016: personal communication).

Ket *dεstij*; Yugh *déstəu* '*inf*. to shoot' (Werner 2002/1: 184) < Yeniseian finite verb *des-t-ij* (Vajda 2014: personal communication):
cf. Northern Tungusic: Ewenki *dïsut-* 'to defend':
> *Southern Ewenki*: Podkamennyi, Nepa *dïsut-*;
>
> cf. Northern Tungusic: Lamut *disut-* ~ *dihut-* ~ *ǰisut-*; Negidal *disut-*; Southern Tungusic: Nanai *ǰïsun-* 'to defend, to regret'; Remaining lgs. – (SSTMJa 1: 208b).

The etymology of the Yeniseian verbs is unknown (Werner 2002/1: 184). According to Vajda (2014: personal communication), the words are compound action nominals of Yeniseian origin.

Southern Ket *it*; Central Ket *īte*; Northern Ket *īti*; Yugh *ĩʰt*; Kott *iti* ~ *ite*; Arin *itin* < Proto-Yeniseian **ĩʰtə* 'tooth' (Vajda & Werner: in preparation):

---

7   The phonetic fluctuation of the initial consonants *j-* ~ *ǰ-* ~ *d'-* is typical for Ewenki dialects, e.g. *jeɣin* ~ *ǰeɣin* ~ *d'eɣin* 'nine', *jelekī* ~ *ǰelekī* ~ *d'elekī* 'ermine', *julēskī* ~ *ǰulēskī* 'forward', etc. (For more fetails and examples, see Vasilevič 1948: 336; Cincius 1949: 211–213).

cf. Northern Tungusic: Ewenki *itte* < *īkte 'tooth':
> *Northern Ewenki*: Ilimpeya *itte*; *Southern Ewenki*: Podkamennyi, Nepa *īkte*;
> cf. Northern Tungusic: Lamut *īt*; Negidal *īkte*; Southern Tungusic: Oroch *ikte*; Udihe *ikte*; Ulcha *ikte*; Orok *ikte*; Nanai *hukte*; Jurchen *wéi-hēi*; Manchu *weihe*; Sibe – (SST-MJa 1: 300a).

From a phonetic perspective, the Yeniseian forms look like Tungusic borrowings. More probably, the resemblance is coincidental, given the lack of evidence that Tungusic words were borrowed into Proto-Yeniseian (Vajda 2014: personal communication).

Conclusion

One of the main goals of my research was to etymologize Yeniseian words, and confirm their Altaic origin. Establishing the existence of early Yeniseian-Altaic linguistic contacts is possible if we first separate and examine the later layer. My monograph firstly deals with later loanwords and may be a starting point for the next step of research.

During the research, I found more than 300 Altaic loanwords; approximately 230 of them are of Turkic origin and around 70 loanwords have Tungusic etymologies. A few number of loanwords are of Mongolic origin, which came through either Siberian Turkic, or Tungusic Ewenki languages. There are clear phonetic, morphological and semantic criteria that help to distinguish loanwords borrowed via Turkic or Tungusic and not directly from Mongolic languages.

One of the important results of my work is the establishment that the Middle Mongol invasion did not reach the Yeniseian people, contrary to what had earlier been assumed. The Mongolic loanwords do not have phonetic criteria characteristic of the Middle Mongol period, e.g.

> the Middle Mongol initial consonant *h*- disappeared, cf. Arin *oo* 'woods' ← Mongolic *oi* 'woods, forest, grove' < *hoi*: Middle Mongol *hoi*; LM *oi*;

> the secondary long vowels developed from *Vocal-Consonant-Vocal* pattern and further shortened, as in Turkic and Tungusic loanwords of Mongolic origin. Cf. Kott *keršo* 'clever' ← Turkic *kärsü* 'clever, talanted' ← Mongolic **kersü* < *kersegüü* 'wise, circumspect, prudent; careful, circumspect, astute'; etc.

The absence of direct Mongolic loanwords shows that the territories where the Yeniseian and Mongolic people lived were not contiguous. The Mongolic loanwords display characteristics of Siberian Turkic or Tungusic Ewenki. Owing to the paucity of examples, it is questionable whether any direct borrowing from Mongolic into Yeniseian languages occurred.

From a statistical point of view, a breakdown of Turkic loanwords in the 29 semantic fields represented in the database reflects a predominance of Kott loans in comparison to loans attested in other Yeniseian languages. Most loanwords are names of wild and domestic animals, terms belonging to household items, and adjectives that express physical and characteristic peculiarities of humans and animals:

	Kott	Assan	Arin	Pump.	Yugh	Ket
Nouns						
Inanimate nature	8	0	8	0	0	0
Metals, minerals	7	3	5	2	1	1
Plants	10	5	6	0	1	1
Wild animals, birds, fishes and insects	15	4	7	1	4	3
Domestic animals	11	7	7	0	0	0
Human and animal body parts	6	1	2	1	4	4
Designation of people	4	0	1	0	1	1
Kinship terminology	1	0	5	1	0	0
Titles	4	0	0	0	1	1
Mythology and religion	5	1	1	0	0	0
Administrative units	1	0	1	0	0	1
Food	6	6	5	0	2	1
Buildings and their parts	4	0	1	0	0	0
Household equipment and tools	18	5	5	0	4	4
Clothing, cloth	4	0	2	0	1	0
Measurement	1	0	1	0	0	0
Taxes and finance	1	0	0	0	0	0
Abstract nouns	3	1	1	0	1	1
Agriculture	4	0	1	0	0	0
Art, writing and entertainment	4	0	0	0	0	0
Military terminology	3	0	1	0	0	0
Adjectives						
Colour names	8	0	0	0	0	0
Qualitative adjectives	9	0	0	0	3	2
Physical and characteristic peculiarities of humans and animals	17	1	3	0	1	1
Adverbs	5	0	0	0	0	0
Numerals	1	0	1	0	0	0
Verbs	4	0	1	0	3	0
Postpositions	1	0	0	0	1	0
Interjections	1	0	0	0	0	0
Total	166	34	65	5	28	21

CONCLUSION

The Tungusic loanwords are mostly found in Ket dialects and Yugh. The source of borrowing clearly were Ewenki dialects: Podkamennyi and Nepa dialects belonging to the Southern Ewenki branch, on the one hand, and Yerbogachon and Ilimpeya dialects of the Northern Ewenki branch, on the other. This fact may be strengthened not only by the logic of geography, but also by phonetic features such as the appearance of sibilant *s in different positions of Tungusic loanwords in Yeniseian. There is only one Tungusic loanword in Kott,[1] which was probably re-borrowed from one Yeniseian variety due to the fact that Tungusic loanwords are absent in Kott.

The table below categorizes this as either borrowed Ket terminology, or as belonging to inanimate nature and household equipment; both categories are nouns:

	Yugh	Ket
Nouns		
Inanimate nature	2	11
Wild animals, birds and insects	3	6
Human and animal body parts	0	2
Designation of people	0	4
Mythology and religion	0	2
Hunting	0	3
Harness and means of conveyance	0	7
Food	0	2
House, household equipment and tools	0	10
Clothing	0	3
Illness, disease	0	1
Monetary units	0	1
Abstract nouns	0	2
Adverbs	0	4
Verbs	1	4
Particles	0	3
Interjections	1	2
Total:	7	67

---

[1] Kott *kaltapen* 'wedge for splitting wood' < *kalta -p-* {?} + Yeniseian *eˑn* 'wedge': *kalta* ← Tungusic: Podkamennyi Ewenki *kalta-* 'to crack, to break up in two parts; to split in half'.

The main outcome of my research is the identification of typical characteristics of Altaic loanwords in Yeniseian. The phonetic criteria include the regular disappearance of vowel harmony, diphthongization of vowels, prothesis, apocope, paragoge, epentheses, gemination of consonants, syncope. Some Turkic and Tungusic loanwords lost internal syllables or added internal -ŋ- or final -t consonants, which atypical for Altaic languages. One of the important phonetic features in Yeniseian is metathesis of consonants. The investigation showed that the metathesis usually happened in Altaic loanwords with nasal and plosive consonants, while in original Yeniseian words it occurred with labial and velar consonants.

From a morphological perspective, Yeniseian suffixes were identified in Altaic loanwords, such as Arin suffix -ok of Russian origin and peculiar for loanwords, as well as the Yeniseian plural suffix -ŋ/-n and the productive Yeniseian nominalizer -s. Yeniseian adjective forming suffixes -Xŋ, -tu, -m and Yeniseian action nominal suffixes in verbs are also found in certain Altaic loanwords. Several Yeniseian names of animals and plants dropped the original Altaic suffixes in word-final position, which can be explained by the monosyllabic structure of the Yeniseian words. The predominant noun-forming technique of Yeniseian is compounding. One of the important results of the research was in establishing the nature or structure of Yeniseian compounds of Turkic and Tungusic origin. The half-affixes of Altaic origin were also explored.

In the field of semantics, the meaning of Altaic loanwords were usually preserved, though in some cases metaphor, synecdoche, widening, narrowing and amelioration happened. A special category includes taboo words connected with hunting animals such as bear, hare, etc.

In the future, it would be important to examine Samoyedic-Yeniseian linguistical contacts, which may be present in the early layer of different loanwords including Altaic.

I hope my research has revealed new results not only for Yeniseian studies, but also for Altaic and Siberian Studies.

References

Afanas'jev, P.S.; Voronkin, M.S. & Alekseev, M.P. (1976): *Dialektologičeskij slovar' jakutskogo jazyka*. Moskva: Nauka.

Alekseenko, E.A. (1960): Kul't medvedja u ketov. *Sovetskaja ėtnografija* 4. 90–104.

Alekseenko, E.A. (1971): Domašnie pokroviteli u ketov. In: *Religioznye predstavlenija i obrjady narodov Sibiri v 19—načale 20 vekov*. Leningrad. 263–274.

Alekseenko, E.A. (1976): Predstavlenija ketov o mire. In: *Priroda i čelovek v religioznyx predstavlenijax narodov Sibiri i Severa (vtoraja polovina 19—načalo 20 vekov)*. 67–105.

Alekseenko, E.A. (1985): Na medvež'jem prazdnike u ketov. *Sovetskaja ėtnografija* 5. 92–97.

Alekseenko, E.A. (1999): *Kety*. Sankt-Peterburg.

Anderson, G. (2003): Yeniseic languages from a Siberian areal perspective. *Sprachtypologie und Universalienforschung* 56 (1–2). 12–39.

Anikin, Je.A. (1990): *Tunguso-man'čžurskie zaimstvovanija v russkix govorax Sibiri*. Novosibirsk.

Anikin, A.E. (2000): *Ėtimologičeskij slovar' russkix dialektov Sibiri: zaimstvovanija iz ural'skix, altajskix i paleoaziatkix jazykov*. Novosibirsk: Nauka.

Anžiganova, O.P. (1992) Kojbal'skij govor xakasskogo jazyka. In: Anžiganova, O.P.; Patačkova, D.F. & Subrakova, O.V. (eds.) *Xakasskaja dialektologija*. Abakan. 51–64.

Apatóczky, Á.B. (2009): *Yiyu (Beilu yiyu). An indexed critical edition of a 16th century Sino-Mongolian glossary*. Kent.

Atkine, V. (1997): The Evenki Language from the Yenisei to Sakhalin. In: Shoji, H. & Janhunen, J. (eds): *Northern Minority Languages: Problems of Survival*. Osaka (Senri Ethnological Studies 44). 109–121.

Avrorin, V.A. (2000): *Grammatika man'čžurskogo pis'mennogo jazyka*. Sankt-Peterburg.

Baskakov, N.A. (1947): Očerk grammatiki ojrotskogo jazyka. In: Baskakov, N. A. & Toščakova, T.M. *Ojrotsko-russkij slovar'*. Moskva. 219–307.

Baskakov, N. A. & Toščakova, T.M. (1947): *Ojrotsko-russkij slovar'*. Moskva: Gosudarstvennoe izdatel'stvo inostrannyx i nacional'nyx slovarej.

Baskakov, N A. & Inkiževa-Grekul, A.I. (1953): *Xakassko-russkij slovar'*. Moskva.

Baskakov, N A. & Inkiževa-Grekul, A.I. (1953a): Xakasskij jazyk. Fonetičeskaja struktura, slovarnyj sostav i grammatičeskij stroj. In: Baskakov, N A. & Inkiževa-Grekul, A.I. *Xakassko-russkij slovar'*. Moskva: Gosudarstvennoe izdatel'stvo inostrannyx i nacional'nyx slovarej. 359–487.

Baskakov, N.A. (1966): *Dialekt černevyx tatar (tuba-kiži), Severnye dialekty altajskogo (ojrotskogo jazyka). Grammatičeskij očerk i slovar'*. Moskva: Nauka.

Baskakov, N.A. (1972): *Dialekty kumandincev (kumandy-kiži). Severnye dialekty altajskogo (ojrotskogo) jazyka. Grammatičeskij očerk, teksty, perevody i slovar'*. Moskva: Nauka.

Baskakov, N.A. (1975): *Dialekt lebedinskix tatar-čalkancev (kuu-kiži). Grammatičeskij očerk, teksty, perevody i slovar'*. Moskva: Nauka.

Baskakov, N.A. & Grekul, A.I. (1975a): Sintaksis slovosočetanij. In: Baskakov, N.A. (ed.) *Grammatika xakasskogo jazyka*. Moskva: Nauka. 278–286.

Bawden, Ch. (1997): *Mongolian-English Dictionary*. London & New-York.

Bektaev, K. (1999): *Bol'šoj kazaxsko-russkij slovar' i russko-kazaxskij slovar'*. Almaty.

Benzing, J. (1955): *Die tungusischen Sprachen. Versuch einer vergleichenden Grammatik*. Wiesbaden.

Birjukovič, R.M. (1984): *Leksika čulymsko-tjurskogo jazyka. Posobie k speckursu*. Saratov: Izdatel'stvo Saratovskogo Universiteta.

Boldyrev, B.V. (1987): *Slovoobrazovanie imen suščestvitel'nyx v tunguso-man'čžurskix jazykax v sravnitel'no-istoričeskom osveščenii*. Novosibirsk.

Boldyrev, B.V. (1994): *Russko-ėvenkijskij slovar'*. Novosibirsk.

Boldyrev, B.V. (2000): *Ėvenkijsko-russkij slovar'*. 1–2. Novosibirsk.

Borgojakov, V.A.; Sarbaševa, S.B. & Tazranova, A.R. (2012): *Altajskij jazyk v sisteme tjurkskix jazykov: učebnoe posobie*. Gorno-Altajsk.

Bouda, K. (1957): Die Sprache der Jenissejer. Genealogische und morphologische Untersuchungen. *Anthropos* 52. 65–134.

Bulatova, N.Ja. (2002): Ėvenkijskij jazyk. In: Neroznak, V.P. (ed.): *Jazyki narodov Rossii. Krasnaja kniga. Ėnciklopedičeskij slovar'-spravočnik*. Moskva. 267–272.

Burykin, A. & Parfenova, O. (2003): Evenkijskij jazyk. In: McConnell, G.D. & Mikhalchenko, V.Yu. (eds.) *Pis'mennye jazyki mira: Jazyki Rossijskoj Federacii. Sociolingvističeskaja enciklopedija*. 1–2. Moskva. 640–666.

Butanaev, V.Ja. (1973): Nekotorye osobennosti xakasskoj leksiki. *Učenye zapiski Xakasskogo naučno-issledovatel'skogo Instituta jazyka, literatury i istorii*. Vypusk 18. 145–148.

Butanaev, V.Ja. (1992): Xakassko-ketskie leksičeskie paralleli. *Journal de la Société Finno-Ougrienne* 84. 21–29.

Butanaev, V.Ja. (1999): *Xakassko-russkij istoriko-ėtnografičeskij slovar'*. Abakan.

Campbell, L. (2011): Review of *The Dene-Yeniseian Connection* ed. by James Kari and Ben A. Potter. *International Journal of American Linguistics* 77. 445–451.

Castrén, A. (1856): *Grundzüge einer tungusischen Sprachlehre nebst kurzem Wörterverzeichniss*. St.-Petersburg.

Castrén, M.A. (1858): *Versuch einer jenissei-ostjakischen und kottischen Sprachlehre*. St.-Petersburg.

Cincius, V.I. (1949): *Sravnitel'naja fonetika tunguso-man'čžurskix jazykov*. Leningrad.

Cincius, V.I. (ed.) (1975): *Sravnitel'nyj slovar' tunguso-man'čžurskix jazykov* 1–2. Leningrad.

Clauson, G. (1972): *An etymological dictionary of Pre-thirteenth-Century Turkish*. Oxford.

Coloo, J. (1988): *BNMAU dax' mongol xelnii nutgiin ayalguunii tol' bičig. Oird ayalguu*. Ulaanbaatar: Ulsyn xevleliin gazar.

Comrie, B. (2003): Yeniseic linguistics at the crossroads. *Sprachtypologie und Universalienforschung* 56 (1–2). 8–11.

Čeremisov, K.M. (1973): *Burjatsko-russkij slovar'*. Moskva.

Čispijakova, F.G. (1992): Istoričeskie plasty v leksike kondomskogo dialekta. In: Anžiganova, O.P.; Patačkova, D.F. & Subrakova, O.V. (eds.) *Xakasskaja dialektologija*. Abakan.

Damdinov, D.G. & Sundueva, Je.V. (2015): *Xamnigansko-russkij slovar'*. Irkutsk.

Darbeeva, A.A. (1996): *Istoriko-sopostovitel'nye issledovanija po grammatike mongol'skix jazykov. Fonetika*. Moskva.

Das, S.Ch. (2000^8): *A Tibetan-English dictionary*. Delhi.

Dmitriev, N.K. & Isxakov, F.G. (1954): *Voprosy izučenija xakasskogo jazyka i jego dialektov. Materialy dlja naučnoj grammatiki*. Abakan.

Doerfer, G. (1963–1975): *Türkische und mongolische Elemente im Neupersischen*. 1–4. Wiesbaden.

Doerfer, G. (1973): Zur Sprache der Hunnen. *Central Asiatic Journal* 17/1. 1–50.

Doerfer, G. (1976): Proto-Turkic: reconstruction problems. *Türk Dili Araştırmaları Yıllığı Belleten* 1975–1976. 1–59.

Doerfer, G. (1978): Classification Problems of Tungus. In: *Tungusica 1*. Wiesbaden. 1–26.

Doerfer, G. (1985): *Mongolo-Tungusica*. Wiesbaden.

Doerfer, G. (2004): *Etymologisch-Ethnologisches Wörterbuch tungusischer Dialecte (vornehmlich der Mandschurei)*. Hildesheim & Zürich & New-York.

Dolgikh, B.O. (1934): *Kety*. Moskva & Irkutsk.

Dolgikh, B.O. (1982): K istorii rodo-plemennogo sostava ketov. In: Alekseenko, Je.A.; Goxman, I.I.; Ivanov, V.V. & Toporov, V.N. (eds.) *Ketskij sbornik*. Leningrad. 84–132.

Donner, K. (1931): Russische Lehnwörter im Jenissei-Ostjakischen. In: *Mélanges de philologie offert à M.J.J. Mikkola*. Helsinki. 1–6.

Donner, K. (1933): *Ethnological notes about the Yenisey-Ostyak (in the Turukhansk Region)*. Helsinki.

Donner, K. (1955): *Ketica. Materialien aus dem Ketischen oder Jenissei-Ostjakischen*. Hrsg. von A.J. Joki. Helsinki. [Mémoires de la Société Finno-ougrienne 108]

Donner, K. (1958): *Ketica II. Supplement*. Hrsg. von A.J. Joki. Helsinki. [Mémoires de la Société Finno-ougrienne 102/2]

Dul'zon, A.P. (1959): Ketskie toponimy Zapadnoj Sibiri. *Učenye zapiski* 18. Tomskij Gosudarstvennyj pedagogičeskij Institut. Tomsk. 91–111.

Dul'zon, A.P. (1961): Slovarnye materialy 17 veka po ketskim narečijam. *Učenye zapiski* 19/2. Tomskij Gosudarstvennyj pedagogičeskij Institut. Tomsk. 152–189.

Dul'zon, A.P. (1962): Drevnie peredviženija ketov po dannym toponimiki. *Izvestija Vsesojuznogo Geografičeskogo obščestva* 6. 474–482.

Dul'zon, A.P. (1966): *Ketskie skazki*. Tomsk.

Dul'zon, A.P. (1968): *Ketskij jazyk*. Tomsk.

Dyrenkova, N.P. (1940): *Šorskij fol'klor*. Moskva—Leningrad.
Dyrenkova, N.P. (1948): *Grammatika xakasskogo jazyka. Fonetika i morfologija*. Abakan.
Engkebatu et al. (1984): *Daɣur kelen-ü üges*. Köke qota.
Erdal, M. (1991): *Old Turkic word formation. A functional approach to the lexicon*. Wiesbaden.
Erdal, M. (2004): *A grammar of Old Turkic*. Leiden & Boston: Brill.
Erdal, M.; Nevskaya, I.; Nugteren, H. & Rind-Pawlowski, M. (2013): *Handbuch des Tschakantürkischen. Teil 1: Texte und Glossar*. Wiesbaden: Harrassowitz.
ĖSTJa (1989): Levitskaja, L.S.; Dybo, A.V. & Rassadin, V.I. (eds.) *Ėtimologičeskij slovar' tjurkskix jazykov. Obščetjurkskie i meztjurkskie osnovy na bukvy «ǰ, ž, j»*. Moskva.
ĖSTJa (1997): Levitskaja, L.S.; Dybo, A.V. & Rassadin, V.I. (eds.) *Ėtimologičeskij slovar' tjurkskix jazykov. Obščetjurkskie i meztjurkskie osnovy na bukvy «k, q»*. Moskva.
ĖSTJa (2000): Levitskaja, L.S.; Dybo, A.V. & Rassadin, V.I. (eds.) *Ėtimologičeskij slovar' tjurkskix jazykov. Obščetjurkskie i meztjurkskie osnovy na bukvy «k»*. Vypusk 2. Moskva.
ĖSTJa (2003): Levitskaja, L.S.; Dybo, A.V. & Rassadin, V.I. (eds.) *Ėtimologičeskij slovar' tjurkskix jazykov. Obščetjurkskie i meztjurkskie osnovy na bukvy «l, m, n, p, s»*. Moskva.
Vasmer, M. (1986-1987): *Ėtimologičeskij slovar' russkogo jazyka*. 1-4. Moskva: Progress.
Fillipova, T.M. (1994): Leksičeskie zaimstvovanija iz tjurkskix v sel'kupskix dialektax. *Journal de la Société Finno-Ougrienne* 85. 41-70.
Futaky, I. (1975): *Tungusische Lehnwörter des Ostjakischen*. Wiesbaden. [Veröffentlichungen der Societas Uralo-Altaica 10]
Futaky, I. (1983): Zur Frage der nganasanisch-tungusischen Sprachkontakte. *Urálisztikai Tanulmányok* 1. Budapest. 155-162.
Futaky, I. (1988): Uralisch und Tungusisch. In: Sinor, D. (ed.) *The Uralic languages: description, history and foreign influences*. Leiden. 781-791. [Handbuch der Orientalistik 8/1]
Georg, S., Michalove, P.A., Ramer, A.M. & Sidwell, P.J. (1998): Telling general linguists about Altaic. *Journal of Linguistics* 35. Cambridge. 65-98.
Georg, S. (2000): Methodologische Bemerkungen zum Problem der äusseren genetischen Beziehungen der jenissejischen Sprachen. In: *XXII Dul'zonovskie čtenija. Sravnitel'no-istoričeskoe i tipologičeskoe izučenie jazykov i kul'tur* 2. Tomsk. 128-139.
Georg, S. (2007): *A descriptive grammar of Ket (Yenisei-Ostyak)*. Kent.
Georg, S. (2008): Yeniseic languages and the Siberian linguistic area. In: A. Lubotsky, A.; Schaeken, J. and Wiedenhof, J. (eds.): *Evidence and counter-evidence. Festschrift Frederik Kortlandt*. Vol. 2. Amsterdam—New York. 151-168.
Georg, S. (2018): Other isolated languages of Asia. In: Campbell, L. (ed.): *Language isolates*. London & New York: Routledge. 139-161.
Golden, P.B. (1992): *An introduction to the history of the Turkic peoples*. (Turcologica 9) Wiesbaden.

Haenisch, E. (1939): *Wörterbuch zu Manghol-un Niuca Tobca'an*. (*Yüan-ch'ao pi-shi*) *Geheime Geschichte der Mongolen*. Leipzig.

Haenisch, E. (1957) *Sinomongolische Glossare* 1. *Das Hua-I ih-yü*. Abhandlungen der Deutschen Akademie der Wissenschaften zu Berlin 1956: 5. Berlin.

Hauer, E. (1952): *Handwörterbuch der Mandschusprache*. 1–3. Wiesbaden.

Helimski, E. [= Xelimskij, E. A] (1982): Keto-Uralica. In: *Ketskij sbornik. Antropologija, etnografija, mifologija, lingvistika*. Leningrad. 238–251.

Helimski, E. [= Xelimskij, E. A] (1985): Samodijsko-tungusskie leksičeskie svjazi i ix etnoistoričeskie implikacii. In: *Uralo-altaistika. Arxeologija, etnografija, jazyk*. Novosibirsk. 206–213.

Helimski, E. [= Хелимский] E.A. (1986): Arhivnye materialy XVIII veka po jenisejskim jazykam. In: Skorik, P.Ja. (ed.) *Paleoaziatskie jazyki*. Leningrad. 179–213.

Helimski, E. (1991): On the interaction of Mator with Turkic, Mongolic, and Tungusic: A rejoinder. *Journal de la Société Finno-Ougrienne* 83. 257–267.

Helimski, E. (1997): *Die Matorische Sprache. Wörterverzeichnis. Grundzüge der Grammatik. Sprachgeschichte*. Szeged.

Helimski, E. (2003): Areal groupings (Sprachbünde) within and across the borders of the Uralic family: a survey. *Nyelvtudományi Közlemények* 100. 156–167.

Jaimova, N.A. (1990): *Tabuirovannaja leksika i évfemizmy v altajskom jazyke*. Gorno-Altajsk.

Janhunen, J. (1977a): Samoyed-Altaic contacts: present state of research. In: *Altaica: Proceedings of the 19th Annual Meeting of the Permanent International Altaistic Conference*. Helsinki. 123–129. [Mémoires de la Société Finno-Ougrienne 158]

Janhunen, J. (1977b): *Samojedischer Wortschatz: Gemeinsamojedische Etymologien*. Helsinki. [Castrenianumin Toimitteita 17]

Janhunen, J. (1980): On glottalization in Sayan Turkic. *Bulletin of the Institute for the Study of North Eurasian Cultures* 13. 23–41.

Janhunen, J. (1989): On the interaction of Mator with Turkic, Mongolic and Tungusic. *Journal de la Société Finno-Ougrienne* 82. 287–297.

Janhunen, J. (1990): *Material on Manchurian Khamnigan Mongol*. Helsinki.

Janhunen, J. (1991): *Material on Manchurian Khamnigan Evenki*. Helsinki.

Janhunen, J. (1996): *Manchuria. An ethnic history*. Helsinki.

Janhunen, J. (1997): The Languages of Manchuria in Today's China. In: Shoji, H. & Janhunen, J. (eds): *Northern Minority Languages: Problems of Survival*. Osaka (Senri Ethnological Studies 44). 123–146.

Janhunen, J. (ed.) (2003): *The Mongolic languages*. London & New-York.

Janhunen, J. (2003): Proto-Mongolic. In: Janhunen, J. (ed.) *The Mongolic languages*. London & New-York. 1–29.

Janhunen, J. (2005): Tungusic: an endangered language family in northeast Asia. *International Journal of the Sociology of Language* 173. 37–54.

Janhunen, J. (2012): The expansion of Tungusic as an ethnic and linguistic process. In: Malchukov, A.N. & Whaley, L.J. (eds.) *Recent advances in Tungusic linguistics*. Wiesbaden: Harrassowitz. 5–16.

Janhunen, J. (2013): The Tungusic languages: A history of contacts. In: *Current Trends in Altaic Linguistics*. A Festschrift for Professor Emeritus Seong Baeg-in on his 80th Birthday. Seoul: Altaic Society of Korea. 17–60.

Jäschke, H.A. (1958): *A Tibetan–English dictionary with special reference to the prevailing dialects to which is added and English-Tibetan vocabulary*. London.

Johanson, L. & Csató, É.Á. (eds.) (1998): *The Turkic languages*. London & New-York.

Johanson, L. (1998) The history of Turkic. In: Johanson, L. & Csató, É.Á. (eds.) *The Turkic languages*. London. 81–125.

Johanson, L. (1998b): The structure of Turkic. In: Johanson, L. & Csató, É.Á. (eds.) *The Turkic languages*. London & New-York. 30–66.

Johanson, L. (2001): *Discoveries on the Turkic linguistic map*. (Swedish Research Institute in Istanbul: Publications 5) Stockholm.

Johanson, L. (2006): Nouns and adjectives in South Siberian Turkic. In: Erdal, M. & Nevskaya, I. (eds.) *Exploring the Eastern frontiers of Turkic*. (Turcologica 60) Wiesbaden. 57–78.

Joki, A.J. (1952): *Die Lehnwörter des Sajansamojedischen*. Helsinki.

Joki, A. (1953): *Wörterverzeichnis der Kyzyl-Sprache*. Helsinki: Druckerei-A.G. der Finnischen Literaturgesellschaft.

Joki, A. (1977): Die Tungusen und ihre Kontakte mit anderen Völkern. *Studia Orientalia* 47. Commentationes in honorem Pentti Aalto. Helsinki. 109–118.

Judaxin, K.K. (1965): *Kirgizsko-russkij slovar'*. Moskva: Sovetskaja ènciklopedija.

Kałużyński, S. (1962): *Mongolische Elemente in der jakutischen Sprache*. Warszawa.

Kałużyński, S. (1982): Einige tungusische Lehnwörter im Jakutischen. *Acta Orientalia Academiae Scientiarum Hungaricae* 36/1–3. 261–269.

Kara, Gy. (1990): Zhiyuan Yiyu. Index alphabétique des mots mongols. *Acta Orientalia Academiae Scientiarum Hungaricae* 44. 279–344.

Kara, Gy. (1998): *Mongol-magyar szótár*. [Mongolian-Hungarian dictionary] Budapest.

Khabtagaeva, B. (2001): Colour names and their suffixes. A study on the history of Mongolian word-formation. *Acta Orientalia Academiae Scientiarum Hungaricae* 54. 85–65.

Khabtagaeva, B. (2009): *Mongolic elements in Tuvan*. Wiesbaden: Harrassowitz.

Khabtagaeva, B. (2010): Mongolic elements in Barguzin Evenki. *Acta Orientalia Academiae Scientiarum Hungaricae* 63 (1). 9–25.

Khabtagaeva, B. (2010/2011): An overview on the Barguzin Evenki dialect. *Ural-Altaische Jahrbücher* 24. 227–258.

Khabtagaeva, B. (2011): Yakut elements of Mongolic origin in Evenki. *Ural-Altaic Studies* 1/4. 93–109.

Khabtagaeva, B. (2015a): Some remarks on Turkic elements of Mongolic origin in Yeniseian. *Studia Etymologica Cracovensia* 20. 111–126.

Khabtagaeva, B. (2015b): Ob altajskih elementah v jenisejskih jazykah. In: Rykin, P. (ed.) *Issledovanija po mongol'skim jazykam*. [Acta Linguistica Petropolitana 11/3. Transactions of the Institute for Linguistic Studies, Russian Academy of Sciences]. St. Petersburg: Nauka. 519–540.

Khabtagaeva, B. (2015c): Metathesis in Yeniseian loanwords of Altaic origin. *Türk Dilleri Araştırmaları* 25.1. *Festschrift für Uwe Bläsing*. 91–107.

Khabtagaeva, B. (2015d): The Turkic compounds in Yeniseian. *Turkic languages* 19. 128–146.

Khabtagaeva, B. (2015e): On the Yeniseian Arin word *teminkur* 'ore'. In: Mańczak-Wohlfeld, E. & Podolak, B. (eds.) *Words and dictionaries. A Festschrift in honour of S. Stachowski*. Krakow. 149–156.

Khabtagaeva, B. (2017): Tungusic loanwords in Yeniseian. In: Szeverényi, S. & Khabtagaeva, B. (eds.) *Uralic and Siberian Lexicology and Lexicography. Proceedings of the 4th Mikola Conference 14–15, November 2014*. [Studia Uralo-Altaica 51]. Szeged: University of Szeged. 75–88.

Khabtagaeva, B. (2017a): *The Ewenki dialects of Buryatia and their relationship to Khamnigan Mongol*. Wiesbaden: Harrassowitz. [Tunguso-Sibirica 41]

Knüppel, M. (2005): Jakutische Elemente in tungusischen Sprachen 1: Jakutisches im Ost-Ewenki (nach S.M. Shirokogorov's Tungus Dictionary) In: Stachowski, F.S.; Siemieniec-Gołaś E.; Pomorska, M. (eds.) *Turks and Non-Turks: Studies on the history of linguistic and cultural contacts*. Kraków. 191–202.

Knüppel, M. (2007): Jakutische Elemente in tungusischen Sprachen 2: Jakutisches im Tumunchanskischen (nach S.M. Shirokogorov's Tungus Dictionary). In: Fenz, H. (ed.) *Strukturelle Zwänge Persönliche Freiheiten. Osmanen, Türken, Muslime: Reflexionen zu gesellschaftlichen Umbrüchen. Gedenkband zu Ehren Petra Klapperts*. Berlin. 235–247.

Knüppel, M. (2008): Jakutische Elemente in tungusischen Sprachen 3: Jakutisches im Negidal (nach S.M. Shirokogorov's Tungus Dictionary). *Central Asiatic Journal* 52/1. 55–63.

Knüppel, M. (2010): Jakutische Elemente in tungusischen Sprachen 4: Jakutisches im Birare (nach S.M. Shirokogorov's Tungus Dictionary). In: Kappler, M.; Kirchner, M.; Zieme, P. (eds.) *Trans-Turkic Studies: Festschrift in Honour of Marcel Erdal*. Istanbul. 463–471.

Kowalevskij, O.M. (1844; 1846; 1849): *Mongol'sko-russko-francuzskij slovar'*. 1–3. Kazan'.

Kőhalmi, K. (1959): Der Mongolisch-kamniganische Dialekt von Dadal Sum und die Frage der Mongolisierung der Tungusen in der Nordmongolei und Transbajkalien. *Acta Orientalia Academiae Scientiarum Hungaricae* 9. 163–204.

Kreinovič, Je.A. (1955): Giljacko-tunguso-man'čžurskie jazykovye paralleli. *Doklady i soobščenija Instituta jazykoznanija AN SSSR* 8. Moskva. 133–167.

Krejnovič, Je.A. (1968a): *Glagol ketskogo jazyka.* Leningrad.

Krejnovič, Je.A. (1968b): O grammatičeskom vyraženii imennyx klassov v glagole ketskogo jazyka. In: Ivanov, V.V.; Toporov, V.N. & Uspenskij, B.A. (eds.) *Ketskij sbornik. Lingvistika.* Moskva. 139–195.

Kurpeško-Tannagaševa, N.N. & Apon'kin, F.Ja. (1993) *Šorsko-russkij i russko-šorskij slovar'.* Kemerovo: Kemerovskoe knižnoe izdatel'stvo.

Laude-Cirtautas, I. (1961): *Der Gebrauch der Farbezeichnungen in den Türkdialekten.* Wiesbaden.

Lebedeva, Ye.P.; Konstantinova, O.A. & Monaxova, I.V. (1979): *Evenkijskij jazyk.* Leningrad: Prosveščenie.

Lessing, F.D. (1996): *Mongolian-English dictionary.* Bloomington.

Levin, M.G. & Potapov, L.P. (eds.) *The peoples of Siberia.* Chicago.

Lewicki, M. (1959): *La langue mongole des transciptions chinoises du 14-e siècle. Le Houa-yi yi-yu de 1389.* 2. *Vocabulaire-index.* Wroclaw.

Ligeti, L. (1935): Mongolos jövevényszavaink kérdése. *Nyelvtudományi Közlemények* 49. 190–271.

Ligeti, L. (1950): Mots de la civilization de Haute Asie en transcription chinoise. *Acta Orientalia Academiae Scientiarum Hungaricae* 1. 141–188.

Ligeti, L. (1960): Les anciens éléments mongols dans le mandchou. *Acta Orientalia Academiae Scientiarum Hungaricae* 10. 231–248.

Ligeti, L. (1962): Un vocabulaire mongol d'Istanboul. *Acta Orientalia Academiae Scientiarum Hungaricae* 14. 3–99.

Ligeti, L. (1963): *Preklasszikus emlékek* 1. *XIII–XIV század.* (Mongol nyelvemléktár I) Budapest.

Ligeti, L. (1964): *A mongolok titkos története.* (Mongol nyelvemléktár III) Budapest.

Ligeti, L. (1965a): *Preklasszikus emlékek* 2. *XIII–XVI század és a XVII század eleje.* (Mongol nyelvemléktár IV) Budapest.

Ligeti, L. (1965b): Le lexique mongol de Kirakos de Gandzak. *Acta Orientalia Academiae Scientiarum Hungaricae* 18. 241–297.

Ligeti, L. (1966): Un vocabulaire sino–ouigour des Ming. *Acta Orientalia Academiae Scientiarum Hungaricae* 19. 117–199; 257–316.

Ligeti, L. (1967): *Preklasszikus emlékek* 3. *Jüan- és Ming-kori szövegek klasszikus átírásban.* (Mongol nyelvemléktár V) Budapest.

Ligeti, L. (1971): *Histoire secrète des mongols.* (Monumenta Linguae Mongolicae Collecta I) Budapest.

Ligeti, L. (1973): *Monuments en écriture 'Phags-pa, Pieces de chancellerie en transcription chinoise.* (Indices Verborum Linguae Mongolicae Monumentis Traditorum III) Budapest.

Ligeti, L. (1986): *A magyar nyelv török kapcsolatai a hongfoglalás előtt és az Árpádkorban.* Budapest.

Malov, S.Je. (1957): *Jazyk želtyx ujgurov. Slovar' i grammatika*. Alma-Ata: Izdatel'stvo Akademii nauk Kazaxskoj SSR.

Mathews, R.H. (1931): *Chinese-English dictionary*. Shanghai. [Revised American edition: 1979]

Menges, K.H. (1955): The South-Siberian Turkic languages I. General characteristics of their phonology. *Central Asiatic Journal* 1. 107–143.

Menges, K.H. (1956): The South-Siberian Turkic languages II. Notes on the Samojed substratum. *Central Asiatic Journal* 2. 161–175.

Menges, K.H. (1958–1959): The South-Siberian Turkic languages III. Tuba (Sojoŋ und Karaġas): 1. Zur Charakteristik einer einzelnen sibirisch-türkischen Gruppe. *Central Asiatic Journal* 4. 90–129.

Menges, K.H. (1959–1960): The South-Siberian Turkic languages III. Tuba (Sojoŋ und Karaġas): 2. Zur Charakteristik einer einzelnen sibirisch-türkischen Gruppe. *Central Asiatic Journal* 5. 97–150.

Menges, K.H. (1959): Das Sojonische und Karagassische. In: Deny, J.; Grönbech, K. & Scheel, H. (eds.) *Philologicae Turcicae Fundamenta* 1. Wiesbaden. 598–640.

Menges, K.H. (1963): Die sibirischen Türksprachen. In: Spuler, B. (ed.) *Handbuch der Orientalistik* 5. *Turkologie*. Leiden-Cologne. 72–138.

Menges, K.H. (1968): *The Turkic languages and peoples. An introduction to Turkic studies*. Wiesbaden.

Mikola, T. (2004): *Studien zur Geschichte der samojedischen Sprachen*. Szeged.

Monier-Williams, M. (1997): *A Sanskrit–English dictionary*. Delhi. (reprint) Mostaert, A. (1977): *Le matériel mongol du Houa I I Iu de Houng-ou (1389)*. Bruxelles.

Nadeljaev, V.M.; Nasilov, D.M.; Tenišev, Ė. R. & Ščerbak, A.M. (eds.) (1969): *Drevnetjurkskij slovar'*. Leningrad.

Nedjalkov, I. (1997): *Evenki*. London & New York.

Nikolaev, R.V. (1985): *Fol'klor i voprosy ėtničeskoj istorii ketov*. Krasnojarsk.

Novgorodov, I.N. (1998): Tunguso-man'čžurskoe vlijanie na dialektnye zony jazyka saxa. In: Voronkin, M.S. (ed.) *Jakutskij jazyk. Dialektologija*. Novosibirsk. 57–68.

Nugteren, H. (2011): *Mongolic phonology and the Qinghai-Gansu languages*. Utrecht.

Nugteren, H. (2012): Diagnostic anomalies? Unusual reflexes of *d in South Siberian Turkic and Western Yugur. In: Erdal, M.; Nevskaya, I. & Menz, A. (eds.) *Areal, typological and historical aspects of South Siberian Turkic*. Wiesbaden. 75–89.

Nugteren, H.; Ragagnin, E. & Roos, M. (2015): On the wandering semantics of Turkic *köt. In: Ragagnin, E. & Wilkens, J. (eds.) *Kutadgu Nom Bitig. Festschrift für Jens Peter Laut zum 60. Geburtstag*. Wiesbaden: Harrassowitz. 337–349.

Ölmez, M. (2007): *Tuwinischer Wortschatz mit altürkischen und mongolischen Parallelen*. Wiesbaden.

Patačkova, D.D. (1992): O roli dialektov v formirovanii nacional'nyx osobennostej xakasskogo jazyka. In: Anžiganova, O.P.; Patačkova, D.F. & Subrakova, O.V. (eds.) *Xakasskaja dialektologija*. Abakan. 14–18.

Pekarskij, E.K. (1959²): *Slovar' jakutskogo jazyka*. 1–3. Moskva.

Pevnov, A.M. (1992): Nivxskij i tunguso-man'čžurskie jazyki: problemy kontaktov. In: B.O. *Pilsudskij—issledovatel' narodov Saxalina. Materialy meždunarodnoi naučnoi konferencii* 2. Južno-Saxalinsk. 25–29.

Pomorska, M. (2004): *Middle Chulym noun formation*. Kraków.

Pomorska, M. (2005): Arabic loanwords in Chulym. *Rocznik Orientalistyczny* 58/1. 141–147.

Pomorska, M. (2012): Notes on Persian loanwords in Chulym. *Mémoires de la Société Finno-Ougrienne* 264. Per Urales ad Orientem. Iter polyphonicum multilingue. Festskrift tillägnad Juha Janhunen på hans sextioårsdag den 12 februari 2012. 299–308.

Poppe, N. (1927): Das mongolische Sprachmaterial einer Leidener Handschrift. *Izvestija Akademii Nauk SSSR*. 1927/12–14: 1009–1040; 1927/15–17: 1251–1274; 1928: 55–79.

Poppe, N. (1930): *Dagurskoe narečie*. Leningrad.

Poppe, N. (1938): *Mongol'skij slovar' Mukaddimat al-Adab*. 1–2. Moskva & Leningrad.

Poppe, N. (1955): *Introduction to Mongolian comparative studies*. Helsinki.

Poppe, N. (1957): *The Mongolian monuments in ḥP'ags-pa script*. Second edition translated by Krueger, J.R. Wiesbaden.

Poppe, N. (1960): *Vergleichende Grammatik der altaischen Sprachen* 1. *Vergleichende Lautlehre*. Wiesbaden.

Poppe, N. (1964): *Grammar of Written Mongolian*. Wiesbaden.

Poppe, N. (1966): On some Ancient Mongolian Loanwords in Tungus. *Central Asiatic Journal* 11. 187–198.

Poppe, N. (1969): On some vowel correspondences in Mongolian loanwords in Turkic. *Central Asiatic Journal* 13.

Poppe, N. (1972): On some Mongolian loan words in Evenki. *Central Asiatic Journal* 16: 2. 95–103.

Porotova, T.I. (2004): Patterns of plural formation in Kott nouns and adjectives. In: Vajda, E.J. (ed.) *Languages and Prehistory of Central Siberia*. Amsterdam & Philadelphia. 129–134.

Pulleyblank, E.G. (1962): The consonantal system of Old Chinese. *Asia Major* 9. 58–144; 206–265.

Rachewiltz, I. de. (2004) *The SH of the Mongols*. Leiden & Boston.

Radloff, W. (1893–1911): *Versuch eines Wörterbuches der Türk-Dialecte*. 1–4. St. Petersburg.

Ragagnin, E. (2011): *Dukhan, a Turkic variety of Northern Mongolia: Description and analysis*. Wiesbaden: Harrassowitz.

Ramstedt, G.J. (1913): Zur Verbstammbildungslehre der mongolisch-türkischen Sprachen. *Journal de la Société Finno-Ougrienne* 28/3.

Ramstedt, G.J. (1935): *Kalmückisches Wörterbuch*. Helsinki.

Ramstedt, G.J. (1952): *Einführung in die altaische Sprachwissenschaft. Formenlehre*. (Mémoires de la Société Finno-Ougrienne 104/2) Helsinki.

Rassadin, V.I. (1971): *Fonetika i leksika tofalarskogo jazyka*. Ulan-Udė.
Rassadin, V.I. (1978): *Morfologija tofalarskogo jazyka v sravnitel'nom osveščenii*. Moskva.
Rassadin, V.I. (1980): *Mongolo-burjatskie zaimstvovanija v sibirskix tjurkskix jazykax*. Moskva.
Rassadin, V.I. (1982): *Očerki po istoričeskoj fonetike burjatskogo jazyka*. Moskva.
Rassadin, V.I. (1995): *Tofalarsko-russkij slovar'. Russko-tofalarskij slovar'*. Irkutsk: Vostočno-sibirskoe knižnoe izdatel'stvo.
Rassadin, V.I. (1996): *Prisajanskaja gruppa burjatskix govorov*. Ulan-Udė.
Rassadin, V.I. (1999): *Stanovlenie govora nižneudinskix burjat*. Ulan-Udė.
Rassadin, V.I. (2013): *Tjurkologičeskie issledovanija. Izbrannoe*. Elista.
Räsänen VEWT = Räsänen, M. (1969): *Versuch eines etymologischen Wörterbuchs der Türksprachen*. Helsinki.
Rjumina-Syrkaševa, L.T. & Kučigaševa, N.A. (1995): *Teleutsko-russkij slovar'*. Kemerovo: Kemerovskoe knižnoe izdatel'stvo.
Romanova, A.V. & Myreeva, A.N. (1962): *Očerki tokkinskogo i tommotskogo dialektov*. Moskva & Leningrad.
Romanova, A.V. & Myreeva, A.N. (1964): *Očerki učurskogo, majskogo i tottinskogo govorov*. Moskva & Leningrad.
Romanova, A.V. & Myreeva, A.N. (1968): *Dialektologičeskij slovar' ėvenkijskogo jazyka. Materialy govorov ėvenkov Jakutii*. Leningrad.
Romanova, A.V.; Myreeva, A.N. & Baraškova, P.P. (1975): *Vzaimovlijanie ėvenkijskogo i jakutskogo jazykov*. Leningrad.
Róna-Tas, A. (1970): Az altaji nyelvrokonság vizsgálatának alapjai. A nyelvrokonság elmélete és a csuvas-mongol nyelvviszony. *Dissertation*. 1–2. Budapest.
Róna-Tas, A. (1991): *An introduction to Turkology*. (Studia uralo-altaica 33) Szeged.
Róna-Tas, A. (1998): The reconstruction of Proto-Turkic and the genetic question. In: Johanson, L. & Csató, É.Á. *The Turkic languages*. London & New-York. 67–80.
Róna-Tas, A. & Berta, Á. (2011): *West Old Turkic. Turkic loanwords in Hungarian*. 1–2. Wiesbaden.
Roos, M. (2000): *The Western Yugur (Yellow Uygur) language. Grammar, texts, vocabulary*. Leiden. [PhD thesis]
Rozycki, W. (1994): *Mongol elements in Manchu*. Bloomington: Indiana University.
Rybatzki, V. (1999): Turkic words for 'steel' and 'cast iron'. *Turkic Languages* 3. 56–86.
Rybatzki, V. (2002): Die Tungusische Metallterminologie. *Studia Etymologica Cracoviensia* 7. 89–126.
Rybatzki, V. (2006): *Die Personennamen und Titel der mittelmongolischen Dokumente. Eine lexikalische Untersuchung*. Helsinki.
Schönig, C. (1997–1998): A new attempt to classify the Turkic languages. *Turkic Languages* 1. 117–133; 262–277; 2: 130–151.
Schönig, C. (1998): South Siberian Turkic languages. In: Johanson, L. & Csató, É.Á. (eds.) *The Turkic languages*. London & New-York. 403–416.

Schönig, C. (2000): *Mongolische Lehnwörter im Westoghusischen*. Wiesbaden.

Schönig, C. (2003): Turko-Mongolic relations. In: Janhunen, J. (ed.) *The Mongolic languages*. London & New-York. 403–419.

Serebrennikov, B.A. & Gadžieva, N.Z. (eds.) *Sravnitel'no-istoričeskaja grammatika tjurkskix jazykov*. Moskva.

Sevortjan, Ė. V. (1974): *Ėtimologičeskij slovar' tjurkskix jazykov. Obščetjurkskie i meztjurkskie osnovy na glasnye*. Tom 1. Moskva.

Sevortjan, Ė. V. (1978): *Ėtimologičeskij slovar' tjurkskix jazykov. Obščetjurkskie i meztjurkskie osnovy na b*. Tom 2. Moskva.

Sevortjan, Ė. V. (1980): *Ėtimologičeskij slovar' tjurkskix jazykov: Obščetjurkskie i meztjurkskie osnovy na v, g, d*. Tom 3. Moskva.

Slepcov, P.A. (1972): *Jakutsko-russkij slovar'*. Moskva.

Stachowski, M. (1992): Persische Etymologien in der Geschichte der jakutischen Wortforschung. *Zeitschrift der Deutschen Morgenländischen Gesellschaft* 142/1. 105–119.

Stachowski, M. (1992/1993): Beiträge zur Kenntnis der arabischen und persischen Lehnwörter in den südsibirischen Türksprachen. *Folia Orientalia* 29. 247–259.

Stachowski, M. (1993): *Dolganischer Wortschatz*. Kraków.

Stachowski, M. (1993a): *Geschichte des Jakutischen Vocalismus*. Kraków.

Stachowski, M. (1995): Etymological studies on Khakas food names. *Folia Orientalia* 31. 147–161.

Stachowski, M. (1996): Über einige altaische Lehnwörter in den Jenissej-Sprachen. *Studia Etymologica Cracoviensia* 1. 91–115.

Stachowski, M. (1997): Altaistische Anmerkungen zum "Vergleichenden Wörterbuch der Jenissej-Sprachen". *Studia Etymologica Cracoviensia* 2. 227–239.

Stachowski, M. & Menz, A. (1998): Yakut. In: Johanson, L. & Csató, É.Á. (eds.) *The Turkic languages*. London & New-York. 417–433.

Stachowski, M. (2004): The origin of the European word for sabre. *Studia Etymologica Cracoviensia* 9. 133–141.

Stachowski, M. (2005): Chronology of some Yakut phonetic changes in the context of 18th century Mongolian loanwords into Yakut. *Rocznik Orientalistyczny* 58/1. 194–203.

Stachowski, M. (2006a): Arabische Lehnwörter in den Jenissej-Sprachen des 18. Jahrhunderts und die Frage der Sprachbünde in Sibirien. *Studia Linguistica Universitatis Iagellonicae Cracoviensis* 123. 155–158.

Stachowski, M. (2006b): Persian Loan Words in 18th Century Yeniseic and the Problem of Linguistic Areas in Siberia. In: Krasnowolska, A.; Maciuszak, K. & Mękarska, B. (eds.) *In the Orient where the gracious light ... Satura Orientalis in honorem Andrzej Pisowicz*. Krakow. 179–184.

Starostin, S.A. (1982): Prajenisejskaja rekonstrukcija i vnešnie svjazi jenisejskix jazykov. In: *Ketskij sbornik. Studia Ketica*. Leningrad. 144–237.

REFERENCES

Starostin, S.A. (1984): Gipoteza o genetičeskix svjazjax sinotibetskix jazykov s jenisejskimi i severnokavkazskimi jazykami. *Lingvističeskaja rekonstrukcija i drevnejšaja istorija Vostoka* 4. Moskva. 19–38.

Starostin, S., Dybo, A. & Mudrak, O. with assistence of Gruntov, I. & Glumov, V. (2004): *Etymological dictionary of the Altaic languages*. Leiden & Boston.

Starostin, S.A. & Ruhlen, M. (online): *Proto-Yeniseian reconstructions, with extra-Yeniseian Comparisons* (available: http://www.merrittruhlen.com/publications.html)

Steingass, F. (1930): *A comprehensive Persian-English dictionary*. London.

Sunik, O.P. (1962): *Glagol v tunguso-man'čžurskix jazykax. Morfologičeskaja struktura i sistema form glagol'nogo slova*. Moskva & Leningrad.

Ščerbak, A.M. (1961): Nazvanija domašnix i dikix životnyx v tjurkskix jazykax. In: Ubrjatova, E.I. (ed.) *Istoričeskoe razvitie leksiki tjurkskix jazykov*. Moskva. 82–172.

Ščerbak, A.M. (1966): O xaraktere leksičeskix vzaimosvjazej tjurkskix, mongol'skix i tunguso-man'čžurskix jazykov. *Voprosy jazykoznanija* 3. 21–35.

Ščerbak, A.M. (1968): O tjurko-mongolo-tungusskix svjazjax v morfologii. *Narody Azii i Afriki* 1. 104–116.

Ščerbak, A.M. (1970): *Sravnitel'naja fonetika tjurkskix jazykov*. Leningrad.

Ščerbak, A.M. (1996): Irregular sound correspondences in Turkic languages conditioned by reborrowing from Mongolian. In: Berta, Á.; Brendemoen, B. & Schönig, C. (eds.) *Symbolae Turcologicae. Studies in Honour of Lars Johanson on his Sixtieth Birthday 8 March 1996*. Stockholm. 199–203.

Ščerbak, A. M. (1997): *Rannie tjursko-mongol'skie jazykovye svjazi (VII–XIV v.v.)*. Sankt-Peterburg.

Tatarincev, B.I. (2000): *Ėtimologičeskij slovar' tuvinskogo jazyka*. 1 tom: a, b. Novosibirsk.

Tatarincev, B.I. (2002): *Ėtimologičeskij slovar' tuvinskogo jazyka*. 2 tom: d, jo, i, j. Novosibirsk.

Tatarincev, B.I. (2004): *Ėtimologičeskij slovar' tuvinskogo jazyka*. 3 tom: k, l. Novosibirsk.

Tatarincev, B.I. (2004): *Ėtimologičeskij slovar' tuvinskogo jazyka*. 4 tom: m, n, o, ö, p. Novosibirsk.

Tenišev, Ė. R. (ed.) (1968): *Tuvinsko-russkij slovar'*. Moskva: Sovetskaja ėnciklopedija.

Tenišev, Ė. R. (ed.) (1984): *Sravnitel'no-istoričeskaja grammatika tjurkskix jazykov. Fonetika*. Moskva.

Tenišev, Ė. R. (ed.) (1988): *Sravnitel'no-istoričeskaja grammatika tjurkskix jazykov. Morfologija*. Moskva.

Tenišev, Ė. R. (ed.) (2001): *Sravnitel'no-istoričeskaja grammatika tjurkskix jazykov. Leksika*. Moskva: Nauka.

Tenišev, Ė. R. (ed.) (2002): *Sravnitel'no-istoričeskaja grammatika tjurkskix jazykov. Regional'nye rekonstrukcii*. Moskva: Nauka.

Timonina, L.G. (1978): Tjurkskie zaimstvovanija v kottskom jazyke. *Sovetskaja tjurkologija* 3. 7–13.

Timonina, L.G. (1979): Kottsko-tjurkskie slovarnye sopostovlenija Karla Bouda. *Sovetskaja tjurkologija* 5. 20–25.

Timonina, L.G. (1982a): K ėtimologii komponenta *il-/al-* v sostave nekotoryx jenisejskix slov. In: Ubrjatova, Je.I. (ed.) *Grammatičeskie issledovanija po jazykam Sibiri*. Novosibirsk.

Timonina, L.G. (1982b): O nekotoryx drevnix jenisejsko-tjurkskix paralleljax v slovoobrazovanii. *Sovetskaja tjurkologija* 1 (janvar'-fevral'). 91–96.

Timonina, L.G. (1985): *Tjurkskie zaimstvovanija v jenisejskix jazykax v sravnitel'no-istoričeskom osveščenii*. PhD thesis. Leningrad.

Timonina, L.G. (1985a): Jenisejskie nazvanija častej tela tjurkskogo proisxoždenija. In: *Struktura samodijskix i jenisejskix jazykov*. Tomsk. 134–142.

Timonina, L.G. (1985b): Nazvanija domašnix životnyx v kottskom jazyke. In: *Voprosy jenisejskogo i samodijskogo jazykoznanija*. Tomsk: Tomskij Gosudarstvennyj Pedagogičeskij Institut. 144–150.

Timonina, L.G. (1986): Jenisejskaja kul'turnaja leksika tjurkskogo proisxoždenija. In: Vall, M.N. (ed.) *Issledovanija po grammatike i leksike jenisejskix jazykov*. Novosibirsk. 69–79.

Timonina, L.G. (2004): On distinguishing loanwords from the original Proto-Yeniseic lexicon. In: Vajda, E.J. (ed.) *Languages and Prehistory of Central Siberia*. Amsterdam & Philadelphia. 135–142.

Todaeva, B.H. (1986) *Dagurskij jazyk*. Moskva.

Toporov, V.N. (1964): O nekotoryx ketsko-sel'kupskix tipologičeskix paralleljax. In: *Voprosy struktury jazyka*. Moskva. 117–129.

Toporov, V.N. (1968): Materialy k sravnitel'no-istoričeskoj fonetike jenisejskix jazykov. 1. Arinsko-jenisejskie sootvetstvija. In: Ivanov, V.V.; Toporov, V.N. & Uspenskij, B.A. (eds.) *Ketskij sbornik. Lingvistika*. Moskva. 277–330.

TSSDAJa = D'ajym, N.A.; Tybykova, A.T.; Tybykova, L.N.; Tydykova, N.N. (2004): *Tematičeskij slovar' severnyx dialektov altajskogo jazyka*. Gorno-Altajsk.

Tumaševa, D.G. (1992): *Slovar' dialektov sibirskix tatar*. Kazan': Izdatel'stvo Kazanskogo universiteta.

Tumurtogoo, D. (2006): *Mongolian monuments in Uighur-Mongolian script (XIII–XVI centuries). Introduction, transcription and bibliography*. Taipei.

Tumurtogoo, D. (2010): *Mongolian monuments in 'Phags-pa script. Introduction, transliteration, transcription and bibliography*. Taipei.

Ubrjatova, Je.I.; Korkina Je.I.; Xaritonov, L.N. & Petrov, N.Je. (1982): *Grammatika sovremennogo jakutskogo literaturnogo jazyka. Fonetika i morfologija*. Moskva.

Vajda, E.J. (2000): *Ket Prosodic Phonology*. Munich.

Vajda, E.J. (2001): Yeniseian *peoples and languages. A history of Yeniseian studies with annotated bibliography and a source guide*. Richmond.

Vajda, E.J. (2003): Ket verb structure in typological perspective. *Sprachtypologie und Universalienforschung* 56 (1–2). 55–92.

Vajda, E.J. (2004): *Ket*. Munich. [Languages of the World/Materials 204]
Vajda, E.J. & Zinn, M. (2004): *Morphological dictionary of the Ket verb*. Tomsk.
Vajda, E.J. (2009): Loanwords in Ket, a Yeniseian language of Siberia. In: Haspelmath, M. & Tadmor, U. (eds.) *Loanwords in the World's languages: a comparative handbook*. Berlin. 471–494.
Vajda, E.J. (2010): Siberian Link with Na-Dene Languages. In: Kari, J. & Potter, B. (eds.) *The Dene-Yeniseian Connection. Anthropological Papers of the University of Alaska* 5. Fairbanks: University of Alaska Fairbanks, Department of Anthropology. 33–99.
Vajda, E.J. (2010a). Ket shamanism. *Shaman* 18/1–2. 131–150.
Vajda, E.J. (2013): Metathesis and reanalysis in Ket. *Tomsk Journal of Linguistics and Anthropology* 1/1. 14–26.
Vajda, E.J. (2015): Yeniseian. In: Stekauer, P. & Lieber, R. (eds.) *Handbook of Derivation*. Oxford: Oxford University Press. 509–519.
Vajda, E.J. (2017): Patterns of innovation and retention in templatic polysynthesis. In: *Handbook of Polysynthesis*, Michael Fortescue, Marianne Mithun, and Nicholas Evans (eds.). Oxford: Oxford University Press. 363–391.
Vajda, E.J. & Werner, H. (in preparation): *Etymological Dictionary of the Yeniseian Languages*.
Vall, M.N. & Kanakin, I.A. (1990): *Očerk fonologii i grammatiki ketskogo jazyka*. Novosibirsk.
Vasilevič, G.M. (1948): *Očerki dialektov ėvenkijskogo (tunguskogo jazyka)*. Leningrad.
Vasilevich, G.M. & Smolyak, A.V. (1955): The Evenks. In: Levin, M.G. & Potapov, L.P. (eds.) *The peoples of Siberia*. Chicago. 620–654.
Vasilevič, G.M. (1958): *Ėvenkijsko-russkij slovar'*. Moskva.
Vasilevič, G.M. (1969): *Ėvenki. Istoriko-ėtnografičeskie očerki (XVIII—načalo XX v.)*. Leningrad.
Vásáry, I. (1971): Käm, an early Samoyed name of Yenisey. In: Ligeti, L. (ed.) *Studia Turcica*. Budapest. 469–482.
Vovin, A. (1993): Towards a New Classification of Tungusic Languages. *Ural-Altaische Jahrbücher* 65. 99–113.
Vovin, A. (2000): Did the Xion-nu speak a Yeniseian language? *Central Asiatic Journal* 44/1. 87–104.
Vovin, A. (2003): Did the Xiong-nu speak a Yeniseian language? Part 2: Vocabulary. In: Sárközi, A. & Rákos, A. (eds.) *Altaica Budapestinensia 2002. Proceedings of the 45th Permanent International Altaistic Conference. Budapest, Hungary, June 23–28, 2002*. Budapest. 389–394.
Vovin, A. (2005): The end of the Altaic controversy. A review article of S. Starostin, A. Dybo & O. Mudrak's Etymological dictionary of the Altaic languages. *Central Asiatic Journal* 49. 71–132.
Vovin, A. (2017): Some Tofalar etymologies. In: Németh, M.; Podolak, B. & Urban, M.

(eds.) *Essays in the History of Languages and Linguistics. Dedicated to Marek Stachowski*. Kraków. 793–801.

Wehr, H. (1994⁴): *Arabic-English dictionary. Dictionary of Modern Written Arabic*. Urbana: Spoken Language Services Inc.

Werner, H. [= Verner, G.K.] (1972): Problema proisxoždenija faringalizacii v tuvinskom i tofalarskom jazykax. *Sovetskaja tjurkologija* 5. 17–24.

Werner, H. [= Verner, G.K.] & Verner, I.G. (1976): Ob affiksal'noj derivacii u jenisejskix suščestvitel'nyx. In: *Jazyki i toponimija* 3. Taganrog. 20–24.

Werner, H. [= Verner, G.K.] (1990): *Kottskij jazyk*. Rostov-na-Donu: Izdatel'stvo Rostovskogo universiteta.

Werner, H. [= Verner, G.K.] (1990b): *Sravnitel'naja fonetika jenisejskix jazykov*. Taganrog.

Werner, H. (1995): *Zur Typologie der Jenissej-Sprashen*. Wiesbaden.

Werner, H. (1997): *Die ketische Sprache*. Wiesbaden.

Werner, H. [= Verner, G.K.] (1997a): Jenisejskie jazyki. In: Volodin, A.P. (ed.) *Jazyki mira. Paleoaziatskie jazyki*. Moskva. 169–177.

Werner, H. [= Verner, G.K.] (1997b): Ketskij jazyk. In: Volodin, A.P. (ed.) *Jazyki mira. Paleoaziatskie jazyki*. Moskva. 177–187.

Werner, H. [= Verner, G.K.] (1997c): Jugskij jazyk. In: Volodin, A.P. (ed.) *Jazyki mira. Paleoaziatskie jazyki*. Moskva. 187–195.

Werner, H. [= Verner, G.K.] (1997d): Kottskij jazyk. In: Volodin, A.P. (ed.) *Jazyki mira. Paleoaziatskie jazyki*. Moskva. 195–203.

Werner, H. (1997e): *Abriss der kottischen Grammatik*. Wiesbaden. [Tunguso-Sibirica 4]

Werner, H. (1997f): *Das Jugische (Sym-Ketische)*. Wiesbaden. [Veröffentlichungen der Societas Uralo-Altaica 50]

Werner, H. (2002): *Vergleichendes Wörterbuch der Jenissej-Sprachen*. 1–3. Wiesbaden.

Werner, H. [= Verner, G.K.] (2002a): *Slovar' ketsko-russkij i russko-ketskij*. Sankt-Peterburg.

Werner, H. (2005): *Die Jenissej-Sprachen des 18. Jahrhunderts*. Wiesbaden.

Zhen-hua, Hu & Imart, Guy (1987): *Fu-yü Gürgïs: A tentative description of the easternmost Turkic language*. Bloomington: Indiana University.

Zikmundova, V. (2013): *Spoken Sibe. Morphology of the inflected parts of speech*. Prague.

Index of the Yeniseian Words

Kott

abičijak 359
agaŋa 48
agel 105, 215, 220, 248
aibič 89, 207, 208, 217, 329, 353
aipiš 89, 207, 208, 217, 329, 353
ajaŋ 149, 208, 216, 219
ajel 105, 219, 315
akāŋa 48
aksax 173, 213, 249
aktur 203, 208, 327, 329, 336
ala 155, 220, 246
alpaka 49, 215, 251, 315
alpan 142, 250
alpeš 101, 209, 218, 250, 356
alpot 95, 211, 247, 250
alpuga 49, 251, 315
alpuka 49, 215, 251, 315
altɨn 32, 207, 216, 249
altun 32, 207, 216, 249
anar 79, 219, 347
arai 190, 220, 314
arak 173, 209, 353
araka 108, 209, 212
arba 39, 207, 250
arɨš 40, 208, 219, 220
arix 165, 207, 215
arkā 108, 332
asa 102, 215
askar 67, 214, 221
askɨr 67, 208, 214, 221
atax 114, 208, 211, 215
ataŋ 119, 208, 209, 211, 213
atkur 203
atuš 68, 347
árɨš 40, 208, 219, 220
áša 102, 215
âgel 105, 215, 220, 248
ânar 79, 219, 347
âpeš 96, 209, 214, 218
âpuš 214
âreš 40, 219, 220
âsa 102, 215
ašâm 163
ašâme 163

bača 92
baha 98, 207, 208, 212, 327
baker 32, 207, 209, 212, 213, 221
baktîr 196, 217, 249, 312
bal 69, 217
baltu 120, 213, 249
balt^{h}u 120, 213, 249
báltō 120, 209, 213, 249
berxen 99, 207, 217, 251
bêlen 166, 207
bik 167, 207, 212, 213
bɨšól 71, 218, 333
bɨšóu 71, 218, 248
boga 70, 209, 213
bolat 33, 207, 208, 211, 220
bolát 33, 207, 208, 211, 220
boru 50, 210, 213, 220, 327
bosarak 156, 218, 330
bôru 50, 210, 213, 220, 327
bušôu 71, 218, 248
butai 41, 214, 248

čik 361
čîk 361
čogár 122
čôgor 157, 209, 213, 217, 246
čukar 122
čukár 122
čûčuk 77, 217

d'era 51
d'ibak 123, 207, 208, 210, 212, 219
d'ida 152, 208, 214
d'ili 144, 342
d'ipak 123, 207, 208, 210, 212, 219
d'ira 51
d'ônaš 90, 318
d'ôrgan 123, 216, 219, 246, 250
d'ôt 362

elor 176, 207, 248
erol 176, 207, 220, 248
eser 177, 207, 218, 340
esirolog 177, 207, 218

êper 167, 207, 209, 219, 342
êti 168, 209, 211, 219

ɛkačačik 34, 344, 358
ɛšjalikitan 41, 328, 342

farpax 45
fôk 80, 214
fôx 80, 214

gobimojb[e]ga 169, 213

hagin'e 116, 214
hagîn'e 116, 214
hagîni 116, 214
hagše 169, 209, 219, 250
hagši 169, 219, 250
hanpen 103, 207, 212, 252, 336, 338
harâ 178, 212, 354
hâra 205, 212, 342, 354
häteäŋ 191
häteäŋôk 191
hîta 42, 209, 212, 214, 216, 351
holanka 53, 212, 220
hônaŋ 363
hôpetal 124, 207, 212, 220, 330
hôptal 124, 207, 212, 220, 250

in 125, 329
iptak 110, 207, 212, 336
ite 367
iti 367
itpak 110, 207, 212
itpák 110, 207, 212
în 125, 329
îre 126, 218, 247, 330
îri 126, 218, 247, 330
īta 179, 215, 219, 246

kabúrgenaŋ 44, 219, 249, 337
kačei 197, 209, 217
kajag 110, 213, 216
kajax 110, 213, 216
kalači 55, 347, 358
kalakai 179, 215, 317, 327, 341
kalakei 179, 215, 317, 327, 341
kaleš 153, 209, 217
kališ 153, 209, 217
kalkul 180, 210, 251, 354

kalôx 82, 207, 210, 213, 220
kalšu 24, 208, 212, 252
kaltapen 282, 309, 350
kaltar 158, 249, 316
kaltum 56, 333, 339, 357
kamagalá 42, 215, 219, 351
kamči 127, 209, 250
kamču 127, 209, 250
kan 90, 216, 247
kankoj 82
kanšá 127, 252, 313
kant^{h}êg 128, 313, 329
kant^{h}êx 128, 215, 313, 329
kapax 84, 210, 213
kapsagai 181, 215, 251, 313
kaptu 129, 249
karaul 144, 354
karâga 57, 330
karei 144, 248, 354
kareš 140, 209, 219
kariš 140, 209, 219
karuj 144, 248, 354
kasak 146, 214, 215
kasax 146, 214, 215
kat 150, 211
káptu 129, 249
kem 26, 217
kep 130, 212, 329
kereunčak 147, 358
keršo 182, 207, 210, 248, 251, 311
koaskir 71, 221, 252
koaš 170, 218
koâš 170, 218
kobur 117, 210, 221
koi 73, 208, 216
kolá 35, 207, 208, 220, 313
kolča 184, 247, 252, 327
kolun 73, 212, 216
komtú 104, 251, 317
konkoj 82
konkorôš 130, 216
kononak 137, 212, 215
kopur 117, 210, 221
korkotni 35, 208, 251
korkôtn 35, 208, 251
korogotn 35, 208, 251
koskun 131, 209, 214, 351
koŋar 159, 209, 216
koŋoroš 130, 216

INDEX OF THE YENISEIAN WORDS 391

kônak   137, 212, 215, 247, 249
kôpur   117, 210, 221
kubúrgenaŋ   44, 208, 219, 249, 337
kukanak   137, 212, 215
kulun   73, 212, 216
kulún   73, 212, 216
kulʲuk   184
kuľuk   210, 220, 352
kumɨš   38, 210, 211, 217, 219, 327
kumuš   38, 211, 217, 219, 327
kuštap parak   198, 213, 333
kuštu   185, 210, 211, 217, 246, 339
kûra   132, 209, 212, 330, 352

mangara   60, 216, 357
mankara   60, 216, 357
mentara   61
min   195, 208, 214, 216
munkan   186, 216, 252, 352
munxan   186, 216, 252, 352

najči   91, 209, 314

obal   104, 208, 214, 220
ogus   74, 208, 210, 212, 218, 327
ô   44, 246, 356
ôpal   104, 208, 214, 220
ôr   75, 221, 247

pačasulema   153, 347
pai   187, 213, 220, 246
pât   62
pêj   361
pʰarpak   45
pʰôk   80, 213, 246

qep   130, 212, 329

saran   323
sâškan   63, 218, 247, 252
sera   112, 209, 218
sihirá   112, 218
šaban   148, 213, 218
šam   163
šar   160, 218, 329
šašin   150, 208, 217, 218, 311
šaška   63, 218, 247, 252
šâr   160, 218, 329
šâškana   63, 218, 247, 252, 330

šera   112, 209, 218
šɨčir   148, 217
širá   112, 209, 218
šoška   77, 217, 252
šugur   188, 208, 215, 218, 352
šurgan   27, 207, 216, 219, 248, 249, 355
šut   112, 210, 211, 218, 246

tabat   64, 207, 219, 327, 334
tagaj   84, 215, 220
takai   84, 215, 220
talkan   113, 211, 216, 249
tarei   138, 328, 355
tarêi   138, 328, 355
taripan   149, 208, 348
tarup   139, 336, 347, 352
tarûp   139, 336, 347, 352
tálgan   113, 211, 216, 250
tátien   29, 347, 358
tâmukol   133, 211, 330, 347
tegteka   65, 210, 250, 330, 351
tʰantu   28, 207, 211, 339
tʰategâtna   192, 211, 352
tipar   29, 207, 210, 217, 340
tîpar   29, 207, 210, 217, 340
toi   151, 208, 246
tokmaxon   66
tor   161, 211
torá   117, 209, 211, 220
toteš   47, 209, 218, 346
tôteäš   47, 209, 218, 346
tui   151, 208, 246
tura   211, 220
turá   117, 209, 211, 220
turkatu   189, 211, 251, 318, 327, 339

una ôjaŋ   193, 208, 210, 216, 217
uŋo   194
uŋôjaŋ   194, 347
ureäk   162, 347
urkan   134
uruk   31, 208, 209, 212, 220, 355
urum   139, 208, 217, 327, 356
ušou   31, 210, 219, 356
ušôx   31, 210, 212, 219, 356

xalpen   364
xep   130, 212, 329

xêp 130, 212, 329
xoxutajut 199, 209, 213, 352

Assan

araka 108, 221–223, 226
ariš 40, 221, 222, 225, 226
arpá 39, 221, 253
asa 102, 224
askɨr 67, 221, 222, 224, 226
askir 67, 221, 222, 224, 226
atîš 68
atůš 68

balat 33, 221–223, 225
balō 120, 222, 253
bej 361
bišol 71, 223, 225, 333
boka 70, 221–223
boru 50, 222, 223, 226, 327
borü 50, 222, 223, 226, 327
bútaj 41, 221, 223, 225, 248

čegar 122
čogár 122

esrolagín 177, 221, 332
esrolokon 177, 221, 332, 336, 338

haj 362

itpák 110, 221, 223

kabɨrgina 44, 221–223, 225, 253, 330
kaburgina 44, 221–223, 225, 253, 330
kai 73, 222, 224
karaul 144, 225, 354
karei 144, 248, 354

karuj 144, 248, 354
kep 130, 223, 329
koi 73, 224
korgoden 35, 222–224, 253
kulún 73, 222–225
kumís 38, 222–225, 327
kumus 38, 222–225, 327
kura 132, 222, 223, 226, 330, 352
kümüs 38, 222–225

mangára 60, 224, 357
mankara 60, 224, 357

pej 361

sir'á 112, 222, 225, 226
šar 76, 221, 225, 226
šarijag 111, 222, 224–226, 344
šut 112, 222–224
šüt 112, 222–224

tabát 64, 221, 225, 327, 334
tagáj 84, 221, 223–225
takaj 84, 221, 223–225
talkán 113, 223, 224, 253
tapat 64, 221, 225, 327, 334
toteš 47, 222, 223, 225, 346
tógaj 84, 221, 223–225
tútaj 41, 223, 225, 248

ug 67, 222, 329

xajp 130, 223, 328, 329

Arin

ajna 100, 231, 232
altin 32, 231, 254
altinok 32, 336
arba 39, 226, 254
argiš 89, 226, 232, 254, 353
askɨr 67, 226, 227, 230, 233

ba[g]akulak 20, 348
bagakulak 229, 230, 233
bajšu 144, 226, 230, 338
balgaš bore 21, 226, 233
balto 120, 226, 228, 249, 254
baltó 120, 226, 228, 249, 254

INDEX OF THE YENISEIAN WORDS

barčol 233, 254
barčol badija 135
belkertura 106, 345
berek 174, 345
berke 174, 175, 253, 345
berketura 106, 345
berkitak 22, 228, 230, 346
berkuštukdu 175, 255, 332, 338, 346
berkutu 174, 339
bi-b'ača 92
bičisagnɨbašu 200
bɨkašeb 360
birka 174, 227, 253, 345
bugá 70, 226, 228–230
bugdaj 41, 230, 232, 254
buturčinok 50, 228, 230, 254, 336

čarba 109, 233, 255

dalaj 23, 230, 233
dolaj 23, 226, 230, 233
džipká 52

in 125, 329
itin 367
itpák 110, 227
itp'ák 110, 227
itpek 110, 227

kaják 110, 226, 229, 231
kajakok 110, 336
kaptɨ 129, 253
kar 25, 227, 229, 233
karananuk 43, 227, 230, 231, 344
karasek 58, 229, 247, 348
kemenenčak 141, 231, 345, 355, 358
kɨlph'an 364
kis 93, 227, 229, 232, 246, 354
kogonek 137, 229, 231, 249
korgoldžín 35, 227, 229, 231, 253, 255
kuburgan 44, 227, 228, 231, 232, 253
-kul 364
kulún 73, 228, 229, 231, 233
kumiš 38, 228, 229, 231, 232, 327
kusku kok 59, 255
kuštuk 175

laj 27, 226, 232, 233

menɨnajči 91, 323
mintora 26, 231, 255, 330, 356
molát 33, 227, 228, 230, 233

ogus 74, 227–229, 232, 327
oj- 346
ojakel'a 93, 232, 247, 346
ojakelbala 93, 346
ojče 94, 346
oo 324
ott 45, 227, 228, 331

paj 361
pajbal 75, 230, 233, 348

qonda 133
qólpas 86, 232, 254, 348

serga 63, 227, 232, 254
sɨrá 112, 227, 232, 233
sulem'a 153, 232
šižir 148, 231
šoška 77, 231, 255

tamkorgolči 35, 348
tebé 64, 227, 232
tegentestek 46, 227–229, 233, 254, 345, 351
teminkur 38, 336
tok 189, 227–229
torgɨjan 66, 226–229, 232, 253
tumantolatɨ 30, 226, 228, 231
tura 117, 228, 233
t'ugal 324

uragā 108, 226, 227, 229, 233
uške 78, 227, 255, 328

xamčook 127, 229, 254, 336
xonta 133

yus 195, 228, 232, 246

Pumpokol

aniŋ   79, 236, 337

baj   361
bɔi   361

fala   95, 234–236
falla   95, 234–236, 331

kun   59, 234, 235, 329
kümüč   38, 234–236

pʰala   95, 234–236
pʰalla   95, 234–236, 331

xaj   362
xórgosin   35, 234, 235, 255

Yugh

ajaŋi̇   105, 236, 237, 241, 315, 330
ajāχi̇n   257, 298, 302, 306, 349
ajāχn   257, 306, 349

badi̇r   97, 247
bat   79, 237–239, 327
bádir   97, 247
báti̇r   97, 247
báŋguˑs   360
baʔt   79, 237–239, 327
bätes   136, 237, 239–241
bēj   361
bérgi̇n   121, 237, 238, 239, 240, 256, 342
bi̇ldʲa   326
bi̇lʲlʲa   326
boŋsi   272, 301, 303, 338
bétes   136, 237, 239–241
bə̄ˑtn   62

číčik   265, 300, 306, 329

déstəu   367
dʲīk   361

eti   168, 237, 238, 241
ēˑt   168, 241, 340

fálgi̇   53, 236, 239, 351
fɔʔχ   80, 237, 239, 246

gɔʔt   81, 237, 238

iʔn   125, 329
iti̇ŋ   338
iti̇ŋsi   179

īˑt   179, 237, 239, 241, 246
iʰt   367

karábr   144, 241, 341
kàńčá   127, 237, 238, 240, 256, 313
kʌčiŋej   55, 237, 238, 240, 241, 333
kitn   42, 237–240, 332, 351
kû   36, 238
kuʔ   36, 238
kuʔo   36, 238, 248
kuʔu   36, 238
kūʰn   59, 238, 329

lagún   286

namčej   294, 299, 340, 356

sáŋa   201, 237, 240, 241, 318, 355
súlʲgej   171, 237, 241, 316, 332

tàli̇n   237
tàliˊn   113, 238, 240
tálli̇n   113, 237, 238, 240, 256
tōˑj   263, 306, 308, 320

uččij   202, 340
ugur   114, 238, 327
unče   204, 238, 328, 336
usn-č-tuj   325
utčij   202, 340
úlʲan   268, 301, 332, 341

χan   90, 239, 240, 247
χap   130, 238, 327, 329
χaʔj   362

INDEX OF THE YENISEIAN WORDS 395

χaʔp 130, 238, 327, 329
χʌlčakŋ 203, 237, 256, 340
χʌlčaŋ 87, 237, 239
χʌ́lčaχan 203, 237, 256, 340
χɨ·l'a 296, 300, 305, 308
χoj 172, 237, 239, 241, 329

χómuljej 266
χóŋɨrɔχ 130, 239, 240
χúmal 266, 340
χúmɨl 266, 340
χúmɨlʲej 340
χúmɨljej 266

Ket

aʁidɛ 258, 307, 349
ajgiddɛ 258, 307, 328, 331, 349
ajgitdɛ 258, 307, 328, 331, 349
alepqaj 293, 298, 300, 305, 309, 328
aluk 277, 299, 305, 307
aqtul 259, 306, 309, 333
áʁses 275, 302, 309, 333, 338, 357
álok 277, 299, 305, 307
áloq 277, 299, 305, 307
álək 277, 299, 305
áləq 277, 299, 305, 307
ána 295, 299, 304
āna 295, 299, 304

baŋgos 360
baŋgu·s 360
baŋos 360
bat 79, 242–244
batɨr 97, 247
báŋa 296, 302, 303, 330, 342
bejetil 271, 302, 303, 306, 321, 333
beʔj 271, 300, 303, 322, 329
bē·j 361
bə·tn 62
bilʲda 326
bilʲdɛ 326
boksel 269, 334
boŋnij 272, 301, 303, 328, 331
bō·ŋ 272, 301, 303, 305, 329

dankɨjaj 281, 299, 304, 310, 349
daŋtakan 259, 304, 328
däʁɔ 365
däŋtiɣin 259, 302, 304
deŋtiɣin 259, 302, 304
dɛstij 367
déʁɔ 365
dib 367
dī·k 361

doʔk 289, 300, 306, 307
dɔgbən 260, 302, 304
dɔktɔraŋ 287, 299, 302, 304, 305, 307, 309

enčil 266, 300, 304, 340
enna 291, 302, 305, 306, 331
ē·t 168, 245, 340
ē·ti 168, 242, 243, 245

gólɔmɔ 285, 299, 303, 305

hál'ga 53, 242, 244, 351
hʌ́gdaŋ 260
hɨlgum 288, 300
hɨtaj 288, 300, 301, 308
hɨ·lʲ 296, 300, 305, 308, 329
huktɛn 276, 301, 310, 337, 357
hulgum 288, 300, 302, 307, 309
húktɛŋ 276, 300, 310, 337, 357
hɔttɔn 282, 305, 308, 331
hɔʔq 80, 242–244, 246
hóttən 282, 308

ɨmejaŋ 277, 300, 350
ɨ·lʲ 88, 242, 245, 329, 354
ɨ·lʲi 88, 242, 245, 354
ilʲt 282, 305
ip 367
ígäj 293, 307, 340
ígij 293, 307, 340
íl'tə 282, 305
ɨt 367
iʔn 125, 329
ɨ̄te 367
ɨ̄ti 367
ɨ̄·t 242, 244–246

kalebel 144, 245, 341
kat sim 292, 305, 307

kànčá 127, 242–244, 256, 313
kʌdaŋ 261, 301, 303, 306
kʌdəŋ 261, 306
kʌndaŋ 292
kä·r 283, 299, 306, 353
kī·tn 42, 242, 244, 332, 351
kolij 284, 299, 306, 322, 350
kɔɣɔ́n 273, 304, 333
kɔjel 284, 299, 306, 350
kɔlɔmɔ 285, 299, 303, 305, 307
kɔ́jil 284, 299, 306, 350
kɔʔt 81, 242, 243
kudab 366
kulgum 288, 300, 302, 309
kútgɨt 280, 300, 301, 307, 321, 332, 334
kùn 59, 242, 243, 329
kuʔ 36, 243
kūn 59, 242, 243, 329
kǔne 59, 242, 243, 329
kǔnə 59, 242–244, 329

lačako 278, 299, 305–307
laɣun 286
laún 286
lɔčik 278, 306, 329
lúčkɔ 278, 299, 332

naravoks 278, 349
naroboks 278, 299, 304, 305, 349
nikkor 326, 331

ogə 301
ôgə 267, 300, 307, 308

ɔkɔŋɔ 292, 302, 307, 330, 355
ɔmɔɣɨn 278, 300, 303, 304, 307
ɔmɔɣuun 320
ɔnéŋ 366

qap 130, 243, 327, 329
qaʔj 362
qaʔp 130, 243, 327, 329
qa·n 90, 243, 244, 247
qʌbdal 281, 308, 350
qʌltaŋ 87, 242, 243
qäpil 270, 300, 303, 305, 307
qɨtet 272, 303, 308, 334, 350

qɨ·l'a 296, 300, 305, 308
qo·j 172, 242, 243, 245, 329
qɔ́lan 261
qɔ́ŋloq 130, 243–245
qúmɨlej 266
qúmlej 266
qùr 274, 307, 329
qùt 274, 307, 329
qǔde 274, 303, 307
qǔre 274, 303, 307

saŋɔl 286, 304, 334
sē·tal 290, 304, 305, 308, 329
sē·til 290, 304, 305, 308, 329
sɔnal 286
sūliŋ 273, 304, 305, 308, 319
sū·ŋ 279, 304, 353

tamtul 262, 349
táĺma 287, 303, 305
tàlɨn 242
tàlɨ´n 113, 243, 244
tállɨn 113, 242–244, 256
táĺma 299
tʌns'uk 276, 301, 303, 310, 329, 357
tɨl 268, 300, 304, 341
tɨ̄l 268, 341
toqtis 262, 301, 309, 338
to·k 341
tō·j 263, 306, 308, 320
tō·ji 263, 308, 320
tə·qt 267, 303, 310, 341
tə·qtə 267, 300, 303, 310, 341

učik 279, 299, 306, 307, 353
ulan-mukŋ 294, 301
ulla 290, 301, 305, 332, 341, 351
ullen 268, 301, 332, 341
ut-qo 294, 301, 358
úkta 297, 299, 309, 321, 333
úlen 268, 301, 341
úlle 290, 301, 305, 332, 341, 351
úĺba 264, 341
úĺĺɔŋ 291, 299, 310
úĺɔŋ 291, 299
u·ĺs' 107, 242, 245, 332, 356

Index of the Turkic Words

ačïn- 359
aða 102, 215, 224
aðğïr 67, 208, 214, 221, 222, 224, 226, 227, 230, 233
agïl 220
ağïl 105, 215, 248, 315, 330
aġu 44, 246, 356
al- 143
āla 155, 220, 246
alp 96
alpaġut 95, 211, 247, 250
altūn 32, 207, 216, 231, 249, 254, 336
andan 363
andïn 363
anïn 193
aŋït 48
āq 48
aqsaq 173, 213, 249
arakï 227, 229, 233
arïġ 165, 207, 215
arïq 353
arït- 136
arpa 39, 207, 221, 226, 250, 253, 254
arqïš 89, 226, 232, 254, 353
aruq 173
at 68, 347
ay- 89
ayïn- 100
ayna 231, 232
āz 191, 315
äčkü 78, 227, 255, 328
äl 88
älig 88, 242, 245, 329, 354
äsür- 177, 207, 218, 221, 336, 338, 340
ätmäk 110, 207, 212, 221, 223, 227
ävir- 207, 209
äβir- 167, 219, 342

baġatur 97, 247
bala 94, 95, 234–236, 331
balïq 53, 236, 239, 242, 244, 351
baltu 120, 209, 213, 222, 226, 228, 249, 253, 254
baqa 20
baqan 116
baqāńaq 360
baqāyaq 360
baqïr 32, 207, 209, 212, 213, 221
bar- 198
baš 86
bāy 75, 144, 187, 213, 220, 226, 230, 246, 338
bäk 167, 207, 212, 213
bärk 22, 106, 174, 253, 345
bät 238, 243
bet 79, 237, 239, 242, 244, 327
biŋ 195, 208, 214, 216
bïčïs 237, 239, 240
bïčïš 136
bïldïrčïn 50
bolat 227, 228, 230, 233
bōq 80, 213, 214, 237, 239, 242–244, 246
bōz 21, 156, 218, 330
bögä 99
bökä 99, 207, 208, 212
böksäg 269
böri 50, 210, 213, 220, 222, 223, 226, 327
budurčun 228, 230
budursïn 50, 336
buġday 41, 214, 221, 223, 225, 230, 232, 248, 254
buqa 70, 209, 213, 221–223, 226, 228–230
buzāġu 71, 218, 223, 225, 248, 333
bür- 121, 342
bürken- 237–240

čāġ 141, 147
čaqïr- 197
čočuq 77, 217, 231, 252, 255

eče 94

ïġač 34, 47
ignä 125, 329

käm 26, 217
kämi 130, 212, 223, 238, 243, 327–329
käpäk 42
kegde 150
kïftu 129
köbürgän 228, 231
kōk 59, 162, 347
köl 364

kömürgän 44
kőń- 248
köŋläk 137, 212, 215, 229, 231, 247, 249
köŋül 184, 247, 252
köprüg 117, 210, 221
köt 81, 237, 238, 242, 243
köβürgän 44, 208, 219, 221–223, 225, 227, 232, 249, 253, 330, 337
kṻč 175, 185, 210, 211, 217, 246, 339
kṻčlüg 175
kṻg 82
külüg 185, 352
külük 210, 220
kümüš 38, 210, 211, 217, 219, 222, 224, 225, 228, 229, 231, 232, 234–236, 327
küń- 37

lāčïn 56
lāġūn 286
lay 226

mal 69, 76, 217
maŋ- 61, 216, 224
mindir 231
munġan 186, 216, 252, 352

nägü 194

oruq 31, 208, 209, 212, 220, 355
ot 45, 227, 228, 331
otāġ 115, 208, 211, 215
otluġ 119
ōy 324
oyna- 150
oyun 150, 208, 216, 219
öč- 202, 340
ögey 93, 94, 232, 247, 346
ögür 75, 221, 247
öküz 74, 208, 210, 212, 218, 227–229, 232, 327
örüm 139, 208, 217, 327, 356
ötgürü 204, 208, 327, 329
ötmäk 110

qaðïġ 214, 215
qaġan 91, 216, 239, 240, 243, 244, 247
qal 55
qamčï 127, 209, 229, 250, 254, 336
qamla- 103, 207, 212, 252, 338
qān 38, 336

qańaq 110, 213, 216, 226, 229, 231, 336
qapaq 84, 210, 213
qara 43, 56, 58, 158, 316
qara- 205, 212
qarġa 57, 330
qariš 140, 209, 219
qašuq 364
qaya 362
qaβïq 42, 351
qïčï 203
qïlčïq 237
qïlïč 153, 209, 217
qïqïr- 198
qïr 25, 227, 229, 233
qīz 93, 227, 229, 232, 246, 354
qoč 71
qočŋār 71, 221, 252
qol 24
qōl 86
qoltuq 87, 237, 239, 242, 243
qōń 73, 208, 216, 222, 224
qoŋrāq 130
qoŋur 159, 216
qoruġjin 35
qoš- 285, 322
qoyuġ 172, 237, 239, 241–243, 245, 329
qučaqla- 198
quðuš- 214
qulaq 20, 82, 181, 207, 210, 213, 220
qulqaq 20, 82, 181
qulun 73, 212, 216, 222–225, 228, 229, 231, 233
qur 132, 209, 212, 222, 223, 226, 330, 352
qut 274, 329
quzġun 59

saban 148, 213, 218
saġïzġan 63, 218, 247, 252, 330
sana- 201, 318, 355
saqïn- 200
sārïġ 111, 160, 218, 329
say 349
sāy 257
siŋäk 58
siŋir 126, 218, 247, 330
sirkä 63, 227, 232, 254
širä 112
sōl 171, 316, 332
sūt 112, 210, 211, 218, 222–224, 246

INDEX OF THE TURKIC WORDS

ta   192
tāġ   23, 29
talqan   113, 211, 216, 223, 224, 237, 238, 240, 242–244, 249, 250, 253, 256
taluy   23
tān   28, 207, 211, 339
tarï-   149, 208, 348
täk   191
täkin   191
täkün   191
tämir   38, 336
täri   138, 139, 328, 347, 355
täβäy   64, 207, 219, 221, 225, 227, 232, 327, 334
tïl   144
tṳ̈t   47
tikän   46, 351
tikänäk   46
tilä-   144
töpö   85
töpü   85
toq   189, 227–229
toqlï   325
torġayaq   228, 229, 232
torgayaq   227, 253
toṅġā   66
toruġ   161, 211
tōy   152, 208, 246
tum   29, 340
tuman   29, 30, 217, 226, 228, 231
tura   106, 117, 209, 211, 220, 228, 233
tṳ̈   65

tüg   65
tükteg   250, 330, 351

uluš   107, 332, 356
uruq   134
üčün   193, 194, 204, 238, 328, 336
ṳ̈gi   67, 222, 329
ügre   114, 238, 327
üšik   31, 210, 212, 219
üšük   210, 356

yāġ   111
yaman   163
yān   79, 219, 236, 337, 347
yarma   109, 233, 255
yat-   362
yavlaq   164
yaxšï   169, 209, 219, 250
yïð   237, 239, 241, 242, 244, 245, 246, 338
yïðïg   215, 219
yïðïġ   179
yïlan   51
yïp   123, 207, 219
yïpaq   208
yitī   168
yitig   168, 209, 211, 219, 237, 238, 241–243, 245, 340
yoġurqan   123, 216, 219, 246, 250
yōl   57
yumaq   43
yumġaq   43
yṳ̈z   195, 228, 232, 246

Index of the Literary Mongolian Words

ada 103
ajirɣ-a(n) 68
alaɣ 156
alban 49, 143, 315
albin 101
almas 101
alta(n) 32
aŋgir 48
arai 190, 314
araki(n) 109
arbai 40
arčiɣul 136
arčiɣur 136
ariki(n) 109
ariɣ 165
ariɣun 165
ayil 105, 315

baɣana 116
baɣatur 98
baǰa 92
balčir 95
balta 120
bayan 188
belen 166
berke 22, 100, 106, 167, 174
beye(n) 271, 321
bilǰuuqai 51
biraɣu(n) 71
boɣ 81
bolud 33
bora 21
boro 21, 157
bögse(n) 269
böke 99, 167
buɣudai 41
bultu 326
buq-a 70
buudai 41

čaɣ 142, 147
čaɣalsu(n) 151, 311
čaɣarsu(n) 151, 311
čaɣasu(n) 151, 311
čar 77
čegčegei 265

čiɣulɣan 273
čirɣ-a 122
čooqor 157
čoqor 157
čuɣlaɣ-a(n) 273, 319

dalai 23

egere- 168
eǰi 95
emegel 279, 320
eregül 176
ermüge(n) 140
esige 78

ɣabsiɣai 182, 314
ɣangsa 128, 313
ɣanǰuɣ-a(n) 129, 313
ɣansa 128, 313
ɣauli 35, 313
ɣoɣomai 169
ɣool 24
ɣoomai 169
ɣuuli 35, 313

gejige 203
güǰege 280, 321

isige(n) 78

ǰarm-a 109
ǰegeke(n) 52
ǰida 152
ǰon 90, 318

kebeli 270
kegürge 117
kei 361
kele(n) 180
kelegei 179, 317
kem 141
kersegüü 183, 311
kir-a 25
kö 37
kög 83
köge 37

INDEX OF THE LITERARY MONGOLIAN WORDS

kögege 37
kögemei 83
kögerge 117
kögürge 117
köke 60, 163
kölüg 185
kömei 83
kömöl 44
kömöli 44
küčü(n) 176, 186
külüg 185

maɣta- 196, 312
mal 69
mangɣus 360
mingɣan 196
möndür 26
muna- 187
munu- 187

način 56
nayiji 91, 314, 323
noqto 133
nökör 326

oi 324
otoɣ 115
örmöge 140
ötege 295

qabtasun 124
qalbaɣ-a(n) 364
qalbuɣ-a 364
qaltar 158, 316
qan 91
qara- 205
qaram 178
qaraɣačai 55
qaraɣul 145
qariyačai 55
qaškir- 197
qaskir- 197
qayiba 284
qayibi 284
qayibu 284
qaɣan 91
qobdu 104, 317
qoki 199
qolba- 285, 322
qolbo- 285, 322

qongqo 131
qongɣor 160
qoni(n) 73
qorɣoljin 36
quča 72
quluɣur 181
qutuɣ 275

sana- 201, 318
sarana 323
sayir 258
selem-e 154
siɣajiɣai 64
siɣur- 27
siɣurɣan 27
simaɣul 58
simuɣul 58
sir-a 161
sirke 63
solongɣ-a 54
sologai 171, 316
soqor 188
sü(n) 113
šaɣajaɣai 64
šar 77
širɣa 161

talqan 114
tari- 149
tegün 192
temege(n) 65
toi 152
toqai 320
toqoi 320
tuɣul 324
tur-a 118
türgen 189, 319

uda- 297, 322
uɣuli 67
uɣurɣa 134
ulus 107
uraqa(n) 135
urɣa(n) 134
uriqa(n) 135
uuli 67
üker 74
ünesü(n) 262
üsü(n) 325

Index of the Ewenki Words

aγī 258, 307, 328, 331, 349
aγī- 258
ajan 257
ajān 257, 306, 349
ala 277
alaγ 277, 299, 305, 307
ali- 293
aliγ 277
alik 277
alipkī- 293, 298, 300, 305, 309, 328
amā 275
amākā 275
amākākse 275, 302, 309, 333, 338, 357
amut 349
āmut 262
argis 90
argiš 90
ayān 298, 302

bā- 296
bāde 80
bān 296, 302, 303, 330, 342
bāter 98
bātur 98
bejetī 271, 302, 303, 306, 333
beye 271, 300, 303, 322, 329
beyetī 321
bu- 272, 328
buksu 269, 334
bunī 272, 301, 303, 305, 328, 329, 331, 338

čičakān 265
čičakūn 265, 300, 306, 329
čičakūtkān 265
čuglan 273
čūha 361
čūhe 361
čūksa 361

dāgwūn 260, 302, 304
dāγ- 260
daγańa 281
daŋajā 299, 304
daŋańā 281
daŋanī 281, 310, 349
ďapka 367

dektekēn 287
dekten 288
delkēn 268
det 328
detkēn 259, 302, 304, 328
dïsut- 367
dilkēn 268, 300, 304, 341
doktokōn 287, 299, 302, 304, 305, 307, 309
dokton 288

elbe- 282
elben 282
elbeptun 282
eltin 305
elwun 282
emegen 278, 300, 303, 304, 307, 320

-gAčin 292, 305, 307
gene- 366
gida 152
golo 285
golomo 285, 299, 303, 305, 307
gūdexe 280
gudï 280
gudiγē 280, 321
gudige 300, 301, 307, 332, 334

haran 282, 308, 331
harān 282
hegdï 288, 300, 301, 308
helin 296, 300, 305, 308
helinǰi 296
hepete 281
hepete tïle 308, 350
hiγin 260
hila 296, 300, 305, 308, 329
holoŋgo 54
hōna 287
honoŋgo 54
horan 282, 305, 308, 331
huγun 261
hug 276
hūg 276
hugdï 276, 300, 301, 310, 337, 357
hugi 267, 300, 301, 307, 308
hugī 267

INDEX OF THE EWENKI WORDS

huglan 319
hulepten 261
huna 279
hute 272, 303, 308, 334, 350

ī- 293
īg 293, 307, 340
īkte 368
ilbe- 282
ilben 282
immen 277, 300, 350
immer 277
inman 277
inmar 277
intilgun 266, 300, 304, 340
itmar 277
itte 368

jalbuka 341
jēŋan 291, 302, 305, 306, 331
jū- 289
jūďēk 289
jūďek 306
jūdek 289, 300, 306, 307
jūkte 259, 306, 309
jūktu 259

kāja 284
kaja 299, 306, 350
kalta- 283, 309, 350
kar 283
kari 283, 306
karje 283, 299, 353
karjen 283
kelkē 289, 300, 302, 307, 309
kēńe- 292
kolbo 284, 299, 306, 322, 350
kolbo- 284
kotï- 366
kotoro- 366
kulin 274
kulitkān 274, 304, 333
kumalāndō 266, 340
kuta 261, 274, 301, 303, 306
kuta- 261
kutu 274, 303, 307, 329

lačako 278
lagun 286

lālbukā 264
ločoko 278, 299, 305–307, 329, 332

mene- 366

nam- 340, 356
nama- 294
namū- 294
namuwčā 294, 299
nara 278, 299, 304, 305, 349
nārā 278
nene- 366
ńalbuka 264
ńūkte 259

ŋenē 366
ŋene- 366
ŋono- 366

ōkīdalā 292
ōkija 292
ōkīlā-dā 292
ōkīmaka 292
ōkin 292, 302, 307, 330, 355
ōkīn-dā 292

seleme 347
selmi 154
sigdilē 290, 304, 305, 308, 329
solga 54
soliγā 54
soloŋgō 54
soloŋo 54
sōna 287, 304, 334
sonoŋgo 54
sōŋa 287, 304, 334
suglān 273, 304, 305, 308, 319
suna 279, 304, 353
šonoŋgō 54

talmī 287, 299, 303, 305
talu 287
tïgde 267
tïgdewkī 267, 300, 303, 310, 341
tïle 281
tïle- 281
tobo 64
toγočī 320
toγor- 320

togoi   263, 308, 320
togoj   306
tokto-   341
tuktï-   262, 301, 309, 338
tuŋsuku   276, 301, 303, 310, 329, 357

ūčak   280, 299, 306, 307, 353
uda-   297, 321

udakta   299, 309, 321, 333
ulanmukī   268, 301, 332, 341
ulle   294
ulme-   294, 301
ūlta   291, 299, 310
ūlta-   291
ulukī   290, 301, 305, 332, 341, 351
utu   295, 301, 358

Printed in the United States
By Bookmasters